SECONDHAND TIME

SECONDHAND TIME

The Last of the Soviets

◆ ◆ ◆

SVETLANA ALEXIEVICH

Translated by Bela Shayevich

RANDOM HOUSE | NEW YORK

Translation copyright © 2016 by Bela Shayevich

All rights reserved.

Published in the United States by Random House, an imprint and division of
Penguin Random House LLC, New York.

RANDOM HOUSE and the HOUSE colophon are registered trademarks of
Penguin Random House LLC.

Originally published in Russian as Время секонд хэнд by Vremya Publishing
House, Moscow, in 2013. Copyright © 2013 by Svetlana Alexievich. This English
translation is published in the United Kingdom by Fitzcarraldo Editions, London.

Library of Congress Cataloging-in-Publication Data

Names: Aleksievich, Svetlana.
Title: Secondhand time : the last of the Soviets / Svetlana Alexievich ; translated by
Bela Shayevich.
Other titles: Vremёiia sekond khçend. English | Secondhand time
Description: New York : Random House, 2016. | First published in Russian in 2013.
Identifiers: LCCN 2016005925| ISBN 9780399588808 (hardback : acid-free paper) |
ISBN 9780399588815 (ebook)
Subjects: LCSH: Post-communism—Russia (Federation) | Russia (Federation)—
Social conditions—1991– | Soviet Union—Social conditions. | Russia (Federation)—
Biography. | Soviet Union—Biography. | Oral history—Russia (Federation) | Oral
history—Soviet Union. | BISAC: HISTORY / Europe / Former Soviet Republics. |
HISTORY / Europe / Russia & the Former Soviet Union.
Classification: LCC DK510.76 .A44913 2016 | DDC 947.086092/2—dc23 LC record
available at lccn.loc.gov/2016005925

Printed in the United States of America on acid-free paper

randomhousebooks.com

8 9

Book design by Mary A. Wirth

Victim and executioner are equally ignoble; the lesson of the camps is brotherhood in abjection.

—DAVID ROUSSET, *The Days of Our Death*

In any event, we must remember that it's not the blinded wrongdoers who are primarily responsible for the triumph of evil in the world, but the spiritually sighted servants of the good.

—FYODOR STEPUN, *Foregone and Gone Forever*

CONTENTS

• • •

CHRONOLOGY:
RUSSIA AFTER STALIN

· · ·

1953: Josef Stalin dies on March 5. On September 14, Nikita Khrushchev becomes First Secretary of the Central Committee of the Communist Party of the Soviet Union (CPSU).

FEBRUARY 1956: Khrushchev delivers a speech to the Twentieth Congress of the CPSU denouncing Stalin's cult of personality and the excesses of his policies. Over the next decades, this speech circulates covertly through *samizdat* and is discussed at closed Party meetings, shocking many. The speech marks the beginning of de-Stalinization and the Khrushchev Thaw, a time of relative liberalization.

NOVEMBER 1956: The Soviet army violently puts down an uprising in Hungary.

NOVEMBER 1957: The Italian publisher Feltrinelli publishes *Doctor Zhivago* by Boris Pasternak. Under pressure from the Soviet authorities, Pasternak is forced to turn down the Nobel Prize in Literature the following year.

NOVEMBER 1962: *One Day in the Life of Ivan Denisovich* by Aleksandr Solzhenitsyn is published in *Novy Mir,* an influential Russian literary magazine. It is the first time that the Soviet labor camps had been written about openly. Nevertheless, a crackdown on dissident groups marks the end of the Thaw.

1964: Khrushchev is removed from power and replaced by Leonid Brezhnev.

1968: The Soviet military invades Czechoslovakia in an attempt to counteract the series of liberalizing reforms known as the Prague Spring reforms, sparking off waves of protests and nonviolent resistance.

1973–1974: Solzhenitsyn's *Gulag Archipelago* is published in the West in Russian and other languages. In February 1974 Solzhenitsyn is expelled from the Soviet Union.

1975: Thirty-five states, including the USSR and the United States, sign the Helsinki Accords, an attempt to improve relations between the Communist Bloc and the West. The document cites respect for human rights and fundamental freedoms such as freedom of speech.

1979: Soviet troops invade Afghanistan.

NOVEMBER 1982: Brezhnev, the General Secretary of the Communist Party from 1964 to 1982, dies of a heart attack. Yuri Andropov, the head of the KGB, succeeds him.

FEBRUARY 1984: Andropov dies of renal failure. Konstantin Chernenko replaces him.

MARCH 1985: Chernenko dies of emphysema. Mikhail Gorbachev becomes General Secretary of the Communist Party and takes steps toward reform, marking the beginning of perestroika. *Novy Mir* commences serialization of *Doctor Zhivago* three years later.

Important reforms undertaken by Gorbachev between 1985 and 1991 under the umbrella of perestroika and glasnost: restitution of land to peasants after sixty years of collectivized agriculture; progressive restoration of political pluralism and freedom of speech, liberation of political prisoners, publication of banned literature; withdrawal of troops from Afghanistan; creation of a new legislative assembly, the Congress of People's Deputies. The Congress elects Gorbachev to the presidency of the Soviet Union for five years and institutes constitutional reforms in March 1990. Strategic Arms Reduction Treaty (START I) agreements are signed with the United States in 1991.

FEBRUARY 1986: Boris Yeltsin becomes a member of the Politburo a few months after being named First Secretary of the Moscow City

Committee (effectively making him the mayor of Moscow). He is removed from the Politburo in 1988.

APRIL 26, 1986: Reactor No. 4 at the Chernobyl nuclear power plant explodes, leading to serious contamination of Soviet territory.

MARCH 1989: Yeltsin is elected to the Congress of People's Deputies.

NOVEMBER 1989: East Berlin permits passage to West Berlin, marking the effective end of the Cold War and the beginning of the reunification of Germany.

DECEMBER 1989: Gorbachev and George H. W. Bush announce the end of the Cold War in Malta.

JUNE 1990: The Congress of People's Deputies of the Republic adopts the Declaration of State Sovereignty of the Russian Soviet Federative Socialist Republic (RSFSR), pitting the Soviet Union against the Russian Federation and other constituent republics and signaling the beginning of constitutional reform in Russia.

MAY 1991: Boris Yeltsin is elected president of the RSFSR.

AUGUST 1991: A group of eight high-ranking officials led by Gorbachev's vice president, Gennady Yanayev, form the General Committee on the State Emergency, the GKChP, and stage an attempted coup of the government. It becomes known as "the putsch." The GKChP issues an emergency decree suspending all political activity, banning most newspapers, and putting Gorbachev, who is on holiday in Foros, Crimea, under house arrest.

Thousands of protesters come out to stand against the putsch in front of the White House, the Russian Federation's parliament building and office of Boris Yeltsin, building barricades to protect their positions. Yeltsin famously addresses the crowd from atop a tank. The Army forces dispatched by the GKChP ultimately refuse to storm the barricades and side with the protesters. After three days, the putsch collapses. Gorbachev returns from Foros, and members of the GKChP are arrested. On August 24, Gorbachev dissolves the Central Committee of the Communist Party of the Soviet Union and resigns as its general secretary.

NOVEMBER–DECEMBER 1991: In the Ukrainian popular referendum on December 1, 1991, 90 percent of voters opt for independence from the Soviet Union.

On December 8, the leaders of Russia, Ukraine, and Belarus secretly meet in western Belarus and sign the Belavezha Accords, declaring the dissolution of the Soviet Union and the establishment of the Commonwealth of Independent States (CIS) in its place. On the night of December 25, 1991, the Soviet flag is lowered for the last time and the Russian tricolor is raised in its place, symbolically marking the end of the Soviet Union. Gorbachev resigns. In a period of great tumult, Yeltsin takes on both the prime ministerial and presidential roles.

The newly independent states of Armenia, Georgia, and Azerbaijan are created and immediately succumb to violent ethnic conflicts. Armenia and Azerbaijan fight over the Nagorno-Karabakh enclave; Abkhazia, South Ossetia, and Adjara fight to secede from Georgia. Dzhokhar Dudayev takes power in Chechnya and proclaims independence.

JANUARY 1992: The liberalization of prices leads to massive, destabilizing inflation, from 200 percent initially to a high of 2600 percent.

AUTUMN 1993: In response to President Yeltsin's attempt to dissolve the parliament, the parliament impeaches Yeltsin and proclaims vice president Alexander Rustkoy president. In events reminiscent of the 1991 putsch, demonstrators congregate at the White House and attempt to storm the Ostankino television tower. On Yeltsin's orders, the army storms the White House and arrests members of the parliament who oppose Yeltsin.

The ten-day standoff between protesters supporting the parliament and army-backed Yeltsin supporters leads to the deadliest street fighting in Moscow since 1917. Estimates place the death toll as high as two thousand casualties.

1994–1995: First Chechen War.

1998: Economic difficulties, which dramatically lowered the quality of life of the population throughout the 1990s, lead to a financial crisis and a brutal devaluation of the ruble.

1999–2000: Second Chechen War. On December 31, 1999, Yeltsin resigns and Vladimir Putin becomes president of the Russian Federation. In 2000, Putin wins his first presidential election against Communist opponent Gennady Zyuganov, firmly establishing his power.

OCTOBER 2003: Oil magnate and prominent liberal Mikhail Khodorkovsky is arrested on charges of tax evasion and fraud, an early casualty of Putin's campaign to drive Yeltsin-era oligarchs out of politics. The imprisonment of Khodorovsky and seizure of his assets marks the beginning of Vladimir Putin's efforts to transfer control of all major Russian industries to his political party, United Russia. This economic takeover, necessitating a great deal of corrupt maneuvering, also leads to the necessity of silencing criticism and dissent in the press. By 2010, most formerly privately owned media enterprises are under government control, including nearly all major television networks. Independent media outlets are almost exclusively relegated to the Internet.

2008: War breaks out between Georgia and South Ossetia. Dmitri Medvedev of United Russia is elected president of the Russian Federation and names Putin prime minister.

DECEMBER 2010: Alexander Lukashenko is reelected for a fourth term as president of Belarus. This leads to protests, which are brutally repressed.

DECEMBER 2011: Prime Minister Putin declares that he will once again run for president in 2012, with Dmitri Medvedev as prime minister; effectively Putin and Medvedev will switch places. This sparks the first major antigovernment protests since the early 1990s. While these are tacitly tolerated, individual activists begin to be arrested and penalized in larger numbers than previously, and the parliament begins to seriously curtail the rights of activist groups and nongovernmental organizations that work in opposition to government policies.

FEBRUARY 2012: Putin is reelected president of Russia with 63 percent of the vote and names Medvedev prime minister. Oppositionists again take to the streets of several major cities to protest; the police arrest hundreds. Putin's government harshly punishes a handful of protesters, intensifying its efforts to repress political dissent in the Russian Federation.

FEBRUARY–MAY 2014: The Maidan protests in Kiev, Ukraine, lead to armed conflict between Ukrainians supporting a pro–European Union political orientation and those who wish to remain under the Russian sphere of influence. After the flight from Ukraine of pro-Moscow president Viktor Yanukovych, Russian forces take over Crimea, which then votes to join Russia in a referendum. At the same time, Russia denies that its forces have entered Ukraine and are providing financial and military support to pro-Russian groups, effectively fueling a civil war in Ukraine. These events spark the biggest East-West showdown since the Cold War, with the United States and its European allies imposing harsh sanctions on Russia.

SECONDHAND TIME

REMARKS FROM AN ACCOMPLICE

◆ ◆ ◆

We're paying our respects to the Soviet era. Cutting ties with our old life. I'm trying to honestly hear out all the participants of the socialist drama . . .

Communism had an insane plan: to remake the "old breed of man," ancient Adam. And it really worked . . . Perhaps it was communism's only achievement. Seventy-plus years in the Marxist-Leninist laboratory gave rise to a new man: *Homo sovieticus.* Some see him as a tragic figure, others call him a *sovok.** I feel like I know this person; we're very familiar, we've lived side by side for a long time. I am this person. And so are my acquaintances, my closest friends, my parents. For a number of years, I traveled throughout the former Soviet Union— *Homo sovieticus* isn't just Russian, he's Belarusian, Turkmen, Ukrainian, Kazakh. Although we now live in separate countries and speak different languages, you couldn't mistake us for anyone else. We're easy to spot! People who've come out of socialism are both like and unlike the rest of humanity—we have our own lexicon, our own conceptions of good and evil, our heroes, our martyrs. We have a special relationship with death. The stories people tell me are full of jarring terms: "shoot," "execute," "liquidate," "eliminate," or typically Soviet varieties of disappearance such as "arrest," "ten years without the right of correspondence,"† and "emigration." How much can we value human life when we know that not long ago people had died by

* This is a widely used pejorative term for one who adheres to Soviet values, attitudes, and behaviors. The word can also refer to the Soviet Union itself. It is a pun on the word for "dustpan."—*Trans.*
† "Ten years without the right of correspondence" is a clause that appeared in official form letters addressed to relatives of political prisoners regarding the status of the arrested, especially during Stalin's purges of the 1930s. It often meant that the person had been executed.

the millions? We're full of hatred and superstitions. All of us come from the land of the gulag and harrowing war. Collectivization, dekulakization,* mass deportations of various nationalities . . .

This was socialism, but it was also just everyday life. Back then, we didn't talk about it very much. Now that the world has transformed irreversibly, everyone is suddenly interested in that old life of ours—whatever it may have been like, it was our life. In writing, I'm piecing together the history of "domestic," "interior" socialism. As it existed in a person's soul. I've always been drawn to this miniature expanse: one person, the individual. It's where everything really happens.

Why does this book contain so many stories of suicides instead of more typical Soviets with typically Soviet life stories? When it comes down to it, people end their lives for love, from fear of old age, or just out of curiosity, from a desire to come face to face with the mystery of death. I sought out people who had been permanently bound to the Soviet idea, letting it penetrate them so deeply that there was no separating them: The state had become their entire cosmos, blocking out everything else, even their own lives. They couldn't just walk away from History, leaving it all behind and learning to live without it—diving headfirst into the new way of life and dissolving into private existence, like so many others who now allowed what used to be minor details to become their big picture. Today, people just want to live their lives, they don't need some great Idea. This is entirely new for Russia; it's unprecedented in Russian literature. At heart, we're built for war. We were always either fighting or preparing to fight. We've never known anything else—hence our wartime psychology. Even in civilian life, everything was always militarized. The drums were beating, the banners flying, our hearts leaping out of our chests. People didn't recognize their own slavery—they even liked being slaves. I remember it well: After we finished school, we'd volunteer to go on class trips to the Virgin Lands,† and we'd look down on the students who didn't want to come. We were bitterly disappointed that the Revolu-

---

* The Stalin-initiated campaign of "liquidating of the kulak class" lasted from 1929 to 1932, entailing the arrest, deportation, and execution of better-off peasants ("kulaks") and their families for the purposes of seizing their property and incorporating it into collective enterprises ("collectivization").
† The Virgin Lands Campaign was an agricultural reform strategy initiated by Nikita Khrushchev in 1953, the purpose of which was to increase crop yields rapidly by

tion and Civil War had all happened before our time. Now you wonder: Was that really us? Was that me? I reminisced alongside my protagonists. One of them said, "Only a Soviet can understand another Soviet." We share a communist collective memory. We're neighbors in memory.

My father would say that he personally started believing in communism after Gagarin went into space. We're the first! We can do anything! That's how he and my mother raised us. I was a Little Octobrist, I sported the pin with the curly-headed boy; I was a Young Pioneer, then a member of the Komsomol.* Disillusionment came later.

After perestroika, we were all impatient for the archives to be unsealed. Finally, it happened. We learned the history that they had been hiding from us . . .

> We need to attract ninety million out of the hundred that populate Soviet Russia. It's impossible to talk to the rest of them—they must be eliminated. (Zinoviev, 1918)
>
> We must hang (and it has to be hanging, so that the people will see) no fewer than 1,000 inveterate kulaks, the rich ones . . . seize their grain, take hostages . . . Make sure that people hear about it one hundred versts† around and tremble from fear . . . (Lenin, 1918)
>
> Moscow is literally dying of hunger. (N. G. Kuznetsov to Trotsky)
>
> That's not hunger. When Titus was taking Jerusalem, Jewish mothers ate their children. When I have your mothers eating their young, then you can tell me you're starving. (Trotsky, 1919)

People read newspapers and magazines and sat in stunned silence. They were overcome with unspeakable horror. How were we supposed to live with this? Many greeted the truth as an enemy. And freedom as well. "We don't know our own nation. We don't understand what the

---

bringing a vast swath of land under cultivation. The Virgin Lands Campaign is also known for the severe food, housing, and machinery shortages faced by its workers.

* Little Octobrists, Young Pioneers, and the Komsomol were Soviet youth organizations that most children joined in school. Children were Little Octobrists from age seven to nine, when they would join the Young Pioneers. At fourteen, children could elect to join the Komsomol, the youth division of the Communist Party.

† Obsolete Russian unit of length, equal to approximately 1.07 kilometers or 0.67 miles.

majority of people think about; we see them, we interact with them every day, but what's on their minds? What do they want? We have no idea. But we will courageously take it upon ourselves to educate them. Soon, we will learn the whole truth and be horrified," my friend would say in my kitchen, where we often sat talking. I'd argue with him. It was 1991 . . . What an incredibly happy time! We believed that tomorrow, the very next day, would usher in freedom. That it would materialize out of nowhere, from the sheer force of our wishing.

From Varlam Shalamov's *Notebooks:** "I participated in the great lost battle for the true reinvention of life." The man who wrote these words spent seventeen years in Stalin's camps. He continued to yearn for the ideals . . . I would divide the Soviets into four generations: the Stalin, the Khrushchev, the Brezhnev, and the Gorbachev. I belong to the last of these. It was easier for my generation to accept the defeat of the communist Idea because we hadn't been born yet when it was still young, strong, and brimming with the magic of fatal romanticism and utopian aspirations. We grew up with the Kremlin ancients, in Lenten, vegetarian times.† The great bloodshed of communism had already been lost to the ages. Pathos raged, but the knowledge that utopia should not be attempted in real life was already ingrained in us.

This was during the first Chechen war . . . At a train station in Moscow, I met a woman from the Tambov area. She was headed to Chechnya to take her son home. "I don't want him to die. I don't want him to kill." The government no longer owned her soul, this was a free person. There were not many of them. More often, people were irritated with freedom. "I buy three newspapers and each one of them has its own version of the truth. Where's the real truth? You used to be able to get up in the morning, read *Pravda,* and know all you needed to know, understand everything you needed to understand." People were slow to come out from under the narcosis of old ideas. If I brought up repentance, the response would be, "What do I have to repent for?" Everyone thought of themselves as a victim, never a will-

---

* Varlam Shalamov (1907–1982) was a Soviet writer and gulag survivor whose *Kolyma Tales,* which circulated in samizdat editions beginning in the middle of the 1960s, is considered a classic of twentieth-century Russian literature.
† Russian and Soviet modernist poet Anna Akhmatova (1889–1966) coined the term "the vegetarian years" to describe a period when her work was merely suppressed and not published, as opposed to the "cannibalism" of Stalin's purges, when Soviets, including many of her fellow poets, were murdered by the millions. It is used colloquially to denote the contrast between Stalinism and what followed.

ing accomplice. One person would say, "I did time, too"; another, "I fought in the war"; a third, "I built my city up from the ruins, hauling bricks day and night." Freedom had materialized out of thin air: Everyone was intoxicated by it, but no one had really been prepared. Where was this freedom? Only around kitchen tables, where out of habit people continued to badmouth the government. They reviled Yeltsin and Gorbachev: Yeltsin for changing Russia, and Gorbachev for changing everything. The entire twentieth century. Now we would live no worse than anyone else. We'd be just like everyone else. We thought that this time, we'd finally get it right.

Russia was changing and hating itself for changing. "The immobile Mongol," Marx wrote of Russia.

The Soviet civilization . . . I'm rushing to make impressions of its traces, its familiar faces. I don't ask people about socialism, I want to know about love, jealousy, childhood, old age. Music, dances, hairdos. The myriad sundry details of a vanished way of life. It's the only way to chase the catastrophe into the contours of the ordinary and try to tell a story. Make some small discovery. It never ceases to amaze me how interesting everyday life really is. There is an endless number of human truths. History is concerned solely with the facts; emotions are outside of its realm of interest. In fact, it's considered improper to admit feelings into history. But I look at the world as a writer and not a historian. I am fascinated by people.

My father is no longer living, so we won't get to finish one of our conversations . . . He claimed that it was easier to die in the war in his day than it is for the untried boys to die in Chechnya now. In the 1940s, they went from one hell to another. Before the war, my father had been studying at the Minsk Institute of Journalism. He would recall how often, on returning to college after vacations, students wouldn't find a single one of their old professors because they had all been arrested. They didn't understand what was happening, but whatever it was, it was terrifying. Just as terrifying as war.

I didn't have many honest, open conversations with my father. He felt sorry for me. Did I feel sorry for him? It's hard to answer that question . . . We were merciless toward our parents. We thought that freedom was a very simple thing. A little time went by, and soon, we too bowed under its yoke. No one had taught us how to be free. We had only ever been taught how to die for freedom.

So here it is, freedom! Is it everything we hoped it would be? We were prepared to die for our ideals. To prove ourselves in battle. Instead, we ushered in a Chekhovian life. Without any history. Without any values except for the value of human life—life in general. Now we have new dreams: building a house, buying a decent car, planting gooseberries . . . Freedom turned out to mean the rehabilitation of bourgeois existence, which has traditionally been suppressed in Russia. The freedom of Her Highness Consumption. Darkness exalted. The darkness of desire and instinct—the mysterious human life, of which we only ever had approximate notions. For our entire history, we'd been surviving instead of living. Today, there's no longer any use for our experience in war; in fact, it'd be best to forget it. There are thousands of newly available feelings, moods, and responses. Everything around us has been transformed: the billboards, the clothing, the money, the flag . . . And the people themselves. They're more colorful now, more individualized; the monolith has been shattered and life has splintered into a million little fragments, cells and atoms. It's like in Dal's dictionary:* free will . . . free rein . . . wide-open spaces. The grand old evil is nothing but a distant saga, some political detective story. After perestroika, no one was talking about ideas anymore—instead, it was credit, interest, and promissory notes; people no longer earned money, they "made" it or "scored" it. Is this all here to stay? "The fact that money is a fiction is ineradicable from the Russian soul," wrote Marina Tsvetaeva.† But it's as though Ostrovsky and Saltykov-Shchedrin‡ characters have come to life and are promenading down our streets.

I asked everyone I met what "freedom" meant. Fathers and children had very different answers. Those who were born in the USSR and those born after its collapse do not share a common experience—it's like they're from different planets.

---

* Vladimir Dal (1801–1872) wrote the most influential Russian dictionary collecting sayings, proverbs, and bywords compiled during his extensive travels through Russia.
† Marina Tsvetaeva (1892–1941) was a Russian and Soviet modernist poet.
‡ Alexander Ostrovsky (1823–1886) was a prominent nineteenth-century Russian realist playwright whose plays depicting the petite bourgeoisie are still among the most performed in Russia today. Mikhail Saltykov-Shchedrin (1826–1889) was a satirist, novelist, and playwright whose works criticized Russian officialdom and the prevailing social order of his day.

For the fathers, freedom is the absence of fear; the three days in August when we defeated the putsch. A man with his choice of a hundred kinds of salami is freer than one who only has ten to choose from. Freedom is never being flogged, although no generation of Russians has yet avoided a flogging. Russians don't understand freedom, they need the Cossack and the whip.

For the children: Freedom is love; inner freedom is an absolute value. Freedom is when you're not afraid of your own desires; having lots of money so that you'll have everything; it's when you can live without having to think about freedom. Freedom is normal.

I'm searching for a language. People speak many different languages: There's the one they use with children, another one for love. There's the language we use to talk to ourselves, for our internal monologues. On the street, at work, while traveling—everywhere you go, you'll hear something different, and it's not just the words, there's something else, too. There's even a difference between the way people speak in the morning and how they speak at night. What happens between two people at night vanishes from history without a trace. We're accustomed to looking at the history of people by day, while suicide is a nighttime state, when a person wavers on the edge between being and non-being. Waking and sleep. I want to understand suicide with the rigor of a person in daytime. Someone once asked me: "Are you worried that you're going to like it?"

We were driving through the Smolensk region when we stopped in front of a store in one of the villages. What familiar faces (I grew up in a village), how beautiful, how good—and what a humiliating, impoverished life they lead! We struck up a conversation. "You want to know about freedom? Have a look around our general store. There's vodka, any kind you like: Standard, Gorbachev, Putinka; heaps of cold cuts and cheese and fish. We even have bananas. What more freedom could you ask for? It's enough for us."

"Did they give you any land?"

"Who's gonna break their back working the land? You want it, you take it. The only guy who took it was Tough Vasya. His youngest kid is eight years old and he's already out there next to his father at the plowtail. If he hires you for a job, watch out—you can't steal, you can't nap. He's a total fascist!"

In "The Legend of the Grand Inquisitor," Dostoevsky stages a debate about freedom. Namely, about the struggle, torment, and tragedy of freedom: "What's the point of delving into that damn good and evil when the cost is so high?" People are constantly forced to choose between having freedom and having success and stability; freedom with suffering or happiness without freedom. The majority choose the latter.

The Grand Inquisitor tells Christ, who has returned to Earth:

Why have You come here to interfere with our affairs? For You have come to interfere with us, and You know it.

For all of Your respect for man, You've acted as though You have ceased to have any compassion for him because You have asked too much of him . . . If You respected him less, You would have asked for less, and this would have been closer to love, for it would have lightened his burden. He is weak and base . . . Is a weak soul to blame for not having the strength to accept such terrible gifts?

There is no more pressing or torturous task for man, having found himself free, than to seek out someone to bow down to as soon as he can . . . someone on whom to bestow that gift of freedom with which this unhappy creature was born . . .

In the nineties . . . yes, we were ecstatic; there's no way back to that naïveté. We thought that the choice had been made and that communism had been defeated forever. But it was only the beginning . . .

Twenty years have gone by . . . "Don't try to scare us with your socialism," children tell their parents.

From a conversation with a university professor: "At the end of the nineties, my students would laugh when I told them stories about the Soviet Union. They were sure that a new future awaited them. Now it's a different story . . . Today's students have truly seen and felt capitalism: the inequality, the poverty, the shameless wealth. They've witnessed the lives of their parents, who never got anything out of the plundering of our country. And they're oriented toward radicalism. They dream of their own revolution, they wear red T-shirts with pictures of Lenin and Che Guevara."

There's a new demand for everything Soviet. For the cult of Stalin. Half of the people between the ages of nineteen and thirty consider Stalin an "unrivaled political figure." A new cult of Stalin, in a country where he murdered at least as many people as Hitler?! Everything Soviet is back in style. "Soviet-style cafés" with Soviet names and Soviet dishes. "Soviet" candy and "Soviet" salami, their taste and smell all too familiar from childhood. And of course, "Soviet" vodka. There are dozens of Soviet-themed TV shows, scores of websites devoted to Soviet nostalgia. You can visit Stalin's camps—Solovki, Magadan—as a tourist. The advertisements promise that for the full effect, they'll give you a camp uniform and a pickaxe. They'll show you the newly restored barracks. Afterward, there will be fishing . . .

Old-fashioned ideas are back in style: the Great Empire, the "iron hand," the "special Russian path." They brought back the Soviet national anthem; there's a new Komsomol, only now it's called Nashi;* there's a ruling party, and it runs the country by the Communist Party playbook; the Russian president is just as powerful as the general secretary used to be, which is to say he has absolute power. Instead of Marxism-Leninism, there's Russian Orthodoxy . . .

On the eve of the 1917 Revolution, Alexander Grin wrote, "And the future seems to have stopped standing in its proper place." Now, a hundred years later, the future is, once again, not where it ought to be. Our time comes to us secondhand.

The barricades are a dangerous place for an artist. They're a trap. They ruin your vision, narrow your pupils, drain the world of its true colors. On the barricades, everything is black and white. You can't see individuals, all you see are black dots: targets. I've spent my entire life on the barricades, and I would like to walk away from them. I want to learn how to enjoy life. To get back my normal vision. But today, tens of thousands of people are once again taking to the streets. They're taking each other by the hand and tying white ribbons onto their jackets—a symbol of rebirth and light. I'm with them.

    I recently saw some young men in T-shirts with hammers and sickles and portraits of Lenin on them. Do they know what communism is?

---

* The youth organization associated with Putin's political party, United Russia; the name means "Our People."

PART ONE

◆

THE CONSOLATION OF APOCALYPSE

SNATCHES OF STREET NOISE AND

KITCHEN CONVERSATIONS

(1991–2001)

◆

ON IVANUSHKA THE FOOL AND
THE MAGIC GOLDFISH

—What have I learned? I learned that the heroes of one era aren't likely to be the heroes of the next. Except Ivanushka the Fool. And Emelya. The beloved heroes of Russian folklore. Our stories are all about good fortune and strokes of luck; divine intervention that makes everything fall right into our laps. Having it all without having to get up from your bed on the stove.* The stove will cook the *bliny,* the magic goldfish will grant your every wish. I want this and I want that . . . I want the fair Tsarevna! I want to live in a different kingdom, where the rivers run with milk and their banks are heaped with jam . . . We're dreamers, of course. Our souls strain and suffer, but not much gets done—there's no strength left over after all that ardor. Nothing ever gets done. The mysterious Russian soul . . . Everyone wants to understand it. They read Dostoevsky: What's behind that soul of theirs? Well, behind our soul there's just more soul. We like to have a chat in the kitchen, read a book. "Reader" is our primary occupation. "Viewer." All the while, we consider ourselves a special, exceptional people even though there are no grounds for this besides our oil and natural gas. On one hand, this is what stands in the way of progress; on the other hand, it provides something like meaning. Russia always seems to be on the verge of giving rise to something important, demonstrating something completely extraordinary to the world. The chosen people. The special Russian path. Our country is full of Oblomovs,† lying around on their couches, awaiting miracles. There are no Stoltzes. The industrious, savvy Stoltzes are despised for chopping down the beloved birch grove, the cherry orchard. They build their factories, make money . . . They're foreign to us . . .

* The Russian stove is a large masonry stove that, to this day, serves as the central and most important feature of rural Russian houses. Stoves are used not only for cooking and heating, they are large enough to accommodate people sleeping on top of them—and they are always the warmest place in the house.
† Hero of the eponymous novel written by Ivan Goncharov published in 1859, Oblomov is an idle aristocrat whose extreme laziness and apathy gave rise to the expression "oblomovism." Stoltz, his friend, is an active and energetic young man.

—The Russian kitchen . . . The pitiful Khrushchyovka* kitchen-
ette, nine to twelve square meters (if you're lucky!), and on the other
side of a flimsy wall, the toilet. Your typical Soviet floorplan. Onions
sprouting in old mayonnaise jars on the windowsill and a potted aloe
for fighting colds. For us, the kitchen is not just where we cook, it's a
dining room, a guest room, an office, a soapbox. A space for group
therapy sessions. In the nineteenth century, all of Russian culture was
concentrated on aristocratic estates; in the twentieth century, it lived
on in our kitchens. That's where perestroika really took place. 1960s
dissident life is the kitchen life. Thanks, Khrushchev! He's the one
who led us out of the communal apartments; under his rule, we got
our own private kitchens where we could criticize the government and,
most importantly, not be afraid, because in the kitchen you were always among friends. It's where ideas were whipped up from scratch,
fantastical projects concocted. We made jokes—it was a golden age
for jokes! "A communist is someone who's read Marx, an anticommunist is someone who's understood him." We grew up in kitchens, and
our children did, too; they listened to Galich and Okudzhava along
with us. We played Vysotsky,† tuned in to illegal BBC broadcasts. We
talked about everything: how shitty things were, the meaning of life,
whether everyone could all be happy. I remember a funny story . . .
We'd stayed up past midnight, and our daughter, she was twelve, had
fallen asleep on the kitchen couch. We'd gotten into some heated argument, and suddenly she started yelling at us in her sleep: "Enough
about politics! Again with your Sakharov, Solzhenitsyn, and Stalin!"
[*Laughs.*]

Endlessly drinking tea. Coffee. Vodka. In the seventies, we had
Cuban rum. Everyone was in love with Fidel! With the Cuban revolution. Che in his beret. A Hollywood star! We talked nonstop, afraid
that they were listening in, thinking they must be listening. There'd
always be someone who'd halt in mid-conversation and point to the
ceiling light or the power outlet with a little grin, "Did you hear that,
Comrade Lieutenant?" It felt a little dangerous, a little bit like a game.

---

* Khrushchyovkas are cheap, prefabricated concrete panel or brick apartment blocks
that started being built in the 1950s, during the administration of their namesake,
Nikita Khrushchev. Though they are cramped and shoddy, they provided many families with their first-ever private apartments.
† Alexander Galich (1918–1977), Bulat Okudzhava (1924–1997), and Vladimir Vysotsky (1938–1990) were singer-songwriters who rose to popularity in the 1960s, primarily among the Soviet intelligentsia. Their songs were known for being anti-Soviet.

We got a certain satisfaction out of leading these double lives. A tiny handful of people resisted openly, but many more of us were "kitchen dissidents," going about our daily lives with our fingers crossed behind our backs . . .

—Today, it's shameful being poor and unathletic—it's a sign that you're not making it. I come from the generation of janitors and security guards. Getting a job like that was a form of internal emigration. You lived your life and didn't pay any attention to what was going on around you, like it was all just the view out the window. My wife and I graduated from the Philosophy Faculty of St. Petersburg (back then, it was Leningrad) State University, then she got a job as a janitor, and I was a stoker in a boiler plant. You'd work one twenty-four-hour shift and then get two days off. Back then, an engineer made 130 rubles a month, while in the boiler room, I was getting 90, which is to say that if you were willing to give up 40 rubles a month, you could buy yourself absolute freedom. We read, we went through tons of books. We talked. We thought that we were coming up with new ideas. We dreamt of revolution, but we were scared we'd never live to see it. In reality, we were completely sheltered, we didn't know a thing about what was actually going on in the world. We were like houseplants. We made everything up, and, as it later turned out, everything we thought we knew was nothing but figments of our imaginations: the West. Capitalism. The Russian people. We lived in a world of mirages. The Russia of our books and kitchens never existed. It was all in our heads.

With perestroika, everything came crashing down. Capitalism descended . . . 90 rubles became 10 dollars. It wasn't enough to live on anymore. We stepped out of our kitchens and onto the streets, where we soon discovered that we hadn't had any ideas after all—that whole time, we'd just been talking. Completely new people appeared, these young guys in gold rings and magenta blazers. There were new rules: If you have money, you count—no money, you're nothing. Who cares if you've read all of Hegel? "Humanities" started sounding like a disease. "All you people are capable of is carrying around a volume of Mandelstam."* Many unfamiliar horizons unfurled before us. The intelligentsia grew calamitously poor. On weekends, at the park by our

---

* Osip Mandelstam (1891–1938) was a Russian and Soviet poet and essayist who died in the gulag.

house, Hare Krishnas would set up a mobile kitchen serving soup and something simple for a second course. The line of the dignified elderly was so long, just thinking about it is enough to give you a lump in your throat. Some of them hid their faces. By then, we'd had two children. We were literally starving. My wife and I became peddlers. We'd pick up four or six cases of ice cream at the factory and take them down to the market, to the most crowded spot. We had no refrigeration, so a few hours in, all the ice cream would be melting. At that point, we'd give it away to hungry kids. They were so happy! My wife did the selling. I'd deliver it, haul it—I was willing to do anything but actually make sales. It felt uncomfortable for a long time.

There was a time when I'd often reminisce about our kitchen days . . . There was so much love! What women! Those women hated the rich. You couldn't buy them. Today, no one has time for feelings, they're all out making money. The discovery of money hit us like an atom bomb . . .

ON HOW WE FELL IN AND THEN
OUT OF LOVE WITH GORBY

—The Gorbachev era . . . Huge crowds of people with radiant faces. Freedom! It was the air we breathed. Everyone hungrily devoured the newspapers. It was a time of great hope—at any moment, we might find ourselves in paradise. Democracy was an exotic beast. Like madmen, we'd run around to every rally: Now we'd learn the truth about Stalin, the gulag. We'd read Anatoly Rybakov's forbidden *Children of the Arbat** and other good books; finally, we'd all become democrats. How wrong we were! A single message rang out from every loudspeaker: Hurry! Hurry! Read! Listen! Not everyone was prepared for all this. Most people were not anti-Soviet; they only wanted to live well. They really wanted blue jeans, VCRs, and most of all, cars. Nice clothes and good food. When I came home with a copy of *The Gulag Archipelago,* my mother was horrified. "If you don't get that book out of my house immediately, I'm kicking you out." Before the war, my grandmother's husband had been shot, but she would say, "I don't feel sorry for Vaska. They were right to arrest him. He had a big mouth."

* Anatoly Rybakov (1911–1998) was a Soviet writer most famous for his anti-Stalinist *Children of the Arbat* tetralogy.

"Grandma, why didn't you tell me before?" I'd ask her. "I hope that my life dies along with me so none of you will have to suffer the consequences." That's how our parents lived, and their parents before them. Then it was all bulldozed over. Perestroika wasn't created by the people, it was created by a single person: Gorbachev. Gorbachev and a handful of intellectuals . . .

—Gorbachev is an American secret agent . . . a freemason . . . He betrayed communism. "All communists to the trash heap, all Komsomol members to the dump!" I hate Gorbachev because he stole my Motherland. I treasure my Soviet passport like it's my most precious possession. Yes, we stood in line for discolored chicken and rotting potatoes, but it was our Motherland. I loved it. You lived in a third world country with missiles, but for me, it was a great nation. The West has always seen Russia as an enemy, a looming threat. It's a thorn in their side. Nobody wants a strong Russia, with or without the communists. The world sees us as a storehouse that they can raid for oil, natural gas, timber, and base metals. We trade our oil for underpants. But we used to be a civilization without rags and junk. The Soviet civilization! Someone felt the need to put an end to it. The CIA . . . We're already being controlled by the Americans . . . They must have paid Gorbachev a tidy sum. Sooner or later, he'll see his day in court. I just hope that that Judas lives to feel the brunt of his nation's rage. I would gladly take him out to the Butovo Firing Range* and shoot him in the back of the skull myself. [*Slams his fist down on the table.*] Happiness is here, huh? Sure, there's salami and bananas. We're rolling around in shit and eating foreign food. Instead of a Motherland, we live in a huge supermarket. If this is freedom, I don't need it. To hell with it! The people are on their knees. We're a nation of slaves. Slaves! Under communism, in the words of Lenin, the cook ran the state; workers, dairymaids, and weavers were in charge. Now our parliament is lousy with criminals. Dollar-rich millionaires. They should all be in prison, not parliament. They really duped us with their perestroika!

I was born in the USSR, and I liked it there. My father was a communist. He taught me how to read with *Pravda*. Every holiday, we'd go to the parades. With tears in our eyes. I was a Young Pioneer, I wore

---

* Between 1936 and 1953, over twenty thousand political prisoners were executed on the Butovo Firing Range as victims of Stalin's purges. It is located just outside of Moscow.

the red kerchief around my neck. Then Gorbachev came, and I never got the chance to join the Komsomol, which I'm still sad about. I'm a *sovok*, huh? And my parents are *sovoks*, and my grandparents, too? My grandfather the *sovok* died defending Moscow in '41 . . . My *sovok* grandmother fought with the partisans . . . The liberals are working off their piece of the pie. They want us to think of our history as a black hole. I hate them all: gorbachev, shevardnadze, yakovlev*— don't capitalize their names, that's how much I hate them all. I don't want to live in America, I want to live in the USSR . . .

—Those were wonderful, naïve years . . . We had faith in Gorbachev like we'll never have faith in anyone ever again. Many Russians were returning from emigration, coming back to their Motherland. There was so much joy in the air! We thought that we'd tear down these barracks and build something new in their place. I got my degree from the Philology Faculty of Moscow State University and started graduate school. I dreamed of working in academia. In those years, I idolized Averintsev,† all of enlightened Moscow sat in on his lectures. We would meet and reinforce one another's delusions that soon, we would find ourselves in a completely different country, and that this was what we were fighting for. I was very surprised when I learned that one of my classmates was moving to Israel. "Aren't you sorry to leave at a time like this? Things are just starting to get good."

The more they shouted and wrote, "Freedom! Freedom!" the faster not only the cheese and salami but also the salt and sugar disappeared from the shelves. Stores stood empty. It was very scary. You could only buy things with ration cards, as though we were at war. Grandma was the one who saved us, she'd spend her days running around the city making sure we got our ration cards' worth. Our whole balcony was covered in detergent, the bedroom was full of sacks of sugar and grain. When they distributed vouchers for socks, my father broke down in

---

* As the minister of foreign affairs from 1985 to 1991, Eduard Shevardnadze (1928–2014) was responsible for many important foreign policy decisions in Gorbachev's administration. He was the president of Georgia from 1992 to 2003. Alexander Yakovlev (1923–2005) was a Soviet politician and historian, sometimes called the "godfather of glasnost." He was one of the main theoreticians behind perestroika.
† Sergey Averintsev (1937–2004) was a philologist, cultural historian, translator, poet, and specialist on antiquity and Byzantine culture. He lectured on Russian spiritual traditions.

tears: "This is the end of the USSR." He felt it coming . . . My father worked in the construction bureau of a munitions factory, he'd worked on missiles; he was crazy about his job. He had two graduate degrees. Then suddenly, instead of missiles, the factory started putting out washing machines and vacuum cleaners. Papa was laid off. He and my mother had been fervent participants in perestroika: They painted posters, distributed flyers, and here's where it got them . . . They were lost. They couldn't believe that this was what freedom looked like. It was impossible for them to come to terms with it. The streets were already filling with cries of "Gorbachev's not worth a pin, long live Yeltsin!" People were carrying around portraits of Brezhnev covered in medals next to Gorbachev covered in ration cards. It was the beginning of the reign of Yeltsin: Gaidar's reforms* and all of that "buy and sell" I can't stand. In order to survive, I had to start traveling to Poland with big bags of light bulbs and children's toys. The train car would be full of teachers, engineers, doctors . . . all of them with bags and sacks. We'd stay up all night talking about *Doctor Zhivago* . . . Shatrov's plays† . . . It was like we were still in a Moscow kitchen.

When I think about my friends from university . . . All of us ended up as anything but philologists: senior executives at advertising agencies, bank tellers, shuttle traders . . . I work at a real estate agency for a woman who comes from the country, a former Komsomol worker. Who owns the businesses today? The mansions on Cyprus and in Miami? The former Party *nomenklatura*.‡ That's where we should look for the party's money . . . As for our leaders, the dissidents of the sixties . . . they'd tasted blood during the war, but they were as naïve as little kids . . . We should have spent our days and nights out on the squares, fighting with all our might to get what we had come for—a Nuremberg trial for the CPSU. We all went home too early. The black marketeers and money changers took power. Contrary to what Marx

---

* Yegor Gaidar (1956–2009) was an economist and the author of a series of controversial "shock therapy" reforms that defined the early post-Soviet Russian economy. As a result of these reforms, which entailed the privatization of all major Soviet industries, most of the largest formerly Soviet enterprises ended up in the hands of a small group of Russian executives who would come to be known as the Russian oligarchs. At the same time, due to reform-related hyperinflation, most Russians' assets and savings were devalued wholesale, landing a large percentage of the population in poverty overnight. Many Russians blame the ensuing high crime rates and low quality of life on Gaidar's reforms.
† Mikhail Shatrov (1932–2010) was a Soviet dissident playwright.
‡ The *nomenklatura* refers to the Soviet government elite.

predicted, after socialism, we're building capitalism. [*Silence.*] But I'm grateful I lived through that era. Communism fell! And that's it, it's gone for good. We live in a different world and see it through different eyes. I'll never forget how freely we breathed in those days . . .

ON FALLING IN LOVE WITH TANKS
UNDER YOUR WINDOWS

—I was so in love, I couldn't think about anything else. It was my entire universe. Then one morning my mother wakes me up: "There are tanks outside! I think there's been an uprising!" Still asleep, I tell her, "Mama, they're just doing training exercises." But oh no! There really were tanks directly outside our windows; I'd never seen tanks that up close before. On TV, they were playing *Swan Lake* . . . My mother's friend ran over, she was very anxious that she hadn't paid her Party dues in several months. She said that at the school where she worked she had stashed a bust of Lenin in the storeroom—what should she do with it now? The lines were drawn immediately: You couldn't do this and you couldn't do that. On the radio, they declared a state of emergency. My mother's friend shuddered at every word: "My God! My God!" My father spat at the television . . .

I called Oleg . . . "Are we going to the White House?"* "Let's go!" So I put on my Gorbachev pin and made some sandwiches. People were quiet on the Metro, everyone anticipated tragedy. Everywhere you looked there were tanks . . . and more tanks . . . The drivers weren't murderers, they were just frightened kids with guilty looks on their faces. Old ladies would feed them hardboiled eggs and *bliny*. What a relief it was to see tens of thousands of people in front of the White House! Everyone was in excellent spirits. We felt capable of anything and everything. We chanted, "Yeltsin! Yeltsin! Yeltsin!" Self-defense squadrons were already forming. They would only let the young join, which the old people really resented. I remember one old man was very upset: "The communists stole my life from me! Let me at least have a beautiful death!" "Step aside, Granddad . . ." Today,

---

* The Russian White House, originally known as the House of the Soviets, is the primary Russian government office and serves as the official office of the Russian prime minister. In 1991 and 1993, it was a locus of protest: first during the 1991 coup d'état and then, in 1993, during the Russian constitutional crisis, when the building was stormed.

they accuse us of fighting for capitalism . . . That's not true! I was defending socialism, but some other kind, not the Soviet kind—that's what I was standing up for! Or at least that's what I thought. It's what we all thought . . . Three days later, when the tanks were rolling out of Moscow, they were different, kinder tanks. Victory! And we kissed and kissed . . .

I'm in my friends' kitchen in Moscow. There are a lot of people here: friends and relatives visiting from the country. We remembered that tomorrow is the anniversary of the August putsch.

—Tomorrow's a holiday . . .
   —What's there to celebrate? It's a tragedy. The people lost.
   —They buried Sovietdom to the music of Tchaikovsky.
   —The first thing I did was get cash and run out to the shops. I knew that no matter what happened, the prices were going up.
   —We got so excited—they're kicking Gorby out! By then, we were pretty fed up with that windbag.
   —The revolution was nothing but a spectacle. A play they put on for the people. I remember the total indifference of anyone you talked to. Everyone was just waiting it out.
   —I called in sick to work and went out to make the revolution happen. I brought every knife I had in the house. I realized that this was war . . . and that I needed weapons . . .
   —I supported communism! Everyone in our family is a communist. Instead of lullabies, my mother would sing us songs of the Revolution. Now she sings them to her grandchildren. "Are you nuts?" I ask her. She replies, "I don't know any other songs." And Grandpa was a Bolshevik . . . And Grandma too . . .
   —Now you're going to go and say that communism was nothing but a pretty little fairy tale. My father's parents disappeared in the Mordovian camps.
   —I went to the White House with my parents. My father said, "Let's go, or else we'll never have salami or good books." We ripped out the cobblestones and built barricades out of them.
   —Today, the people have come to their senses. Attitudes toward the Communists are changing. You don't have to hide it anymore . . . I worked at the Komsomol District Committee. On the first day, I

took all the Komsomol membership cards, unused stationery, and pins home and hid them in the basement. There was so much stuff that later on, we had nowhere to store the potatoes. I didn't know what I needed it all for, but I imagined them coming to shut us down and destroying everything. To me, these were precious symbols.

—We could have ended up killing each other—God protected us!

—Our daughter was giving birth. I went to see her, but all she wanted to know was, "Is there going to be a revolution, Mama? Is civil war breaking out?"

—I graduated from military academy and served in Moscow. If they had given us the orders to arrest someone, we wouldn't have even thought twice, we'd have done it. Many of us would have even relished following those orders. We were sick of all the turmoil. Everything used to be cut and dried, things were done by the book. There was order. That's how army people like to live. In fact, that's how everyone likes to live.

—I'm afraid of freedom, it feels like some drunk guy could show up and burn down my dacha at any moment.

—What are we doing arguing about ideas, friends? Life's too short. Let's drink!

August 19, 2001, the tenth anniversary of the August putsch. I'm in Irkutsk, the capital of Siberia, where I do brief interviews with people on the street.

Question: What would have happened if the putschists had won?
     Answers:
—They would have saved a great country from ruin.

—Look at China, where the Communists are still in power. China has developed into the second-largest economy in the world . . .

—Gorbachev and Yeltsin would have been put on trial for betraying the Motherland.

—They would have drowned the country in blood and filled the camps to capacity.

—They wouldn't have betrayed socialism. We wouldn't have been split into rich and poor.

—There wouldn't have been a war in Chechnya.

—No one would have ever dared to say that the Americans defeated Hitler.

—I stood in front of the White House myself. I feel like I was cheated.

—What would have happened if they'd pulled off the putsch? Well, when you think about it, they did! They may have taken down the Iron Felix,* but the Lubyanka† is right where it always was. We're building capitalism under the leadership of the KGB.

—My life wouldn't have been any different . . .

HOW STUFF BECAME WORTH AS MUCH AS WORDS AND IDEAS

—The world shattered into dozens of colorful little pieces. We were so terribly eager for the gray Soviet everyday to turn into a scene from an American movie! Not many people reflected on how we'd rallied in front of the White House. Those three days may have shaken the world, but we remained unshaken . . . Two thousand people will go out and demonstrate, and the rest will ride past them, looking at them like they're idiots. We drank a lot, we always do, but back then, we drank even more. Society stopped dead in its tracks: Where to next? Will there be capitalism, or maybe some good kind of socialism? Capitalists are fat and scary—that's what they'd been telling us since we were little kids . . . [*She laughs.*]

Our country was suddenly covered in banks and billboards. A new breed of goods appeared. Instead of crummy boots and frumpy dresses, we finally got the stuff we'd always dreamed of: blue jeans, winter coats, lingerie, decent dishware . . . Everything bright and beautiful. Our old Soviet stuff was gray, ascetic, and looked as if it

---

* Felix Dzerzhinsky (1877–1926), also known as Iron Felix, was responsible for creating and developing the Soviet secret police. The "Iron Felix" also refers to a gargantuan statue of Dzerzhinsky that stood on Lubyanka Square in Moscow from 1958 to 1991, when it was removed following the failed coup. Many statues of Dzerzhinsky remain standing throughout the former Soviet Union, where towns and streets and squares continue to bear his name.

† The Lubyanka is an infamous Moscow prison that also served as the KGB headquarters in Soviet times. Its name is synonymous with the horrors perpetrated by the Soviet secret police, especially during Stalin's purges of the 1930s. Today, it houses the directorate of the Federal Security Bureau of the Russian Federation, the FSB.

had been manufactured in wartime. The libraries and theaters stood empty. Markets and stores had taken their place. Everyone decided that they wanted to be happy and they wanted it now. We were all like children discovering a new world . . . Eventually, we stopped fainting at supermarkets . . . A guy I know went into business. He told me about how the first time he shipped in a thousand cans of instant coffee, people bought them up in a matter of days. He used the profits to buy a hundred vacuum cleaners, and those went just as quickly. Coats, sweaters, this and that—if you're selling, they're buying! Everyone was making themselves over, getting a whole new wardrobe. New furniture and appliances. Remodeling their dachas . . . They wanted pretty little fences and charming roofs . . . When my friends and I start remembering this stuff, we die laughing . . . Savages! We were completely impoverished people. We had to relearn how to live from scratch. In Soviet times, you were allowed to have a lot of books but not an expensive car or house. We had to learn how to dress, cook good food, drink juice and eat yogurt in the morning . . . Before, I had hated money, I didn't know what it was. My family never talked about it—it was considered shameful. We grew up in a country where money essentially did not exist. Like everyone else, I would get my 120 rubles a month and that had been enough. Money appeared with perestroika. With Gaidar. Real money. Instead of "Our Future is Communism," the signs began exclaiming, "Buy now!" If you want to, you can travel. See Paris . . . Spain . . . fiesta . . . bullfighting. . . . When I read about it in Hemingway, I'd been sure that I'd never see any of it with my own eyes. Back then, books replaced life . . . This was the end of our nightly kitchen vigils and the beginning of making money then making more money on the side. Money became synonymous with freedom. Everyone was completely preoccupied with it. The strongest and most aggressive started doing business. We forgot all about Lenin and Stalin. And that's what saved us from another civil war with Reds on the one side and Whites on the other. Friends and foes. Instead of blood, there was all this new stuff . . . Life! We chose the beautiful life. No one wanted to die beautifully anymore, everyone wanted to live beautifully instead. The only problem was that there wasn't really enough to go around . . .

—In Soviet times, the word had a holy, magical significance. Out of inertia, the intelligentsia still sat in their kitchens discussing Pasternak, making soup without putting down their Astafiev and Bykov,* but all the while, life kept demonstrating that none of that mattered anymore. Words no longer meant anything. In 1991, our mother came down with acute pneumonia and had to be hospitalized. She came home a hero, having spent her convalescence talking away in the ward. She told everyone about Stalin, the assassination of Kirov, Bukharin† . . . People were prepared to listen to her day and night. In those days, everyone wanted to have their eyes opened. She was recently in the hospital again, but this time, she never said a word. It's only been five years, but things are completely different now. Instead of her, the star of the ward was the wife of a big-time businessman. Her stories had everyone hypnotized . . . She talked about their house—three hundred square meters! All of their help: a cook, a nanny, a driver, a gardener . . . Their vacations to Europe—the museums are nice, of course, but you should see the boutiques! Those boutiques! This ring has this many carats, this one has that many . . . And her pendants, and gold clip-on earrings . . . It was standing room only! Nothing about the gulag or anything of the kind. That's all in the past. What's the point of arguing with old people?

Out of habit, I would go into the used bookstore where the full two-hundred-volume sets of the World Classics Library and Library of Adventures now stood calmly, not flying off the shelves. Those orange bindings, the books that had once driven me mad. I'd stare at their spines and linger, inhaling their smell. Mountains of books! The intelligentsia were selling off their libraries. People had grown poor, of course, but it wasn't just for the spare cash—ultimately books had disappointed them. People were disillusioned. It became rude to ask, "What are you reading?" Too much about our lives had changed, and these weren't things that you could read about in books. Russian novels don't teach you how to become successful. How to get rich . . . Oblomov lies on his couch, Chekhov's protagonists drink tea and complain about their lives . . . [*She falls silent.*] There's a famous Chinese curse: "May you live in interesting times." Few of us remained

---

* Viktor Astafiev (1924—2001) and Vasil Bykov (1924—2003) were both prominent Soviet novelists who wrote candidly about social realities and war.
† Sergey Kirov (1886—1934) was an early Bolshevik leader whose assassination, believed by many to have been ordered by Stalin, served as one of the pretexts for the Great Purge that followed. Nikolai Bukharin (1888—1938) was a Bolshevik revolutionary who worked closely with Lenin and Trotsky. He was executed by Stalin, who saw him as a rival, as part of the Great Purge.

unchanged. Decent people seem to have disappeared. Now it's teeth and elbows everywhere . . .

—You want to talk about the nineties . . . I wouldn't call it a beautiful time, I'd say it was revolting. People's minds flipped 180 degrees. Some couldn't handle it, they went crazy, the psych wards were overflowing. I visited a friend of mine in one of them. One guy was screaming, "I'm Stalin! I'm Stalin!" while another one screamed, "I'm Berezovsky! I'm Berezovsky!" The whole ward was filled with these Stalins and Berezovskys.* Outside, there was always gunfire in the streets. A huge number of people were killed. Shootouts every day. You have to make it, you have to snatch it—get your hands on it before anyone else can snag it! Some people went broke, others went to jail. Down from the throne, straight into the gutter. On the other hand, it was cool to see all that happening right before your eyes . . .

People were lining up at the banks eager to try their hands at business: They wanted to open bakeries, sell electronics . . . I stood in one of those lines myself. It surprised me how many of us were there. Some woman in a knit beret, a boy in a tracksuit, this big guy who looked like he might have done time . . . For over seventy years, they'd told us that money wasn't happiness, that the best things in life were free. Like love, for example. But the minute someone from the podium said "Sell and prosper!" all of that went out the window. Everyone forgot the Soviet books. These people were nothing like the ones I'd been staying up all night with, strumming the guitar. I barely knew three chords. The only thing they had in common with the kitchen folk was that they were also sick of the red calico flags and all that flotsam: the Komsomol meetings, political literacy classes. Socialism had treated the people like they were dummies . . .

I know full well what it means to dream. My whole childhood, I begged for a bicycle, and I never did get one. We were too poor. In school, I sold blue jeans on the side; in college, it was Soviet war uniforms and memorabilia. Foreigners loved that stuff. Your run-of-the-mill black market goods. In Soviet times, you could get three to five years for that if they caught you. My father would chase me around the house with his belt, screaming, "You profiteer! I spilled blood defending Moscow only to raise a little shithead!" Yesterday, it was

---

* Boris Berezovsky (1946–2013) was one of the first Russian oligarchs.

crime—today, it's business. You buy nails in one place, heel caps some-
place else, put them together in a plastic bag and sell them as a set, like
new. That's how you bring home the bacon. I was making sure that we
always had a full fridge while my parents kept waiting for them to
come for me. [*He laughs.*] I sold household appliances. Pressure cook-
ers, steamers. I would go to Germany and haul back truckloads of
that stuff. And it would all sell out . . . I kept a computer box full of
cash in my office—that was the only way I could feel like I really had
money. You keep taking bills out of it, but there's always more inside.
At a certain point, I felt like I'd already bought everything I'd ever
wanted: wheels, an apartment . . . a Rolex . . . I remember the intoxi-
cation . . . You can make all of your dreams come true, all of your secret fantasies. I learned a lot about myself: First of all, I have bad taste;
second of all, I'm completely neurotic. I'm just no good with money. I
didn't know that you're supposed to put big money to work, that it
can't just lie there. Money is a test, like power or love . . . I had this
dream . . . so I went to Monaco. Lost big at a casino in Monte Carlo,
it was really a lot of money. Things were slipping away from me . . . I'd
become the slave of my box. Is there money in there or not? How
much? There had to keep being more and more. I lost interest in everything that I used to be interested in. Politics, protests . . . Sakharov
died. I went to pay my respects. A hundred thousand people gathered
at his funeral . . . Everybody was weeping, and I wept, too. The other
day, I read about him in the paper, "a great Russian holy fool died,"
and I thought to myself that he probably died just in time. Solzhenitsyn came back from America, and everyone fell at his feet. But he
didn't understand us, and we didn't understand him. He was a foreigner. He'd returned to Russia but found Chicago in its place . . .

What would I have been if not for perestroika? An engineer with a
pathetic salary. [*He laughs.*] Now I own an optometrist's office. A few
hundred people, counting the children, grandmothers, grandfathers,
all depend on me. You, you delve into yourselves, you reflect on your
lives . . . I don't have that problem. I work day and night. I bought all
new, cutting-edge equipment, sent my doctors to France for training.
But I'm not an altruist, I make good money. I'm a self-made man. I
started out with three hundred dollars in my pocket . . . If you saw
what my first business partners looked like, you'd pass out from fear.
Gorillas! With ferocious stares! They're not around anymore, those
guys went extinct like the dinosaurs. I used wear a bulletproof vest;
I've been shot at. If someone eats worse salami than I do, I don't care.

All of you wanted capitalism. You dreamt of it! Don't go crying now
that you've been lied to . . .

ON HOW WE GREW UP AMONG VICTIMS
AND EXECUTIONERS

—One night we were walking home from the movies and stumbled on
a man lying in a pool of blood. There was a bullet hole in the back of
his trench coat and a cop standing over him. That was the first time I'd
ever seen someone who'd been murdered. Pretty soon, it became a familiar sight. We live in a big building with twenty entrances. Every
morning, they'd find another body in the courtyard—eventually, we
stopped being shocked. Real capitalism was here. With blood. I
thought that I'd be disturbed, but I wasn't. After Stalin, we have a different relationship to murder. We remember how our people had killed
their own . . . the mass murder of people who didn't understand why
they were being killed . . . It's stayed with us, it's part of our lives. We
grew up among victims and executioners. For us, living together is
normal. There's no line between peacetime and wartime, we're always
at war. Turn on the TV, everyone's speaking in prison camp slang:
the politicians, the businessmen, even the president; kickbacks, bribes,
siphoning . . . Human life—you can just spit and rub someone out.
Just like in prison . . .

—Why didn't we put Stalin on trial? I'll tell you why . . . In order
to condemn Stalin, you'd have to condemn your friends and relatives
along with him. The people closest to you. I'll tell you about my own
family. My father was arrested in 1937 and, thank God, came back
after doing ten years in the camps. He returned eager to live. He himself was amazed that he still wanted to after everything that he'd seen.
This wasn't the case with everyone, not by a long shot . . . My generation grew up with fathers who'd either returned from the camps or the
war. The only thing they could tell us about was violence. Death. They
rarely laughed and were mostly silent. They drank . . . and drank . . .
until they finally drank themselves to death. The other option . . . the
people who were never arrested spent their whole lives fearing arrest.
This wouldn't be for a month or two, it would go on for years—years!
And if they didn't get time, they'd wonder, "Why did they arrest everybody but me? What am I doing wrong?" They could put you in

prison or they could put you to work for the NKVD* . . . The party requests, the party commands. It's not a pleasant choice to have to make, but many were forced to make it. As for the executioners . . . the everyday ones, not the monsters . . . our neighbor Yuri turned out to have been the one who informed on my father. For nothing, as my mother would say. I was seven. Yuri would take me and his kids fishing and horseback riding. He'd mend our fence. You end up with a completely different picture of what an executioner is like—just a regular person, even a decent one . . . a normal guy . . . They arrested my father, then a few months later, they took his brother. When Yeltsin came to power, I got a copy of his file, which included several informants' reports. It turned out that one of them had been written by Aunt Olga . . . his niece. A beautiful woman, full of joy . . . a good singer . . . By the time I found out, she was already old. I asked her, "Aunt Olga, tell me about 1937." "That was the happiest year of my life. I was in love." My father's brother never returned. Vanished. We still don't know whether it was in jail or the camps. It was hard for me, but I asked her the question that had been tormenting me, "Aunt Olga, why did you do it?" "Show me an honest person who survived Stalin's time." [*He is silent.*] Then there was Uncle Pavel who served in the NKVD in Siberia . . . When it comes down to it, there is no such thing as chemically pure evil. It's not just Stalin and Beria,† it's also our neighbor Yuri and beautiful Aunt Olga . . ."

It's May 1. On this day, communists march through the streets of Moscow by the thousands. The capital "reddens" once again, filling with red flags, red balloons, and red T-shirts with hammers and sickles. Portraits of Lenin and Stalin soar over the crowd. More Stalins than Lenins. The signs read, "We'll see your capitalism dead and

---

* The NKVD, a precursor to the KGB, was the central Soviet law enforcement agency from 1934 to 1946. It contained both the public police force and the secret police. The NKVD was responsible for carrying out Stalin's Terror, including mass executions, arrest and torture of political prisoners, and running the gulag system. It was also responsible for foreign espionage. Its predecessor was the Chekha secret police force formed in 1917 by Lenin's decree.

† Lavrentiy Beria (1899–1953), the chief of the NKVD from 1938 to 1946, was responsible for significantly expanding the gulag system, overseeing the exile of many ethnic minorities from their native lands, and supervising the Soviet atom bomb project. He was arrested and executed shortly after Stalin's death.

buried!" "Red banners advance on the Kremlin!" Regular Moscow watches from the sidewalk as Red Moscow barrels down the road. Skirmishes flare up at the crowd's edges; here and there, they escalate into fistfights. The police are incapable of untangling these two Moscows. I barely have time to write down everything I hear . . .

—Bury Lenin already, and without any honors.

—You American lackey! What did you sell out our country for?

—You're idiots, brothers . . .

—Yeltsin and his gang robbed us blind. Drink! Prosper! One day, it'll all come crashing down . . .

—Are they afraid of telling the people outright that we're building capitalism? Everyone is prepared to pick up a gun, even my housewife mother.

—You can get a lot done with a bayonet, but sitting on one is uncomfortable.

—I'd like to run over all of those damn bourgeois with a tank!

—Communism was dreamt up by that Jew, Marx . . .

—There's only one person who can save us, and that's Comrade Stalin. If only he'd come back for just two days . . . he'd have them all shot, and then he can once again be laid to rest.

—And glory be, Dear Lord! I'll bow down before all of the saints . . .

—You Stalinist bitches! The blood on your hands hasn't even had a chance to dry yet. What did you murder the Tsar's family for? You didn't even spare the kids.

—You can't build a Great Russia without a Great Stalin.

—You've filled the people's brains with shit . . .

—I'm a simple man. Stalin didn't touch regular people like me. No one in my family was affected, and all of them were workers. It was the bosses' heads that flew, regular people lived regular lives.

—You red KGB goons! Soon enough, you'll start saying that the only camps we had were Young Pioneer camps. My grandfather was a street sweeper.

—And mine was a land surveyor.

—Mine was an engine driver . . .

• • •

A rally begins in front of the Belorussky Railway Station. The crowd burts into applause and cries of "Hurrah! Hurrah! Glory!" At the end, the whole square sings a song to the tune of the "Warszawianka," the Russian "Marseillaise," but with new lyrics: "We'll cast off these liberal chains / Cast off this bloody criminal regime." After that, packing up their red flags, some hurry toward the Metro, while others line up in front of the kiosks for pastries and beer. The real party begins. There's singing and dancing. An old lady in a red kerchief twirls and stomps her feet around an accordion player, singing, "We're merrily dancing / Around a big tree. / In our Motherland, / We are happy and free. / We're merrily dancing / And singing our song / The one who we sing for / Is Comrade Stalin . . ." By the very entrance of the Metro, I can still hear snatches of a drunken folk ditty: "All the bad stuff can fuck off! And the good stuff fuck right on!"

ON THE CHOICE WE MUST MAKE BETWEEN GREAT HISTORY AND BANAL EXISTENCE

It's always noisy by the beer stand. All sorts of people gather there. You can meet a professor, a working stiff, a student, a homeless man . . . They drink and philosophize. The conversation is always about the same thing—the fate of Russia. And communism.

—I'm a drinking man. Why do I drink? I don't like my life. I want to do an impossible somersault and, with the help of alcohol, transport myself to another place where everything is good and beautiful.

—For me, it's more of a concrete question: Where do I want to live, in a great country or a normal one?

—I loved the empire . . . Life after the fall of the empire has been boring. Tedious.

—A great Idea demands blood. Today, nobody wants to go off and die somewhere. Fighting in some war. It's like that song: "Money, money, money everywhere, / Money everywhere, gentlemen . . ." But if you insist that we do have a goal, then what is it exactly? That everyone drive a Mercedes and have tickets to Miami?

—Russians need something to believe in . . . Something lofty and luminous. Empire and communism are ingrained in us. We seek out heroic ideals.

—With socialism, the people were participating in History . . . They were living through something great . . .

—Fucking shit! Look at us, we're so soulful, we're so special.

—We've never had democracy. What kind of democrats would you and I make?

—The last great event in our lives was perestroika.

—Russia can either be great or not exist at all. We need a strong army.

—What do I need a great country for? I want to live in a small one like Denmark. No nuclear weapons, no oil, no gas. So no one would ever hit me over the head with their pistol. Maybe then even we would learn to shampoo our sidewalks . . .

—Communism is too great an undertaking . . . We're always either demanding a constitution or Sevruga caviar with a side of horseradish . . .

—I am so envious of the people who had an ideal to live up to! Today, we are living without one. I want a great Russia! I don't remember it, but I know it existed.

—We used to live in a great country where we stood in line for toilet paper . . . I remember the smell of Soviet cafeterias and grocery stores all too well.

—Russia will save the world! That's how it will save itself!

—My father lived to the age of ninety. He said that not a single good thing happened in his entire life; he was always at war. That's all we're capable of.

—God is the infinite within us . . . We are created in His likeness and image . . .

ON EVERYTHING

—I was 90 percent Soviet . . . I couldn't understand what was going on. I remember seeing Gaidar on TV saying, "Learn how to sell . . . The market will save us . . ." You buy a bottle of mineral water on one corner and sell it on another—that's business. The people listened, bewildered. I would come home, lock the door, and weep. All of it scared my mother so much, she ended up having a stroke. Maybe they wanted to do something good, but they didn't have enough compassion for their own people. I'll never forget the rows of elderly begging along the road. Their worn-out little hats, their jackets that had been mended too many times . . . I would run to and from work with my eyes down, afraid of looking at them. I worked at a perfume factory. Instead of money, they paid us in perfume . . . makeup . . .

—There was a poor girl in our class whose parents had died in a car crash. She lived with her grandmother. All year long, she wore the same dress to school every day. No one felt sorry for her. It's surprising how fast being poor became shameful . . .

—I don't have any regrets about the nineties. It was an exciting, tumultuous time. Even though I'd never been interested in politics or even read the papers, I ended up running for deputy. Who were the foremen of perestroika? Writers, artists . . . poets . . . You could have collected autographs at the First Congress of the People's Deputies of the USSR. My husband is an economist, and it would drive him up the wall: "Poets are capable of setting people's hearts on fire with words. You're going to end up with a revolution on your hands—and then what? How are you going to build democracy? Who's going to do it? I can already see what your efforts are leading to." He laughed at me. We ended up getting divorced because of it . . . But as it turned out, he was right . . .

—Things got scary, so the people turned to the Church. Back when I still believed in communism, I didn't need church. My wife goes to services with me because in church, the priest will call her "little dove."

—My father was an honest communist. I don't blame the Communists, I blame communism. I still can't decide how to feel about Gorbachev . . . or that Yeltsin . . . You forget about the long lines and empty stores faster than you do about the red flag flying over the Reichstag.

—We triumphed. But over whom? And for what? You turn on the TV, and they're playing a movie about the Reds beating the Whites. You flip the channel, and it's the Whites beating the Reds. Sheer schizophrenia!

—We're always talking about suffering . . . That's our path to wisdom. People in the West seem naïve to us because they don't suffer like we do, they have a remedy for every little pimple. We're the ones who went to the camps, who piled up the corpses during the war, who dug through the nuclear waste in Chernobyl with our bare hands. We sit atop the ruins of socialism like it's the aftermath of war. We're run down and defeated. Our language is the language of suffering.

I tried to talk about this with my students . . . They laughed in my face: "We don't want to suffer. That's not what our lives are about." We haven't understood a thing about the world we'd only recently been living in and yet we're already living in a new one. An entire civilization lies rotting on the trash heap . . .

TEN STORIES IN A RED INTERIOR

◆

ON THE BEAUTY OF DICTATORSHIP AND THE MYSTERY OF BUTTERFLIES CRUSHED AGAINST THE PAVEMENT

◆

Elena Yurievna S.,
third secretary of the district party committee,
49 years old

There were two of them waiting for me: Elena Yurievna, with whom I'd arranged to meet, and her friend Anna Ilinichna M., who was visiting from Moscow. She immediately joined the conversation. "I've been waiting for someone to explain what's going on to me for a long time." Their stories had nothing in common except for the significant proper nouns: Gorbachev, Yeltsin. But each of them had her own Gorbachev and her own Yeltsin. And her own version of the nineties.

ELENA YURIEVNA

Is it really already time to tell the story of socialism? To whom? Everyone around is still a witness. To be perfectly honest, I'm surprised that you've come all this way just to see me. I'm a communist, part of the *nomenklatura* . . . No one wants to listen to us anymore . . . everyone wants to shut us up. Lenin was a gangster, and don't even mention Stalin . . . We're all criminals, even though there isn't a single drop of blood on my hands. Still, we've been branded, every last one of us . . .

Perhaps fifty or a hundred years from now they'll be able to write objectively about the way of life we called socialism. Without all the tears and obscenities. They'll unearth it like ancient Troy. Until recently, you weren't allowed to say anything good about socialism. In the West, after the fall of the Soviet Union, they realized that Marxism wasn't really over, it still needed to be developed. Without being worshiped. Over there, he wasn't an idol like he'd been for us. A saint! First we worshiped him, then we anathematized him. Crossed it all out. But science has also caused immeasurable suffering—should we eliminate scientists? Curse the fathers of the atom bomb, or better yet, start with the ones who invented gunpowder? Yes, start with them . . . Am I wrong? [*She doesn't give me a chance to answer her question.*] You're on the right track, leaving Moscow. You could say that you've come to the real Russia. Walking around Moscow, you might get the impression that we're a European country: the luxury cars, the restaurants . . . those golden cupolas gleaming! But listen to what the people talk about in the provinces . . . Russia isn't Moscow, Russia is Samara, Tolyatti, Chelyabinsk—some Bumblepinsk . . . How much can you really learn about Russia from sitting around in a Moscow kitchen? Going to parties. Blah, blah, blah . . . Moscow is the capital of some other nation, not the country beyond the ring road.* A tourist paradise. Don't believe Moscow . . .

You come here and right away, it's perfectly clear, "Now, this is the *sovok*." People live very poorly, even by Russian standards. They blame the rich and resent everyone. Blame the government. They feel that they've been lied to, that no one had told them that there was going to be capitalism; they thought that socialism was just going to get fixed. The life that we'd all been used to, which is to say the Soviet way of life. While they were out at demonstrations, tearing their vocal chords chanting "Yeltsin! Yeltsin!," they were robbed. The plants and factories were divvied up without them. Along with the oil and the natural gas—everything that came to us, as they say, from God. But they've only just understood. Back in 1991, everyone was joining the revolution. Going off to be on the barricades. They wanted freedom, and what did they get? Yeltsin's gangster revolution . . . My friend's son was almost killed for his socialist views. "Communist" has become an insult. The boys who hang out in the courtyard nearly murdered one of their own. Their friend. They had been sitting around on the benches with their guitars and talking, saying that pretty soon, they'd be marching on the Communists, hanging them from the lampposts. Mishka Slutzer is a well-read boy, his father worked on the district

* The ring road is a major freeway encircling Moscow which served as Moscow's administrative boundary until the 1980s.

Party committee. He quoted G. K. Chesterton, "A man without some kind of dream of perfection is quite as much of a monstrosity as a noseless man . . ." And for that they beat him . . . kicked him with their heavy boots. "You little kike! Who brought about the Revolution in 1917!" I remember the way people's eyes gleamed at the beginning of perestroika, I'll never forget it. They were prepared to lynch the Communists, to send us all to prison camps . . . Volumes of Gorky and Mayakovsky piled up in the dumpsters . . . people would drop the complete works of Lenin off at the paper recycling center. And I would take them home . . . Yes! I'll admit it! I recant nothing! I'm not ashamed of anything! I never changed my colors, repainting myself from red to gray. You'll meet people like that—if the Reds come to power, they welcome the Reds; if it's the Whites, they'll greet the Whites with open arms. People performed incredible transformations: Yesterday they were communists, today they're ultra-democrats. Before my very eyes, "honest" communists turned into religious liberals. But I love the word "comrade," and I'll never stop loving it. It's a good word. *Sovok?* Bite your tongue! The Soviet was a very good person, capable of traveling beyond the Urals, into the furthest deserts, all for the sake of ideals, not dollars. We weren't after somebody else's green bills. The Dnieper Hydroelectric Station, the Siege of Stalingrad, the first man in space—that was all us. The mighty *sovok!* I still take pleasure in writing "USSR." That was my country; the country I live in today is not. I feel like I'm living on foreign soil.

I was born Soviet . . . My grandmother didn't believe in God, but she did believe in communism. Until his dying day, my father waited for socialism to return. The Berlin Wall had fallen, the Soviet Union was crumbling, but he clung to his hope. He stopped talking to his best friend because he had called the flag a red rag. Our red flag! Red calico! My father fought in the Russo-Finnish War, he never understood what he'd been fighting for, but they told him to go, so he went. They never talked about that war, they called it the "Finnish campaign," not a war. But my father would tell us about it . . . In hushed tones. At home. On rare occasions, he would look back on it. When he was drinking . . . The setting of his war was winter: the forests and meter-deep snows. The Finns fought on skis, in white camouflage uniforms; they'd always appear out of nowhere, like angels. "Like angels"—those are my father's words . . . They could take down a detachment, an entire squadron, overnight. The dead . . . My father recalled how the dead always lay in pools of blood; a lot of blood seeps out of people killed in their sleep. So much blood, it would eat through the meter-deep snow. After the war, my father couldn't even bear to butcher a chicken. Or a rabbit. He couldn't stand the sight of a dead animal or the warm smell of blood. He had a fear of large trees with full crowns because they were the kinds of trees that the Finnish snipers would hide in—they called them "cuckoos." [*She is silent.*] I want to add . . . this is my opinion . . . After the Victory, our little town was flooded with flowers, people went flower crazy. The most important flowers were dahlias, you had to keep the bulbs alive through the winter and not let them freeze. God forbid! People would swaddle them, tucking them in like they were little babies. Flowers grew in front of people's houses, behind their houses, around the wells, along the fences. People were hungry for life. After living in fear for so long, they needed to celebrate. But eventually, the flowers disappeared; there's nothing left of that now. But I remember . . . I just remembered them . . . [*Silence.*] My father . . . My father only saw six months of combat before being taken prisoner. How did they capture him? They were advancing over a frozen lake while the enemy's artillery shot at the ice. Few made it across, and those who did had just spent their last strength swimming through freezing water; all of them lost their weapons along the way. They came to the shore half-naked. The Finns would stretch out their arms to rescue them and some people would take their hands, while others . . . many of them wouldn't accept any help from the enemy. That was how they had been trained. My father grabbed one of their hands, and he was dragged out of the water. I remember his amazement: "They gave me schnapps to warm me up. Put me in dry clothes. They laughed and clapped me on the shoulder, 'You made it, Ivan!' " My father had never been face to face with the enemy before. He didn't understand why they were so cheerful . . .

The Finnish campaign ended in 1940 . . . Soviet war prisoners were exchanged for Finns. They were marched toward each other in columns. On their side, the Finns were greeted with hugs and handshakes . . . Our men, on the other hand, were immediately treated like enemies. "Brothers! Friends!" they threw themselves on their comrades. "Halt! Another step and we'll shoot!" The column was surrounded by soldiers with German Shepherds. They were led to specially prepared barracks surrounded by barbed wire. The interrogations began . . . "How were you taken prisoner?" the interrogator asked my father. "The Finns pulled me out of a lake." "You traitor! You were saving your own skin instead of the Motherland." My father

also considered himself guilty. That's how they'd been trained . . .
There was no trial. They marched everyone out on the quad and read
the entire division their sentence: six years in the camps for betraying
the Motherland. Then they shipped them off to Vorkuta to build a
railway over the permafrost. My God! It was 1941 . . . The Germans
were moving in on Moscow . . . No one even told them that war had
broken out—after all, they were enemies, it would only make them
happy. Belarus was occupied by the Nazis. They took Smolensk. When
they finally heard about it, all of them wanted to go to the front, they
all wrote letters to the head of the camp . . . to Stalin . . . And in response, they were told, "Work for the victory on the home front, you
bastards. We don't need traitors like you at the front." They all . . .
Papa . . . he told me . . . All of them wept . . . [*Silence.*] Really, that's
who you should be talking to . . . Alas, my father is gone. The camp
cut his life short, and so did perestroika. He suffered so much. He
couldn't understand what had happened. To the country, to the Party.
Our father . . . After six years in the penal colony, he forgot what an
apple was or a head of cabbage . . . Sheets and pillows . . . Three times
a day, they would give them thin gruel and a single loaf of bread split
among twenty-five men. They slept with a log under their heads and a
wooden plank on the ground for a mattress. Papa . . . He was a strange
man, not like the others . . . Incapable of striking a horse or a cow or
kicking a dog. I always felt bad for him. The other men would make
fun of him: "What kind of man are you? You're a girl!" My mother
would cry over the fact that he . . . well, that he wasn't like other people. He would pick up a head of cabbage and stare at it . . . Or a tomato . . . When he first came back, he was totally silent, he wouldn't
tell us anything. It wasn't until about ten years later that he finally
started talking. Never before . . . Yes . . . At a certain point, while he
was in the camp, his job had been transporting dead bodies. There
would be ten to fifteen fresh corpses a day. The living returned to the
barracks on foot, the dead were pulled back on sleds. They were ordered to remove their clothing, so the dead men lay naked on the sleds,
"like jerboas." My father's words . . . It's coming out all muddled . . .
because of my feelings . . . It's all so upsetting . . . For the first two
years in the camp, none of them thought that they would survive.
Those who'd been sentenced to five or six years would talk about
home, but those who got ten to fifteen never mentioned it. They never
brought up anyone, not their wives or their kids. Their parents. "If
you started thinking about your loved ones, you wouldn't survive," my

father explained. We waited for him . . . "Papa will come back, and he won't even recognize me . . ." "Daddy . . ." I would look for any excuse to say the word "Papa." Then, one day, he returned. Grandma saw a man in a soldier's cloak standing by our gate: "Who are you looking for, soldier?" "You don't recognize me, Mama?" Grandma fainted on the spot. That was Papa's homecoming . . . He came back frozen to the bone, he could never get his hands or his feet warm. My mother? Mama would say that my father came back from the camps gentle, although she had been worried, she'd heard scary stories about people coming back mean. Papa wanted to enjoy life. His motto was, "Man up—the worst is yet to come."

I forgot . . . I forgot where this happened . . . Where was it? The transit camp? They were crawling around a large yard on their hands and knees eating grass. Men with dystrophy and pellagra. You couldn't complain about anything with my father around. He knew that in order to survive, you only needed three things: bread, onions, and soap. Just those three things . . . that's all . . . They're no longer with us, our parents, their generation . . . But if any of them are still around, they should be put in museums, kept under glass so that no one can touch them. They went through so much! After my father was rehabilitated,* they paid him two months' wages for all of his suffering. For a long time, a large portrait of Stalin continued to hang in our home. A very long time . . . I remember it well . . . My father didn't hold a grudge, he considered it all to be a product of his era. Those were cruel times. A powerful nation was being built. And they really did build it, plus they defeated Hitler! That's what my father would say . . .

I grew up a serious girl, a real Young Pioneer. Today, everyone thinks that they used to force people into the Pioneers. I'm telling you: No one was forced to do anything. All of the kids dreamed of becoming Young Pioneers. Of marching together. To drums and horns. Singing Young Pioneer songs: "My Motherland, I'll love forever / Where else will I find one like her?" "The eagle nation has millions of chicks, and we are our nation's pride . . ." There was a stain on our family name because my father had been in the camps. My mother was scared that I wouldn't be accepted into the Pioneers right away or even at all.

* After Stalin's death in 1953, former political prisoners—or their families, if the prisoners were deceased—could apply for "rehabilitation" in order to be officially absolved of their crimes. Those who were not formally rehabilitated faced difficulties with employment and education, as did the members of their family.

I really wanted to be with everyone else. I had to be . . . "Who are you for, the sun or the moon?" the little boys would interrogate me in class. You had to be on your toes! "For the moon!"—"Correct! For the Soviet Union." Because if you said, "For the sun," you would get, "For that damn Japan!" They'd laugh and tease you. The way we swore was "Pioneer's honor," or we gave "Lenin's word." The most sacred oath was "Stalin's word." My parents knew that if I gave them Stalin's word, I couldn't possibly be lying. My God! It's not Stalin I remember, it's our life . . . I joined a club and learned how to play the accordion. Mama got a medal for being a shock worker.* It wasn't all misery . . . barracks life . . . In the camp, my father met a lot of educated people. He never met people that interesting anywhere else. Some of them wrote poems; the ones who did were more likely to survive. Like the priests who would pray. My father wanted all of his kids to go to university. That was his dream. And all of us—there are four of us— ended up with degrees. But he also taught us how to plow, to mow the grass. I know how to load a cart with hay and how to make a haystack. "Anything can come in handy," Papa believed. And he was right.

Now I want to remember it all . . . I want to understand what I've lived through. And not just my own life, all of our lives . . . our Soviet life . . . Overall, I'm not impressed with my people. And I'm not impressed with the Communists either, our Communist leaders. Especially nowadays. All of them have grown petty and bourgeois, all of them chase after the good life, the sweet life. They want to consume and consume. Grab hold of whatever they can! The Communists aren't what they used to be. Now we have Communists who make hundreds of thousands of dollars a year. Millionaires! An apartment in London, a palace in Cyprus . . . What kind of communists are these? What do they believe in? If you ask them, they'll look at you like you're an idiot. "Don't tell us your Soviet fairy tales. Anything but that." What a great country they destroyed! Sold it off at bargain prices. Our Motherland . . . So that some of us could go traipsing around Europe berating Marx. The times are as terrifying as they were under Stalin . . . I stand behind everything I'm saying! Will you write all this down? I don't believe you . . . [*And looking at her, I can*

* The shock worker movement, which originated in the 1920s, pushed workers in all Soviet industries to strive to dramatically overfulfill production quotas, surpassing norms and pushing Soviet industrialization forward at the fastest pace possible. Especially productive shock workers were rewarded with certificates and held up as examples to others in order to spur "socialist emulation."

tell that she doesn't.] We don't have district or regional Party committees anymore. We've left the Soviet regime in the dust. And so what do we have in its place? The boxing ring, the jungle . . . Thieves running the country . . . They grabbed furiously, racing for the biggest piece of the pie. My God! Chubais,* "the foreman of perestroika" . . . Now he goes around bragging, giving lectures around the world, saying that in other countries, it took centuries to build capitalism, while here we did it in three years. They carved it up with surgical precision . . . And if anyone was a thief, God bless them, maybe their grandchildren will turn out decent. Ugh! And these are the democrats . . . [*Silence.*] They put on American suits and did what their Uncle Sam told them to do. But American suits don't fit them right. They sit crooked. That's what you get! It wasn't freedom they were after, it was blue jeans, supermarkets . . . They were fooled by the shiny wrappers . . . Now our stores are filled with all sorts of stuff. An abundance. But heaps of salami have nothing to do with happiness. Or glory. We used to be a great nation! Now we're nothing but peddlers and looters . . . grain merchants and managers . . .

Gorbachev came to power . . . He started talking about the return of Leninist principles. Excitement filled the air. The people had been waiting for change for a long time. Back in the day, they'd believed in Andropov† . . . Yes, he was KGB, but . . . how can I explain it? People no longer feared the Communist Party. At the beer stand, the men might curse the Party, but no one would dare to say anything about the KGB . . . No way! It was ingrained in them . . . They knew the iron fist, the red-hot iron, the iron rod . . . Those boys would get everyone in line. I don't mean to repeat clichés, but Genghis Khan ruined our gene pool . . . and serfdom played its part as well . . . We're used to the idea that everyone needs a good whipping, that you won't get anything done without flogging people. That was Andropov's point of departure—tightening the screws. Everyone had let their hair down: They started skipping work to go to the movies, the bathhouse, the store. Drinking tea instead of working. So the police started doing

---

* Anatoly Chubais (1955–) was responsible for directing privatization in Russia under the Yeltsin administration and introducing the voucher privatization system. He is one of the richest businessmen in Russia.
† Yuri Andropov (1914–1984) ran the KGB from 1967 to 1982 and succeeded Leonid Brezhnev as General Secretary of the Communist Party from November 1982 until his death in February 1984. His successor, Konstantin Chernenko (1911–1985), lasted only a year. He was replaced after his death by Gorbachev.

raids and roundups. They would check documents and grab the slack-
ers right off the street, at the cafés, in the shops, notify their places of
work, fine them and get them fired. But Andropov was very ill. He
died soon into his term. We kept burying them, one after the other.
Brezhnev, Andropov, Chernenko . . . A very popular joke before Gorbachev came to power: "Transmitting a message from TASS news
agency. You're going to laugh, but another general secretary of the
CPSU has passed away . . ." Ha, ha, ha . . . People laughed away in
their kitchens, while we laughed in ours. In that little patch of freedom. Kitchen talk . . . [*Laughs.*] I remember how, during these conversations, we'd turn up the TV or the radio. There was a whole art to it.
We'd teach one another the tricks, so that the KGB agents who tapped
our phones wouldn't be able to make anything out. You turn the dial
to the end—old telephones had little holes for numbers that you could
turn—and then you stick a pencil in it so that it locks . . . You can hold
it down with your finger, too, but your finger gets tired . . . You probably know that one? Do you remember it? If you needed to say something "secret," you had to get two or three meters away from the
phone, from the receiver. Bugging and snitching were everywhere—
from the bottom to the very top. At the district committee, we would
try to guess who the informant was. As it later turned out, I had suspected a totally innocent person, and there wasn't just one informant,
there had been several. None of them were people I would have ever
suspected . . . One was a cleaning lady. A kind, friendly, and unfortunate woman. Her husband was an alcoholic. My God! Even Gorbachev himself . . . the General Secretary of the Central Committee of
the CPSU . . . I read an interview with him where he described how
during confidential discussions in his office, he'd do the same thing,
he'd also turn the TV or radio up to full volume. The oldest trick in
the book. For serious conversations, he'd have people come out to his
dacha. And when they were there . . . they would go to the woods,
strolling and talking. The birds wouldn't inform on them . . . Everyone was afraid, even the people that everyone was afraid of. I was
afraid, too.

The last years of the Soviet Union . . . What do I remember? The
ever-present shame. I was ashamed of Brezhnev plastering himself in
medals and stars, ashamed that people had taken to calling the Kremlin a comfortable retirement home. I was ashamed of the empty store
shelves. We were meeting and even surpassing production quotas, but
somehow the stores were completely empty. Where was our milk? Our

meat? I still don't understand where it all went. Stores would run out of milk within an hour of opening. After noon, the sales clerks just stood there behind clean, empty display cases. The only things on the shelves were three-liter jars of birch juice and packages of salt, which were always wet for some reason. Canned sprats. And that was it! If they put out salami, it'd be sold out in seconds. Hot dogs and *pelmeni* were delicacies. At the district committee, they were always divvying up some lot—this factory gets ten refrigerators and five fur coats, that collective farm gets two Yugoslav furniture sets and ten Polish purses. They would ration out pots and lingerie . . . pantyhose . . . The only thing that could hold a society like this together was fear. Extreme conditions—execute and imprison as many people as possible. But the socialism of Solovki and the White Sea Canal* project was over. We needed a new kind of socialism.

Perestroika . . . There was a moment when people wanted to turn to us again. They were joining the party. Everyone had great expectations. Back then, everyone was naïve, on the left and on the right—the communists and the anti-Soviets alike. Everyone was a romantic. Today, we're ashamed of our former naïveté. People worship Solzhenitsyn. The great Elder of Vermont! It wasn't just Solzhenitsyn, there were many other people who understood that we couldn't go on the way we were. Caught in a web of lies. And the communists—I don't know whether or not you believe me—we weren't blind to it, either. There were a number of good and decent people among the communists. Sincere. I personally knew people like this, especially outside of the cities. People like my father . . . My father wasn't accepted into the Party, he'd suffered at its hands, but he kept on believing in it. He believed in the Party and in our country. Every morning, he'd start his day by reading *Pravda* from cover to cover. There were more communists without Party membership cards than those who had them; many people were convinced communists in their souls. [*Silence.*] At all the parades, they carried banners reading, "The People and the Party Are One!" Those words weren't make-believe, they were the truth. I'm not agitating for anything, I'm just trying to describe the way things really were. Everyone has already forgotten . . .

---

* The White Sea Canal or Belamorkanal project endeavored to join the White Sea to the Baltic. It was the first major Soviet construction project that employed forced labor. A total of 126,000 prisoners worked on the canal from 1931 to 1933, an estimated 25,000 of whom died during its construction. Although it was touted as a great Stalinist achievement, the canal is too shallow for most seagoing vessels.

Many people had joined the Party as an act of conscience, and not out of careerism or some other pragmatic consideration like, "If I'm not a Party member and I steal, they'll put me in jail, but if I join the Party and steal, they'll just kick me out of the Party." I get indignant whenever people start talking about Marxism with disdain and a knowing smirk. Hurry up and toss it on the trash heap! It's a great teaching, and it will outlive all persecution. And our Soviet misfortune, too. Because . . . there are a lot of reasons . . . Socialism isn't just labor camps, informants, and the Iron Curtain, it's also a bright, just world: Everything is shared, the weak are pitied, and compassion rules. Instead of grabbing everything you can, you feel for others. They say to me that you couldn't buy a car—so then no one had a car. No one wore Versace suits or bought houses in Miami. My God! The leaders of the USSR lived like mid-level businessmen, they were nothing like today's oligarchs. Not one bit! They weren't building themselves yachts with champagne showers. Can you imagine! Right now, there's a commercial on TV for copper bathtubs that cost as much as a two-bedroom apartment. Could you explain to me exactly who they're for? Gilded doorknobs . . . Is this freedom? The little man, the nobody, is a zero— you'll find him at the very bottom of the barrel. He used to be able to write a letter to the editor, go and complain at the district Party headquarters about his boss or poor building maintenance . . . About an unfaithful husband . . . A lot of things about the system were stupid, I don't deny it, but who will even listen to the man in the street today? Who needs him? Remember the Soviet place names—Metallurgists Avenue, Enthusiasts Avenue, Factory Street, Proletariat Street . . . The little man was the most important one around . . . You say it was all just talk and a cover-up—today, no one even attempts to disguise their disdain for him. You're broke? Go to hell! Back to your cage! They're renaming the streets: Merchant, Middle Class, Nobleman Street . . . I've even seen "Prince's salami" and "General's wine." A cult of money and success. The strong, with their iron biceps, are the ones who survive. But not everyone is capable of stopping at nothing to tear a piece of the pie out of somebody else's mouth. For some, it's simply not in their nature. Others even find it disgusting.

With her . . . [*She nods in the direction of her friend.*] We argue, of course . . . She wants to prove to me that true socialism demands perfect people who simply do not exist. That it's nothing but a crazy ideal . . . a fantasy . . . There's no way our people are going to trade in their faded foreign currency and passports with Schengen visas for

Soviet socialism. But that's not what I believe in, anyway. I think humanity is headed toward socialism. Toward justice. There is no other way. Look at Germany, France . . . There's the Swedish model. What values does Russian capitalism espouse? Hating the underdogs, the people who haven't made millions and don't drive Mercedes. Instead of the red flag, it's Christ is risen! And the cult of consumerism . . . People don't fall asleep thinking of anything lofty, instead they mull over how they didn't buy this or get that. Do you really think that this country fell apart because people learned the truth about the gulag? That's what people who write books think. People . . . Regular people don't care about history, they're concerned with simpler things: falling in love, getting married, having kids. Building a house. Our country fell apart from the deficit of women's boots and toilet paper, because of the fact that there were no oranges. It was those goddamn blue jeans! Today, the shops resemble museums. Theaters. And people want me to believe that rags from Versace and Armani are all that a person needs. That they're enough. That life is nothing but pyramid schemes and promissory notes. That freedom is money and money is freedom. While our lives aren't worth a kopeck. Well, and . . . well, and . . . you know . . . I can't even find the words . . . I feel sorry for my little granddaughters. I pity them. That's what gets beaten into their heads every day on TV. I don't agree with it. I was and remain a communist.

We take a short break. The eternal tea, this time with the hostess's homemade cherry jam.

It was 1989 . . . By then, I was the third secretary of the district Party committee. I was recruited to work in the Party from the school where I'd taught Russian language and literature. My favorite writers, Tolstoy, Chekhov . . . When they first offered me the job, I was intimidated. What a huge responsibility! But I didn't hesitate for a moment, I had a real burst of desire to serve the Party. That summer, I went home for the holiday . . . I don't usually wear jewelry, but I had bought myself this cheap necklace. When she saw me, my mother exclaimed, "You look like a Tsaritsa." She was so impressed—and it wasn't the necklace that impressed her! My father said, "None of us will ever come asking you for favors. You need to have a clean conscience before the people." My parents were so proud! So happy! And I . . . I . . .

What did I feel? Did I believe in the Party? To tell you the truth, I did. And I still do. Come what may, I will never throw out my Party membership card. Did I believe in communism? I'll be honest with you, I'm not going to lie: I believed in the possibility of life being governed fairly. And today . . . as I've already told you . . . I still believe in that. I'm sick of hearing about how bad life was under socialism. I'm proud of the Soviet era! It wasn't "the good life," but it was regular life. We had love and friendship . . . dresses and shoes . . . People hungrily listened to writers and actors, which they don't do anymore. The stadium poets have been replaced by psychics and magicians. People believe in sorcerers, just like in Africa. Our Soviet life . . . you could say that it was an attempt at creating an alternative civilization. If you want to put it in dramatic terms . . . The power of the people! I can't calm down about it! Where are you going to see a Metro station devoted to dairymaids, lathe operators, or engine drivers today? They're nowhere to be seen—they're not in the newspaper, they're not on TV, and they're nowhere near the Kremlin when they're handing out medals and awards. They're not anywhere anymore. Everywhere you look, you see our new heroes: bankers and businessmen, models and prostitutes . . . managers . . . The young can adapt, while the old die in silence behind closed doors. They die in poverty, all but forgotten. My pension is fifty dollars a month . . . [*She laughs.*] I've read that Gorbachev's is also fifty dollars a month . . . They say that the Communists "lived in mansions and ate black caviar by the spoonful. They built communism for themselves." My God! I've shown you around my "mansion"—a regular two-bedroom apartment, fifty-seven square meters. I haven't hidden anything from you: my Soviet crystal, my Soviet gold . . .

—But what about the special clinics and food rations, "internal queues" for apartments and government-issued dachas? The Party sanatoriums?

—Honestly? All of that existed . . . it did . . . But mostly up there . . . [*Points up.*] I was always at the bottom, on the lowest rung. On the bottom with the people. Always in full view. The fact that this was the case in some places . . . I don't argue with that . . . I couldn't deny it! Just like you, that's what I read about in newspapers during perestroika . . . About how the children of the secretaries of the Central Committee would fly out to Africa to go big-game hunting. How they'd buy up diamonds . . . But still, it's nothing compared to how "new Russians" live today. With their yachts and their castles. Take a look at the houses they've built for themselves all around Moscow. Palaces! Two-meter-thick stone fences, electric fences, security cameras. Armed guards. They're like penal colonies or top-secret military bases. What, is computer genius Bill Gates living there? Or world chess champion Garry Kasparov? That's how the victors live. There was no official civil war, but there are victors. They're behind those stone fences. Who are they hiding from? The people? The people thought that they'd overthrow the Communists and usher in a new golden age. Life in paradise. Instead of free people, we now have all these . . . with their millions and billions . . . Gangsters! They shoot each other in broad daylight . . . Even out here, a businessmen's balcony was shot to pieces. They're not afraid of anyone. Flying around in their private jets with their gilded toilets and bragging about it to boot. I saw it with my own eyes, on TV . . . One of them was showing off his watch that cost as much as a bomber jet. Another one, his diamond-studded mobile phone. And no one—no one!—will shout from the rooftops that this is all shameful. Revolting. We used to have Uspensky and Korolenko. Sholokhov* wrote Stalin a letter in defense of the peasants. Today I want to . . . You're the one asking the questions, but now I want to ask you: Where is our true elite? Why is it that every day I'm reading Berezovsky and Potanin's opinions on any and every topic instead of Okudzhava . . . or Iskander† . . . What happened that made you guys give up your seats for them? Your university departments . . . You were the first ones to chase after the crumbs from the oligarchs' table. To run to their service. The Russian intelligentsia never used to pander to the rich. Now there's no one left—no one will speak for the soul except for the priests. Where are the former supporters of perestroika?

Communists of my generation had very little in common with Pavka Korchagin.‡ They weren't like the first Bolsheviks with their

---

* Gleb Uspensky (1843–1902) was a writer close to the People's Will Movement. Vladimir Korolenko (1853–1921) was a Ukrainian writer and journalist who opposed Tsarism and defended the oppressed. Mikhail Sholokhov (1905–1984) wrote the celebrated novel *And Quiet Flows the Don.*

† Vladimir Potanin (1961–) is a Russian businessman, banker, and former vice president of the Russian Federation (1996–1997). In 2011, his fortune was estimated by *Forbes* to be $17.8 billion. Fazil Iskander (1929–) is a poet and writer of Abkhazian origin.

‡ Pavel "Pavka" Korchagin is the protagonist of Nikolai Ostrovsky's socialist realist novel *How the Steel Was Tempered* about a young Bolshevik fighting in the Civil War of 1918–1921. His name is synonymous with the idealized Soviet war hero.

briefcases and revolvers, all that was left of the forefathers was their army jargon: "soldiers of the Party," "the labor front," "the battle for harvest." We no longer felt like the soldiers of the Party, we were its public servants. Clerks. We had our sacred rites: "the bright future," a portrait of Lenin in the assembly hall, a red banner in the corner. Sacred rites, rituals . . . But soldiers were no longer in demand, what we needed were administrators: "Go, go, go," and if not, then "You can leave your Party membership card on the desk." If they tell you to do something, you do it. You report. The Party isn't an army squadron, it's an apparatus. A machine. A bureaucratic machine. They rarely hired people who'd studied the humanities, the Party hadn't trusted them since Lenin's times. Of the intellectual class, Lenin wrote, "It's not the brains of the nation—it's the shit." There weren't many other people like me there—philologists, that is. The cadres were culled from the ranks of engineers and livestock specialists—experts in machinery, meat and grain, not humanities. The feeder schools for the Party administration were agricultural institutes. They needed the children of workers and peasants. People from the people. It reached absurd extremes: A veterinarian was more likely to work for the Party than a physician. I never met a single lyricist or physicist. What else? Subordination like in the army . . . The rise to the top was slow, rung by rung: you began as the lecturer of the district Party office, then it was the head administrator of the Party office . . . the instructor . . . the third secretary . . . the second secretary . . . It took me ten years to get to the top. Today, junior research associates and lab administrators run the country; the collective farm deputy or electrician can become president. Instead of running the collective farm, it's straight to the head of state! This kind of thing only happens during a revolution . . . [*A rhetorical question addressed either to me or herself.*] I don't know what to call what happened in 1991 . . .

Was it a revolution or counterrevolution? Nobody even attempts to explain what country we're living in. What is our national idea now, besides salami? What exactly are we building? We advance toward the victory of capitalism. Is that it? For one hundred years, we castigated capitalism: It's a monster, a fiend . . . Now we're proud that we're going to be like everyone else. But if we become like everyone else, who will care about us anymore? The "God-bearing" people . . . the hope of all of progressive humanity . . . [*Sarcastically.*] Everyone thinks of capitalism the same way that they—until very recently—had thought of communism. They're dreaming! They're passing judgment

on Marx . . . blaming the idea . . . A murderous idea! I, for one, blame
the executors. What we had was Stalinism, not communism. And now
it's neither socialism nor capitalism. Neither the Eastern model nor
the Western. Neither empire nor a republic. We're dangling like . . . I
won't say it . . . Stalin! Stalin! They're burying him, all right . . . Or at
least they're trying to . . . But they can never quite get him all the way
under the ground. I don't know how it is in Moscow, but around here,
people put portraits of him on their dashboards. On buses. Long-
distance truckers tend to be particularly fond of him. In the generalis-
simo uniform . . . The people! The people! What about them? The
people said, "Make us a truncheon and an icon." Both. Like you would
out of wood . . . Whatever you carve, that's what you'll end up with . . .
Our lives reel between barracks and bedlam. Right now, the pendu-
lum is in the middle. Half of the country is waiting for a new Stalin
to come and put things in order. [*She is silent again.*] We . . . of
course . . . At the district Party committee, we too had our share of
conversations about Stalin. The Party mythology, passed down from
generation to generation. Everyone loved talking about how things
had been during the Master's reign . . . Stalin-era practices included,
for instance: The heads of Central Committee sectors would be served
tea and sandwiches, while the lecturers were only served tea. Then
they introduced the position of deputy sector administrator. What to
do? They decided to serve them tea without sandwiches but on a white
napkin. So they'd be distinguished . . . They'd gotten to the top of
Mount Olympus, they were among the gods and heroes, now all that
was left was to squeeze into a spot at the feeding trough . . . That's
how it's always been—from Caesar's court to Peter the Great's. And
that's how it always will be. Take a good look at your beloved democrats . . . They seized power and took off running—toward what?
Toward the trough. Toward the horn of plenty. The trough's been the
downfall of more than one revolution. Before our very eyes . . . Yeltsin
fought against special privileges and called himself a democrat; now
he likes it when they call him Tsar Boris. He's like the Godfather
now . . .

   I recently reread Ivan Bunin's *Cursed Days*. [*She takes the book
down from the shelf, finds the bookmark and reads from it.*] "I remember the old man who worked in front of the gates of the building
where the *Odessa News* bureau used to be. It was the first day of the
Bolshevik uprising. A gang of boys ran up to the gates with heaps of
Izvestias hot off the presses, shouting, 'Odessa bourgeois are required

to pay an indemnity of 500 million!' The worker sputtered, choking on rage and Schadenfreude: 'It's not enough! It's not enough!' " Remind you of anything? It reminds me of the Gorbachev years . . . The first uprisings . . . When the people started pouring out into the streets making all sorts of demands—one day it would be bread, the next, freedom . . . then vodka and cigarettes . . . The terror! So many Party workers ended up having strokes and heart attacks. We lived "surrounded by enemies," as the Party had taught us, "in a besieged fortress." We were preparing for world war to break out . . . Our greatest fear was nuclear war—we never saw our nation's demise coming. We didn't expect it . . . not in the slightest . . . We'd gotten used to the May and October parades, the posters, "Lenin's Work Will Live On for Centuries," "The Party Is Our Helmsman." Then suddenly, instead of a parade procession, it was a primordial mob. These weren't the Soviet people anymore, they were some other people that we didn't know. Their posters were totally different: "Put the Communists on Trial!" "We'll Crush the Communist Scum!" I immediately thought of Novocherkassk . . . The information was classified, but we all knew what happened there . . . how during Khrushchev's time, hungry workers had protested and were shot. Those who didn't die were sent off to labor camps; their relatives still don't know where they went . . . And here . . . it's perestroika . . . You can't shoot them or put them in camps. You have to negotiate. Who among us could have gone out into the crowd and addressed the people? Initiated a dialogue . . . agitated . . . We were *apparatchiks,* not orators. I, for instance, gave lectures in which I denounced the capitalists and defended blacks in America. I had the full set of Lenin's collected works in my office, all fifty-five volumes . . . But who really read them? People flipped through them while cramming for tests in college: "Religion is the opiate of the masses," "All worship of a divinity is necrophilia."

There was a sense of panic . . . The lecturers, instructors, and secretaries of district and regional Party committees, all of us were suddenly scared of visiting workers at factories and students in their dormitories. We were afraid of the phone ringing. What if somebody asked about Sakharov or Bukovsky*—what would we tell them? Are they the enemies of the Soviet state or not anymore? What was the of-

* Vladimir Bukovsky (1942–) is a famous dissident who spent many years in prison, labor camps, and psychiatric hospitals before being exchanged for a Chilean communist in 1976. Andrei Sakharov (1921–1989) was a Russian nuclear physicist best known as a Soviet dissident and human rights activist. He won the Nobel Peace Prize in 1975.

ficial line on Rybakov's *Children of the Arbat* and Shatrov's plays? There were no orders from above . . . Before, they would tell you when you'd fulfilled an assignment and successfully enforced the Party line. Teachers were striking in demand of higher salaries, a young director in some factory workers' club was putting on a forbidden play . . . My God! At a cardboard factory, the workers had pushed the director out in a cart, shouting and breaking glass. At night, a monument of Lenin was wrapped in a metal cable and toppled, now passersby were making obscene hand gestures at it. The Party was at a loss . . . I remember what it was like to be at a loss . . . People sat in their offices with their blinds shut. Day and night, a reinforced police detachment guarded the Party headquarters. We were afraid of the people while, out of inertia, the people were still scared of us. And then they stopped being afraid . . . People started gathering on the squares by the thousands . . . I remember one poster that said "Give us 1917! A Revolution!" I was shocked. It was some trade school students holding it . . . Kids . . . Babies! One day, parliamentarians showed up at the district Party committee headquarters demanding, "Show us your special stores! You always have plenty of food to eat while our children are fainting from hunger at school." They found neither mink coats nor black caviar in our cafeteria, but they still wouldn't believe us: "You're deceiving the simple people!" Everything went into motion. The ground started shaking. Gorbachev was weak. He stalled. On one hand, he was for socialism. But then again, he also wanted capitalism . . . His biggest concern seemed to be being liked in Europe. And in America. Over there, they'd all applaud him, "Gorby! Gorby! Oh Gorby!" He babbled up perestroika . . . [*Silence.*]

Socialism was dying in front of our very eyes. And those boys of iron had come to take its place.

ANNA ILINICHNA

It wasn't that long ago, but it's as though it happened in another era . . . a different country . . . That's where we left our naïveté and romanticism. Our trust. No one wants to remember it now because it's unpleasant; we've lived through a lot of disappointment since then. But who could say that nothing has changed? Back then, you couldn't even bring a Bible over the border. Did you forget that? When I'd come visit them from Moscow, I'd bring my relatives Kaluga flour and noodles as presents. And they would be grateful. Have you forgotten? No one stands in line for sugar or soap anymore. And you don't need a ration card to buy a coat.

With Gorbachev, it was love at first sight! Today, they disparage him: "He betrayed the USSR!" "He sold our country out for pizza!" But I remember how amazed we were. Shocked! We finally had a normal leader. One we didn't have to be ashamed of! We would tell one another the stories of how he'd stopped his motorcade in Leningrad and went out into the street, or how he refused to accept an expensive gift at a factory. During a traditional dinner, all he had to drink was a cup of tea. He smiled. Gave speeches without reading from a piece of paper. He was young. None of us believed that the Soviet state would ever fall apart, that salami would magically appear in the stores, that you wouldn't have to stand in a kilometer-long line to buy a foreign-made bra anymore. We were used to getting everything through connections: from subscriptions to the World Classics Library to chocolates to tracksuits from the GDR. Being friendly with the butcher so he would save you a piece of meat. Soviet rule seemed eternal. We thought that there would be enough of it left over for our children and grandchildren! It ended abruptly, when no one expected it to. Today, it's clear that Gorbachev himself didn't see it coming. He wanted change, but he didn't know how to change things. No one was prepared. No one! Not even the people who tore down the wall. I'm a regular technician. No hero . . . and no Communist . . . Because of my husband, who is an artist, I fell in with a bohemian crowd when I was young. Poets and artists . . . There were no heroes among us, no one was brave enough to become a real dissident and risk doing time in jail or a psych ward for their beliefs. We lived with our fingers crossed behind our backs.

We sat in our kitchens criticizing the Soviet government and cracking jokes. We read *samizdat*. If someone got their hands on a new book, they could show up at your door at any hour—even two or three in the morning—and still be a welcome guest. I remember that nocturnal Moscow life so well . . . It was special . . . It had its own heroes . . . its cowards and traitors . . . Its own enchantment! It's impossible to explain it to the uninitiated. Most of all, I can't explain how enchanted we were with it all. And there's something else I can't explain . . . It's this . . . Our nocturnal life . . . had nothing in common with how we lived during the day. Nothing! In the morning, we would all go to work and transform into average Soviet citizens. Just like

everyone else. Slaving away for the regime. Either you were a conformist or you had to go work as a street cleaner or a watchman, there was
no other way to preserve yourself. And then when we got home from
work . . . We'd once again be sitting in the kitchen drinking vodka and
listening to the forbidden Vysotsky. Catching the Voice of America
through the crackling of the jamming static. I still remember that
beautiful crackling. There were the endless love affairs. Falling in love,
getting divorced. At the same time, many of us considered ourselves
the nation's conscience, believing that we had the right to teach our
people. But what did we really know about them? What we'd read in
Sketches from a Hunter's Album? The things we'd learned from Tur-
genev and other "authors of village life"? Valentin Rasputin . . . Vasily
Belov* . . . I didn't even understand my own father. I'd yell at him,
"Papa, if you don't return your Party card, I won't talk to you anymore!" My father would cry.

Gorbachev had more power than a Tsar. Unlimited power. Then he
went and said, "We can't go on like this." Those were his famous
words. So the country turned into a debating society. People argued at
home, at work, on public transport. Families fell apart over political
disagreements, children would fight with their parents. One of my
girlfriends got into such a big fight about Lenin with her son and
daughter-in-law, she kicked them out. They had to spend a whole winter in a cold dacha outside of Moscow. The theaters grew empty, everyone was at home glued to their televisions. They were broadcasting
the First Congress of the People's Deputies of the USSR. Before that,
there had been the whole hullaballoo around electing those deputies.
The first free elections! Real elections! There were two candidates in
our ward: some Party bureaucrat and a young democrat, a university
lecturer. I still remember his last name—Malyshev . . . Yuri Malyshev.
I recently happened to learn that he's in agribusiness now, selling tomatoes and cucumbers. Back then, he was a revolutionary. You should
have heard his seditious speeches! It was unbelievable! He said that
Marxist-Leninist literature had low horsepower . . . that it reeked of
mothballs . . . He demanded the repeal of the sixth article of the
Constitution—the article that decrees the leading role of the Communist Party. The cornerstone of Marxism-Leninism . . . I listened and

* Valentin Rasputin (1937–2015) and Vasily Belov (1932–2012) were novelists closely
associated with the so-called Village Prose movement, which espoused an idealized
version of rural Russian village life and became increasingly associated with Russian
nationalism in the 1970s and 1980s.

couldn't imagine any of it coming true. Pipe dreams! Who would allow us to even get near it? Everything would fall apart . . . It was the glue holding everything together . . . That's how zombified we all were. I spent years scrubbing away my Soviet mentality, dredging it out of myself by the bucketful. [*She is silent.*] Our team . . . There were about twenty of us volunteers who would go around to people's homes in our neighborhood after work, campaigning for him. We made posters: "Vote for Malyshev!" And can you imagine? He won! By a large margin. Our first-ever victory! Afterward, we nearly lost our minds from the live Congress broadcasts—the deputies were even more frank than we were in our own kitchens, saying things we wouldn't dare say any further than two meters away from our kitchens. Everyone got sucked into the broadcasts like drug addicts. Stuck to the screen. Now Travkin would show them! Really show them! And Boldyrev? Now he's going to—that's the spirit!

An indescribable passion for newspapers and magazines took hold of us—circulation numbers skyrocketed into the millions. Periodicals became more popular than books. In the morning, in the Metro, day in and day out you'd find entire subway cars reading. Even the people standing up. Passengers would swap newspapers. Total strangers. My husband and I had twenty subscriptions between us—an entire one of our monthly salaries went exclusively toward that. After work, I would rush home to get into my house clothes and start reading. My mother died recently, but when she was still alive, she would lament, "I'm dying like a rat at the dump." Her one-bedroom apartment was like a reading room: Magazines and newspapers lay piled on the shelves, in the closet, on the floor, in the hallway. The precious *Novy Mir* and *Znamya* . . . *Daugava* . . . Boxes of clippings everywhere. Really big boxes. I ended up taking them all to the dacha. I feel bad throwing them out, but who would I give them all to? They're nothing but pulp paper now! But all of them had been read and reread. Underlined in red and yellow pencil. The most important things in red. I think I have like a half-ton of those periodicals. Our whole dacha is crammed with that stuff.

Our faith was sincere . . . Naïve . . . We thought that any minute now . . . there were buses idling outside waiting to take us away to democracy. We'd finally leave behind these run-down Khrushchyovkas and move into beautiful houses, build autobahns to replace these broken-down roads, and we'd all turn into respectable people. No one searched for rational proof that any of this would really happen. There was none. What did we need it for? We believed in it with our hearts, not our reason. At the district polling stations, we voted with our hearts, as well. No one told us what exactly we were supposed to do: We were free now and that was that. When you're stuck in an elevator, the only thing you think about are the doors opening—you're ecstatic when they finally open. Pure euphoria! You don't think about how you're supposed to be doing something . . . You're breathing it in with your whole chest . . . You're already happy! My friend married a Frenchman who worked at the Moscow consulate. She'd always be telling him to look at all the energy we Russians have. "All right, but can you tell me exactly what all this energy is for?" he'd ask her. And neither she nor I could answer him. I'd say, "The energy is pulsing, and that's it." I was seeing living people, living faces all around me. Everyone was so beautiful in those days! Where had all these people come from? Only yesterday you couldn't find them anywhere.

At home, our TV was always on . . . We watched the news every hour. I had just had my son, and I'd always bring the radio whenever I went outside with him. People would walk their dogs clutching their radios. We laugh at our son now, saying he's been into politics since he was a baby, but really, he has no interest in any of that. He listens to music, studies languages. Wants to see the world. Other things are important to him. Our children aren't like us. What are they like? Their own time, each other. Back then, we were so excited, "Hurry! Sobchak* is speaking at the Congress!" And everyone would immediately drop whatever they were doing and run over to the TV. I liked seeing Sobchak in some beautiful, probably velvet jacket, his tie in a "European" knot. Sakharov up on the podium . . . So socialism can have a "human face"? There it is . . . For me, it was the face of the scholar Dmitry Likhachev, not General Jaruzelski.† If I said "Gor-

---

* Anatoly Sobchak (1937–2000) was a university professor, coauthor of the constitution of the Russian Federation, and the first democratically elected mayor of St. Petersburg (1991–1996). A mentor to Vladimir Putin and Dmitry Medvedev, he was forced into exile in Paris to escape legal proceedings initiated against him by his successor.
† Dmitry Likhachev (1906–1999) was a Russian intellectual, literary historian, and author of more than a thousand scholarly works who devoted his life to defending his country's Christian and cultural heritage; having survived four years in the camps, Likhachev was rehabilitated and appointed to the staff of the Institute of Russian Literature in Leningrad, where he became known as the doyen of Russian medieval literature. He was revered as a guardian of national culture and a moral authority. General Wojciech Jaruzelski (1923–2014) was the First Secretary of the Polish United Workers' Party from 1981 to 1989, and as such, he was the final leader of the People's Republic of Poland.

bachev," my husband would add, "Gorbachev . . . and Raisa Maxi-movna, too." It was the first time we'd ever seen the wife of a general secretary we didn't have to be embarrassed of. She had a beautiful figure and dressed well. They loved each other. Someone brought over a Polish magazine that said that Raisa was chic. We were so proud! Endless rallies . . . The streets were drowning in flyers. When one rally ended, another one began. People kept going and going, all of us truly believing that all we had to do was show up at the right place, and we would finally hear some truth. We thought that the right people were searching for the right answers . . . A mysterious new life awaited us, and everyone was eager to see it. We all believed that the kingdom of freedom was right around the corner . . .

But life just kept getting worse. Very soon, the only thing you could buy was books. Nothing but books on the store shelves . . .

ELENA YURIEVNA

August 19, 1991 . . . I got to the district Party office. As I walked down the corridor, I could hear how in all of the offices, on all of the floors, all of the radios were on. The receptionist told me that the first secretary wanted to see me. I went into his office. His TV was on at full volume, his face dark; he was sitting by the radio, switching between Radio Liberty, Deutsche Welle, the BBC . . . whatever he could get. On his desk, there was a list of the members of the State Committee on the State of Emergency—the GKChP . . . the Gang of Eight, as they would later be called. "The only respectable one is Varennikov," he told me. "He's a General, he's seen action. He fought in Afghanistan." The second secretary came in . . . then the head of the Organizational Department . . . We started talking: "How awful! There will be blood. We're going to be drowning in blood." "Not everyone, just the ones who deserve it." "It's high time to rescue the Soviet Union." "There'll be a pile of bodies." "There you have it, Gorby is finished. Finally, sane people, generals, are going to take power. The chaos will come to an end." The first secretary announced that the morning planning meeting was canceled—what was there to report on? There were no orders from above. In front of us, he called the police headquarters: "Have you heard anything?" "Nope." We talked some more about Gorbachev—either he's sick or he's been arrested. All of us were more inclined to believe a third version, that he'd run off to America with his family. Where else could he have gone?

That's how we spent the rest of the day, shackled to our phones and our televisions. It was unnerving: Who was going to end up running the country? We waited. I'll be honest with you, we did nothing but wait. It was like Khrushchev's removal. We'd read the memoirs . . . Naturally, our conversations all revolved around the same things . . . What freedom? Our people need freedom like a monkey needs glasses. No one would know what to do with it. All these stalls and kiosks . . . they don't sit well with us. I just remembered how a few days ago, I ran into my former driver. Through some major connections, he'd ended up with a job at the district committee after the army. For a while, he was terribly happy. But then the times changed, cooperatives became legal,* and he left us. Went into business. When I saw him again, I barely recognized him: He had a buzz cut, a leather jacket, a tracksuit. I take it that that's their uniform. He bragged about making more money in one day than the first secretary of the district Party commit- tee made in a month. His was a no-fail enterprise: blue jeans. He and a friend rented out a launderette and turned it into an acid-washed jeans factory. Their technique couldn't have been simpler (necessity is the mother of invention): They'd toss regular, boring jeans into a solu- tion of bleach or chlorine, add broken-up bricks, and boil them for a couple hours. The jeans end up covered in all sorts of stripes, designs, patterns—abstract art! Then they'd dry them and stick on a label that said "Montana." I had a chilling realization: If nothing changes, then pretty soon, these jeans-mongers will be the ones running our govern- ment. NEP men!† And although it seems absurd, they will be the ones to feed us and dress us, too. They'll build their factories up from the basements . . . And that's what actually ended up happening. It all came true! Today, that guy is a millionaire or a billionaire (for me, a million and a billion are equally crazy figures) and a deputy in the Duma to boot. He has a house on the Canary Islands . . . and another one in London . . . In Tsarist times, Herzen and Ogarev were the ones

---

* Instituted by the 1988 Law on Cooperatives, these were the first Soviet privately owned businesses since the abolition of the New Economic Policy in 1928. Though they were heavily taxed and regulated, many people took advantage of them to start their own businesses in the service sector, manufacturing, and foreign trade.

† This was a colloquial name for those who enriched themselves during the New Economic Policy established by Lenin in the early 1920s in order to repair the USSR's economy.

living in London. Today it's them . . . our "new Russians" . . . Jeans, furniture, and chocolate moguls. Oil magnates.

At nine P.M., the first secretary gathered us all in his office again. The head of the district KGB briefed us. He told us about the mood among the people. According to him, the people supported the GKChP. They weren't outraged by the putsch. Everyone was fed up with Gorbachev . . . Ration cards for everything but salt . . . No vodka . . . The KGB boys had gone around town recording people's conversations. The arguments in queues.

". . . It's a coup! What's going to happen with our country?"

". . . There's been no uprising at my house—bed's in the same place it was last night. The vodka's no different."

". . . So that's it for freedom."

". . . Uh-huh. The freedom to stand in line for socks."

". . . Someone must have really wanted some gum to chew and some Marlboros to smoke."

". . . It's high time! The country's on the verge of ruin."

". . . Gorbachev is a Judas. He wanted to sell out the Motherland for dollars."

". . . The blood's about to flow . . ."

". . . We can't do anything around here without bloodshed . . ."

". . . In order to save the country . . . the Party . . . we need jeans. Nice lingerie and salami—not tanks."

". . . So you want the good life? Good luck! Forget about it!"

[*She is silent.*] In a word, the people were waiting. Just like we were. By the end of the day, there were no detective novels left in the Party bureau library. [*She laughs.*] What we should have been reading is Lenin, not detective novels. Lenin and Marx. Our apostles.

I remember the GKChP press conference . . . Yanaev's trembling hands. He stood there making excuses: "Gorbachev deserves all due respect . . . He's my friend . . ." Looking around with his eyes full of terror . . . my heart sank. These weren't the people who could set things right . . . They weren't the ones we'd been waiting for. They were just little cogs . . . Your run-of-the-mill party *apparatchiks* . . . Save the country! Save communism! There was no one to do it . . . On TV: a sea of people on the streets of Moscow. An ocean! Storming the Moscow-bound trains and commuter rails. Yeltsin on the tank. Handing out leaflets . . . Chanting "Yeltsin! Yeltsin!" Triumph! [*She nervously fingers the edge of the tablecloth.*] This tablecloth is made in China . . . The world is chock-full of Chinese goods. China is where

the GKChP triumphed . . . As for us? We're a third world country.
Where are the people who cried "Yeltsin! Yeltsin!" now? They thought
that they'd be living like people in the U.S. and Germany, but they
ended up living like the people in Colombia. We lost . . . we lost our
country . . . Back then, there were fifteen million of us communists!
The Party could have . . . It was sold out . . . Out of fifteen million
people, not a single leader emerged. Not one! While the other side had
its leader—Yeltsin! We stupidly let it all slip through our fingers! Half
of the country was waiting for us to win. We were no longer one nation, we had already split into two.

The people who'd called themselves communists suddenly started
confessing that they'd hated communism from the day they were born.
They returned their Party membership cards. Some showed up and
handed in their Party cards in silence, others slammed the door behind
themselves. People would toss them in front of the district Party headquarters at night, stealing away like thieves. If you're going to do it, at
least give up communism with a clean conscience! But no, they did it
in secret. Every morning, the yardsmen would collect the discarded
Party membership cards and Komsomol certificates from around the
courtyard and bring them all to us. They'd gather them by the bag full,
in big, plastic bags . . . What were we supposed to do with all that
stuff? Where were we supposed to take it? There were no orders. No
signals from above. Instead, there was dead silence. [*Falls deep in
thought.*] Those were the times . . . when people started changing everything . . . absolutely everything. Starting over from scratch. Some
left, changing homelands. Some changed their convictions and principles. Others changed their possessions, buying all new stuff for their
homes. Throwing out everything old and Soviet, and replacing it with
everything new and imported . . . The shuttle traders had already
brought it all over: electric kettles, telephones, furniture . . . refrigerators . . . Mountains of goods materialized out of God knows where.
"I have a Bosch washing machine." "I bought a Siemens TV." Every
conversation was sprinkled with words like "Panasonic," "Sony,"
"Philips" . . . I ran into my neighbor: "I'm embarrassed that I'm so
excited because of a German coffee grinder . . . but I'm just so happy!"
It had only been moments ago—just a moment ago—that she'd spent
the night waiting in line to get her hands on a volume of Akhmatova.
Now she was head over heels for a coffee grinder. Some piece of
junk . . . People threw away their Party membership cards like they
were just trash. It was hard to believe . . . The whole world had trans-

formed in a matter of days. Tsarist Russia, as you can read in the memoirs, slipped away in three days, and the same went for communism. A matter of days. It boggles the mind . . . There were also the kind of people who hid their membership cards, stashing them away just in case. I was recently at a house where they took down a bust of Lenin from the storage cabinet to show me. They're holding on to it for a rainy day . . . The communists will come back, and they'll be the first ones to pin the red bow on once more. [*She is silent for a long time.*] I had hundreds of declarations of resignation from the Party piled on my desk . . . Soon enough, they were all rounded up and taken out to the trash. To rot at the dump. [*She looks for something in the folders on the table.*] I saved a few . . . One day, a museum will ask me for them. They'll come looking . . . [*She begins reading from them.*]

"I was a devoted Komsomol member . . . I joined the Party with a sincere heart. Today, I wish to say that the Party no longer has any power over me . . ."

"The times have led me into confusion . . . I used to believe in the Great October Revolution. After reading Solzhenitsyn, I realized that the 'beautiful ideals of communism' were all drenched in blood. It was all a lie . . ."

"Fear forced me to join the Party . . . Leninist Bolsheviks executed my grandfather, then Stalin's communists massacred my parents in the Mordovian camps . . ."

"On behalf of myself and my deceased husband I hereby resign from the Party . . ."

You had to live through this . . . and not drop dead from the horror. People stood in line outside the district Party headquarters like it was a store. They were queuing up to return their Party membership cards. A woman got in to see me, she was a dairywoman. In tears, she entreated me, "What do I do? What am I supposed to do? In the newspapers, it says that we're supposed to throw out our Party membership cards." She justified herself, saying that she had three children, she had to think of them. Someone was spreading rumors that the Communists were going to be put on trial. Exiled. That they were already fixing up the old barracks in Siberia . . . A new shipment of handcuffs had come into the police headquarters . . . Someone saw them being unloaded out of covered trucks. Dreadful stuff! And then there were the real communists. The ones still devoted to the Idea. A young teacher . . . Not long before the putsch, he'd been accepted into the Party, but he hadn't been issued a membership card yet. "You're going to get shut down soon," he said. "Issue me a membership card. Otherwise, I'll never get one." In that moment, people showed their true colors. A man who had fought at the front came to the offices covered in war medals with an icon hanging around his neck! He returned his Party membership card, which he had gotten at the front, saying, "I don't want to be in the same party as that traitor Gorbachev!" Truly, truly . . . people's characters were revealed. Friends and strangers alike. Even relatives. Before, when I'd run into them, it'd be, "Oh hello, Elena Yurievna!" "How's your health, Elena Yurievna?" Suddenly, if one of them saw me, they'd cross the street to avoid me. The principal of the best school in the district . . . Not long before all of this happened, we'd held an academic Party conference at his school on Brezhnev's novels, *Malaya Zemlya* and *Rebirth*. He'd read an excellent paper on the leading role of the Communist Party during the Great Patriotic War . . . and on the leadership of Comrade Brezhnev in particular . . . I had presented him with a certificate from the district Party committee. A loyal communist! A Leninist! My God, it hadn't even been a month . . . He saw me on the street and started in on me: "Your time is up! You'll have to answer for all of it! First of all, for Stalin!" I couldn't breathe, I was so hurt . . . He was saying that to me? To me! Me, whose father had been in the camps . . . [*It takes her a few minutes to calm down.*] I never liked Stalin. My father forgave him, but I didn't. I could never forgive him . . . [*Silence.*]

The rehabilitation of so-called politicals began after the Twentieth Party Congress.* After Khrushchev's speech . . . while all of this . . . All this was happening during Gorbachev's time . . . I was appointed the director of the district committee on the rehabilitation of the victims of political repressions. I know the position was initially offered to our public prosecutor and then to the second secretary, but both of them had turned it down. Why? Probably out of fear. People are still scared of anything having to do with the KGB. But I didn't even think twice, I said yes right away. My father had been a victim. What did I have to be afraid of? The first time, they took me down to some basement . . . Tens of thousands of folders . . . One "case" is two

* The Twentieth Party Congress, held on February 14–25, 1956, is famous for Nikita Khrushchev's speech denouncing the dictatorship of Stalin, which rocked the *nomenklatura* and eventually the entire Soviet Union. The meeting was classified, but in the subsequent months and years, transcripts of it were released to district and regional Party committees to be discussed at closed meetings and eventually made the rounds as forbidden *samizdat*.

sheets long, another one's an entire thick volume. I learned of how, in 1937, there had been a plan . . . quotas . . . for "exposing and rooting out enemies of the people," just as in the eighties, they were lowering the quotas for people who could be rehabilitated district- and region-wide. The plan needed to be fulfilled and exceeded. It was all in Stalin's style: the meetings, the pressure, the admonishments. More, more . . . [*She shakes her head.*] At night, I would sit there and read them, going through volumes of these documents. To be perfectly honest . . . Honestly . . . It made my hair stand on end. Brother informed on brother, neighbor on neighbor . . . because they'd gotten into an argument about their vegetable patch, or over a room in the communal apartment. Someone sang a rhyme at a wedding, "We should thank Stalin, our brother, he put all our feet in rubber." That was enough. On one hand, the system was butchering people, but on the other hand, the people didn't show one another much mercy, either. The people were ready . . .

A regular communal apartment . . . Five families live there—twenty-seven people in total. Sharing one kitchen and one bathroom. Two of the neighbors are friends: One of them has a five-year-old daughter and the other one is single with no kids. In communal apartments, people were always spying on one another, listening in on each other's conversations. The people with ten-square-meter rooms envied the ones with twenty-five. Life . . . that's just how it is . . . And then, one night, a Black Maria—a police van—shows up . . . They arrest the woman with the five-year-old daughter. Before they take her away, she has a chance to cry out to her friend, "If I don't come back, please look after my little girl. Don't let them take her to an orphanage." So that's what happened. The neighbor took the child in, and the building administration gave her a second room . . . The girl started calling her Mama . . . Mama Anya . . . Seventeen years went by . . . And seventeen years later, the real mother returned. She kissed her friend's hands and feet in gratitude. If this were a fairy tale, this is where the story would end, but in real life, the ending was very different. Without a "happily ever after." When Gorbachev came to power, after they unsealed the archives, they asked the former camp inmate whether she wanted to see her file. She did. So she went down to look at it, opened the folder . . . and the very first page was an informant's report. Familiar handwriting . . . It was her neighbor's, Mama Anya's . . . She'd been the one who'd informed on her . . . Do you understand any of this? I don't. And that woman couldn't, either. She went home and hanged herself. [*Silence.*] I'm an atheist. I have a lot of questions for God . . . I remember . . . I remember my father's words: "It's possible to survive the camps, but you can't survive other people." He'd also say, "You die today, I'll die tomorrow—the first time I heard these words wasn't in the camps, it was from our neighbor Kaprusha . . ." Kaprusha spent his whole life arguing with my parents over our chickens; he hated that they walked all over his vegetable patch. He'd run around in front of our windows waving a hunting rifle . . . [*She is silent.*]

On August 23, they arrested the members of the GKChP. Minister of Internal Affairs Pugo shot himself . . . after shooting his wife . . . The people celebrated: "Pugo shot himself!" Marshal Akhromeyev hanged himself in his Kremlin office. There were a handful of other ghastly deaths . . . The head administrator of Central Committee Affairs, Nikolay Kruchina, fell out of a fifth-floor window . . . Were these suicides or murders? To this day, we don't know. [*Silence.*] How do we go on? How can we go out? If you leave the house, you might run into someone. In those days . . . I had already been living alone for several years. My daughter had married an officer and moved to Vladivostok. My husband died of cancer. At night, I would come home to an empty apartment. I'm not a weak person . . . but I would have all sorts of thoughts . . . dark thoughts . . . They'd float up. I'll be honest with you . . . it occurred to me . . . [*Silence.*] For a while, we continued showing up to work. We'd lock ourselves in our offices and watch the news on TV. Waiting. Hoping for something to happen. Where was our party? Lenin's invincible party! The world had collapsed . . . We got a phone call from a collective farm: men with whips and pitchforks, hunting rifles—whatever they could find—had gathered in front of the farm's administrative offices in order to defend the Soviet state. The first secretary told them, "Send everyone home." We got scared . . . We were all scared . . . While the people were resolute. I know a handful of stories like that. But we were too scared to do anything . . .

And then finally the day came . . . We got a phone call from the district executive committee, "We have to shut you down. You have two hours to gather your things and leave." [*She is too upset to speak.*] Two hours . . . two . . . A special commission showed up to seal the doors . . . Democrats! Some locksmith, a young journalist, and that mother of five . . . I recognized her from the demonstrations. From her letters to the district committee . . . to our newspaper . . . She lived in a barracks house* with a large family. She gave speeches everywhere she could demanding a real apartment. She cursed the Communists. I'd remembered her face . . . This was her moment of triumph . . . When they got to the first secretary's office, he threw a chair at them. In my office, one of the members of the commission went up to the window and demonstratively ripped off the blinds. So that I wouldn't take them home? My god! They made me open my handbag . . . A few years later, I ran into that mother of five on the street, I even remembered her name just now, Galina Avdey. I asked her, "So did you ever get your apartment?" She shook her fist in the direction of the regional administration offices: "Those bastards lied to me, too." And so on . . . What else? A crowd was waiting for us outside of the building. "Put the communists on trial! Send them off to Siberia!" "If only we had a machine gun to shoot through all these windows!" I turned around and saw two tipsy men standing behind me—they were the ones who'd been talking about a machine gun . . . I said, "Just remember that I'll shoot back." A policeman stood by pretending that he didn't hear anything. I knew that policeman personally.

The whole time I felt like . . . I felt like I could hear ominous noises following me. I wasn't the only one living that way . . . The daughter of our Party instructor was approached by two girls from her class in school, who told her, "We're not going to be friends with you. Your father worked in the district Party headquarters." "My father is a good man." "A good father wouldn't have worked there. We were at a demonstration yesterday . . ." Fifth graders† . . . children . . . and already they're Gavroches, prepared to hand soldiers ammunition. The first secretary had a heart attack. He died in the ambulance, he didn't even make it to the hospital. I thought that it would be like the old days, lots of wreaths, an orchestra, but instead—nothing and no one. A handful of people walked behind the coffin, a small group of his comrades. His widow had a hammer and sickle carved on his tombstone along with the opening lines of the Soviet anthem: "The unbreakable Union of free republics . . ." People laughed at her. All the while, I kept hearing those ominous noises . . . I thought I was going

---

* Barracks were another Soviet solution to communal housing, especially on the outskirts of major cities and in factory towns. They were constructed as temporary buildings, but many people ended up settling in them permanently.
† Soviet children typically began first grade at the age of seven. The Soviet school system went up to the tenth grade. Fifth graders would be eleven or twelve years old.

to lose my mind . . . A woman I didn't know accosted me at the store, getting into my face: "Are you happy now, commies, you squandered the country to shit!"

What saved me? Phone calls . . . phone calls from my friends. "If they ship you off to Siberia, don't be scared. It's pretty there." [*She laughs.*] She'd been on a tour and liked it. My cousin from Kiev called: "Come stay with us. I'll give you your own keys. You can hide out at our dacha. No one will find you there." "I'm not a criminal," I told her. "I'm not about to go into hiding." My parents called me every day: "What are you doing?" "Pickling cucumbers." I spent my days boiling jars. Pickling and pickling. Not reading the papers or watching TV. I read detective novels, I'd finish one book and immediately start the next one. Television was terrifying, and so were the newspapers.

For a long time, no one would give me a job . . . Everyone thought that we'd divvied up the Party money and that each of us had ended up with a chunk of an oil pipeline or, at the very least, a small gas station. I have no gas station, no store, not even a kiosk. They call the privately owned kiosks "*komki*" now. *Komki,* shuttle traders . . . The great Russian language has grown unrecognizable: "voucher," "exchange rate corridor," "IMF tranche" . . . It's like we speak a foreign language now.

I went back to teaching. I reread my beloved Tolstoy and Chekhov with my students. How are the others? My comrades met various fates . . . One of our Party instructors killed himself . . . The director of the Party bureau had a nervous breakdown and spent a long time in the hospital recovering. Some went into business . . . The second secretary runs a movie theater. One district committee instructor became a priest. I met up with him recently and we talked for a long time. He's living a second life. It made me jealous. I remembered . . . I was at an art gallery. One of the paintings had all this light in it and a woman standing on a bridge. Gazing off into the distance . . . There was so much light . . . I couldn't look away. I'd leave and come back, I was so drawn to it. Maybe I too could have had another life. I just don't know what it would have been like.

ANNA ILINICHNA

I woke up from the clamor . . . I opened the window: They'd come into Moscow! The capital was filled with tanks and armored vehicles full of troops! The radio! Quick—turn on the radio! The radio was broadcasting an address to the Soviet people: "A deadly danger looms over our Motherland . . . The country is plunging into a maelstrom of violence and lawlessness . . . We must wipe the streets clean of criminal elements . . . Put an end to this time of troubles . . ." It was not clear whether Gorbachev had stepped down from office for health reasons or if he'd been arrested. I called my husband, who was at the dacha: "There's been a coup d'état. The power is in the hands of . . ." "You idiot! Hang up the phone, they're going to come for you!" I turned on the TV. All of the channels were playing *Swan Lake*. But I was seeing flashes of very different images—we're all the children of Soviet propaganda: Santiago in Chile . . . the presidential palace burning . . . Salvador Allende's voice . . . The phone calls began: The city was full of military equipment, tanks standing on Pushkin Square, in Theater Square . . . My mother-in-law was visiting. She got terribly scared: "Don't go outside. I've lived through a dictatorship, I know what this means." But I didn't want to live under a dictatorship!

After lunch, my husband came back from the dacha. We sat in our kitchen, smoking like chimneys. We were afraid that our phone was tapped, so we put a pillow on top of it. [*She laughs.*] We'd read our fill of dissident literature. We'd heard enough stories. It had all finally come in handy . . . They'd given us a little air, now everything was going to go on lockdown again. They'd chase us back into the cage, rub us into the asphalt . . . We'd be like butterflies crushed against the pavement . . . We'd just been discussing Tiananmen Square, talking about the recent developments in Tbilisi, how they'd dispersed a demonstration with shovels. The storming of the television tower in Vilnius . . . "While we were sitting around, reading Shalamov and Platonov," my husband said, "civil war has broken out. People used to argue in their kitchens and go to demonstrations, now we're going to start shooting each other." That was the mood . . . It felt like catastrophe was at hand . . . We never turned off the radio, we kept turning the dial, but every station was just playing music, classical music. Then, suddenly, a miracle! Radio Russia started working again: "The legally elected President has been forced to resign . . . There has been a cynical attempt at a putsch . . ." That's how we found out that thousands of people were already out in the streets. Gorbachev was in danger . . . To go or not to go—there was no question. We had to go! My mother-in-law tried to talk me out of it at first, like, "Think of your child, are you crazy, where are you running off to?" I didn't say anything. She saw we were getting ready to go: "Since you're such huge idiots, at least bring some baking soda solution with you so you can wet cloths and put them over your faces if they start gassing you." I made a three-liter jar of baking soda solution and ripped up one of our sheets. We took all the food we had in the house, I dug all of the cans out of the pantry.

Many people were, like us, headed down to the Metro . . . While others were standing in line for ice cream or buying flowers. We walked past a group of friends laughing . . . I overheard someone say, "If I can't go to the concert tomorrow because of the tanks, I'll never forgive them." A man in his underwear came running toward us with a shopping bag full of empty bottles. He caught up with us: "Can you show me the way to Stroitelnaya Street?" I told him where he should turn right, then head straight. He said thanks. The only thing he cared about was getting those bottles down to the recycling center. Were things any different in 1917? Some people were shooting while others were dancing at balls. Lenin on the armored train . . .

ELENA YURIEVNA

A farce! They played out a farce! If the GKChP had won, we'd be living in a different country. If Gorbachev hadn't been too much of a coward . . . If they hadn't been paying people in tires and dolls. Shampoo. If a factory made nails, they'd pay the workers in nails. If it was soap, then it was soap. I tell everyone: look at the Chinese . . . They have their own path. They're not dependent on anyone, they don't try to imitate anyone. Today, the whole world is afraid of China . . . [*She turns to me with a question again.*] I'm sure you're just going to get rid of everything I'm saying.

I promise her that there will be two stories. I want to be a cold-blooded historian, not one who is holding a blazing torch. Let time be the judge. Time is just, but only in the long term—not in the short term. The time we won't live to see, which will be free of our prejudices.

ANNA ILINICHNA

You could laugh at the way we were and call it a musical comedy. Mockery is in style these days. But everything that happened was in earnest. Sincere. It was all real and we were all real. Unarmed men and women stood in front of the tanks, prepared to die. I sat on those barricades and saw those people. They'd come from all over the country. There were some old Muscovite ladies, God's dandelions, they'd bring meat patties, warm potatoes wrapped in towels. They gave everyone something to eat . . . including the men in the tanks. "Eat your fill, boys. Just don't shoot. Are you really going to shoot at us?" The soldiers had no idea what was going on . . . When they opened up the hatches and climbed out of their tanks, they were shocked. All of Moscow was there! Girls would climb on top of the tanks and hug and kiss them. Feed them rolls. Soldiers' mothers whose sons had died in Afghanistan wept, begging them, "Our children died on foreign soil, are you planning on dying here in your own country?" Some major . . . When the women surrounded him, he couldn't handle it any more, he screamed, "I have kids, too! I'm not going to shoot anyone! I swear, I won't! We're not going to go against our own people!" So many funny and touching things happened, things that reduced us to tears. Suddenly, shouts swept the crowd: "Does anyone have any Validol? Someone is ill!" The pills materialized instantly. A woman had come with her child in a stroller (what would my mother-in-law think!) and she got out a diaper in order to draw a red cross on it. But with what? "Who has lipstick?" People started tossing their lipsticks at her— cheap stuff and Lancôme, Dior, Chanel . . . No one was filming it, no one recorded these details, and it's too bad. Really, too bad. The elegance, the beauty of the event . . . All of that comes later, with the banners and the music . . . That's what gets cast in bronze . . . In real life, everything is broken down, filthy, and lilac: people spending the night around the fire, sitting directly on the ground, on newspapers and flyers. Hungry and angry. They swore and drank, but there were no drunks. Some people came by with salami, cheese, and bread. Coffee. They said that these were cooperative owners . . . businessmen . . . I even glimpsed a couple of jars of red caviar. Those disappeared into people's pockets. Others were handing out free cigarettes. A guy sitting next to me was covered in prison tattoos—a real tiger! Rockers, punks, students with guitars. And professors. Everyone all together. The people! Those were my people! I ran into my friends from college who I hadn't seen in fifteen years, if not more. Some of them lived in Vologda, others in Yaroslavl . . . But they'd all gotten on the train to come to Moscow! To defend something that was sacred to all of us. In the morning, we took them home with us. We washed, ate breakfast, and then we all went back out there. At the Metro exit, people were handing out metal rods and rocks. "Paving stones are the weapons of the proletariat," we laughed. We built barricades, overturned trolley-buses, cut down trees.

There was already a tribune. They hung posters over it: "No to the Junta!" "The People Aren't Dirt Under Your Feet." Speakers addressed the crowd through a megaphone. Simple people and famous politicians alike would begin their speeches with regular words. Then, a few minutes in, those words would no longer be enough and they would all start swearing. "We're going to take these shitheads and . . ." Obscenities! Good old Russian obscenities. "Their time is up . . ." And then the great and mighty Russian language! Obscenities like war cries. A language everyone could understand. That was the spirit of the moment. Those minutes of pure exaltation! So powerful! The old words weren't enough and we didn't yet know new ones . . . The whole time, we were waiting to storm the White House. The silence, especially at night, was unfathomable. Everyone was unbearably tense. Thousands of people—and silence. I remember the smell of gasoline being poured into bottles. It smelled like war . . .

The people there were good people! Excellent people! Today, they write about the vodka and the drugs, as though there were no revolution to speak of, just some drunks and druggies going off to the barricades. Lies! Everyone had come to die honorably. We were all well aware that this machine had been grinding people into sand for seventy years . . . Nobody thought that it would break down so easily . . . Without major bloodshed. There were rumors that they'd mined the bridge, that any moment now they were going to gas us. A medical school student instructed us on what to do in case they gassed us. Every half hour, the situation changed. We got some terrifying news: Three people had been run over by a tank and died . . . But nobody flinched, no one left the square. It was incredibly important to be there, no matter how things turned out. No matter how much disappointment awaited us. We lived through it . . . That's who we were! [She cries.] In the morning, there were shouts of "Hurrah! Hurrah!" echoing through the square. Then cursing again . . . tears, shouting . . . Through the grapevine, we learned that the army had gone over to the side of the people, the special forces from the Alpha division had refused to participate in an assault. The tanks were leaving the capital . . . When they announced that the putschists had been arrested, people began embracing—there was so much joy! We'd won!

We'd defended our freedom. Together, we'd done it. We could do any-thing! Dirty, wet from the rain, we lingered, not wanting to go home. We wrote down each other's addresses. Swore to remember each other, to become friends. The policemen in the Metro were extremely polite—never before or since have I seen such polite policemen.

We won . . . Gorbachev returned from Foros* to an entirely differ-ent country. People were walking around the city smiling at one an-other. We won! That feeling stayed with me for a long time . . . I walked around, going over everything in my mind, scenes flashing in front of my eyes . . . How someone had shouted, "Tanks! The tanks are coming!" and everyone took one another's hands and made a human chain. It had been two or three in the morning. The man next to me took out a packet of cookies: "Anyone want a cookie?" and ev-eryone took one. For some reason, we were all laughing. We wanted cookies—we wanted to live! But I . . . Still, to this very day . . . I'm glad I was there. With my husband and my friends. Everyone was very sincere back then. I feel sorry for us . . . Sad that we're not like that anymore. I used to think about it all the time.

Parting ways, I ask them how they've managed to remain friends, which, as it turned out, they had been since college.

—We agreed never to talk about these things. We have no interest in hurting each other's feelings. We used to get into fights, stop talking. Sometimes, we wouldn't speak to each other for years on end. But all that has passed.

—Now we only ever talk about our children and grandchildren. What we're growing at our dachas.

—When our friends get together . . . Not a word about politics. Everyone came to this by their own path. We all live together: the gen-tlemen and the comrades. Reds and Whites. But no one wants any more shooting. There's been enough blood.

---

* The August putsch took place while Gorbachev was in Foros, in Crimea.

ON BROTHERS AND SISTERS, VICTIMS AND EXECUTIONERS ... AND THE ELECTORATE

◆

Alexander Porfirievich Sharpilo,
retired, 63 years old

AS TOLD BY HIS NEIGHBOR,
MARINA TIKHONOVNA ISAICHIK

Strangers, what do you want, coming here? People keep coming and coming. Well, death never comes for no reason, there's always a reason. Death will find a reason.

He burned alive on his vegetable patch, among his cucumbers . . . Poured acetone over his head and lit a match. I was sitting here watching TV when suddenly I heard screaming. An old person's voice . . . a familiar voice, like Sashka's . . . and then another, younger voice. A student had been walking past, there's a technical college nearby, and there he was, a man on fire. What can you say! He ran over, started trying to put him out. Got burned himself. By the time I got outside, Sashka was on the ground, moaning . . . his head all yellow . . . You're not from around here, what do you care? What do you need a stranger's grief for?

Everyone wants a good look at death. Ooh! Well . . . In our village, where I lived with my parents before I was married, there was an old man who liked to come and watch people die. The women would shame him and chase him away: "Shoo, devil!" but he'd just sit there. He ended up living a long time. Maybe he really was a devil! How can you watch? Where do you look . . . in what direction? After death, there is nothing. You die and that's it—they bury you. But when you're alive, even if you're unhappy, you can walk around in the breeze or stroll through the garden. When the spirit leaves, there's no person left, just the dirt. The spirit is the spirit and everything else is just dirt. Dirt and nothing else. Some die in the cradle, others live until their hair goes gray. Happy people don't want to die . . . and those who are loved don't want to die, either. They beg to stay longer. But where are these happy people? On the radio, they'd said that after the war was over, we would all be happy, and Khrushchev, I remember, promised . . . He said that communism would soon be upon us. Gorbachev swore it, too, and he spoke so beautifully . . . it had sounded so good. Now Yeltsin's making the same promises. He even threatened to lie down on the train tracks . . . I waited and waited for the good life to come. When I was little, I waited for it . . . and then when I got a little older . . . Now I'm old. To make a long story short, everyone lied and things only ever got worse. Wait and see, wait and suffer. Wait and see . . . My husband died. He went out, collapsed, and that was that—his heart stopped. You couldn't measure it or weigh it, all the trouble we've seen. But here I am, still alive. Living. My children all scattered: My son is in Novosibirsk, and my daughter stayed in Riga with her family, which, nowadays, means that she lives abroad. In a foreign country. They don't even speak Russian there anymore.

I have an icon in the corner and a little dog so that there's someone to talk to. One stick of kindling won't start a fire, but I do my best. Oh . . . It's good of God to have given man cats and dogs . . . and trees and birds . . . He gave man everything so that he would be happy and life wouldn't seem too long. So life wouldn't wear him down. The one thing I haven't gotten sick of is watching the wheat turn yellow. I've gone hungry so many times that the thing I love best is ripening grain, seeing the sheaves sway in the wind. For me, it's as beautiful as the paintings in a museum are for you . . . Even now, I don't hanker after white bread—there's nothing better than salted black bread with sweet tea. Wait and see . . . and then wait some more . . . The only remedy we know for every kind of pain is patience. Next thing you know, your whole life's gone by. That's how it was for Sashka . . . Our Sashka . . . He waited and waited and then he couldn't take it any longer. He got tired. The body lies in the earth, but the soul has to answer for everything. [*She wipes her tears.*] That's how it is! We cry down here . . . and when we die, we cry then, too . . .

People have started believing in God again because there is no other hope. In school, they used to teach us that Lenin was God and

Karl Marx was God. The churches were used to store grain and stock-pile beets. That's how it was until the war came. War broke out . . . Stalin reopened the churches so prayers would be said for the victory of Russian arms. He addressed the people: "Brothers and sisters . . . My friends . . ." And what had we been before that? Enemies of the people . . . Kulaks and kulak sympathizers . . . In our village, all of the best families were subjected to dekulakization; if they had two cows and two horses, that was already enough to make them kulaks. They'd ship them off to Siberia and abandon them in the barren taiga for-est . . . Women smothered their children to spare them the suffering. Oh, so much woe . . . so many tears . . . more tears than there is water on this Earth. Then Stalin goes addressing his "brothers and sis-ters" . . . We believed him. Forgave him. And defeated Hitler! He showed up with his tanks . . . gleaming and iron-plated . . . and we defeated him anyway! But what am I today? Who are we now? We're the electorate . . . I watch TV, I never miss the news . . . We're the elec-torate now. Our job is to go and vote for the right candidate then call it a day. I was sick one time and didn't make it to the polling station, so they drove over here themselves. With a red box. That's the one day they actually remember us . . . Yep . . .

We die how we lived . . . I even go to church and wear a little cross, but there has never been any joy in my life, and there isn't any now. I never got any happiness. And now even praying won't help. I just hope that I get to die soon . . . I hope the heavenly kingdom hurries up and comes, I'm sick of waiting. Just like Sashka . . . He's in the graveyard now, resting. [*She crosses herself.*] They buried him with music, with tears. Everyone wept. Many tears are shed on that day, people feel sorry for you. But what's the point of repenting? Who can hear us after death? All that's left of him are two rooms in a barracks house, a vegetable patch, some red certificates, and a medal: "Victor of Social-ist Emulation." I have a medal just like that in my cabinet. I was a Stakhanovite* and a deputy. There wasn't always enough to eat, but there were plenty of red certificates. They'd hand you one and take your picture. Three families live together in this barracks. We moved

---

* The Stakhanovite movement was a campaign initiated in the 1930s to stimulate in-dustry by encouraging workers to surpass production quotas, following the example of coal miner Alexey Stakhanov, who was said to have mined 102 tons of coal in less than six hours, fourteen times his quota. Like the shock worker movement, this was also an example of "socialist emulation"—seeing who can work hardest for the com-mon good.

in when we were young, we thought it would only be for a year or two, but we ended up spending our entire lives here. And we'll die in this barracks, too. For twenty, for thirty years . . . people were on the waiting list for an apartment, putting up with this . . . Then, one day, Gaidar comes and laughs in our faces: So go ahead and buy one! With what money? Our money evaporated . . . one reform, then another . . . We were robbed! What a country they flushed down the toilet! Every family had had two little rooms, a small shed, and a vegetable patch. We were exactly the same. Look at all the money we made! We're rich! We spent our whole lives believing that one day, we would all live well. It was a lie! A great big lie! And our lives . . . better not to remember what they were like . . . We endured, worked and suffered. Now we're not even living anymore, we're just waiting out our final days.

Sashka and I were from the same village . . . Here, near Brest. We used to spend evenings together on our bench reminiscing. What else is there to talk about? He was a good man. He didn't drink, he wasn't a drunk . . . No-o-o . . . Even though he lived alone. What's an old bachelor to do? He'd drink a little—take a nap . . . drink a little more . . . I walk around the courtyard. Pace. I walk and think: Earthly life isn't the end. Death gives the soul some open space . . . Where is he? In his final moments, he thought of his neighbors, he didn't forget us. The barracks is old, they built it right after the war, the wood's dried out. It would have caught fire like paper, gone up in flames in an instant! In the blink of an eye! It would have burned down to the ground, to a pile of ashes . . . He wrote a note to his children: "Raise your children right. Farewell," and left it in a visible place. And then he went out into the garden . . . onto his vegetable patch.

Oh! Oh! So . . . what can you do . . . The ambulance came, they laid him out on a stretcher, but he hopped off, he wanted to walk. "What have you done, Sashka?" I followed him to the ambulance. "I'm sick and tired of living. Call my son, tell him to come to the hospital." He could still talk . . . His jacket was burnt, his shoulder was all white and clean. He left five thousand rubles . . . That used to be good money! He took it out of his savings account and left it next to his note. His life savings. Before perestroika, that kind of money could buy you a car, a Volga. The most expensive model! But today? It was only enough for a new pair of boots and a funeral wreath. That's our life! He lay there on the stretcher turning black . . . turning black right before my eyes . . . The doctors also took that kid who'd found him, who'd grabbed my wet sheets off the clothesline (I'd washed them that day) and thrown them on top of him. A stranger . . . just a student . . . He was passing by and suddenly saw a man in flames. Sitting in his vegetable patch, hunched over and on fire. Smoldering. Silent! That's how he described him later, "Silent and burning." Burning alive . . . In the morning, his son knocked on my door: "Papa is dead." Lying in his coffin . . . his head covered in burns and his hands . . . Black, all black . . . His hands had been golden! He used to be able to do anything. He was a carpenter, a mason. Everyone around here has something to remember him by—a table, a bookcase, shelves . . . Sometimes he would stand there in the courtyard and plane wood into the night. I can see him now, standing there and planing. He loved wood. He could recognize the type of wood by its smell, from a single shaving. Every kind of tree, he told me, has its own smell, and the strongest-smelling wood is pine. "Pine smells like good tea, and maple has a happy smell." He worked until his dying day. The proverb is true: While the chain's in your hands, the bread's in your teeth. There is no surviving on today's pensions. I work as a nanny, raising other people's children. They give me a kopeck, I buy sugar and cheap bologna. What can you afford on our pensions? You get yourself some bread and milk, and then there isn't enough left over for slippers. It's just not enough. Old people used to sit on the benches in their courtyards, carefree. Prattling. Not anymore . . . Some collect empty bottles around town, others stand in front of the church, begging . . . Some sell sunflower seeds or cigarettes at the bus stop. Ration cards for vodka. A person got trampled here in the liquor aisle. Trampled to death. Vodka is worth more than—what's it called?—that American dollar. You can buy anything with vodka. You can use it to pay the plumber and the electrician, too. Otherwise, they won't even come. So . . . Well . . . Life went by . . . The only thing money can't buy is time. Weep before God or not, you can't buy it. That's just the way it is.

Sashka made the decision to stop living. He didn't want to go on. Returned his ticket back to God himself . . . Oh! Lord! The police keep coming and coming. Asking questions . . . [*She pauses to listen.*] There it goes, the train whistle . . . That's the Moscow train—Brest-Moscow. I don't even need a watch. I get up with the whistle of the Warsaw train—six in the morning. Then it's the Minsk train, and then the first train to Moscow . . . They sound different in the morning and at night. Sometimes I'll listen to them all night long. When you get older, sleep evades you . . . Who do I have to talk to now? I sit on the bench alone . . . I would console him: "Sashka, find yourself a good woman. Get married." "Lizka will come back. I'll wait for her." I hadn't seen her in seven years, not since she left him. She got involved with some sort of officer. She was young, much younger than him. He was crazy about her. She beat her head against the coffin: "I'm the one who ruined Sashka's life." Oh! Well . . . Love isn't a hair, you can't just pull it out. And no ritual can make it stick. Why cry over it? Who's going to hear you underground . . . [*Silence.*] Oh, Lord! You can do whatever you want before you're forty, you can even sin. But after forty, you have to repent. Then God will forgive you.

[*She laughs.*] You're still writing? Go on, keep writing. I'll tell you more stories . . . I've had more than my share of grief . . . [*She raises her head.*] Look there . . . The swallows have come! It's going to get warm soon. The truth is, a journalist has already come here and talked to me . . . asked me all about the war . . . I would give everything I have to prevent a war. There's nothing more terrifying than war! We were under fire from German guns, our houses cracking apart in flames. Our gardens burning. Oh Lord! Sashka and I would talk about the war every day . . . His father went missing in action, his brother died fighting with the partisans. They herded the prisoners into Brest—throngs of people! Drove them down the roads like they were horses, then kept them in fenced-in lots where they'd drop dead and lie there like garbage. All summer long, Sashka would go there with his mother to look for his father . . . He'd start telling me . . . and wouldn't be able to stop. They looked for him among the living and the dead. No one was afraid of death anymore, it was an everyday occurrence. Before the war, we'd sing, "From the taiga to the British sea, / There's nothing more mighty than the Red Army . . ." We sang it proudly! Spring came, the ice melted . . . it all broke apart . . . and the whole river behind our village was choked with corpses. Naked, blackened, only their belts shining. Belts with little red stars. There's no sea without water and no war without blood. God gives men life, but during a war, anyone can take it away . . . [*She weeps.*] I pace and pace the courtyard. Marking time. Sometimes, I feel like Sashka is standing there behind me. I'll hear his voice. Then I turn around and there's no one there. What can you do . . . Well . . . What have you done, Sashka? What a painful path you chose! Maybe there's one good thing: You burned on Earth, so it won't be like that in heaven. You've done your suffering. There must be somewhere where they keep all our tears . . . How will he be greeted there? Down here, the invalids crawl, the paralyzed lie there, the deaf get by. It's not up to us to decide . . . We're not the ones in charge . . . [*She crosses herself.*]

I will never forget the war . . . The Germans invaded our village . . . Young and cheerful. With so much noise! They arrived in huge vehicles and their three-wheeled motorcycles. I'd never even laid eyes on a motorcycle before. All we had at the collective farm were these one-and-a-half-ton trucks with wooden beds, these machines that were low to the ground. You should have seen those German trucks! They were as tall as houses! Their horses—not horses, but mountains. They painted a message on the wall of our schoolhouse: "The Red Army has abandoned you!" We started living under German rule . . . There were a lot of Jews in our village: Avram, Yankel, Morduch . . . They rounded them all up and took them out to the *shtetl*. They'd brought their pillows and blankets, but they were all killed right away. They rounded up every Jew in the district and shot them all in a single day. Tossed them into a pit . . . thousands of them . . . thousands . . . People said that for three days afterward, their blood kept rising to the top of the pit . . . like the ground was breathing . . . it was alive . . . Now there's a park there. A place of recreation. You can't hear anyone from beyond the grave. No one can scream . . . So, that's what I think . . . [*She cries.*]

I don't know . . . How did it happen? Did they come to her, or did she find them in the forest? Our neighbor hid two little Jewish boys in her barn—adorable kids. Real cherubs! Everyone was shot, but they hid. They managed to run away. One was eight, and the other one was ten. My mother would bring them milk . . . "Children, hush," she told us. "Not a word of this to anyone." In my neighbor's family, there was an old, old grandfather, he remembered the other war with the Germans, the first one . . . He'd feed the boys and weep: "Oh, children, they'll capture you and torture you. If I could stand to do it, you'd be better off if I killed you myself." Those were his words . . . And the devil hears everything . . . [*She crosses herself.*] Three Germans showed up on a black motorcycle with their big black dog. Someone had informed on them . . . There are always people willing to do things like this, people whose souls are black. They're alive, but it's like they are soulless . . . Their hearts are just medical, not human hearts. They have no pity for anyone. The kids ran into the field, into the grain . . . The Germans sent their dog in after them . . . Afterward, their remains had to be gathered up shred by shred . . . There were nothing but rags left of them . . . nothing to bury, no one even knew their last names. Then the Germans tied our neighbor to their motorcycle and made her run until her heart burst . . . [*She no longer wipes her tears.*] In times of war, people fear one another. People they know and strangers alike. Say something during the day, and the birds will hear—speak at night, and the mice will. My mother taught us prayers. Without God, even a worm can swallow you.

On May 9 . . . our holiday* . . . Sashka and I would each have a drink . . . and a cry. It gets hard to swallow your tears . . . So, well, what can you do . . . At the age of ten, he became the man of the house, taking the place of his father and brother. When the war ended, I turned sixteen. I went to work at a cement factory, I had to help my mother. We'd drag fifty-kilo sacks of cement; load sand, stone chips, and equipment onto big trucks. But I wanted to go to school . . . We hauled loads and plowed with the cow . . . The cow would wail from the burden . . . And what did we have to eat? What did we eat? We ground up acorns and gathered pinecones in the forest. Still, I held fast to my dreams. Throughout the entire war, I'd dreamed of finishing school and becoming a teacher . . . The last day of war was so nice, it was warm . . . Mama and I went out into the field. Suddenly, a policeman galloped by on a warhorse: "Victory! The Germans have signed the capitulation!" He was dashing through the fields shouting, "Victory! Victory!" People ran into the village. Yelling, crying, swearing. Most of all crying. But the very next day, we all began wondering, "What's going to happen to us now?" Our houses stood empty, nothing but wind in our barns. Cups made of tin cans . . . cans left behind by the German soldiers . . . Candles in used cartridges. During the war, we had forgotten all about salt, our bones had gone soft. When the Germans were retreating, they took our pig and caught the last of our chickens. Before that, partisans had taken our cow away in the night . . . My mother hadn't wanted to give it up, so one of the partisans shot up at the ceiling. They carried off Mama's sewing machine and her dresses, too. Were they partisans or just burglars? They had guns . . . So, well, what can you do . . . ? People always want to live, even during wartime. You'll learn a lot from living through a war . . . There is no beast worse than man. It's men who kill other men, not bullets. People kill people . . . Ah, my dear girl!

* Victory Day. The Germans surrendered late at night on May 8, 1945, so it is celebrated on May 9 with the time adjusted to Moscow time. The choice of May 9 as Victory Day was also a way to emphasize the fact that the victory was the USSR's and Stalin's and not that of the Western powers.

Mama called the fortune teller . . . The fortune teller told her, "Everything will turn out fine." We had nothing to give her. My mother found two beets in the cellar and thought it was enough, and the fortune teller did, too. I went to apply to the teacher training college like I had dreamed. I had to go there and fill out an application. I answered all of the questions and then I got to the one that said, "Were you or any of your relatives prisoners of war or under occupation?" I answered that yes, of course we were. The director called me into his office: "Young lady, please take your documents and go." He'd fought at the front and lost one of his arms. He had an empty sleeve. That's how I learned that we . . . everyone who'd survived the occupation . . . were unreliable elements. We were now under suspicion. No one was calling us brothers and sisters anymore . . . It took forty years for them to remove that question from the application form. Forty years! By the time they took it out, my life was already over. "And who abandoned us to the Germans?" "Hush, my girl, quiet . . ." The director closed the door so that no one would hear. "Hush . . . hush . . ." What can you do to escape your fate? It's like drawing blood from a stone . . . Sashka applied to the military academy. In his application, he wrote that his family had lived in occupied territory and that his father had gone missing in action. He was rejected outright . . . [*She is silent.*] Is it all right that I keep talking about myself, telling you my life story? All of our lives were the same. I just hope that they don't put me away for telling you all this. Is the Soviet government still in power or is it entirely gone?

For all the grief, I forget the good . . . When we were young and in love. I had a great time at Sashka's wedding . . . He loved his Lizka, he courted her for a long time. Worshiped the ground she walked on! He went all the way to Minsk to get her a real wedding veil. After the wedding, he lifted her up and carried her into the barracks . . . That's one of our old traditions . . . the groom is supposed to carry the bride like a baby so that the *domovoi** doesn't notice her. So he doesn't get his eye on her. The *domovoi* doesn't take to strangers, he always tries to get rid of them. He's the true master of the house, you have to get on his good side. Oh . . . [*She gestures dismissively.*] Nobody believes in anything anymore. Not in the *domovoi* and not in communism. People live without any kind of faith! Maybe they still believe in love . . .

---

* House goblin of Russian folklore.

"Bitter! Bitter!"* we cried at Sashka's wedding table. How did people drink back then? There was a single bottle for the entire table, ten people—nowadays you need a bottle for every guest. You used to have to sell the cow to pay for a wedding feast for your child. He really loved his Lizka . . . but it's impossible to make someone love you back. So, well, what can you do . . . She crept around like a cat. After their children grew up, she left him, and didn't look back. I said to him, "Sashka, find yourself a good woman. You'll take to drink." "I'll just have a few sips, watch some ice skating, and go to bed." When you sleep alone, not even the blanket can warm you. Even heaven will make you sick if you're alone. He drank, but he never overdid it. No . . . he never overdid it, not like other people do. Oh! One of our neighbors here . . . He'll drink Gvozdika eau de cologne, aftershave, methylated spirits, cleaning fluid . . . Believe it or not, he's still alive! A bottle of vodka costs as much as a coat used to. And something to snack on? Half a kilo of salami is half a month's pension. Drink up that freedom! Eat it up! What a country they surrendered. An empire!! Without a single shot fired . . . The thing I don't understand is, Why didn't anyone ask us? I spent my life building a great nation. That's what they told us. They promised.

I felled timber, dragged railway ties on my back . . . My husband and I even worked in Siberia, at a communist construction site. I remember the names of the rivers: the Yenisei, the Biryusa, the Mana . . . We worked on the Abakan-Taishet Railway. They shipped us there in freight cars: two levels of hammered-together bunks, no mattresses, no linens, and your fist for a pillow. A hole in the floor of the train car . . . and for more serious needs, there was a bucket screened off with a sheet. The train would stop in a field, we'd pile up whatever straw we found and that would be our beds. There was no light in the train cars. But the whole ride there, we sang Komsomol songs! Until we went hoarse! It was a seven-day journey, but we made it! The wild taiga, snow as high as a man. Soon, we all came down with scurvy, all our teeth went loose. Lice. And the production quotas—oh-ho! The men who hunted would go after bear. That was the only time we had meat, otherwise it was just kasha and more kasha. I still remember

---

* It's Russian custom for wedding guests cry "Bitter!" during toasts, and when they do, the bride and groom must kiss. The idea is that the guests are bemoaning the bitterness of their vodka, which must be sweetened with the sight of the couple's kisses.

that you should only shoot a bear in the eye. We lived in barracks
without showers or baths. In the summer, we'd go into town to wash
ourselves in the fountain. [*She laughs.*] If you feel like listening, I'll tell
you more . . .

I forgot to tell you about how I got married . . . I was eighteen. I
was already working at the brick factory. They'd closed down the cement factory, so I went over to the brick factory. I started out as a clay
worker. Back then we would dig out the clay by hand, with shovels . . .
Then we'd unload the trucks and spread the clay out in even layers to
let it "ripen." Half a year later, I was already pushing loaded carts
from the brick press to the oven, bringing raw bricks in and baked, hot
bricks out. We'd take the bricks out of the ovens ourselves—they were
unbelievably hot! You'd handle four to six thousand bricks a shift, up
to twenty tons. Only women worked there. And girls . . . There were
men, too, but the men generally worked the machines. Were behind
the wheel. One of them started courting me. He'd come up to me,
laugh . . . Then he started putting his hand on my shoulder. One time
he said to me, "Will you come with me?" And I said, "Yes," without
even asking him where we were going. That's how we got recruited to
go to Siberia. To build communism! [*She is silent.*] And today . . .
ah . . . well . . . Turns out it was all in vain . . . All of our suffering was
in vain . . . It's terrible to admit it and even worse to live with it. All of
our grueling labor! We built so much. Everything with our own hands.
The times we lived through were so hard! When I was working at the
brick factory . . . One morning, I overslept. After the war, if you were
late to work . . . even ten minutes late, they could send you to prison.
The foreman saved me: "Tell them I sent you down to the quarry . . ."
If someone had informed on me, he would have been charged as well.
After '53, they stopped punishing lateness like that. After Stalin died,
people started smiling again; before that, they lived carefully. Without
smiles.

But . . . what's the point of remembering all this? It's as good as
collecting the nails after a fire. Everything burned down to the ground!
Our whole life . . . Everything that was once ours is now gone . . .
We built and built . . . Sashka spent time in the Virgin Lands. That's
where he built communism! The bright future. He said that in winter they'd sleep in tents without any sleeping bags. In all their clothes.
He almost froze his hands off . . . but he was still proud! "Down the
winding roads, / Hello, virgin soil!" He had a Party membership card,

a little red book with a picture of Lenin on it, and he treasured it. He was a deputy and a Stakhanovite, just like me. Our lives went by just like that, they simply flew by. Without leaving a trace, you won't find any traces of us anywhere . . . Yesterday, I stood in line for three hours for milk and in the end, there wasn't enough. They brought a package full of gifts from Germans to our building: grain, chocolate, soap . . . For the victors from the vanquished! I don't need any care packages from Germans. No . . . I refused to take any of it. [*She crosses herself.*] The Germans and their dogs . . . the fur on their dogs glistening . . . When they came through the forest, we hid in the swamp. Up to our necks in water. Women, children. And the cows alongside the people. Silent. The cows were silent, just like the people. They understood everything. I don't want any German cookies or candy! Where are my just deserts? The fruits of my labor? That's what we believed! We believed that one day, we'd live to see the good life. Just wait and see, wait and suffer . . . Yes, wait and see . . . We spent our whole lives shuttling between bunkers, dormitories, and barracks.

What can you do? That's how it is . . . You can live through anything except death. You won't live through death . . . For thirty years, Sashka toiled away at the furniture factory. Backbreaking labor. A year ago, they had a retirement party for him, presented him with a watch. But he wasn't left without work. People would come to him with odd jobs, one after the other. Yep . . . And still, he wasn't happy. He was sick and tired. Stopped shaving. Thirty years of working at the same factory, that's half a lifetime! It was like a second home to him. His coffin came from the factory, too. A rich man's coffin! All polished and lined with velvet. These days, only gangsters and generals get buried in coffins that nice. Everyone wanted to touch it—a sight unseen! When they were carrying the coffin out of the barracks, we scattered grain across the threshold. We do that so that things will be easier on the living who are left behind. Our old customs . . . We put the coffin in the courtyard. One of his relatives said, "Kind people, forgive him." "God will forgive him," everyone replied. What's there to forgive? We lived together so well, we were like family. If you don't have something, I'll give it to you, if I run out of something, you'll bring it to me. We liked celebrating holidays together. We were building socialism, and now on the radio they say that socialism is over. But we're . . . we're still here . . .

The trains clatter . . . and clatter . . . Strangers, what do you need here? What? All deaths are different . . . I had my first son in Siberia, he came down with diphtheria and just like that, he was gone. I keep on living. Yesterday, I went down to Sashka's grave and sat there with him. I told him about Lizka's weeping, how she'd banged her head on the coffin. Love doesn't count the years . . .

We'll all die . . . And everything will be all right.

ON CRIES AND WHISPERS . . .
AND EXHILARATION

◆

Margarita Pogrebitskaya,
doctor, 57 years old

My favorite holiday was always November 7* . . . A big and bright
day . . . The most vivid impression from my childhood was the military parade on Red Square . . .

I'd sit on my father's shoulders with a red balloon tied to my wrist.
Up in the sky, over the marching columns, loomed the huge portraits
of Lenin and Stalin . . . Marx . . . Garlands and bouquets of red, blue,
and yellow balloons. Red everywhere. My favorite color in the world.
The color of the Revolution and of the blood spilled in its name . . .
The Great October Revolution! Today, they're calling it a military
coup, the Bolshevik conspiracy . . . the Russian catastrophe . . . Saying
Lenin was a German agent and the Revolution was brought about by
deserters and drunken sailors. I cover my ears, I don't want to hear it!
It's more than I can take . . . My whole life, I've believed that we were
the luckiest people on earth, born in the most beautiful and extraordinary country in the world. There's no other one like it! We have Red
Square, the Spasskaya Tower clock, that the whole world sets its time
to. That's what my father told me . . . and my mother and grandmother . . . "November 7 is a red-letter day . . ." The night before, my
whole family would stay up late making flowers out of crepe paper,
cutting out cardboard hearts. Coloring them in. In the morning, my

* The Bolshevik uprising, which turned into the October Revolution, took place the
night of October 24–25, 1917, according to the Julian calendar, which is November
6–7 according to the Gregorian calendar that was subsequently adopted in the USSR.
Known as the Day of the October Revolution, it was celebrated with military parades
attended by most citizens.

mother and grandmother would stay home preparing the holiday dinner. We always had guests. They'd bring us wine and cakes in string
bags . . . Back then, we didn't have plastic bags . . . My grandmother
would bake her famous *pirozhki* stuffed with cabbage and mushrooms,
and my mother would work her magic on Olivier salad and prepare
her essential meat in aspic. As for me, I got to be with my father!

There were many people out in the street, and all of them had red
ribbons on their coats and jackets. Red flags blazing in the wind, the
military brass band playing. Our leaders at the rostrum . . . and the
song:

> World capital, our capital
> Like the Kremlin's stars you glow
> You're the pride of the whole cosmos,
> Granite beauty, our Moscow . . .

I wanted to keep shouting "Hurrah!" The loudspeakers cried,
"Glory to the workers of the Likhachev factory, twice awarded the
orders of Lenin and the Red Banner! Hurrah, comrades!" "Hurrah!
Hurrah!" "Glory to our heroic Leninist Komsomol . . . to the Communist Party . . . to our glorious veterans . . ." "Hurrah! Hurrah!"
Beauty! Ecstasy! People wept, overwhelmed with joy . . . The brass
band played marches and songs of the Revolution:

> He was ordered to move westward,
> She was sent the other way,
> Komsomol men marched away toward
> Battle in the civil war . . .

I remember all the words to every single song, I haven't forgotten a
thing, I sing them all the time. I sing them to myself. [*She begins to
quietly sing.*]

> Vast is my beloved country
> Full of forests, fields, and rivers.
> I know there's none other like her
> Where a man can breathe so freely . . .

I recently found our old records in the closet, so I took the record
player down from the storage cabinet and spent the whole evening

reminiscing. The songs of Dunaevsky and Lebedev-Kumach—we used to adore them! [*She is silent.*] And there I am, high up in the sky. My father lifts me up . . . higher and higher . . . The most important moment comes: Powerful vehicles pulling covered missiles, tanks, and artillery are about to roar down the cobblestones of Red Square. "Remember this moment for the rest of your life!" my father shouts over the noise. And I know that I will! On the way home, we'd stop into the store and I would get my favorite lemon soda, Buratino. That day, I was allowed to have anything I wanted: toy whistles, rooster lollipops . . .

I loved Moscow at night . . . the lights . . . When I was eighteen . . . Eighteen! I fell in love. The moment I realized that I was in love—guess where I went. That's right, I went to Red Square. The first thing I wanted to do was spend those moments in Red Square. The Kremlin walls, black spruces dusted with snow, Alexander Gardens shrouded in snowdrifts. As I took it all in, I knew that I would be happy. I would definitely be happy!

My husband and I recently visited Moscow. And for the first time . . . For the first time, we didn't go to Red Square. We didn't pay our respects. For the first time . . . [*She has tears in her eyes.*] My husband is Armenian, we got married when we were in college. He had a blanket, I had a cot, and that's how we began our life together. After graduating from the Moscow Medical Academy, we were assigned to work in Minsk. All of my friends went off to different places: One went to Moldavia, another to Ukraine, a third to Irkutsk. We called the people who were sent to Irkutsk Decembrists.* It's all the same country, go wherever you please! There were no borders back then, no visas or customs. My husband wanted to return to his homeland, Armenia. "We'll go to Lake Sevan, you'll see Ararat. Try real Armenian *lavash*," he promised me. But we were offered jobs in Minsk. So we decided: "Let's go to Belarus!" "Okay!" We were young, we had our whole lives ahead of us, we thought that we'd have enough time to do everything. We came to Minsk and ended up liking it here. There's nothing but lakes and forests all around. They are the forests, swamps, and backwoods of the partisans; fields are rare among all these trees. Our children grew up out here, their favorite foods are *draniki* and

---

* Many of the Decembrists, a group of young aristocrats who had organized a small but resonant uprising against the Tsar, were exiled to Irkutsk in 1825. Others were executed.

mochanka. "They fry the taters, they boil the taters . . ." Their second favorite dish is Armenian *khash* . . . Still, every year, we'd go on a family trip to Moscow. How could we not? I couldn't live without it, I had to walk around Moscow. Breathe the air. I waited . . . I couldn't wait for those first moments when our train would pull into Belorussky Station and the march would play over the loudspeaker; my heart would jump at the words: "Comrade passengers, our train has arrived in the capital of our Motherland, the Hero-City Moscow!" "Roiling, mighty, undefeatable / My Moscow, my country, I love you most of all . . ." That's the music you disembark to.

But then . . . Where are we? We were greeted by a strange, unfamiliar city . . . The wind blew dirty wrappers and scraps of newspaper down the sidewalks, beer cans rattled underfoot. At the train station . . . and by the Metro . . . everywhere you went, you saw gray rows of people peddling lingerie and sheets, old shoes and toys, loose cigarettes. Like in war movies. I'd never seen anything like it except in those movies. On beds of torn paper, in cardboard laid directly on the ground, you'd find salami, meat, and fish. In some places, it'd be covered in tattered cellophane; in others, it lay bare. And Muscovites were buying it all. Bargaining. Knitted socks, napkins. Nails and food and clothes, all side by side. People speaking Ukrainian, Belarusian, Moldavian . . . "We came from Vinnytsia . . ." "We're from Brest . . ." So many poor people . . . Where had they all come from? Invalids . . . Like in the movies . . . That's all I have to compare it to, old Soviet films. It felt like I was watching a movie . . .

On the Old Arbat, my beloved Arbat, I found peddlers selling *matryoshka* dolls, samovars, icons, and portraits of the Tsar and the royal family. Portraits of White Guard generals—Kolchak and Denikin,* next to busts of Lenin . . . There were all sorts of *matryoshkas:* Gorbachev *matryoshkas,* Yeltsin *matryoshkas.* I didn't recognize my Moscow. What city was this? Right there on the asphalt, on top of some bricks, an old man sat playing the accordion. He was wearing his medals, singing war songs, with a hat full of change at his feet. Our favorite songs: "The fire burns bright in the little stove, / Sap drips down the logs, like tears . . ." I wanted to go up to him . . . but he was already surrounded by foreigners . . . They started snapping pictures

---

* Alexander Kolchak (1874–1920) was a polar explorer and commander in the Imperial Russian Navy who was internationally recognized as the ruler of Russia during the Russian Civil War. Anton Denikin (1872–1947) was a leading general of the Whites in the Russian Civil War. He lived out his final two decades in France.

of each other in front of him. Shouting things at him in Italian, French, and German. Clapping him on the shoulder: *"Davai! Davai!"* They were in high spirits, clearly having a lot of fun. Why wouldn't they be? People used to be so scared of us . . . and now . . . Here you go! Nothing but piles of junk, an empire gone up in smoke! Next to all the *matryoshkas* and samovars, there was a mountain of red flags and pennants, Party and Komsomol membership cards. And Soviet war medals! Orders of Lenin and the Red Banner. Medals! "For Valor" and "For Military Service." I touched them . . . caressed them . . . I couldn't believe my eyes! I simply couldn't! "For defending Sebastopol," and "For Defending the Caucasus." All of them were real. Precious. Soviet army uniforms, jackets, and greatcoats . . . peaked caps with red stars . . . being sold for dollars . . . "How much?" my husband asked, pointing at the "For Valor" medal. "Twenty dollars. Or, for you, I'll do a grand—one thousand rubles." "And the Order of Lenin?" "One hundred dollars." "And your conscience?" My husband was prepared to fight him. "Are you nuts? What rock have you been living under? These are relics from the era of totalitarianism." Those were his words . . . Like these were just refuse, but the foreigners liked them, Soviet symbols are in style over there, so now they were hot commodities. I screamed . . . called a policeman over . . . I was yelling, "Look! Look . . . Ahh!" The policeman confirmed it, "These are relics of the totalitarian era . . . We only arrest people for drugs or pornography . . ." But isn't a Party membership card for ten dollars pornography? The Order of Glory . . . or this: a red flag with a portrait of Lenin being sold for dollars. It felt like we were on some kind of film set. Like we were being pranked. We'd come to the wrong place. I stood there and wept. Next to us, Italians tried on military greatcoats and caps with red stars. *"Horoshow! Horoshow!"* À *la Russe* . . .

The first time I went to the Lenin Mausoleum was with my mother. I remember it was raining, a cold autumn rain. We had to stand in line for six hours. The steps . . . the twilight . . . the wreaths . . . A whisper: "Step in. Don't dally." I couldn't see anything through my tears. But Lenin . . . he seemed to be glowing . . . I was little, and I told my mother, "Mama, I'm never going to die." "Why do you say that?" my mother asked. "Everyone dies. Even Lenin died." Even Lenin . . . I don't know how to talk about any of this, but I have to. I want to. I'd like to talk, but I don't know who to talk to. What do I want to talk about? About how incredibly lucky we were! Now I am fully convinced of it. We grew up poor and naïve, but we never knew it and didn't envy anyone. We went to school with cheap pencil cases and forty-kopeck pens. In the summer, you put on some canvas shoes, spiff them up with tooth powder, and they're pretty! In the winter, it'd be rubber boots, the cold would burn the soles of your feet—it was fun! We believed that tomorrow would be better than today and the day after tomorrow better than yesterday. We had a future. And a past. We had it all!

We loved our Motherland, our love for her was boundless, she was everything to us! The first Soviet car—hurrah! An illiterate worker unlocked the secret to making our own Soviet stainless steel—victory! The fact that everyone in the world had already known this secret for a long time is something we only found out later. Back then: We're going to be the first to fly over the North Pole, we're going to learn how to control the Northern Lights! We'll change the course of the mightiest rivers . . . We'll irrigate the endless deserts . . . Faith! Faith! Faith! Something higher than reason. I would wake up to the sound of the national anthem instead of an alarm clock: "Unbreakable Union of free republics, / For ages, united by Mighty Rus . . ." We sang a lot in school. I remember our songs . . . [*She sings.*]

Our fathers dreamt of joy and freedom.
For this, they battled more than once.
Braving war, Lenin and Stalin,
Built our Fatherland for us . . .

At home, we remembered how . . . When the anthem played on the radio the day after I was accepted into the Young Pioneers, I leapt up and stood on my bed at attention. The Pioneer oath: "I hereby am joining the ranks . . . in the presence of my comrades . . . I solemnly swear to passionately love my Motherland . . ." At home, we celebrated. The smell of the pies baked in my honor filled the air. I always wore my red Pioneers' kerchief, I would wash it and iron it every morning so that it never had a single wrinkle. Even when I was already in college, I continued tying my scarves in a Pioneers' knot. My Komsomol membership card . . . I still have it . . . I pretended to be a year older so that they would let me join sooner. I loved walking through the streets, you could always hear the radio . . . The radio was our life, it was everything. You'd open the window and music would pour in, the kind of music that made you want to get up and march around your apartment. Like a soldier . . . It might have been a prison, but I was warmer in that prison. That's what we were used to . . . Even today, when we stand in line, we huddle close to one another and try to be together. Have you noticed that? [*Again, she starts to quietly sing.*]

Stalin is our warrior glory,
Stalin is the joy of youth,
Singing, battling, victorious
Our nation follows Stalin's path . . .

And yes! Yes! Yes! My greatest dream was to die! To sacrifice myself. Give myself away. The Komsomol oath: "I am prepared to give up my life if my nation should need it." These weren't just words, that's what we were really taught. If we saw a column of soldiers marching down the street, everyone would stop . . . After the Victory, the soldier became an extraordinary figure . . . When I was entering the Party, in my application, I wrote, "I know and accept the Party Program and Regulations. I am prepared to devote all of my energy, and, if necessary, to give my life to my Motherland." [*She examines me carefully.*] And what do you think of me? That I'm an idiot? That I'm infantile . . . ? Some of the people I know . . . they have outright laughed at me: emotional socialism, the ideals on paper . . . That's what I look like to them. Stupid! Down syndrome! You're "an engineer of human souls."* You want to comfort me? Our writers are more than just writers. You're teachers. Spiritual leaders. That's how it used to be; it's not like that anymore. Many people go to church these days. There are very few believers among them, the majority are just sufferers. Like me . . . traumatized . . . I'm not a believer in the canonical sense, but I do believe with my heart. I don't know the prayers, but I pray . . . Our priest is a former officer, his sermons are always about the army, the atom bomb. The enemies of Russia and Masonic conspiracies. But I want to hear about something else, something totally different . . . Not that. But that's all there is, everywhere you turn . . . So much hatred . . . There's nowhere for the soul to hide from it. I turn on the TV, and it's the same thing, nothing but denunciations. Everyone rejecting the past. Cursing it. My favorite director, Mark Zakharov, whom I don't love and trust liked I used to . . . He burned his Party membership card and they showed it on TV . . . He did it in public. This isn't

---

* A well-known phrase of Stalin's describing writers and other cultural workers.

theater! This is life! My life. How can you treat it like that? My life . . .
I don't need these spectacles . . . [*She weeps.*]

I've fallen behind . . . I'm one of the people who's fallen behind . . .
Everyone else transferred from the train that was hurtling toward socialism onto the train racing to capitalism. I'm late . . . People laugh at
the *sovok:* He's trash, he's a dope. They laugh at me . . . Now the Reds
are the monsters and the Whites are knights. My heart and mind rebel,
I can't accept it on a physiological level. I won't allow the thought in.
I can't, I'm incapable . . . I embraced Gorbachev, even though I criticized him . . . He was . . . Now it's clear to me that, like the rest of us,
he was a dreamer. An ideas man. You could call him that. But I wasn't
prepared for Yeltsin . . . for Gaidar's reforms. All our money disappeared at the snap of his fingers. Our money and our lives along with
it . . . In the blink of an eye, everything became worthless. Instead of
the bright future, they started telling us to get rich, love money . . .
Bow down to this beast! The people were not prepared. No one had
even dreamed of capitalism, I can tell you that about myself, I definitely had not . . . I liked socialism. The Brezhnev years . . . Vegetarian
times . . . I wasn't around for the cannibalism. Pakhmutova had a
song: "Under the wing of the airplane, the green sea of the taiga
sings . . ." I was prepared to make close friends with and build "blue
cities."* To dream! "I know, there'll be a city . . ." "There'll be a garden city here . . ." I loved Mayakovsky. Patriotic poems and songs.
They were so important back then. They meant so much to us. No one
can convince me that we were given life just to eat and sleep to our
hearts' content. That a hero is someone who buys something one
place and sells it down the road for three kopecks more. That's what
they want us to believe now . . . It turns out that everyone who had
given up their lives for others had been a fool. Everyone who'd died for
lofty ideals. No! No! Yesterday, I was standing in line at the store . . .
An old woman in front of me kept counting the change in her wallet.
She ended up buying one hundred grams of the cheapest salami . . .
"Dog salami" . . . and two eggs. I know her, too . . . Her whole life,
she'd worked as a teacher.

I can't get excited about this new life! I'm not going to do well, I'm
never going to be happy on my own. Alone. And life keeps pulling and
pulling me into this muck. Down to the earth. My children already live

---

* In a 1960s Soviet pop song of the same name, "blue cities" are the dream cities of
the future.

according to these new laws. They don't need me anymore, I seem ridiculous. My whole life . . . I was going through papers and came across my teenage diary: my first love, my first kiss, and pages and pages about how much I loved Stalin, how I was prepared to die just to see him. Notes of a madwoman . . . I wanted to throw it away, but I just couldn't bring myself to. I hid it. I'm scared, I hope no one finds it. They'd mock me and laugh at me. I didn't show it to anyone . . . [*She is silent.*] I remember many things that can't be explained rationally. I'm a rare specimen! A therapist's dream . . . isn't that right? You're very lucky to have found me . . . [*She laughs and cries at the same time.*]

Ask me . . . You have to ask how these things coexisted: our happiness and the fact that they came for some people at night and took them away. Some people disappeared, while others cried behind the door. For some reason, I don't remember any of that. I don't! I remember how the lilacs blossomed in the spring, and everyone outside, strolling; the wooden walkways warmed by the sun. The smell of the sun. The blinding mass demonstrations: athletes, the names of Lenin and Stalin woven from human bodies and flowers on Red Square. I would ask my mother this question, too . . .

What do we remember about Beria? About the Lubyanka? My mother was silent on this . . . She once told me the story of how one summer, after a vacation to Crimea with Papa, they were returning to Moscow through Ukraine. It was the 1930s, during collectivization . . . There was a huge famine in Ukraine, they call it Holodomor. Millions of people died . . . Entire villages . . . No one was left to bury anyone. Ukrainians were killed because they didn't want to join collective farms. They were starved to death. Now I know about it . . . They used to have the Zaporozhian Sich,* the people remembered freedom . . . The soil there is so fertile you can stick a stake in and it'll grow into a tree. And yet they were dying . . . dropping dead like cattle. They had everything taken away from them, down to the last poppy pod. They were surrounded by troops like in a concentration camp. Now I know . . . One of my friends at work is Ukrainian, she heard about it from her grandmother . . . How in their village, a mother killed one of her children with an axe, cooked him and fed

* The Zaporozhian Sich was an autonomous Cossak polity from the sixteenth through the eighteenth centuries in the lower Dnieper River region. It fell to the Russian empire in 1775 but remains a symbol of the ongoing struggle for Ukrainian independence from Russia.

him to the others. Her own child . . . All of this really happened. Parents were afraid to let their kids out of their yards because people hunted them like cats and dogs. They'd dig up earthworms in their gardens and eat them. Those who had the strength would crawl into town to the train tracks. Waiting for passengers to toss them bread crusts from passing trains . . . Soldiers would kick them, beat them with their gun butts . . . The trains rushed by at full speed. Conductors would shut the windows, batten down the blinds. No one asked anyone about anything. They'd go straight back to Moscow. Bearing wine and fruit, showing off their tans, talking about the sea. [*Silence.*] I loved Stalin . . . I loved him for a long time. I kept loving him even when they started writing that he was short, red-headed, and had a lame hand. That he shot his wife. After he was dethroned. Thrown out of the Mausoleum. I kept loving him all the same.

I was a Stalin girl for a long time, a very long time. Yes . . . that's how it was! With me . . . with us . . . With that life gone, I'm left empty-handed. I have nothing . . . a pauper! I was proud of our neighbor Vanya, he was a real hero! He returned from the war without any legs. He pushed himself around in a homemade wooden wheelchair. Called me "my Margaritka" and fixed everyone's boots and felt boots. When he was drunk, he'd sing, "My dearest brothers and sisters / I heroically did battle . . ." A few days after Stalin died, I saw him, and he went, "What do you know, Margaritka, that you-know-what finally croaked . . ." That's what he said—about my Stalin! I tore my felt boots out of his hands: "How dare you? You're a hero! With a medal." For two days, I deliberated: I'm a Young Pioneer, so it's my duty to go to the NKVD and tell them about what Vanya said. I have to file a report. This was a very serious matter—it really was! Like Pavlik Morozov,* I was capable of informing on my own father . . . my mother . . . I could have done it. Really, I was ready! Then, coming home from school, I found Vanya lying on the ground, drunk in the

---

* Pavlik Morozov (1918—1932) was a young peasant boy who became a Soviet martyr, a hero of Soviet mythology. According to the legend, during collectivization Pavlik allegedly informed on his own father for forging documents. His father was executed, but Pavlik's relatives took revenge on him and murdered him in retribution. They were then killed by a firing squad. This story, immortalized in song, verse, plays, and even an opera, was held up as an example of loyalty to the Party to Soviet children, encouraging the youth to hold their Motherland above all else—even their families. The story is likely apocryphal.

building entrance. He'd tumbled off his wheelchair and couldn't get up. I took pity on him.

That's how I am . . . I would sit there with my ear pressed to the radio listening to the hourly updates on Comrade Stalin's health. Crying. With my whole heart. That happened! That's how it was! These were Stalin's times . . . and we were Stalin's people . . . My mother is from the gentry. A few months before the Revolution, she'd married an officer who ended up fighting in the White Guard. They parted ways in Odessa: He emigrated with the remains of Denikin's shattered troops, but she couldn't leave her paralyzed mother behind, so she stayed. The Cheka* arrested her as the wife of a White Guard soldier. The investigator in charge of her case fell in love with her. Somehow he managed to save her, but in return, he forced her to marry him. He'd come home drunk after work and beat her over the head with a pistol. Eventually, he disappeared somewhere. That's my mother . . . She was a true beauty, she adored music, spoke several languages, and was crazy for Stalin. Whenever he was unsatisfied with anything, she would threaten my father: "I'll go to the district Party committee and tell them what kind of communist you really are." And my father . . . my father took part in the Revolution . . . In 1937, he was repressed†. . . . But they soon let him out because a prominent Bolshevik who knew him personally intervened on his behalf. Vouched for him. But they wouldn't let him back into the Party. It was a blow he would never recover from. In jail, they'd knocked his teeth out and crushed his skull. Still, my father didn't change his stripes, he remained a communist to the end of his life. Explain that to me . . . Do you think that these people are idiots? Simpletons? They're not—they were smart, educated people. My mother read Shakespeare and Goethe in the originals, my father graduated from the Timiryazev Agricultural Academy. And what about Blok . . . Mayakovsky . . . Inessa Armand?‡ My

---

* The Cheka was the Soviet secret police, established by Lenin in 1917 and first led by Felix Dzerzhinsky, a predecessor to the NKVD and, in turn, the KGB. Officers of the secret police were colloquially known as "Chekisty" or Chekists until the fall of the Soviet Union.

† "Repression" is a Soviet term broadly covering a process that may include a person's being denounced—at meetings, assemblies, and in the press—as well as their expulsion from public life, arrest, and execution.

‡ Inessa Armand (1874–1920) was a prominent French-Russian communist politician who joined the Bolsheviks and fought for women's equality in the Communist Party.

idols . . . My heroes . . . the ones I grew up with . . . [*She falls into thought.*]

At a certain point, I learned how to fly a plane. The plane we learned to fly would shock you: How did we manage to stay alive? Instead of wings, it had these handmade wooden planks wrapped in burlap. You flew it with a gear stick and a pedal. But it was so amazing to fly—seeing the birds, the earth from above. It makes you feel like you have wings! The sky changes you . . . the heights transform you . . . Do you understand what I'm getting at? I'm talking about our old life. I don't feel sorry for myself, I feel bad for everything we used to love . . .

I've recounted everything honestly . . . and I don't even know why it's shameful to talk about all this now . . .

When Gagarin went into space . . . People went out into the streets laughing, embracing, and crying. Strangers. Workers came out of their factories, still in their jumpsuits; medics in white caps, throwing them up into the sky: "We're the first! Our man is in space!" It was an unforgettable moment! It took your breath away, the awe. To this day, I get excited when I hear the song:

> We don't dream of cosmodromes
> It's not all that azure ice
> But the grass around our homes
> We dream of green, green grass . . .

The Cuban revolution . . . Young Castro . . . I shouted, "Mama! Papa! They won! Viva Cuba!" [*She sings.*]

> Cuba my love!
> Island of the crimson dawn,
> The song is heard around the world,
> Cuba, my true love!

Veterans from the Spanish Civil War would come to our school. We sang "Grenada" with them: "I left my home, I went to fight, / To win Grenada for the peasants . . ." I had a photo of Dolores Ibárruri*

---

* Isidora Dolores Ibárruri Gómez (1895–1989)—known as "La Pasionaria"—was a Republican heroine of the Spanish Civil War and communist politician of Basque origin, known for her famous slogan "¡No Pasarán!" during the Battle for Madrid in November 1936.

hanging over my desk. Yes . . . we dreamed of Grenada . . . and then of Cuba . . . Some decades later, a new generation of boys spoke in those same fervent tones, only now it was about Afghanistan. We were easy to fool. But still, still . . . I won't forget it! I'll never forget how the whole tenth grade* left to volunteer to work on the Virgin Lands. They marched off in a column, in backpacks, with banners flying. Some of them carried guitars. "There go true heroes," I thought. Many of them later returned sick. They never made it to the Virgin Lands, they were sent to the taiga somewhere to build a railway, dragging rails on their backs, waist-deep in ice water. There wasn't enough machinery . . . All they had to eat were rotten potatoes, so all of them came down with scurvy. But they did it! There was a girl, too, seeing them off, brimming with admiration. That girl was me. My memories . . . I refuse to give them up for anyone: not the communists, not the democrats, not the brokers. They're mine! All mine! I can go without many things: I don't need a lot of money, expensive food, or fancy clothes . . . a nice car . . . In our Zhigulis, we drove across the whole Union: I saw Karelia, Lake Sevan, the Pamir mountains. All of it was our Motherland. My Motherland, the USSR. I can do without a lot of things, the only thing I can't do without is the past. [*She is silent for a long time. Such a long time that I have to call her back.*]

Don't worry . . . I'm fine . . . I'm fine now . . . For the time being, I've been staying home . . . petting the cat, knitting mittens. Simple things like knitting help most of all . . . What kept me from going all the way? I never hit bottom . . . No . . . As a doctor, I could clearly picture how it would all turn out . . . in graphic detail . . . Death is hideous, it's not pretty. I've seen people who've hanged themselves . . . In their final moments, they have orgasms, or they get covered in urine or feces. Gas turns people blue, purple . . . Just the thought of it is awful to a woman. I couldn't harbor any illusions about a beautiful death. But something throws you for a loop, triggers you, sends you flying . . . You're in a fit of despair. There's a pulse and a rhythm . . . and then a sudden burst of energy . . . It's hard to restrain yourself. Pull the emergency brake! Stop! I somehow managed to stop myself in time. I chucked out the clothesline. Ran into the street. Got soaked in the rain, which was so beautiful after all that—it was so good getting soaked! [*Silence.*] For a long time, I didn't say a word to anyone . . . I spent eight months in bed, terribly depressed. I forgot how to walk.

* Tenth grade was the final year of Soviet secondary school.

Then, finally, I got up. Learned to walk again. I am . . . I am once again on solid footing . . . But I was really sick . . . deflated like a balloon . . . What am I talking about? Enough! That's enough . . . [*She sits and weeps.*] Enough . . .

1990 . . . Fifteen people were living in our three-bedroom apartment in Minsk, plus a newborn. First, my husband's relatives arrived from Baku, his sister with her family and his cousins. They weren't visiting, they came with the word "war" on their lips. They entered the house shouting, their eyes dulled . . . It was autumn or maybe winter . . . I remember that it was already cold out. Yes, they came in the autumn, because that winter, there were even more of us. That winter, my sister . . . My sister, her family, and her husband's parents came from Dushanbe, Tajikistan. That's how it happened . . . like that . . . People slept everywhere—in summer, even out on the balcony. And . . . They didn't talk, they screamed . . . about how they'd fled their homes with war at their heels. Burning the soles of their feet. And they . . . All of them were like me, they were Soviets . . . completely Soviet people. One hundred percent! And proud of it. Then suddenly, it had all been taken out from underneath them. Gone! They woke up one morning, looked out the window, and there was a new flag. Suddenly finding themselves in another country. They became foreigners overnight.

I listened. And listened. They talked . . .

". . . It was such an amazing time! Gorbachev came to power . . . Then, all of a sudden, there was shooting outside. Dear Lord! Right in the capital! In Dushanbe . . . Everyone sat in front of their TVs, anxious not to miss the latest updates. We had a women's collective in our factory, it was predominantly Russian. I asked them, 'Girls, what's going to happen?' 'A war is starting, Russians are already getting killed.' A few days later, a store was robbed in the middle of the day . . . And then another . . ."

". . . In the first months, I cried, but then I stopped. The tears dry up quickly. Most of all, I was afraid of men, the ones I knew as much as the ones I didn't know. That they could drag me into a building, into a car . . . 'Pretty lady! Hey lady, let's fuck . . . ' A neighbor girl had been raped by her classmates. Tajik boys we knew. Her mother went to see one of their families. 'What did you want, coming here?' they shouted back at her. 'Go back to your Russia. Pretty soon there won't be any of you Russians left here. You'll be running away in your underwear.'"

". . . Why did we move out there? We were on a Komsomol trip, building the Nurek Dam and an aluminum plant . . . I studied Tajik: *chaikhana, piala, aryk, archa, chinara* . . . They called us 'Shuvari.' Russian brothers."

". . . I still have dreams about the pink hills, the almond trees in bloom. I wake up in tears . . ."

". . . In Baku . . . We lived in a nine-story building. One morning, they took all the Armenian families out into the courtyard . . . Everyone gathered around them, and every single person there went up to us and hit us with something. A little boy—five years old—came up to me and hit me with a toy shovel. An old Azerbaijani woman patted him on the head . . ."

". . . Our Azerbaijani friends hid us in their basement. They covered us in junk and boxes. At night, they'd bring us food . . ."

". . . I was running to work one morning, and I saw dead bodies lying there on the street. Just lying there or leaning against the wall—sitting there, propped up as though they were alive. Some had been covered in tablecloths, others hadn't. There hadn't been time. The majority of them were naked . . . both the men and the women . . . The ones who were sitting up hadn't been undressed—it must have been too hard to move them . . ."

". . . I used to think that Tajiks were like little kids, totally harmless. In a matter of just six months, maybe even less than that, Dushanbe became unrecognizable, and so did the people. The morgues were filled to capacity. In the mornings, before they were absorbed into the asphalt, there'd be puddles of coagulated blood . . . like gelatin . . ."

". . . For days, people walked by our house carrying posters that read, 'Death to the Armenians! Death!' Men and women. A furious mob, not a single human face among them. The newspapers were filled with ads: 'Trading a three-bedroom apartment in Baku for any apartment in any Russian city . . . ' We sold our apartment for three hundred dollars. Like it was a refrigerator. And if we hadn't sold it that cheap, they could have killed us . . ."

". . . With the money we got for our apartment, we bought a Chinese down jacket for me and a pair of warm boots for my husband. Furniture, dishes, rugs . . . We left all of that behind . . ."

". . . We lived without gas or electricity . . . without running water . . . The prices at the market were awful. They opened a new kiosk next to our building. All they sold were flowers and funeral wreaths . . ."

". . . One night, someone painted the words, 'Be afraid, you Russian bastards! Your tanks won't help you!' on the wall of the building across from ours. Russians were being removed from administrative positions . . . They'd shoot you from around the corner . . . The city quickly grew as filthy as a *kishlak*.* It became a foreign city. No longer Soviet . . ."

". . . They could kill you for anything . . . If you hadn't been born in the right place, if you didn't speak the right language. If someone with a machine gun simply didn't like the looks of you . . . How had we lived before then? On holidays, our first toast had always been, 'To friendship,' and *'es kes sirum em'* ('I love you' in Armenian). Or *'Man sani seviram'* ('I love you' in Azerbaijani). We'd lived happily side by side . . ."

". . . Regular people . . . Our Tajik friends would lock their sons up, they wouldn't let them out of the house, so no one could teach them or force them to kill."

". . . We decided to leave . . . We were already on the train, the steam was billowing out from under the wheels. The final moments before departure. Someone starting shooting at the wheels with a machine gun. Soldiers had to make a corridor to protect us. If it weren't for the soldiers, we wouldn't have even made it onto the train alive. Today, when I see war on TV, I can immediately smell that smell . . . the smell of fried human flesh . . . a sickening, sweet candy smell . . ."

Six months later, my husband had his first heart attack. And another six months later, his second. His sister had a stroke. All of it was making me lose my mind . . . Have you heard of how hair goes crazy? It becomes coarse, like fishing line. The hair is the first to go . . . Who can bear it? Little Karina . . . By day, she was a normal kid, but when it would start getting dark outside, she'd begin trembling. She screamed, "Mama, don't go! If I fall asleep, they'll kill you and Papa!" I would run to work in the morning and pray to be hit by a car. I'd never gone to church before, but after that, I started spending hours on my knees: "O Holy Mother of God! Can you hear me?" I stopped sleeping, couldn't eat anymore. I'm no politician, I don't know anything about politics. I'm simply a person who lives in fear. What else did you want to ask me? I've told you everything . . . That's all!!

* A Central Asian village.

ON THE LONELY RED MARSHAL AND THREE DAYS OF FORGOTTEN REVOLUTION

◆

Sergey Fyodorovich Akhromeyev (1923–1991),
marshal of the Soviet Union, Hero of the Soviet Union (1982),
chief of the General Staff of the Soviet Armed Forces (1984–1988).
Laureate of the Lenin Prize (1980).
In 1990, he was named advisor to the president of
the USSR on military affairs.

FROM INTERVIEWS ON RED SQUARE IN DECEMBER 1991

—I was a student . . . It all happened so fast. Three days, and the revolution was over . . . On the news, they reported that the Gang of Eight had been arrested . . . Minister of Internal Affairs Pugo shot himself, Marshal Akhromeyev hanged himself . . . At home, we discussed it for a long time. I remember my father saying, "They're war criminals. They should have met the same fate as the German generals, Speer and Hess." We were all waiting for our Nuremberg . . .

We were young . . . Revolution! When people went out into the streets to stand up against the tanks, for the first time in my life I felt proud of my country. Before that, there'd been Vilnius, Riga, Tbilisi. In Vilnius, the Lithuanians defended their television tower, we'd seen it all on TV. And what were we, sheep? People who had never done anything like that before, who'd been sitting there, venting their frustration in their kitchens, all went out into the streets. They stepped outside . . . My friend and I grabbed our umbrellas in case it rained and also to use as weapons. [*She laughs.*] I was proud of Yeltsin when he stood on the tank. I felt like he was my president. Mine! Real! There were lots of young people there. Students. All of us had grown up reading Korotich's *Ogonyok,* the dissident writers of the sixties.* It felt like a war zone . . . Someone was screaming into a megaphone, a male voice was begging: "Girls, please leave. There's going to be shooting and lots of corpses." A man near me sent his pregnant wife home. She was crying, "Why are you staying?" "This is how it has to be."

I forgot to mention something really important . . . about how that day had begun . . . In the morning, I woke up because my mother was wailing. Inconsolable. She asked my father, "What's a state of emergency? What do you think they've done to Gorbachev?" My grandmother ran back and forth between the TV and the radio in the kitchen: "Was anyone arrested? Shot?" My grandmother was born in 1922. Her whole life, people had been shot and executed. Arrested. That was all she'd ever known . . . After my grandma passed away, my mother revealed a family secret. She lifted the curtain . . . those blinds . . . In 1956, my grandfather was returned to my mother and grandmother from the camps. He came back a bag of bones. From Kazakhstan. He was so weak, someone had had to escort him home. And they kept the fact that he was her father, her husband, a secret from everyone . . . They were afraid . . . They told people that they weren't that close, that he was a very distant relative. This went on for several months, and then they put him in the hospital. That was where he hanged himself. I need to . . . I have to come to terms with this somehow, with this knowledge. I need to understand it . . . [*She repeats herself.*] Find some way to live with it . . . My grandmother's greatest fear was a new Stalin and another war. Her whole life, she'd been anticipating arrest and starvation. She grew onions in egg cartons on the windowsill, fermented huge pots of cabbage. Stockpiled sugar and butter. Our storage cabinets were glutted with grains. Pearl barley. She always told me, "Don't say anything! Nothing!" Keep your mouth shut in school . . . in university . . . That's how I was raised, those were the people I grew up with. We had no reason to love the Soviet regime. All of us were for Yeltsin! My friend's mother wouldn't even let her out of the house: "Over my dead body! Can't you see that all of that is back?" We'd been studying at the Patrice Lumumba Peoples' Friendship University. People from all over the world studied

* *Ogonyok* was an influential weekly magazine that reached its pinnacle of popularity during perestroika under editor-in-chief Vitaly Korotich, who pushed a pro-capitalist, pro-American editorial agenda. "Writers of the sixties" refers to the post-Stalinist generation who came to prominence during the Thaw.

there, many of them had come to the USSR expecting the land of balalaikas and atom bombs. We were offended. We wanted to live in a different country . . .

—I was a metal worker at a factory . . . I was in the Voronezh region when I found out about the putsch. Visiting my aunt. All that shouting about the greatness of Russia—total bullshit. Phony patriots! Sitting in front of their zombie box. They should come see what it's like fifty kilometers outside of Moscow . . . Look at the houses, see how people really live. Their drunken parties . . . There's practically no men in the village; they've all died out. They're like a bunch of horned beasts— they drink themselves to death. Until they collapse. And they'll drink anything flammable: from cucumber aftershave to gasoline. First they drink, and then they brawl. In every household, there's someone who's either doing time or has already been to prison. The police can't cope. Only the women don't give up, they keep digging in their vegetable gardens. The few men who don't drink have long since gone to Moscow in search of work. The only farmer in the village had had his house burned down by arsonists three times before getting the hell out of there! Cut and run! They hated him with a passion . . . this visceral hatred . . .

Tanks in Moscow, barricades . . . In the village, no one was particularly worried about any of it. They didn't fret. Everyone was much more concerned with potato beetles and cabbage moths. Those beetles are tough to get rid of . . . The only things the young men care about is munching on sunflower seeds and girls. And where they'll score a bottle for the night. But overall, the people supported the putschists. From what I gathered, not all of them were communists, but everyone wanted to live in a great country. They were afraid of change because every time there had ever been change, the people had always gotten screwed. I remember what my grandfather used to say: "Our lives used to be shitty, really shitty, and then shit got worse and worse." Before and after the war, people out there lived without any passports. They didn't issue them to people in the country because they didn't want them in the cities. They were slaves. Under house arrest. They came back from the war covered in medals, they'd conquered half of Europe! But they wouldn't even give them passports.

When I got back to Moscow, I found out that all my friends had been on the barricades. That they'd taken part in that fracas. [*He laughs.*] I could have gotten a medal . . .

◆ ◆ ◆

—I'm an engineer . . . Who's that Marshal Akhromeyev? Crazy for the
sovok. I lived in the *sovok* and have no desire to go back there. He was
a fanatic, sincerely devoted to the communist Idea. My enemy. Just
hearing him speak filled me with rage. I knew that he was a person
willing to fight to the very end. His suicide? Clearly an extraordinary
act that inspires respect. You have to respect death. But I ask myself,
"What if they had won?" Look through any textbook . . . Not a single
coup in history went off without terror, everything always ends in
blood. With tongues torn out and eyes gouged out. Like the Middle
Ages. You don't have to be a historian to know that . . .

One morning on television I heard about "Gorbachev's inability to
run the country due to serious illness . . ." Then I saw tanks in front
of my house . . . I called my friends, and all of them were for Yeltsin.
Against the Junta. So let's go defend Yeltsin! I opened the fridge, put a
piece of cheese in my pocket. There were crackers on the table, so I
grabbed a handful of crackers. How about a weapon? I needed something . . . There was a kitchen knife on the table. I held it in my hand
for a moment, but then I put it back. [*He grows thoughtful.*] And what
if . . . what if they would have won?

Now, on TV, they show you things like Maestro Rostropovich* arriving from Paris and sitting there with a machine gun, girls giving
soldiers ice cream . . . a bouquet resting on a tank . . . My images are
different . . . Moscow grandmothers giving soldiers sandwiches and
taking them to their apartments so they could pee. They ordered a
tank division into the capital without providing any rations or bath-
rooms. The boys' skinny necks sticking out of the hatches and their
eyes huge, full of terror. They didn't understand a thing. By the third
day, they were sitting on top of the tanks, hungry and angry. Half
asleep. Women surrounded them: "Darling boys, are you really going
to shoot at us?" The soldiers were silent, but an officer barked, "If they
give the orders, we'll shoot." As though they'd been blown away by a
strong wind, the soldiers vanished back into the hatches. That's how it
was! My memories aren't like the photos . . . We stood there arm in
arm, awaiting attack. There were rumors that soon they'd gas us, that

---

* Mstislav Rostropovich (1927–2007) was a Soviet and Russian cellist and conductor.
He left the Soviet Union in 1974 and did not return until 1990. In November 1989,
Rostropovich famously played a Bach cello suite as the Berlin Wall collapsed around
him.

there were snipers on the roofs . . . A woman with military decorations pinned to her shirt came up to us: "Who are you defending? The capitalists?" "Yes, and what about you, Auntie? We're standing up for our freedom." "I fought for the Soviet regime—for workers and peasants. Not kiosks and cooperatives. If I had a machine gun right now . . ."

It was all hanging on by a thread. The smell of blood was in the air. I don't remember it being a celebration . . .

—I'm a patriot . . . Let me have my say. [*A man in an open shearling coat with a massive cross around his neck approaches us.*] We're living in the most shameful era of our entire history. Ours is the generation of cowards and traitors. That's how our children will remember us. "Our parents sold out a great country for jeans, Marlboros, and chewing gum," they'll say. We failed to defend the USSR, our Motherland. An unspeakable crime. We betrayed everything! I will never get used to the Russian tricolor flag, I will always see the red banner in front of my eyes. The banner of a great nation! Of the great Victory! What had to have happened to us . . . the Soviet people . . . to make us close our eyes and run to this motherfucking capitalist paradise? They bought us with candy wrappers, display cases full of salami, colorful packaging. They dazzled and sweet-talked us. We traded everything we had for cars and rags. Don't tell me any fairy tales . . . about how the CIA took down the Soviet Union or Zbigniew Brzezinski's* machinations . . . Why didn't the KGB take down America? It wasn't the stupid Bolsheviks that fucked up the country, and not even the bastard intelligentsia that destroyed it so that they could go on trips abroad and read *The Gulag Archipelago* . . . Don't go looking for a Judeo-Masonic conspiracy. We did it ourselves. With our own hands. We dreamed of having a McDonald's with hot hamburgers, we wanted everyone to be able to buy themselves a Mercedes, a plastic VCR. We wanted pornos in the kiosks . . .

Russia needs a strong hand. An iron hand. An overseer with a stick. Long live the mighty Stalin! Hurrah! Hurrah! Akhromeyev could have been our Pinochet . . . our General Jaruzelski . . . It was a great loss . . .

◆ ◆ ◆

* Zbigniew Brzezinski (1928–) was Jimmy Carter's National Security Advisor from 1977 to 1981. He was particularly reviled by the Soviet establishment for his firm stance with the USSR as well as his Polish origins.

—I'm a communist . . . I supported the putschists, or rather, the USSR. I was a fervent supporter because I liked living in an empire. As the famous song goes, "My beloved land is vast . . ." In 1989, I was sent to Vilnius on a business trip. Before I left, the chief engineer of the factory, who had recently been there, called me into his office and warned me, "Don't speak Russian to them. They won't even sell you a box of matches if you ask for them in Russian. Do you remember Ukrainian? Speak Ukrainian." I could hardly believe my ears—what was this nonsense? He instructed me: "Be careful in the cafeterias, they're capable of poisoning you or putting powdered glass in your food. They see you as an occupier now, understand?" I still believed in the Friendship of the Peoples* and all of that other stuff. The Soviet brotherhood. I didn't believe him until I got to the station in Vilnius. I stepped out onto the platform . . . and from the very first moment, I was given to understand that when they heard me speaking Russian, I was in a foreign country. As an occupier. From filthy, backward Russia. Russian Ivan, the barbarian.

And then there was that whole song and dance . . . I heard about the putsch one morning while I was at the store. I ran home, turned on the TV: Had they killed Yeltsin? Who controlled the television tower? What about the army? My friend called me: "Those sons of bitches are going to tighten the screws again. We'll all be nuts and bolts." I was enraged: "I support them all the way. I'm for the USSR!" He instantly changed tack: "Down with Mikhail the Marked! Off to Siberia with him!" Do you understand? That's how you had to talk to people. Convince them. Get them on your side. The first order of business should have been taking over the Ostankino Television Tower† and broadcasting the message twenty-four hours a day: "We're going to save the country! The Soviet Motherland is in danger! Hurry up and get rid of the Sobchaks, Afanasievs,‡ and all the rest of those traitors!" The people would have stood behind it.

---

* The Friendship of the Peoples was a cultural policy introduced by Stalin in 1935 in order to consolidate the national identities of Russian and non-Russian groups within the USSR. Its image of an international socialist brotherhood lived on in Soviet propaganda to the very end, which compounded the trauma of the reemergence of nationalism in soon-to-be former Soviet republics at the fissure of the Soviet empire.
† The Ostankino Television Tower, completed in 1967, is a radio and television broadcasting tower in Moscow. It remains the tallest standing structure in Europe.
‡ Dmitry Afanasiev (1969–) is a leading contemporary Russian corporate lawyer who has served on the board of Norilsk Nickel, the world's leading producer of nickel and palladium.

I don't believe that Akhromeyev killed himself. A combat veteran couldn't have hanged himself with a piece of string . . . with the ribbon from a cake box . . . like some prison inmate. That's how they do it in jail cells—sitting down, with their knees bent. In solitary. It's not part of the military tradition. Officers look down on nooses. It wasn't a suicide, it was murder. He was killed by the same people who killed the Soviet Union. They were afraid of him—Akhromeyev had a lot of clout in the army, he could have organized resistance. The people weren't disoriented yet, they weren't as disengaged as they are now. Everyone still lived the same way and read the same newspapers. It wasn't like today, when the grass is always greener on the other side.

But then . . . I saw it myself . . . young guys putting ladders up to the Central Committee of the Communist Party building on Staraya Square. No one was guarding it anymore. Tall fire ladders. They climbed up . . . and with hammers and chisels, they started removing the gold letters "CC CPSU." Other guys on the ground sawed them up and gave away the pieces as mementos. They took apart the barricades. Pieces of barbed wire also became souvenirs.

Those are my memories of the fall of communism . . .

EXCERPTS FROM THE CASE FILES OF THE INVESTIGATION

On 24 August 1991, at 21:50, in bureau office No. 19A in Corpus 1 of the Moscow Kremlin, the security officer on duty, Koroteyev, discovered the body of Marshal of the Soviet Union Akhromeyev, Sergey Fedorovich (born 1923), at that time, an advisor to the President of the USSR.

The corpse was discovered in a sitting position under the windowsill of the office. It was leaning against the wooden grate covering the radiator. The corpse wore the uniform of the Marshal of the Soviet Union. No harm had been done to the uniform. Around the corpse's neck, there was a slipknot made of synthetic twine folded over twice. The noose went around the entire circumference of the neck. The upper end of the noose was attached to a handle on the window frame with scotch tape. No injuries other than those associated with the hanging were found on the corpse . . .

Examination of the contents of the desk revealed five notes left on top of it in a visible place. All of the notes were handwritten. They were found in a neat pile. The inventory that follows was recorded in the order in which the notes were stacked . . .

Akhromeyev requested the first note be given to his family. In it, he informed them that he had decided to commit suicide. "My primary duty has always been war and serving the citizenry. You came second. Today, for the first time, I am putting my duty to you first. I implore you to live through these days with courage. Support one another. Do not give enemies cause to gloat . . ."

The second note was addressed to Marshal of the Soviet Union S. Sokolov. It contained a request that Sokolov and army general Lobov assist in the funeral preparations and that they not abandon the members of Akhromeyev's family in these difficult times.

The third note contained a request to pay back a debt to the Kremlin cafeteria and included a fifty-ruble bill.

The fourth note was not addressed to anyone in particular: "I cannot go on living while my Fatherland is dying and everything I heretofore considered to be the meaning of my life is being destroyed. My age and my life's accomplishments give me the right to die. I fought until the end."

The final note was found separately. "I am no specialist in suicide. The first attempt (at 9:40) was unsuccessful, the cord snapped. I am gathering my strength for a second attempt . . ."

Graphological analysis determined that all of the notes were written in Akhromeyev's hand . . .

His youngest daughter, Natalia, with whose family Akhromeyev spent his final night, said: "Even before August, we'd often ask my father if a military coup d'état was possible here. Many people were unhappy with the course that Gorbachev's perestroika had taken—they didn't like all his babble, his weakness, the one-sided concessions he'd made in Soviet-American disarmament talks. They were deeply unsatisfied with the deteriorating economic situation. But my father didn't like these conversations, he was confident: 'There's not going to be any coup. If the army wanted a coup, it would all be over in two hours. Here in Russia, you're not going to get anything done by force. Getting rid of an incompetent leader isn't our biggest problem. The question is what happens next.' "

On August 23, Akhromeyev had not stayed late at the office. The family ate dinner together. They bought a big watermelon and spent a long time around the table. According to his daughter, Akhromeyev spoke openly. He confessed that he was anticipating arrest. No one in the Kremlin was talking to him anymore. "I understand," he said, "that it will make things difficult for you. There's going to be a lot of mud-slinging directed at our family. But I could not have done things any differently." His daughter asked him if he regretted coming to Moscow. Akhromeyev replied, "If I hadn't come, I would have never forgiven myself."

Before going to bed, Akhromeyev promised his granddaughter that he would take her to the park with the swing set the following day. He worried about who was going to pick up his wife, who was due to arrive from Sochi the following morning. He asked to be notified as soon as she landed and ordered a car for her from the Kremlin garage.

His daughter called him at 9:35 in the morning. He sounded normal . . . Knowing her father's character, his daughter does not believe that her father's death was a suicide . . .

EXCERPTS FROM THE FINAL REPORTS

. . . I swore allegiance to the Union of Soviet Socialist Republics . . . and I spent my entire life serving my country. What am I supposed to do now? Whom should I serve? Thus, while I live and breathe, I will continue to fight for the Soviet Union . . .

Vzglyad, television show, 1990

Now they're casting it all in a dark light . . . Denying everything that happened in our country after the October Revolution. Yes, when Stalin was in power, there was Stalinism. Yes, there were repressions, violence against the people, I don't deny any of it. All of that happened. Nonetheless, it needs to be investigated and assessed fairly and objectively. For instance, there is no need to convince me of these things, I was alive for them. I personally witnessed how people worked back then, with what conviction . . . Our task is not to smooth things over or conceal them. There is nothing to hide. Considering what happened in our country and what everyone already knows, how could anyone even think of playing hide and seek? When it comes down to it, we won the war against fascism, we didn't lose it. We have the Victory.

I remember the thirties . . . People like me came of age in those years. Tens of millions of us. And we consciously built socialism. We were prepared to make any and all necessary sacrifices. I don't agree with General Volkogonov, who wrote that the only thing that existed in those pre-war years was Stalinism. He is an anticommunist. Today, the word "anticommunist" is no longer considered derogatory. It's simply that I am a communist and he is an anticommunist. I am an anticapitalist, and he . . . I don't know what he is: Does he stand behind capitalism or not? This is no more than a statement of fact. And an ideological disagreement. I am not only criticized but downright berated for calling him a "turncoat." Until recently, Volkogonov defended the Soviet order and the communist ideals alongside me. Then, suddenly, he made a radical switch. Let him explain why he broke the army oath himself . . .

Many people today have lost their faith. I would say that the chief one among them is Boris Nikolayevich Yeltsin. The Russian president had, after all, once been the secretary of the Central Committee of the Communist Party of the Soviet Union and a candidate for the Politburo. Now, he openly says that he doesn't believe in socialism and communism, that he believes that everything the Communists did was wrong. He's turned into a militant anticommunist. And there are others like him. In fact, there are more than a handful of them. But you're talking to me . . . I am, in principle, opposed . . . I see a threat to our country's existence, it is as clear as day. The danger is as great as it was in 1941 . . .

N. Zenkovich, *The Twentieth Century:*
The Top Brass in the Years of Upheaval (Olma Press, 2005)

In the 1970s, the USSR produced twenty times more tanks than the United States.

A question from G. Shakhnazarov, aide to General Secretary of the Communist Party of the USSR M. Gorbachev (in the 1980s): Why do we need to manufacture so many weapons?

Answer from the Chief of General Staff S. Akhromeyev: Because, at the cost of great sacrifices, we've built first class factories, just as good as the ones the American's have. Would you have them stop their work to start manufacturing pots and pans instead?

Yegor Gaidar, *The Fall of the Empire*
(The Russian Political Encyclopedia, 2007)

◆ ◆ ◆

On the ninth day of the First Congress of the People's Deputies of the USSR, flyers were distributed among the deputies claiming that in an interview with a Canadian newspaper, Sakharov had declared, "During the war in Afghanistan, Soviet helicopters shot at Soviet soldiers who had been surrounded by the enemy so that they couldn't surrender and be taken prisoner . . ."

The First Secretary of the Cherkassk Municipal Committee of the Komsomol and Afghan war veteran S. Chervonopisky approached the podium. He had no legs, so people helped him to the tribune. He read a message on behalf of Afghan war veterans: "Mr. Sakharov claims that there is evidence that Soviet helicopters shot at Soviet soldiers . . . We are gravely concerned about the unprecedented defamation of the Soviet Army in the mass media. To the depths of our souls, we are disturbed by this irresponsible, incendiary statement from the famous scientist. We consider it a malevolent attack on our army, an insult to its worthiness and honor. It is yet another attempt to rend the holy unity of the army, the people, and the Party . . . [*Applause.*] Over 80 percent of those gathered here today are communists. But not once, including in the report from Comrade Gorbachev, has the word 'communism' been uttered. Regardless, the three words that we need to fight for with the strength of the whole world behind us are the State, the Motherland, and Communism . . ."

[*An ovation. All deputies stand except for the democrats and the Metropolitan Alexey.*]

A teacher from Uzbekistan: Comrade Academician! With this single act, you have canceled out all the good you have ever done. You have insulted the entire army and all of our fallen soldiers. I hereby express the deepest contempt for you . . .

Marshal Akhromeyev: What Academician Sakharov said is a lie. Nothing of the sort happened in Afghanistan. I say this holding myself fully accountable for my words. First, I myself served in Afghanistan for two and a half years; second, as the first deputy of the chief of the General Staff and then the chief of General Staff, I have been involved in Afghanistan affairs every day, and thereby am aware of every single directive issued on every single day of combat operations. It never happened!

V. Kolesov, Perestroika: A Chronicle, 1985–1991
(Lib.ru. Contemporary Literature Publishing House)

◆ ◆ ◆

. . . Comrade Marshal, how does it make you feel to know that you received the title of Hero of the Soviet Union for Afghanistan? Academician Sakharov gave a number: There were one million Afghan casualties . . .

—Do you think I'm happy I received the Hero's Star? I followed orders, but all I found was blood . . . dirt . . . As I have said on more than one occasion, the military top brass was against that war, well aware that we were getting ourselves involved in combat operations that would take place in difficult, unfamiliar conditions. We feared that the whole Islamic world would rise up against the USSR. That we would lose face in Europe. We were told firmly, "Since when do our generals interfere in politics?" We lost the battle for the Afghan people. But our army is not to blame . . .

From a television news interview, 1990

I am reporting on the degree of my involvement in the criminal actions of the State Committee on the State of Emergency.

On August 6 of this year, in accordance with your orders, I went on leave to the military sanatorium in Sochi, where I remained until August 19. Before my departure and, during my stay at the sanatorium, until the morning of August 19, I knew nothing about the orchestration of a conspiracy plot. No one even hinted at its organization or the identity of its organizers, which is to say that I played no part in neither its preparation nor realization. The morning of August 19, upon hearing the statements of the aforementioned Committee on television, I independently made the decision to fly to Moscow. At 8 P.M., I met G. I. Yanaev. I told him that I supported the program as described by the Committee in its address to the people and, as an advisor to the acting President of the USSR, I proposed my participation. G. I. Yanaev approved, but, citing his workload, scheduled our next meeting for 12 o'clock on August 20. He said that the Committee did not have any organized information on the current state of affairs, and that it would be best if I prepared a report . . .

On the morning of August 20, I met with O. D. Baklanov, who had been given the same assignment. We decided to work together . . . We created a working group with representatives from various agencies and organized the collection and analysis of data regarding the situation. This working group ended up preparing two reports, one by 9 P.M. on August 20 and the other by the morning of August 21, both of which were discussed at the Committee meeting.

In addition to this, on August 21, I worked on the preparation of G. I. Yanaev's address to the Presidium of the Supreme Soviet of the USSR. On the evening of August 20 and the morning of August 21, I participated in the Committee meetings. To be precise, I participated in the proceedings that took place in the presence of invited parties. These were the activities that I participated in on August 20–21 of the present year. Additionally, on August 20, at approximately 3 P.M., at his request, I met with D. T. Yazov at the Ministry of Defense. He told me that the situation was growing complicated and expressed doubts regarding the plan's success. After our conversation, he asked me to accompany him to a meeting with Deputy Minister of Defense General V. A. Achalov, where they were developing a plan for taking over the building of the Supreme Soviet of the RSFSR. He listened to V. A. Achalov for three minutes, only learning about the composition of forces and the projected duration of operations. I did not ask anyone any questions.

Why had I come to Moscow on my own initiative—no one had summoned me from Sochi—and begun working with the Committee? I was, after all, certain that this venture would be defeated and, upon my arrival in Moscow, felt even more sure of this. Since 1990, I had been convinced, just as I am convinced today, that our country is headed toward ruin. Soon, it will be dismembered. I was searching for a way to loudly declare this. I believed that my participation in facilitating the work of the Committee and the consequent involvement with these proceedings would provide me with the opportunity to speak about this openly. Though it may sound unconvincing and naïve, this is the case. There were no ulterior motives for my decision . . .

Letter to USSR President M. S. Gorbachev, August 22, 1991

Gorbachev is important, but the Fatherland is more important still! We must at least leave our trace so that history may show that there was resistance to the death of such a great state. Let history decide who was right and who is to blame . . .

From a notebook, August 1991

N.'S ACCOUNT

This was a rare witness. From of the holy of holies—the Kremlin, the chief citadel of communism. A witness to the life that was hidden from us, its inner workings as tightly guarded as the lives of Chinese emperors. The gods on Earth. It took a long time to convince him to speak to me.

N. requested that his name and position remain confidential due to his role in the Kremlin. Initially, he only agreed to be interviewed over the phone.

. . . What does history have to do with it? You want the facts "fried up"? Served spicy, with some extra sauce? Everyone's thirsty for blood, the people want fresh meat. These days, even death is a commodity. Everything is for sale. The man on the street will be over the moon, what a good jolt of adrenaline . . . It's not every day that an empire falls. There it is, lying face down in the mud! All bloody! And it's not every day that a Marshal of the empire kills himself . . . Hangs himself from a Kremlin radiator.

. . . Why did he leave us? His country disappeared, and he went along with it: He no longer saw his place here. He . . . here's what I think . . . He saw where things were headed. How socialism was going to be eviscerated. Idle chatter would end in blood. Gangsterism. How they'd start toppling the monuments. The Soviet idols going for scrap, to the salvage lots. They'd start threatening Communists with Nuremberg . . . and who would be the judges? Communists putting other Communists on trial—those who left the Party on Wednesday prosecuting the ones who'd left it on Thursday. How Leningrad would be renamed . . . The cradle of the Revolution . . . How it would become fashionable to use obscenities when discussing the Communist Party, how everyone would start cursing it. How people would walk down the street with posters reading, "The Communist Party is kaput!" "Rule, Boris!" Thousands of people at demonstrations . . . and what ecstatic faces! Their country was dying, and there they were, celebrating. Smash the state! Tear it down! For us, this kind of thing is always a cause for celebration . . . A real holiday! They only had to say the word "Attack!" and there would have been pogroms . . . "Kikes and commissars against the wall!" The people were waiting for it. They would have welcomed the opportunity, gone after the old men, hunted them down. I would find flyers on the ground with the addresses of leading Central Committee workers—last names, house and apartment numbers; see pictures of them posted in every possible location. In case you run into one of them, so that you'll recognize him. The Party *nomenklatura* would run from their offices with plastic bags, string bags full of their things. Many of them were afraid to sleep at home, they hid at their relatives' houses. We knew the score . . . We knew how things had gone down in Romania. They'd shot Ceaușescu and his wife,* rounded up Chekists and Party elites and executed them all. Buried them in ditches . . . [*A long pause.*] As for him . . . He was an idealist, a romantic communist. He believed in the "glittering peaks of communism." He took all that literally. He thought that communism was forever. It's embarrassing to admit this now . . . It sounds dumb . . . [*A pause.*] He could not abide what was happening. He saw the young predators stirring . . . the pioneers of capitalism . . . Instead of Marx and Lenin, they had their minds on dollars . . .

. . . What kind of putsch was this, with no shots fired? The army beat a hasty retreat out of Moscow, like cowards. After the members of the GKChP were arrested, he waited for them to come for him and lead him away in handcuffs. Out of all of the aides and advisors to the president, he was the only one who had supported the putschists. Openly supported them. The rest just held their breath. Waiting it out. The bureaucratic apparatus is a machine capable of major maneuvering . . . anything for the sake of survival. Principles? Bureaucrats have no convictions, principles, or any of those muddled metaphysical ideals. The most important thing is holding on to your seat, keeping your palms greased. Bureaucracy is our hobby horse. Lenin himself considered bureaucracy a greater threat than Denikin. The only thing that's valued is personal loyalty—never forget who owns you, whose hand is feeding you. [*A pause.*] No one knows the truth about the GKChP. Everyone lies. So . . . that's that . . . In reality, it was all a big game. We will never know the whole truth about its players and the behind-the-scenes machinations. The foggy role of

---

* Nicolae Ceaușescu (1918–1989) was General Secretary of the Romanian Communist Party from 1965 to 1989. When the regime collapsed, Ceaușescu and his wife were hastily tried and convicted by a special military tribunal on charges of genocide and sabotage of the Romanian economy in an hour-long court session on December 25. They were executed on the same day by firing squad. Video footage and photographs of the rushed show trial and the dead Ceaușescus were released in numerous countries in the West two days after their execution.

Gorbachev . . . What did he say to journalists when he came back from Foros? "I'll never tell you everything anyway." And he really won't! [*A pause.*] Perhaps this was another reason for his departure. [*A pause.*] Hundreds of thousands of demonstrators . . . this had a profound effect. It became impossible to maintain the status quo. It wasn't himself that he was afraid for . . . He couldn't come to terms with the fact that all of it would be stamped underfoot, entombed in concrete: the Soviet order, the great industrialization of our nation . . . the Victory . . . That it would turn out that the cruiser *Aurora* had never fired to signal the beginning of the storm of the Winter Palace, and that the Winter Palace had never been stormed at all . . .

They blame the times . . . Our era is evil. Empty. We're drowning in flashy rags and VCRs. Where is our great country? The way we are now, we'd never triumph over anyone. Gagarin wouldn't have even gotten off the ground.

I was taken by complete surprise when, at the end of one of our conversations, he said, "All right, you can come see me in person." We met on the following day at his home. He wore a black suit and tie despite the heat. The Kremlin uniform.

Have you talked to . . . [*He names several prominent people.*] And what about . . . [*Another name that's been on everyone's lips for a long time.*] Their version of events—that he was killed—I don't buy it. There are rumors going around about witnesses . . . facts . . . They say the cord wasn't right, that it's too thin, that it could have only been used to strangle him, and that the key was left in the outer lock of the office door . . . People say all sorts of things . . . Everyone likes a palace intrigue. I'll tell you something else: Witnesses can be manipulated, too. They're not robots. They are manipulated by television, newspapers, friends, corporate interests . . . Who has the real truth? As far as I understand, the truth is something that's sought out by specially trained experts: judges, scholars, priests. Everyone else is ruled by ambition and emotions. [*A pause.*] I've read your books . . . You shouldn't put so much stock in what people say, in human truth . . . History records the lives of ideas. People don't write it, time does. Human truth is just a nail that everybody hangs their hats on.

. . . You have to begin with Gorbachev. Without him, we'd still be living in the USSR. Yeltsin would have been the first secretary of the regional Party committee in Sverdlovsk, and Yegor Gaidar would be

editing economics articles in *Pravda* and believing in socialism. Sobchak would still be lecturing at the University of Leningrad . . . [*A
pause.*] The USSR would have lasted a long time yet. A colossus with
feet of clay? Total nonsense! We were an Almighty Superpower that
called the shots in many countries. Even America was afraid of us.
There weren't enough pantyhose and blue jeans? To win a nuclear
war, you need the latest in missiles and bomber aircraft, not pantyhose. And we had them. First-class weapons. We could have won any
war. The Russian soldier is not afraid to die. In this, we're Asiatic . . .
[*A pause.*] Stalin created a state that was impossible to puncture from
below; it was impenetrable. But from above, it was vulnerable and defenseless. No one thought that they would start destroying it from the
top, that the top leaders would be the ones to betray it first. *Pererozh-
dentsy!** The general secretary turned out to be the chief revolutionary, installed in the Kremlin. Our state proved easy to destroy from
the top. Harsh discipline and Party hierarchy worked against it. It's a
unique case in history . . . it's as if Caesar himself had initiated the fall
of the Roman Empire . . . No, Gorbachev is no pygmy; he's no toy in
the hands of circumstances, and he's not a CIA agent . . . But who is he?

"Communism's undertaker," "traitor of the Motherland," "Nobel
Laureate," and "bankrupter of the Soviet Union"; the "sixties
dissident-in-chief," "the perfect German," "the prophet," and "little
Judas"; "the great reformer," "the great actor," "the great Gorby," and
"Gorbach"; "the man of the century," "Herostratus"† . . . All that
rolled up into one.

. . . Akhromeyev prepared for his suicide for several days: He wrote
two of his suicide notes on the 22nd, one on the 23rd, and then his last
one on August 24. What happened that day? August 24 was the day
that they announced Gorbachev's declaration of resignation from the
position of General Secretary of the Central Committee of the Communist Party of the Soviet Union and his call for the self-dissolution
of the Party. "We must make a difficult but honest decision." The general secretary went out without a fight. He did not appeal to the people and the millions of communists . . . Instead, he betrayed them. He

---

* This term originated in the 1930s to describe people who have been "reborn" or
"regenerated" under the influence of the bourgeois milieu, ideologically gone over to
the side of the enemies of socialism.

† Herostratus was a fourth-century B.C. arsonist who burned down the Temple of
Artemis at Ephesus in Ancient Greece, one of the Seven Wonders of the Ancient
World.

gave everyone up. I can only guess what Akhromeyev had felt in those moments. It's not impossible and, in fact, it's quite likely that on his way to work, he saw the flags being removed from the government buildings. From the towers of the Kremlin. What could he have felt? As a communist . . . a man who had fought at the front . . . his whole life had lost meaning . . . I can't imagine him participating in our new way of life. Non-Soviet life. Sitting on the presidium under a Russian tricolor flag instead of the red Soviet flag. Under a Tsarist eagle instead of a portrait of Lenin. He simply doesn't fit into the new interior. He was a Soviet Marshal . . . You understand? So-vi-et!!! That and nothing else. Only that . . .

He wasn't comfortable in the Kremlin. An odd man out, a black sheep . . . He couldn't get used to it, he'd always said that "honest, selfless camaraderie only exists among soldiers." His whole life, all of it . . . He spent his entire life in the army. Among army men. Half a century. He first put on a uniform at the age of seventeen. That's a long sentence! Life! He moved into his Kremlin office after resigning from the position of the Chief of the General Staff. He wrote his letter of resignation himself. First of all, he thought that it was important to leave at the right time (he'd seen his share of hearses) and make way for the next generation. At the same time, he'd started butting heads with Gorbachev. Just like Khrushchev, who only ever referred to the generals as "spongers," Gorbachev didn't like the army. We were a military nation, 70 or so percent of the economy was, in one way or another, tied to the military. Our best minds worked for it . . . physicists, mathematicians . . . All of them helped develop tanks and bombs. And our ideology was also militarized. But Gorbachev was profoundly civilian. Previous general secretaries had all seen combat, while his background was the Philosophy Department of Moscow State University. "Are you preparing to fight?" he would ask the top brass. "I'm not. And there are more generals and admirals in Moscow alone than there are in the whole world combined." Before him, no one had dared to speak to the top command like that, they used to be the most important people in government. The minister of defense, not the minister of economics, was always the first to address the Politburo; the number of weapons manufactured used to be more important than the number of VCRs. And that's why a VCR cost as much as an apartment. Then everything changed . . . So of course the top brass revolted. We need a large and powerful military, our territory is enormous! We have borders with half of the world! People respect us as long as we're strong, but if we become weak, no "new way of think-ing" will convince anyone of anything. Akhromeyev reported to him personally on many occasions . . . That was the major disagreement between them . . . I won't go into the petty conflicts or anything like that. Words familiar to every Soviet had vanished from Gorbachev's speeches: "the machinations of international imperialism," "counter-strike," "overseas big wigs" . . . he got rid of all that. All he had were the "enemies of glasnost" and "enemies of perestroika." He cursed in his office (he was an old hand at that!) and called them all fuckwits. [*A pause.*] "Dilettante," "The Russian Gandhi" . . . That's not even the most biting stuff that was going around the Kremlin in those days. Naturally, members of the old guard were in shock and presaged di-saster: He's going to drown and take everyone else down with him. For America, we were the "Evil Empire," they were threatening us with Crusades, "Star Wars" . . . Meanwhile, our chief of state was playing the Buddhist monk, "the world is a common home for humanity," "change without violence or bloodshed," "war is no longer a continu-ation of politics," and so on. Akhromeyev fought for a long time, but eventually, he got tired. At first, he thought that people were giving false reports to the higher-ups, deceiving them, but then it dawned on him that this was treason. So he made a statement. Gorbachev ac-cepted his resignation, but he would not let him go. He made him his advisor on military affairs.

. . . It was dangerous tinkering with this edifice. Stalinist, Soviet, call it what you will . . . Our state has always been in a state of mobi-lization. From its inception. It was not built for peacetime. Again . . . you think we weren't capable of spitting out some trendy women's boots and pretty bras? Plastic VCRs. It would have been child's play. But we had other objectives . . . And the people? [*A pause.*] The people want simple things. A surplus of ginger-snaps. And a Tsar! Gorbachev didn't want to be Tsar. He refused. Compare him to Yeltsin . . . When, in 1993, he felt the presidential seat begin to rock underneath him, he kept his wits about him and gave orders to fire on the parliament. The Communists had been too sheepish to shoot in '91 . . . Gorbachev ceded power without any bloodshed. But Yeltsin fired from the tanks. He went into battle. So that's that . . . and the people supported him. Our country has a tsarist mentality, it's subconsciously tsarist. Ge-netically. Everyone needs a Tsar. Ivan the Terrible, as they call him in Europe, who drowned Russian cities in blood and lost the Livonian War, is remembered with fear and awe. The same goes for Peter the

Great and Stalin. While Alexander II, the Liberator . . . the Tsar who gave Russia freedom, who abolished serfdom . . . he was murdered. The Czechs can have their Vaclav Havel, but we don't need a Sakharov in charge here, we need a Tsar. The Tsar, the Father of the Russian people! Whether it's a general secretary or a president, it has to be a Tsar. [*A long pause.*]

He shows me his notebook with quotations from the Marxist classics. I write down a quote from Lenin: "I would live in a pigsty as long as it was under Soviet rule." I confess that I haven't read Lenin.

. . . And then there's something else . . . there's another story to air . . . This conversation is, as they say, between friends. There was a chef at the Kremlin. All the members of the Politburo would order herring, *salo,* black caviar—Gorbachev preferred kasha. Salads. He asked not to be served black caviar: "Caviar goes well with vodka, but I don't drink." He and Raisa Maximovna dieted and fasted. He was nothing like any of the general secretaries who had come before him. He loved his wife in a tender, entirely un-Soviet manner. They'd take walks together, holding hands. Yeltsin, on the other hand, needed a pickle and a shot of vodka first thing in the morning. Now that's Russian. [*A pause.*] The Kremlin is a terrarium. I'll tell you a story . . . only don't use my last name . . . let me be an anonymous source . . . I'm retired . . . Yeltsin put his team together, and they swept the "Gorbachevites" out; one way or another, he got rid of everyone. That's why I'm sitting here with you—because I'm retired. Otherwise, I'd be as silent as a partisan. I'm not afraid of the tape recorder, but it does bother me. Just out of habit, you know. We were so heavily scrutinized; it was like being in an X-ray machine . . . [*A pause.*] It might seem like a little thing, but it's telling . . . Akhromeyev moved to the Kremlin and right away, he refused the raise they offered him, even though it was several times his former salary. He asked to keep what he had: "It's enough for me." Who's the Don Quixote here? And who would call Don Quixote sane? When the Central Committee and the government passed the decree on the compulsory relinquishment of any foreign gifts worth over five hundred rubles to the government (the war on special privileges had begun), he was the first and one of the only people to actually comply. Kremlin mores: serve, scratch backs, know who to inform on, and when to laugh at somebody's joke. Whom to say hello to and whom to acknowledge with a slight nod.

Calculating everything in advance . . . Where is your office? Is it close to the president's office, is it on the same floor? If not, you don't count, you're small-time . . . What kind of phones do you have? Do you have a *Vertushka*?* What about a telephone labeled "President," a direct line to "Himself"? Did they give you a car from the special garage?

. . . I'm reading Trotsky's *My Life*. It takes you behind the scenes of the Revolution . . . Today, everyone blames Bukharin. His motto, "Prosper and accumulate," is apt. Timely. "Bukharchik" (as Stalin christened him) proposed to "grow into socialism." He called Stalin "Genghis Khan." But he's also an equivocal figure . . . He was prepared, like everyone else, to hurl people into the inferno of international revolution without counting the bodies. To educate with executions. Stalin didn't invent that . . . All of them were military people—after the Revolution, the civil war. After all that bloodshed . . . [*A pause.*] Lenin once said that revolutions come when they want to, not when we want them to. Indeed . . . so . . . Perestroika, glasnost . . . We all let it slip through our fingers . . . Why? The upper echelons of the government had their share of smart people. They read Brzezinski . . . But their attitude was that they'd patch it up, give some parts of it a fresh coat of paint, and keep going. They didn't understand how sick our people were of everything Soviet. It's not that they had much faith in the "bright future," but they believed that the people believed in it . . . [*A pause.*] No, Akhromeyev wasn't murdered . . . Let's ditch the conspiracy theories. His suicide was like a parting shot, a bold statement of the most essential fact: We were hurtling into an abyss. We had a great nation, it was victorious in a terrifying war, and it was collapsing. China didn't fall. And neither did North Korea, where the people were starving to death. While little socialist Cuba stood, we were falling. And we weren't defeated by tanks and missiles, we were destroyed by our own greatest strength: our spirit. The system and the Party rotted from the inside. And maybe, that's why . . . that may have also contributed to why he did it . . .

. . . He was born in a remote Mordovian village and lost his parents when he was very young. He went to war while still a naval cadet. As a volunteer. On Victory Day, he was in the hospital with total nervous exhaustion, weighing thirty-eight kilograms. [*A pause.*] A tortured, sick, and dead tired army had triumphed. Emaciated, coughing. With spinal injuries and arthritis, gastric ulcers . . . That's how I remember

* A special kind of telephone used exclusively for internal Kremlin communication.

the victory . . . He and I are from the same generation, we're the people who lived through the war. [*A pause.*] He rose from cadet to the very peak of the military pyramid. The Soviet state gave him everything: the highest military rank of Marshal, the Hero's Star, the Lenin Prize . . . All that bestowed on a boy from a simple peasant family, and not some crown prince. From the middle of nowhere. The USSR gave thousands of people like him a chance. Poor, simple people . . . And he loved the Soviet state back.

The doorbell rings. An acquaintance of his enters. They discuss something for a long time in the hall. When N. returns, I can tell that he's somewhat upset and not as eager to talk; luckily, a little while later, he becomes engaged again.

We used to work together . . . I invited him to join us, but he refused: These are Party secrets, it's forbidden to reveal them. Why let outsiders in on them? [*A pause.*] I wasn't a friend of Akhromeyev's, but I knew him for many years. No one else took up the cross to try to save the country. Only him. The rest of us were too busy fussing over our personal pensions and doing whatever we could to hold on to our government dachas. I have to say something about this . . .

. . . Before Gorbachev, our people only saw their leaders on the Mausoleum rostrum: muskrat fur hats and stony faces. A joke: "Why have muskrat hats disappeared?" "Because the *nomenklatura* reproduces faster than muskrats." [*He laughs.*] More jokes were told in the Kremlin than anywhere else. Political jokes . . . anti-Soviet . . . [*A pause.*] "Perestroika" . . . I don't remember exactly when, but I think that the first time I heard that word was from foreign journalists while I was abroad. Here, we were more likely to say "acceleration" and "the Leninist path." Abroad, the Gorbachev boom was in full swing, the whole world had caught Gorbymania. They called everything that went on here perestroika. All the changes. Wherever a motorcade bearing Gorbachev went, thousands of people lined up along the road. Tears, smiles. I remember all that . . . the people started loving us! The fear of the KGB dissipated, and, most importantly, they put an end to all of that nuclear insanity . . . For that, the world was grateful to us. For decades, everyone had been terrified of nuclear war, even children. We got used to watching one another from the trenches.

Through the crosshairs . . . [*A pause.*] In European countries, they started teaching Russian. Restaurants started serving Russian food: borscht, *pelmeni* . . . [*A pause.*] I worked in Canada and the U.S. for ten years. When I came home during Gorbachev's tenure in office, I met a great many sincere and honest people who wanted to take part in everything. The last time I'd seen people like that, with faces like that, was when Gagarin went into space . . . Gorbachev had a lot of ideological allies, but very few among the *nomenklatura*. Or the Central Committee, or the regional committee . . . They called him the "Resort Secretary," because they had brought him to Moscow from Stavropol where general secretaries and members of the Politburo liked to go on vacation. The "mineral water secretary" and "son of a juice" because of his antialcohol campaign. The dirt on him was accumulating: While visiting London, he didn't go to Marx's grave . . . Unheard of! He came back from Canada singing its praises, saying how nice it was there. This was nice, that was nice . . . While here . . . you know what it's like here . . . Someone couldn't help themselves: "Mikhail Sergeyevich, it'll be that way here, as well, in a hundred years or so." "That's pretty optimistic." Incidentally, he was always trying to provoke people . . . [*A pause.*] I read an essay by a so-called democrat who said that the war generation . . . which is to say, us . . . was in power too long. We won the war, rebuilt the country, and after that, we should have left because we had no conception of how to live in peacetime. And that was the reason why we fell behind in the world . . . [*He snarls.*] "The Chicago Boys"* . . . "The boys in pink shorts"† . . . Where has our great country gone? If this had been a war, we would have won. If there had been a war . . . [*He takes a long time to regain his composure.*]

. . . Gorbachev became more and more like an evangelist instead of a general secretary. He was a TV star. Soon enough, everyone got sick of his sermons: "back to Lenin," "a leap into developed socialism" . . . It made you wonder: What have we been building, then, "underdeveloped socialism"? What did we have . . . [*A pause.*] I remember that

---

* A group of Chilean economists, educated at the University of Chicago, who worked toward instituting a liberal economy under Pinochet's dictatorship. The term was later used to designate economists in favor of a "shock therapy" approach in the former Soviet Union.

† Pejorative name for Gaidar's team, which had embarked on reforming the most profound tenets of the Soviet economy. This pejorative term was subsequently used to designate supporters of liberal economics.

abroad, we saw a different Gorbachev who barely resembled the Gorbachev we knew at home. Over there, he felt free. His jokes landed, he articulated his thoughts clearly. At home, he played the game, walked the line. And these things made him appear to be weak. And a windbag. But he was not weak. And he wasn't a coward, either. None of that is true. He was a shrewd, calculating politician. Why were there two Gorbachevs? If he'd been as open at home as he was abroad, the elders would have instantly torn him to pieces and eaten him alive. And there's another reason. He . . . it seems to me . . . had stopped being a communist a long time ago. He no longer believed in it . . . Either secretly or subconsciously, he was a social democrat. He didn't advertise it, but everyone knew that when he was young, he was a student at Moscow State University with Alexander Dubček, the leader of the Prague Spring, and his comrade-in-arms Zdeněk Mlynář. They were friends. In his memoirs, Mlynář wrote that when they were read Khrushchev's address to the Twentieth Party Congress at a closed Party meeting at the university, they were so shocked, they spent the whole night wandering Moscow. In the morning, on Lenin Hills, like Herzen and Ogarev before them, they swore to devote their lives to fighting Stalinism.* [A pause.] Those are the roots of perestroika . . . It came out of Khrushchev's thaw . . .

. . . We've already broached this topic . . . From Stalin to Brezhnev, our country's leaders had all seen battle. Lived through the Terror. Their psychological makeup was forged under conditions of violence. In constant fear. They couldn't forget 1941 . . . the Soviet Army's humiliating retreat to Moscow. How soldiers were sent into battle empty-handed and told that they'd win their weapons in combat. They didn't count the people, but they did count the rounds of ammunition. It's understandable . . . It makes sense that people with these kinds of memories believed that in order to defeat the enemy, we needed to keep pumping out tanks and fighter jets. The more the better. There ended up being enough weapons for the USSR and America to destroy one another a thousand times over. And yet they kept making more. Then a new generation came to power. Gorbachev's entire team was made up of the children of the war years . . . The joy of peace had

---

* In 1840, young poet and activist Nikolay Ogarev (1813–1877) and philosopher and writer Alexander Herzen (1812–1870) made an oath to one another on Moscow's Sparrow Hills (in Soviet times, renamed "Lenin Hills") to devote their lives to fighting for freedom in Russia. Both men ended up becoming prominent advocates for social reform, which led to their exile in Western Europe.

been impressed on them . . . Marshal Zhukov overseeing the Victory Parade on a white steed . . . It was a new generation and a different world. While the older generation didn't trust the West and saw it as an enemy, the younger one yearned for the Western way of life. Of course Gorbachev spooked the elders! They were disturbed by his talk of "building a nuclear-weapon-free world"—goodbye, postwar doctrine of the "balance of fear." He said that "there can be no victors in nuclear war," so we started cutting back on defense, reducing the size of the military. The first-rate ammunitions plants were slated to start putting out pots and juicers . . . Was that how it was going to be? There was a moment when the top brass generals were practically at war with the administration. Specifically, with the general secretary. They couldn't forgive him for the loss of the Eastern Bloc, our retreat from Europe. Especially from the GDR. Even Chancellor Kohl was taken aback by Gorbachev's lack of calculation: We were offered huge sums of money to exit Europe and he refused them. His naïveté was astonishing. Russian simplicity. That's how much he wanted to be loved . . . To have French hippies wearing T-shirts with his face on them . . . He represented our country's interests worthlessly and humiliatingly. The army was forced to withdraw into the forests, into the Russian fields. Officers and soldiers lived in tents. In mud huts. Perestroika . . . It was like war, it was no renaissance . . .

During the Soviet-American disarmament talks, Americans always got exactly what they wanted. In his book, *Through the Eyes of a Marshal and Diplomat,* Akhromeyev describes the debates about the Oka missile (known in the West as the SS-23). It was a new missile, no one else had anything like it, and the American side intended to destroy it. However, it didn't fall under the terms of their agreement, which dictated the destruction of medium-range missiles with a radius of 1000–5500km, and smaller ones, with a range of 500–1000km. The Oka's range was 400km. The Soviet General Staff made an offer to the Americans: All right, let's play fair and ban all missiles starting with a 400km range instead of 500km. But then the Americans would have had to sacrifice their modernized Lance-2 missiles, which had a range of 450–470km. A drawn-out behind-the-scenes battle . . . Behind the backs of the military, Gorbachev personally decided to destroy the Oka. That was when Akhromeyev made his famous statement: "And while we're at it, maybe we should ask for political asylum in Switzerland and never come home?" He couldn't participate in the annihilation of something he'd devoted his life to . . . [*A pause.*] The world became unipolar; now, it belongs to America. We became weak, we were pushed to the sidelines. Turned into a third-rate defeated country. We won World War II, but we lost World War III. [*A pause.*] For him . . . this was unbearable . . .

. . . December 14, 1989 . . . Sakharov's funeral. Thousands of people in the streets of Moscow. According to police records, between seventy and one hundred thousand. Yeltsin, Sobchak, Starovoitova* standing next to the coffin . . . American consul Jack Matlock wrote in his memoirs that while the presence of these people at the funeral of the "symbol of the Russian revolution" and "the nation's chief dissident" was to be expected, he was surprised "to see Marshal Akhromeyev, in full uniform, standing modestly in the crowd." While Sakharov was alive, they'd been enemies, irreconcilable opponents. [*A pause.*] But Akhromeyev came to pay his respects. No one else from the Kremlin came except for him. No one else from the General Staff . . .

. . . They'd allowed a little freedom, and the petit bourgeois started coming out of the woodwork. For Akhromeyev, an ascetic man, uninterested in money, this came as a blow. Straight to the heart. He couldn't believe that we could have capitalism here. With our Soviet people, our Soviet history . . . [*A pause.*] I can still see the image of a pale young woman running around the government dacha where Akhromeyev lived with his family of eight, crying, "Take a look: two refrigerators and two televisions! Who is this Marshal Akhromeyev that he should have two televisions and two refrigerators?" Today they're silent, not a peep . . . when all the previous records for dachas, apartments, cars, and other privileges have long since been broken. Luxury automobiles, Western office furniture, vacations in Italy instead of Crimea . . . Our offices had Soviet furniture, we drove Soviet cars. We wore Soviet suits and boots. Khrushchev comes from a mining family . . . Kosygin from peasant stock† . . . All of them, as I've already said, had seen war. Their life experience was, admittedly, limited. It wasn't just the people, but also their leaders who lived behind the Iron Curtain. All of us lived as though we were in an aquarium . . . [*A pause.*] And again . . . maybe this is incidental, but Marshal Zhu-

---

* Galina Starovoitova (1946–1998) was a Russian politician and ethnographer who supported democratic reforms in Russia. She was murdered in her apartment building during the Yeltsin administration.
† Alexei Kosygin (1904–1980) was chairman of the Council of Ministers (the effective head of the Soviet government) from 1964 to 1980.

kov's postwar fall from grace didn't just happen because Stalin envied his glory, it was also because of all of the German carpets, furniture, and hunting rifles they found at his dacha. Even though all of that stuff could have easily fit into two cars. A Bolshevik shouldn't have that much junk . . . These days, it sounds ridiculous. [*A pause.*] Gorbachev loved luxury. In Foros, they built him a dacha with Italian marble, a German tile stove . . . sand for the beach shipped in from Bulgaria . . . Not a single Western leader had anything like it. Gorbachev's dacha made Stalin's Crimean dacha look like a dormitory. The general secretaries changed with the times . . . and so did their wives . . .

Who stood up for communism? Neither the professors nor the secretaries of the Central Committee. Instead, it was people like Leningrad chemistry teacher Nina Andreyeva who threw herself into defending communism. Her article, "I Cannot Forsake My Principles," made a lot of noise. Akhromeyev wrote, too . . . gave speeches . . . He told me, "We have to fight back." They'd call him and threaten him, telling him he was a war criminal because of Afghanistan. Few people knew that he'd actually been against the war in Afghanistan. And he never took diamonds or any other precious gems out of Kabul, or paintings from the national museum, not like the other generals. They were always attacking him in the press . . . for getting in the way of the "new historians," who needed to prove that we had nothing, that our past was nothing but a wasteland. And that there had been no Victory. Just antiretreat detachments and penal units.* That the war had been won by prisoners, they were the ones who had marched into Berlin under gunfire. What Victory? They blanketed Europe in corpses . . . [*A pause.*] The army was insulted and denigrated. Could an army like this have won in '91? [*A pause.*] And could the Marshal have lived through it?

Akhromeyev's funeral . . . Relatives and a handful of friends stood around the grave. There was no military salute. *Pravda* didn't even print the obituary of the former chief of General Staff of an army numbering four million. The new Minister of Defense Shaposhnikov (the former Minister Yazov had been jailed along with the other putschists) was, I believe, preoccupied with taking over Yazov's apart-

---

* Antiretreat detachments were placed behind troops to prevent desertion by immediately executing any deserters. During World War II, penal units were military units made up of NKVD prisoners.

ment, from which they were urgently evicting Yazov's wife. Selfish interests. But . . . I want to say . . . This is important . . . Say what you will about the motives of the putschists, they were not in it for themselves. They weren't out for profit . . . [*A pause.*] People whispered about Akhromeyev in the Kremlin corridors: "He didn't bet on the right horse." The bureaucrats rushed to Yeltsin's side . . . [*He repeats my question.*] The concept of honor? Don't ask me naïve questions! Good people are going out of style . . . His obituary appeared in the American magazine *Time*. It was written by Admiral William J. Crowe, who had been the chairman of the Joint Chiefs of Staff (Akhromeyev's equivalent) in Reagan's administration. They had met many times during military negotiations. And he respected Akhromeyev for his faith, although it was foreign to him. The enemy paid his respects . . . [*Pause.*]

Only a Soviet person can understand another Soviet person. I wouldn't have talked to anyone else . . .

FROM THE AFTERLIFE

On September 1, in Moscow, Marshal of the Soviet Union S. F. Akhromeyev was buried in the Troyekurovsky Cemetery for High-Ranking Persons (a branch of Moscow's Novodevichy Cemetery).

On the night between September 1st and September 2nd, unknown parties excavated Akhromeyev's grave, along with the adjacent grave of Lieutenant-General Srednev, who had been buried the previous week. Investigators speculate that Srednev's grave was unearthed first, apparently by mistake. The grave robbers made off with Akhromeyev's Marshal's uniform with its gold braid, and his Marshal's cap, which, according to military tradition, had been nailed to the coffin. Along with his numerous medals and decorations.

Investigators are confident that Marshal Akhromeyev's grave was not desecrated for political reasons but for financial gain. The uniforms of high-ranking military officials are in especially high demand among antiques dealers. A Marshal's uniform is bound to go like hotcakes . . .

Kommersant newspaper, September 9, 1991

FROM INTERVIEWS ON RED SQUARE IN DECEMBER 1991

—I'm a construction worker . . .

Before August 1991, we lived in one country, and afterward, we lived in another. Before that August, my country was called the USSR.

Who am I? I'm one of those idiots who defended Yeltsin. I stood in front of the White House, ready to lie down in front of a tank. People went out into the streets on the crest of a wave, on a surge. But they were out there to die for freedom, not capitalism. I consider myself a person who's been deceived. I don't need this capitalism we've been led to . . . that they slipped us . . . Not in any form, neither the American model nor the Swedish. I didn't start a revolution to get my hands on someone else's dough. We shouted "Russia!" instead of "USSR!" I'm sorry that they didn't disperse us with water cannons or roll a couple of machine guns onto the square. They should have arrested two or three hundred people and the rest would have gone into hiding. [*A pause.*] Where are the people who called us out onto the square today? "Down with the Kremlin mafia!" "Freedom tomorrow!" They have nothing to say to us. They ran off to the West, now they're over there badmouthing socialism. Sitting around in Chicago laboratories. While we sit here . . .

Russia . . . they've wiped their feet with it. Anyone who wants to can smack her in the face. They turned it into a Western junkyard full of worn-out rags and expired medicine. Garbage! [*Obscenities.*] A trough full of raw materials, a natural gas tap . . . The Soviet regime? It wasn't ideal, but it was better than what we have today. Worthier. Overall, I was satisfied with socialism: No one was excessively rich or poor, there were no bums or abandoned children . . . Old people could live on their pensions, they didn't have to collect bottles and food scraps off the street. They wouldn't look at you with searching eyes, standing there with outstretched palms . . . We've yet to count how many people were killed by perestroika. [*A pause.*] Our former life has been smashed to smithereens, not a single stone was left standing. Pretty soon, I won't have anything to talk about with my son. "Papa, Pavlik Morozov is a moron. Marat Kazei* is a freak," my son says to me, when he comes home from school. "But you taught me . . ."

* Marat Kazei (1929–1944), a Young Pioneer who joined the partisans at the age of thirteen and was posthumously given the title of Hero of the Soviet Union for killing himself with a hand grenade in a standoff with Germans. For Pavlik Morozov, see note on p. 100.

I taught him the same things that I had been taught. The right things. "That horrible Soviet upbringing . . ." That "horrible Soviet upbringing" taught me to think about people other than myself. About the weak and the suffering. Nikolai Gastello* was my hero, not those magenta sports coats with their philosophy of only looking out for themselves—their own skin, their own wallets. "And please, Papa, don't start in with that the spirit stuff, that humanism mumbo jumbo." Where did he pick that up? People are different now . . . Capitalists . . . You have to understand, that's what he learns from the world, he's twelve years old. I'm not an example for him anymore.

Why did I defend Yeltsin? He won a million supporters just for saying that the *nomenklatura*'s special privileges should be revoked. I was ready to pick up a machine gun and shoot at the Communists. I was convinced . . . We didn't understand what they were preparing for us in its place. What they were slipping us. An enormous lie! Yeltsin spoke out against the Reds and signed up with the Whites. It was a calamity . . . The question: What did we want? Gentle socialism, humane socialism . . . And what did we get? On the streets, it's bloodthirsty capitalism. Shooting. Showdowns. People figuring out who runs the kiosk and who owns the factory. The gangsters have risen to the top . . . Black marketeers and money changers have taken power . . . Enemies and predators all around. Jackals! [*A pause.*] I can't forget . . . I can't forget how we stood in front of the White House . . . Whose chestnuts were we pulling from the fire? [*Obscenities.*] My father was a real communist. A righteous man. He was the Party organizer at a big factory. Fought in the war. I said to him, "Freedom's here! We're going to be a normal, civilized country . . ." And he replied, "Your children will be servants. Is that what you really want?" I was young and dumb . . . I laughed at him. We were terribly naïve. I don't know why things turned out like this. I really don't. It's not what we wanted. We had something completely different in mind. Perestroika . . . there was something epic about it. [*He pauses.*] A year later, they shut down our design bureau, and my wife and I ended up out on the street. How did we survive? First, we took all of our valuables to the market. The crystal, the Soviet gold, and our most precious possessions, our books. For weeks on end, we'd eat nothing but mashed potatoes. Then I went into "business." I started selling ciga-

---

* Nikolai Gastello was a Russian aviator and the first Soviet pilot to conduct a suicide attack by an aircraft, earning him the title of Hero of the Soviet Union.

rette butts. A liter jar of butts . . . or a three-liter jar of butts . . . My wife's parents (college professors) collected them off the street, and I would sell them. And people would buy them! Smoke them. I smoked them myself. My wife cleaned offices. At a certain point, she sold *pelmeni* for some Tajik. We paid dearly for our naïveté. All of us . . . Now, my wife and I raise chickens, and she never stops weeping. If only we could turn back time . . . And don't give me a hard time for saying that . . . This isn't some nostalgia for gray salami for two rubles and twenty kopecks . . .

—I'm a businessman . . .

Those goddamn communists and KGB goons . . . I hate communists. Soviet history is the NKVD, the gulag, SMERSH.* The color red makes me want to throw up. Those red carnations . . . My wife bought herself a red blouse and I asked, "Have you lost your mind?" I consider Stalin as bad as Hitler, I demand Nuremberg trials for those Red bitches. Death to the Red dogs!

Everywhere, we're surrounded by five-pointed stars. The Bolshevik idols remain standing on the squares. When I walk down the street with my kid, he asks me: "Who's that?" That's a monument to Rosa Zemlyachka, who flooded Crimea with blood. She loved to personally execute young White officers . . . What am I supposed to tell him?

As long as that mummy—the Soviet pharaoh—remains in Red Square under that pagan burial mound, we'll continue to suffer. We're cursed . . .

—I work at a deli . . .

My husband could tell you about it . . . Where is he? [*She looks around.*] What good am I? All I do is make pastries . . .

1991? We were good people back then . . . Beautiful people. We weren't a mob. I saw a man dancing. Dancing and shouting "F—the Junta! F—the Junta!" [*She covers her face with her hands.*] Oh, don't write that down! Oh no! You can't take back what's been said, but that word shouldn't be printed. He wasn't a young man, either . . . and he

---

* SMERSH was a counterespionage unit tasked with identifying and punishing spies and traitors during the war. It was, essentially, an instrument of terror within the army.

was dancing. We beat them and we were celebrating. They say they already had kill lists prepared. Yeltsin would go first . . . I saw them all on TV the other day. That junta . . . a gang of not-too-bright old men. For those three days, there was a sense of terrible despair: Could this really be the end? Visceral fear. That spirit of freedom . . . everyone felt it . . . and the fear of losing it. Gorbachev is a great man . . . He opened the floodgates . . . People loved him, but not for long. Pretty soon, everything about him was irritating: how he talked, what he said, his mannerisms, his wife. [*She laughs.*] "Through the land gallops a troika: Mishka, Raika, perestroika." Compared to Naina Yeltsina . . . People like her more because she's always standing behind her husband. Raisa would sidle up to him or even get in front of him. Our custom is that either you're the Tsaritsa, or you stay out of the Tsar's way.

Communism is like prohibition: It's good in theory, but it doesn't work. That's what my husband says . . . The Red saints, they were . . . Take Nikolai Ostrovsky*—a saint! But consider how many people they killed. Russia really exhausted its limit for blood in all the wars and revolutions. There's no strength left over for any more blood, any more madness. The people have suffered enough. Now they go shopping, picking out drapes and lace curtains, wallpaper, choosing between different kinds of frying pans. They like everything colorful because it all used to be so gray and ugly. We're as giddy as kids at the sight of a washing machine with seventeen settings. My parents are gone: My mother for seven years now, and my father for eight, but I still haven't used up all of the matches my mother stockpiled. We still have their grain. And their salt. Mama would buy everything she could (back then, we would say "procure" rather than "buy") and stash it away for a rainy day . . . Now we go to the markets and stores like they're museums—there's loads of everything. You want to spoil yourself, indulge. It's therapeutic. We're all so sick . . . [*She falls into thought.*] How much did a person have to suffer to have hoarded that many matches? I can't bear to call what we have a petit bourgeois mentality. Materialism. It's therapy . . . [*She is silent.*] As time goes on, people are forgetting the putsch. They've grown embarrassed. The feeling of victory is long gone. Because . . . I didn't want the Soviet government to be destroyed. Thinking back on how we destroyed it—

* Nikolai Ostrovsky (1904–1936) was a Soviet social realist writer best known for his novel *How the Steel Was Tempered.*

gleefully! . . . But I lived there for half of my life . . . you can't just erase that . . . Everything in my head is built around Soviet structures. I would have to work very hard to change that. People don't remember the bad things too often anymore, now they're just proud of the Victory and the fact that we were the first ones in space. The empty stores—that's all been forgotten . . . It's hard to imagine all that considering how it is now . . .

Right after the putsch, I went to visit my grandfather in the country . . . I couldn't put the radio down for even a second. In the morning, we went out to dig plant beds. Every five minutes, I'd throw down my shovel: "Listen to this, Grandpa . . . Yeltsin's speaking . . ." Then again: "Grandpa, did you hear that?" My grandfather put up with it until he couldn't take it any more. "Why don't you dig a little deeper and stop listening to all that blather. Our salvation is in the soil, the only thing it depends on is the potatoes." Grandpa was a wise man. In the evening, our neighbor came by. I brought up Stalin. Our neighbor: "He was a good man, but he lived too long." My grandfather: "And I outlived that bastard." And there I was, still walking around with my little radio. Trembling with excitement. The worst part of the day was when the deputies would take their lunch break. The action stopped.

. . . What do I have? What was I left with? A huge library, tons of books and records—all of them! And my mother's, too; she had a PhD in chemistry, I have her books and her collection of rare minerals. A burglar broke into her house once . . . She woke up in the middle of the night to see a young thug standing in the middle of her apartment (it was a one-room apartment). He opened the closet and started throwing everything out of it. Hurling things on the floor, cursing: "Damn intelligentsia . . . You don't even have a decent fur coat . . ." He ended up slamming the door and leaving. She had nothing for him to steal. That's our intelligentsia for you. Their legacy. Meanwhile, people are building themselves villas, buying expensive cars. My whole life, I've never seen a single diamond . . .

Life in Russia is like fiction. But I want to live here, among Soviet people . . . And watch Soviet films. They might be full of lies and made-to-order for the government, but I love them. [*Laughs.*] God forbid my husband sees me on TV . . .

—I'm an officer . . .

Now I would like to say my piece. [*He's a young man, around twenty-five.*] Write this down: I am a Russian Orthodox patriot. I serve Our Lord. And I serve Him zealously, with the help of prayer. Who sold Russia out? The Jews. The Rootless. The kike has made God weep many times over.

The worldwide conspiracy . . . What we're dealing with is a conspiracy against Russia. The Dulles plan . . . I don't want to hear it—don't tell me it's a hoax! Silence! CIA director Allen Dulles's plan . . . "After sowing chaos, we will imperceptibly substitute their values for false ones. We will find like-minded individuals, our allies within Russia . . . We will turn the youth into cynics, vulgarians, cosmopolitans. That's how we'll get our way . . ." Do you understand? The Jews and the Yanks are our enemies. Dumb Yankees. President Clinton's speech at a secret meeting of the American political elite: "We have achieved what President Truman set out to do with the atom bomb . . . We have bloodlessly eliminated the country that was America's greatest competitor for world domination . . ." How long will our enemies soar over us? Jesus said, "Fear not nor be dismayed, be strong and of good courage." God will have mercy on Russia and lead her to mighty glory through suffering . . .

[*I can't stop him.*]

. . . In '91 I graduated from military academy with two stars. A junior lieutenant. I was so proud, I never took off my uniform. A Soviet officer! A defender! Then, after the putsch failed, I started reporting to work in civilian clothes and changing there. Otherwise, any old man might come up to me at the bus stop, demanding, "Why didn't you defend the motherland, boy? You son of a bitch! You took an oath." Officers served hungry. On our monthly salary, all you could afford was a kilogram of cheap salami. I ended up quitting the army. For a while, I worked nights, doing security for prostitutes. Now I'm a security guard for a company. Kikes! They're the root of all evil . . . A Russian has nowhere to turn to. They crucified Christ . . . [*He shoves a flyer at me.*] Here, read this . . . All these Sobchaks and Chubaises and Nemtsovs* . . . Neither they, nor the police, nor the army can defend you from the righteous rage of the people. "Haim, did you hear—there's going to be a pogrom." "I'm not scared. It says I'm Russian on

---

* Boris Nemtsov (1959–2015) was a prominent politician under Boris Yeltsin, holding several important government posts. He later became an outspoken critic of Vladimir Putin and was assassinated in Moscow in February 2015.

my passport." "You idiot, they beat your face, not your passport." [*He crosses himself.*]

I'm for Russian law in the Russian land! The names of Akhromeyev, Makashov and other heroes . . . flying on our banners! God will not abandon us . . .

—I'm a student . . . Akhromeyev? Who is that? Where's that from?

—The putsch . . . the August revolution . . .

—Sorry . . . Never heard of it . . .

—How old are you?"

—Nineteen. I'm not interested in politics. That spectacle is foreign to me. But I like Stalin. Now he's interesting. Compare today's politicians to a leader in a military greatcoat. Who comes out looking better? That's the thing . . . I don't need a mighty Russia. I am not about to pull on some stupid boots and hang a machine gun around my neck. I don't want to die! [*He is silent for a moment.*] The Russian dream: a suitcase in your hand, and get the fuck out of Russia! Go to America! But I don't want to move there just to spend my whole life as a waiter. I need to think.

ON THE MERCY OF MEMORIES AND THE LUST FOR MEANING

◆

Igor Poglazov, eighth grader,
14 years old

AS TOLD BY HIS MOTHER

This feels like betrayal . . . I am betraying my feelings, betraying our lives. Our words . . . They were only ever intended for us, and here I am letting a stranger in. Is this stranger a good or a bad person? It doesn't matter anymore. Will they understand me or not . . . I remember there was a woman selling apples at the market who would tell anyone who listened about how she'd buried her son. Then and there, I promised myself that would never be me. My husband and I never talk about it; we weep, but each of us do it in private so that the other one doesn't see. A single word is enough to make me break down. The first year, I couldn't get ahold of myself at all: Why? What made him do it? I want to think . . . I console myself: He wouldn't leave us like that . . . he just wanted to try it out, have a look . . . They're so curious when they're that age: What is going on over there? Especially boys . . . After he died, I combed through his notebooks, his poems. Scoured them like a bloodhound. [*She cries.*] A week before that Sunday . . . I was standing in front of the mirror brushing my hair . . . He came up to me, put his arms around my shoulders, and we stood there like that, looking in the mirror and smiling. "Igor," I pressed myself against him, "You're so handsome. It's because you're a love child. Born of a great love." He hugged me even tighter: "Mama, you are, as usual, incomparable." I get a chill every time I wonder whether that day, when we were standing in front of the mirror, he was already thinking about it . . . Was he thinking about it then?

Love . . . It feels strange to say that word out loud. To remember that there's such a thing as love. There was a time when I thought that love was greater than death . . . that it was more powerful than anything else in the world. My husband and I met in tenth grade. The boys from the neighboring school came to our school for a dance. I don't remember our first evening together because I didn't see Valik, my husband; he saw me but didn't come up to me. He didn't even see my face, just my silhouette. But it was as though he heard a voice telling him, "This is your future wife." That's what he later confessed to me . . . [*She smiles.*] Maybe he made it up? He's a dreamer. But magic was always with us, it has always carried me through the world. I was happy, insanely happy, irrepressible—that's the way I used to be. I adored my husband, but I also liked to flirt with other men, it was like a game for me. You walk along, they look at you, and you like being looked at—so what if they fall just a tiny bit in love with you? "And what have I done to deserve all these gifts?" I'd often sing along with my beloved Maya Kristallinskaya. I ran through life, and now I sometimes regret that I don't remember it all because I'll never be that happy ever again. You need a lot of energy for love, and I'm a different person now. I've grown ordinary. [*She is silent.*] Sometimes I'll be in the mood, but more often than not, it's unpleasant to remember the way I used to be . . .

Igor was three or four . . . I was bathing him. "Mama, I love you like the fail Tsalina." We'd had to fight hard for the letter *r* . . . [*She smiles.*] You can live on things like this, it's what I live on now. The mercy of my memories. I pick up every crumb . . . I'm a schoolteacher, I teach Russian language and literature. A typical scene from our home life: I'm at my books, he's in the pantry. While he's getting the pots, pans, spoons, and forks I prepare for the next day's lesson. He's grown up. I sit and write and he sits at his desk writing, too. He learned how to read very young. And how to write. When he was three, we memorized poems by Mikhail Svetlov: "Kakhovka, Kakhovka—my darling rifle . . . / Fly, hot bullet, fly!" I have to pause here and explain . . . I wanted him to grow up to be strong and brave, so the poems I'd pick out for him were all about heroes and war. The Motherland. Then, one day, my mother took me by surprise: "Vera, quit reading him those war poems. The only game he ever plays is war." "But all little boys like to play war." "Yes, but what Igor likes is when people shoot at him and he falls down. He likes to die! He is so eager to fall over dead, he seems to enjoy it so much it scares me. I hear him shouting to the other boys, 'Shoot me and I'll fall.' Never the other way around." [*After a long pause.*] Why didn't I listen to my mother?

I gave him military toys: a tank, tin soldiers, a sniper rifle . . . He was a boy, he needed to become a warrior. The instructions for the sniper rifle read, "A sniper must kill calmly and selectively . . . First, he must get to know the target . . ." For some reason, this was considered normal, it didn't frighten anyone. Why? We had a war mentality. "If tomorrow war should break out, if tomorrow we must depart . . ." I can't find any other explanation. Today, it's less common for children to be given swords and guns . . . Bang! Bang! But back then . . . I remember how surprised I was when one of the teachers at school told me that in Sweden I think it was, they'd outlawed war-related toys. How are you supposed to raise a man? A defender? [*Her voice breaks.*] "Keep your eye on death, on death / You poor singer and rider . . ." At every single gathering, without fail . . . Within five minutes, we'll be remembering the war. We're constantly singing war songs. Is there anyone else in the world like us? The Poles lived under socialism, too, and the Czechs, and the Romanians, but none of them are quite like this . . . [*Silence.*] I don't know how I'm going to survive. What should I hang on to? What . . .

[*Her voice suddenly drops to a whisper. But to me, it feels like she's screaming.*]

. . . When I close my eyes, I see him lying there in the coffin . . . But we were so happy . . . Why did he decide that death was a beautiful thing . . . ?

. . . My friend took me to a seamstress: "You have to sew yourself a new dress. Whenever I'm depressed, I have a new dress made . . ."

. . . In my dreams, someone keeps stroking my head . . . The first year, I would run off to the park to scream . . . I'd frighten the birds . . .

He's ten years old, no, probably eleven . . . After a long day at school, I barely make it home with two big shopping bags. I come in. Both of them are on the couch—one with a newspaper and the other one with a book. The apartment's a huge mess—unbelievable! There's a mountain of unwashed dishes . . . You can imagine how happy they are to see me! I pick up the broom. Barricade myself with chairs. "Get out of here!" "Never!" "Eenie, meenie, miney, mo—which one of you should I thrash first?" "Mamochka-devotchka, don't be angry," Igor gets out first, he's already as tall as his father. "Mamochka-devotchka" is what he called me at home. He made it up . . .

In the summer, we'd usually go south, "to see the palm trees that

live closest to the sun." [*Happily.*] I remember words . . . our words . . .
We were fixing to warm up his stuffy nose. It'd leave us in debt until
March, we'd have to scrimp and save: first course—*pelmeni,* second
course—*pelmeni,* and with tea—*pelmeni.* [*Silence.*] I remember a
brightly colored travel ad for sunny Gurzuf. And the sea . . . Rocks
and sand bleached by the sea and the sun. I still have lots of photos, I
have to hide them from myself. I'm scared . . . They kill me inside. I
immediately break down . . . One time, we tried to go on vacation
without him. We made it halfway before turning back. "Igor!" we
burst into the house. "You're coming with us! We can't go without
you!" With a cry of "Hurray!" he jumped up on me, wrapping his
arms around my neck. [*After a long pause.*] We can't go on without
him . . .

Why didn't our love stop him? I used to believe that love could do
anything. Again, I'm . . . again . . .

It's in the past . . . He's not with us anymore . . . For a long time, I
was simply in a daze. "Vera," my husband called out to me. I didn't
hear him. "Vera . . ." No response. Then suddenly, hysterics! I started
screaming, stamping my feet, yelling at my mother, my beloved
mother, "You monster, you Tolstoyan monster! And you raised us to
be freaks just like you! What did we hear from you our whole lives?
You have to live for others . . . for a higher purpose . . . throw yourself
under a tank, go down in an airplane for your Motherland. The rum-
ble of the Revolution . . . Heroic death . . . We were taught that death
is more beautiful than life. That's why we grew up to be monsters and
freaks. And that was how I raised Igor. It's all your fault! Your fault!!!"
My mother crumpled and suddenly became very small. A little old
lady. It was like a knife in my heart. For the first time in many days, I
actually felt pain. Before that, even when someone on the trolleybus
put a heavy suitcase down directly on my toes, I didn't feel anything.
It wasn't until my toes swelled up that night that I remembered the
suitcase. [*She cries.*] I should pause here and tell you about my
mother . . . My mother is from the generation of the pre-war intelligentsia. She's one of the people whose eyes sparkled with tears whenever the Internationale played. She lived through the war and never
forgot how a Soviet soldier had hung a red flag on the Reichstag. "Our
country was victorious in such a horrible war!" Ten, twenty, forty
years passed . . . and she would still repeat those words to us like an
incantation. Like a prayer . . . It was her prayer. "We had nothing, but
we were happy!" My mother's conviction in this was absolute. There

was no arguing with her. She loved Leo Tolstoy, "the mirror of the Russian Revolution,"* for *War and Peace,* and because the Count wanted to give everything he owned to the poor in order to save his soul. My mother wasn't alone, all of her friends were like this, too—the first generation of Soviet intelligentsia who had grown up on Chernyshevsky, Dobrolyubov, Nekrasov† . . . on Marxism . . . Could you imagine my mother sitting down and embroidering something or going out of her way to decorate our house with porcelain vases or little elephant figurines . . . Never! That would be a pointless waste of time. Petit bourgeois nonsense! The most important thing is spiritual labor . . . Books . . . You can wear the same suit for twenty years, two coats are enough to last a lifetime, but you can't live without Pushkin or the complete works of Gorky. You're part of the grand scheme of things, there's a grand scheme . . . That's how they lived . . .

. . . There's an old cemetery in the center of our town. Full of trees. Lilacs. People stroll through it like it's a botanical garden. Not many old people go there, so the young laugh and kiss. Play their stereos . . . One night, he came home kind of late: "Where have you been?" "I went to the cemetery." "What made you suddenly want to go to the cemetery?" "It's interesting. You get to look people who are no longer there in the eye."

. . . I opened the door to his room . . . He was standing at full height on the windowsill; our windowsills aren't sturdy or level. We live on the sixth floor! I froze. I couldn't even scream, it was like when he was little and he would climb out onto the skinniest branch in a tree or up onto the high old wall of the ruined church: "If you feel like you can't hold on anymore, just fall toward me." I didn't scream or cry because I didn't want to startle him. I crept back out of his room along the wall. Five minutes later, which felt like an eternity to me, I went in again—he'd hopped down and was walking around the room like normal. I jumped on him, kissing him, hitting him, shaking him, "Why? Tell me, why?" "I don't know. I just wanted to see what it was like."

. . . One morning, I saw funeral wreaths outside of the next building over. Someone had died. All right, so they died and that's that. I came home from work and found out from his father that he had gone over there. I asked him, "Why? We don't know those people." "It was a young woman. She lay there so beautiful. And I had thought death

---

* As Leo Tolstoy was called in a 1908 essay by Lenin.
† Progressive writers from the nineteenth century.

was a scary thing." [*She is silent.*] He was circling it . . . Something was pulling him toward the beyond . . . [*Silence.*] But that door is closed . . . We don't have access to the other side.

. . . He'd nestle into my lap: "Mama, what was I like when I was little?" I'd start telling him . . . how he'd waited up for Father Christmas by the door. He would ask what bus he could take to the Thrice-Ninth Kingdom, the Thrice-Ninth Country.* He saw a Russian stove in a village and waited all night for it to take off running like in the fairy tale. He was very trusting . . .

. . . I remember how one time, there was already snow on the ground . . . He ran up to me: "Mama! I kissed someone today!" "You kissed someone?" "Yep. I went on my first date." "And you didn't tell me you were going?" "I didn't have time. I told Dimka and Andrei and the three of us went together." "Is that how you go on dates, three at a time?" "I was too scared to go alone." "So how were the three of you all on a date?" "It was great. She and I walked around the slide holding hands and kissing while Dimka and Andrei stood guard." Oh Lord! "Mama, can a fifth grader marry a ninth grader†? I mean, if it's really love . . ."

But that . . . that . . . [*She weeps for a long time.*] I can't talk about it . . .

It was our favorite month, August. We'd gone out to the country, we were inspecting a spider web. Laughing . . . and laughing, and laughing . . . [*She is silent.*] Why do I keep on crying? We had a whole fourteen years together . . . [*She cries.*]

I was cooking in the kitchen with the window open. I heard him talking to his father on the balcony. Igor said, "Papa, what's a miracle? I think I've understood. Listen . . . Once upon a time, there was an old man and woman and they had a little chicken, Ryaba. The chicken laid an egg, but not just any old one, a gold one. The old man struck it and struck it, but he still couldn't crack it. The old woman struck it and struck it, but she still couldn't crack it. A mouse ran by, swatted its tail, and the egg cracked when it fell. The old man cried and the old woman cried as well . . ." His father said, "From a logical perspective, it's completely absurd. They struck it and struck it and couldn't crack it, and then suddenly, they're in tears! But how many years—centuries,

* Russian fairy tale locale.
† As previously noted, according to the Soviet education system, a fifth grader would have been eleven or twelve and a ninth grader fourteen or fifteen.

even—have children listened to this fairy tale like it's poetry." Igor said, "I used to think that you could understand everything with reason, Papa." "There are many things you can't understand with reason. For instance love." "And death," Igor said.

From a very young age, he wrote poems . . . On his desk, in his pockets, under the couch, I would find pages and pages covered in his writing. He would lose them, abandon them, forget all about them. Sometimes, I couldn't even believe that he'd written them: "Did you really write this?" "What does it say?" I read it back to him: "People go to each other's houses, / Animals go to each other's houses . . ." "Well, that's an old one. I've already forgotten it." "What about these lines?" "Which ones?" I read them: "Only on branches that are scarred / Can you find the dew of the stars . . ." When he was twelve, he wrote that he wanted to die. He wanted love and death—his two desires. "You and I are betrothed / With blue water . . ." More?! Here: "I am not yours, silvery clouds / I am not yours, blue snows . . ." He'd read them to me. He would! But teenagers write about death all the time . . .

Poems always filled our home, like speech: Mayakovsky, Svetlov . . . My beloved Semyon Gudzenko:

> When going to their deaths, they sing.
> Before that, you can cry.
> In battle, the most fearful time
> Is waiting to attack.

Do you remember that? Of course it's in there . . . Why even ask? We all grew up with it. Art loves death, especially our art. The cult of martyrdom and death is in our blood. Life for aortic rupture* . . . "Oh, those Russians, they don't like to die their own deaths!" wrote Gogol. And Vysotsky sang: "Let me stand a little longer on the edge . . ." On the edge! Art loves death, but there's also French comedy. Why is it that we have so little comedy? "Advance, for the Motherland!" "The Motherland or Death!" I taught my students: Lighting the way for others, I am "consumed in the service of others." I taught them about the feat of Danko,† who ripped his heart out of his chest and lit the way for others. We never talked about life . . . No, hardly . . .

---

* A reference to Osip Mandelstam's famous poem "After Long-fingered Paganini," which was adapted into song by Vladimir Vysotsky.
† "Danko's Burning Heart," an 1895 short story by Maxim Gorky.

Hero! Hero! Hero! Life consisted of heroes . . . victims and executioners . . . There were no other kinds of people. [*She screams. She cries.*]
Going to school is torture. The children wait for me . . . They want
words and feelings . . . What should I tell them? What can I say to
them?

All this happened . . . Here's exactly what happened . . . Late one
night I was in bed reading *The Master and Margarita* by Bulgakov (it
was still considered a dissident book, I had been given a *samizdat*
copy). I got to the final pages . . . Remember? Margarita asks for the
Master's release, and Woland, the spirit of Satan, says, "There's no
need to shout it from the mountaintops, he's gotten used to avalanches
and it won't disturb him. There's no need for you to intervene on his
behalf, Margarita, because he has already been summoned by the one
that he so longed to speak to . . ." Some strange force flung me into
the neighboring room, to the couch where my son was sleeping. I got
down on my knees and started whispering, like a prayer, "Igor, don't
do it. My darling, don't do it. Don't do it!!!" I started doing what I was
no longer allowed to do since he had grown big, kissing his hands and
feet. He opened his eyes: "Mama, what are you doing?" I immediately
recovered: "Your blanket slipped off. I was just fixing it." He fell back
asleep. And I . . . I didn't understand what had gotten into me. When
he was happy, he'd tease me, calling me a will-o'-the-wisp. I went
through life light on my feet.

His birthday was coming up, and New Year's Eve . . . Some of our
friends had promised to get us a bottle of champagne—there wasn't
much you could buy at the store in those days, you had to procure everything by other means. Through connections. Through friends and
friends of friends. We managed to find some smoked salami, chocolates . . . You were very lucky if you somehow got your hands on a kilo
of tangerines in time for New Year's Eve! Good find! Tangerines
weren't just fruit, they were an exotic delicacy, only the New Year
smelled like tangerines. People spent months getting together the delicacies for their New Year's Eve table. This time, I had stashed away a
can of cod liver and a piece of salmon. All of it ended up being served
at his wake . . . [*Silence.*] No, I don't want to end my story so quickly.
We had a whole fourteen years together. Ten days short of fourteen
years . . .

One time, I was cleaning out the storage cabinet and found a folder
full of old letters. When I was in the hospital after giving birth, my
husband and I would write each other letters and notes every day,

sometimes several times a day. We read them aloud and laughed . . . Igor was seven. He couldn't wrap his mind around how he could have not existed while his father and I did. I mean, he existed, we would talk about him in the letters all the time: The baby turned over, he just kicked me . . . He's moving . . . "But I died once, and then I came back to you, right?" The question made me go cold. But children—they talk like that sometimes . . . like philosophers, poets . . . I should have followed him around, writing down the things he'd say: "Mama, Grandpa died. That means they've buried him in the ground and he's growing now . . ."

He already had a girlfriend in the seventh grade. It was serious. "Don't go and marry your first love—or some salesgirl!" I threatened him. I had already gotten used to the idea that I would eventually have to share him with someone else. I was steeling myself. My friend has a son, too, the same age as Igor. She once confessed to me: "I don't know my daughter-in-law yet, but I already hate her." That's how much she loves her son. She can't even imagine giving him up to another woman. What would have happened to us? To me? I don't know . . . I loved him . . . I loved him like crazy . . . No matter how hard my day had been, as soon as I opened the door to our apartment, it was as though a light was shining on me from somewhere. Not "from somewhere," from love.

I had two nightmares. In the first one, he and I were drowning. He was a good swimmer, and once, I'd dared to swim out as far as him. When I turned around to swim back I realized that I wouldn't have the strength to get to shore. I grabbed onto him with a death grip. He screamed, "Let go of me!" "I can't!" I held onto him, I was pulling him down. He was able to wrest himself out of my grip and started nudging me toward the shore. Holding me up and pushing me. That's how he and I made it out. The same thing happened in the dream, only I never let him go. We neither drowned nor made it out of the water. We just wrestled in place . . . In the second dream, it started raining, but I could feel that it wasn't rainwater coming down, it was dirt. Sand. It started to snow, but I could already tell by the sound that it wasn't snow, it was dirt. The shovel drove into the ground like a heart beating, crunch-crunch, crunch-crunch . . .

Water . . . He was fascinated by water . . . He loved lakes, rivers, wells. Especially the sea. He wrote a lot of poems about water. "The quiet star has gone white like the water. Now it's dark." Another one:

"And only water flowing . . . Silence." [*A pause.*] We don't go to the sea anymore.

The final year . . . We often had family dinners. Naturally, the conversation would revolve around books. We'd read *samizdat* together. *Doctor Zhivago,* Mandelstam's poems . . . I remember an argument we had about what a poet was. What is a poet's fate in Russia? Igor's opinion: "A poet has to die early or else he's not a poet. An old poet is just silly." That . . . I missed that, too . . . I didn't think anything of it. Everything was always spilling and spilling out of me like I was Santa's sack . . . Almost every Russian poet has poems about his homeland. I know a lot of them by heart. I'd recite my beloved Lermontov: "I love the Fatherland, but with a strange love." And Esenin: "I love you, my meek homeland . . ." I was overjoyed after I bought a copy of Blok's letters. An entire little volume of them! In a letter to his mother that he wrote upon returning from abroad, he said that our Motherland had immediately displayed her swinish mug and holy visage . . . I put the emphasis on the holy visage, of course . . . [*Her husband comes into the room. He puts his arm around her and sits down.*] What else? Igor went to Moscow to visit Vysotsky's grave. He shaved his head, which made him look a lot like Mayakovsky. [*She turns to her husband.*] Do you remember that? How I yelled at him? He had incredible hair.

The last summer . . . He was tan. Big and strong. He passed for an eighteen-year-old. That summer, the two of us went to Tallinn. It was his second time there, so he showed me around, took me down every alleyway. We went through a whole load of money in three days. We were staying in some dormitory. One night, we came back from a walk, holding hands, laughing. We opened the door and went up to the attendant. She didn't want to let us in. "Ma'am, bringing a man here after 11 o'clock is forbidden." I whispered to Igor, "Go upstairs, I'll be up in a minute." He went and I hissed, "How dare you! That's my son." Everything was so much fun! So great! And then all of a sudden, one night, while we were there . . . I got scared. I was terrified that I would never see him again. Like the fear of something new. Nothing had even happened yet.

His last month . . . My brother had died. There aren't many men in my family, so I took Igor along with me to help out. If I had known . . . He was inspecting it, eyeing death . . . "Igor, move the flowers. Bring the chairs here. Go buy some bread." Doing mundane activities side by side with death . . . it's dangerous . . . You risk confusing the two. I can see this clearly now . . . The hearse arrived. All of the relatives got in, but my son wasn't there. "Igor, where are you? Come here." He got in, but there was no room for him to sit down. All these strange signs . . . Was it the car starting that jolted him? The hearse started, and for a moment, my brother's eyes flipped open. That's a bad omen—it means that there will be another death in the family. I immediately got scared for my mother, she has a bad heart. As the coffin was being lowered into the ground, something fell in with it . . . That's not good, either . . .

His last day . . . The last morning. While I was getting ready, I felt him standing in the doorway, bracing the frame with both hands and watching, studying me. "What are you doing? Go do your homework. I'll be back soon." He silently turned away and went to his room. After work, I met up with a friend. She'd knitted him a fashionable sweater, it was my birthday present to him. I brought it home. When I showed it to my husband, he even admonished me: "Don't you think that he's a little too young to wear such fancy clothes?" For dinner, I made his favorite chicken patties. He usually asked for seconds, but that day, he picked at them and left them on his plate. "Did something happen at school?" He said nothing. I started crying, a rain of tears. It was the first time in many years that I was crying that hard, I hadn't even cried like that at my brother's funeral. And it scared him. He got so scared, I started comforting him. "Try on the sweater." He put it on. "Do you like it?" "A lot." A little while later, I looked in on him, he was lying on his bed and reading. In the other room, his father was typing away at the typewriter. I had a headache, so I fell asleep. They say that people sleep more soundly during a fire . . . I left him reading Pushkin . . . Timka, our dog, lay sleeping in the hall. He didn't bark or whine. I don't remember how much time passed, but eventually I opened my eyes and saw my husband sitting next to me. "Where's Igor?" "He locked himself in the bathroom. He's probably in there muttering poems to himself." A wild, mute fear flung me out of bed. I ran over, I knocked, I banged on the door. I hit it and kicked it. Silence. I called to him, I screamed, I begged. Silence. My husband went to find a hammer or an axe. He broke down the door . . . And there he was, in his old pants, a sweater, slippers . . . hanging from some belt . . . I grabbed him and carried him in my arms. He was soft and warm. I started giving him CPR. Called an ambulance.

How had I slept through it? Why hadn't Timka felt it? Dogs are so sensitive, their hearing is ten times better than ours. Why . . . I sat there and stared. The paramedics gave me a shot and I collapsed. In the morning, they woke me up. "Vera, get up. You won't forgive yourself if you don't." "I'm going to give you a good thrashing for that prank. You're going to get it from me," I thought. And then I realized that there was no one to thrash anymore.

He lay there in his coffin . . . In the sweater I'd given him for his birthday . . .

I didn't start screaming right away, it took a few months . . . But there were no tears. I could scream, but I couldn't cry. It was only when, one day, after I had a glass of vodka, that the tears finally came. I started drinking to make myself cry . . . throwing myself on people . . . We spent two days in one of our friends' apartments without leaving the house. Now I understand how hard that had been on them, how much we tormented them. We needed to escape our house . . . The kitchen chair he usually sat on broke, but I wouldn't touch it. The chair stayed right where it was—what if he didn't like me throwing away something he loved? Neither of us could bear to open the door to his bedroom. Twice, we tried to move, we'd have the documents prepared, raise people's hopes, pack our belongings. And then I wouldn't be able to leave. I felt like he was in there somewhere, I just couldn't see him . . . But he was there. I roamed the shops, picking out clothes for him: Those pants are his color, that shirt. It was some spring . . . I've lost track of which one . . . I came home and told my husband, "Guess what? A man got a crush on me today. He wanted to ask me out." And my husband said, "I'm so happy for you, Verochka. You're coming back . . ." I was endlessly grateful to him for those words. I want to tell you about my husband . . . He's a physicist. Our friends joke: "You guys are lucky, you got a physicist and lyricist blended in one." I loved him . . . Why "loved" and not "love"? Because I don't know this new person yet, the "me" who survived. I'm afraid . . . I'm not ready . . . I won't ever be able to be happy again.

One night, I lay there with my eyes open. Suddenly, I heard a ringing. I clearly heard the doorbell ring. In the morning, I told my husband about it. "I didn't hear anything," he said. That night, it happened again. I was awake, I looked at my husband, he had been woken up by it. "Did you hear that?" "I did." We both got this feeling like we weren't alone in the apartment. Timka was running around in circles by the bed as though he was chasing someone. I nodded off somewhere, into some kind of warm realm. And I had this dream . . . I don't know where we were, but Igor appeared to me in the sweater that we buried him in. "Mama, you call to me but you don't understand how hard it is for me to come to you. Stop crying." I touched him, he felt soft. "Were you happy at home?" "Very." "And over there?" He had no time to answer before disappearing. From that night on, I stopped crying. After that, he would only appear in my dreams as a little boy. But I kept waiting for an older version of him to come so I could talk to him . . .

This was not a dream. I had only just shut my eyes . . . The door to our bedroom swung open, and an adult Igor, whom I had never seen before, stepped in, just for an instant. From the look on his face I could tell that he was indifferent to everything that was going on down here. Our conversations about him, our memories. He's very far from us now. And I can't bear the thought that our connection is severed. I can't handle it . . . I thought about it for a long time . . . And I decided to have another baby. I wasn't supposed to, I was too old, the doctors were afraid for me, but I did it anyway. I had a girl. We treat her as though she's not our daughter but Igor's. I'm afraid of loving her the way I loved him . . . I can't love her like that. I'm crazy! Insane! I cry all the time, I keep going to the cemetery. Our little girl is always with me, but I can't stop thinking about death. This can't go on. My husband thinks that we need to leave. Go to another country. Change everything: the scenery, the people, the alphabet. Our friends keep telling us to move to Israel. They call us all the time: "What's keeping you there?" [*She's practically screaming.*] What's keeping us? What?!

I have this terrifying thought: But what if Igor were to tell you a completely different story? Completely different from mine . . .

AS TOLD BY HIS FRIENDS

"That amazing glue was holding everything together"

We were really young . . . Adolescence is a nightmare, I don't know why they say it's a wonderful time. You're irrational, you're awkward, you're doing everything in your power to stand out, you're vulnerable from all sides. But your parents still think of you as a little kid, they're still molding you. It's like you're under some kind of bell jar where no one can reach you. It feels like . . . I remember the feeling very vividly . . . It was like when I was in the hospital, in an isolation ward, behind glass. With some sort of infection. Your parents pretend (that's how it feels) that they want to be with you, but in reality, they live in an entirely different world. They're off somewhere . . . It's like they're close, but actually, they're very far away . . . Parents have no clue how serious everything is to their kids. First love is terrifying. Fatally dangerous. My friend thought that Igor had killed himself out of love for her. So dumb! Little girl nonsense . . . All of the girls were in love with him. Oh! He was so beautiful and he acted as though he were older than all of us, but it also felt like he was very lonely. He wrote poems. A poet is supposed to be standoffish and lonely. To die in a duel. We were all full of childish ideas.

Those were Soviet times . . . Communist. We were raised on Lenin, fiery revolutionaries, so fiery, we didn't consider the Revolution an error and a crime. Although we weren't into that Marxist-Leninist stuff either. The Revolution was something abstract to us . . . Most of all, I remember the holidays and the anticipation leading up to them. I remember it all very vividly . . . Huge crowds of people out in the streets. Words roaring from the loudspeakers: There were some who believed in them wholeheartedly, others who believed only some of them, and some who didn't believe them at all. But overall, everybody seemed happy. There was music everywhere. My mother was young and beautiful. Everyone was together . . . I remember all this as happiness . . . Those smells, those sounds . . . The bang of the typewriter keys, the morning cries of the milkmaids who would come into town from the countryside, "Mo-lo-ko! Mo-lo-ko!" Not everyone had a refrigerator, so people kept jars of milk out on their balconies. String bags full of raw chickens hung from the window frames. People decorated their windows, filling the space between two windowpanes with glittery cotton and green apples. The stray cat smell wafting up from the basements . . . And how about the inimitable bleach and rag smell of Soviet cafeterias? These things may seem unrelated, but for me, they have all merged into a single sensation. A unified feeling. Freedom has different smells . . . different images . . . Everything about it is different. One of my friends, after her first trip abroad—this was already when Gorbachev was in power . . . she returned with the words, "Freedom smells like a good sauce." I remember my first supermarket, it was in Berlin: a hundred different kinds of salami, a hundred different cheeses. It was baffling. Many discoveries awaited us after perestroika, countless new thoughts and new sensations. They haven't even been described yet, let alone integrated into history. We don't yet know how to articulate them . . . But I'm getting ahead of myself . . . jumping from one era into the next . . . The outside world would be revealed to us later. Back then, we only dreamed of it . . . About the things we didn't have, the things we wanted . . . It felt nice to dream of a world we knew nothing about. We dreamed . . . and meanwhile, we lived our Soviet lives by a unified set of rules that applied to everyone. Someone stands at the podium. He lies, everyone applauds, but everyone knows that he's lying, and he knows that they know that he's lying. Still, he says all that stuff and enjoys the applause. We had no doubts that our generation would go on living that way, so all we ever sought were sanctuaries. My mother listened to the forbidden Galich . . . and I listened to Galich, too . . .

I also just remembered how we tried to go to Moscow for Vysotsky's funeral. The police were kicking people like us off the commuter trains . . . We yelled back at them, "Save our souls! / We're going crazy, suffocating . . ." "Undershot. Overshot. Undershot. The artillery shoots at their own . . ." It was a scandal! Our headmaster ordered us to show up to school with our parents. My mother came, and she conducted herself perfectly. [*She falls into thought.*] We lived in our kitchens . . . The whole country lived in their kitchens. You'd go to somebody's house, drink wine, listen to songs, talk about poetry. There's an open tin can, slices of black bread. Everyone's happy. We had our own rituals: kayaks, tents, hikes. Songs by the campfire. There were common symbols by which we recognized one another. We had our own fashions, our own jokes. Those secret kitchen societies are long gone. And gone with them is our friendship, which we had thought was eternal. Yes . . . Our minds were tuned to the eternal . . . and there was nothing holier than friendship. That amazing glue was holding everything together . . .

In reality, none of us lived in the USSR, we each lived in our own social circle. The hikers clique, the climbers group . . . After class, we'd hang out at this housing department office, and they ended up letting us use one of their rooms. We put together a drama club, I acted in it. There was a literature club. I remember Igor reading us his poems. He imitated Mayakovsky and was incredibly intense. His nickname was "The Student." Adult poets would come and speak openly with us. From them, we learned the truth about the Prague Spring. The war in Afghanistan. And what . . . what else? We learned how to play guitar. You had to! In those days, playing guitar was a top priority. We were prepared to listen to our favorite poets and singer-songwriters on our knees. Poets attracted entire stadiums full of people. They had to police them with mounted officers. The word was the deed. Standing up at a meeting and telling the truth was so dangerous, it was as good as a deed. Going out onto the square . . . It was all such a rush, so much adrenaline, we were so earnest. The word was everything . . . It's difficult to believe it now. These days, you have to do something, not just say it. You can say absolutely whatever you want, but the word has no power at all. We'd like to have faith in something, but we can't. No one cares about anything anymore, and the future is shit. That's not how it used to be . . . Oh! Poems, poems . . . Words, words . . .

[*She laughs.*] In tenth grade, I had an affair. He lived in Moscow. I went to see him, we only had three days. In the morning, at the station, we picked up a mimeographed copy of Nadezhda Mandelstam's memoirs, which everyone was reading at the time. We had to return the book the next day at four in the morning. Hand it off to someone on a train passing through town. For twenty-four hours, we read without stopping—we only went out once, to get milk and a loaf of bread. We even forgot to make out, we just handed the pages to one another. All of this happened in some kind of fever, a stupor . . . All because you're holding this particular book in your hands . . . because you're reading it . . . Twenty-four hours later, we ran through an empty city back to the train station; the public transit wasn't even running yet. I remember the city that night, walking together with the book in my purse. We handled it like it was a secret weapon . . . That's how ardently we believed that the word could change the world.

The Gorbachev years . . . Freedom and coupons. Ration cards, coupons for everything: from bread to grain to socks. We'd stand in line for five or six hours at a time . . . But you're standing there with a book that you hadn't been able to buy before. You'd know that in the evening, they were going to play a previously forbidden movie on TV that had been kept on the shelf for the past ten years. It was so cool! Or all day long, you'd think about how at ten, *Vzglyad* was going to come on TV . . . Its hosts, Alexander Lyubimov and Vladislav Listiev, became national heroes. We were learning the truth . . . that there hadn't just been a Gagarin, there'd been a Beria . . . In reality, for me, I'm just a twit, freedom of speech would have been enough because, as it soon turned out, at heart, I'm a Soviet girl. Everything Soviet went deeper in us than we'd ever imagined. All I really wanted was for them to let me read Dovlatov and Viktor Nekrasov* and listen to Galich. That would have been enough. I didn't even dream of going to Paris and strolling through Montmartre . . . Or seeing Gaudí's Sagrada Família . . . Just let us read and talk. Read! Our little Olga got sick, she was just four months old, she'd come down with an acute bronchial obstruction. I was losing my mind from worry. She and I went to the hospital, and I couldn't put her down for a second, she would only calm down when I was holding her upright. Sitting upright in my arms. I kept pacing and pacing with her, back and forth through the corridors. And if I managed to get her to sleep for even a half hour, what do you think I would do? Even though I was beyond exhausted . . . Guess! I always had *The Gulag Archipelago* under my arm, and I would immediately open it and start reading. In one arm, my baby is dying, and with my free hand, I'm holding Solzhenitsyn. Books replaced life for us. They were our whole world.

Then something happened . . . We came down to earth. The happiness and euphoria suddenly broke. Into a million little pieces. I quickly realized that the new world wasn't mine, it wasn't for me. It required another breed of person. Kick the weak in the eyes! They raised the ones from the bottom up to the top . . . All in all, it was a revolution . . . But this time, with worldly ends: a vacation home and a car for everyone. Isn't that a little petty? The streets were filled with these bruisers in tracksuits. Wolves! They came after everyone. My mother had worked at a sewing factory. It happened so fast . . . They shut down the factory . . . My mother would sit at home all day sewing underwear. All her friends sewed underwear too, every apartment you walked into, that's what they'd be doing. We lived in a building the factory had built for its workers, so everyone in the whole building was sewing bras and underwear. Swimsuits. En masse, they all cut the labels off all their old clothes . . . And they would ask their friends to do it too, to snip the labels off their clothes—preferably imported clothes—so that they could sew them onto those swimsuits of theirs. Then, in small groups, the women would travel through Russia with bags full of their homemade goods. They called it "Underwear Tourism." By then, I was in grad school. [*Happily.*] I remember . . . it was so funny . . . In the university library and the dean's office, they kept

---

* Sergei Dovlatov (1941–1990) and Viktor Nekrasov (1911–1987) were Soviet dissident writers who were not officially published in the USSR. They both emigrated in the 1970s.

barrels of pickles and pickled tomatoes, mushrooms, and cabbage. They sold the pickles and used the proceeds to pay the professors. Or suddenly the whole department would be flooded with oranges. Or stacks of men's dress shirts . . . The great Russian intelligentsia did what it could to survive. People remembered the old recipes . . . what they ate during the war . . . In the hidden corners of the parks and on sloping plots off the railroad tracks, people planted potatoes. Does eating nothing but potatoes for weeks on end count as going hungry? What about when it's nothing but sauerkraut? I will never be able to eat that again for as long as I live. We learned to make chips out of potato peels and would pass around this wonderful recipe: Throw some peels into boiling sunflower oil and add a generous pinch of salt. There was no milk, but there was plenty of ice cream, so that's what we made porridge with. Would I still eat that today?

The first thing to go was friendship . . . Suddenly, everyone was too busy, they had to go out and make money. Before, it had seemed like we didn't need money at all . . . that it had no bearing on us. Suddenly, everyone saw the beauty of green bills—these were no Soviet rubles, they weren't just play money. Bookish boys and girls, us house plants . . . We turned out to be ill suited for the new world we'd been waiting for. We were expecting something else, not this. We'd read a boatload of romantic books, but life kicked and shoved us in another direction. Instead of Vysotsky, it was Kirkorov* now. Pop! That says it all . . . Not long ago, some people came over and we were hanging out in my kitchen, which doesn't happen too often anymore. We had a debate: would Vysotsky sing for Abramovich?† People had differing opinions. The majority were positive that yes, he would. The next question was how much he would charge.

Igor? In my mind's eye, I still see him as Mayakovsky. Beautiful and lonely. [*She is silent.*] Have I explained anything to you? I wonder whether I managed to get anything across . . .

"The market became our university"

It's been so many years, but I still wonder why. What made him decide to do it? We were friends, but the decision was totally his . . . his

---

* Filip Kirkorov (1967–) is a Russian pop singer.
† Roman Abramovich (1966–) is a Russian oligarch whose fortune, in 2003, was estimated to be around $10.2 billion.

alone . . . What can you say to somebody standing on the ledge? What? When I was that age, I thought about suicide too. Why? I don't know. I loved my mother and father . . . my brother . . . Everything was all right at home. But still, I was drawn to it. Somewhere out there, there's something else. What? Something . . . just over there . . . Like a whole world that's brighter, more meaningful than the one that you live in, like something more important is happening just over our horizon. Out there, you can even touch the mystery that you can't get close to otherwise, that you can't tune into with reason. And you want to so badly . . . Let me just try it . . . try getting up on your windowsill . . . jumping off the balcony . . . But you're not trying to die, you want to rise up. You believe you're about to take flight. It feels like you're in a dream . . . in a trance . . . When you come to, you remember a light, a sound . . . and that it had felt good . . . that you felt so much better than you do down here . . .

Our group of friends . . . Leshka was part of it, too . . . He just recently died of an overdose. Vadim got sucked into the nineties. Got into the book business. It had started out as a joke, a pipe dream, but as soon as he had money coming in, a racket showed up, these boys with revolvers. He was always either buying them off or running from them—he'd sleep in the woods, up in the trees. In those years, they didn't bother with beatings, more often, they'd just murder you. What ever happened to him? He disappeared without a trace . . . The police still haven't found him. They must have buried him somewhere. Arkady hightailed it to America: "I'd rather live under a bridge in New York City." Just Ilyusha and I were left . . . Ilyusha had fallen in love and gotten married. While poets and artists were still in style, his wife had tolerated his eccentricities. Then brokers and accountants became the fashion and she left him. He fell into a major depression. The moment he steps outside, he has a panic attack. He shakes from fear. Now he stays home. Like an overgrown child living with his parents. Ilyusha keeps writing his poetry—a cri de coeur . . . When we were kids, we used to all listen to the same tapes and read the same Soviet books. Ride the same bicycles . . . Everything was simpler in our old life: one pair of boots for all seasons, one coat, one pair of pants. We were raised like young warriors in ancient Sparta: If the Motherland called, we'd sit on a hedgehog for Her.

. . . It was some military holiday . . . They walked our preschool class to the monument to the heroic Young Pioneer Marat Kazei. "Look, children," our teacher said. "This young hero blew himself up with a hand grenade and took a whole lot of fascists down with him. When you grow up, you have to be just like him." You mean we have to blow ourselves up with grenades? I don't actually remember this, but my mother told me the story . . . That night, I wept bitterly: I would have to die and lie somewhere all alone, without my mom and dad. The fact that I was crying already meant that I was no hero . . . I ended up getting sick.

. . . When I was in school, I dreamt of getting into the brigade that guarded the Eternal Flame in the center of town. They only accepted the very best students. They'd sew them military overcoats, hats with earflaps, and issue them army gloves. It wasn't an annoying obligation, it was a great honor. Meanwhile, we listened to Western music, jockeyed for blue jeans; at that point, we already had them . . . A symbol of the twentieth century, right up there with the Kalashnikov. My first pair of jeans said "Montana" on the label—it was so cool! But at night, I would still dream of hurling myself at the enemy with a hand grenade . . .

. . . My grandma died, so my grandpa moved in with us. He was a career officer, a lieutenant colonel. He had a lot of medals and decorations, and I'd always be bugging him: "Grandpa, what did they give you this medal for?" "For defending Odessa." "What was your special achievement?" "I defended Odessa." That was all I could get out of him. I'd get frustrated. "Come on, Grandpa, tell me about something noble and lofty." "You want to know something noble and lofty, go to the library. Take out a book and read it." My grandpa was great, we got along really well, we had this great chemistry. He died in April, but he'd wanted to live until May. Until Victory Day.

. . . When I was sixteen, I was summoned to the conscription office. "Which of the services would you like to join?" I told the enlistment officer that when I graduated, I would volunteer to go fight in Afghanistan. "Idiot," he said. But I prepared for a long time: I learned how to parachute, studied machine guns . . . We are the last Young Pioneers of the Land of Soviets. Always be prepared!

. . . A boy from our class was about to move to Israel . . . They called an all-school assembly to try to talk him out of it: If your parents want to leave, they can go. We have good orphanages, you can finish school there and remain in the USSR. He was considered a traitor. They kicked him out of the Komsomol. The next day, our whole class was going on a trip to harvest potatoes at a collective farm. He showed up, and they led him off the bus. At assembly, the principal warned everyone that whoever corresponded with him would have a hard time graduating. After he left, we all started writing him letters as a group . . .

. . . During perestroika . . . Those same teachers told us to forget everything they'd ever taught us and start reading the papers. We started studying newspapers in class. The graduation test for history was canceled, we didn't have to memorize all those Party Congresses after all. For the last October demonstration, they still handed out posters and portraits of the leaders, but for us, it just felt like Carnival in Brazil.

. . . I remember people walking around empty stores with bags full of Soviet currency . . .

I went to university . . . At that point, Chubais was lobbying for privatization vouchers, promising that one voucher would buy you two Volgas when in reality, these days, it's worth about two kopecks. What an exciting time! I handed out flyers in the subway . . . Everyone dreamt of a new life . . . Dreams . . . People dreamt that tons of salami would appear at the stores at Soviet prices and members of the Politburo would stand in line for it along with the rest of us. Salami is a benchmark of our existence. Our love for salami is existential . . . Twilight of the idols! The factories to the workers! The soil to the peasants! The rivers to the beavers! The dens to the bears! Mexican soap operas were the perfect replacement for Soviet parades and live broadcasts of the First Congress of People's Deputies. I stayed in college for two years and then dropped out. I feel sorry for my parents because they were told flat out that they were pathetic *sovoks* whose lives had been wasted for less than a sniff of tobacco, that everything was their fault, beginning with Noah's Ark, and that now, no one needed them anymore. Imagine working that hard, your whole life, only to end up with nothing. All of it took the ground out from underneath them, their world was shattered; they still haven't recovered, they couldn't assimilate into the drastically new reality. My younger brother would wash cars after class, sell chewing gum and other junk in the subway, and he made more money than our father—our father who was a scientist. A PhD! The Soviet elite! When they started selling salami at the privately owned stores, all of us ran over to ogle it. And that was when we saw the prices! This was how capitalism came into our lives . . .

I got a job as a freight handler. Real happiness! My friend and I would unload a truck of sugar and get paid in cash plus a sack of sugar each. What was a sack of sugar in the nineties? An entire subsistence! Money! Money! The beginning of capitalism . . . You could become a millionaire overnight or get a bullet to the head. When they talk about it today, they try to frighten you: There could have been a civil war, we were teetering on the edge of ruin! It didn't feel like that to me. I remember when the streets emptied out and there was nobody left on the barricades. People stopped subscribing to or even reading the newspapers. The men hanging out in the courtyard berated Gorbachev and then Yeltsin for hiking up the vodka prices. They'd gone after their golden calf! Wild, inexplicable avarice took hold of everyone. The smell of money filled the air. Big money. And absolute freedom—no Party, no government. Everyone wanted to make some dough, and those who didn't know how envied those who did. Some sold, others bought . . . Some "covered," others "protected." When I made my first "big bucks," I took my friends out to a restaurant. We ordered Martini vermouth and Grand Piano vodka—the crème de la crème! I wanted to feel the weight of the glass in my hand, imagine that I was one of the beautiful people. We lit up our Marlboros. Everything was just like we'd read about in Remarque. For a long time, we modeled ourselves after those images. New stores, new restaurants . . . They were like stage sets from a different life . . .

. . . I sold fried hot dogs. Those brought in crazy money . . .

. . . I shipped vodka to Turkmenistan . . . I spent a whole week in a sealed freight car with my business partner. We had our axes ready, plus a crowbar. If they found out what we were bringing into the country they would have killed us! On the way back, we carted a shipment of terrycloth towels . . .

. . . I sold toys. One time, I sold off an entire lot wholesale for a truckload of carbonated beverages, traded that for a shipping container of sunflower seeds, and then, at a butter plant, traded it all in for butter, sold half of the butter, and traded the other half for frying pans and irons . . .

. . . Now I have a flower business. I learned how to "salt" roses: you put heat-treated salt at the bottom of a cardboard box—you need a layer at least a centimeter thick—and then you put half-blossomed flowers into it and pour some more salt on top of them. You put a lid on the box and put it all in a big plastic bag. Tie it up tight. Then, a month or a year later, you take them out, wash them off . . . Come by any day, any time. Here's my card . . .

The market became our university . . . Maybe it's going too far to call it a university, but an elementary school for life, definitely. People would visit it like they were going to a museum. Or to the library. Boys and girls stumbled around with crazed expressions, like zombies among the stalls . . . A couple stops in front of some Chinese epilators, and she explains the importance of epilation: "Don't you want that? For me to be like . . ." I don't remember the name of the actress . . . Say it was Marina Vlady or Catherine Deneuve. Millions of new little boxes and jars. People would bring them home as though they were sacred texts and, after using their contents, they wouldn't throw them out, they'd display them in a place of honor on their bookshelves or put them in their china cabinets behind glass. People read the first glossy magazines as though they were the classics, with the reverent faith that behind the cover, directly under that packaging, you'd find the beautiful life. There were kilometer-long queues outside of the first McDonald's, stories about it on the news. Educated, intelligent adults saved boxes and napkins from there and would proudly show them off to guests.

I have this good friend . . . His wife slaves away at two jobs, while he has too much pride to work: "I'm a poet. I am not about to go out and sell pots and pans. It's gross." Back in the day, he and I, like everyone else, would walk around chanting, "Democracy! Democracy!" We had no idea what all that would lead to. No one was itching to peddle pots and pans. And now, there's no choice: You either feed your family or you hang on to your *sovok* ideals. It's either/or, no other options . . . You can write poems, strum the guitar, and people will pat you on the shoulder: "Well, go on! Go on!" But your pockets are empty. The people who left? They sell pots and pans and deliver pizza, but in other countries . . . Assemble boxes at cardboard factories . . . That kind of thing is not considered shameful like it is here.

Did you understand what I've been trying to tell you? I've been talking about Igor . . . About our lost generation—a communist upbringing and a capitalist life. I hate guitars! You can have mine if you want.

ON A DIFFERENT BIBLE AND A
DIFFERENT KIND OF BELIEVER

◆

Vasily Petrovich N.,
member of the Communist Party since 1922,
87 years old

Well, yes, I wanted to . . . but then the doctors brought me back. Did they understand where they were bringing me back from? I am, of course, an atheist, but in my old age, I've become an unreliable one. You're face to face with . . . The thought that it's time to go . . . somewhere else . . . It makes you look at things differently . . . yes . . . At earth and sand . . . I can't look at regular sand anymore without being overcome with emotion. I've been old for a long time now. The cat and I sit by the window. [*The cat is on his lap. He's petting it.*] Sometimes, we'll turn on the TV . . .

And of course, I never thought I'd live to see the day when they'd start erecting monuments to the White generals. Who were the heroes in my day? Red commanders . . . Frunze, Shchors* . . . Now it's Denikin and Kolchak . . . Even though there are people still alive today who remember how the Kolchakites would hang us from the lampposts. The Whites have finally won . . . Is that what it is? I fought and fought and fought. For what? I built and built . . . What did I build? If I were a writer, I would write a memoir myself. The other day I listened to a radio show about my factory. I was its first director. They were talking about me as though I were already dead. Except . . . I'm alive . . . It didn't even occur to them that I could still possibly be here. Yes!

* Mikhail Frunze (1885–1925) was a Soviet army officer and military theorist. He is regarded as one of the fathers of the Red Army. Nikolay Shchors (1895–1919) was a Red Army Commander renowned for his courage during the post-Revolution civil war.

Indeed . . . [*The three of us laugh. His grandson is with us, listening.*] I feel like a forgotten artifact in a museum vault. Some dusty pottery shard. We had a great empire—stretching from sea to sea, from beyond the Arctic to the subtropics. Where is it now? It was defeated without a bomb. Without Hiroshima. It's been conquered by Her Majesty Salami! The good chow won! Mercedes-Benz. The people don't need anything else, don't even offer it to them. They don't need it. Only bread and circuses for them! And that truly is the most important discovery of the twentieth century. The response to all of the famous humanists and Kremlin dreamers. While we, my generation . . . We had great plans. We dreamt of worldwide revolution: "To the grief of all bourgeois / Through the world, we'll spread the fire." We wanted to build a new world where everyone would be happy. We thought that it was possible, I sincerely believed in it! Completely sincerely! [*He has a coughing fit and becomes short of breath.*] This asthma's killing me. Hold on . . . [*He pauses.*] I've lived long enough . . . I've lived long enough to see the future we had dreamed of. The future we died and killed for. There was so much blood . . . Our own and other people's . . .

Go and die without reproach!
Your death won't be in vain,
When the blood runs from under him . . .
The heart tired of hate can't learn to love . . .

[*He is surprised.*] I still remember . . . I haven't forgotten! My senility hasn't wiped it all out yet. Not entirely. We memorized poems in our political literacy classes. How many years has it been? I'm afraid to count . . .

What astonishes me? Destroys me? The ideals have been trampled underfoot! Communism has been anathematized! Everything was smashed to smithereens! I'm nothing but a doddering old fool. A bloodthirsty maniac, a serial killer . . . Is that how it is? I've been alive too long, it's no good living this long. You shouldn't . . . no, really, you shouldn't . . . It's dangerous living too long. My time was up before my life could end. You have to die along with your era. Like my comrades . . . They all died young, at twenty or thirty years old. And they died happy. With faith! With Revolution in their hearts, as we'd say in those days. I envy them. You wouldn't understand this, but I envy them. "Our young drummer died . . ." He died gloriously! For a great cause! [*He falls into thought.*] I always lived side by side with death, but I never thought about it very much. Then, this summer, they took me out to our dacha and I kept staring at the ground . . . It seemed alive to me . . .

—"Death and killing—aren't they one and the same? You lived among murderers."

[*Irritably.*] For questions like that . . . They'd grind you into labor camp dust. It'd either be the North or execution—not much of a choice. In my day, people didn't ask those kinds of questions. We didn't have questions like that! We . . . imagined a just life without rich or poor. We died for the Revolution, and we died idealists. Wholly uninterested in money . . . My friends are long gone, I'm all alone. None of the people I used to talk to are around anymore. At night, I talk to the dead . . . And you? You don't understand our feelings or our words: "grain confiscation campaign," "foodgroups," "disenfranchisee," "committee of the poor" . . . "repeater" . . . "defeatist." It's Sanskrit to you! Hieroglyphics! Old age means, first and foremost, loneliness. The last old man I knew—he lived in the adjacent courtyard—died five years ago, or maybe it's been even longer . . . seven years ago . . . I'm surrounded by strangers. People come from the museum, the archive, the encyclopedia . . . I'm like a reference book, a living library! But I have no one to talk to . . . Who would I like to talk to? Lazar Kaganovich* would be good . . . There aren't many of us who are still around, and even fewer who aren't completely senile. He's even older than me, he's already ninety. I read in the papers . . . [*He laughs.*] In the newspaper, it said that the old men in his courtyard refuse to play dominos with him. Or cards. They drive him away: "Fiend!" And he weeps from the hurt. Ages ago, he was a steel-hearted People's Commissar. He'd sign the execution lists, he sent tens of thousands of people to their deaths. Spent thirty years by Stalin's side. But in his old age, he doesn't even have anyone to play dominoes with . . . [*After this, he speaks very quietly. I can't tell what he's saying, I only catch a few words.*] It's scary . . . Living too long is scary.

. . . I'm no historian, I never even studied the humanities. Although

---

* Lazar Kaganovich (1893–1991) worked closely with Stalin and was one of the leading political figures behind collectivization and the purges. After occupying several high-ranking posts, he fell into relative disfavor after 1957.

for a time, I did run a theater, our city theater. Wherever the Party assigned me, I served. I was totally devoted to the Party. I don't remember very much of my life, only work. The whole country was a construction site, a blast furnace, a forge! People don't work that hard anymore. I would get three hours of sleep a night. Three hours . . . We were fifty or a hundred years behind the most developed countries. An entire century. Stalin's plan was to catch up within fifteen or twenty years. Stalin's famous Great Leap Forward. And we knew that we could do it! People don't believe in anything anymore, but back then, we really did. People were prepared to believe in anything. Our mottos: "We'll destroy industrial ruin with our Revolutionary dreams!" "The Bolsheviks must master technology!" "We'll catch up with capitalism!" I didn't live at home, I lived at the factory . . . at the construction site. You know . . . At two, three in the morning, the phone could ring. Stalin never slept, he went to bed late, so we didn't sleep, either. The administrative cadres. From the top down to the bottom. My hard work earned me two medals and three heart attacks. I was the director of a tire factory, the head of a construction trust, and from there, I was transferred to a meatpacking plant. Put in charge of the Party Archive. After my third heart attack, they gave me the theater. Our era—my era—was a great era! Nobody lived for himself. That's why it hurts . . . A charming young lady was interviewing me the other day. She started "enlightening" me about how terrifying the years I lived through had been. She'd read about them in books—but I lived through them! That's where I come from. I'm a man of my era. And here she was telling me, "You were slaves. Stalin's slaves." You little snot! I was no slave! No way! Even today, when I am gnawed by doubt . . . I know that I was no slave. People's heads are full of mush. Everything's been mashed together: Kolchak and Chapayev,* Denikin and Frunze . . . Lenin and the Tsar . . . It's a Red and White salad. Kasha. They're tap dancing on their graves! It was a great time! We will never live in such a big and strong country again. I cried when the Soviet Union collapsed. They began cursing us immediately. Slandering. The consumer triumphed. The louse. The worm.

My homeland is October. Lenin, socialism . . . I loved the Revolution! There is nothing more precious to me than the Party! I was in the

---

* Vasily Chapayev (1887–1919) was a celebrated Red Army Commander whose exploits were later novelized and, in 1934, adapted into a wildly popular film. Chapayev and his aide-de-camp Petka would later become recurring characters in Soviet jokes.

Party for seventy years. My Party membership card is my Bible. [*He begins declaiming the Internationale.*]

> We will smash the world of violence
> Down to its foundations, then
> Build our new world over the ruins.
> The former nobody shall rule . . .

We wanted to create Heaven on Earth. It's a beautiful but impossible dream, man is not ready for it. He is not yet perfect enough. Well . . . From Pugachev* to the Decembrists, down to Lenin himself, everyone dreamt of equality and brotherhood. Without the idea of fairness, it'll be a different Russia with different people. A completely different country. We aren't over communism yet. Don't get your hopes up. And the world isn't over it, either. Man will always dream of the City of the Sun.† Even when he was still living in caves, walking around in animal skins, he was already hungry for justice. Remember our Soviet songs and films . . . the dream in them! The faith . . . A Mercedes is no kind of dream . . .

His grandson will remain silent the whole time we're talking. In response to my questions, all he'll contribute to the conversation are a handful of jokes.

A joke from his grandson

It's 1937. Two Old Bolsheviks‡ are sitting in a jail cell. One says to the other, "It looks like we're not going to live to see communism, but surely our children will!" The other: "Yes, our poor children!"

◆ ◆ ◆

* Yemilyan Pugachev (1742–1775) was a pretender to the throne who led a Cossack insurrection against Catherine the Great.
† *The City of the Sun* is a work of utopian fiction by philosopher Tommaso Campanella, written in 1602 describing a theocratic society where goods, women, and children are all shared.
‡ Party members who had joined before the 1917 Revolution came to be known as "Old Bolsheviks." Many of them were tried and executed during Stalin's purges.

—I've been old for a long time . . . Old age is interesting, too. You come to realize that man is an animal . . . You suddenly see a lot of the animal in yourself . . . It's that time in your life, as Ranevskaya* would say, when the candles on your birthday cake cost more than the cake itself, and half of your urine goes off to the lab. [*He laughs.*] Nothing can save you from old age—no medals, no decorations. There's no escaping it . . . the refrigerator buzzes, the clock ticks. And nothing else happens. [*The conversation turns to his grandson, who is in the kitchen making tea.*] Kids these days . . . All they think about is the computer. When he was in ninth grade, this grandson, he's the youngest one, told me, "I'll read about Ivan the Terrible, but I don't want to read about Stalin. I'm sick of your Stalin!" They don't know anything, but they're already sick of it all. Fed up with it! Everyone curses 1917. "Idiots!" they call us. "Why did they have to have a revolution?" But the things I remember . . . I remember people with fire in their eyes. Our hearts were on fire! No one believes me! But I still have my wits about me . . . I remember . . . Yes . . . Those people didn't want anything for themselves, it wasn't like today, when everyone puts himself first. A pot of cabbage soup . . . a little house, a little garden . . . It was about the collective "we"! We! We!!! Sometimes my son's friend stops in to see me, he's a university professor. He goes abroad, lectures out there. We argue until we're hoarse. I tell him about Tukhachevsky,† and he responds that as a Red Army commander he gassed peasants in Tambov and hanged sailors in Kronstadt. "First," he says, "you shot the aristocrats and priests. That was in 1917. And then, in 1937, you all shot each other . . ." They've even gotten to Lenin. I won't let anyone have Lenin! I'll die with Lenin in my heart! One moment . . . hold on . . . [*Has a severe coughing fit that makes it difficult to understand what he's saying.*] We used to expand our fleet, conquer outer space, but today, it's nothing but mansions and yachts . . . I have to admit that a lot of the time, I don't think about anything at all. Are my bowels working or not? That's what you need to know first thing in the morning. That's what the end of your life is like.

* Faina Ranevskaya (1896–1984) was a famous actress known for her strong character and propensity to speak her mind. Some of her expressions have become proverbial.
† Mikhail Tukhachevsky (1893–1937) was a second lieutenant in the Tsarist army during World War I and joined the Bolsheviks in 1918. He commanded the Red Army offensive against Poland in 1920 and put down the Kronstadt uprising in 1921. Named a Marshal of the Soviet Union in 1935, he was a victim of the purges and was executed in 1937.

. . . We were eighteen, twenty years old. What did we talk about? We talked about the Revolution and love. We were Revolution fanatics. But we also spent a lot of time arguing about Alexandra Kollontai's *Love of Worker Bees,* which was very popular at that time. The author defended free love, that is, love without anything superfluous . . . "Like drinking a glass of water."* Without the sighs and flowers, no jealousy or tears. Kissing and love letters were considered bourgeois prejudices. A true revolutionary was supposed to reject the urges to practice these rituals. We even held meetings about it. Our views were divided: some were for free love, but with "the wild cherries"—that is, with feelings, while others were against any "wild cherries" at all. I was for "the wild cherries," or at least in favor of kissing. Yes! Really . . . [*He laughs.*] I'd fallen in love—I was courting my future wife. How did I court her? We'd read Gorky together: "A storm! A storm is coming! The dumb penguin meekly hides his fat body in the cliffs . . ." Were we naïve? Perhaps. But what we did was also beautiful. Beautiful, goddammit! [*He laughs like a young person. I notice how handsome he still is.*] Dances . . . regular dances . . . We considered them bourgeois. We would put dances on trial and punish the Komsomol members who danced or brought their girlfriends flowers. For a while, I even presided over an antidancing tribunal. Because of this "Marxist" conviction of mine, I never did learn how to dance. I later repented. I could never dance with a beautiful woman, I'm like a bear! We'd have Komsomol weddings. No candles, no wreaths. No priests. Instead of icons, portraits of Marx and Lenin. My bride had long hair, so she cut it all off before the wedding. We hated beauty. It wasn't right, of course. You could say that we overdid it . . . [*Another coughing fit. He waves at me, signaling me not to turn off the tape recorder.*] It's all right, it's fine . . . I don't have the time to put this off . . . Pretty soon, I'll be decomposing into phosphorus, calcium, and so on. Who else will you find to tell you the truth? All that's left are the archives. Pieces of paper. And the truth is . . . I worked at an archive myself, I can tell you firsthand: Paper lies even more than people do.

What was I talking about? I was talking about love . . . my first wife . . . When our son was born, we named him October. In honor of

* Alexandra Kollontai (1872–1952) was a Russian revolutionary who went on to become the most prominent woman in early Soviet politics. She is best known for her work for women's emancipation. "Like drinking a glass of water" is a famous expression from Kollontai's book on communist morality in sexual relations.

the tenth anniversary of the Great October Revolution. I wanted us to have a daughter, too. "You must really love me if you want a second child," my wife teased. "And what will we name this daughter of ours?" I liked the name Lyublena, a combination of *lyublyu* ("I love") and Lenin. My wife wrote out all of her favorite girls' names: Marxana, Stalina, Engelsina, Iskra . . . Those were the most fashionable names of the day. That piece of paper just sat there on the table . . .

The first Bolshevik I ever saw was a man who'd showed up at my village one day, this young student in a soldier's overcoat. He made a speech on the square by the church. "Today, some people go around in leather boots, while others only have bast shoes. When the Bolsheviks come to power, everyone will be equal." The men shouted at him, "How?" "A wonderful time will come when your wives wear silk dresses and high-heeled shoes. There will no longer be rich and poor. Everyone will be happy." My mother would get to wear a silk dress, my sister would be in heels. I'd go to school . . . everyone would live like brothers and sisters, everyone would be equal. How can you not fall in love with a dream like that! Poor people, those who had nothing, believed the Bolsheviks. They won the support of the youth. We walked through the streets crying, "Melt down the church bells! Turn them into tractors!" The only thing we knew about God was that there was no God. We mocked the priests, and at home we destroyed icons. Instead of sacred processions, we held demonstrations with red banners . . . [*He stops.*] Have I told you all this already? Senility . . . I'm old . . . I've been old for a long time . . . Anyway . . . Marxism became our religion. I felt lucky to be alive at the same time as Lenin. We'd get together and sing "The Internationale." When I was fifteen or sixteen, I was already in the Komsomol. A communist. A soldier of the Revolution. [*Silence.*] I'm not afraid of death. At my age, it's just unpleasant . . . And it's only unpleasant to me because someone is going to have to deal with my body. All that hassle with the corpse . . . I went to a church once to meet the priest. He told me, "You need to confess." I'm really old . . . It won't be long until I see whether there's a God or not for myself. [*He laughs.*]

We were half-famished, half-naked, but we went to *subbotniks** all

---

* *Subbotniks* were officially designated days for volunteer work, typically Saturdays, that were first instituted in 1919. Citizens would work together to clean streets, fix public amenities, collect recyclables, and other such activities. In some places, the tradition is carried on to this day.

year round, even in the winter. It was freezing! All my wife had was a light jacket, plus she was pregnant. We were at the depot, loading coal and timber, pushing it in wheelbarrows, and a young woman we didn't know was working alongside us. She turned to my wife: "Your jacket is so thin. Do you own anything warmer?" "No." "You know what, I have two. I had a good coat and then I also got a new one from the Red Cross. Give me your address, I'll come by with it this evening." That evening, she brought us a coat, but it wasn't her old one—she had brought us her new one. She didn't know us, but it was enough that we were Party members like her. It meant that we were like brothers and sisters. There was a blind young woman in our building, she'd been blind since childhood, but she would cry if we didn't bring her along to *subbotniks*. Even if she wasn't able to help out much, she could at least sing Revolutionary songs with us!

My comrades . . . They're all underground now . . . The inscriptions on their tombstones read: Member of the Bolshevik Party since 1920 . . . 1924 . . . 1927 . . . Even after you die, it's important to know what you believed in. They would bury Party members separately, wrapping the coffins in red calico. I remember the day Lenin died . . . What? How could Lenin be dead? It can't be! He was a saint . . . [*He has his grandson take a number of small busts of Lenin down from a shelf and shows them to me. They're bronze, iron, porcelain.*] I ended up with an entire collection. All of them were gifts. And yesterday . . . They said on the radio that Lenin's hand was sawed off from the monument in the center of town in the middle of the night. Traded in for scrap . . . for kopecks. It used to be an icon. An idol! Now, he's nothing but scrap metal. They buy and sell him by the kilogram . . . And yet, I'm still alive . . . Communism is denigrated! Socialism trashed! People say to me, "But who could take Marxism seriously today? Marx's place is in the history textbooks." And who among you can say you've ever read the later works of Lenin? That you know all of Marx? There's early Marx . . . and Marx at the end of his life . . . What people today disparage as socialism has no relation to the socialist idea. The Idea is not to blame. [*His coughing once again makes it difficult to understand him.*] The people have lost their history . . . They've been left without faith . . . No matter what you ask them, they answer with blank stares. The bosses have learned how to cross themselves and balance candles in their right hands like they're glasses of vodka. They brought back the moth-eaten two-headed eagle . . . Holy banners and icons . . . [*Suddenly his speech is completely distinct.*] My final wish is that you record the truth. But my truth, not yours. So that my voice may live on . . .

[*He shows me his photographs, occasionally commenting.*]

. . . They brought me to the Commander. "How old are you?" he asked. "Seventeen," I lied. I wasn't even sixteen yet. That was how I enlisted in the Red Army. They gave us cloth to wrap our feet in and red stars for our hats. There weren't any *budyonovkas,** but they did hand out red stars. What kind of Red Army would we be without red stars? And they gave us guns. We felt like we were the defenders of the Revolution. There was hunger all around, epidemics everywhere. Fever . . . typhoid fever, trench fever . . . But we were happy . . .

. . . Someone had dragged a piano out of a destroyed manor house . . . They'd left it standing in the garden, in the rain. Cowherds would herd their cattle close to it and try to play it with sticks. People had gotten drunk and burned down the estate. Looted it. But who needed a piano?

. . . We blew up a church . . . I can still hear the cries of the old women, "Children, don't do it!" they begged us. Grabbed onto our ankles. The church had stood there for two hundred years. A prayed-in place, as they say. They built the municipal public toilet over the ruins. And forced the priests to work there as cleaning men. Washing out the shit. Today . . . of course . . . Today, I understand . . . But back then, it was fun . . .

. . . Our comrades lay dead in the field . . . They had stars carved into their foreheads and chests. Red stars. Their stomachs had been cut open and filled with dirt: You want land, here you go! For us, it was victory or death! Let us die as long as we know what we're dying for.

. . . By the river, we'd seen some White Officers impaled by bayonets. "Their Excellences" had grown black in the sun. They had epaulettes sticking out of their stomachs . . . Their stomachs were stuffed with epaulettes. I don't feel sorry for them! I've seen as many dead people as I've seen living . . .

—Today, it's sad for everyone, the Reds and Whites alike. I feel sorry for everyone.

—You feel sorry for them . . . Sorry for them? [*It felt like this could*

* A peaked felt hat that became an essential part of the Red Army uniform during the Russian Civil War, named after Semyon Budyonny, a close ally of Stalin's responsible for organizing the powerful Red Cavalry.

be the end of our conversation.] Well, yes, of course . . . "universal human values" . . . "abstract humanism" . . . I watch TV, I read the papers. For us, mercy was a priest's word. Kill the White vermin! Make way for the Revolution! A slogan from the first years of the Revolution: We'll chase humanity into happiness with an iron fist! If the Party says so, I believe the Party! I do.

. . . The town of Orsk, near Orenburg. Freight trains full of kulak families rolling through night and day. On their way to Siberia. We were guarding the station. One time, I opened the doors of one of the train cars: A half-naked man was hanging from a belt in the corner. The mother was cradling the little one in her arms, while her older boy sat on the floor next to her eating his own shit with his hands like it was kasha. "Shut that door!" the Commissar shouted at me. "That's the kulak bastard! There's no room for them in our new life!" The future . . . It was supposed to be beautiful . . . It will be beautiful later . . . I believed that! [*He's practically screaming.*] We believed in a beautiful life. Utopia . . . it was utopia . . . And how about you? You have your own utopia: the market. Market heaven. The market will make everyone happy! Pure fantasy! The streets are filled with gangsters in magenta blazers, gold chains hanging down to their bellies. Caricatures of capitalism, like the cartoons in *Krokodil.** A farce! Instead of the dictatorship of the proletariat, it's the law of the jungle: Devour the ones weaker than you, and bow down to the ones who are stronger. The oldest law in the world . . . [*A coughing fit. He catches his breath.*] My son wore a *budyonovka* with a red star . . . When he was little, it was his favorite ever birthday present. I haven't gone to the stores in a long time. Do they still sell *budyonovkas*? They were popular for a long time. They were still around when Khrushchev was in power. What's in style these days? [*He attempts a smile.*] I've fallen behind the times, of course . . . I'm ancient. My only son is dead. I'm living out my final days with my daughter-in-law and grandchildren. My son was a historian and a convinced communist. And my grandchildren? [*Smirking.*] My grandchildren read the Dalai Lama. Instead of *Capital,* they have the *Mahabharata.* The Kabbalah . . . Now everyone believes in something different. Yep . . . that's how it is . . . People always want to believe in something. In God or in technological progress. In chemistry, polymers, a cosmic consciousness. Today it's the market. So all right, we'll eat our fill, and then what? When I go into

---

* A popular Soviet satirical magazine.

my grandchildren's room, everything in there is foreign: the shirts, the jeans, the books, the music—even their toothbrushes are imported. Their shelves are lined with empty cans of Coke and Pepsi. Savages! They go to the supermarkets like they're museums. They think it's cool, celebrating their birthday at McDonald's! "Grandpa, we went to Pizza Hut!" Mecca! They ask me, "Did you really believe in communism? How about aliens?" I dreamt of war on the palaces, peace to the cottages—they want to become millionaires. Their friends come over and I overhear them saying things like: "I would rather live in a weak country where there's yogurt and good beer." "Communism is the dregs." "The Russian path is monarchy. God save the Tsar!" They play songs: "Everything will be all right, Lieutenant Golytsyn / The Commissars will get what they deserve . . ."* And yet, I'm still alive. I'm here to see it all . . . It's really happening, I haven't lost my mind . . . [*He looks at his grandson, who remains silent.*] There's loads of salami at the store, but no happy people. I don't see anyone with fire in their eyes.

A joke from his grandson

A professor and an Old Bolshevik are at a séance. The professor: "From the very beginning, communism was based on an error. Remember the song, 'Our train is flying forward, / The next stop is the commune . . . '" The Old Bolshevik: "Of course I do. What's the problem?" "Trains don't fly."

—First they arrested my wife. She went to the theater and didn't come back. I got home from work and found my son sleeping on a little rug in the hall next to the cat. He'd waited and waited for Mama until he finally fell asleep. My wife worked at a shoe factory. She was a Red engineer. "Something strange is going on," she'd told me. "They've taken all my friends. For some kind of treason . . ." "You and I are innocent, so no one is coming for us." I was sure of it. Absolutely positive . . . Sincerely! I was a Leninist, then a Stalinist. Until 1937, I was a Stalinist. I believed everything Stalin said and did. Yes . . . The greatest, the most brilliant leader of all eras and peoples. Even after Bukha-

---

* A White Guard song that saw a resurgence in popularity in the Soviet Union in the 1980s.

rin, Tukhachevsky, and Blyukher* were all pronounced enemies of the people, I still believed him. It seems stupid now, but I thought that Stalin was being deceived, that traitors had made their way to the top. The Party would sort it all out. But then they arrested my wife, an honest and dedicated Party warrior.

Three days later, they came for me . . . The first thing they did was sniff inside the oven: Did it smell like smoke, had I burnt anything in there recently? There were three of them. One walked around the apartment picking things out for himself: "You won't be needing this anymore." He took down the clock from the wall. I was shocked . . . I hadn't expected that . . . At the same time, there was something human about it that gave me hope. This human nastiness . . . yes . . . So these people have feelings, too. The search lasted from 2 A.M. until morning. There were lots of books in the house and they flicked through each and every one of them. Rifled through all of our clothes. Cut the pillows open . . . It gave me a lot of time to think. Trying to remember, feverishly . . . By then, there was a mass incarceration going on. People were being taken away every day. It was pretty frightening. They'd take someone away, and everyone would be silent about it. It was useless asking what had happened. At the first interrogation, the investigator explained, "You're automatically guilty because you failed to inform on your wife." She was already in jail . . . During the search, I racked my brains, scrutinizing every last detail . . . I only remembered one thing . . . At the most recent citywide Party conference, they read a salutation to Comrade Stalin, and the whole auditorium had stood up. A storm of applause: "Glory to Comrade Stalin—the organizer and inspiration behind our victories!" "Glory to Stalin!" "Glory to our Leader!" Fifteen minutes . . . Half an hour . . . Everyone kept turning and looking at one another, but no one wanted to be the first to sit down. So we all just stood. And then, for some reason, I sat down. It was mechanical. Two plainclothes officers went up to me: "Comrade, why are you sitting?" I jumped up! I jumped like I'd been scalded. During the break, I kept looking around. Waiting for them to come up and arrest me on the spot. [*A pause.*]

The search ended toward morning. They ordered me to pack my bags. The nanny woke my son. Before I left, I managed to whisper to

---

* Vasily Blyukher (1889–1938) was a high-ranking officer in the Red Army who presided over the tribunal that condemned Tukhachevsky before he himself was arrested and executed as a spy in 1938.

him, "Don't tell anyone about your mother and father." That's how he survived. [*He pulls the tape recorder toward himself.*] Record this while I'm still alive . . . "S.A." . . . "Still alive" . . . That's what I write on cards. Although there's no one to send them to anymore . . . People often ask me, "Why did you keep silent?" "It was the times." I thought that the traitors were to blame—Yagoda, Yezhov*—not the Party. It's easy to judge us fifty years later. To laugh . . . mock us old fools . . . but in those days, I marched in step with everyone else. And now, there's nobody left . . .

. . . I spent a month in solitary confinement. A stone coffin—wider at the head, more narrow at the feet. I tamed a raven that would come to my window by feeding it grains of barley from the gruel. Ravens have been my favorite birds ever since. At war . . . After the battle, all is silent. They've collected the wounded, only the dead are left on the battlefield. Only the raven flies, there are no other birds in the sky.

. . . They called me in for an interrogation two weeks later. Was I aware that my wife had a sister living abroad? "My wife is an honest communist." An informant's report lay on the investigator's desk, signed by—I couldn't believe it!—our neighbor. I recognized his handwriting. His signature. He'd been my comrade, you could say, since the days of the civil war. A soldier, high-ranking. He was even a little in love with my wife; I was jealous about it. Yes, jealous . . . I loved my wife so much . . . my first wife . . . The investigator related our conversations back to me in great detail. I saw that I was right, it really had been that neighbor . . . All of those conversations had taken place in front of him . . . My wife's story goes like this: She'd come from a town near Minsk. A Belarusian. After the Brest-Litovsk peace treaty, part of Belarus went to Poland. That's where her parents ended up. Along with her sister. Her parents died soon afterwards, but her sister would write to us, "I would rather end up in Siberia than stay here in

---

* Genrikh Yagoda (1891–1938) served as the director of the NKVD from 1934 to 1936 and oversaw the show trials of Lev Kamenev and Grigory Zinoviev, which heralded the Great Purge. He was demoted in 1936, arrested in 1937, and executed in 1938 after being found guilty of wrecking, espionage, Trotskyism, and conspiracy. His successor, Nikolai Yezhov (1895–1940), ran the NKVD until 1938, presiding over mass arrests and executions during the Great Purge, before he too was arrested, tried, and executed.

Poland." She was desperate to live in the Soviet Union. In those days, communism was very popular in Europe. In fact, it was popular all over the world. A great many people believed in it. Not only simple people—also the Western elite. Writers: Aragon, Barbusse . . . The October Revolution was the "opiate of the intellectuals." I remember reading that somewhere . . . I read a lot these days. [*He pauses.*] My wife was an "enemy." So they needed to pin some "counterrevolutionary activity" on her . . . They wanted to fabricate an "organization," an "underground terrorist cell." "Who would your wife socialize with? Who did she hand off the plans to?" What plans? I denied everything. They beat me. Stomped on me with their boots. All of them, people we thought we trusted. I had a Party membership card and so did they. And my wife had a Party membership card, too.

   . . . I ended up in a group cell with fifty people. They would take us out to use the toilet twice a day. And what about the rest of the time? How can you explain this to a lady? There was a big pail by the entrance . . . [*Angry.*] Try taking a shit in front of a cell full of people! They'd feed us herring and wouldn't give us any water. Fifty people . . . all English and Japanese spies . . . an illiterate old man from the country . . . He was in there for starting a fire in a stable. A student was in for telling a joke: "A portrait of Stalin hangs on the wall. The lector reads a report on Stalin, then the choir sings a song about Stalin, and finally, an actor declaims a poem about Stalin. What's the occasion? An evening commemorating the hundredth anniversary of Pushkin's death." [*I laugh, he doesn't.*] The student got ten years in the camps without the right of correspondence. There was a chauffeur who had been arrested because he looked like Stalin. And he really did. The director of a laundry, a non-Party member barber, a lapidary . . . More uneducated people than anyone else. But there was also a folklore scholar. At night, he'd tell us all fairy tales . . . children's fairy tales . . . Everyone would listen. The folklore specialist had been informed on by his own mother. She was an Old Bolshevik. She brought him cigarettes just once before they transferred him to the camps, and that was that. Yes . . . An old Socialist Revolutionary* was in there with us, and he was openly happy: "I'm so glad that you Com-

---

* The Socialist Revolutionary Party played an active role in the fall of Tsarism but was systematically destroyed by the Bolsheviks following the October Revolution, with many of its members executed or deported.

munists are in here with me and you can't understand a thing, either."
A counterrevolutionary! I thought that the Soviet regime had been dissolved. And that Stalin was gone.

A joke from his grandson

A railway station . . . Hundreds of people. A man in a leather jacket is
desperately searching for someone. He finds him! He goes up to the
other guy, who is also wearing a leather jacket. "Comrade, are you in
the Party?" "Yes, I'm in the Party." "In that case, can you tell me where
the bathroom is?"

—They confiscated everything: my belt, my scarf, they yanked out my
bootlaces, but you can still kill yourself. The thought occurred to me.
It did . . . I thought of asphyxiating myself with my pants or the rubber waistband from my underwear. They beat me in the stomach with
a bag of sand. Everything came out of me like I was a worm. They'd
hang me from hooks like it was the Middle Ages! Everything is leaking
out of you, you're no longer in control of your bodily functions. Leaking out of everywhere . . . enduring this pain . . . it's completely humiliating. It's easier just to die . . . [*He catches his breath.*] I met my
old comrade in the prison . . . Nikolai Verkhovets, a Party member
since 1924. He taught at a worker's school. He'd been among friends,
in a tight circle . . . Someone was reading *Pravda* aloud, and it said
that the Bureau of the Central Committee had held a hearing on the
fertilization of mares. Then he went and made a joke about how the
Central Committee had nothing better to do than worry about mare
fertilization. They came for him that same night. Slammed his fingers
in a door and broke them like they were pencils. They'd keep him in a
gas mask for days at a time. [*Silence.*] I don't know how to talk about
these things today . . . All in all, it was barbarism. Humiliating. You're
nothing but a piece of meat . . . lying in a pool of urine . . . Verkhovets
got a sadist for an interrogator, but not all of them were sadists. They
would be given their quotas from above, quotas to fulfill for capturing
enemies—monthly and annual. They'd change over, drink tea, call
home, flirt with the nurses who were called in when someone lost consciousness from the torture. They had regular hours, shifts . . . Meanwhile, your whole life has been turned upside down. That's how it
went . . . The investigator in charge of my case had been a school

principal, and he'd try to convince me, "You're a naïve person. We'll put you down and the protocol will say that you were killed during an escape attempt. You know what Gorky said: If the enemy doesn't surrender, he will be eliminated." "I'm not an enemy." "You have to understand: The only kind of person that isn't a threat to us is a repentant man—a ruined man." He and I would discuss this . . . The second interrogator was a career officer. You could tell that he didn't feel like filling out all that paperwork. They were always writing something down. One time, he gave me a cigarette. People would be in there for long stretches. Months. The victims and executioners would get involved in human . . . well, you wouldn't quite call them human, but they were nonetheless some sort of relationships. It wasn't mutually exclusive . . . "Sign this." I read the protocol. "I never said that." They beat me. They really put their hearts into those beatings. And in the end, all of them ended up getting shot themselves. Or sent to the camps.

One morning they came for me . . . Opened the door to the cell, ordered me to come out. I was just in my shirt, I wanted to get dressed. "No!" They led me into some sort of basement. The interrogator was waiting for me there with a piece of paper: "Will you sign it—yes or no?" I refused. "In that case, get up against the wall!" Pow! A bullet flew over my head . . . "Will you sign it now?" Pow! That happened three times. Then they led me back through some kind of labyrinth . . . Who knew that the prison had so many basement cells! I'd never even suspected it. They led prisoners around in a way that would prevent them from seeing anything or recognizing anyone. If someone was coming toward you, the guard would bark, "Face to the wall!" But I was experienced, I always managed to peek. That's how I saw my old boss from Red commander training. And my former professor from Soviet Party school . . . [*He is silent.*] Verkhovtsev and I were open with one another: "Criminals! They're destroying the Soviet regime. They will answer for this." A few times, his interrogator was a woman. "When they torture me, she becomes beautiful. Do you understand? In those moments, she's beautiful." He was an impressionable man. He's the one who told me that in his youth, Stalin had written poems . . . [*He closes his eyes.*] Even today, I will still wake up in the middle of the night in a cold sweat: I could have been assigned to work for the NKVD. And I would have done it. I had a Party membership card in my pocket. A little red book.

◆ ◆ ◆

The doorbell rings. A nurse is here. She measures his blood pressure, gives him a shot. The whole time, although it's disjointed, the conversation continues.

. . . One time I thought, "Socialism doesn't solve the problem of death." Of old age. The metaphysical meaning of life. It overlooks it. Only religion has answers to those questions. Yes . . . In 1937, for conversations like this, I would have . . .

. . . Have you ever read Aleksander Belyayev's *The Amphibian Man?* In an attempt to make him happy, a brilliant scientist turns his son into an amphibian man. But his son is lonely under the sea. He wants to be like everyone else, to live on land, fall in love with a regular girl—but it's too late. And so he dies. But the father had thought that he'd solved a great mystery . . . That he was God! That's the response to all the great utopians!

. . . It was a beautiful idea! But what are you going to do with human nature? Man hasn't changed since the days of ancient Rome . . .

[*The nurse leaves. He shuts his eyes.*]

Hold on, I'm going to finish my story . . . I have enough strength for another hour. Let's keep going . . . I spent almost a year in prison. I was preparing for my trial. For the penal colony. I was surprised, I wondered why they were dragging their feet. As far as I can tell, there was no rhyme or reason to it. Thousands of cases . . . Chaos . . . A year later, a new investigator summoned me. My case was being reviewed. And then they released me, dismissing all charges. So it had been a mistake after all. The Party believed me! Stalin was a great puppetmaster . . . Right around then, he'd dismissed the "bloody dwarf," People's Commissar Yezhov. They put him on trial and shot him. Rehabilitations began. The people let out a sigh of relief: The truth had finally reached Stalin . . . But this was only a brief interlude before a new era of bloodshed . . . A game! But everyone had believed it. And so had I, I believed it too. I said goodbye to Verkhovets . . . He held up his broken fingers: "I've been in here for twelve months and seven days. No one is going to let me out now. They're too scared." Nikolai Verkhovets . . . Party member since 1924 . . . Shot in 1941, as the Germans advanced on the city. NKVD officers shot all the prisoners they didn't evacuate in time. They released the common criminals, but all the "politicals" were subject to liquidation as traitors. The Germans entered the city and opened the prison gates to find a pile of corpses.

Before they could begin decomposing, the Germans herded civilians in to have a look at the handiwork of their Soviet regime.

I found my son living with strangers, the nanny had taken him out to the country. He'd started stuttering and was afraid of the dark. The two of us began a new life together. I tried to get any news I could about my wife. At the same time, I applied to get reinstated in the Party. I wanted my Party membership card back. New Year's Eve . . . We'd decorated a tree. My son and I were expecting guests. The door-bell rang. I opened the door. A poorly dressed woman stood on the threshold. "I've come to send greetings from your wife." "She's alive!" "She was alive a year ago. I used to work with her in a pigsty. We'd steal frozen potatoes from the pigs, and thanks to that, we didn't starve to death. I have no idea whether or not she's still alive." She didn't stay for long. And I didn't try to keep her, either. Our guests were supposed to arrive at any minute. [*He is silent.*] The bells rang. We opened the champagne. Our first toast was "To Stalin!" Yes . . .

1941 . . .

Everyone cried, but I jumped for joy—war! I'll go to war! At least they'll let me fight. They have to send me. I started asking to be sent to the front. For a long time, they refused. I knew the recruitment officer, he told me, "I can't do it. I have instructions not to enlist any 'ene-mies.'" "Who's an enemy? Me, an enemy?" "Your wife is serving time in the camps under Article 58 for counterrevolutionary activity." Kiev fell . . . German troops were advancing on Stalingrad . . . I envied ev-eryone in an army uniform—they got to defend the Motherland! Young women went to the front—why not me? I wrote a letter to the district Party committee: Either shoot me or send me to the front! Two days later, they sent a notice telling me to report to the assembly point at 2400 hours. The war was my savior . . . It was my only chance to win back my good name. I was relieved.

. . . I remember the Revolution. I'm sorry, but what came later is foggier. I don't remember the war as well, even though chronologi-cally, it was more recent. I remember that nothing had changed. The only thing was that toward the end of the war, we got new weapons—Katyusha rocket launchers took the place of rifles and sabers. As for the soldier's life, it was the same as ever. Nothing but barley soup and wheat kasha to eat for years at a time; we'd wear the same dirty linens for months. Never wash. Sleep on the bare ground. Could we have won if we had been any different?

. . . I went into the fray . . . They were shooting at us with machine guns! Everyone hit the dirt. Then they started in with the howitzer, which outright rips people to shreds. The commissar fell down next to me: "What are you lying here for, you counterrevolutionary! Advance! Or I'll shoot you myself!!!"

. . . Near Kursk, I ran into my one-time interrogator, the former school principal. I had the thought, "Well, you bastard, you're mine now. I'll kill you during battle, and no one will ever know." I wanted to . . . yes, I did. But I never got the chance. We even had an exchange. "We share a Motherland." Those were his words. He was a brave man. A hero. He died at Königsberg. What can I say . . . I'm not going to lie . . . I thought that God had done my job for me.

I came home twice wounded, with three decorations and medals. They called me into the district Party committee, "Unfortunately, we will not be able to return your wife to you. She's died. But you can have your honor back . . ." And they handed me back my Party membership card. And I was happy! I was so happy . . .

[*I tell him that I will never understand that—never. He loses his temper.*]

You can't judge us according to logic. You accountants! You have to understand! You can only judge us according to the laws of religion. Faith! Our faith will make you jealous! What greatness do you have in your life? You have nothing. Just comfort. Anything for a full belly . . . Those stomachs of yours . . . Stuff your face and fill your house with tchotchkes. But I . . . my generation . . . We built everything you have. The factories, the dams, the electric power stations. What have you ever built? And we were the ones who defeated Hitler. After the war, whenever anyone had a baby, it was such a great joy! A different kind of happiness than what we'd felt before the war. I could have wept . . . [*He closes his eyes. He's tired.*] Ahhh, we were believers. And now, they've passed the verdict on us: You believed in utopia . . . We did! My favorite novel is Chernyshevsky's *What Is to Be Done?* Nobody reads it anymore. It's boring. People only read the title, the eternal Russian question: What is to be done? For us, this book was like the catechism. The textbook for the Revolution. People would learn entire pages of it by heart. Vera Pavlovna's fourth dream . . . [*He recites it like a poem.*] "Houses made of crystal and aluminum . . . Crystal palaces! Lemon and orange groves in the cities. There are almost no elderly, people get old very late in life because life is so wonderful. Machines do all the work, people just drive and control them. The machines sow seeds and knit . . . The fields are thick with verdure and bounty. Flowers as tall as trees. Everyone is happy. Joyful. Everyone goes around in fine clothes, men and women alike, leading free lives of labor and pleasure. There's enough space and work for everyone. Is this really us? Can this really be our Earth? And everyone will live this way? The future is bright and wonderful . . ." Get out of here . . . [*He gestures in the direction of his grandson.*] He giggles at me . . . To him, I'm a little old fool. That's how we live now.

—Dostoevsky had a response to Chernyshevsky: "Go on and build your crystal palace, but I will throw a stone at it. Not because I'm hungry and living in a cellar, but just because—out of my own free will . . ."

[*He gets angry.*]

—You think that communism was like an infectious disease, as they write in today's newspapers? That it was brought over in a sealed train car from Germany?* Nonsense! The people revolted. There was no Tsarist "golden age" like the one that's suddenly being remembered today. Fairy tales! Like the ones about how we fed America with our grain and decided the fate of Europe. The Russian soldier died for everyone—that's the truth. But the way people lived . . . In my family, there was one pair of snow boots for five children. We ate potatoes with bread and, in the winter, without bread. Just potatoes . . . And you ask me where communists came from.

I remember so much . . . and for what? Huh? For what? What am I supposed to do with all of this? We loved the future. The people of the future. We'd argue about when the future was going to come. Definitely in a hundred years, we thought. But it seemed too far away for us . . . [*He catches his breath.*]

[*I turn off the tape recorder.*]

Good. It's better without the tape recorder . . . I need to tell someone this story . . .

I was fifteen. Red Army troops had come to our village. On horseback. Drunk. A subdivision. They slept until evening, and then they rounded up all the Komsomol members. The Commander addressed us, "The Red Army is starving. Lenin is starving. While the kulaks are hiding their grain. Burning it." I knew that my mother's brother, Uncle Semyon, had taken sacks of grain into the woods and buried them. I was a Komsomol youth, I'd taken the oath. That night, I went to the

* An allusion to Lenin's pivotal journey from Germany to Russia in 1917 in a sealed train car.

troops and led them to where he'd buried the grain. They got a whole cartload. The Commander shook my hand: "Hurry up and grow up, brother." In the morning, I woke up to my mother screaming, "Semyon's house is on fire!" They found Uncle Semyon in the woods, the soldiers had cut him to pieces with their sabers . . . I was fifteen. The Red Army was starving . . . and Lenin . . . I was afraid to go outside, I sat in the house, weeping. My mother figured out what had happened. That night, she handed me a feedbag and told me, "Leave, son! Let God forgive your miserable soul." [*He covered his eyes with his hand. But I could still see he was crying.*]

I want to die a communist. That's my final wish.

In the nineties, I published a part of this confession. My protagonist let someone read it, consulted with somebody else, and they convinced him that the publication of this story in its entirety would "show the Party in a negative light," which was his greatest fear. After he died, they found his will. His large, three-bedroom apartment in the center of the city was not bequeathed to his grandsons but to "serve the needs of my beloved Communist Party, to which I owe everything." They even wrote about it in the evening paper. No one could understand it anymore. Everyone laughed at the crazy old man. They never did put a monument on his grave.

Now I have decided to publish his story in full. It belongs to history more than it does to any one individual.

ON THE CRUELTY OF THE FLAMES
AND SALVATION FROM ABOVE

◆

Timeryan Zinatov,
front-line veteran, 77 years old

Timeryan Khabulovich Zinatov was one of the heroic defenders of the Brest fortress, which bore the initial brunt of the Nazi incursion on the morning of June 22, 1941.

He is of Tatar nationality. Before the war, he was a cadet (42nd sniper unit of the 44th rifle division). In the first days of defending the fortress, he was taken prisoner after being wounded. Twice, he attempted escape from German concentration camps, and his second attempt was successful. He finished the war as he started it, in the field forces as a private. He was awarded the Order of the Patriotic War (Second Level) for defending the Brest Fortress. After the war, he traveled the entire country working for construction projects in the far north as well as on the Baikal-Amur Mainline railway. After retiring, he remained in Siberia, in Ust-Kut.

Even though Ust-Kut is thousands of kilometers away from Brest, Timeryan Zinatov would visit the fortress every year, bringing cakes to the museum staff. Everyone knew him. Why did he visit so often? Like his friends from his regiment who would meet him here, he only felt truly safe at the fortress. Here, nobody ever doubted that these veterans were our nation's true—and not imaginary—heroes. At the fortress, no one dared to say anything like, "If you hadn't won, we'd be drinking Bavarian beer and living in Europe." Those damn perestroikites! If they only understood that if their grandfathers had not been victorious, we would have been a country of housemaids and swineherds. Hitler wrote that Slavic children should only be taught to count to one hundred.

The last time Zinatov came to Brest was in September 1992. Everything was the same as ever: He met with his friends with whom he'd fought at the front, and they strolled through the fortress grounds. Naturally, he noticed that the stream of visitors had grown appreciably thinner. It had become fashionable to slander our Soviet past and its heroes . . .

Finally, the time came for them to go their separate ways. On Friday, he said goodbye to everyone, telling them that he was going home over the weekend. None of them even suspected that this time, he had come to the fortress to stay forever.

When the museum staff arrived on Monday morning, they received a phone call from the transportation police office: The defender of the Brest fortress, survivor of the bloody battle of 1941, had thrown himself under a train.

Someone will be sure to recall how the neatly dressed old man with the suitcase had spent a long time standing on the platform. Among his possessions, investigators found seven thousand rubles he had brought from home in order to cover his funeral expenses and a suicide note cursing the Yeltsin-Gaidar administration for the humiliating and impoverished way of life they'd brought about. And for their betrayal of the Great Victory. He asked to be buried in the fortress.

Here's an excerpt from his suicide note:

"If I had died from my wounds during the war, I would have known that I'd died for my Motherland. Today, I'm dying from leading a dog's life. Have them write that on my tombstone . . . And please don't consider me insane . . .

"I'd rather die standing up than on my knees, begging for my pauper's pittance, only to extend my old age and go to my grave with an outstretched palm! Thus, my esteemed friends, do not judge me too harshly, put yourselves in my shoes. I am leaving behind the means, if I am not robbed, that will, I hope, suffice for my burial . . . I don't need a coffin. Bury me in what I'm wearing, that will be good enough. Just don't forget to put the certificate of my status as a defender of the Brest fortress in my pocket for posterity. We were heroes and now, we're dying in poverty! Farewell. Do not mourn a lone Tatar who sin-

glehandedly protests on behalf of everyone: 'I die, but I do not surrender! So long, my Motherland!' "

After the war, in the underground passages of the Brest fortress, an
inscription was found scratched into the walls: "I die, but I do not surrender. So long, my Motherland! 22. VII. 41." The Central Committee
declared this line an emblem of the courage of the Soviet people and
their devotion to the mission of the CPSU. Surviving defenders of the
Brest fortress maintained that the author of this inscription was none
other than Timeryan Zinatov, a cadet and non-Party member, but
communist ideologues preferred to have it attributed to the fallen Unknown Soldier.

The Brest municipal administration has decided to cover the costs
of the funeral. The budget for the hero's burial was provided for by the
clause for "the ongoing maintenance of public amenities . . ."

—*Communist Party of the Russian Federation, The System Perspective, No. 5*

Why did Timeryan Zinatov, an old soldier, throw himself under a
train? I'll begin from afar . . . with a letter to *Pravda* written by Victor
Yakovlevich Yakovlev, a veteran from Leningrad village in Krasnodar
Krai. Yakovlev had fought in the Great Patriotic War, defending Moscow in 1941, and participated in the Moscow parade in honor of the
fifty-fifth anniversary of the Victory. He had been moved to write by a
serious grievance.

Recently, he and a friend—a former colonel and fellow war veteran—
had gone to Moscow. For the occasion, they had worn their parade
jackets, decorated with medal ribbons. After a long, tiring day in the
noisy capital, they returned to Leningrad Station, where they searched
for a place to sit while waiting for their train. Not finding any free
seats, they went into a mostly empty hall where they saw a café with
soft chairs. As soon as they sat down, a young woman who had been
serving drinks ran up to them and rudely pointed to the exit. "You're
not allowed to be in here. This room is business class only!" I quote
from Yakovlev's letter: "Enraged, I replied, 'So speculators and thieves
can be in here but we can't? Is it like how it used to be in America,
"Entrance Forbidden to Negroes and Dogs"?' " What else was there to
say when everything was already crystal clear? We turned around and

left. But I still managed to catch a glimpse of a few of these so-called businessmen—thieves and swindlers—sitting there munching, chomping, drinking . . . The fact that we spilled blood here has already been forgotten. These bastards, those Chubaises, Vekselbergs, and Grefs[*] have robbed us of everything—our money, our honor. Our past and our present. Everything! And now they shave our grandsons' heads, turn them into soldiers, and send them off to defend their billions. I want to know: What were we fighting for? We sat in the trenches, up to our knees in water in the autumn; in brutal winter frosts, up to our knees in snow; without changing our clothes or getting any real sleep for months on end. That's how it was at Kalinin, Yakhroma, Moscow . . . We weren't divided into rich and poor back then . . ."

Of course, you could say that the veteran is mistaken, that not all businessmen are "thieves and speculators." But let's take a look at our postcommunist nation through his eyes, at the condescension of the new masters, their disgust with "the men of yesterday," who, as they write in their glossy magazines, "reek of poverty." According to the authors of these publications, this is how the celebratory gatherings in great halls smell on Victory Day, where, once a year, veterans are invited to hear hypocritical panegyrics in their honor. In reality, nobody needs them anymore. Their ideas of fairness are naïve. Along with their devotion to the Soviet way of life . . .

At the beginning of his presidency, Yeltsin swore that he would lie down on the train tracks if he allowed our quality of life to decline. Well, the quality of life here hasn't simply declined, it has bottomed out. Nonetheless, Yeltsin is still with us. And the one who lay down on the tracks was the old soldier Timeryan Zinatov, who died in protest in the autumn of 1992 . . .

—Website of the newspaper *Pravda*, 1997

CONVERSATIONS FROM AROUND THE TABLE AT THE WAKE

According to our customs, the dead go into the ground and the living, to the table. Many people had come, some from afar: from Moscow, Kiev, Smolensk . . . All of them wore their decorations and medals

---

[*] Viktor Vekselberg (1958–) is a Ukrainian-born Russian billionaire who owns the Renova Group conglomerate. Herman Gref (1964–), minister of economics and trade for Russia from 2000 to 2007, is now CEO of the largest Russian bank, Sberbank.

like they would have on Victory Day. They spoke about death the
same way they spoke about life.

—To our fallen comrade! A bitter gulp. [*All rise.*]

   —May he rest in peace . . .

   —Oh Timeryan, Timeryan Khabulovich . . . He was hurt. All of us are deeply hurt. We were used to socialism. To our Soviet Motherland, the USSR. Now we all live in different countries, under new regimes. With different flags. Not our victorious red calico. I ran away from home to fight at the front when I was seventeen . . .

   —Our grandchildren would have lost the Great Patriotic War. They have no ideals and no great dream.

   —They read different books and watch different movies.

   —You tell them about it, but to them it sounds like a fairy tale. They ask you, "Why would soldiers die to save the regiment banner? Couldn't they just sew a new one?" We fought, we killed—and for whom? For Stalin? It was for you, you idiots!

   —Maybe we should have surrendered and licked the Hun's boots . . .

   —As soon as they brought us my father's death notice, I asked to be sent to the front.

   —They're robbing our Soviet Motherland blind, selling it off piece-meal . . . If we had known that this was how the wind would blow, we might have thought twice . . .

   —My mother died in the war, and my father died before that, from tuberculosis. I've been working since I was fifteen. At the factory, they'd give us half a loaf of bread a day and that was it. The bread was made of cellulose and glue. One day, I fainted from hunger. And then it happened again. I went down to the conscription office: "Please don't let me die like this. Send me to the front." They approved my request. The people leaving and the ones sending them off had wild eyes! There was a whole freight car full of us girls. We sang, "Girls, the war has reached the Urals, / Girls, is our youth really gone?" At the stations, the lilacs were blooming. Some girls laughed while others wept . . .

   —All of us supported perestroika. And Gorbachev. But not what came out of all that . . .

   —Gorbach is an enemy agent . . .

   —I didn't understand what Gorbachev was talking about . . . All those words I'd never heard before . . . What kind of candy was he promising us? But I liked listening to him . . . The problem is that he turned out to be weak, he gave up our nuclear suitcase without a fight. And our Communist Party along with it.

—Russian people need the kind of idea that gives them goose bumps and makes their spines tingle.

—We were a great country . . .

—To our Motherland! To Victory! Cheers! [*They clink glasses.*]

—Now they put stars on veterans' memorials, but I remember how we used to bury our boys during the war . . . We'd throw whatever was left of them into shallow graves, sprinkle some dirt over them, and immediately, the orders would come: "Forward! Forward!" And we'd advance. Toward the next battle. And the next pit full of corpses. We retreated and advanced from grave pit to grave pit. They'd bring in reinforcements and two or three days later, they were already corpses. Only handfuls of people survived. The lucky ones! Toward the end of '43, we finally learned how to fight. Started doing it right. After that, fewer people would die. That's when I finally made friends . . .

—I spent the whole war on the front lines and came out without a single scratch—nothing! And I'm an atheist at that. I walked to Berlin . . . I saw inside the lion's den . . .

—We'd go into battle with one rifle for every four men. When they kill the first one, the second one grabs the rifle, after the second one, the next one. Meanwhile, the Germans all had brand-new machine guns.

—At first, the Germans were condescending. They'd already conquered Europe. Marched into Paris. They thought that they'd take care of the USSR in a matter of two months. When their wounded were taken prisoner, they'd spit in our nurses' faces. Rip off their bandages. Scream "Heil Hitler!" But by the end of the war, it was "Russian, don't shoot! Hitler kaput!"

—Most of all, I was afraid of a shameful death. If someone turned coward and ran, the Commander would shoot them on the spot. It happened all the time . . .

—What can I say . . . We had a Stalinist upbringing: We'll go off to fight on foreign soil, and "From the taiga to the British seas / There's none mightier than the Red Army . . ." There will be no mercy for the enemy! The first days of the war . . . I remember them as a total nightmare . . . We were surrounded. Everyone had the same question: What's happening? Where's Stalin? Not a single one of our planes was in the sky . . . People buried their Party and Komsomol membership cards and took to wandering the forest paths . . . All right, that's enough, you shouldn't write about this . . . [*He pushes away the tape recorder.*] The Germans disseminated their propaganda, their loud-speakers worked around the clock: "Surrender, Russian Ivan! The German army will guarantee you life and bread." I was prepared to shoot myself. But what if there's no ammo to do it with . . . Well . . . We were kids, little soldiers, all of us eighteen, nineteen years old . . . Commanders were hanging themselves left and right. Some used their belts, others used whatever they could find . . . Their bodies swung from the pine trees. It was the end of the world, dammit!

—The Motherland or death!

—Stalin had a plan—the families of those who surrendered would be sent to Siberia. But there were three and a half million prisoners of war! You couldn't send them all into exile! That whiskered cannibal!

—That cursed year, 1941 . . .

—Tell the whole truth. You're allowed to now . . .

—I'm not accustomed to doing that sort of thing . . .

—At the front, we were afraid of speaking openly with one another. A lot of people had been arrested before the war . . . and during the war . . . My mother worked at a bread factory, and one day, during an inspection, they found breadcrumbs on her gloves. That was enough to constitute sabotage. They sentenced her to ten years in prison. I was at the front, my father was at the front, so my younger brothers and sisters had to go live with my grandmother. They'd beg her, "Granny, don't die before Papa and Sashka (that's me) come back from the war." My father went missing in action.

—What kind of heroes are we? No one ever treated us like heroes. My wife and I raised our kids in barracks and after that, all we got was a room in a communal apartment. Today, it's kopecks . . . Tears instead of pensions. On television, they show us the Germans. They're doing pretty well for themselves! The defeated are living one hundred times better than the victors.

—The Lord doesn't know what it's like for the little man.

—I was, I am and will remain a communist! Without Stalin and Stalin's Party, we would have never triumphed. To hell with you, democrats! I am afraid of wearing my war medals out. "You senile old fool, where did you serve? At the front or in the prisons and the camps?" That's what I hear from the young people. They guzzle beer and jeer at us.

—I propose we return the monuments to our leader, the great Stalin, to their former places. They hide them in the back alleys like they're garbage.

—So put one up at your dacha . . .

—They want to rewrite the history of the war. They're just waiting for all of us to croak so they can do it.

—All in all, we're nothing but *Sovieticus cretinus* now . . .

—Russia was saved by its size. The Urals, Siberia . . .

—The most terrifying part was going into combat. The first five, ten minutes . . . Those who went in first had no chance of making it out alive. The bullet will find its hole. Forward, communists!

—To the military might of our Motherland! [*They clink glasses.*]

—Nobody wanted to kill anyone. It's unpleasant. But you get used to it, you learn . . .

—I joined the Party at Stalingrad. I wrote a notice: "I want to be in the first line of our Motherland's defenders . . . I will not spare my young life . . ." They rarely gave foot soldiers medals. I have one, though, "For Valor."

—My war wounds have made themselves felt . . . I became an invalid, but I'm still holding on.

—I remember how we captured two Vlasovites* . . . One of them said, "I was avenging my father . . ." His father had been shot by the NKVD. The other one: "I didn't want to die in a German concentration camp." They were young, the same age as us. After you've talked to someone, looked them in the eye, it's hard to kill them . . . The next day, we were all interrogated by agents from the secret police division, "Why were you talking to traitors? Why didn't you shoot them right away?" I started making excuses . . . The special agent slammed his revolver on the desk: "You motherfucker, who do you think you are? One more word out of you and . . ." No one had any pity for the Vlasovites. The tank drivers would tie them to their tanks, start them up and go in opposite directions, tearing the men to pieces . . . Traitors! But were all of them really traitors?

—We were more afraid of the special police agents than we were of the Germans. Even the Generals were scared of them . . .

—Fear . . . All through the war, fear reigned . . .

---

* Followers of General Andrey Vlasov (1901–1946), who, on being imprisoned by the Germans in 1942, defected and founded the Russian Liberation Army, a group of predominantly Russian forces who fought under German command.

—If it weren't for Stalin . . . Without an "iron hand," Russia would have never survived.

—I wasn't fighting for Stalin, I was fighting for the Motherland. I swear on the lives of my children and grandchildren that I never once heard people shouting, "For Stalin!"

—You can't win a war without soldiers.

—God damn it . . .

—The only thing to fear is God. He is the judge.

—If God exists . . .

[*They sing in chorus, a slightly discordant chorus.*]

And so, we need just one victory!

One for all, no matter the cost . . .

A MAN'S STORY

—My whole life, I've kept my arms at my sides! I didn't dare breathe a word of any of this to anyone. Now, I'll tell you my story . . .

I remember, when I was little, I was always afraid of losing my father . . . Fathers were taken away at night; they'd vanish into thin air. That's how my mother's brother, Felix, disappeared . . . He was a musician. He was taken away for something very stupid . . . total nonsense . . . He was at a store with his wife and he said, "The Soviet regime has been around for twenty years, and they still can't make a decent pair of pants." Today, they say that everyone was against it, but I'll tell you—the people supported the mass arrests. Take my mother . . . Her own brother was in prison, but she still maintained, "They made a mistake with our Felix. They have to sort that out. But people need to be punished, look at all the crime all around us." The people supported those policies . . . Then the war came! After the war, I was afraid of ever remembering it . . . My war . . . Afterward, when I tried to join the Party, they wouldn't accept me: "What kind of communist are you if you were in the ghetto?" I kept my mouth shut. Never said a word . . . There was a girl named Rozochka in our partisan division, this pretty Jewish girl, she'd brought books with her. Sixteen years old. The commanders took turns sleeping with her . . . They'd crack jokes about her: "She still has little kid hair down there, ha ha . . ." Rozochka ended up pregnant. So they took her off deep into the woods and shot her like a dog . . . People had kids, of course, there was a forest full of healthy men. The usual practice was that when a child was born, it would immediately be taken to a village. Left at a farmstead. But who would take a Jewish baby? Jews had no right to have kids. I returned from a mission. "Where's Rozochka?" "What do you care? This one's gone, there'll be another one to take her place." Hundreds of Jews who'd escaped from the ghettos had gone into the forest. Peasants would capture them and give them up to the Germans in exchange for a bag of flour, a kilogram of sugar. Write that down . . . I've held my silence for long enough . . . A Jew spends his whole life afraid. No matter where the stone falls, it hits him.

We didn't make it out of Minsk as it went up in flames because of my grandmother . . . Grandma had seen the Germans in 1918 and tried to convince us all that the Germans were an educated people who would not touch civilians. A German officer had been quartered at their home, and every night he had played the piano for them. My mother started vacillating: Should we leave or not? Because of that piano playing, naturally . . . We ended up losing a lot of time. One day, the German motorcycles rode into the city. Some people welcomed them in traditional costume—embroidered shirts, bearing bread and salt. Joyously. Many thought that that because the Germans were here, we'd finally get to lead normal lives. A lot of people hated Stalin and now they could stop concealing it. So many new and strange things emerged at the outbreak of war . . .

That was when I first heard the word "kike." Our neighbors started knocking on our door and shouting, "That's it, kikes, your days are numbered! You'll answer for what you did to Christ!" I was a Soviet boy. I had completed fifth grade, I was twelve. I couldn't fathom what they were talking about. Why were they saying those things? I still don't understand it . . . I come from a mixed family: My father was a Jew, and my mother was Russian. We celebrated Easter, but in a special way: My mother would tell us that it was the birthday of a very special person and bake a cake. For Passover (when the Lord took mercy on the Jews), my father would bring matzo over from my grandmother's. The times were such that we didn't advertise it . . . You had to keep quiet.

My mother sewed yellow stars onto our clothes . . . For several days, none of us could bear to go out. We were ashamed . . . I'm old, but I still remember how it felt, how embarrassing it was. There were leaflets lying around all over the ground in the city: "Liquidate the Commissars and Jews," "Save Russia from the Bolshevikike Regime."

Someone slid one of those leaflets under our door . . . It all happened so fast . . . Rumors started spreading that American Jews were collecting gold to bail all of the Jews out of Europe and bring them to America, that Germans loved order but hated Jews, so Jews would have to spend the war in ghettos . . . People attempted to make sense of what was going on . . . to catch onto a thread . . . Even hell is something that people will try to understand. I remember . . . I remember how we moved into the ghetto like it was yesterday. Thousands of Jews marched through the city . . . With children, with pillows. It's funny: I brought my butterfly collection with me. It's funny now . . . The residents of Minsk spilled out onto the sidewalk to watch: Some were curious, others were full of malicious glee, but a number of them were in tears. I didn't look around much, I was afraid of seeing one of the boys I knew. I was ashamed . . . I remember the constant shame . . .

My mother took off her wedding ring, wrapped it in a handkerchief, and told me where to take it. That night, I crawled under the barbed wire . . . A woman was waiting for me at the place where my mother had sent me. I gave her the ring, and she poured out some flour for me. In the morning, we realized that instead of flour, she'd given us chalk. Whitewash. That's how we lost my mother's ring. We didn't have any other valuables . . . We started bloating from hunger . . . Peasants with big sacks hung out outside of the ghetto day and night, waiting for the next pogrom. Whenever Jews were taken away to be shot, they'd let them in so they could loot their abandoned homes. The Polizei searched for valuables, while the peasants took anything they could find. "You won't need any of it anymore," they'd assure us.

One day, the ghetto went quiet like it usually did before a pogrom. Even though not a single shot had been fired. That day, there wasn't any shooting . . . Vehicles arrived, lots of vehicles . . . Kids in nice suits and boots, women in white pinafores, and men with expensive suitcases poured out of them. Their suitcases were incredible! All of them spoke German. The guards and convoy troops were at a loss, especially the Polizei. They didn't scream or beat anyone with their batons, they kept their growling dogs on their leashes. It was pure theater, a play . . . it felt like we were in a play . . . That same day, we learned that these were Jews they'd brought over from Europe. We started calling them the Hamburg Jews because the majority of them had come from Hamburg. They were disciplined, obedient. They didn't attempt to outsmart or trick the guards, they didn't hide in any of the secret spots . . . They were doomed . . . They looked down on us. We were poor, badly dressed. We weren't like them . . . we didn't speak German . . .

All of them were shot. Tens of thousands of those so-called Hamburg Jews . . .

That day . . . it's all a fog . . . How did they kick us out of the house? How did they transport us? I remember the big field on the edge of the forest . . . They selected the strongest men and ordered them to dig two big pits. Deep. While the rest of us stood there and waited. First, they tossed all the little kids into one of the pits . . . they started burying them . . . Their parents didn't even weep or beg. Everyone stood there in total silence. Why, you ask? I've given it a lot of thought . . . When a wolf pounces on you, you don't try to talk to it, you don't beg for your life. Or if a wild boar charges you . . . The Germans looked down into the pit and laughed, threw candy in it. The Polizei were dead drunk . . . Their pockets were stuffed with wristwatches . . . They buried the children alive . . . Then they ordered everyone else to jump into the other pit. We stood there, my mother, my father, my little sister and I. Our turn came . . . The German in charge noticed my mother was Russian and gestured to her: "You're free to go." My father shouted, "Run!" But she grabbed onto him, clutched at me: "I have to be with you." All of us pushed her away, we begged her to leave . . . but she was the first one of us to jump into the pit . . .

And that's all I can remember . . . I regained consciousness when I felt something sharp strike my leg. I cried out in pain. Somebody whispered, "Sounds like one of them's alive." Men were digging through the pit with shovels, removing the shoes and boots from the corpses . . . Taking everything they could find. They helped me out. I sat on the edge of the pit and waited and waited . . . It was raining. The ground was very warm. They cut me off a hunk of bread, "Run, kikeling. Maybe you'll survive."

The nearest village was deserted . . . Not a soul around, but the houses were intact. I wanted to eat, but there was no one to beg for food. I wandered through the village alone. On the side of the road, I'd see a rubber boot, a pair of galoshes . . . a kerchief . . . Behind the church, there were charred bodies. Blackened corpses. It smelled like gasoline and frying . . . I ran back into the forest. I lived off mushrooms and berries. One day, I came upon an old man chopping wood. He gave me two eggs. "Don't set foot in the village," he warned me. "The men will tie you up and turn you over to the commanding officers. They just caught two little Jews that way."

One day, I fell asleep and woke up to a bullet flying over my head. I leapt up, "Germans?" It was these two young guys on horseback. Partisans! They laughed and started arguing: "What do we need a little kike for? Let's go . . ." "Let the Commander decide." They brought me to the regiment encampment, put me in a separate mud hut.* Had someone stand guard over me . . . I was summoned for an interrogation: "How did you come to find yourself in this regiment? Who sent you?" "No one sent me. I climbed out of a mass grave." "But maybe you're a spy?" They punched me in the face twice and threw me back into the mud hut. Toward evening, they pushed another two Jews in there with me, young men in nice leather jackets. From them, I learned that they don't accept Jews into partisan regiments unless they come with weapons. If you don't have a weapon, you have to bring them gold, some gold object. They had a gold watch and a cigarette case— they even showed me. They demanded to see the Commander. Soon, they were taken away. I never saw them again . . . but that cigarette case did end up in our Commander's possession . . . and one of the leather jackets. I was saved by a friend of my father's, Uncle Yasha. He was a cobbler, and cobblers were considered as valuable as doctors. I became his assistant . . .

Yasha's first piece of advice: "Change your last name." My last name is Friedman, so I became Lomeiko. His second piece of advice: "Keep your mouth shut, or else you'll get a bullet in the back. No one will be held accountable for killing a Jew." That's how it was . . . War is a swamp, it's easy to get stuck in it and hard to get out. Another Jewish saying: "When the wind is strong, the trash rises to the top." Nazi propaganda had infected everyone, and the partisans were anti-Semitic, too. There were eleven of us Jews in the regiment . . . and then there were five . . . People would intentionally have conversations in front of us like, "What kind of warriors are you? They lead you off like sheep to the slaughter . . ." "Kike cowards . . ." I held my silence. I had a friend in battle, this hotheaded guy named David Greenberg. He'd talk back to them, stand up for himself. He ended up getting shot, and I know exactly who killed him. Today, that guy's a hero, strutting around, showing off his medals. Acting all heroic! He murdered two Jews for allegedly sleeping on duty. And another one for the brand-new Parabellum pistol he coveted . . . Where could you run to?

---

* A common forest dwelling dug into the earth; it is at least partially underground and has a thatched roof.

The ghetto? I wanted to defend my Motherland . . . avenge my family . . . And the Motherland? The partisan commanders had secret instructions from Moscow: Don't trust the Jews, don't let them into the regiments, annihilate them. They considered us traitors. We learned the truth about all of this thanks to perestroika.

You feel sorry for people . . . But horses . . . Do you know how horses die? Horses don't hide like other animals: dog, cats, and even cows will run off somewhere, while horses just stand around waiting to be killed. It's hard to watch . . . In the movies, cavalry soldiers charge in whooping, brandishing sabers over their heads. Nonsense! Pure fantasy! There were some cavalrymen in our regiment for a little while, but they disappeared pretty quickly. Horses can't walk through deep snow, let alone gallop—they get caught in snowdrifts. Meanwhile, the Germans had motorcycles—two-wheelers, three-wheelers; in winter, they'd put them on skis. They'd ride by laughing, shooting our horses and riders. Some of them would take pity on beautiful horses—many of them must have been country boys . . .

The orders: Burn down the Polizei hut, along with the family . . . It was a big family: a wife, three kids, a grandma and grandpa. At night, we surrounded them. Nailed the door shut . . . Drenched the house in gasoline and set it on fire. We could hear them screaming inside. The little boy tried to climb out the window. One partisan wanted to shoot him, but another one stopped him. They threw him back into the fire. I was fourteen, I didn't understand a thing . . . All I could do was try to remember it. And now, I told you the story . . . I don't like the word "hero." There are no heroes in war. As soon as someone picks up a weapon, they can no longer be good. They won't be able to.

I remember a blockade . . . The Germans decided to clear out their rear units and set their SS divisions on the partisans. They hung lights on their parachutes and started bombing us day and night. After bombing, they'd shell us. Their division was retreating in small groups, they were evacuating their wounded, they'd gag them and put special muzzles on their horses. They were leaving everything behind, even domestic livestock, who ran after their retreating owners. Cows, sheep . . . we were forced to shoot them all. The Germans got so close we could hear them, "Oh Mutter, Oh Mutter" . . . Smell their cigarettes. Each of us had a final bullet . . . but it's never too late to die. One night, three of us were left behind as the rear guard. We cut open the belly of a dead horse, tossed everything out of it, and climbed in.

We spent two days like that, listening to the Germans go back and forth. Shooting at them from time to time. Finally, the forest was completely silent. We climbed out covered in blood, guts, and shit . . . half-insane. It was night . . . We saw the moon . . .

You should know that the birds helped us, too . . . When a magpie hears a stranger coming, it will always squawk. Give out a warning signal. They'd gotten used to us; the Germans smelled different: They wore cologne, washed with scented soap, smoked cigarettes; their overcoats were made of excellent military baize, their boots well polished. While we only had hand-rolled tobacco, our feet were wrapped in rags, our shoes made of woven cowhide and strapped to our feet with belts. They had woolen undergarments . . . We'd strip their dead down to their underwear! Our dogs would eat their hands and faces. Even animals got sucked into the war . . .

Many years have passed . . . half a century . . . but I've never forgotten that woman. She had two kids. Little ones. She'd hidden a wounded partisan in her cellar. Someone informed on them . . . They hanged the entire family in the middle of the village. The children first . . . Her screams! They weren't human, they were animal . . . Should people risk making such sacrifices? I couldn't tell you. [*Silence.*] Today, people who weren't there write about the war. I don't read any of it . . . Forgive me, but I can't . . .

We liberated Minsk . . . For me, that was the end of the war. I was too young, they wouldn't let me enlist in the army. I was fifteen. Where was I supposed to live? Strangers had moved into our apartment. They tried to get rid of me: "You dirty kike . . ." They didn't want to give anything back: neither our apartment nor our things. They'd gotten used to the idea that us Jews were gone for good . . .

[*A discordant chorus.*]

The fire burns bright in the little stove
Sap drips down the logs, like tears
In the mud hut, the accordion sings
About your smile and eyes . . .

—The people weren't the same after the war. I myself came home crazed.

—Stalin didn't like our generation. He hated us. We'd tasted freedom. For us, the war meant freedom! We'd gone to Europe and seen how people lived there. When I would walk past a monument of Stalin on my way to work, I'd break into a cold sweat: What if he could read my thoughts?

—"Back to the stables!" they told us. And so we went.

—The democraps! They've destroyed everything . . . now we're rolling around in shit . . .

—I've forgotten everything . . . even love . . . but I still remember the war . . .

—I fought with the partisans for two years. In the forest. After the war, for seven years, eight years . . . I couldn't even look at men. I'd seen too much! I had this apathy. My sister and I went to a sanatorium. People courted her, she'd go dancing, but all I wanted was peace and quiet. I ended up marrying late. My husband was five years younger than me. He was like a little girl.

—I went to the front because I believed everything they wrote in *Pravda*. I fired guns. I had this passionate desire to kill! Kill! It used to be that I wanted to forget it all but couldn't, now it disappears on its own. One thing I remember is that in war, death smells different . . . Murder has a particular smell. When it's not a lot of people, but just one lying there, you start to wonder: Who was he? Where is he from? Someone out there must be waiting for him . . .

—Near Warsaw, an old Polish woman brought me her husband's clothes: "Take everything off. I'll wash it. Why are you all so filthy and thin? How did you manage to win the war?" How did we manage to win?!

—Oh, please . . . Put away those violins . . .

—We won, indeed. But our great victory didn't make our country great.

—I'll remain a communist until my dying day . . . Perestroika is a CIA operation to destroy the USSR.

—What stayed with me? The most hurtful part was how much the Germans hated us. Our way of life, our daily lives . . . Hitler called the Slavs rabbits . . .

—The Germans invaded our village. It was spring. On the very next day, they started building plant beds and a toilet. The old people still talk about how those Germans planted flowers . . .

—In Germany, we'd go into people's homes: The closets were filled with so much high-quality clothing, so many linens and knick-knacks. Heaps of dishes. Before the war, they'd been telling us that people were suffering under capitalism. Then we saw it all for ourselves and said nothing. Try praising a German lighter or bicycle—they'll slap you with Article 58 for anti-Soviet propaganda. For a brief while, they let us send packages home: A general could send fifteen kilograms, an officer ten, and a private five. We flooded the post office. My mother wrote me, "We don't need any more packages from you. Your packages will get us all killed." I'd sent them lighters, watches, some silk fabric . . . huge chocolate bars . . . so big that they'd thought they were soap . . .

—No German women between the ages of ten and eighty were left unfucked! The generation born there in 1946 are "the Russian people."

—War erases everything . . . It already has . . .

—Here it is—victory! Victory! Throughout the whole war, people fantasized about how well they would live afterward. They celebrated for two or three days, and then they wanted something to eat, they needed clothes to wear. They wanted to live again. But there was nothing to be had. Everyone walked around in German uniforms. Adults and children alike. They'd mend them and re-mend them. We bought bread with ration cards, waiting in kilometer-long lines. Rage hung in the air. You could get killed over nothing.

—I remember . . . the clamor, all day long . . . Invalids rolling around on homemade boards with ball-bearing wheels. The roads were paved with cobblestones. They lived in basements and sub-basements. They'd get wasted and lie around in the gutters. Beg. Trade their medals for vodka. They'd roll up to the bread line pleading, "Please let me buy a little piece of bread." But the lines were full of exhausted women, "You're alive, my husband is in his grave." They'd chase them away. When life got a little better, people started outright hating the invalids. No one wanted to be reminded of the war, everyone was busy living in the here and now. One day, all the invalids were cleared out of the city. Policemen caught them and tossed them into cars like they were piglets. Swearing, squealing, yelping . . .

—We had an Invalids' Home in our town. Full of young men without arms, without legs. All of them with medals. You could take one home . . . They issued an order permitting it. Many women yearned for masculine tenderness and jumped at the opportunity, some wheeling men home in wheelbarrows, others in baby strollers. They wanted their houses to smell like men, to hang up men's shirts on their clotheslines. But soon enough, they wheeled them right back . . . They weren't toys . . . it wasn't a movie. Try loving that chunk of man. He's mean, hurt, and he knows he's been betrayed.

—Oh, Victory Day . . .

A WOMAN'S STORY

—I'll tell you about my love . . . The Germans rode into our village in big cars, the tops of their helmets gleaming. Young, cheerful. They pinched the girls. At first, they paid for everything: chicken, eggs. No one believes me, but it's the honest truth! They paid with deutsche marks . . . What did I care about the war? I was in love! I only had one thing on my mind: When was I going to see him? He'd come and sit next to me on the bench and look at me, unable to look away. Smiling. "What are you smiling about?" "Oh, nothing . . ." Before the war, we'd gone to school together. His father died of tuberculosis, his grandfather was declared a kulak, and they sent him and his family off to Siberia. He remembered how his mother would dress him up as a little girl and tell him that if they ever came for them, he should run to the station, jump on a train, and leave. His name was Ivan . . . He always called me "my Lyubochka . . ." That was the only name he had for me . . . It wasn't in the stars for us, we weren't destined to be happy together. The Germans came, and soon after, his grandfather returned. He came back full of hatred, of course. Alone. He'd buried the whole family in exile. He told stories of how they'd taken them down Siberian rivers, unloaded them in the depths of the taiga. Gave them a single saw and axe for twenty or thirty people. They'd eat leaves, gnaw on bark . . . His grandfather despised the communists! Lenin and Stalin! As soon as he returned, he started taking his revenge. He'd point them out to the Germans: This one's a communist . . . and that one . . . Those men would be taken off somewhere . . . It took me a long time to understand what the war was . . .

I remember the two of us washing a horse in the river. The sun! We dried the hay, and it smelled so good to me! I didn't know anything, I'd never felt that way before. I'd been a simple, ordinary girl, and then I fell in love. I had this prophetic dream . . . Our river was not very deep, but I saw myself drowning in it. I was sucked in by the undertow, and suddenly I was underwater. I didn't understand how or with what, but someone started lifting me up, pushing me up to the surface, except for some reason, I was naked. I swam back to the shore. It had been night, and now it was morning. Many people—our entire village—were standing on the shore. I stepped out of the water naked, completely naked . . .

One of our neighbors had a gramophone, so that was where we young people hung out. We danced. Told fortunes about who we would and wouldn't marry using the Book of Psalms, pinesap, beans . . . With sap, the girl had to go into the forest and find an old pine; a young one wouldn't do because it had no memory. No powers. All of this is real! I still believe in it today . . . With the beans, we'd put them into little piles and count them: odds, evens. I was eighteen. Again, of course, they don't write about this kind of thing in books, but . . . our lives were better under German rule. The Germans reopened the churches, dissolved the collective farms, and redistributed the land—two hectares per person, one trailer for every two farmers. They established a firm tariff: In autumn, we'd give them grain, peas, potatoes, and one pig per household. They'd get their due, and we'd keep the rest. Everyone was satisfied. Under Soviet rule, we'd been poor. The brigadier would put down a tally mark for every workday. In autumn, in payment for all our workdays, we'd get a big fat nothing! Now we had meat and butter. It was a totally different life! The people were happy that they had gotten their freedom. We started living according to German rules . . . If you don't feed your horse, you'll get whipped. If you don't sweep the road in front of your yard . . . I remember the conversations: We got used to the communists, now we'll get used to the Germans. We'll learn to live the German way of life. That's how it was . . . It's all so vivid to me, to this day. At night, everyone was afraid of the "forest people" who would come into our homes uninvited. One night, they came to our house: One had an axe, and the other one was carrying a pitchfork. "Hand over the *salo*, mother. And the moonshine. Don't make too much noise." I'm telling you how it happened in real life, not how they write about it in books. At first, people didn't like the partisans . . .

We set a wedding date . . . After Dozhinki, the harvest festival. After we'd finished working the fields, and the women had laid a wreath on the final sheaf. [*She is silent.*] My memory grows dimmer, but my soul has not forgotten a thing . . . The rain started after dinner. Everyone ran in from the fields, and my mother came crying, "Oh Lord! Oh Lord! Your Ivan has signed up with the police. You'll be the wife of a Polizei." "No! I can't be!" My mother and I wept. In the evening, Ivan came over. He sat down, not daring to raise his eyes. "Ivan, my darling, why didn't you think of us?" "Lyubka . . . My Lyubochka . . ." His grandfather had forced him into it. The old devil! He threatened him: "If you don't sign up with the police, they'll ship you off to Germany. Then you can say goodbye to your Lyubka! Forget about her!" His grandfather had his own dreams . . . he wanted his daughter-in-law to be German . . . The Germans played their propaganda films about Germany, about how good life was over there. A lot of the younger boys and girls believed it. They'd leave. Before setting off, they'd throw them goodbye parties. A brass band would play. Then they'd board the trains in their little shoes . . . [*She gets pills out of her purse.*] My health isn't that good anymore . . . The doctors say that medicine is powerless to help me . . . I'm going to die soon. [*Silence.*] I want my love to live on. I won't be here anymore, but people will be able to read about it . . .

War raged all around us, but we were happy. For a year, we lived together as man and wife. I got pregnant. Our house was right next to the railway station. The German divisions would head to the front, their soldiers all young and full of life. Belting out their songs. They'd see me and shout, "Mädchen, kleines Mädchen!" And laugh. Then there were fewer and fewer young soldiers—old ones took their place. The young ones had been joyful; these ones were somber. Their excitement had run out. The Soviet army was beating them. "Ivan," I'd ask him. "What will become of us?" "There's no blood on my hands. I've never shot anyone." [*Silence.*] My children don't know about any of this, I've never confessed it to them. Maybe at the very end, right before I die . . . I'll tell you one thing, though: Love is a kind of poison.

Two houses down from us, there was another guy who liked me, he'd always ask to dance with me. I was the only one he ever danced with. "Let me walk you home." "I already have a chaperone." He was a good-looking guy . . . Went off into the forest and joined the partisans. People who'd seen him said that he now wore a *kubanka* hat with a red ribbon on it. One night, there was a knock at our door. "Who is it?" "Partisans." That guy and another, older one, had come to see us. My suitor started in: "How have you been, Mrs. Polizei? I've been wanting to call on you for a long time now. Where's that little husband of yours?" "How should I know? He didn't come home today. He's probably spending the night at the garrison." Suddenly, he grabbed my arm and threw me against the wall: You German puppet, you floor rag . . . He called me a—I can't say it but it starts with *w* and told me to go f . . . Told me I'd gone with a German toady, kulak spawn, and pretended to be a virgin with him. That's when he made to reach for his gun. My mother fell to her knees in front of him: "Go ahead and shoot, boys. When I was young, I was close with your mothers. Let's give them something to cry about, too." My mother's words had an effect on them. They talked among themselves and left. [*Silence.*] Love is something very bitter . . .

The front kept advancing, getting closer and closer. You could hear shooting at night. One night, the guests returned. "Who is it?" "Partisans." My suitor comes in, and there's another one with him. He brandishes his gun, "This is what I used to kill your husband." "It's not true! It can't be true!" "You don't have a husband anymore." I thought that I would kill him . . . that I would claw his eyes out . . . [*She is silent.*] In the morning, they brought me my Ivan . . . lying on a sled. On top of an overcoat . . . His eyes were shut, his face was like a little child's. He'd never killed anyone . . . I believed him! And I still do! I rolled around on the floor, wailing. My mother was scared that I'd go crazy and that my child would be stillborn or sick. She ran to get the wise woman, Baba Stasa. "I know your trouble," she told my mother, "but I am powerless here. Have your daughter pray to God." And she told us what to do . . . When Ivan was taken to the cemetery, I would have to walk in front of the coffin, instead of behind it with everyone else. Up to the very cemetery gates. Through the entire village . . . By the end of the war, many men had disappeared into the forest. Gone partisaning. There'd been a death in every family. [*She cries.*] And so I walked . . . in front of the Polizei's coffin . . . I walked in front of it, and my mother walked behind it. All of the people came out of their houses, leaned on their gates and watched us pass, but no one said a single unkind word. They just looked at me and wept.

The Soviets returned to power . . . and that suitor of mine found me again. He showed up on horseback: "They're interested in you." "Who?" "What do you mean, who? The authorities." "I don't care where I die. Let them send me to Siberia." "What kind of mother are you? You have a child." "You know whose it is . . ." "I'll marry you anyway." And so I married him. The man who murdered my husband. I had his child, my daughter . . . [*She cries.*] He loved both of our children the same, my son and his daughter. I won't speak ill of him on that account. As for me . . . I . . . was always covered in bruises, I went around with bloody contusions. At night, he'd beat me, and in the morning, he'd get on his knees and beg my forgiveness. He was burned up by some violent passion . . . jealous of my dead husband. In the morning, while everyone else was still asleep, I would already be up. I needed to be up as early as possible, before he could wake up, so that he wouldn't embrace me. At night, every single window would be dark, but I'd still be up working in the kitchen. All of my pots sparkled. I waited for him to fall asleep. We lived together like that for fifteen years, and then he got very ill. He died in the course of a single autumn. [*She weeps.*] It's not my fault . . . I never wished for him to die. The moment came . . . the final moment . . . He'd been lying with his face to the wall, and then he turned to me, "Did you ever love me?" I didn't say anything. He started laughing like he'd laughed the night he'd showed me his gun . . . "You're the only woman I've ever loved. I loved you so much I wanted to kill you when I found out I was going to die. I asked Yashka (that's our neighbor who prepares animal hides) for poison. I couldn't stand the thought that I'd be dead and you'd find somebody else. You're too beautiful."

He lay there in his coffin . . . and it felt like he was laughing. I was afraid to go up to him. But I was supposed to kiss him.

[*The chorus starts up.*]

Rise up, you mighty nation,
To fight the fatal fight . . .
Let righteous rage boil like a swelling wave.
Rise up, there is a war on
A holy war to fight . . .

—We're going out with aching hearts . . .

—I told my daughters: When I die, just let the music play. Don't let anyone say anything.

—After the war, the German prisoners lugged stones. Rebuilt our town. Starving. They begged for bread. But I couldn't bear to give them even a tiny piece. Sometimes, this is what I remember . . . that detail . . . It's strange the kind of things that stay with you . . .

There are flowers on the table and a big portrait of Timeryan Zinatov. This whole time, it seemed like I could hear his voice among the chorus, like he was right there with us.

FROM ZINATOV'S WIFE'S STORY

—There isn't much I remember . . . Our home, our family, he was never very interested in us. Always going on and on about the fortress. He couldn't forget the war . . . He taught our kids that Lenin was a good man, that we were building communism. One day, he came home from work clutching a newspaper: "Let's go to the great construction site. Our Motherland is calling us." Our children were still very little. Let's go and that's that. Our Motherland commands us to . . . and that's how we ended up working on the Baikal-Amur Mainline . . . Building communism . . . We really did build it, too! We believed that everything was ahead of us! Ardent believers in the Soviet regime, we were. From the bottom of our hearts. But then we got old. Glasnost, perestroika . . . We sit here and listen to the radio. Communism doesn't exist anymore . . . where did communism go? No more communists, either . . . It's impossible to understand who's in charge up there. Gaidar picked everyone clean. The people have been left homeless . . . Some steal from their factories or collective farms . . . others swindle . . . That's how people get by these days. But my guy . . . he lived up in the clouds, he was always up there somewhere. Our daughter works at a pharmacy. One day, she brought home some medications to sell on the side so she could make a little bit of extra money. How did he find out? Did he pick up the scent? "Shame on you! Terrible shame!" he yelled. He kicked her out. I couldn't get him to calm down. Other veterans take advantage of their benefits . . . They're entitled to them, after all . . . "Go down there," I implored him. "Maybe they'll give you something." He started screaming at me, "I fought for the Motherland, not benefits." He'd lie awake at night with his eyes open, completely silent. I'd call his name, but he wouldn't answer me. Eventually, he stopped speaking to us altogether. He was beside himself. But he wasn't upset for us, his family—he was upset on behalf of everyone. The entire nation. That's the kind of man he was. I saw my share of grief with him . . . I'll tell you the truth, speaking to you as a woman, not as a writer . . . I couldn't understand him . . .

One day, he dug up the potatoes, put on his best clothes, and went off to his fortress. He didn't even leave us a note. He addressed his final statement to the state, to strangers. To us, he said nothing. Not a single word . . .

ON THE SWEETNESS OF
SUFFERING AND THE TRICK OF
THE RUSSIAN SOUL

◆

THE STORY OF A LOVE AFFAIR

Olga Karimova, musician,
49 years old

No, no, it's impossible . . . I can't go through with it. I thought that one day, I'd tell someone the story . . . But right now, I can't . . . Now is not that time. It's all under lock and key, walled up and plastered over. Done . . . secreted away in a sarcophagus . . . I put it all in a sarcophagus . . . It's not on fire anymore, but there's still some kind of chemical reaction going on. Crystals forming. I'm afraid of disturbing it. I'm scared . . .

My first love . . . can I really call it that? My first husband . . . it's a beautiful story. He pursued me for two years. I really wanted us to get married because I needed all of him, I didn't want him to go anywhere. All mine! I can't even fathom why I wanted him so much. Just to spend every minute together, never be apart, fight and fuck and fuck and never stop fucking. He was the first man I'd ever been with. The first time it was just this . . . interesting, hmmm . . . like, what's going on here? Same thing the second time . . . And in general, it's kind of mechanical . . . You know, the body . . . the body, the body . . . That's all it really is! It went on like that for six months. It didn't seem like it was particularly important to him that I was me, he could have found himself something else. And then, for some reason, there we were, getting married . . . I was twenty-two. We went to conservatory together, we did everything together. And then it happened . . . Something opened up inside me, except I missed the exact moment . . . when I fell in love with the male body. And now I had one all to myself . . . It was a beautiful story, it could have either gone on forever or ended in half an hour. So . . . I left him. Left him of my own accord. He begged me to stay. But for some reason, I was set on leaving. I was sick of him . . . Dear Lord, I was so sick of him! I was already pregnant, with a big belly . . . What did I need him for? We fucked, we fought, and then I'd cry. I didn't have any patience back then. I didn't know how to forgive.

I stepped out of the house, closed the door behind me, and felt a rush of real joy that I was leaving. Leaving him forever. I went to my mother's, he ran after me, it was the middle of the night, he was in total shock: I was pregnant, unhappy all the time for no apparent reason, what did I want from him? Huh? What else did I want? I turned over a new leaf . . . I was happy when I got him and happy when I got rid of him. My life has always been like a change jar. It's full, then it's empty, then it's full again, then it's empty again.

Anya's birth was beautiful . . . I liked it so much. First, my water broke . . . I was on one of my long, many-kilometer walks, when, in the middle of the forest, my water broke. I didn't really know what to do—was I supposed to go to the hospital right that minute? I waited until evening. It was winter—it's hard to imagine now—forty degrees below zero. The bark on the trees had cracked from the cold. Finally, I decided to go. The doctor took a look and said, "You're going to be in labor for two days." I called home: "Mama, bring me some chocolate. It's going to take a while." Before her morning rounds, a nurse popped in: "The head's already sticking out! I'm calling the doctor." So there I was in the stirrups . . . They told me, "Any minute now. Hang in there." I don't remember how much time went by. But it was fast, very fast . . . and then they were holding up this strange little clump to show me: "It's a girl." They put her on the scale, she was four kilograms. "You don't have a single tear. She took pity on her Mama." Oh, when they brought her to me the next day, her eyes were just giant pupils, black and swimming all around. After that, I couldn't see anything else . . .

My new, totally different life began. I liked how I started looking after I gave birth. Overall, I instantly became more beautiful . . . Anya took her place immediately, I adored her, but for some reason, it felt like she had nothing to do with men. With the fact that she had a father. It was like she'd fallen from the sky! From heaven. She learned to talk, and people would ask her, "Anya, do you have a daddy?" "I have Granny for a daddy." "Do you have a doggy?" "I have a hamster for a doggy." That's how the both of us are . . . My whole life, I've been afraid of suddenly not being me. Even at the dentist, I tell them, "Don't give me a shot. I don't want to be numbed." My feelings are my feelings, whether they feel good or hurt, I don't want to be unplugged from myself. Anya and I liked each other. And then the two of us met him . . . Gleb . . .

If it hadn't been him, I would have never married again. I had everything: a child, a job, freedom. Suddenly, he came along . . . Awkward, practically blind. Chronically short of breath . . . Letting a person with that much baggage into my life—he'd done twelve years in Stalin's camps . . . They'd taken him when he was still just a kid, sixteen years old. His father, a high-ranking Party official, had been executed, and his mother had frozen to death in a barrel full of water. Somewhere far away, off in the snows. Before him, I'd never thought about those things . . . I was a Young Pioneer, in the Komsomol . . . Life was beautiful! Exhilarating! What made me go for him? What was it about him? Time passes, and pain develops into knowledge. It's pain and it's knowledge, as well. It's been five years since he passed away . . . five . . . and I'm sad that he never knew me as the person I am today. I understand him a lot better now, I'm finally mature enough for him, and he's gone. For a long time, I couldn't bear living alone. I had absolutely no will to live. It's not that I'm afraid of solitude, I just don't know how to live without love. I need the pain . . . the pity . . . Without that, I'm lost, the way I get scared when I've swum out too far into the sea. Out there, I'm alone . . . It's dark in those depths . . . I don't know what's down there . . .

[*We sit talking on a terrace. The leaves are rustling, then it starts raining.*]

You know how beach romances go, they don't last long. They're flings. Like life, but in miniature. They sparkle and fade, it's pretty. Like what we don't get to have in real life and what we really want. That's why people love traveling so much . . . meeting people . . . so I'd braided my hair, I was wearing a blue polka dot dress that I'd bought the day before we left at a children's store. The sea . . . I like to swim out pretty far, there's nothing in the world I love more than swimming. In the morning, I'd do my exercises under a white acacia. One day, a man walked by, just a regular man, totally normal-looking, not young. He noticed me, and for some reason it made him very glad. He stood there watching me: "Would you like me to come over and read you some poems this evening?" "Maybe, I'm about to go on a long swim!"

"I'll wait for you." So he waited for me for several hours. He read poorly, constantly fixing his glasses. But it was touching. I saw . . . I saw what he was feeling . . . Those movements, those glasses, that nervousness. I've completely forgotten what poems they were. And why should that be so important? It was raining then, too. It started raining. I remember that . . . I haven't forgotten a thing. The feelings . . . Our feelings are like some sort of separate entities—suffering, love, tenderness. They have lives of their own, they don't depend on us. For some unknown reason, you suddenly choose one person over another, even though the other one might be better. Or without even realizing it, you're suddenly part of another person's life. You don't know it yet, but they've already found you . . . They've sent out their signal . . . "I've been waiting for you." With those words, he met me the following morning. And for some reason, something in his voice made me believe him, even though I wasn't at all ready for this. Quite the opposite. But everything around me had transformed . . . It wasn't love yet, but it felt like I had suddenly been given a lot of something. Two people had gotten through to each other. The signals had been received. I swam far out into the sea. When I came back in, he was waiting for me. Again, he told me, "We're going to be happy together." And for some reason, I believed him again. In the evening, we drank champagne. "This is red sparkling wine, but it cost as much as regular champagne." I thought that was funny. He made eggs. "I have a strange relationship with eggs. I buy ten in one go, fry two at a time, but for some reason, there's always one left over." He'd say sweet little things like that.

Everyone would look at us and ask, "Is that your grandpa? Your father?" I always wore a short dress . . . I was twenty-eight. Later on, he grew handsome. After we got together. I think I know the secret . . . It's a door that can only be opened with love . . . only love . . . "I thought about you." "What did you think about me?" "I wanted us to go somewhere together. Far, far away. And I didn't need anything but to feel you next to me. That's how tender my feelings are, I just want to look at you and walk beside you." We spent many happy hours together, as happy as children. "Maybe we'll go away to an island and lie there on the sand." Happy people are always like children. They need to be protected, they're delicate and funny. Vulnerable. That's how he and I were, I don't know how else it could have possibly been. That's how it was with him—although with a different person, it might have been different. It's whatever you make of it . . . "Unhappiness is the best teacher," as my mother used to say. And you want happiness. I'd wake up in the middle of the night wondering, "What am I doing?" I felt crazy, and from that tension ... I ... I had ... "The back of your head is always tense," he told me. What am I doing? Where am I falling? It's an abyss.

... The breadbox ... As soon as he saw bread, he'd start methodically devouring it. In any quantity. There must never be left-over bread. It's your ration. So he'd eat and eat it, finishing however much there was. I didn't understand it at first ...

... He told me about school ... In history classes, they'd open their textbooks and draw prison bars over the portraits of Marshals Tukhachevsky and Blyukher. The principal had told them to. While singing and laughing. Like it was a game. After class, kids would beat him up and write "Son of an enemy of the people" on his back in chalk.

... One step out of line and they'd shoot you; if you made it to the forest, wild animals would tear you to shreds. At night, in the barracks, other prisoners could murder you. Just for the hell of it, just like that. Without a word ... nothing ... It was camp life, every man for himself. I had to understand that ...

... After the Leningrad Blockade* broke, a transit of Blockade survivors arrived in the camp. They were like skeletons ... nothing but flesh and bone ... Barely human. They were in for stashing away ration cards for fifty grams of bread (the daily allotment) that had been issued to their dead mother or dead child ... People would get six years for that. For two days, the camp was terrifyingly silent. The guards ... even they were silent ...

... For a while, he worked in a boiler room ... Someone was looking out for the kid. The stoker was a philology professor from Moscow, his job was pushing the logs in on a wheelbarrow. They'd argue about whether someone who quoted Pushkin could be capable of shooting unarmed people. Someone who listened to Bach ...

But why him? Why him specifically? Russian women love finding these unfortunate men. My grandmother was in love with someone, but her parents were marrying her off to somebody else. She really

---

* The Leningrad Blockade lasted from September 8, 1941, to January 27, 1944. Nazi troops had the city surrounded, effectively cutting citizens off from supply lines and paths of escape. As a result, nearly a million of the city's residents died, mainly of starvation, as they were forced to survive on minuscule rations and whatever else they were desperate enough to eat.

didn't like the guy, she didn't want to be with him in the least! Lord! She'd decided that when the priest in the church would ask her whether she was marrying him of her own free will, she would say no. But the priest had gotten drunk beforehand, so instead of asking her like he was supposed to, he just said, "Be nice to him, he froze his feet off in the war." After that, she had no choice but to marry him. That's how my grandmother ended up spending the rest of her life with my grandfather, even though she never loved him. It's a great caption, summing up our whole lives . . . "Be nice to him, he froze his feet off in the war." Was my mother happy? Mama . . . My father came back from the war in '45 . . . destroyed, drained. Sick from his wounds. Victors! Only their wives really knew what it was like to live with a victor. My mother would cry day and night after my father returned. It took years for those victors of ours to get re-accustomed to civilian life. Get used to it. I remember my father's stories, how at first, just the mention of "fire up the sauna" and "go fishing" would set him off. Our men are martyrs, all of them are traumatized, either from war or from prison. From life in the camps. War and prison are the two most important words in the Russian language. Truly Russian words! Russian women have never had normal men. They keep healing and healing them. Treating them like heroes and children at the same time. Saving them. To this very day. Women still take on that same role. The Soviet Union has fallen . . . and now we have the victims of the fall of the empire. Of the collapse. The gulag had made Gleb brave. It was like a badge of honor: I survived! I endured that! The things I saw! But I still write books and kiss women . . . He was proud. While the men today walk around with fear in their eyes. Nothing but fear . . . They're downsizing the army, the factories are at a standstill . . . The markets are full of engineers and doctors peddling their wares. PhDs. There are so many of them—everywhere you look, you see people who've been thrown off the train. They sit on the curb waiting for something to happen. My friend's husband was a pilot, a squadron commander. They put him in the reserves. As soon as she lost her job, she learned a new trade—she used to be an engineer, now she's a hairdresser. Meanwhile, he's at home drinking his pain away, drinking because he was a pilot, a battle veteran with Afghanistan under his belt, and now he has to make his kids kasha. That's how it goes . . . He's angry at everyone. Furious. He went down to the conscription office, begged them to send him anywhere at all to fight, on a special mission, but they turned him away. There are plenty of men just like him. We have thousands of out-of-work army men, people who only know the gun and the tank, unsuited for any other kind of life. Our women are forced to be stronger than our men. They travel the world with their giant checkered bags. From Poland to China. Buying and selling. Carrying the weight of their entire households, the children and old folks, too. Plus their husbands. Plus the entire nation. It's hard to explain this to an outsider. Practically impossible. My daughter is married to an Italian . . . His name is Sergio, he's a journalist. When they come stay with me, he and I have our kitchen dialogues. In Russian . . . We'll talk until morning. Sergio thinks that Russians love to suffer, that that's the trick of the Russian soul. For us, suffering is "a personal struggle," "the path to salvation." Italians aren't like that, they don't want to suffer, they love life, which they believe is given to them to enjoy, not suffer through. We don't think like that. We rarely talk about joy . . . about how happiness is an entire world. An amazing world! With so many little nooks, windows, doors that you need lots of little keys for. We're always drawn down dark, Buninesque alleys.* Like . . . my daughter and Sergio will come home from the supermarket, and he'll be carrying the grocery bags. In the evening, she can play piano while he makes dinner. For me, it was nothing like that: He'd try to take the bags from me, and I'd grab them away, "I'll do it. You shouldn't." He'd come into the kitchen, and I'd tell him, "This isn't your place. Off to your desk." I always shone with reflected light.

A year passed, maybe more . . . It was time for him to come home with me. You know, to meet everyone. I warned him that my mother was nice, but my daughter wasn't always . . . she wasn't like other children. I couldn't guarantee that she'd give him a warm welcome. Oh, my Anya . . . She'd put everything up to her ear: her toy, a rock, a spoon . . . Most children put everything in their mouth, but what she wanted to know was, "How does it sound?" I started teaching her music pretty early, but she was a weird kid, as soon as I'd put on a record she'd turn around and leave the room. She didn't like other people's music, she was only interested in what she heard inside her head. So there he was, Gleb, very shy, with a bad haircut, they'd cut it too short—not particularly attractive. And he'd brought over records. He started telling the story of how he'd gone here and there . . . how he'd gotten his hands on those records. But with Anya's hearing . . . she doesn't care about words, she listens to . . . intonations . . . Right

---

* *Dark Alleys* is the title of Ivan Bunin's 1943 collection of short stories.

away, she took the records from him: "What wondelful wecords." Just like that . . . A little while later, she put me in a tough spot: "How can I not call him Papa?" It wasn't that he'd been trying to get her to like him, he just liked spending time with her. They fell in love at first sight . . . I was even a little jealous, thinking they loved each other more than they loved me. I managed to convince myself that I played a different role . . . [*She is silent.*] He asked her, "Anya, do you stutter?" "I'm not good at it anymore, but I used to be great." You won't get bored around the two of them. You could write down everything she said. So: "How can I not call him Papa?" We were at the park. Gleb had stepped away to buy cigarettes, and when he came back, "So what are you girls talking about?" I winked at her—don't you dare, it's too stupid. But she goes, "You tell him then." What was I supposed to do? What could I say? I confessed: She's scared of accidentally calling you Papa. He replied, "It's not a simple matter, but if you really want to, you can go ahead." "But watch out," my Anya grew serious, "I have another papa, but I don't like him. And Mama doesn't love him." That's how she and I have always been. We burn bridges. By the time we were walking home, he was already Papa. She ran down the street, shouting, "Papa! Papa!" The next day in preschool she announced to everyone, "My papa is teaching me how to read." "And who's your papa?" "His name is Gleb." The next day, her friend had news for her: "Anya, you're not telling the truth, that's not a papa. He's not your real papa." "The other one is the one who wasn't real, this one is." It's useless arguing with Anya, he was Papa now, and as for me? I wasn't his wife yet . . . No . . .

I had a vacation from work . . . I went away again. He ran down the platform after the train and waved to me for a long, long time. But I'd barely boarded the train before I met someone. There were these two young engineers from Kharkov who were also headed to Sochi. Lord! I was so young! The sea. The sun. We swam, we kissed, we danced. Everything was easy and free because the world was simple—the cha-cha-cha, the *kazachok*—I was in my element. Somebody loved me . . . Someone carried me around in his arms . . . For two hours, he carried me up a mountain. Young muscles, youthful laughter. Sitting around the bonfire until dawn . . . I had a dream . . . The ceiling opened up above me. The sky was blue . . . I saw Gleb . . . He and I were walking somewhere. We walked along the seashore, but the pebbles weren't the kind that are smooth, polished by the waves. We were stepping on sharp rocks, as sharp as nails. I was wearing shoes, but he was barefoot. "When you're barefoot," he explained, "you can hear better." But I knew that really, he was in pain. The pain made him float up into the sky . . . He soared above me . . . I saw him flying away. For some reason, his hands were folded over his chest, like a dead person's . . . [*She stops.*]

Good Lord! I'm crazy . . . I shouldn't tell anyone about these things. More often than not, I feel like I've been very lucky . . . So happy! I went to see him in the cemetery . . . I remember, as I was walking around, it felt like he was somewhere nearby. And I was so overwhelmingly happy, I wanted to cry from the joy. Cry. They say the dead don't come back to us. Don't believe that.

My vacation came to an end, and I went home. The engineer escorted me all the way back to Moscow. I'd promised to tell Gleb everything . . . I went to see him . . . There was a diary on his desk all covered in scribbling, the wallpaper in his office, and even the newspapers were all scrawled in four little letters: I . . . G . . . I . . . O . . . Upper case, lower case, print, cursive—he wrote them everywhere. Ellipses . . . ellipses . . . I asked him, "What is this?" He decoded it for me: "I guess it's over?" So we were breaking up, and I had to somehow explain it to Anya. We went to pick her up, but she wanted to finish her drawing. There wasn't time, we put her in the car, and she sat there wailing. He was already used to how crazy she was, he saw it as a sign of her talent. This was a family scene: Anya's crying, he's comforting her, and I'm sitting between them . . . The way he looked, the way he was looking at me . . . and I . . . It was only a moment . . . an instant . . . I realized what a terribly lonely person he was. Terribly! And . . . I had to marry him . . . I had to . . . [*She breaks down.*] We're so lucky we didn't miss each other. That I didn't pass him by. What amazing luck! He gave me a whole life! [*She bursts into tears.*] So I married him . . . He was scared, he was afraid because he'd already been married twice. Those women had betrayed him, got tired of him . . . And you can't blame them . . . Love is hard work. For me, it's primarily work. We didn't have a wedding, I never got a white dress. It all went off modestly. I had always dreamed of having a wedding and a white dress, of throwing a bouquet of white roses off a bridge. That's what my dreams had been like.

He didn't like being questioned . . . He had this bravado . . . always trying to make light of everything . . . this prisoner's habit of hiding everything serious behind jokes. The bar is higher for them. For instance, he never said the word "freedom"—it was always "the out-

side." "Here I am on the outside." At rare moments, he'd tell stories . . .
But he'd tell them so vividly, so avidly . . . I could just feel the happiness he'd taken out of there: like when he'd gotten his hands on some
tire scraps and tied them to his felt boots. When they were transferred,
he was so happy to have them! Another time, they'd gotten half a sack
of potatoes . . . And somewhere "on the outside," while they were
working . . . somebody had given him a big hunk of meat. That night,
in the boiler room, they made soup: "And it was just so good! So wonderful!" When they released him, they gave him a reparation payment
for his father. They told him, "We owe you for the house, the furniture . . ." It ended up being a lot of money. He bought a new suit, a
new shirt, new shoes, a camera, and went out to the best restaurant in
Moscow, the National, where he ordered the most expensive things on
the menu, and cognac and coffee with their signature dessert. At the
end, when he'd eaten his fill, he asked someone to take a picture of
him at the happiest moment of his life. "Then, when I got back to my
apartment," he recalled, "I caught myself thinking that I didn't feel
any happiness. In that suit, with that camera . . . Why wasn't there any
happiness? At that moment, the tires and that soup in the boiler room
came back to me—now that was real happiness." And we'd try to examine it . . . like . . . what makes happiness? He wouldn't have given
up his years in the camp for anything in the world . . . he wouldn't
have changed a thing about his life . . . That was his secret treasure
trove, his wealth. He was in the camps from when he was sixteen until
he was almost thirty . . . Count that up . . . I asked him, "But what if
they'd never arrested you?" He'd make jokes to avoid answering, "I
would have been an idiot zooming around in a bright red sports car.
The latest model." Only at the end . . . the very end, when he was in
hospital . . . For the first time, he discussed it with me in earnest. "It's
like when you go to the theater. From your seat in the audience, you see
a beautiful fairy tale—a carefully decorated set, brilliant actors, mysterious light, but when you go backstage . . . As soon as you step into
the wings, you see broken planks, rags, unfinished and abandoned
canvases . . . empty vodka bottles, food scraps. There's no fairy tale.
It's dark and filthy . . . It's like I'd been taken backstage . . . Do you
understand?"

. . . They threw him in with the criminals. He was just a boy . . .
No one will ever know what happened to him in there . . .

. . . The indescribable beauty of the Great North! Silent snows . . .
and the light on the snow, even at night . . . To them, you're just a

beast of burden. They trudge you out into nature and then bring you back at night. "Trial by beauty," he called it. His favorite saying was, "His trees and flowers turned out much better than His people did."

. . . About love . . . How it happened to him for the first time . . . They were working in the forest. A column of women was being led past them on their way to work. The women saw the men and stopped dead in their tracks, refusing to go any further. The convoy commander yelled, "Forward! Keep moving!" But the women held their ground. "Forward, dammit!" "Citizen commander, let us go see the men, we can't stand it anymore. Or we'll scream!" "Are you nuts? You've lost your minds! You're possessed!" They stood there: "We're not going anywhere." The orders: "You have half an hour. Disperse!!!" In the blink of an eye, the column shattered. But they all came back on time. On the dot. They came back happy. [*She is silent.*] Where does true happiness lie?

. . . He wrote poems in there. Someone informed on him to the head of the camp, "He's been writing." The head of the camp called him in: "Write me a love letter in verse." He remembered what that man had asked him to write but was too shy to tell me. The head of the camp had a lover somewhere out in the Urals.

. . . His journey home, he rode on the top bunk. The train took two weeks across all of Russia. That whole time, he lay there on the top bunk, afraid of coming down. He would only smoke at night. He was scared that his travel companions would offer him something to eat and he'd break down in tears. Tell them everything. And they'd find out he'd come from the camps . . . Distant relatives of his father's took him in. They had a young daughter. He hugged her, and she broke down in tears. There was something about him . . . He was an insanely lonely person . . . even with me. I realize that even with me, he was lonely . . .

He proudly told everyone, "I have a family now." Every day, he was enthralled by our regular family life; he was very proud of it. But the fear . . . no matter what, the fear . . . He didn't know how to live without it. Sheer terror. He'd wake up in the middle of the night drenched in sweat, afraid that he wouldn't finish his book (he was writing a book about his father), that he wouldn't get a new translation to do (he was a technical translator from the German), that he wouldn't be able to provide for his family. What if I suddenly left him . . . First, it was fear, then came the shame for being afraid. "Gleb, I love you. If you wanted me to become a ballerina, I would do it. I would go to the ends of the Earth for you." He survived the camps, but in normal, civilian life a cop pulling him over was enough to give him a heart attack . . . a phone call from the building management . . . "How did you make it out of there alive?" "My parents loved me a lot when I was little." We're saved by the amount of love we get, it's our safety net. Yes . . . only love can save us. Love is a vitamin that humans can't live without—the blood curdles, the heart stops. I was a nurse, a nanny . . . an actress . . . I was everything for him.

I consider us lucky . . . It was an important time—perestroika! It felt like a celebration. Like any moment now, we would take off flying. Freedom was in the air we breathed. "Gleb, your time has come! You can write about everything and publish it." Most of all, it was their time . . . The era of the sixties dissidents . . . Their triumph. I saw him so happy: "I lived to see the total victory of anticommunism." His most important dream had come true: Communism collapsed. Now they'll take down the Bolshevik monuments and get Lenin's sarcophagus off Red Square; the streets won't be named after murderers and executioners anymore . . . It was a time of great hope! The sixties dissidents—people can say what they like about them, but I love them all. Were they naïve? Romantics? Yes!!! He read the papers all day long. In the morning, he'd run down to the Publisher's Union kiosk by our house with a big shopping bag. He listened to the radio and watched TV nonstop. Everyone was a bit nuts at the time. Free-dom! The word itself was intoxicating. We'd all grown up on *samizdat* and *tamizdat*.* We were children of the word. Literature. You should have heard how we talked! Everyone used to speak so well! I would be cooking lunch or dinner, and he'd be next to me with a newspaper, reading to me, "Susan Sontag: Communism is Fascism with a Human Face," "And this . . . listen . . ." That's how we read Berdyaev, Hayek†. . . How had we lived before those books and newspapers? If only we'd known . . . Everything would have been different . . . Jack London has a story about this: You can live in a straightjacket, you just have to suck it up and get used to it. You can even dream. That's how we'd always lived. So how were we going to live now? I didn't know, but I imagined that

---

* Wheras *samizdat* designates the clandestine or illegal production and circulation of literature within the Soviet Union, *tamizdat* specifically refers to Russian writings that were published abroad and smuggled back into the USSR.
† Nikolai Berdyaev (1874–1948) was a Russian philosopher who emigrated to France in 1920. Friedrich Hayek (1899–1992) was an Austrian liberal philosopher and essayist.

all of us were going to live well. There were no doubts in my mind . . .
After he died, I found a note in his diary: "I'm rereading Chekhov . . .
'The Shoemaker and the Devil.' A man sells his soul to the devil in
exchange for happiness. What kind of happiness does the cobbler
imagine for himself? Here's what it looks like: Riding in an open car-
riage wearing a new jacket and calf boots, next to a fat, large-breasted
woman, holding a ham in one hand and a big bottle of bread wine in
the other. He doesn't need anything else . . ." [*She falls into thought.*]
Apparently, he had his doubts . . . but we'd been so desperate for
something new. Something full of kindness and light and justice. We
were so excited, running around to every protest and rally . . . Before
that, I'd been afraid of crowds. Of the mob mentality. I had always felt
alienated from the crowd, those parades marching through the streets.
The banners. But now, I liked all of it . . . such familiar faces all
around—I'll never forget those faces! I miss that time, and I know a lot
of other people do, too. Our first trip abroad. To Berlin. Hearing us
speaking Russian, two young German women approached our group.
"Are you Russian?" "Yes." "Perestroika! Gorby!" And they hugged us.
Now I wonder, where did those faces go? Where are those beautiful
people I saw in the streets in the nineties? Did they really all leave?

   . . . When I found out he had cancer, I was up all night, in tears,
and in the morning, I ran to the hospital to see him. He was sitting on
the windowsill, all yellow and very happy. He was always happy whenever his life changed. First, it was the camps, then it was exile, then
freedom, and now this . . . Death was just another change of circumstances . . . "Are you afraid I'm going to die?" "Yes." "Well, first of all,
I never promised you I wouldn't. Second of all, it won't be that soon."
"Are you sure?" As usual, I believed him. I immediately wiped away
my tears and convinced myself that once again, it was time to help
him. After that, I didn't cry . . . Up until the very end, I didn't cry . . .
I would come to the ward in the morning and that's when our regular
life would begin. We used to live at home and now we lived in the hospital. We got to spend another six months together in the oncology
ward . . .

   He didn't read much. More often, he'd tell me stories . . .

   He knew who had informed on him. This boy . . . He'd been in a
study group with him at the House of Young Pioneers. Either he did it
of his own accord, or they forced him to, but he had written a letter
criticizing Comrade Stalin and defending his father, an enemy of the
people. At the interrogation, the investigator showed him that letter.

His whole life, Gleb was afraid . . . afraid that the informant would find out that he knew . . . When someone told him that the guy's kid was disabled, he got scared—what if that was retribution? For a while, we even lived in the same neighborhood and would run into each other all the time—on the street, at the store. We'd say hello. After Gleb died, I told one of our mutual friends . . . She couldn't believe it. "N.? How could he? He always speaks so highly of Gleb and talks about how they were friends when they were kids." I realized I shouldn't have said anything. It's as simple as that: knowing these things is dangerous. But he was aware . . . Other former camp inmates came by very infrequently, he didn't seek them out. Whenever they came over, it made me feel like I didn't belong, like they'd all come from some place where I didn't exist. They knew more about him than I did. I saw that he had another life . . . which also made me realize that a woman can talk about her humiliating experiences, but a man can't. It's easier for a woman to discuss them because somewhere deep inside of herself, she's prepared to endure violence—take the sex act itself . . . Every month, a woman begins her life anew. These cycles . . . nature helps her along. Many of the women who have done time in the camps are single. I have not met many couples where both the man and the woman did time. The secret of the camps doesn't bring people together, it cuts them off from one another. His friends from there called me "child" . . .

"Is it interesting listening to us?" Gleb would ask me after the guests left. "What kind of question is that?" I'd get offended. "Do you know what I'm afraid of? Back when this was interesting, we had gags in our mouths, but now that we can tell our whole story, it's like it's too late. Nobody wants to hear about it anymore. They don't want to read about it. People bring manuscripts about the camps to publishers and they're returned to them unread. 'Again with the Stalin and Beria? It's not a commercially viable project. The readers have had their fill.' "

. . . Dying wasn't new to him . . . He wasn't afraid of this little death . . . Criminal brigade leaders used to take away prisoners' bread and lose it at cards, and the prisoners would be forced to eat asphalt. Tarmac. A lot of people died that way—their stomachs would get glued shut. But he'd just stop eating and only drank.

. . . One boy tried to escape . . . He made a run for it on purpose so that they would shoot him. In the snow . . . in the sun . . . excellent visibility. They shot him in the head, dragged him back to camp with a rope, then put him up in front of the barracks—take a good look at him! They had him up there for a long time . . . until the spring.

. . . It was election day . . . There was a concert at the polling station. The camp choir performed. Political prisoners, Vlasovites, prostitutes, pickpockets, all of them singing about Stalin: "Stalin is our banner! Stalin is our joy!"

. . . At a transfer station, he met a girl. She told him what an investigator had once said to her while trying to talk her into signing a confession, "You'll end up in hell . . . But you're beautiful, some higher-up is sure to like you. That can be your salvation."

. . . Spring was especially terrifying. Nature is full of changes, everything coming to life . . . It's better never to ask anyone how much time they have left in their sentence. In spring, any sentence is an eternity. The birds are flying overhead, but no one lifts their eyes to admire them. In spring, prisoners don't look at the sky . . .

I looked back at him from the doorway, and he waved at me. When I returned a few hours later, he'd lost consciousness. He was begging someone, "Hold on. Hold on." But eventually, he stopped and just lay there. Three more days. I got used to that, too. There he is, lying there, and here I am, living. They brought in a bed for me and put it next to his. So, on the third day . . . It had gotten difficult to give him intravenous injections. He was getting blood clots . . . I had to give the doctors permission to stop treatment, it wouldn't hurt him, he wouldn't feel anything. And then he and I were left alone. No more machines, no more doctors, no one came in to check on us anymore. I lay down next to him. It was cold. I got under the blanket with him and fell asleep. When I woke up, for a moment I thought we were asleep at our house and that the balcony door had opened for some reason . . . like he just hadn't woken up yet . . . I was afraid of opening my eyes. When I did, I remembered exactly where we were. I started fussing over him . . . I got up, put my hand on his face: "Ahhh . . ." He heard me. The agony began . . . and I sat there. Holding his hand, I listened to his final heartbeat. Afterward, I sat with him like that for a long time . . . I called the nurse, and she helped me get his shirt on. It was light blue, his favorite color. I asked her, "Can I stay here?" "Sure, go ahead. You're not afraid?" What was there to be afraid of? I knew him like a mother knows her child. By morning, he was beautiful . . . The fear had evaporated from his face, the tension dissipated, all the frenzy of life had dispersed. And I noticed his subtle and elegant features. The face of an Oriental prince. So that's what he was like! That's what he was really like! I never knew that about him.

His one request: "Write that I was a happy man on my tombstone. That I was loved. The most terrible torment is not being loved." [*Silence.*] Our lives are so short . . . just a flash! I remember how in her old age, my mother would look out at the garden in the evenings . . . Her eyes . . .

[*We spend a long time sitting in silence.*]

I can't . . . I don't know how to live without him . . . Men have started pursuing me again. Bringing me flowers.

[*The next day, she calls me unexpectedly.*]

I cried all night long . . . wailed from the pain . . . All this time, I'd been escaping, fleeing, running from it. I'd barely made it out alive . . . and then, yesterday, I had to go back there again. You brought me back to that place . . . I'd been walking around all bandaged up and when I started removing the bandages, it turned out that nothing had healed. I thought I would have new skin under there, but there's nothing. No scar tissue. The pain hasn't gone anywhere . . . Everything is right where I left it . . . I'm afraid of handing it off to someone. No one can possibly handle it. It's too much for ordinary hands . . .

THE STORY OF A CHILDHOOD

Maria Voiteshonok, writer,
57 years old

I'm an *osadnik*. I was born to an exiled Polish *osadnik* officer ("osadnik" is Polish for "settler." They received land in the Eastern Borderlands* after the Polish-Soviet war of 1921). Then, in 1939, in accordance with a secret protocol in the Molotov-Ribbentrop Pact, Western Belarus became part of the USSR, and thousands of *osadnik* colonists and their families were resettled to Siberia for being "dangerous political elements" (as specified in a note from Beria to Stalin). But this is Big History. I have my own little history . . .

I don't know when my birthday is . . . or even what year I was

---

* The Eastern Borderlands refers to the territory covered by present-day Western Ukraine, Belarus, and Latvia, which were a part of Poland in the interwar years (1918–1939).

born . . . With me, everything is approximate. I never found any documents. I exist, but I don't. I don't remember anything, but I remember everything. I think my mother was pregnant with me when they were leaving. Why do I think that? Because train whistles always upset me . . . and the smell of railway sleepers . . . the way people cry at train stations. I can take a good brand-name train, but whenever a freight train goes by, I'm in tears. I can't handle seeing cattle cars, hearing the cries of the animals . . . that was the kind of train that took us away; I know although I wasn't born yet. Still, I was there. I don't see faces in my dreams or narratives . . . My dreams are all sounds and smells . . .

The Altai Krai. The town of Zmeinogorsk, on the banks of the Zmeyevka River . . . The exiles were unloaded outside of town. Next to the lake. We moved into the dirt. Into mud huts. I was born underground, and it's where I grew up. The soil has always smelled like home to me. Water's dripping from the ceiling—a clump of dirt falls down and bounces toward me. That's a frog. But I was little, I didn't know that you were supposed to be afraid of these things. I slept with two little goats on a warm spread of goat droppings . . . My first word was "b-a-a-a" . . . The first sound I made, instead of "ma" . . . or "mama." My older sister Vladya recalled how surprised I was when I learned that goats don't talk like we do. I was confused, I thought they were our equals. We shared a world, it seemed indivisible. I still don't feel the difference between us, the distinction between man and animal. I always talk to them . . . they understand me . . . and the beetles and spiders do, too. They were all around me . . . Such colorful beetles, it was as though they'd been painted. My toys. In spring, we'd go out into the sunshine together, crawling through the grass in search of food. Warming ourselves. In winter, we'd go dormant like the trees, hibernating from hunger. I had my own school, humans weren't my only teachers. I can hear the trees and the grass, too. For me, there's nothing more interesting than animals, they're truly fascinating. How can I cut myself off from that world, from those smells . . . ? I simply can't. Finally, the sun would come out! Summer! I'd go above ground . . . The beauty all around me was blinding, and no one had to cook anyone anything. On top of that, everything was singing, all the colors were out. I tasted every single little blade of grass, every leaf, each flower . . . every little root. One time, I ate so much henbane I nearly died. I remember entire tableaux . . . Bluebeard Mountain and the blue light spilling down it . . . That light . . . it was coming from the left, down the slope. Lighting the mountain from top to bottom . . . Those sights! I'm afraid that I don't have the talent to convey it all. Resurrect it. Words are only a supplement to our emotional states. Our feelings. Bright red poppies, turk's cap lilies, peonies . . . All of them spread out before me. Right under my feet. Or another image . . . I'm sitting next to a house. A sunspot is creeping down the wall . . . it's so many different colors . . . Constantly changing. I sat there for a long, long time. If it weren't for those colors, I would have probably died. I simply wouldn't have survived. I don't remember what we ate . . . If we had any kind of real food at all . . .

In the evenings, I would see the blackened people marching. Black clothes, black faces. They were exiles coming home from the mines . . . All of them looked exactly like my father. I don't know whether or not my father loved me. Did anyone love me?

I have very few memories . . . There aren't enough of them. I root around in the darkness trying to unearth anything I can. It doesn't happen very often . . . It's very rare that I will suddenly remember something that I didn't remember before. My memories are bitter, but they always make me happy. I'm terribly happy whenever a new one floats up.

I can't remember anything about the winter . . . In winter, I would never leave our mud hut. Day was the same as night. Nothing but twilight. Not a single spot of color . . . Did we own anything other than bowls and spoons? No clothes . . . For clothes, we would wrap ourselves in rags. Not a single spot of color. Shoes . . . What did we have by way of shoes? Galoshes, I remember galoshes . . . I had galoshes, too, they were big and old, like Mama's. They had probably been hers . . . I got my first coat in the orphanage, as well as my first pair of mittens. A little hat. I remember Vladya's face barely growing whiter in the darkness . . . She would lie there and cough for days on end, she'd gotten sick in the mines, tuberculosis. I already knew that word. Mama wouldn't cry . . . I don't remember Mama ever crying. She didn't talk very much, either, and eventually, she stopped talking altogether. When the coughing subsided, Vladya would call me over: "Repeat after me . . . This is Pushkin." I would recite: "The frost and sun, a gorgeous day! You're dreaming still, beautiful friend!" I tried to picture winter. How it had been for Pushkin.

I'm a slave of the word . . . I have an absolute belief in words. I always expect to hear the words I've been waiting for, even from strangers, even more so from strangers. With strangers, you can harbor hopes. I feel like I want to say something . . . and then I decide to . . . I'm ready. When I start telling someone, afterwards, I can't find anything in the place I've been describing. It's drained, the memories have fled. It instantly transforms into a hole. Afterwards, I have to wait a long time for the memories to come back to me. That's why I usually keep silent. I am refining everything within myself. The paths, the labyrinths, the burrows . . .

The scraps . . . Where had those bits of fabric come from? They were many different colors, a lot of them magenta. Someone had brought them to me and I sewed little people out of them. I would cut off pieces of my hair to make them hairdos. They were my friends . . . I'd never seen a doll, I didn't know a thing about them. By then, we lived in the town, but not in a house—we lived in a basement. With one little blacked-out window. We even had an address: 17 Stalin Street. Just like other people . . . like everyone else . . . We had an address now, too. I would play with a girl there . . . The girl lived in a real house, not a basement. She wore dresses and shoes while I was still in my mother's galoshes . . . I brought my scraps over to show her, they looked even prettier on the street than they had in the basement. The girl asked me for them, she wanted to trade me something, but I wouldn't do it for anything in the world! Her father came home. "Don't play with that pauper girl," he scolded her. I saw that they had cast me out. I had to make a quiet retreat, get out of there as soon as I could. Of course, these are the words of an adult, not children's thoughts. But the feeling . . . I remember the feeling . . . It's so painful, you don't even feel hurt or sorry for yourself, it's like you suddenly have a lot of freedom. But there's no self-pity . . . When there's still some self-pity left, it means that you haven't gone so far that you've left humanity behind. But once you have, you don't need people anymore, you're self-sufficient. I went too far . . . It's difficult to hurt my feelings. I hardly ever cry. I laugh at all the regular kinds of pain, women's problems . . . For me, it's all play-acting . . . in the play that is life. But whenever I hear a child crying . . . I can never walk past a poor person . . . I will never just walk past them. I remember that smell, the odor of tragedy . . . I pick up the wavelength, I'm still tuned in to those frequencies. That's the smell of my childhood. My diapers.

I remember walking with Vladya. We were carrying a down shawl . . . a beautiful object intended for some other world. She'd made it for a customer. Vladya knew how to knit, and that was the money we lived on. The woman paid us, and then she said, "Let me cut you a bouquet." A bouquet—for us? We're standing there, two beggar girls in some kind of respectable setting . . . Cold and hungry . . . And here she is giving us flowers! The only thing we ever thought about was bread, but this person saw that we were capable of thinking about other things as well. You're locked up, walled in by your circumstances, and suddenly, someone cracks the window . . . Lets in some fresh air. It turns out that besides bread, besides food, people were capable of giving us flowers! It meant that we really were no different than anyone else. We . . . were like everyone else . . . This broke the rules: "Let me cut you a bouquet." She wasn't going to pick them or gather them, she was going to cut them for us from her garden. From that moment on . . . maybe that was the key for me, it opened the door . . . My world turned upside down. I remember that bouquet . . . It was a big bouquet of cosmos . . . I always plant them at my dacha now. [*We're actually at her dacha. There's nothing but trees and flowers all around.*] I recently went to Siberia, to Zmeinogorsk. I went back . . . I looked for our street . . . our house, our basement . . . but the house was gone, it had been demolished. I asked everyone: "Do you remember us?" One old man remembered that yes, there was a beautiful girl who had lived in a basement there, she was sick. People remember beauty more than they remember suffering. The reason that woman had given us the bouquet was also because Vladya was beautiful.

I went to the cemetery . . . Near the gates, there was a guardhouse with boarded-up windows. I knocked for a long time. The guard came out, he was blind . . . What kind of omen was this? "Would you mind pointing out where they buried the exiles?" "Oh . . . over there . . ." and he waved his hand up and down. Some people led me out to the furthest corner . . . There was nothing but grass there . . . Nothing else left. That night I couldn't sleep, I felt like I was suffocating. I was having a spasm . . . It felt like someone was choking me . . . I ran away from the hotel and went to the station. I walked through the empty town. The station house was closed. I sat down on the tracks and waited for morning. A guy and a girl were sitting on the banks of the railway. Kissing. It finally got light out. The train came. An empty tram car . . . We got in: me and four men in leather jackets with shaved heads. They looked like convicts. They started offering me bread and pickles. "Wanna play some cards?" I wasn't afraid of them.

Not long ago, I was on the trolleybus and suddenly remembered . . . Vladya used to sing this song: "I went searching for my darling's grave / But her grave is hard to find . . ." Turns out that it also used to be Stalin's favorite song . . . he'd cry whenever he heard it. I immediately stopped liking it. Friends would come to see Vladya, they'd invite her out to dances. I remember all of that . . . I was already six or seven. I saw how instead of a waistband, they'd sew wires into their underwear. So that no one could rip them off. There were only exiles out there . . . convicts . . . There were a lot of murders. I knew about love already. There was a good-looking guy who would come to see Vladya when she was sick. She'd be lying there in rags, coughing. But the way he would look at her . . .

It's all very painful, but it's mine. I'm not running from my past . . . I can't say that I've accepted everything, that I'm grateful for the pain. There needs to be another word for how it makes me feel. I won't be able to find it right now. I know that when I'm in this state, I'm far away from everyone. Alone. I have to get a handle on the suffering, own it completely, find my way out of it, and also come back from it with something new. It's such a victory, it's the only meaningful thing to do. That way, you're not left empty-handed . . . Otherwise, why descend into hell?

Someone led me up to the window: "Watch, they're taking your father away . . ." A woman I didn't recognize was pulling something along on a sled. Someone or something . . . wrapped in a blanket and tied up with rope. Soon afterwards, my sister and I buried our mother. We were left all alone. Vladya could barely walk by then, her legs would give out. Her skin peeled off like paper. Someone brought her a bottle . . . I thought it was medicine, but it was actually some kind of acid. Poison. "Don't be scared . . ." She called me over and handed me the bottle. She wanted us to poison ourselves together. I took it and threw it into the stove. The glass shattered . . . The stove was cold, there hadn't been anything in there for a long time. Vladya burst into tears: "You're just like our father." Somebody found us . . . maybe her friends? Vladya was unconscious . . . They sent her to the hospital and me to the orphanage. My father . . . I want to remember him, but no matter how hard I try, I can't see his face. His face isn't anywhere in my memory. Later on, I saw what he looked like when he was young, my aunt showed me a photograph. It's true . . . I do look like him . . . That's our connection. My father married a beautiful peasant girl. From a poor family. He wanted to make a fancy lady out of her, but my mother always wore a kerchief pushed down low on her forehead.

She was no lady. In Siberia, my father didn't live with us for very long . . . He moved in with another woman. I had already been born . . . I was a punishment! A curse! No one had the strength to love me. My mother didn't have it, either. It's built into my cells: her despair, her pain . . . The lack of love . . . I can never get enough love, even when somebody loves me, I don't believe it, I need constant proof. Signs. I need them every day. Every minute. I'm hard to love, I know . . . [*She is silent for a long time.*] I love my memories . . . I love my memories because everyone is alive in them. I have everyone: my mother, my father, Vladya . . . I always need to sit at a long table. With a white tablecloth. I live alone, but I have a big table in my kitchen. Maybe they're all here with me . . . Sometimes I'll be walking along, and suddenly I'll imitate someone else's gesture. It's not mine . . . It's Vladya's, or Mama's . . . I'll think that our hands are touching . . .

When I was in the orphanage . . . In the orphanage, they kept *osadnik* orphans until the age of fourteen, then they would send them off to work in the mines. By the time they were eighteen, they'd all have tuberculosis . . . just like Vladya . . . That was our destiny. Vladya told me that somewhere far away, we had a home. But it was very far away. Aunt Marylya was still out there, our mother's sister . . . an illiterate peasant. She went around asking about us. Strangers wrote letters on her behalf. I still can't understand it . . . How? How did she do it? A notice came to the orphanage to send me and my sister to such and such an address. To Belarus. The first time, we didn't make it all the way back to Minsk, they took us off the train in Moscow. Everything happened for a second time: Vladya had a fever and ended up in the hospital; I was quarantined. After the quarantine, I was transferred to a temporary foster care center, which was in a basement that smelled like chlorine. Strangers . . . I'm always living among strangers . . . My whole life. But my aunt kept writing . . . and writing . . . Six months later, she found me again in the foster care center. Again, I heard the words "home" and "aunt." They took me to the train . . . A dark train car, with only the corridor lit. Full of people's shadows. There was a teacher escorting me. We got to Minsk and bought a ticket to Postavy . . . I knew the names of all those towns. Vladya had entreated me: "Remember them. Remember that our estate is called Sovchino." From Postavy we walked to Gridki . . . my aunt's village . . . We sat down by the bridge to rest. A neighbor biked by on his way home from the night shift. He asked who we were. We said that we'd come to see

Aunt Marylya. "Yes," he said, "you're going the right way." And then he must have told my aunt that he'd seen us . . . because she came running toward us . . . I saw her and said, "That lady looks like my mother." And that was it.

I had a shaved head, I sat on the long bench at Uncle Stakha's house, my mother's brother. The door was open, and through the doorway, I watched the people keep coming and coming . . . stopping there just to stare at me, speechless . . . It was completely unreal! No one spoke. They just stood there staring and weeping. In total silence. The whole village came . . . and they covered my tears with their tears, everyone wept with me. All of them had known my father, some of them had even worked for him. Oftentimes afterward I would hear: "At the collective farm, all we get are tally marks, but Antek (my father) would always pay us." Here it was, my legacy. They'd moved our house from our farmstead to the central collective farm, it's still the village council building. I know everything about those people, in fact, I know more than I would like to. The same day the Red Army soldiers loaded our family into a cart and drove us off to the station, these same people . . . Azhbeta, Yuzefa, Matei . . . had gone to our house and taken everything they could carry. Dismantled the outbuildings. Down to the very last planks. Dug up the new garden. The apple saplings. My aunt ran over . . . All she managed to grab was a planter to remember us by . . . I don't want to think about these things, I chase them out of my memory. I remember how the whole village nannied me, everyone carried me around in their arms. "Come see us, Manechka, we picked some mushrooms . . ." "Let me pour you some milk, sweetie . . ." The very next day after I arrived, my face broke out in hives. My eyes were burning. I couldn't even open them. They would lead me by the hand to wash my face. Everything inside of me was sick. It all started dying off, burning off, so that I could look at the world with new eyes. It was my transition from that life to this one . . . Now, when I walked down the street, everyone would stop me: "Oh what a beautiful girl! Ah, what a girl!" Without those words, my eyes would have been like a dog's who'd been dragged out of a hole in the ice. I can't imagine how I would have looked at people . . .

My aunt and uncle lived in a storage shed. Their house had burned down in the war, so they'd built themselves a shed to live in, thinking that it would be temporary, but it ended up staying there for good. It had a thatched roof and a little window. *"Bulbochka"* growing in a

corner (my aunt's words)—not *"bulba"* but *"bulbochka"**—and a
piglet squealing in another. No floorboards, just dirt covered in sweet
flag and straw. Soon, Vladya was brought there, too. She lived for a
little while longer and then she died. She was glad that she got to die
at home. Her last words were, "What's going to happen to Manechka?"

Everything I know about love I learned in my aunt's storage
shed . . .

"Oh my little birdie . . ." my aunt would coo. "My buzzy . . . my
little bee . . ." I was always pawing her, bugging her. I couldn't believe
it . . . Somebody loved me! I was loved! You're growing, and someone
is appreciating your beauty—what a luxury! All of your little bones
straighten out, your every muscle. I danced the Russian dance, the
yablochko, and the sailor's dance for her. I'd been taught those dances
in exile . . . I sang her songs:

There's a road off the Chuya highway.
Many drivers will go down that way . . .

I'll die and they'll bury me here,
My mother will weep bitter tears,
Though my wife may find another man,
For Mama, there'll be no other son . . .

In the course of a day, you can run around until your feet turn black
and blue. We didn't have any shoes. You go to bed, and your aunt
wraps your feet in the hem of her nightgown to warm them. She'd
swaddle me. You can lie there somewhere near her stomach . . . It's like
being in the womb . . . And that's why I don't remember anything evil.
I've forgotten it all . . . It's hidden away in some distant place. In the
morning, I would be woken up by my aunt's voice: "I made potato
pancakes. Have some." "Auntie, I want to sleep more." "Eat some and
then you can go back to sleep." She understood that food, *bliny,* were
like medicine to me. Pancakes and love. My uncle Vitalik was a shepherd, he carried a whip over his shoulder and had a long birch-bark
pipe. He went around in his military jacket and breeches. He'd bring
us "feed" from the pasture—there'd be some cheese and a piece of
salo—whatever the women gave him while the animals grazed. Holy

---

* "Bulba" is Belarusian (and Ukrainian) for potato. "Bulbochka" is the diminutive.

poverty! It didn't mean anything to them, they weren't upset or in-sulted by it. All of this is so important to me . . . so precious. One of my friends complains, "I can't afford a new car . . ." another, "I dreamt of it my whole life, but I never did manage to buy myself a mink coat . . ." When people say those kinds of things to me, it's like they're speaking from behind glass . . . The only thing I regret is not being able to wear short skirts anymore . . . [*We laugh.*]

My aunt had a unique voice . . . She warbled like Edith Piaf. People would ask her to sing at their weddings. And whenever anyone died. I would always come with her . . . Running alongside her. I remem-ber . . . she would stand near the coffin, stand there for a long time . . . Then, at a certain point, she would somehow break off from everyone else and go up to the body. She'd approach slowly . . . after she realized that no one else could say the final words. Everyone wanted to, but they didn't know how. And so she'd begin: "Why have you left us, An-nechka . . . You left the bright day and dark night behind . . . Who is going to walk around your yard . . . and kiss your children? Who will greet the cow when she's comes home in the evening?" Very quietly, she'd find the words . . . Everything was mundane and simple, and that's what made it truly lofty. And sad. There was some sort of ulti-mate truth in those simple words. Something final. Her voice would tremble . . . and then everyone else would start weeping. They'd forget that the cow hadn't been milked, that their husband was drunk at home. Their faces changed, they'd stop fidgeting, and light would shine through their eyes. Everyone wept. I was shy . . . And I felt sorry for my aunt. She'd come home feeling ill: "Oh, Manechka, my little head is pounding." That was the kind of heart my aunt had . . . I'd run home from school and see her through the little window holding a needle the size of her finger, darning our rags and singing, "You can put out a fire with water / But nothing will extinguish love . . ." My whole life is lighted by these memories . . .

The remains of our estate . . . all that was left of our house were the stones. But I can feel their warmth, I'm drawn to them. I go there like you visit a grave. I could spend the night in our field. I walk care-fully, watching my step. There are no people, but there is life. The hum of life, all sorts of living beings . . . I walk around afraid of destroying someone's home. I can make a home for myself anywhere, like a bug. I have a cult of domesticity. I need there to be flowers, it needs to be beautiful . . . I remember in the orphanage, when they led me to the room where I was going to live with all the white beds . . . I scanned the room looking to see if there was a bed by the window. Would I have my own cabinet? I was searching for my home.

Now . . . How long have we been sitting here talking? Meanwhile, a storm has come and gone, my neighbor stopped by, the phone rang . . . Those things also affected me, I responded to them as well. But the only things that will go down on paper are my words . . . There won't be anything else: no neighbor, no phone calls . . . Things I didn't say but which flashed through my memory, making their presence felt. Tomorrow, I might tell this story completely differently. The words remain, but I'll have moved on. I have learned to live with this. I know how. I keep going and going.

Who gave me all of this? All of it . . . Was it God or people? If God gave it to me, then He chose well. Suffering brought me up . . . It's my art . . . my prayer. So many times, I've wanted to tell someone all of it. To speak my fill. But no one has ever wanted to know: "And then what . . . and then what?" I've always waited for someone, whether it be a good or bad person, to come and listen to my story—I don't know who exactly I had in mind, but I was always waiting for someone. My whole life, I've been waiting for someone to find me and I would tell them everything . . . and they would keep asking, "And then what? And then what?" Now, people have started blaming socialism, Stalin, as though Stalin had God-like powers. Everyone has their own God—why didn't they speak up? My aunt . . . Our village . . . I also remember Maria Petrovna Aristova, a respected teacher who'd visit our Vladya in the hospital in Moscow. We weren't related to her or anything . . . She's the one who brought Vladya back to our village, who carried her home . . . Vladya couldn't walk anymore. Maria Petrovna would send me pencils and candy and write me letters. And in the temporary foster center, when they were washing and disinfecting me . . . I was sitting on a high bench . . . all covered in foam. I could have slipped and broken my bones on the cement floor. I started slipping . . . sliding down . . . and a woman I didn't know . . . a nanny . . . caught me in her arms and embraced me: "My little chickadee."

I saw God.

ON A TIME WHEN
ANYONE WHO KILLS BELIEVES THAT
THEY ARE SERVING GOD

◆

Olga V., surveyor, 24

It was morning. I was on my knees, begging, "Oh Lord! I'm ready now! I want to die right now!" Even though it was morning . . . and the day was just beginning . . .

Such a powerful desire . . . to die! So I went down to the sea. Sat down on the sand. Tried to talk myself into believing that there was no need to fear death. Death is freedom . . . the waves kept crashing and crashing against the shore. Then night came, and then it was morning again. The first time, I couldn't decide. I wandered along the shore, listening to the sound of my voice: "God, I love you! Oh Lord . . ." "*Sara bara bzia bzoi* . . ." That's Abkhazian. So many colors all around me, so many sounds, but there I was, ready to die.

I'm Russian. I was born in Abkhazia and lived there for a long time. In Sukhumi. Until I was twenty-two. Until 1992, when the war broke out. If the water catches fire, how do you put it out? That's what Abkhazians say about war . . . Everyone took the bus together, went to the same schools, read the same books, lived in the same country, and all learned the same language, Russian. Then suddenly they were all killing each other: Neighbor killing neighbor, classmate killing classmate. Brother killing sister! And they were warring right there, right in front of their own homes . . . How long ago had it been? Only a year before that, two . . . We'd been living like brothers, everyone was in the Komsomol and a communist. In my papers for school, I'd write, "Brothers forever . . ." "Unbreakable union . . ." Killing someone! It's not heroic, it's more than a crime . . . It's too awful! I saw it—it's impossible to comprehend—I still can't make sense of it. I'll tell you about Abkhazia, I truly loved it there . . . [*She stops.*] And I still do, no matter what . . . I love it. In every Abkhazian home, there's a dagger hanging on the wall. When a boy is born, relatives give him a dagger and some gold. Next to their daggers, they hang their drinking horns. Abkhazians drink wine out of horns like they're glasses. You can't put your horn down until you've drunk everything in it, down to the last drop. According to Abkhazian custom, the time you spend with guests around the table doesn't count toward your lifespan because you're drinking wine and enjoying yourself. So how does the time you spend murdering count? Shooting people . . . Well, how? I spend a lot of time thinking about death now.

[*She lowers her voice to a whisper.*] The second time . . . there was no stopping me. I locked myself in the bathroom . . . I practically scratched my fingernails off, down to bloody nubs. I kept scratching, digging my nails into the wall, into the clay, into the chalk, but at the last moment, I suddenly wanted to live again. And the cord snapped . . . In the end, I'm alive, I can pinch myself. The only thing is, I can't stop thinking about it . . . about death.

When I was sixteen, my father died. Ever since, I've hated funerals . . . that music . . . I don't understand, why do people put on such a show? I sat next to the coffin and even then, I knew that this wasn't my father, that my father wasn't there. It was just a cold body. A shell. The first nine days, I kept having the same dream . . . Someone was calling to me . . . calling me to come . . . but I didn't understand: Where was I supposed to go? To whom? I started thinking about my relatives . . . I'd never even met a lot of them, never knew them, most of them had died before I was even born. But suddenly I saw my grandmother. My grandmother died a long, long time ago, we don't even have any pictures of her left, but I recognized her in my dream. Everything is different where they are . . . They exist but they don't exist, they're not covered by anything like we are by our bodies. They have nothing to protect them. I saw my father. He was still cheerful, earthly, completely familiar. All of the other people were kind of . . . kind of . . . Like I had known them but forgotten. Death is a beginning . . . the beginning of something . . . We just don't know what. I keep thinking about it. I want to break out of this captivity, I want to hide. And it wasn't even that long ago when I would dance in the morning in front of the mirror, thinking "I'm young and beautiful! I'm going to have fun! I'm going to love!"

The first one . . . He was this really good-looking Russian guy . . . really very handsome! As the Abkhazians would say, "A man for his seeds." He had a little dirt sprinkled on him, he was wearing sneakers and an army uniform. The next day, someone had taken his sneakers. He was lying there dead . . . and then, and then what? What happens underground? Under our feet, beneath our soles . . . down there or up in the sky . . . What happens up there in the sky? It was summer all around, and the waves were crashing. The cicadas were singing. My mother had sent me out to the store. And there he lay, killed. Trucks full of weapons rolled through the streets, people handing out machine guns like they were loaves of bread. I saw refugees, someone pointed them out to me and told me that these were refugees, which made me remember that long-forgotten word. I'd only ever read it in books. There were a lot of refugees: Some came in cars, others on tractors, some on foot. [*Silence.*] Can we talk about something else? Like about movies . . . I love movies, but I prefer ones from the West. Why? Because nothing in them resembles our lives, not in the least. Which means I can make up whatever I want . . . dream up an entire world, put on another face when I'm sick of my own. My body, even my hands . . . My body's not enough for me, I'm too restricted by all this. I keep having the same body, always the same one, while inside, I'm constantly changing; I keep being different . . . I'm listening to my words and thinking that I can't be saying these things because I don't know these words and I'm dumb and only like buttered rolls . . . Because I haven't loved yet. Haven't had kids. And yet I'm saying these things . . . I don't know why I'm saying all this. Where did it come from? The next one was a young Georgian . . . He was lying in the park. There was a spot with a little sandy area, and he was lying on the sand. He just lay there looking up . . . and no one moved him, he stayed there for a long time. When I saw him, I knew that I had to run . . . I had to get out of there. But where could I run to? I made a run for the church . . . There was nobody there. I got down on my knees and prayed for everyone. Back then, I didn't know how to pray, I hadn't learned how to talk to Him yet . . . [*She digs around in her purse.*] Where are my pills . . . I can't! I'm not supposed to get upset . . . After all that, I got sick. They took me to the psychiatrist. I'd be walking down the street . . . and suddenly I'd want to scream . . .

Where would I like to live? Inside my childhood . . . Back then, it was just me and my mother in our little nest. Save us . . . Lord, save the trusting and blind! In school, I loved books about war. And movies

about it. I imagined that it was a beautiful thing. That it made everything vivid . . . That life during a wartime was something brilliant. I
was even sad that I was a girl and not a boy: If there was ever a war,
they wouldn't let me fight. I don't read books about war anymore.
Even the best ones . . . Books about war are all full of lies. War is filthy
and terrifying. I'm not sure anymore, is it even possible to write about
it? I'm not talking about trying to capture the whole truth, I mean
writing anything about it at all? Talking about it . . . How can you
ever be happy afterward? I don't know, I'm lost. My mother would put
her arms around me: "What are you reading, daughter?" "*They Fought
for the Motherland,* by Sholokhov. It's about war . . ." "Why do you
read those books? They're not about life, daughter. Life is something
else . . ." Mama loved books about love . . . My mother! I don't even
know if she's alive. [*Silence.*] At first, I thought that I couldn't live
there anymore . . . in Sukhumi . . . But it turns out that I can't live
anymore at all. And books about love won't save me. Although love
does exist, I know it does. I know . . . [*For the first time, she smiles.*]

It was the spring of 1992 . . . Our neighbors Vakhtang and
Gunala—he's Georgian and she's Abkhazian—sold their home and
their furniture and got ready to leave. They came to say goodbye.
"There's going to be a war. Go to Russia if you have anyone there." We
didn't believe them. The Georgians were always making fun of the
Abkhazians, and the Abkhazians didn't like the Georgians, either.
Oh . . . the jokes! [*She laughs.*] "Can a Georgian go into space?" "No."
"Why not?" "Because all the Georgians would die of pride, and the
Abkhazians would die of envy." "Why are Georgians so short?" "It's
not that the Georgians are short, it's that the Abkhazians' mountains
are too tall." They laughed at each other, but they lived side by side.
They tended their vineyards. Made wine . . . For Abkhazians, wine-
making is like a religion. Every winemaker has his own secret. May
went by, then June . . . the beach season began . . . the first berries . . .
What war? My mother and I didn't think about the war, we were busy
pickling, making jam. Every Saturday, we went to the bazaar. The Abkhazian bazaar! Those smells, the sounds . . . It smells like wine barrels and cornbread, sheep's cheese, and roasted chestnuts. The subtle
scent of cherry plums and tobacco—pressed tobacco leaves. Cheeses
hanging . . . *matsoni,* my favorite yogurt . . . Vendors beckon custom-
ers in Abkhazian, Georgian, and Russian—in every language, it's
"*Vai-vai,* sweetie. You don't want it, don't buy it, but come here and
try it." There hadn't been bread anywhere in the city since June. That

Saturday, my mother decided to stock up on flour . . . We were on the bus, a friend of ours sat down next to us with her son. At first, he was playing, but then he burst into tears and started crying so loudly, it was as though someone had frightened him. Suddenly, the woman turned to us: "Were those gunshots? Can you hear that? Are those gunshots?" What a crazy question! When we got to the bazaar, we saw a mob of people running toward us, all panicked. Chicken feathers flying, rabbits underfoot, ducks . . . No one ever remembers the animals . . . how they suffer . . . but I remember a wounded cat. A cockerel squawking in pain, he had a shard of something sticking out from under his wing . . . I really am crazy, huh? I think about death too much, it's all I ever do these days . . . And suddenly, the screaming! That screaming . . . Not just one person screaming, but a whole mob of people, and all of them screaming. Armed men, in civilian clothes but holding machine guns, chasing down women, snatching their handbags, taking whatever they had: "Give me that . . . Take those off . . ." "Are those convicts?" my mother whispered to me. We got off the bus and saw Russian soldiers. "What's going on?" my mother asked them. "Don't you understand?" a lieutenant answered. "This is war." My mother is a big coward, she fainted. I dragged her into the inner courtyard of the nearest building. Someone from one of the apartments brought down a pitcher of water. They were bombing somewhere nearby . . . The sound of explosions . . . "Women! Women! Do you need any flour?" This young guy appeared out of nowhere holding a sack of flour, wearing a blue smock like freight loaders wore, only he was all white, covered in flour. I burst out laughing, but my mother said, "Let's get some. Maybe this really is a war." So we bought some flour from him. Gave him our money. Afterward, it dawned on us that we'd just bought stolen goods. From a looter.

I lived among those people . . . I knew their habits, their language . . . I loved them. But where had these other ones come from? So fast! So inhumanly fast! Where had all of this been lying dormant? Where . . . who will answer these questions? I took off my gold cross and hid it in the flour, where I also hid the wallet with the money. Like an old woman . . . I knew exactly what to do. How? I carried the ten kilograms of flour all the way home, like five kilometers. I walked calmly . . . If someone had killed me right then, I wouldn't have had time to get scared. But the people I saw . . . many of them were running from the direction of the beach . . . Tourists . . . Panicked and in tears. While I was calm . . . Probably I was in shock? It would have been better if I had been screaming . . . screaming like everyone else . . . That's what I think now. We stopped to take a break by some railway tracks. There were these young men sitting on the rails: Some of them had black ribbons tied around their heads, others had white ones. All of them had guns. They even teased me, cracked jokes. Not far from them, smoke was rising up from the hood of a truck . . . The driver was behind the wheel, murdered. In a white shirt . . . When we caught sight of him, we took off running through a mandarin grove. I was all covered in flour . . . "Put that down! Leave it!" my mother begged me. "No, Mama, I can't. War has broken out and there's nothing to eat at home." All of these images . . . A Zhiguli came toward us. We tried flagging it down. The car went past us so slowly, it was like it was part of a funeral procession. There was a guy and a girl in the front seat and a woman's corpse in the back. Terrifying . . . but for some reason, not as terrifying as I had imagined it would be . . . [*She is silent.*] I want to think about this all the time. Think and think. Right by the sea, there was another Zhiguli, its windshield shattered . . . a puddle of blood and women's shoes on the ground next to it . . . [*She is quiet.*] I'm sick, of course . . . sick . . . Why can't I forget anything? [*A silence.*] I wanted to hurry! Hurry up and get home, get to some familiar place. Run somewhere . . . flee. And suddenly, this booming . . . war from above! Green military helicopters—and on the ground, tanks. They weren't moving in a column—they came one by one, with soldiers holding machine guns sitting on top of them. Georgian flags unfurled in the wind. The column advanced chaotically: Some tanks moved quickly, while others were stopping at kiosks. The soldiers would hop down and break the locks off with their gun butts. They took champagne, candy, soda, cigarettes. Behind the tanks, there was an Ikarus bus full of chairs and mattresses. What were the chairs for?

At home, we rushed to the TV . . . They were broadcasting a symphony concert. Where's the war? The war was not being televised . . . Before going to the market, I'd prepared cucumbers and tomatoes for pickling. I'd sterilized the jars. And when we got home, I started filling them. I needed something to do to keep myself busy. In the evening, we watched the Mexican soap opera *The Rich Cry, Too*. It's about love.

Morning. We woke up extremely early from the rumbling. Military machines were moving down our street. People had come out to watch. One of the vehicles came to a halt in front of our house. The crew was Russian. I understood what they were: mercenaries. They called out to my mother: "Give us water, Mama." My mother brought them water and some apples. They drank the water but wouldn't touch the apples. They said, "Somebody poisoned one of our men with apples yesterday." I ran into a girl I knew on the street: "How are you? Where's your family?" She walked right past me as though she didn't know me. I ran after her and grabbed her by the shoulders: "What's wrong with you?" "Don't you understand? It's dangerous to speak to me because of my husband—my husband is a Georgian." But I . . . I had never thought about whether her husband was an Abkhazian or a Georgian! What did I care? He was an excellent friend. I hugged her as hard as I could! That night, her brother had showed up at her house in order to kill her husband. "Then you can kill me, too," she'd told him. Her brother and I had gone to the same school. We were friends. I wondered what I would do if I saw him. What would we say to one another?

A few days later, our whole street buried Akhrik . . . Akhrik was an Abkhazian boy I knew. He was nineteen. He'd gone to see his girlfriend one evening and gotten stabbed in the back. His mother walked behind his coffin. One moment she'd be weeping, the next, she was laughing. She'd lost her mind. Only a month ago, we'd all been Soviet, now we were a Georgian, an Abkhazian . . . an Abkhazian, a Georgian . . . a Russian . . .

Another guy I knew lived on the next street over . . . I knew him by sight; I didn't know his name, just his face. We'd say hi to each other. By all appearances, a normal guy. Tall, good-looking. He killed his old teacher, a Georgian. Killed him for teaching him Georgian in school. He'd given him bad grades. How could he do that? Can you understand it? In Soviet school, everyone was taught that all men are friends . . . friends, comrades, and brothers. When my mother heard about it, her eyes got very small, and then they got huge . . . Dear Lord, protect the trusting and blind! I spend hours on my knees in church, praying. It's quiet there . . . although it's always full of people now, all praying for the same thing . . . [*Silence.*] Do you think you'll be able to? Are you hoping that it's possible to write about this? You are, aren't you? Well, go ahead and hope . . . I don't have any hope.

I would wake up in the middle of the night, call out to my mother . . . My mother would be lying there with her eyes open, too. "I was never as happy as I was in my old age. And then, all of a sudden, we're in the middle of a war." Men are always talking about war, they like weapons—young and old alike . . . while women like to remember love stories. Old women tell stories of how they were young and beautiful. Women never talk about war . . . They just pray for their men. My mother would go see the neighbors and every time, she'd come home petrified. "They burned a stadium full of Georgians in Gagra." "Mama!" "I also heard that the Georgians have been castrating Abkhazians." "Mama!" "They bombed the monkey house . . . Then, one night, the Georgians were chasing someone thinking it was an Abkhazian. They wounded him and heard him scream. Then the Abkhazians stumbled upon him and thought it was a Georgian. So they started chasing him and shot at him. Finally, when it started getting light out, they realized that all along, it had been a wounded monkey. So then all of them—the Georgians and the Abkhazians—declared a ceasefire and rushed over to save it. If it had been a human, they would have killed him . . ." There was nothing I could say to her. I prayed for everyone. I turned to God: "They walk around like zombies, convinced that they're doing good. But is it possible to do good with a machine gun and a knife? They go into people's homes and if they don't find anyone, they'll shoot the livestock or the furniture. You'll go into town and see a cow lying in the middle of the street with her udders full of bullet holes . . . shot-up jars of jam . . . They can't stop shooting. Make them see reason!" [*She is silent.*] The TV broke, we only got sound, no picture . . . Moscow was somewhere very far away.

I would go to church and talk there . . . I'd talk and talk . . . Whenever I saw anyone in the street, I'd stop them and talk to them. Eventually, I started talking to myself. My mother would be sitting next to me, listening, and suddenly I'd realize she was asleep. She'd get so tired, she'd fall asleep on her feet. She'd be washing the apricots and fall asleep. While I was all wound up, talking and talking, about what I heard from other people and what I'd seen myself . . . How a Georgian, a young Georgian, threw down his machine gun and started screaming, "What have we come to? I came here to die for my Motherland! Not to steal other people's refrigerators! Why are you going into strangers' homes and stealing their refrigerators? I came here to die for Georgia . . ." They led him away, stroking his head. Another Georgian stood up straight and walked toward the people shooting at him: "Abkhazian brothers! I don't want to kill you, don't shoot me." He was shot from behind by his own comrades. And then . . . I don't know whether it was a Russian or a Georgian, but he jumped under a military vehicle with a hand grenade. Shouting something. No one could make out what he was trying to say. The vehicle was full of burning Abkhazians . . . They were screaming, too. [*She is silent.*] Mama, Mama . . . My mother covered every windowsill in our house with flowers. She did everything in her power to try to save me. She'd tell me, "Look at the flowers, darling! Look at the sea!" My mother is very special, she has an exceptional heart . . . She'd confess to me, "I wake up so early, the sun is just coming through the leaves, and I think to myself, 'If I go look in the mirror right now, how old will I be?'" She suffered from insomnia, her feet hurt, she'd worked at a cement plant for thirty years, but in the morning, she wouldn't remember how old she was. She'd get up, brush her teeth, look at herself in the mirror and see an old woman staring back . . . Then she'd make breakfast and forget. I would always hear her singing . . . [*She smiles.*] My mother . . . my sweet friend . . . The other day, I had a dream about leaving my body . . . I rose way up into the sky . . . it felt so good.

I can't remember what came earlier and what happened later. I don't remember . . . at first, the looters wore masks. They'd pull black stockings over their faces. But pretty soon, they stopped bothering. You'd see one walking by, holding a crystal vase in one hand, a machine gun in the other, and a rug draped over his back. They took TVs, washing machines . . . women's furs, dishware . . . Nothing was sacred, they'd pick through children's toys in bombed-out houses . . . [*She lowers her voice to a whisper.*] Now, when I see a regular knife at the store, a normal kitchen knife, it makes my skin crawl . . . I never used to think about death. I went to school, then medical college. I'd study and get crushes. I'd wake up in the middle of the night and lie in bed dreaming. When was that? It seems so long ago . . . I don't remember anything from that life anymore. I remember other things . . . how they cut off a boy's ears so that he wouldn't listen to Abkhazian songs. They cut off this other guy's you know what . . . so that his wife wouldn't have his kids. There are nuclear missiles out there, airplanes and tanks, but people still get stabbed with knives. They run pitchforks through them, chop them up with axes . . . It would have been better if I had lost my mind . . . at least I wouldn't remember anything. A girl on our street hanged herself . . . She was in love with this guy, and he'd married somebody else. They buried her in a white dress. No one could believe it: How could she die for love at a time like this? Maybe if she had been raped . . . I remember my mother's friend Sonya. One night, they butchered her neighbors . . . a Georgian family she'd been close to. And their two little kids. Sonya would spend all day in bed with her eyes closed, refusing to go outside. "My girl, why go on living?" she'd ask me. I spoon-fed her soup; she couldn't swallow anything.

In school, they had taught us to love armed men . . . Defenders of the Motherland! But these, they weren't like that . . . and it wasn't that kind of war. They were all just boys, boys with machine guns. When they're alive they're terrifying, and when they're lying there dead, they're helpless—you feel sorry for them. How did I survive? I . . . I . . . I like thinking about my mother. How in the evenings, she would spend a long time brushing her hair . . . "One day," she promised, "I'll tell you about love. But I'll tell you the story as though it happened to another woman and not me." She and my father had really loved one another. It was true love. My mother had been married to another man before him. Then, one day, while she was ironing his shirts and he was eating dinner—and this could have only happened to my mother— she suddenly declared, "I'm not going to have your children." So she got her things and left. Some time later on, my father appeared . . . He'd tag along behind her, waiting for hours for her outside her house, getting frostbite on his ears in the winter. He'd just walk beside her, admiring her. And then, one day, he kissed her . . .

My father died on the eve of the war . . . it was heart failure. One evening, he sat down in front of the television and died. As if he just stepped out . . . "So, little girl, when you grow up," my father had big plans for me. And—and—and . . . [*She bursts into tears.*] Then it was just me and my mother. My mother, who is afraid of a mouse, who can't sleep if she's home alone. She would cover her head with a pillow to block out the war . . . We sold all of our valuables: the TV, my father's gold cigarette case—a sacred item, we held onto it for a long time—my gold cross. We'd decided to leave, but in order to leave Sukhumi, you had to bribe the officials. The military and the police both needed to be paid off, which meant you needed a lot of cash! The trains had stopped running. The last ships had left long ago, with refugees packed onto their holds and decks like sardines. We ended up only having enough money for one ticket . . . one one-way ticket to Moscow. I didn't want to leave without my mother. For a month, she begged, "Go, my little girl. Go!" But I wanted to go to the hospital, take care of the wounded . . . [*Silence.*] They didn't let me take anything on the plane except for my purse with my papers in it. No clothes, not even the pies my mother had baked. "You have to understand, we're operating under wartime conditions." The man going through customs next to me was dressed in civilian clothes, but the soldiers all addressed him as "Comrade Major" and loaded his suit-cases for him, these big cardboard boxes. They loaded his cases of wine and mandarins onto the airplane themselves. I cried . . . In fact, I cried the whole way there. A woman with two little boys comforted me—one was her son, and the other one was her neighbor's. Both of the boys were bloated from hunger. I didn't want to go . . . I didn't want to leave, not for anything . . . My mother tore me away from her, pushed me onto the plane. "Mama, where am I going?" "You're going home. To Russia."

Moscow! Moscow . . . I spent my first two weeks in Russia living at the railway station. People like me . . . there were thousands of us at all of the train stations in Moscow—Belorussky station, Savelovsky, Kievsky. Whole families, with children and old people. From Armenia, Tajikistan, Baku . . . living on the benches and on the floor. Cooking their food there. Washing their clothes. There are outlets in the bath-rooms, and next to the escalators . . . You pour some water into a basin, stick in an electric heating wand, throw in some noodles, a little meat—soup's ready! Porridge for the kids! I think that all of the rail-ways stations in Moscow must have reeked of canned food and *khar-cho* soup. Pilaf. Children's urine and dirty diapers. People would dry them on the radiators, on the windows. "Mama, where am I going?" "You're going home. To Russia." So there I was, at home. No one had been expecting us. No one came to meet us. Nobody paid any atten-tion to us at all, nobody asked any questions. Today, all of Moscow is nothing but one great big railway station. A caravanserai. My money ran out very fast. Twice, men tried to rape me: The first time it was a soldier and the second time, a policeman. The policeman pulled me up off the floor in the middle of the night. "Where are your docu-ments?" He started dragging me to the police room. His eyes were crazed . . . I screamed my head off! Apparently, that scared him . . . he ran off shouting, "You little idiot!" During the day, I would wander the city . . . I stood on Red Square . . . In the evenings, I'd roam the gro-cery stores. I was always hungry; one time, a woman bought me a meat pie. I didn't ask her to . . . She had been eating and she saw me watching her eat. She took pity on me. Just that one time . . . but I will remember that "one time" for the rest of my life. She was an old, old woman. Poor. I was willing to go anywhere, do anything rather than sit at the station . . . sit there thinking about food and my mother. Two weeks went by like that. [*She cries.*] At the train station, you could oc-casionally find a piece of bread in the trash, a gnawed chicken bone . . .

That's how I lived until one day my father's sister showed up. We hadn't had any contact with her for a long time—was she dead or alive? She's eighty. All I had was her phone number. I called every day, and no one ever answered. It turned out that she'd been in the hospital. I'd been positive that she was dead.

It was a miracle! I had been waiting for it and then it happened. My aunt came to get me: "Olga! Your aunt from Voronezh is waiting for you in the police room." Everything suddenly went into motion, everyone was abuzz . . . The whole station wanted to know: Who had come? Who was getting picked up? What last name? Two of us ran over to see: There was another girl with the same last name but a different first name. She'd come from Dushanbe. She cried so hard when she found out it wasn't her aunt . . . That she wasn't the one being taken home . . .

Now I live in Voronezh . . . I work odd jobs, wherever they'll hire me—I've been a dishwasher at a restaurant, a security guard at a construction site, I sold fruit for this Azerbaijani until he started hitting on me. Right now, I'm a surveyor. It's a temporary position, of course, which is too bad—it's interesting work. My diploma from the medical college was stolen at the railway station in Moscow. Along with all of my mother's photos. My aunt and I go to church together. I kneel and beg: "Oh Lord! I'm ready now—please take me! I want to die right now!" Every time I go, I ask Him: Is my mother dead or alive?

Thank you . . . Thank you for not being afraid of me. For not turning away like the others. For listening. I don't have any girlfriends here, no boys pursuing me. I talk and talk . . . About how they lay there, so young and handsome . . . [*She has a crazy smile.*] Their eyes open . . . with their eyes wide open . . .

Six months later, I got a letter from her: "I'm joining a monastery. I want to live. I will pray for everyone."

ON THE LITTLE RED FLAG AND
THE SMILE OF THE AXE

◆

Anna M., architect,
59 years old

But, but . . . I . . . I can't go on like this anymore. The last thing I remember was a scream. Whose? I don't know. Was it mine? Or was it
the neighbor screaming? She had smelled gas in the stairwell. Called
the police. [*She stands up and walks over to the window.*] It's autumn.
The leaves were just recently yellow . . . Now they're black from all the
rain. Even during the day, the light seems very far away. It's dark already in the morning. I turn on all the lamps and keep them on all day
long. I can never get enough light . . . [*She returns and sits down across
from me.*]

First, I dreamed that I'd died. I saw a lot of people die when I was
little, but later on I forgot about it all . . . [*She wipes her tears.*] I don't
understand why I'm crying. I already know everything, I know everything about my own life . . . I dreamt that a whole lot of birds were
circling over me. Beating their wings against the window. When I woke
up, it felt like someone was standing right by my head. That someone
had stayed. I wanted to turn to see who it was, but I felt this fear, like
a premonition, that I absolutely should not do that. I absolutely must
not! [*She is silent.*] I'm talking about something else . . . I'd wanted to
talk about something else first . . . not this right away. You asked about
my childhood . . . [*She covers her face with her hands.*] I can smell it
already, the sweet smell of coltsfoot . . . I see the mountains and the
wooden tower with the soldier on top—in winter he wears a sheepskin
coat and in spring it's an overcoat. And the metal beds, so many metal
beds, all side by side. Side by side . . . I used to think that if I told
someone about this, afterward I would have to run away from that

person and never see them again. It's all so much my own . . . hidden
so deep inside of me. I never lived alone. First, I lived in the camp in
Kazakhstan, it was called Karlag, and after the camp, in exile. I've
lived in an orphanage, a dormitory, a communal apartment . . . always
surrounded by many, many other bodies; other eyes. I got my own
place for the first time when I was forty. They gave my husband and me
a two-bedroom apartment, our children were already grown up. I
would run over to the neighbors' out of sheer habit, like I had in the
dormitory, to borrow bread, salt, or matches. People didn't like me
because of that. But I had never lived alone before, I couldn't get used
to it . . . I always wanted letters. I was always waiting for envelopes to
arrive! I still do that . . . One of my friends writes me regularly, she
moved to Israel to live with her daughter. She wants to know how
things are over here, what life is like after socialism . . . What is our life
like? You walk down a familiar street and see a French boutique, German, Polish—all of the stores' names are in foreign languages. Foreign
socks, shirts, boots . . . cookies and salami . . . You can't find anything
that's our own, Soviet, anywhere. All I hear is that life is a battle, the
strong defeat the weak, and this is the law of nature. You have to grow
some horns and hooves, a thick skin, no one needs weaklings anymore. Everywhere you go it's elbows, elbows, and more elbows. This
is fascism, this is the swastika! I'm in shock . . . and despair. This is
not my world! It's not for me! [*Silence.*] If I had someone beside me . . .
anyone . . . my husband? He left me. And I keep on loving him . . .
[*Suddenly, she smiles.*] We got married in the spring, when the wild
cherries were in bloom and the lilacs were budding. And when he left
me, it was also spring. But he comes sometimes . . . he comes to me in
my dreams and can't bear to part with me . . . He keeps talking and
talking about something. But during the day, I'm going deaf from the
silence. Going blind. The past is like another person to me, a living
being . . . I remember when *Novy Mir* published Solzhenitsyn's *One
Day in the Life of Ivan Denisovich,* everyone was reading it. They were
all so shocked! Their conversations! I didn't understand why everyone
was so surprised and suddenly so interested. To me, it was all very
familiar territory and totally normal: the inmates, the camp, the
bucket . . . The penal colony.

In 1937, my father was arrested, he'd been a railway worker. My
mother flew into action, went to see everyone that she could, did everything possible to prove him innocent, demonstrate that it had been
a mistake. She forgot all about me. Forgot I was there. When she fi-

nally remembered, she tried to get rid of me, but it was too late. She drank all sorts of poison, took boiling hot baths. And . . . As a result, she ended up giving birth to me prematurely . . . but still, I survived. For some reason, I keep on surviving. It's happened so many times now! Soon, my mother was also arrested, and I was taken into custody along with her—you can't leave a baby alone in an apartment. I was just four months old. My mother had arranged to send my two older sisters to my father's sister's house in the country, but then a notice arrived from the NKVD ordering her to send them back to Smolensk. The authorities were waiting for them at the station. "Your children will live in an orphanage. Maybe that way they'll grow up to be in the Komsomol." They didn't even give us the address. By the time we found them, they were already married with kids. Many, many years later . . . In the camp, until I was three, I lived with my mother. Later, my mother recalled how often little children would die in there. In the winter, they would collect the dead children in big barrels and leave them like that until spring. By then, their bodies would be gnawed away by rats. They would wait to bury them in spring . . . that is, what remained of them. After the age of three, children would be taken away from their mothers and moved into the children's barracks. I start remembering things from the age of four . . . no, it was probably almost five. In episodes . . . In the morning, we would see our mothers through the barbed wire fence: They would be counted and led off to work. They would lead them out of the colony, out to where we weren't allowed to go. When people asked me, "Where are you from, little girl?" I would say, "From the colony." "The outside" was another world, something incomprehensible, frightening, which didn't exist for us. It was a desert out there, nothing but sand and dry scrub. I thought that the desert reached to the very edge of that world, that there was no way of life other than ours. Our soldiers guarded us, and we were proud of them. They had stars on their hats . . . I had a little friend named Rubik Tsirinsky. He'd lead me to the mamas through an opening under the barbed wire fence. When everyone else lined up to be marched to the cafeteria, he and I would hide behind the door. "You don't like kasha, right?" Rubik would ask me. I was always hungry, and I adored kasha, but I was prepared to do anything to see my Mama. So we would crawl to the barracks to see the mamas, but the barracks would be empty because all the mamas were at work. We knew they wouldn't be there, but we would go anyway sneaking around, exploring every corner. The metal beds, the metal canister for drinking water, the tin cup hanging from a chain—all of that smelled like mamas. It smelled like earth and mamas . . . Sometimes, we would find other people's mamas in there, lying on their beds and coughing. Someone's Mama would be coughing up blood . . . Rubik told me that was Tomochka's Mama, she was the littlest one out of all of us. That Mama died shortly afterward. And then Tomochka died, too, and for a long time, I wondered, "Whom should I tell that Tomochka died?" Since her Mama was dead as well . . . [*She falls silent.*] Many, many years later I remembered this . . . My mother didn't believe me: "You were only four." I told her that I remembered her walking around in canvas boots with wooden soles and a large tunic sewn from these little scraps of fabric. That surprised her, as well. It made her cry. I remember . . . I remember the aroma of a slice of melon that my mother had brought me. It was the size of a button, wrapped in a rag. And how one time, the boys called me over to play with a cat, but I didn't know what a cat was. The cat had come from the outside, there were no cats in the colony, they couldn't survive in there because there were no leftovers for them to eat, we would pick up every last crumb. We were always looking under our feet for something to eat. We ate grasses, roots, licked pebbles. We really wanted to give the cat some sort of treat, but we didn't have anything, so we'd feed it our spit after dinner—and it would eat it! It would! I remember how another time, my mother tried to pass me a piece of candy. "Anya, take this candy!" she'd called to me through the wire. The guards chased her away . . . she fell down . . . They grabbed her by her long black hair and dragged her through the dirt. I was so frightened, I didn't have the slightest idea of what candy was. None of the children knew what candy was. Everyone got scared and realized that they needed to hide me, so they pushed me into the middle of our little cluster. The other kids would always put me in the middle, "Because our Anya is always falling over." [*She weeps.*] I don't know why I'm crying . . . I already know all this . . . I know what my life was like. But there you go . . . What was I talking about? I didn't finish the thought . . . Right? I didn't finish?

There was more than one fear . . . There were many fears, both great and small. We were afraid of growing up, afraid of turning five. At five, they'd take us away to the orphanage, and we knew that this was somewhere far away—far away from the mamas. As I now recall, they took me to orphanage number eight in village number five. Everything was numbered, and instead of streets, they called them "lines": the first line, the second line . . . They loaded us onto a truck and took us away. The mamas ran after us, grabbing on to the bumper, shouting, crying. I remember that the mamas were always crying while we children cried very rarely. We were not crybabies, and we didn't fool around. We didn't laugh. I only learned how to cry at the orphanage. At the orphanage, they beat us hard and often. They'd tell us, "We can beat you and even kill you because your mothers are enemies." We didn't know our fathers. "Your mother is bad." I don't remember the face of the woman who kept repeating this to me. "My mother is good. My mother is beautiful." "Your mother is bad. She is our enemy." I don't remember whether she'd say the word "kill," but it was something like that . . . They'd say something along those lines. Frightening words . . . terrifying. Yes . . . I was too scared to even remember them. We didn't have teachers or tutors—we never even heard of them—we had commanders. Commanders! All of them with long rulers . . . They would beat us for doing things wrong and also, just because . . . they'd just beat us. I wanted them to beat me so hard there'd be holes in my body, and they would have to stop beating me. I never got any holes, but I was covered in infected wounds. I was so happy when that happened . . . My friend Olechka had metal clamps in her spine so they weren't allowed to beat her. Everyone was jealous of her . . . [*She looks out the window for a long time.*] I've never told anyone any of this. I was afraid . . . What was I afraid of? I don't know . . . [*She falls into thought.*] We loved the night . . . We'd spend our days waiting for it to come. Dark, dark night. At night, Miss Frosya, the night guard, would come sit with us. She was nice and would tell us the story about Alyonushka and Little Red Riding Hood, bringing us wheat in her pocket and giving a couple of grains to whoever was crying. Lilechka cried more than everyone else; she cried in the morning and cried at night. All of us had scabies, fat red boils on our stomachs, but Lilechka also had blisters in her armpits and they'd burst from being full of pus. I remember that the children would inform on one another, it was encouraged. Lilechka did it more than anyone else . . . The climate in Kazakhstan was harsh—in the winter, it would be 40 degrees below zero, and in the summer, it was 40 above. Lilechka died in the winter. If only she had made it until there was grass again . . . In the spring, she wouldn't have died. She wouldn't have . . . [*She falls silent in the middle of a word.*]

We were taught . . . above all, we were taught to love Comrade Stalin. The first letter we ever wrote was addressed to him in the Kremlin. Here's how it happened . . . Once we'd learned the alphabet, they handed out white sheets of paper and dictated a letter to our most benevolent, most beloved leader. We loved him so much, we really believed that he would answer our letters and send us presents. Lots of presents! We'd stare at his portrait and think he was so handsome. The most handsome man in the world! We even argued over who would give up more years of their life for a day of Comrade Stalin's. On May Day, they handed out little red flags, and we walked around happily waving them. I was the shortest one, so I was always the last in line, worried I wouldn't get a flag. What if there weren't enough? They kept repeating, "Your Motherland is your mother! Your Motherland is your mother!" But every adult we ever met, we'd ask, "Where is my Mama? What is my Mama like?" No one knew . . . the first Mama came for Rita Melnikova. She had an incredible voice. She sang us a lullaby:

Sleep, my little darling, sleep.
All of the lights have gone out
None of the doors squeak,
Even the mouse is asleep . . .

We didn't know this song, so we learned it. We begged her: more, more. I don't remember what else she sang us; by the time she finished, we were all asleep. She told us our mamas were good, our mamas were beautiful. All mamas are beautiful. She said all of our mamas sang this song. We waited for them . . . and then we'd get terribly disappointed—she hadn't told us the truth. Other mamas came and they were not beautiful, they were sick and they didn't know how to sing. We cried, we sobbed . . . We weren't crying because we were so happy to see them, we cried out of disappointment. Ever since then, I've disliked untruths . . . I don't like to daydream. She shouldn't have consoled us with those stories, we shouldn't have been lied to and told that our mamas were alive when they were actually dead. Because later on it would turn out . . . that there was no beautiful Mama, or there was no Mama at all . . . None!

All of us were very quiet kids. I don't remember our conversations. I remember touching . . . My friend Valya Knorina would touch me, and I would know what she was thinking because all of us thought the same things. We all knew each other in intimate detail: who wet their bed, who screamed in their sleep, who couldn't pronounce their *r*'s. I would always straighten out one of my teeth with a spoon. There were forty metal beds in one room . . . In the evening, they'd order us: "Palms together, hands under your cheeks, and everyone on your right side." And we were supposed to do all that all together. Everyone! That was community—maybe it was savage, maybe we were like cockroaches, but that's how I was brought up. That's still the way I am today . . . [*She turns away from me to face the window so I can't see her face in these moments.*] We'd lie there at night and then we'd all start to cry . . . All of us in chorus: "All of the good mamas have come already . . ." One girl said, "I hate my Mama! Why won't she come for me?" I was also upset at my mother. And in the morning, we would all sing . . . [*She immediately bursts into song.*]

> With gentle light, the morning paints
> The ancient Kremlin walls.
> The whole Soviet nation
> Awakens with the dawn . . .

It's a pretty song. To me, it's still pretty.

May Day! Our favorite holiday in the world was May 1. On that day, they would give us new coats and dresses. All of the coats and all of the dresses were identical. You'd start breaking yours in, leaving your mark on it, just one little knot or crease to show that it's yours . . . a part of you. We were told that our Motherland is our family and that it was thinking of us. Before the May 1 assembly, we would carry a big red banner out into the courtyard. To the beating of a drum. One time—it was a miracle! A general came to wish us a happy holiday. For us, all men were either soldiers or officers, but here he was, a real general. His pants had the special piping. We climbed up on the tall windowsill to catch a glimpse of him getting into his car and waving to us. "Do you know what having a father is like?" Valya Knorina asked me that evening. I didn't. And neither did she. [*She is silent.*] We had Stepka . . . He'd wrap his arms around himself as though he was dancing with someone and twirl down the corridor. Dancing with himself. We thought it was funny, but he never paid any attention to any of us. And then one morning he suddenly died, he wasn't sick, but he died. In an instant. We thought about him for a long time . . . They said that his father was a big-time army official, very high up—a general, too. After that, I started getting blisters in my armpits, the kind that burst. It was so painful, I'd weep from the pain. Igor Korolev kissed me in the storeroom. We were in fifth grade. I started getting better. I survived . . . again! [*Her voice breaks, she's almost screaming.*] Does anyone care about any of this anymore? Show me—who? It hasn't been useful or interesting to anyone for a long time. Our country doesn't exist anymore, and it never will, but here we are . . . old and disgusting . . . with our terrifying memories and poisoned eyes. We're right here! But what's left of our past? Only the story that Stalin drenched this soil in blood, Khrushchev planted corn in it, and everybody laughed at Brezhnev. But what about our heroes? In the papers, they've started writing that Zoya Kosmodemyanskaya had schizophrenia as a result of childhood meningitis and had a known propensity for arson. That she was just mentally ill. Alexander Matrosov* was drunk: That's why he threw himself in front of a German machine gun and not because he wanted to rescue his comrades. Pavka Korchagin is no longer a hero . . . They're Soviet zombies! [*She calms down a little.*] But to this day, I still have dreams about the camp. I still get upset whenever I see German Shepherds, I'm afraid of anyone in military uniform . . . [*Through tears.*] I can't go on like this . . . I turned on the gas, all four burners . . . shut the windows and pulled the blinds down. I don't have anything left that would . . . that would make me afraid to die . . . [*She is silent.*] When you still have something holding you back . . . like the smell of a baby's head . . . I don't even have any trees under my windows . . . just roofs . . . [*Silence.*] I put a bouquet on the table, turned the radio on . . . In the final moments, as I was lying there . . . I was already lying on the floor . . . all of my thoughts were from the camp. Despite everything else that ever happened to me . . . I saw myself walking through the camp gates . . . They were metal gates, so they slammed shut behind me with a loud clank. I'm free, I've been released. I walked along talking to myself: No matter what, don't look back! I was terrified that someone would catch up with me and make me go back. That for some reason, I'd have to go back there. I walked a little ways and saw a birch tree by the road . . . just a regular birch . . . I ran up to it and put my arms around it, pressed my whole body against it. There was a bush next to it, and I embraced the bush, too. There was so much joy my first year out . . . Everything made me happy! [*She is silent for a long time.*] My neighbor smelled gas . . . The

* Zoya Kosmodemyanskaya (1923–1941) was a Soviet partisan murdered by Nazis during World War II after setting fire to a number of horse stables and houses occupied by a German calvary regiment. She became a martyr and Hero of the Soviet Union. Alexander Matrosov (1924–1943) was a Soviet infantry soldier who threw himself onto a German machine gun.

police broke down the door . . . When I came to in the hospital, my first thought was, "Where am I? Am I back in the camp?" As though my whole other life hadn't happened, like there'd been nothing at all between the camp and the hospital. First, I heard sounds, then I felt pain . . . Everything hurt: every single motion, swallowing air, lifting a finger, opening my eyes. The whole world was my body. And then the world spread out and grew taller, I saw the nurse standing over me in her white uniform, her white kerchief . . . It took me a long time to come back to life. A girl was dying in the bed next to mine, she died over the course of several days, lying there with all these tubes coming out of her. There was a tube in her mouth, so she couldn't even scream. For some reason, they couldn't save her. Looking at all those tubes, I pictured everything in detail: I'm lying there like that . . . I'm dead . . . but I don't realize that I've died and no longer exist. Because I've already been to the other side . . . [*She stops.*] Are you sick of listening to me? No? You can tell me . . . I can shut up . . .

Mama . . . My mother came for me in the beginning of sixth grade. She'd ended up doing twelve years in the camps, we were together for three of them, and separated for nine. Now, we were being shipped off for resettlement, they had granted us permission to go together. It was morning . . . I was walking through the yard when I heard someone calling to me, "Anechka! Anyutochka!" No one ever called to me like that, no one ever called me by my name. I saw a woman with black hair and screamed, "Mama!!!" She embraced me with a bone-rattling cry, "Daddy!" She'd call me that—when I was little, I'd looked a lot like my father. Bliss! So many feelings, so much joy! For several days, I was beside myself; I've never been so overcome with happiness before or since. Such a rush of feelings . . . But soon . . . very soon, it turned out that my mother and I didn't understand one another. We were like strangers. I was eager to join the Komsomol and combat all the invisible enemies plotting to destroy this very best life of ours. My mother would just look at me and weep . . . She said nothing. She was always afraid. In Karaganda, they issued us documents and dispatched us to the town of Belovo for resettlement. It's far out, past Omsk. The farthest reaches of Siberia . . . It took us a month to get there. We kept riding and riding, waiting and changing trains. At every stop along the way, we were required to check in with the local NKVD authorities, and they'd always tell us to keep going, sending us farther and farther away from the capital. We weren't allowed to settle in the border zone, we couldn't live near any defense enterprises or major cities, the list of places we weren't allowed to live went on and on. I still can't stand to see the lights on in people's windows in the evening. They'd kick us out of train stations at night, and we'd be forced to walk the streets. Through snowstorms, in the freezing cold. We'd see the lights on in the windows, there were people inside, living in warmth, heating up their tea. We had to knock on people's doors . . . that was the scariest part . . . No one wanted to let us spend the night. "We smell like convicts . . ." my mother would say. [*She cries without even realizing it.*] In Belovo, we rented "an apartment," except it was in a mud hut. Then we moved into our very own mud hut. I came down with tuberculosis, I was so weak I couldn't stand; I had this terrible cough. It was September . . . All of the other children were getting ready to start school, and there I was, unable to walk. They admitted me to the hospital. I remember how someone was always dying. Sonechka died, Vanechka, Slavik . . . I wasn't afraid of the dead, but I didn't want to die myself. I embroidered beautifully, I drew, and everyone praised me, "What a talented girl. You ought to be in school." And I wondered, "Then why should I die?" By some miracle, I survived . . . One day, I opened my eyes, and there was a bouquet of wild cherry blossoms on the cabinet. From whom? It made me realize that I was going to live . . . I'm going to live! I returned to our mud hut. While I'd been in the hospital, my mother had had another stroke. I hardly recognized her . . . She'd turned into an old woman. That same day, she was hospitalized. At home, I didn't find a single crumb of food, not even a whiff of it. I was too shy to say anything to anyone . . . Finally, they found me on the floor, barely breathing. Someone brought me a mug of warm goat milk. That's everything, everything . . . everything . . . Every story I can remember about myself is about how I kept dying and surviving . . . and then dying again. [*She turns away toward the window again.*] I regained some of my strength . . . The Red Cross bought me a ticket and put me on a train. They sent me to my hometown of Smolensk, to an orphanage. That was my homecoming. [*She cries.*] I don't know why . . . Why am I crying? I know everything about my life already . . . I know it all too well.

In the orphanage—that's where I turned sixteen . . . I started making some friends, boys started courting me . . . [*She smiles.*] Good-looking boys pursued me. Older ones. The thing about me was that whenever anyone liked me, I'd get scared. It was scary that someone was paying attention to me. That they'd noticed me. It was impossible to try to go out with me because I would always bring a friend along on dates. Even if someone asked me out to the movies, I'd refuse to go alone. I took two girlfriends with me on my first date with my future husband. He wouldn't let me forget that for a long time . . .

The day Stalin died . . . the whole orphanage was marched into the courtyard carrying a red banner. For the entire duration of the funeral, we stood outside "at attention"; it went on for six or eight hours. Some kids fainted. I cried . . . I had already come to terms with living without my mother, but how could I go on without Stalin? How would I live . . . For some reason, I was afraid that war was going to break out. [*She cries.*] Mama . . . Four years later . . . I was already studying at the architecture college . . . My mother finally returned from internal exile. This time, she was back for good. She came with a wooden suitcase containing a zinc roasting pan (which I still have, I can't bear to throw it away), two aluminum spoons, and a tangle of torn stockings. "You're a bad housekeeper," my mother admonished me. "You don't know how to darn holes." I knew how to darn, it's just that the holes in her stockings were beyond darning. No handicraft could fix them! I had a stipend of eighteen rubles, and my mother had a pension of fourteen. We were in heaven: We could eat as much bread as we wanted and there would still be enough money left over for tea. I had one tracksuit and one calico dress I had sewn for myself. In autumn and winter, I went to college in the tracksuit. And to me, it seemed like . . . from my perspective, we had everything we could ever want. Whenever I went into a normal home, with a normal family, I would get tense—what was all that stuff for? So many spoons, forks, cups. The simplest things would confound me . . . the very basics. For instance, why would anyone need two pairs of shoes? I'm still indifferent to possessions, to domesticity. Yesterday, my daughter-in-law called: "I'm trying to find a brown gas stove." They remodeled, and now she's looking for everything brown for her kitchen—furniture, curtains, dishes—she wants it to look like a foreign magazine. She spends hours on the phone. Her apartment is full of advertisements and newspapers, she reads all the classified ads she can find. "I want that! And that . . ." Everyone used to have very basic furniture, people lived simply. And now? Everyone's turned into stomachs . . . bellies . . . I want! I want! I want! [*She waves her hand dismissively.*] I don't go to my son's house very often. Everything at their place is new and expensive. It's like an office. [*She is silent.*] We're strangers . . . We're family, but strangers . . . [*Silence.*] I want to remember what my mother was like when she was young. But I don't remember her as a young woman . . .

I only remember her sick. We never once hugged or kissed, never exchanged any affectionate words. I don't remember that ever happening . . . Our mothers lost us twice: the first time, when we were taken from them as children; the second time, when they came back to us and we were already grown up. Their children had turned into strangers, they'd been swapped . . . Another mother had raised them: "Your Motherland is your mother . . . your mother . . ." "Little boy, where is your father?" "He's still in prison." "And your mother?" "In prison already." We could only imagine our parents as being in prison. Somewhere far, far away . . . never nearby. There was a time where I wanted to run away from my mother and go back to the orphanage. How could I! How . . . She didn't read newspapers and didn't go to parades; she didn't even listen to the radio. She didn't like the songs that made my heart leap out of my chest . . . [*She sings quietly.*]

And the enemy will never force you
To bow your mighty crown
My beloved capital,
My golden Moscow . . .

I always wanted to be out in the street. I went to all the military parades, I loved big sporting events. I still remember that high! You march in step with everyone else, you're part of something bigger than yourself . . . something huge. That's where I was the happiest. I wasn't happy with my mother. And I will never be able to fix that. Mama died very soon after she came home. I was only affectionate with her after she was already dead. When I saw her in her coffin, I was suddenly filled with so much tenderness! Such powerful love! She lay there in her old felt boots . . . She didn't own any regular shoes or sandals, and mine wouldn't fit onto her swollen feet. I said so many sweet words to her, confessed so much—could she hear me? I kissed her and kissed her. Told her how much I loved her . . . [*She cries.*] It felt like she was still with me . . . I believed it . . .

[*She goes to the kitchen. Pretty soon, she calls to me, "Dinner's on the table. I'm always alone, it'll be nice to at least share a meal with someone."*]

You should never go back to the past. Because . . . Yes . . . But me, I practically ran there! I was dying to go. Fifty years . . . For fifty years,

I kept returning to that place . . . In my thoughts, I was there day and night . . .

Winter . . . Most often, my dreams were of winter . . . It was so freezing cold, there were no dogs or birds anywhere. The air is brittle like glass, the smoke from the chimneys rises straight up into the sky in a column. Or it would be the end of the summer, after the grass stops growing, and everything is covered in a heavy coat of dust. Finally, I . . . I decided to make the trip. By then, it was perestroika. Gorbachev, the rallies . . . Everybody was out in the streets. Celebrating. You can write about whatever you want, shout whatever you want wherever you want. Free-dom! Free-dom! No matter what awaited us, the past was finally over. We were waiting for something new to emerge . . . Impatience was in the air . . . then we'd get afraid again. For a long time, I was scared of turning on the radio in the morning: What if suddenly it was all over? Like they'd abruptly canceled the whole program? For a long time, I couldn't believe it was real. I thought they were going to come in the middle of the night and take everyone down to the stadium like they did in Chile . . . One stadium would be enough for the smart alecks, the rest would shut up on their own. But they never came . . . They didn't take anyone away. Instead, they started publishing people's gulag memoirs in the newspapers. Their photographs. Their eyes! The people's eyes in those photos! It was like they were staring back at you from the afterlife . . . [*She is silent.*] So I decided that I wanted to . . . I had to go there! Why? I don't know. But I had to . . . I took time off work. The first week went by, the second week . . . I couldn't do it, I kept putting it off: I had to go to the dentist, I hadn't finished painting the balcony door. All sorts of excuses. One morning . . . it was morning . . . I was painting the balcony door and I said to myself, "Tomorrow I'm going to Karaganda." I remember, I said it out loud to myself, and I realized that I was really going to do it. I was going and that was that. What's Karaganda? Pure barren steppe for hundreds of kilometers around, burnt out in the summer. During Stalin's time, they built dozens of camps on this steppe: Steplag, Karlag, Alzhir . . . Peschanlag . . . They herded in hundreds of thousands of prisoners. Soviet slaves. Then, after Stalin died, they took down the barracks and barbed wire and ended up with a city. The city of Karaganda . . . I'm going . . . That's it! It was a long journey. On the train, I met a woman, a teacher from Ukraine. She was looking for her father's grave, this was her second trip to Karaganda. "Don't worry," she informed me. "They're used to strange people arriving from all over the world just to talk to the stones." She had a letter from her father with her, the only letter he ever sent from camp, ". . . No matter what, there's nothing in the world better than the red banner . . ." That was how it ended . . . with those words. [*She falls into thought.*] That woman . . . She told me about how her father had signed a document testifying that he was a Polish spy. The interrogator had turned over a stool, hammered a nail into one of its legs, made her father sit on it and spun him around. That's how he got his way. "Fine, I'm a spy." The interrogator: "For whom?" Now it was her father's turn to ask, "Where do spies come from?" They gave him a choice—he could either be German or Polish. "Say that I'm Polish." He knew two phrases in Polish, *"dziękuję bardzo"* and *"wszystko jedno."** Just those two phrases. As for me . . . I don't know a single thing about my father. One time, my mother let slip that he had gone mad from the torture in prison. Apparently, he started singing all the time . . . There was also a young man with us in our compartment. The Ukrainian teacher and I talked all night long. Wept . . . In the morning, he looked at us and said, "It's all awful! Like some kind of horror movie!" He was eighteen, maybe twenty years old. Lord! We lived through so much and have no one to tell the story to. We tell one another . . .

I got to Karaganda . . . Someone started cracking jokes: "Step out! Step out with your belongings!" Some laughed, others cried. At the station, the first words I heard were *"Shalava . . . kurva . . . lyaga-vye . . ."†* The familiar language of the camps. I instantly remembered all those words . . . Instantly! I froze. I couldn't stop shaking inside; the whole time I was there, I shook. Of course, I didn't recognize the town itself, but just beyond the city limits, after the last houses, the familiar landscape began. I recognized everything . . . the dry needle-grass, the white dust . . . an eagle soaring up high in the sky. And the names of the villages were familiar—Volnyj, Sangorodok. All former camps. I thought I'd forgotten, but I still remembered. An old man sat down next to me on the bus and noticed that I wasn't from around there. "Who are you looking for?" "Well," I began, "there used to be a camp here." "Oh, the barracks? They dismantled the last of those buildings two years ago. People built themselves sheds and saunas out of the bricks. Took the soil back to their dachas for planting. Put camp

---

* *Dziękuję bardzo* and *wszystko jedno:* "Thank you very much" and "Doesn't matter."
† Prison slang for "prostitute . . . slut . . . snitches . . ."

wire around their gardens. My son's place is out there. It's so, you know, unpleasant . . . In the spring, the snows and rains leave bones sticking out of their potato patches. No one is squeamish about that sort of thing around here because they're so used to it. There are as many bones as stones in this soil. People just toss them out to the edge of their property, stamp them down with their boots. Cover them up. It happens all the time. Just stick your hand in the dirt, run your fingers through it . . ." It felt like the wind had been knocked out of me. Like I had passed out. Meanwhile, the old man turned to the window and pointed: "Over there, behind that store, they covered over the old cemetery. Behind that bathhouse, too." I sat there, unable to breathe. What had I expected? That they had erected pyramids? Mounds of Glory?* The first line is now the street named after someone or other . . . Then the second line . . . I looked out the window, but I couldn't see anything, I was blinded by tears. Kazakh women were selling their cucumbers and tomatoes at every bus stop . . . pails of blackcurrants. "Fresh from the berry patch. From my own garden." Lord! My God . . . I have to say that . . . It was physically difficult for me to breathe, something was going on with me out there. In a matter of just a few days, my skin dried out, my nails started chipping off. Something was happening to my entire body. I wanted to fall down on the ground and lie there. And never get up. The steppe . . . it's like the sea . . . I walked and walked until finally, I collapsed. I fell next to a small metal cross that was up to the crossbeam in the earth. Screaming, in hysterics. There was no one around . . . just the birds. [*After a short pause.*] I was staying in a hotel. In the evening, the restaurant was filled to the gills . . . People drank vodka. I had dinner there one night . . . Two men sitting at my table got into an argument, shouting at each other until they were hoarse. The first one said, "No matter what, I'm still a communist. We were supposed to build socialism. How could we have broken Hitler's spine without Magnitka and Vorkuta†?" The second one: "I've been talking to the local elderly . . . All of them worked or served—I don't know the right word for what they did—in the camps. They were the cooks, the guards, special agents. There was no other work out here, and those jobs paid well: salaries, rations, outfitting. That's what they call it, 'work.' For them, the

---

* Burial mounds of "glory" and "immortality" were erected in the 1960s across the Soviet Union to commemorate the fatalities of World War II.
† Magnitka was the name given to the famous Magnitogorsk steel factory built by camp inmates. Vorkuta was an infamous forced labor camp.

camps were work! A job! And here you are talking about crimes against humanity. Sin and the soul. It wasn't just anyone doing time, it was the people. And the ones sentencing them and guarding them were the people, too—not foreign workers, not people brought in from outside—they were the very same people. Our own men. Kin. Today, you see everybody putting on the striped uniform. Now, everyone's the victim and Stalin alone is to blame. But think about it . . . it's simple arithmetic . . . Millions of inmates had to be surveilled, arrested, interrogated, transported, and shot for minor transgressions. Someone had to do all this . . . and they found millions of people who were willing to . . ." The waiter brought them bottle after bottle . . . I sat there listening . . . I listened! And they kept drinking and drinking without getting drunk. I sat there, chained to the spot, I couldn't leave . . . The first one: "I was told that after the barracks were already empty, shut down, screams and moans could still be heard coming from them in the middle of the night, carried by the wind . . ." The second one: "That's all myth. They've started crafting the mythology. Our entire tragedy lies in the fact that our victims and executioners are the same people." And again: "Stalin entered the Russia of the wooden plow and left it with the atom bomb . . ." For three days and three nights, I didn't get a moment of sleep. During the day, I roamed and roamed the steppe. Crawled through it. Until dark, until the streetlights came on.

One day, a man gave me a lift back into town. He was around fifty, or maybe older, my age. He'd clearly been drinking and was apparently feeling talkative. "You're looking for graves? I understand. You could say that we live in a cemetery. But we . . . the long and short of it is that people around here don't like remembering the past. It's taboo! The older generation has died out, our parents, and the ones still alive keep their mouths shut. It's that Stalinist upbringing. Gorbachev, Yeltsin . . . That's all today . . . Who knows what tomorrow will bring. Where the wind will blow . . ." One thing led to another, and I learned that his father had been an officer "with epaulettes." When Khrushchev was in power, he'd wanted to leave the area, but they wouldn't let him move. Everyone had to sign confidentiality agreements on the nondisclosure of state secrets—both the people who did time and the ones who kept them in. The guards. No one was allowed to leave, they all knew too much. He heard that they didn't even allow the guards who convoyed prisoner trains to get away. Working out here, they'd avoided having to fight in the war. But if they'd fought, they could have gone home afterward—there was no way out for them after serving here. The penal colony, the system, swallowed them up forever. The only ones who could get out after serving their sentences were the common criminals and convicts. The gangsters. The rest ended up staying, all together, sometimes living in the same building, sharing a courtyard. "This life of ours ain't pretty!" was his refrain. He remembered a story from his childhood . . . How a group of ex-cons conspired to murder a former camp guard for being a beast. When they were drunk, they'd fight and gang up on each other. His father drank like a devil. He'd get wasted and weep: "Dammit! I've spent my whole life with my mouth clamped shut. We're nothing but dust . . ." Night. The steppe. The two of us riding through it—the daughter of a victim and the son of . . . what should I call him? An executioner? A small-time executioner . . . The big-time executioners can't do without the little ones, you need a lot of people who are willing to do the dirty work. And so we'd crossed paths . . . What did we talk about? We talked about how neither of us knew anything about our parents, about how they'd kept silent until their very deaths. Taken their secrets with them to their graves. But apparently, something about me got to him, and it really upset him. He told me his father never ate fish because fish, he said, were willing to eat human flesh. If you throw a naked man into the sea, a few months later, there will be nothing but bones left of him. All white. How exactly did he know this? When he was sober, he never said a word, but when he was drunk, he swore up and down that all he ever did was push paper. His hands were clean . . . His son wanted to believe him, but then why didn't he eat fish? Fish nauseated him . . . After his father's death, he found documents certifying that for several years, he'd served near the Sea of Okhotsk. There were camps out there, too . . . [*She is silent.*] Drunk . . . His tongue was loose . . . He stared at me so hard, it even sobered him up. And once he sobered up, he got scared. I realized he was scared. Suddenly, he became surly, and shouted something like, "Enough digging up the dead! Enough!" I realized . . . that these people, the children . . . they'd never been forced to sign anything, but they knew full well that they had better keep their mouths shut. He offered his hand in parting. I wouldn't take it . . . [*She cries.*]

I searched. Until the very last day, I kept searching . . . And on the last day, somebody told me, "Go see Katerina Demchuk. The old crone's going to be ninety soon, but she still remembers everything." They led me to where she lived, pointed her out to me. It was a brick house with a tall fence. I knocked on the gate. She came out . . . older than time, half-blind. "Someone told me that you used to work at the orphanage?" "I was a teacher." "We didn't have teachers, we had commanders." She said nothing. She stepped away from her fence and started watering her vegetable patch with a hose. I stood there . . . not moving . . . I refused to leave! Reluctantly, she led me into her house: a cross with a crucified Christ in her upper chamber; an icon in the corner. I remembered her voice . . . not her face, but her voice . . . "Your mother is an enemy. We can beat you and even kill you." I recognized her! But maybe I'd just really wanted to? I could have not asked, but I did: "Maybe you remember me? Perhaps . . ." "No, no . . . I don't remember anyone. You were all very small and grew poorly. We were just following orders." She put tea on, brought me cookies . . . I sat there listening to her complaints: Her son was an alcoholic and her grandsons drank, too. Her husband had died a long time ago, and her pension was pitiful. Her back hurt. It's boring being old. And that was it! I thought about it: Here we are after fifty years . . . We meet again . . . I imagined that it was really her . . . That's what I imagined was happening . . . We were finally face to face again—and so what? I too had lost my husband; my pension is also pitiful. My back hurts. Nothing but old age. [*She is silent for a long time.*]

The next day, I went home . . . What's left? Confusion and resentment . . . Only who am I upset at? The steppe keeps surfacing in my dreams; one day, it's covered in snow, the next, in red poppies. On the former site of one barracks there's a café, on another, dachas. Cows grazing. I shouldn't have gone back. No! We weep so bitterly, we suffer so much, and for what? What was the point of all that? So twenty, fifty more years will go by . . . and all of it will be stamped into dust, as though we never even existed. All that'll be left of us will be a couple of lines in a history textbook. A paragraph. Solzhenitsyn and history according to Solzhenitsyn are going out of style. People used to be put in jail for *The Gulag Archipelago*, they read it in secret, typed copies of it up on their typewriters, wrote it out by hand. I believed . . . I believed that if thousands of people read it, everything would change. People would repent, tears would be shed. But what happened instead? Everything that had been written and hidden away in desk drawers was published; everything that people thought about in secret was said aloud. And then?! These books lie around on book piles gathering dust. While people run past them . . . [*She is silent.*] We exist, but we don't exist . . . Even the streets I used to live on are gone. There used to be a Lenin Street. Everything is different now: the stuff, the people, the money. There are new names for it all. We used to be "comrades," now we are "ladies and gentlemen," except that we "ladies and gentlemen" seem to be struggling. Everyone is searching for their aristocratic roots. That's what's in fashion! Princes and counts are coming out of the woodwork. Before, people were proud of being from long lines of workers and peasants. Now everyone crosses themselves and keeps the fasts. They have serious discussions about whether or not monarchy will save Russia. They adore a Tsar that every college girl was making fun of in 1917. This country is foreign to me. It's foreign! It used to be that when people came over, we'd talk about books, plays . . . Now it's who bought what? What's the exchange rate? And the jokes. Nothing is sacred anymore, people will laugh at anything. Everything's funny. "Papa, who's Stalin?" "Stalin was our chief." "But I thought only savages had chiefs." Somebody calls up Armenian radio: "What's left of Stalin?" Armenian radio answers, "All that's left of Stalin are two changes of underwear, a pair of boots, a couple of army jackets, one of them for special occasions, and four rubles and forty kopecks of Soviet money. And, oh yeah, an enormous empire." The second question: "How did the Russian soldier manage to reach Berlin?" "By not being brave enough to retreat." I've stopped seeing my friends. I don't even go outside very much. What's out there? The triumph of Mammon! No values are left except for the power of the purse. And me? I'm poor, we're all poor. My entire generation, the former Soviet nation . . . no bank accounts, no property. All of our things are Soviet, no one will give us a single kopeck. Where is our capital? All we have is our suffering, everything that we went through. I have two certificates on regular pieces of paper ripped out of a student notebook: "Rehabilitated . . ." and "Rehabilitated . . . due to the absence of a crime . . ." One for my mother and one for my father. There was a time . . . I used to be proud of my son . . . He was in the air force, he served in Afghanistan. Now he sells things at the market . . . A Major with two combat decorations—a street peddler!!! It used to be called speculation; today, it's known as business. He crates vodka, cigarettes, and skis out to Poland and comes back with clothes. Junk! He goes to Italy with amber and returns with plumbing fixtures: toilets, taps, plungers. Yuck! There's never been a single salesman in our family! They were detested! I may be a chunk of *sovok* . . . But it's better than all this buying and selling . . .

So, I admit it . . . I used to like people more. The people before were our people . . . I lived with that country for its entire history. I don't care about the one that exists now, it's not mine. [*I can tell that she's tired. I turn off the tape recorder. She hands me a sheet of paper with her son's phone number on it.*] You asked for this . . . my son will tell you his version . . . He has his own story. There's a gulf between us . . . I realize . . . [*Through tears.*] Now go. I want to be alone.

HER SON'S STORY

For a long time, he wouldn't let me turn on the tape recorder. And then, out of the blue, he suggested it himself: "This, you should record . . . It's not just family squabbles, fights between fathers and sons. This is history with a capital 'H' . . . Don't use my last name. I'm not afraid of anything, but it's unpleasant for me."

. . . You already know everything . . . But what can we say about death? Nothing intelligible . . . It's unknowable!

. . . I still like old Soviet films, there's something about them that you won't find in today's movies. I liked that certain something ever since I was a kid. I can't put it into words. I was into history, I read a lot, everyone read a lot back then. I read about the Chelyuskinites and Chkalov* . . . Gagarin and Korolev† . . . but it was a long time before I learned anything about 1937. One day, I asked my mother, "Where did my grandfather die?" and she fainted. My father told me, "Never ask your mother about that again." I was a Little Octobrist, a Young Pioneer, whether I believed in it or not didn't matter. Maybe I did? More likely, I didn't think twice about it . . . The Komsomol. Songs by the campfire: "If it suddenly turns out that your friend / Is not friend, but not quite foe . . ." And so on . . . [*He lights a cigarette.*] My dream? I dreamed of becoming a soldier. Of flying! It's prestigious and mag-

---

* The Chelyuskinites were the polar explorers aboard the SS *Chelyuskin,* a Soviet steamship tasked with testing the possibility of traveling the Northern Maritime Route through the Arctic without an icebreaker. The failed 1933 expedition resulted in the unlikely survival of its crew. Famed Russian aviator Valery Chkalov (1904–1938) was named a Hero of the Soviet Union.
† Sergei Korolev (1907–1966) was a Soviet rocket scientist and rocket designer who oversaw the Sputnik project and Yuri Gagarin's space flight. He was the leading figure behind the Soviet space project.

nificent. All of the girls were dying to marry an army man. My favorite
author was Aleksandr Kuprin.* An officer! In an elegant uniform . . .
Dying a heroic death! Fraternal debauchery. Friendship. All of that
seemed very attractive when I was young and impressionable. And my
parents supported me. I was raised on Soviet books: "Man is higher,"
"Mankind! That has a proud sound." They wrote about a man that
didn't exist . . . who doesn't exist in nature. I still can't understand it,
why were there so many idealists back then? Now they've all vanished.
What kind of idealism can the Pepsi Generation have? They're prag-
matics. I finished military school and served in Kamchatka. On the
border. Out where there's nothing but snow and volcanoes. The one
thing I've always loved about my country is the nature. The landscape.
Now that's really something! Two years later, they sent me for training
at a military academy, and I graduated with honors. More little stars!
A career! There would have been a gun salute at my funeral . . . [*Pro-
vocatively.*] And now? There's been a change of scenery . . . The Soviet
major is now a businessman. I sell Italian plumbing fixtures . . . If
someone had prophesied this ten years ago, I wouldn't have even bothered punching that Nostradamus, I would have just laughed in his
face. I was totally Soviet—it's shameful to love money, you have to love
a dream. [*He lights a cigarette and falls silent.*] It's too bad . . . You
forget a lot . . . You forget because it all goes by too fast. Like a kalei-
doscope. First, I fell in love with Gorbachev, then I was disillusioned.
I went to demonstrations and shouted alongside everyone else,
"Yeltsin—Yes! Gorbachev—No!" I screamed, "Down with Article 6!"
I even put up flyers. We talked and read and read and talked. What did
we want? Our parents wanted to say and read whatever they wanted.
They dreamt of humane socialism . . . with a human face. And young
people? We . . . we also dreamt of freedom. But what is it? Our idea of
freedom was purely theoretical . . . We wanted to live like they do in
the West. Listen to their music, dress like them, travel the world. "We
want change . . . change . . ." sang Viktor Tsoi.† We had no clue what
we were hurtling toward. We just kept on dreaming . . . Meanwhile,
the only things on sale at the store were three-liter jars of birch juice
and sauerkraut. Bags of bay leaves. We had ration cards for noodles,

---

* Aleksandr Kuprin (1870–1938) was a novelist best known for *The Duel*, a 1905 realist novel on life as a soldier in the Tsar's army. After the Revolution, Kuprin emigrated
to France, but returned to the Soviet Union in 1936.
† Viktor Tsoi (1962–1990) was a Soviet musician, leader of the underground post-
punk band Kino.

butter, grain . . . tobacco . . . You could get killed in the vodka line! But they published the forbidden Platonov, Grossman . . . They took the troops out of Afghanistan. I got out alive, I thought that all of us who had fought there were heroes. We returned to our Motherland only to discover that it was gone! Instead of the Motherland, we found ourselves in a new country that didn't give a damn about us! The army fell apart and people started flinging mud at army men. Murderers! We were no longer defenders—now we were murderers. They blamed us for everything from Afghanistan to Vilnius to Baku. All the bloodshed was our fault. It became unsafe to walk around in your uniform at night, you could get beaten up. People were angry because there was no food or anything else at the stores. No one understood what was going on. In our regiment, the planes weren't flying for lack of fuel. Combat crews sat grounded, beating each other at cards, chugging vodka. An officer's monthly pay was only enough for ten loaves of bread. One of my friends shot himself. Then another . . . People ditched the army, scattering in every direction. Everyone had families to feed. I have two kids, a cat and a dog . . . How to live? We switched the dog from meat to cottage cheese, while we ate nothing but kasha for weeks on end. All of this gets wiped clean from your memory . . . Yes, it's important to write it down while there are still people around who remember it. Officers . . . we'd work the night shift, unloading train cars, or as security guards. Laying asphalt. The people working alongside me were PhDs, doctors, surgeons. I even remember a pianist from the symphony. I learned how to lay ceramic tile and install armored doors. And so on, and onwards . . . It was the dawning of the age of business . . . Some people imported computers, others "cooked" jeans . . . [He laughs.] Two men decide to start a business together: One is going to buy a cistern of wine, and the other one's going to sell it. They shake on it! One goes looking for money, and the other one wonders where he's going to find a cistern of wine. It's a joke, and it's the truth. People like that would come see me, too: wearing beat-up sneakers, trying to sell me a helicopter . . . [A pause.]

But we made it out alive! We survived—and the country survived! So what do we know about the soul? Only that it exists. For me and my friends, everything worked out all right. One of them runs a construction business, another one has a little grocery store—cheese, meat, salami; a third one sells furniture. Some have capital abroad, others have houses in Cyprus. One used to be an academic, another one, an engineer. They're smart, educated people. In the papers, they portray "new Russians" in ten-kilo gold chains with gold bumpers and silver wheels on their cars. That's all bullshit! Successful businesses are run by all sorts of people, but never idiots. So we'll get together . . . bring expensive cognac, but drink vodka. We get drunk and by morning, we're putting our arms around each other and belting out Komsomol songs at the top of our lungs: "Komsomol youth, volunteers . . . / Our mighty friendship is our strength . . ." We remember the trips we took "digging potatoes" and funny anecdotes from army life. In short, we reminisce about the Soviet era. Do you understand? Our conversations always end the same way: "It's a mess out there. We need a Stalin." Even though all of us, as I've already told you, have made it. What's that about? Take me, for example . . . November 7 is still a holiday to me. On that day I celebrate something great. And I miss something, I miss it enormously. Actually, to be perfectly honest . . . On the one hand, it's nostalgia, but on the other hand, it's fear. Everyone wants to leave, get the hell out of this country. Make the big bucks and clear out. What about our children? They all want to study accounting. But ask them about Stalin . . . that past has been severed clean! To give you a rough idea . . . I gave my son Solzhenitsyn to read, and it made him laugh. I'd hear him laughing while reading it! For him, the accusation of being a triple agent seems ridiculous. "Papa . . . There wasn't a single literate interrogator, they misspelled every word. They couldn't even spell 'execution' right . . ." He will never understand me or my mother because he didn't spend a single day of his life in the Soviet Union. My mother—my son—me . . . we all live in different countries, even though they're all Russia. The ties that bind us are ghastly. Ghastly! Everyone feels lied to . . .

. . . Socialism is alchemy. It's an alchemical concept. We were hurtling forward and ended up God knows where. A joke: "Where do I sign up for the Communist Party?" "At the psychiatrist's." While they—our parents, my mother—want to feel like they led important, not worthless lives, believing in the things that are worth believing in. But what do they have instead? From all sides, they hear that their lives were total shit, that they never had anything but their terrible missiles and tanks. They were prepared to defeat any enemy. And they could have done it! But without a war, it all collapsed. No one can understand why. That's something we need to think about . . . but no one ever taught us how to think. All anyone remembers is fear . . . and fear is all anyone talks about. I read somewhere that fear is also a form of love. I bet that's a quote from Stalin . . . Today, the museums stand empty while the churches are full. It's because all of us need therapists. Psychotherapy sessions. Do you think that Chumak and Kashpirovsky* heal people's bodies? They heal souls. Hundreds of thousands of people sit in front of their televisions and listen to them like they're hypnotized. It's a drug! The terrifying loneliness . . . the sense of abandonment . . . From the taxi driver to the office clerk to the People's Artist† and the scholar. Everyone is terribly lonely. And on and on . . . like that . . . Life has completely transformed. The world is now divided into new categories, no longer "White" and "Red," or those who did time and the ones who threw them in jail, those who've read Solzhenitsyn and those who haven't. Now it's just the haves and have-nots. You don't like that? No, of course not . . . And as for me, I don't like it, either. You, and even I . . . we were romantics . . . And how about those naïve sixties dissidents? A cult of earnest people . . . They thought that as soon as communism fell, the Russian man would drop everything and learn how to live with freedom. Instead, he went out and learned how to live. Really live! Try everything, lick it, take a bite of it. Eat good food, wear nice clothes . . . travel . . . see palm trees and the desert. Camels . . . Instead of burning and burning out, eternally running somewhere with a torch and a pickaxe. No, all Russians wanted was to live like other people . . . in France and Monaco . . . Because you never know what might happen! They gave us land, but they can take it away. They let us do business, but they might still put us in jail. They'll take away the factory and the little grocery, too. That fear keeps drilling away at our brains. Boring holes into us. What history?! It's time to hurry up and make some money. No one thinks about anything great . . . or sublime . . . We've had it up to here with greatness! We want something on the human scale. Normal. Mundane . . . you know, everyday stuff! It's enough to remember the great stuff occasionally, after a little vodka . . . We were the first ones in space . . . and manufactured the best tanks in the world. But there was no detergent or toilet paper. Those goddamn toilets always leaked! People would wash plastic bags and hang them out to dry on their balconies. Having a VCR was tantamount to having your own personal helicopter. A guy in jeans didn't inspire envy, just aesthetic interest—what an exotic novelty! That's the price we paid. The price

---

* Alan Chumak and Anatoly Kashpirovsky were rival television faith healers who enjoyed widespread popularity at the end of the 1980s and beginning of the 1990s, during the years of the Soviet collapse.
† An honorary title awarded to outstanding performers in the arts.

for all those missiles and spaceships. For great history! [*A pause.*] I've been running my mouth . . . Everyone's so eager to talk these days, but no one listens to one another . . .

. . . In the hospital, there was a woman in the bed next to my mother . . . When I walked into the room, she was the first person I'd see. One time, I watched her trying to tell her daughter something, but she couldn't form the words: m-ma . . . m-mu . . . Her husband came, and she tried to tell him, but that didn't work either. She turned to me: m-ma . . . Then she reached for one of her crutches and—do you understand—she started hitting her IV drip with it. Beating the bed . . . She didn't care what she was hitting, or breaking . . . She desperately wanted to speak . . . but who can you to talk to these days? Tell me: who? A person can't live in a vacuum . . .

. . . My whole life, I adored my father. He's fifteen years older than my mother, he fought in the war. But the war didn't crush him like it did so many others, it didn't shackle him to itself as the most significant event in his life. He still hunts and fishes. Dances. He's been married twice, and both times to beautiful women. My childhood memories . . . We were headed to the movies, and my dad grabbed my arm: "Look at how beautiful your mother is!" He never harbored that savage war valor like other men do after seeing combat. "A shot. A hit. The meat spilled out of him like it was coming out of a meat grinder." He remembers innocent things. Trifles. How on Victory Day, he and a friend went to a village to see some girls and ended up taking two Germans prisoner. The Germans had climbed into an outhouse and were hidden up to their necks in it. It seemed like a pity to shoot them! After all, the war was over. They'd had their fill of shooting. But it was impossible to get up close to them . . . My father got lucky: He could have been killed in the war, but he wasn't. Before the war, they could have arrested him, but they didn't. He had an older brother, Uncle Vanya. He hadn't been as lucky . . . When Yezhov was head of the NKVD, in the thirties, they sent him to the Vorkuta mines. Ten years without the right of correspondence. His wife, tormented by her coworkers, jumped out of a fifth-story window. Their son grew up with his grandmother. But Uncle Vanya made it back alive . . . He came back with a withered hand, toothless, his liver enlarged. He went back to work at the same factory, at the same job, in the same office, same desk . . . [*He lights another cigarette.*] He sat across from the guy who'd informed on him. Everyone knew it . . . and Uncle Vanya knew it, too—that that was the guy who had informed on him . . . but nothing changed: They attended meetings and demonstrations together. Read *Pravda,* voiced support for the Party's policies and the government. On holidays, they sat at the same table drinking vodka. And so on . . . that's us! Our life! That's what we're like . . . Imagine a victim and an executioner from Auschwitz sitting side by side in the same office, getting their wages out of the same window down in accounting. With identical war decorations. And now, with the same pensions . . . [*He is silent.*] I am close to Uncle Vanya's son. He doesn't read Solzhenitsyn, there isn't a single book about the camps at his house. The son had waited for his father, but the man who came back was somebody else . . . the husk of a man . . . Crushed and crumpled. He didn't last long. "You don't understand what it means to be afraid," he'd tell his son. "You don't understand . . ." With his own eyes, he'd seen an interrogator, this enormous guy, stick a prisoner's head in the shit bucket and hold him down until he drowned in it. As for Uncle Vanya . . . they'd strip him naked and hang him from the ceiling, pour spirits of ammonia into his nose, his mouth—every orifice in his body. The investigator pissed in his ear, screaming: "Names! . . . Give me names!" So Uncle Vanya named names . . . and signed everything. And if he hadn't given him names and signed the confessions, his head would have been the one in the shit bucket. Afterward, he ran into some of the people he'd named in the barracks . . . "Who informed on us?" they'd wonder. Who could have done that? Who . . . I'm no judge. And you're no judge, either. Uncle Vanya would be carried back to his cell on a stretcher, drenched in blood and piss. Covered in his own shit. I don't know when a person stops being human. Do you?

. . . It's very sad about our elderly, of course . . . They collect bottles at the stadiums, sell cigarettes in the Metro at night. Pick through the garbage dumps. But our elderly are no innocents . . . That's a terrifying thought! Seditious. I'm scared just thinking it. [*He is silent.*] But I will never be able to talk about this with my mother . . . I've tried . . . She goes into hysterics!

[*He wants to end the conversation, but for some reason he changes his mind.*]

. . . If I had read this story somewhere or heard it from someone, I wouldn't have believed it. But all sorts of things happen in real life . . . things out of a bad detective novel. My encounter with Ivan D. . . . Do you need his last name? For what? He's dead. His children? The son doesn't answer for the father—that's an old proverb . . . Yes, and his children are old men themselves. The grandchildren and great-grandchildren? I don't know about the grandchildren, but the great-grandchildren, they don't even know who Lenin is . . . Grandfather Lenin is all but forgotten. He's nothing but a statue now. [*A pause.*] Let me tell you about my encounter with him . . . I had just been promoted to lieutenant and was about to get married to his granddaughter. We'd already bought the wedding rings and her dress. Anna . . . that was her name. Pretty, right? [*He lights another cigarette.*] She was his granddaughter . . . He adored her. At home, everyone jokingly called her "The Doted Toad." He'd made it up . . . it meant that she was adored. And she looked like him, too—even a lot, I'd say. I come from a normal Soviet family, our whole lives, we lived from kopeck to kopeck, while these people had crystal chandeliers, Chinese porcelain, rugs, new Zhigulis. Everything was first class! There was an old Volga, too, that the old man refused to sell. And so on . . . I was already living with them in that apartment. In the mornings, we'd drink tea in the dining room, out of cups in silver cup holders. It was a big family— sons-in-law, daughters-in-law . . . One of the sons-in-law was a professor. Whenever the old man got angry at him, he'd always say the same thing: "People like you . . . I would have them eating their own shit!" Yep, that was a nice touch . . . but I never put it together . . . I didn't get it! Later on, I remembered. Afterward . . . Young Pioneers would come see him and write down his stories. They got his photographs for the museum. By the time I was around, he was already ailing, so he'd stay home. But before that, he'd speak at schools, tie red kerchiefs around the necks of the excellent students. He was an honored veteran. Every holiday, there'd be a big congratulatory card in the mailbox, every month, a special ration of groceries. One time, I went with him to pick up the ration . . . In some strange basement, we were handed a stick of *cervelat,* a jar of pickled Bulgarian cucumbers and tomatoes, imported canned fish, a jar of Hungarian ham, peas, canned cod liver . . . In those days, these were all scarce goods! Privileges! He took a liking to me right off the bat: "I like army men, and I hate suits." He showed me all of his expensive hunting rifles: "I'll leave these to you." Every wall of their giant apartment was covered in deer antlers; taxidermied animals stood on the bookshelves. Hunting trophies. He was a passionate hunter; for ten years or so, he'd been the head of the city hunting and fishing society. What else? He told a lot of war stories . . . "In combat, shooting at a distant target is one thing. Anyone can do that . . . but taking someone out when they're right there . . . Three meters away from you . . ." He was always saying stuff like that. You never got bored with him. I liked the old man.

I was on vacation and went to see them . . . The wedding was right around the corner. It was the middle of summer. We were all living together at their big dacha. It was one of the old dachas, not just the regulation four hundred square meters of land. I don't remember exactly how big it was, but they had a piece of the woods, too. Old pines. Only top-ranking officials got dachas like that. For special services. Prominent academics and writers. And him . . . Whenever I'd wake up, the old man would already be out in the garden. "I have the soul of a peasant. I came to Moscow from Tver in bast shoes." Most evenings, he'd sit alone on the terrace smoking. It was no secret: They'd discharged him from the hospital to die—he had terminal lung cancer. He didn't quit smoking. He came back from the hospital with a Bible: "I've been a materialist my whole life, but now, in the face of death, I've come to God." Some nuns who took care of the gravely ill had given him the Bible in the hospital. He read it with a magnifying glass. Before dinner, he'd read the papers, and after his post-dinner nap, war memoirs. He'd collected an entire library of memoirs: Zhukov, Rokossovsky.* He liked remembering his own life, too . . . How he'd seen Gorky and Mayakovsky in the flesh . . . the Chelyuskinites. He often said, "The people want to love Stalin and celebrate May 9." I'd argue with him: It was perestroika, the spring of Russian democracy . . . I was just a kid! One day, it was just the two of us, everyone else had gone to the city. Two men in an empty dacha. A carafe of vodka. "I don't give a damn about the doctors! I've lived my fill." "So should I pour you one?" "Go ahead." And so it began . . . I didn't understand right away . . . It didn't immediately occur to me that what we needed was a priest. The man was coming to terms with death . . . not immediately . . . At first, it was the regular conversation that people were having in those days: socialism, Stalin, Bukharin. Lenin's political last testament, which Stalin had hidden from the Party . . . We talked about everything that was in the air and in the papers. We drank. We got good and drunk! Pretty soon, he had gotten worked up: "You little snot! All young and green . . . Listen up! The last thing we want is for

* Georgy Zhukov (1896–1974), Marshal of the Soviet Union, was the most important Soviet military commander during World War II. Konstantin Rokossovsky (1896–1968) was among the most prominent Red Army commanders during World War II, a Marshal of Poland and of the Soviet Union.

our men to have freedom. They'll piss it all away!! You understand?"
Then swearing. A Russian can't convince another Russian of anything
without obscenities. I'm taking them out. "Get that through your
skull . . ." I, of course . . . I was in shock. In shock! He was going all
out: "These arm-waving liberals ought to be handcuffed and taken out
to chop timber. Get some pickaxes into those hands. You need fear.
Without fear, everything will fall apart in the blink of an eye." [*A long
pause.*] We picture monsters with horns and hooves. But there he was,
by the looks of it, a regular person sitting there . . . just a normal person . . . blowing his nose, sick, drinking vodka . . . I think . . . that was
the first time it occurred to me—that the victims stick around and
testify while the executioners hold their silence. They disappear, they
go down some invisible hole. They have no last names, no voices. They
vanish without a trace, and we know nothing about them.

In the nineties, while the executioners were still alive . . . they got
spooked . . . The name of the interrogator who'd tortured Academician Vavilov* flickered through the papers. I remember it, Alexander
Khvat. They printed a couple more names. All of them started panick-
ing that the archives would be unsealed, that they'd remove the "confidential" stamp. They got nervous. No one paid much attention to it,
there aren't any special statistics, but there were dozens of suicides.
All over the country. They wrote it off as another consequence of the
fall of the empire, blamed it on the general impoverishment . . . but I'd
hear about the suicides of rather well-off, decorated old men. Without
apparent cause. They all had one thing in common: All of them had
served the regime. Some of them suddenly heard the voice of their
consciences, some of them got scared that their families would find
out. They lost their nerve. Were stricken with terror. They couldn't
comprehend what was going on, why a vacuum had suddenly formed
around them . . . They were loyal hounds! Faithful service dogs! Of
course, not all of them flinched . . . In *Pravda,* or maybe it was *Ogonyok,* I don't remember, they published a letter from a former correc-
tions officer. That one wasn't afraid! He described all of the illnesses
he'd accumulated from working in Siberia where he'd guarded "the

* Nikolai Vavilov was a prominent Russian and Soviet botanist and geneticist. Although he was a brilliant scientist, because his beliefs ran counter to Stalin's anti-
genetics campaign, he was arrested in 1940 and died of starvation in 1943. In the
1960s, he was rehabilitated and hailed as a hero of Soviet science. A star and a moon
crater were named after him and his brother, Sergei Vavilov, a physicist who went on
to win the Nobel Prize.

enemies of the people" for fifteen years. He hadn't spared his health . . .
The work, he complained, had been strenuous: In the summer, the
mosquitos would eat him alive, and the heat was unbearable; in the
winter, it was the brutal cold. The "little jackets"—I remember, he
wrote "little jackets"—distributed to the soldiers were thin, while the
real bosses went around in sheepskin coats and felt boots. These days,
he said, you see the enemies they didn't manage to exterminate daring
to show their faces . . . It's sheer counterrevolution! The letter seethed
with hatred . . . [*A pause.*] Former inmates responded immediately . . .
They weren't afraid anymore. They spoke up. They wrote about how
inmates could be stripped naked, tied to trees, and overnight, the gnats
would eat them down to their bones. In winter, when it was forty
below zero, an inmate who didn't complete his daily quota could be
doused with water. Dozens of icy statues would be left standing outside like scarecrows until the spring . . . [*A pause.*] No one was ever
put on trial! Not a single one of them! The executioners lived out their
final days as respected pensioners . . . What can I say? Don't ask anyone to repent. Don't make things up about what our people are like,
saying that Russians are so good at heart. No one is prepared to repent. It's a great feat, repentance. Even when I go to church, I don't
have it in me to confess. It's hard . . . and really, people only ever feel
sorry for themselves. Not anyone else. Anyway . . . the old man was
furiously pacing the terrace, screaming . . . The things he was telling
me made my hair stand on end. By then, I already knew a lot. I'd read
Shalamov . . . But here, there was a little bowl of candy on the table, a
bouquet . . . It was this completely idyllic scene. And that contrast
made the reality all the starker. I was both scared and curious. More
curious than scared, to be perfectly honest. I wanted to . . . You always
want to look down into the abyss. Why? That's just the way we are.

". . . When I was hired by the NKVD, I was terribly proud," he
said. "First time they paid me, I bought myself a nice suit . . .

". . . What was the work like . . . What can you compare it to? It's
something like war. But for me, the war was like a vacation. You shoot
a German, he screams in German. These people screamed in Russian . . . They're practically your own people . . . It was easier to shoot
Lithuanians and Poles. But the ones screaming in Russian, 'Cretins!
Idiots! Hurry up and finish!' Shit . . . !!! We were always covered in
blood, we'd have to wipe our hands on our hair. Sometimes, they gave
us leather aprons. That's what work was like. The job. You're young . . .
Perestroika! Perestroika! You believe the babblers . . . They can shout,

'Freedom! Freedom!' all they like. Run around the squares . . . The axe is right where it always was. The axe will survive the master . . . Don't forget that! Shit . . . !!! I'm a soldier. When I was told to march, I marched. When I was told to shoot, I shot. If they give you the orders, you'll go, too. You *will* go!!! I was killing enemies. Vermin! You get a document: Sentenced to 'the highest measure of social protection.' It's a verdict from the state . . . The work—God forbid! If you don't get him the first time, he'll fall down squealing like a pig . . . vomiting blood . . . It's especially unpleasant to shoot a laugher. They've either gone crazy, or they really hate you. There was wailing and cursing from all sides. You can't eat beforehand . . . I couldn't . . . I was always thirsty. Water! Water! Just like when you're hungover . . . Shit . . . !!!! Toward the end of our shifts, they would bring us two buckets: a bucket of vodka and a bucket of cologne. They'd bring the vodka in after the shift was over, not before. Have you read that anywhere? It's the truth . . . They write all sorts of things these days. Make a lot of stuff up . . . We'd wash ourselves with cologne from the waist up. Blood is pungent, it's a special kind of smell . . . a little like the smell of semen . . . I had a German Shepherd, and it wouldn't go near me after work. Shit . . . !!! What are you sitting there all silent for? You're still green, you haven't seen anything yet . . . Listen! It didn't happen often, you know, but sometimes, we'd get an officer who liked to kill . . . People like that would soon be transferred out of the firing corps. We didn't like people like that. There were a lot of country boys like me. Country boys are tougher than city folk. More resilient. More used to death: some had slaughtered boars, others calves, everyone had killed a chicken before. With death, it's something you have to get used to . . . The first few days of work, you just watched. Troops were simply present at executions, or they would transport the condemned. There were cases of people going insane immediately. They couldn't handle it. It's a subtle art . . . Even with killing a rabbit, you have to be in the habit, not everyone can do it. Shit . . . !!! You put a person on their knees and then you have to shoot them practically point-blank, into the left side of the head, behind the left ear. By the end of my shift, my arm would be hanging down like a whip. The worst was my index finger. We had a plan to fulfill, like at any other place. Like at a factory. At first, we couldn't meet our quotas. We physically couldn't do it. So they called some doctors in. Had a consultation. It was decided that two days a week, the troops would get massages. They'd massage our right hands and index fingers. They absolutely had to massage our index fingers because they're under the greatest strain during shooting. My only work-related injury is that I'm deaf in my right ear from shooting from the right side . . .

". . . They would issue us certificates: 'For performing special Party and government missions,' 'For dedication to the mission of the Party of Lenin and Stalin.' I have a whole cupboard full of these awards, all printed on excellent paper. Once a year, they would send me and my family to a good sanatorium. Great food . . . lots of meat, medical treatment . . . My wife didn't know anything about what I did. It was top secret, important work—that's all she knew. I married for love.

". . . During the war, we were trying to save ammunition. If we were by the sea, we'd pack a barge tight as a can of sardines. It wouldn't be screaming coming from the hold, but a beastly roar . . . 'Our proud Varangian never surrenders / No one seeks mercy here . . . ' The hands of each of the condemned were bound with wire, and a stone would be tied to their feet. If it was calm weather, a calm sea, you could watch them sinking for hours . . . What are you looking at me for? You little punk! What are you looking at? Shit . . . !!! Pour me another! That was our job. Work . . . I'm telling you this so that you understand: The Soviet state cost us dearly. It needs to be guarded. Preserved! At night, we'd go back to the sea, and the barges would be empty. Dead silence. Everyone had the same thought: as soon as we set foot on the shore, they'll . . . Shit . . . !!! For years, I kept a wooden suitcase ready under my bed: a change of underwear, a toothbrush, a razor. I slept with a gun under my pillow . . . always prepared to put a bullet through my forehead. Everyone lived like that in those days! Soldiers and marshals alike. In that, we were equals.

"When war broke out, I immediately asked to be sent to the front. It's not that frightening to die in battle. At least you know that you're dying for the Motherland. It's all very straightforward. I liberated Poland and Czechoslovakia . . . Shit . . . !!! I finished my tour of duty in Berlin. I have two decorations and medals. Victory! Then . . . what happened was, after the Victory, I was arrested. The special service agents had the lists prepared ahead of time. For Chekists, there are only two ways out of the service: Either you die by the enemy's hand or at the hands of the NKVD. They gave me seven years. And I did all seven. To this day, I still wake up like I did at the camps, at six on the dot. What was I in for? They never told me. What was I in for?! Shit . . . !!!"

[He nervously crumples the empty pack of cigarettes.]

Maybe he was lying. But no, of course he wasn't lying . . . It didn't seem like it . . . I don't think so. In the morning, I made up some excuse, some nonsense, and left. I ran! Called off the wedding. Uh-huh, yep . . . How could I marry her? I couldn't go back to that house. I couldn't! I went to my regiment. My fiancée . . . she didn't understand what had happened. She wrote me letters . . . suffered . . . and I did, too. But that's not what we're talking about right now. This isn't about love—that's another story. I want to understand—and you want to understand, as well—what kind of people they were. Right? After all, a murderer is an interesting kind of person. No matter how you cut it, a murderer can't be just a regular guy. You're drawn to him. It pulls you in . . . Evil is mesmerizing. There are hundreds of books about Hitler and Stalin. What were they like as children, with their families, with the women they loved . . . ? Their wine and their favorite cigarettes . . . We're interested in every last detail. We want to understand . . . Tamerlane, Genghis Khan, who were they? Who? And the millions of people like them . . . miniature copies . . . They also committed atrocities and only handfuls of them lost their minds. While the rest led normal lives: kissing girls and playing chess . . . Buying toys for their kids . . . Each one of them thinking, "That isn't me." I wasn't the one putting those people on the rack or blowing their brains out, that wasn't me back there putting sharpened pencils through women's nipples. It's not me, it's the system. Even Stalin . . . even he'd say, "I'm not the one who decides, it's the Party." He taught his son: You think that I'm Stalin—you're wrong! That's Stalin! And he'd point to the portrait of himself hanging on the wall. Not at himself, but at his portrait. Meanwhile, for decades, the death machine worked nonstop . . . Its logic was brilliant: The victims are accused of being executioners and then, in the end, the executioners themselves become the victims. As though it wasn't just people running it . . . Things are only that perfect in nature. The flywheel turns, but there's no one to blame. No one! Everyone wants to be pitied. Everyone is a victim. Everyone is at the bottom of the food chain. There! I was young, I got scared, I was bewildered. Today, I would have asked him more questions . . . I need to know these things . . . Why? I'm afraid. Knowing what I know about people, I'm afraid of myself. Scared. I'm an ordinary man . . . weak . . . I'm black and white and yellow . . . I'm all sorts of things. In Soviet school, they taught us that by himself, man is good, he's great. And even today, my mother still believes that it is only terrible circumstances that make him terrible, but man is essentially good! That's just not how it is. It's not! No . . . Man vacillates between good and evil for his entire life. Either you're stabbing someone in the nipples with a pencil, or you're getting stabbed . . . Take your pick! Go ahead! It's been so many years, but I still can't forget it . . . He shouted, "I watch TV, I listen to the radio. It's the rich and poor all over again. Some people gorge themselves on caviar, buy islands and private jets, while others can't afford a loaf of white bread. This won't last long around here! People will once again acknowledge Stalin's greatness. The axe is right where it always was . . . The axe will survive the master. Mark my words . . . You asked how long a man is a man, how long can he hang on? I'll tell you: The leg of a Viennese chair in the anus or a nail to the scrotum, and he's gone. Ha ha . . . no longer a man . . . just some crap on the floor!"

[*Taking his leave.*]

They've shaken up our entire history . . . Thousands of revelations, tons of truth. For some, the past is a trunk of flesh and a barrel of blood. For others, it's a great era. We butt heads in our kitchens every day. But soon enough, the next generation is going to come of age . . . the young wolves, as Stalin called them. They'll be grown soon . . .

[*He attempts to leave, but suddenly resumes talking.*]

I recently saw these old snapshots online—just these regular-looking war-era photos, if you don't know who they are of. It's an SS brigade from Auschwitz, officers and privates. Lots of girls. They took pictures at parties, while they were out strolling. Young people having fun. [*A pause.*] And how about the photos of our own Chekists that you see at museums? Take a close look at them sometime: You'll see their handsome and inspired faces. For a long time, we were taught that these people were saints . . .

I would like to leave this country or at least get my kids out of here. We're going to leave. The axe will survive the master . . . I never forgot those words . . .

A few days later, he called me and forbade me to publish his story. Why? He refused to explain. Later, I found out that he and his family had emigrated to Canada. When, after another ten years, I reconnected with him, he finally agreed to let me publish it. He said, "I'm glad I left in time. For a while, people liked Russians, now they're afraid of us again. Aren't you?"

PART TWO

◆

THE CHARMS
OF
EMPTINESS

SNATCHES OF STREET NOISE AND
KITCHEN CONVERSATIONS

(2002–2012)

◆

ABOUT THE PAST

—Yeltsin's nineties . . . how do we remember them? They were a happy time . . . a crazy decade . . . terrifying years . . . the age of fantastical democracy . . . the fatal nineties . . . hands down, a golden age . . . the age of self-denunciation . . . mean and hard times . . . a bright dawn . . . aggressive . . . turbulent . . . That was my time . . . It wasn't for me!!

—We pissed away the nineties! We're not going to have an opportunity like that again, at least not anytime soon. Everything started out so well in '91! I'll never forget the faces of the people I stood with in front of the White House. We were triumphant, we were powerful. We wanted to live. We were intoxicated by freedom. But now . . . now I see it all in a different light . . . We were so naïve, it's disgusting! Brave, honest, and naïve. We believed that salami was spontaneously generated by freedom. We too are to blame for everything that happened afterward . . . Of course, Yeltsin is also responsible, but so are we . . .

I think that it all started that October. October 1993 . . . "Bloody October," "Black October," "The Second Coup"* . . . That's what they call it . . . Half of Russia was pulling forward, while the other half was pulling back. Back toward dreary socialism. The damned *sovok*. The Soviet regime refused to surrender. The "Red" parliament refused to be subordinate to the president. That's how I saw it back then . . . My wife and I had helped the cleaning woman in our building—she was from somewhere around Tver—with money on more than one occasion, and we gave her all of our furniture after renovating our apartment. But on the morning when it all started, she noticed my Yeltsin pin, and instead of saying, "Good morning!" she

---

* In reaction to the dissolution of parliament, some conservative deputies locked themselves in the White House after having deposed Yeltsin to have him replaced with General Alexander Rutskoy. Yeltsin decreed a state of emergency on October 3 and ordered the storming of the White House the next day. Several hundred people died. The state of emergency was lifted on October 18. On November 5, Yeltsin presented a constitutional amendment reinforcing presidential powers, which was adopted on December 12.

told me, her voice full of malice, "Your time is running out, you bourgeois pig," and turned away. I didn't see that coming. Where had this hatred come from? What did she hate me for? The situation was the same as it had been in '91 . . . On TV, I saw the White House burning, the tanks firing . . . tracer bullets in the sky . . . the storming of the Ostankino Television Tower . . . General Makashov* in a black beret screaming, "No more of your mayors or misters or monsters." And hatred . . . hatred . . . It began to smell like civil war. Like blood. From the White House, General Rutskoy† outright called for war: "Pilots! Brothers! Get your planes in the air! Bomb the Kremlin! There's a gang of criminals in there!" Seemingly overnight, the city filled with military vehicles. Mysterious men in camouflage. That's when Yegor Gaidar addressed "Muscovites and all Russians who hold democracy and freedom sacred," asking them to come to the White House to stand up for Yeltsin. It was exactly like 1991 . . . We went down there . . . I went . . . There were thousands of us . . . I remember running forward in a crowd of people. I tripped and fell onto a sign reading, "For a Bourgeois-Free Russia!" The image of what awaited us if General Makashov won flashed before my eyes . . . I saw a wounded young man; he couldn't walk, so I carried him. "Which side are you on?" he asked me. "Are you for Yeltsin or Makashov?" He supported Makashov, which meant we were enemies. "Go to hell!" I swore at him. What else? We split off into Reds and Whites again with an alarming speed. There were dozens of wounded lying by the side of the ambulance. All of them—for some reason, I remember this very clearly—had worn-out boots; all of them were simple people. Poor people. I was questioned there as well: "Who did you drag here—is he one of us or one of them?" People who weren't "one of us" were put to the back of the line; they lay bleeding on the asphalt . . . "What's wrong with you? You're insane!" "But aren't these our enemies?" Something had happened to everyone in the course of those two days . . . something in the

---

* Albert Makashov (1938–) was one of the fomenters of the so-called Second Putsch. After the rebellion was suppressed, he and other leading opposition figures were arrested. He was amnestied in 1994 and elected to the Duma as a Communist Party deputy in 1995.

† Alexander Rutskoy (1947–), vice president of Russia before the October 1993 crisis, constitutionally proclaimed himself president in opposition to Yeltsin on September 22. Once Yeltsin's forces had seized back control, Rutskoy was arrested and imprisoned until the 1994 amnesty proclaimed by the new Duma.

air was off. The people around me were totally different, they had very little in common with the people with whom I'd stood in front of the White House two years before. They were carrying spikes made of sharpened plumbing fixtures . . . real machine guns, which people were handing out from the back of a truck . . . War! It was real this time. They were piling up the dead next to a phone booth . . . The corpses were also in worn-out boots . . . Meanwhile, not far from the White House, the cafés were still open, and people were still drinking beer as though nothing was happening. Gawkers hung out on their balconies watching it all like it was a play. And suddenly, right in front of me, I saw two men carrying a TV out of the White House. With telephone receivers hanging out of their coat pockets . . . The looters were cheerfully being shot at from above. Probably by snipers. Sometimes they would hit them, other times they would hit the TVs . . . There was the constant sound of gunfire in the streets . . . [*He falls silent.*] After it was all over, when I got home, I found out that our neighbor's son had been killed. The kid was twenty. He had been on the other side of the barricades . . . It had been one thing when we argued with them in our kitchen, but shooting . . . How did it happen? I never wanted that . . . When you're part of a mob, the mob is a monster. A person in a mob is nothing like the person you sit and chat with in the kitchen. Drinking vodka, drinking tea. I'm never demonstrating again, and I won't let my sons do it, either . . . [*He is silent.*] I still can't wrap my mind around it: Were we defending freedom or participating in a military coup? I have my doubts . . . hundreds of people died . . . No one but their families remembers them. "Woe to him who is building a city by blood . . ."* [*Silence.*] And what if General Makashov had won? There would have been even more bloodshed. Russia would have collapsed. I don't have the answers . . . Until 1993, I believed in Yeltsin . . .

My sons were little boys back then, they've grown up since. One of them is even married. Several times, I tried . . . I wanted to tell them about 1991 . . . 1993 . . . but they're not interested. Their eyes would glaze over. The only question they have for me is, "Papa, why didn't you get rich in the nineties, back when it was so easy?" As though the only people who didn't get rich were the armless and dumb. Your cre-

---

* Archpriest Avvakum quoting the Old Testament in the address of the Russian Orthodox clergy to the State Duma following the events of October 3–4, 1993.

tin ancestors . . . kitchen impotents . . . We were too busy running around to protests. Sniffing the air of freedom while the smart ones divvied up the oil and gas . . .

—Russians are the kind of people who get swept up in things. For a while, they were swept up in communism, furiously working to manifest it in real life with a religious fanaticism. Eventually, they got tired of it, and grew disillusioned. They decided to reject the old world, shaking its ashes off of their feet. It's very Russian to start over from the smoking ruins. So once again, we're drunk on seemingly new ideas. Forward, toward the triumph of capitalism! Soon, we'll be living as well as they do in the West! Rose-colored dreams . . .

—The living is better.

—And for some people, it's gotten a thousand times better.

—I'm fifty years old . . . I try not to be a *sovok,* but I'm not very good at it. I work at a private company and hate the owner. The way they split up the big pie of the USSR, their pirate privatization, just doesn't sit well with me. I don't like the rich. They're always showing off their palaces on TV, their wine cellars . . . They can bathe in breast milk in gold bathtubs for all I care! What do I need to see that for? I don't know how to live with them. It hurts. It's humiliating. And I'm not going to change. I lived under socialism for too long. Life is better now, but it's also more revolting.

—I'm amazed at how many people are still rooting for the Soviet regime.

—What's there to talk about with *sovoks?* We just have to sit tight until they all die out and then remake everything the way we think it ought to be. The first order of business is getting that mummy Lenin out of the mausoleum. What Asiatic nonsense! It lies there like a hex . . . that rotting carcass . . .

—Calm down, comrade. You know that people speak much more kindly about the USSR these days than they did twenty years ago. I recently visited Stalin's grave, and there were mountains of flowers there. Red carnations.

—The devil knows how many people were murdered, but it was our era of greatness.

—I don't like the way things are today, I'm not thrilled about it. But I don't want to return to the *sovok,* either. I'm not champing at the bit to go back in time. Unfortunately, I can't remember anything ever being good.

—I would like to go back. I don't need Soviet salami, I need a country where people are treated like human beings. We used to say "simple people" and now they say "the simplefolk." Can you feel the difference?

—I grew up in a dissident family . . . in a dissident kitchen . . . My parents knew Sakharov, they distributed *samizdat*. Along with them, I read Vasily Grossman, Yevgenia Ginzburg, Dovlatov, listened to Radio Liberty. In 1991, I was, of course, in front of the White House, in a human chain, prepared to sacrifice my life to prevent the return of communism. Not a single one of my friends was a communist. For us, communism was inextricably linked with the Terror, the gulag. A cage. We thought it was dead. Gone forever. Twenty years have passed . . . I go into my son's room, and what do I see but a copy of Marx's *Das Kapital* on his desk, and Trotsky's *My Life* on his bookshelf . . . I can't believe my eyes! Is Marx making a comeback? Is this a nightmare? Am I awake or am I dreaming? My son goes to the university, he has a lot of friends, and I've started eavesdropping on their conversations. They drink tea in our kitchen and argue about *The Communist Manifesto* . . . Marxism is legal again, on trend, a brand. They wear T-shirts with pictures of Che Guevara and Lenin on them. [*Despairingly.*] Nothing has taken root. It was all for naught.

—Here's a joke to lighten the mood . . . It's the Revolution. In one corner of a church, Red Army men are drinking and partying; in another, their horses are eating oats and pissing on the floor. The psalmist runs over to the hegumen: "Father, how dare they do this in our holy temple!" "It's not so bad. They'll stick around for a while and then they'll move on. When their grandchildren grow up, that's when it'll really get bad." And here they are, fully grown . . .

—There's only one way out for us—we have to return to socialism, only it has to be Russian Orthodox socialism. Russia cannot live without Christ. The Russian people's happiness has never had anything to do with money. That's the difference between the "Russian idea" and the American Dream.

—Russia doesn't need democracy, it needs a monarchy. A strong and fair Tsar. The first rightful heir to the throne is the Head of the Russian Imperial House, the Grand Duchess Maria Vladimirovna, and then her heirs.

—Berezovsky suggested Prince Harry . . .

—Monarchy is madness! Doddering antiquity!

—The unbelieving heart is weak and unfortified before sin. The

Russian people will renew themselves through the search for God's truth.

—I only liked perestroika when it first started. If someone had told us back then that a KGB lieutenant-colonel would end up as president . . .

—We weren't prepared for freedom . . .

—Liberty, equality, and fraternity are words that have spilled an ocean of blood.

—Democracy! That's a funny word in Russia. "Putin the Democrat" is our shortest joke.

—Over the course of these past twenty years, we've found out a lot about ourselves. Made a lot of discoveries. We learned that Stalin is secretly our hero. Dozens of books and movies have been made about him, which people avidly read and watch. And debate. Half of the country dreams of Stalin—and if half of the country is dreaming of Stalin, he's bound to materialize, you can be sure of it. They've dragged all of the evil dead back out of hell: Beria, Yezhov . . . They've started writing that Beria was a talented administrator, they want to rehabilitate him, because under his leadership, the Russian atom bomb was built . . .

—Down with the Chekists!

—What's next, a new Gorbachev or the next Stalin? Maybe it'll be the swastika? *Sieg Heil!* Russia has gotten up off her knees. Now is a dangerous time because Russia should have never been humiliated for so long.

ON THE PRESENT

—The Putinist 2000s . . . What are they like? Overcast . . . gray . . . brutal . . . Chekist . . . glamorous . . . stable . . . sovereign . . . Russian Orthodox . . .

—Russia is, has always been, and will always be an empire. We're not just a big country, we're the Russian civilization. We have our own path.

—Even today, the West fears Russia . . .

—Everyone needs our natural resources, especially Europe. Open up any encyclopedia: we're seventh in the world for oil reserves, and in Europe, in first place for natural gas. We have some of the largest reserves of iron ore, uranium ore, tin, copper, nickel, cobalt . . . and diamonds and gold, silver and platinum—Mendeleev's entire table of elements! One Frenchman even said to me, "Why do you say everything belongs to you, doesn't the world belong to everyone?"

—At the end of the day, I'm an imperialist, yes. I want to live in an empire. Putin is my president! Today, it's shameful to call yourself a liberal, just like it used to be shameful to call yourself a communist. The men by the beer stand could break your face in for that.

—I hate Yeltsin! We believed in him, and he led us in a totally strange direction. This is no democratic paradise. We ended up in a place that's even more terrifying than the one we came from.

—Our problem isn't Yeltsin or Putin, the problem is that we're slaves. Our slavish little souls! Our slave blood! Take a look at the New Russian . . . He climbs out of his Bentley, money spilling out of his pockets, but he's still a slave. A big boss runs the whole operation, "Everyone back to the stable!" And everyone goes.

—I was watching a talk show . . . "Are you worth a billion?" asked Mr. Polonsky.* "No?! Then go fuck yourself!" I'm one of the people whom the honorable oligarch told to go fuck himself. I come from a normal family: My father's an alcoholic, my mother breaks her back for kopecks at a nursery school. To them, we're just shit; we're nothing but manure. I go to various political meetings. I sit in with the patriots, the nationalists . . . I listen to their speeches. The day will come when somebody will hand me a rifle. And I'll take it.

—Capitalism isn't taking root here. The spirit of capitalism is foreign to us. It never made it out of Moscow. We don't have the proper climate for it in the rest of the country. And we're not the right people. The Russian man isn't rational or mercantile, he'll give you the shirt off his back, but sometimes he'll steal. He's elemental, more of a watcher than a doer. He can get by on very little. Accumulating money isn't for him, saving bores him. He has a very acute sense of fairness. We're a Bolshevik people. And finally, Russians don't want to just live, they want to live for something. They want to participate in some great undertaking. You'll sooner find a saint here than an honest and successful man. Read the Russian classics . . .

—Why is it that when our people go abroad, they have a fine time assimilating into the capitalist way of life? But when they're at home, they like to talk about "sovereign democracy," a separate Russian civi-

---

* Sergei Polonsky (1972–) is a young Russian real estate mogul who came to be an influential figure in the 2000s.

lization, and how "there's no foundation for capitalism in the Russian way of life"?

—Our capitalism is all wrong . . .

—Abandon all hope for any other kind of capitalism . . .

—It's like Russia has capitalism but no capitalists. There are no new Demidovs or Morozovs* . . . The Russian oligarchs aren't capitalists, they're just thieves. What kind of capitalists can you fashion out of former communists and Komsomol members? I don't feel sorry for Khodorkovsky.† Let him rot on his prison bunk. I'm only sorry that he's the only one doing time. Someone ought to be held responsible for what I lived through in the nineties. I was robbed blind. My job was taken away. The capitalist revolutionaries: Gaidar, a.k.a. the Iron Winnie the Pooh, Ginger Chubais . . . They ran experiments on living people like they were some kind of mad scientists . . .

—I went out to the country to visit my mother. The neighbors told me that the night before, someone had burned the farmer's house down. The people had made it out alive, but the livestock were all killed. The village drank for two days straight in celebration. And you call this capitalism . . . What we have is a socialist people living under capitalism . . .

—Under socialism, I was promised that there was a place in the sun for everyone. Now they're singing a different tune: If we live according to Darwin's laws, we will enjoy abundance. Abundance for the fittest. But I'm one of the weak. I'm not a fighter . . . There was a plan for me and I was used to living according to plan: school, college, family. My husband and I will save up for an apartment in a cooperative, and after the apartment, we'll save up for a car . . . Then they canceled that plan. Threw us to the wolves of capitalism . . . I have a degree in engineering, I worked at the design institute that everyone called the "women's institute" because it was all women. You sit there and stack papers all day. I liked to keep things neat, in tidy little piles. I would have sat there my whole life, but then they started downsizing . . . They didn't touch the men, there weren't that many of them, or single mothers, or women who only had one or two years left before retirement. They posted lists, and I saw my last name on one of them . . .

* Famous industrialists and businessmen from the pre-Revolutionary period.
† Mikhail Khordorkovsky (1963–), formerly the richest oligarch in Russia, was imprisoned after coming into conflict with Putin and since his release in 2013 has been living in exile.

What was I going to do now? I was completely lost. I'd never been taught how to live by Darwin's laws.

For a long time, I continued to harbor hopes of finding a job in my field. I was an idealist in the sense that I didn't know my place in the world, my true worth. I still miss the girls from my department—the girls in particular, our chatter. Work came second; socializing, our banter, came first. We'd have tea about three times a day, and everyone would talk about what was going on in their lives. We celebrated all the holidays, all our birthdays . . . and now . . . I go to the employment office. No results. Nothing but jobs for painters and plasterers. . . . My friend, she and I went to college together, she's a housekeeper for this businesswoman, she walks her dog . . . essentially, she's a servant. She used to cry from the humiliation, but now she's used to it. I couldn't do it.

—Vote for the communists, it's cool.

—In the end, a sane person can't understand Stalinists. A hundred years of flushing Russia down the drain, and now they're crying "Glory to the Soviet Cannibals!"

—Russian communists haven't been real communists for a long time now. Private property, which they have indeed recognized, is irreconcilable with the communist Idea. I can say the same thing about them that Marx said about his disciples: "All I know is that I'm not a Marxist." Heine put it even better: "I have sown dragon's teeth and reaped only fleas."

—Communism is the future of mankind. There is no alternative.

—On the gates of the Solovki prison camp there was a Bolshevik motto: "With an Iron Fist, We Will Chase Humanity into Happiness." That's one recipe for saving humanity.

—I have no desire to go out into the street and try to accomplish anything. It's better to do nothing. No good, no evil. What's good today will turn out to have been evil tomorrow.

—There's nothing more terrifying than an idealist . . .

—I love my Motherland, but I am not going to stay here. I could never be as happy as I would like here.

—I might be an idiot, but I don't want to leave, even though I can.

—I'm not going anywhere, either. It's more fun to live in Russia. Europe doesn't have this kind of pulse.

—It's better to love our Motherland from afar . . .

—Today, it's embarrassing to be Russian . . .

—Our parents lived in the country of victors, we live in the country that lost the Cold War. We have nothing to be proud of!

—I'm not about to take off . . . I have a business here. I can tell you with certainty that it's possible to live well in Russia as long as you stay out of politics. All of these rallies for freedom of speech, against homophobia—I don't give a rat's ass about any of that . . .

—Everyone's talking about revolution . . . how Rublevka's* growing vacant . . . The rich are fleeing abroad and taking their capital with them. They're shuttering their palaces, "For Sale" signs are everywhere you look. They sense that the people are resolutely determined. But no one is going to give anything up of their own free will. That's when the Kalashnikovs are going to have to do the talking . . .

—Some people are shouting "Russia for Putin!" Others are shouting "Russia without Putin!"

—And what's going to happen when oil prices fall or oil becomes obsolete?

May 7, 2012. On television, Putin's ceremonial motorcade makes its way to the Kremlin for his inauguration through a completely empty Moscow. No people, no cars. A city perfectly cleared. Thousands of policemen, soldiers, and OMON troops posted in front of every Metro exit and building. The capital, swept clean of Muscovites and the eternal Moscow traffic jams. A dead city.

After all, this isn't a true Tsar!

ON THE FUTURE

More than a century ago, Dostoevsky finished writing The Brothers Karamazov. *He wrote of the eternal "Russian boys" who will always debate "the big questions, nothing less: Is there a God, is there immortal life? As for those who don't believe in God, they take up the subjects of socialism and anarchism, remaking humanity according to a new model. Don't they see that all they'll end up with is the devil? It's always the same questions, no matter how they are posed."*

---

* Rublevka is the unofficial name for a prestigious residential area in the southwestern suburbs of Moscow. It is known for its expensive gated communities, which are populated with Russia's elite.

The specter of revolution is once again haunting Russia. On December 10, 2011, a hundred thousand people came out to demonstrate on Bolotnaya Square. Since then, protests against the current regime have not stopped. What are the "Russian boys" chewing over today? What will they choose this time around?

—I go to protests because it's time they stop treating us like chumps. Bring back free elections, you lowlifes! The first time one hundred thousand people assembled on Bolotnaya Square, no one imagined that there would be that many of us. We kept putting up with it, and then, at a certain point, the lies and lawlessness went off the charts: Enough! Everyone watches the news on TV, reads articles online. People are talking about politics. Being part of the opposition is fashionable. But I'm afraid . . . afraid that we're all just blowhards . . . We stand on the square, chant, and then we go home to our computers and fool around online. All that remains is, "Good job, us!" I've already encountered this: When it came time to make posters and hand out flyers for an upcoming demonstration, everyone ducked out and took off . . .

—I used to stay away from politics. My job and my family were enough for me, I didn't see the point of marching through the streets. I was more attracted to the theory of small deeds: I volunteered at a hospice; when there were forest fires outside of Moscow, I brought clothes and groceries to the victims. It was a different kind of experience . . . Meanwhile, my mother was always in front of the television. She was sick of the liars and crooks with a Chekist past, she'd tell me everything. We went to the first protest together, even though my mother is seventy-five years old. She's an actress. Just in case, we brought flowers. We thought they wouldn't shoot at people holding flowers!

—I wasn't born in the USSR. If I don't like something, I go out on the street and protest. I don't just run my mouth off in the kitchen before going to bed.

—I'm afraid of revolution . . . I know there's going to be a Russian uprising, senseless and merciless. But I'd be ashamed to sit things out at home. I don't need a "new USSR" or "a renewed USSR" or "the true USSR." I won't abide Putin and Medvedev sitting down and deciding: Today you're the president, and tomorrow it's me. I'm not having any of that swill. We're not just cattle, we're the people. At demonstrations, I see people I've never seen at protests before: Alongside the veteran dissidents of the sixties and seventies, there are a lot of students who, until recently, were wholly indifferent to all that propaganda they push on the idiot box . . . like the ladies in mink coats and the kind of young men who'd show up to protests in their Mercedes. Just yesterday, all they cared about was money, clothes, and comfort, but then it turned out that this wasn't enough. It's simply not enough for them anymore. And the same goes for me. It's not the hungry marching, it's the well-fed. Posters . . . our folk art . . . "Putin, leave of your own free will!" "I didn't vote for these bastards, I voted for other bastards!" I liked a poster that said, "You can't even imagine us." We weren't about to storm the Kremlin, we just wanted to declare who we were. As we were leaving, we chanted, "We'll be back."

—I'm a Soviet person, afraid of everything. Even ten years ago, I would have never gone out onto the square. Today, I don't miss a single rally. I went to the demonstrations on Sakharov Prospekt and Novy Arbat. I was part of the White Ring.* I'm learning how to be a free person. I don't want to die the way I am now, all Soviet. I'm dredging the Sovietness out of myself by the bucketful . . .

—I go to demonstrations because my husband does . . .

—I'm not young. I want to live to see a Russia without Putin.

—I've had it up to here with the Jews, the Chekists, and the homosexuals . . .

—I'm a leftist. My conviction is that it's impossible to achieve anything nonviolently. I'm thirsty for blood! Without blood, we can't ever get anything major done. Why are we in the streets? I am standing here waiting to storm the Kremlin. This isn't a game anymore. We should have taken the Kremlin a long time ago instead of going around shouting. Give me the orders to pick up a crowbar and pitchfork! I'm ready.

—I'm here with my friends . . . I'm seventeen. What do I know about Putin? I know that he does judo and has the eighth dan in it. And that's basically all I know about him . . .

—I'm no Che Guevara, I'm a wimp, but I haven't missed a single rally. I want to live in a country I'm not ashamed of.

—I'm the kind of person who has to be on the barricades. It's how I was raised. After the Spitak earthquake in 1988, my father volunteered to go to Armenia to help with the relief effort. Because of that,

---

* An anti-Putin protest during which opponents to the regime formed a human chain in the center of Moscow in 2012.

he died early. Heart attack. Since I was little, instead of a father, all I've had is a photograph. To protest or not to protest—everyone has to decide for themselves. My father went of his own accord . . . It was his choice . . . My friend had wanted to come to Bolotnaya with me, and then she called me up: "I thought about it, and I have a little kid." Well, I have my elderly mother. When I leave the house, she sucks down the Validol. But I go anyway . . .

—I want my children to be proud of me . . .

—I need to be here for my own self-respect . . .

—We have to try to do something . . .

—I believe in revolution . . . Revolution is long, hard work. In 1905, the first Russian revolution ended in failure and defeat. But twelve years later, in 1917, it took off so forcefully that it shattered the Tsarist regime to smithereens. We're going to have our own revolution!

—I'm going to the rally, are you?

—I for one got fed up with 1991 . . . 1993 . . . I don't want any more revolutions! First of all, revolutions are rarely velvet, and second of all, I have experience: Even if we win, it will be the same as it was in 1991. The euphoria will quickly fade. The battlefield will go to looters. Gusinskies,* Berezovskies, and Abramoviches will all show up . . .

—I'm against the anti-Putin demonstrations. It's a lot of hullabaloo in the capital. Moscow and Petersburg support the opposition, but everywhere else, the people stand with Putin. Do we really live so poorly? Aren't things better than they were before? It's scary to risk losing what we have. The suffering we endured in the nineties is still fresh in everyone's minds. No one is eager to smash it to pieces all over again, spilling a lot of blood along the way.

—I am not a huge fan of the Putin regime. We're sick of the little Tsar, we want rotating leaders. Change, of course, is necessary, but not a revolution. And when people fling asphalt at the police, I don't like that, either . . .

—The State Department is behind it all. The Western puppet-masters. We already cooked up one perestroika according to their recipes, do you remember how that turned out? We ended up totally stuck in the mire! I don't go to those demonstrations, I go to Putin rallies! Rallies for a strong Russia!

—The picture has changed completely a number of times over the past twenty years. And what have we ended up with? "Putin, leave!

* Vladimir Gusinsky (1952–) is a Russian media tycoon.

Putin, leave!" is just the latest mantra. I don't want to participate in that kind of spectacle. So what if Putin leaves? Some new autocrat will come take the throne in his place. People will go on stealing, same as before. We'll still have the filthy entranceways, the abandoned elderly, the cynical bureaucrats, and the brazen traffic cops . . . Bribing officials will still be considered a matter of course . . . What's the point of changing governments if we don't change ourselves? I don't believe in the possibility of any kind of democracy here. We're an oriental nation . . . feudal . . . with clergy instead of intellectuals . . .

—I don't like crowds . . . the herd . . . A crowd doesn't decide anything, individuals do. The government made sure that there were no flashy personalities at the top. The opposition doesn't have a Sakharov or Yeltsin. This "snow" revolution hasn't produced any heroes. Where's their platform? What are they going to do? They'll come out to the streets and shout . . . and then that same Nemtsov or Navalny[*] will tweet about how they're on vacation in the Maldives or Thailand. That they're enjoying Paris. Imagine Lenin going on a jaunt to Italy or skiing in the Alps after a demonstration in 1917 . . .

—I don't go to the demonstrations, and I don't vote. I don't harbor any illusions . . .

—Are you aware that besides you people, there's also a Russia? All the way out to Sakhalin . . . Russia doesn't want any revolutions—not an "orange" one, or a "rose" one, or even this "snow revolution."[†] Enough revolutions! Leave the Motherland alone!

—I don't give a damn about tomorrow . . .

—I don't want to march alongside communists and nationalists, next to Nazis . . . Would you march alongside the KKK wearing their hoods and carrying crosses? No matter what wonderful objective a march may have. We're dreaming of different Russias!

—I don't go to the rallies . . . I'm afraid of getting hit over the head with a club . . .

—We need to pray, not go to demonstrations. The Lord sent us Putin . . .

—I don't like the revolutionary banners outside my window. I'm for evolution . . . building something . . .

---

[*] Alexei Navalny (1976–) is a prominent blogger, an anti-corruption campaigner, and a leading opponent of the Putin regime.
[†] The Orange Revolution was a series of protests in Ukraine in 2004 and 2005; the Rose Revolution took place in Georgia after protests in 2003. The "snow revolution" was one of the names for the anti-Putin protests that swept Moscow in 2011 and 2012.

—I don't go to demonstrations . . . and I'm not going to justify myself for not participating in a political spectacle. These demonstrations are nothing but cheap theatrics. People have to make up their minds to live according to the teachings of Solzhenitsyn, without lies. Otherwise, we're not moving forward a single millimeter. We'll just keep going around in circles.

—I love my Motherland the way it is . . .

—I have excluded the government from my areas of interest. My priorities are my family, my friends, and my business. Have I explained myself?

—But aren't you an enemy of the people, citizen?

—Something is bound to happen. And soon. It's not a revolution yet, but you can smell the ozone in the air. Everyone is waiting: Who, what, when?

—I just started living well. Let me live a little!!!

—Russia is sleeping. Don't even dream about change.

TEN STORIES IN THE ABSENCE OF AN INTERIOR

◆

ON ROMEO AND JULIET . . . EXCEPT THEIR NAMES WERE MARGARITA AND ABULFAZ

◆

Margarita K., Armenian refugee,
41 years old

Oh! That's not what I'm talking about . . . that's not what I want to talk about . . . I want to talk about other things . . .

I still sleep with my arms behind my head, an old habit from my years of being happy. I used to love life so much! I'm Armenian, but I was born and grew up in Baku. On the seashore. The sea . . . my sea! I left, but I still love the sea. People and everything else disappointed me, the sea is the only thing I still love. I always see it in my dreams—gray, black, and violet. And lightning bolts! The way the lighting dances with the waves. I used to love staring off into the distance, watching the sun set in the evening. It would get so red toward nightfall, it seemed to sizzle as it descended into the water. The rocks would get warm in the course of the day, warm rocks, like living beings. I loved to look at the sea in the morning and during the day, in the evening and at night. At night, the bats would come out, and I was always so scared of them. Cicadas sang. A sky full of stars . . . You won't see that many stars anywhere else. Baku is my favorite city—my very favorite, in spite of everything! In my dreams, I often find myself strolling through Governor's Park or Nagorny Park. I go up on the fortress wall . . . Everywhere you go, you could see the sea, the ships, and the oil rigs. My mother and I liked to go to *chaikhanas** and drink red tea.

* Traditional Central Asian teahouses.

[*She has tears in her eyes.*] My mother lives in America now. She weeps and misses me. I live in Moscow . . .

In Baku, we lived in a big building. It had a large courtyard, with mulberries growing in it, white mulberries. They were so good! Everyone lived together like one big family—Azerbaijanis, Russians, Armenians, Ukrainians, Tatars. Miss Clara, Miss Sarah . . . Abdulla, Ruben . . . The most beautiful woman was Silva, she was a stewardess on international flights, she'd fly to Istanbul. Her husband, Elmir, was a taxi driver. She was Armenian and he was Azerbaijani, but no one ever gave it a second thought, I don't remember any discussion of their nationalities. The world was divided up differently: Is someone a good or bad person, are they greedy or kind? Neighbor and guest. We were from the same village, the same town . . . everyone had the same nationality—we were all Soviet, everyone spoke Russian.

The most beautiful holiday, everyone's favorite, was Navruz. Navruz Bayram is the celebration of the arrival of spring. People waited for it all year long, it's celebrated for seven days. During Navruz, people didn't close their gates or doors . . . no lock and keys day or night. We'd make bonfires . . . bonfires burned on the roofs and in the courtyards. The whole city was filled with bonfires! People would throw fragrant rue into the fire and ask for happiness, saying *"Sarylygin sene, gyrmyzylygin mene"*—"My hardships to you, my happiness to me." *"Gyrmyzylygin mene . . ."* Anyone could go into anyone else's house—and everyone would be welcomed as a guest, served milk pilaf and red tea with cinnamon or cardamom. And on the seventh day, the most important day of the holiday, everyone came together at one table . . . We would all carry our tables into the courtyard and make one long, long table. This table would be covered in Georgian *khinkali,* Armenian *boraki* and *basturma,* Russian *bliny,* Tatar *echpochmak,* Ukrainian *vareniki,* meat and chestnuts Azeri-style . . . Miss Klava would bring her signature "herring under a fur coat" and Miss Sarah her stuffed fish. We drank wine and Armenian cognac. And Azerbaijani cognac. We sang Armenian and Azerbaijani songs. And the Russian "Katyusha": "The apple and pear trees were in bloom . . . The mists swam over the river . . ." Finally, it would be time for dessert: *bakhlava, sheker-churek . . .* To me, these are still the most delicious things in the world! My mother was the best at making sweet pastries. "What magical hands you have, Knarik! What light dough!" The neighbors would always praise her.

My mother was close with Zeinab, and Zeinab had two daughters and a son, Anar, who was in the same class as me at school. "You'll marry your daughter to my Anar," Zeinab would joke. "Then we'll be relatives." [*She talks to herself.*] I'm not going to cry . . . There's no need to cry . . . When the pogroms on Armenians began . . . Zeinab, our sweet Auntie Zeinab and her son Anar . . . We fled, and kind people hid us . . . While we were gone, they took our refrigerator and television in the night . . . our gas stove and our new Yugoslavian wall cabinet . . . Anar and his friends ran into my husband and beat him with iron rods. "What kind of Azerbaijani are you? You're a traitor! You live with an Armenian woman—our enemy!" My friend took me in to live with her, she hid me up in her attic . . . Every night, they would unseal the attic, feed me, and then I would have to go back up there, and they would nail the door shut. Dead shut. If anyone found me, they'd kill me! When I came out of hiding, my bangs had gone gray . . . [*Very quietly.*] I tell people: No need to cry about me . . . but here I am crying . . . When we were in school, I had a crush on Anar, he was good-looking. One time, we even kissed . . . "Hello, Queen!" He'd wait for me at the gates of our school. "Hello, Queen!"

I remember that spring . . . Of course I remember it, but I don't think about it too often these days . . . Not very often. Spring! I had completed special courses and gotten a job as a telegraph operator. At the Central Telegraph office. People would stand at the window: One woman is crying, her mother just died, the next one is laughing, she's getting married. Happy birthday! Happy golden anniversary! Telegrams, telegrams. Calling Vladivostok, Ust-Kut, Ashkhabad . . . It was a fun job. Never boring. Meanwhile, I waited for love . . . When you're eighteen, you're always waiting for love. I thought that love only came once, and you understand that it's love instantaneously. But the way it happened was funny, it was really funny. I didn't like how he and I met. In the morning, I usually walked right through security, everyone knew me, so no one would ever ask for my ID: Hi, hi, no questions. Then, one day: "Your ID, please." I was dumbfounded. There was this tall, handsome guy standing in front of me, not letting me through. "But you see me every day." "Your ID, please." It just so happened that that day, I had forgotten my ID. I dug around in my purse, but it turned out that I didn't have any of my documents with me. They called my boss . . . I got chewed out . . . I was so mad at that security guard! And he . . . I was working the night shift, and he and his friend came by to have tea with me. Imagine that! He brought me pastries filled with jam, they don't make them like they used to, they were so good, but it was scary to bite into them because you never knew what side the filling was going to come out of. We laughed! But I didn't talk to him because I was still mad. A few days later, he found me after work. "I got tickets to the movies. Wanna come?" They were tickets to my favorite comedy, *Mimino,* starring Vakhtang Kikabidze. I'd seen it ten times already, I knew the whole thing by heart. It turned out that he did, too. We walked along quoting lines, testing one another: "I'll let you in on something smart, just don't get mad at me." "How am I supposed to sell this cow if everyone around here knows her?" So we fell in love . . . His cousin had big greenhouses, he sold flowers. Abulfaz always brought me roses, red and white . . . There are even lilac-colored roses, they look like they're dyed, but they're real. I fantasized . . . I'd often dreamed of love, but I didn't know how hard my heart could beat, how it could feel like it was jumping out of my chest. On the wet beach, we'd leave our writing on the sand . . . "I love you!" in giant letters. And ten meters further along, "I love you!!!" again. Back then, there were these vending machines all over town that dispensed soda water. They'd have cups attached to them by chains, and everyone would drink out of the same cup. You'd rinse it out and drink from it. We went up to one of the vending machines, but there was no cup attached to it, and the next one didn't have a cup, either. I was thirsty! We'd sung, shouted, and laughed so much when we were by the sea—I was thirsty! For a long time, magical, improbable things kept happening to us, and then, one day, they stopped. Yes, yes, I promise, it's the truth! "Abulfaz, I want to drink! Think of something!" He looked at me, raised his hands to the sky, and began muttering. He muttered at the sky like that for a long time . . . Suddenly, from behind the overgrown fences and shuttered kiosks, this drunk appeared out of nowhere and handed over a cup: "For a be-a-u-ti-ful girl, I can spare it."

And that sunrise . . . Not a soul around, just the two of us. The fog rolling in from the sea. I was barefoot, the fog rose up from the asphalt like steam. And then another miracle! The sun suddenly came out! Light . . . so much light . . . as though it was the middle of a summer day. My dress, wet from the dew, dried instantly. "You look so beautiful right now!" And you . . . you . . . [*She has tears in her eyes.*] I tell other people not to cry . . . But I . . . I keep remembering everything . . . remembering . . . but every time, there are fewer voices and fewer dreams. Back then, I really dreamed, I was always up in the clouds . . . Floating through life! Only it never happened. We never got our happy ending: the white dress, the wedding march, a honeymoon. Soon, all too soon . . . [*She stops.*] I wanted to say something . . . something . . . but I keep forgetting the simplest words. I've started forgetting things . . . I wanted to say that soon, so very soon after that, people started hiding me in their basements. I lived in attics, I turned into a cat . . . a bat. If only you could understand . . . if only you could know how scary it is to hear somebody screaming in the middle of the night. A lone scream. When a lone bird cries out in the middle of the night, it's enough to make anyone shudder. Can you imagine how it feels when it's a human screaming? I lived with a single thought: I love him, I love him, and again, I love him. I couldn't have survived otherwise, I wouldn't have been able to bear it. How could I—the horror! I only came down from the attic at night, the drapes were as thick as blankets. One morning, they opened the attic and said, "Come out! You're saved!" Russian troops had entered the city . . .

I think about that . . . I think about it even in my sleep—when did it all begin? 1988 . . . People started gathering on the square, dressed in all black, singing and dancing. They danced with knives and daggers. The telegraph building was near the square, it all happened right before our eyes. We flooded out onto the balcony and watched. "What are they shouting?" I asked. "Death to the infidels! Death!" This went on for a long time, a very long time . . . many months . . . They started chasing us away from the windows: "Girls, it's dangerous. Go to your desks, and don't get distracted. Do your work." At lunchtime, we'd usually drink tea together, and then, one day, the Azerbaijani girls suddenly started sitting at one table and the Armenian girls at another. It all happened in the blink of an eye, do you understand? I for one could not understand it at all, I just couldn't. I couldn't believe any of it for a long time. I was in love, wrapped up in my feelings . . . "Girls! What happened?" "Didn't you hear? The boss said that pretty soon, only pure-blooded Muslim girls are going to be working for him." My grandmother had survived the Armenian pogrom of 1915. I remember when I was little, she would tell me about it: "When I was a little girl like you, they murdered my father, my mother, and my aunt. And all of our sheep . . ." My grandma always had sad eyes. "Our neighbors were the ones who did it . . . Before that, they had been normal—you could even say good—people. We all sat around the same table on holidays . . ." I thought that it had all been so long ago . . . Could something like that really happen today? I asked my mother: "Mama, did you notice that the boys in the courtyard have stopped playing

war and started playing killing Armenians? Who taught them that?"
"Quiet, daughter. Or the neighbors will hear you." My mother was
always crying. She just sat there and wept. Once, I saw the children
dragging some dummy through the courtyard and poking it with
sticks, children's daggers. "Who's that?" I called over little Orkhan,
Zeinab's grandson. "That's an old Armenian woman. We're killing
her. Auntie Rita, what are you? Why do you have a Russian name?"
My mother had named me . . . Mama liked Russian names. Her whole
life, she'd dreamed of seeing Moscow . . . My father had abandoned
us, he lived with another woman, but he was still my father. I went to
him with the news: "Papa, I'm getting married!" "Is he a good guy?"
"Very. But his name is Abulfaz . . ." My father didn't say anything, he
wanted me to be happy. But I had fallen in love with a Muslim . . . he
prayed to a different God. My father said nothing. And then Abulfaz
came to our house: "I want to ask for your hand." "But why are you
here alone without your groomsmen? Where are your relatives?"
"They're all against it, but I don't need anyone but you." And I . . . I
didn't need anyone else, either. What could we do with our love?

The things happening all around us were very different from what
was happening inside of us . . . radically different. At night, the city
was chillingly quiet . . . How can it go on like this, I can't stand it.
What is all this—the horror! During the day, people weren't laughing
anymore, they weren't joking around, they'd stopped buying flowers.
It used to be that there was always someone walking down the street
with a bouquet. People kissing here and there. Now the same people
were walking down the street avoiding one another's gaze . . . Something loomed over everyone and everything, some sort of forebod-
ing . . .

I can't remember everything precisely anymore . . . the situation
changed from day to day. Today, everyone knows about Sumgait . . .
it's only thirty kilometers outside of Baku . . . The first pogrom happened there. One of the girls we worked with was from there. One day,
after everyone had gone home, she started staying at the telegraph office. She'd spend the night in the storeroom. She walked around in
tears, wouldn't even look out the window, and didn't speak to anyone.
We asked her what was wrong, she wouldn't say. And when she finally
opened her mouth and started telling us . . . I wished I'd never
heard . . . I didn't want to hear about those things! I didn't want to
hear anything! What was going on! What is this—how could they!
"What happened to your house?" "It was looted." "What happened to

your parents?" "They took my mother out into the courtyard, stripped her naked, and threw her on the fire! And then they forced my pregnant sister to dance around the fire . . . Then, after they killed her, they dug the baby out of her with metal rods . . ." "Shut up! Shut up!" "My father was hacked to pieces with an ax . . . My relatives only recognized him by his shoes . . ." "Stop! I'm begging you!" "Men, young and old, in groups of twenty or thirty, got together and started breaking into the houses where Armenian families lived. They killed and raped daughters in front of their fathers, wives in front of husbands . . ." "Stop it! Just cry instead." But she wouldn't cry. She was too scared . . . "They torched cars. At the cemetery, they knocked over tombstones with Armenian last names on them. They even hate the dead . . ." "Hush! Are people really capable of such things?!" All of us became afraid of her . . . Meanwhile, on television, on the radio, and in newspapers, there wasn't a single word about Sumgait. All we had were rumors . . . Much later, people would ask me: "How did you survive? How could you go on living after all that?" Spring came. Women put on their light dresses . . . It was so beautiful all around us, and yet there was so much terror! Do you understand . . . ? And the sea.

I was preparing for our wedding . . . My mother pleaded, "Daughter, think about what you're doing." My father said nothing. Abulfaz and I would walk down the street together, sometimes we would run into his sisters: "Why did you tell me she's ugly? Look at what a cute little girl she is." Whenever they saw us, they'd whisper those kinds of things to each other. Abulfaz! Abulfaz! I begged him: "We should get married, but do we really need to have a big wedding?" "What's wrong with you? My people believe that a person's life consists of just three days: the day you're born, the day you get married, and the day you die." He had to have a proper wedding. Without a wedding, we couldn't be happy. His parents were against it—categorically against it! They gave him no money for the wedding and wouldn't even return the money he'd earned himself. But everything had to be done according to custom, according to the traditions . . . Azerbaijani traditions are beautiful, I love them. The first time the groomsmen come, they are heard out and sent away, and only on the second try do they get an agreement or rejection. That's when they drink wine. Then it's the groom's job to buy a white dress and a ring, and bring them to the bride's house in the morning. And it has to be on a sunny day . . . because you have to convince happiness to stay, you have to ward off the forces of darkness. The bride accepts the gifts and thanks the groom, kissing him in front of everyone. She wears a white shawl over her shoulders, a symbol of her purity. On the wedding day, the couple is brought gifts by both sides of the family, they receive a mountain of gifts that are placed on large trays and tied with red ribbons. They also blow up hundreds of balloons and fly them over the bride's house for several days afterward, the longer the better, it means that their love is strong and mutual.

My wedding . . . our wedding . . . all of the gifts from both the bride's side and the groom's side were purchased by my mother . . . and the white dress and the gold ring, too. At the table, before the first toast, members of the bride's family are supposed to get up and praise the bride and the groom's parents, the groom. My grandfather spoke about me, and when he was finished, he asked Abulfaz, "And who is going to say something about you?" "I'll say it myself," he replied. "I love your daughter. I love her more than life itself." The way he said that got everyone on his side. They threw small change and rice at us, for happiness and wealth. And then . . . there's another part . . . when the relatives from one side are supposed to stand up and bow to the relatives from the other side and vice versa. Abulfaz stood alone . . . as though he were kinless . . . "I'll have your baby and then you won't be alone anymore," I vowed in my head. Solemnly. He knew, I'd confessed to him long before, that I had been very sick as a child and the doctors had told me that I must never give birth. And he agreed to that, too, anything just to be with me. But I . . . At that moment, I decided that I would have his baby anyway. Even if it meant that I would die, the child would live.

My Baku . . .

The sea . . .

The sun . . .

It's not my Baku anymore . . .

There were no doors in the entrances, the spaces where the doors had been were covered in plastic . . .

. . . Men or teenagers . . . I was too terrified to remember . . . were beating—murdering—a woman with a fence post. Where had they found them in the city? She lay on the ground not making a sound. When passersby saw what was happening, they'd turn the corner and walk down another street. Where were the police? The police had disappeared . . . I would go days without seeing a single policeman. At home, Abulfaz was nauseated. He was a kind man, very kind. But where had those other people come from, the ones out on the street? A man covered in blood came running toward us . . . His coat, his hands all covered in blood . . . He was clutching a long kitchen knife, the kind people use to cut herbs. He had this triumphant, maybe even happy look on his face . . . "I know that guy," said the girl standing with us at the bus stop.

. . . Something inside me died in those days . . . I lost a part of myself . . .

. . . My mother quit her job . . . It became dangerous to walk down the street, people instantly saw that she was an Armenian. I didn't have that problem, only under one condition: I could never bring any of my documents out with me. None of them! Abulfaz would pick me up from work, and we'd walk home together so that no one would have a chance to suspect that I was Armenian. Anyone could come up to you and demand to see your passport. "Hide. Leave," our neighbors, the old Russian ladies, warned us. The younger Russians had already left, abandoning their apartments and nice furniture. Only the old women remained, those kind-hearted Russian grandmas . . .

. . . I was already pregnant . . . Under my heart, I carried a child . . .

The bloodbath in Baku went on for several weeks. Or at least that's what some people say, others say it was longer . . . They didn't just kill Armenians, they also killed the people who hid them. My Azerbaijani friend hid me, she had a husband and two kids. One day . . . I swear! I'll come back to Baku and bring my daughter to their house: "This is your second mother, daughter." They had these thick drapes . . . thick as a coat . . . They'd had them sewn especially for me. At night, I would come down from the attic for an hour or two . . . We spoke in whispers, but I absolutely had to be talked to. Everyone understood: They needed to talk to me so that I wouldn't go dumb and lose my mind. So that I wouldn't miscarry or start wailing in the night like an animal.

I remember our conversations very well. Afterward, I would spend all day up in the attic going over them in my head. I was alone . . . All I saw was a thin ribbon of sky through a crack . . .

". . . They stopped old Lazar in the street and started beating him . . . 'I'm a Jew,' he insisted. By the time they found his passport, he was already seriously injured."

". . . People get killed for their money and just because . . . They seek out the homes of well-off Armenians . . ."

". . . They killed everyone who lived in this one building . . . The youngest girl climbed a tree to escape . . . so they shot at her like she was a little bird. It's hard to see at night, they couldn't get her for a long time, it made them angry . . . They kept firing. Finally, she fell at their feet . . ."

My friend's husband was an artist. I love his work, he painted portraits of women and still lifes. I remember how he'd go up to the bookshelves and rap on the spines: "We have to burn them all! Burn them to hell! I don't believe in books anymore! We thought that good would triumph over evil—nothing of the kind! We'd argue about Dostoevsky . . . Yes, those are the characters who are always with us! Walking among us. They're right here!" I didn't know what he was talking about—I'm a simple girl, a commoner. I didn't go to university. All I knew was how to cry and wipe my tears . . . For a long time, I had believed that I lived in the best country in the world, among the very best people. That's what they'd taught us in school. He was terribly upset, it was all incredibly hard on him. He ended up having a stroke and becoming paralyzed . . . [*She stops.*] I need to be silent for a moment . . . I'm shaking . . . [*After a few minutes, she continues.*] And then Russian troops entered the city. I could go home . . . My friend's husband was bedridden, he could only move one of his arms, and barely. He embraced me with that arm: "I thought about you all night long, Rita, and about my life. For many years, practically my whole life, I've railed against the communists. Now I have my doubts: so what if those old mummies ruled over us, pinning medal after medal onto one another, and we couldn't go abroad, read forbidden books, or eat pizza, the food of the gods? That little girl . . . she would have still been alive, no one would have been shooting at her . . . like she was a bird . . . You wouldn't have had to hide in the attic like a mouse . . ." He died soon afterward, just a little while later. Many people died in those days, a lot of good people. They couldn't take it anymore.

The streets filled with Russian troops. Military equipment. Russian soldiers, just boys . . . what they saw made them faint . . .

I was eight months pregnant. My due date was coming up. On nights when I was in pain, we'd call an ambulance, but as soon as they heard my Armenian last name, they'd hang up on us. They wouldn't accept us into any maternity clinics, not the neighborhood one . . . not anywhere. They'd open my passport and right away, it was, "Sorry, no room." No room! Nowhere and no way, simply no way. My mother found an old midwife, a Russian woman, one who had helped her give birth a long, long time ago . . . She found her living in a small village on the edge of town. Her name was Anna . . . I don't remember her patronymic. Once a week, she'd come to our house, examine me, and tell us that labor wouldn't be easy. My contractions started in the middle of the night . . . Abulfaz ran out to flag a cab, we couldn't reach one by phone. The taxi driver came and saw me: "What is she, Armenian?" "She's my wife." "I'm not taking you anywhere." My husband broke down in tears. He took out his wallet and waved all his money at the man, his entire month's pay: "Take it . . . I'll give you everything . . . Just save my wife and child." We got in the car . . . all of us . . . My mother came, too. We went to the village where Anna lived, to the hospital where she worked part-time. To supplement her pension. She had been waiting for us; they put me on the table immediately. I was in labor for a long time, seven hours . . . There were two of us giving birth that night: me and an Azerbaijani woman. They only had one pillow, and they gave it to her, so my head was very low the whole time, in a painful and uncomfortable position . . . My mother stood in the doorway. They kept trying to kick her out, but she wouldn't leave. What if they tried to steal the baby . . . What if? Anything could have happened . . . In those days, anything was possible. I gave birth to a girl . . . They only brought her to me once, showed her to me, and then they wouldn't bring her again. They let the other mothers, all Azerbaijani, breastfeed their babies, but not me. I waited for two days. And then . . . along the wall, clinging to it for support . . . I crept to the room where they kept the newborns. It was completely empty except for my little girl, the doors and windows were all shut. I felt her temperature, she was burning up, all hot. Just then, my mother came . . . "Mama, we're taking the baby and leaving. She's already sick."

My daughter was sick for a long time. An old doctor, long retired, treated her. A Jew. He went around helping Armenian families. "They're killing Armenians just for being Armenian the same way they once killed Jews just for being Jewish," he said. He was very, very old. We named our daughter Ira . . . Irinka . . . We decided that she should have a Russian name, it might protect her. The first time Abulfaz held her, he cried. He wept with joy . . . There was joy in those days, as well. Our joy! Around then, his mother got sick . . . He started going to see his family all the time. When he'd come back from seeing them . . . I won't be able to find the words . . . for how he was when he'd come back. It was like he was a stranger with a face I didn't recognize. Of course, I was scared. There were tons of refugees flooding the city, Azerbaijani families fleeing Armenia. They showed up empty-handed, without anything, exactly the same way Armenians fled Baku. And they told the same stories. Oh! It was all identical. They spoke about Khodjali, where there had been a pogrom on Azerbaijanis. About how the Armenians had murdered them, throwing women out of windows . . . cutting people's heads off . . . pissing on the dead . . . No horror film can scare me now! I've seen so much and heard so much—too much! I couldn't sleep at night, I kept turning and turning it over in my mind—we simply had to leave. We just had to! We couldn't go on like this, I couldn't. Run . . . run to forget . . . and if I had stayed, I would have died. I'm sure I would have died . . .

My mother left first . . . After her, it was my father with his second family. Then me and my daughter. We had false documents, passports with Azerbaijani last names . . . It took us three months to buy the tickets, that's how long the lines were! When we got on the airplane, there were more cases of fruit and cardboard boxes of flowers than passengers. Business! Business was booming. In front of us, there were these young Azerbaijanis who drank wine the whole way there. They said they were leaving because they didn't want to kill anyone. They didn't want to go to war and die. It was 1991 . . . The fighting in Nagorno-Karabakh was in full swing . . . Our fellow passengers confessed: "We don't want to lie down under a tank. We're not ready." In Moscow, our cousin came to meet us at the airport . . . "Where's Abulfaz?" "He'll be here in a month." My relatives got together that evening. Everyone begged me: "Talk, please talk, don't be scared. Silent people get sick." A month later, I started talking, even though I thought I'd never talk again. That I'd shut up for good.

I waited, and waited . . . and waited . . . Abulfaz didn't join us in a month . . . or six months. It took him seven years. Seven years . . . seven . . . If it hadn't been for my daughter, I wouldn't have made it. My daughter saved me. For her sake, I held on with all my strength. In order to survive, you need to find at least the thinnest thread . . . In order to survive waiting that long . . . It was morning, just another morning . . . He stepped into our apartment and embraced us. Then he just stood there. One minute he was standing there in the entrance, and the next, I was watching him collapse in slow motion. Moments later, he was lying on the floor, still in his coat and hat. We dragged him to the sofa and rested him on top of it. We got so scared: We had to call a doctor, but how? We weren't registered to live in Moscow, we didn't have insurance. We were refugees! As we were trying to figure out what to do, my mother burst into tears. My daughter was in the corner, staring with wild eyes . . . We'd waited for Papa for so long, and now, here he was, dying. Finally, he opened his eyes: "I don't need a doctor, don't worry. It's over! I'm home." I'm going to cry now . . . Now I'm going to cry . . . [*For the first time in our entire conversation, she breaks down in tears.*] How could I not cry? For a month, he followed me around the apartment on his knees, kissing my hands. "What are you trying to say?" "I love you." "Where have you been all this time?"

. . . They stole his passport . . . and after he got a new one, they did it again . . . It was all his relatives' fault . . .

. . . His cousins came to Baku . . . They'd been forced out of Yerevan where they'd lived for several generations. Every night, they'd tell stories . . . always making sure that he could hear . . . A boy had been skinned alive and hanged from a tree. They'd branded a neighbor's forehead with a hot horseshoe . . . And then, and then . . . "And where do you think you're going?" "To be with my wife." "You're leaving us for our enemy. You're no brother of ours. You're not our son."

. . . I'd call him . . . They'd say, "He's not home," and tell him that I'd called and said I was getting remarried. I kept calling and calling. His sister would answer the phone: "Forget this phone number. He's with another woman now. A Muslim."

. . . My father . . . He wanted me to be happy . . . He took away my passport and gave it to some guys to put a stamp in it certifying that I was divorced. To falsify my documents. They wrote something in it, washed it off, tried to fix it, and in the end, they made a hole in my passport. "Papa! Why did you do that? You know I love him!" "You love our enemy." My passport is ruined, it's not valid anymore . . .

. . . I read Shakespeare's *Romeo and Juliet* . . . two enemy families, the Capulets and the Montagues. It's about my life . . . I understood everything, every word . . .

I didn't recognize my daughter. She started smiling from the moment she saw him, "Papa! Papochka!" She was little . . . Before he came home, she'd take his photos out of the suitcase and kiss them. But only when she thought I wasn't looking . . . so I wouldn't cry . . .

But this is not the end . . . You think that's it? The end? Oh no, not yet . . .

. . . We live here as though we're at war . . . Everywhere we go, we're foreigners. Spending time by the sea would cure me. My sea! But there's no sea anywhere near here . . .

. . . I was a cleaning woman in the Metro, I scrubbed toilets. I dragged bricks and sacks of concrete at a construction site. Right now, I clean at a restaurant. Abulfaz renovates apartments for rich people. Nice people pay him, bad people cheat him. "Get the hell out of here, *churka!** Or we'll call the police." We're not legally registered to live here . . . we have no rights . . . There are as many of us here as there are grains of sand in the desert. Hundreds of thousands of people fled their homes: Tajiks, Armenians, Azerbaijanis, Georgians, Chechens . . . They escaped to Moscow, the capital of the USSR, only now it's the capital of another country. You won't find our nation anywhere on the map . . .

. . . My daughter finished school a year ago . . . "Mama, Papa . . . I want to continue my education!" But she doesn't have a passport . . . We live like transients. We rent from an old lady, she moved in with her son and rents us her one-bedroom apartment. The police knock on the door wanting to check our documents . . . and we freeze like mice. Once again, we're living like mice. They'll send us back—but to where? Where can we go? They can kick us out in twenty-four hours! We don't have the money to buy them off . . . and we're not going to find another apartment as good as ours. Everywhere you go, you see ads that say, "Will rent an apartment to a Slavic family," "Will rent to a Russian Orthodox family. Others need not apply."

. . . We never leave the house at night! If my daughter or husband are late, I take valerian. I beg my daughter not to wear too much makeup or flashy dresses. They killed an Armenian boy, they stabbed a Tajik girl to death . . . they stabbed an Azerbaijani. We used to all be Soviet, but now we have a new nationality: "person of Caucasian descent." In the morning, I run to work. I never look young men in the eye because I have dark eyes and black hair. On Sundays, if we leave the house, we'll stroll through our own neighborhood, not straying far from our house. "Mama, I want to go to the Arbat. I want to walk around on Red Square." "We can't go there, daughter. That's where the skinheads hang out. With swastikas. Their Russia is for Russians. Not for us." [*She falls silent.*] No one knows how many times I've wanted to die.

---

* Russian racial slur for a person from the Caucasus region or Central Asia.

. . . My little girl . . . Since childhood, she's heard the words *"churka,"* "darkie" . . . When she was very little, she didn't understand. When she'd come home from school, I'd kiss her and kiss her so she would forget those awful words.

All the Armenians left Baku for America. They were taken in by a foreign country . . . My mother, my father, and many of our relatives moved there. I went to the American embassy myself. "Tell us your story," they said. I told them about my love . . . They were silent; for a long time, they didn't say anything. Young Americans, they were very young. Then they started discussing it among themselves: Her passport is all messed up, and it's weird, where was her husband for seven years? Is he really her husband? The story is too terrifying and beautiful to believe. That's what they said. I know a little English . . . I realized that they didn't believe me. But I have no proof other than my love for him . . . Do you believe me?

"I believe you . . ." I tell her. "I grew up in the same country as you. I believe you!" [*And both of us cry.*]

ON PEOPLE WHO INSTANTLY TRANSFORMED AFTER THE FALL OF COMMUNISM

◆

Ludmila Malikova,
technician, 47 years old

AS TOLD BY HER DAUGHTER

On a time when everyone lived the same way

Do you know Moscow well? It was in the Kuntsevo district . . . We had a three-room apartment in a five-story building, we got it when we took my grandma in. After my grandpa died, she lived alone for a long time, but then she began to decline, and we decided that we should all live together. I was excited, I loved my grandma. We'd go cross-country skiing, play chess. She was an amazing grandma! As for my father . . . I had one, but he didn't live with us for long. He started screwing up, getting drunk with his buddies all the time, so Mama asked him to leave . . . He worked at a restricted-access military manufacturing plant . . . I remember how when I was little, my father would come over on weekends and bring me presents, candy and fruit. He always tried to make it the very biggest pear, the biggest apple. He wanted to amaze me. "Close your eyes, Yulia—*voilà!*" He had this beautiful laugh . . . but later on, my father disappeared . . . The woman he lived with after us—she was a friend of my mother's—kicked him out, too. She got sick of his benders. I don't know whether or not he's alive, but if he were alive, he would be looking for me . . .

Until I was fourteen, we led a cloudless existence. Until perestroika . . . We did just fine until capitalism arrived, and they started talking about "the market" on TV. No one understood what it was exactly, and no one was explaining anything, either. It all started with being allowed to badmouth Lenin and Stalin. Mostly, it was young people who did the badmouthing, older people kept silent, they would get off the trolleybus if they heard someone deriding the Communists. Like at school—our young math teacher was against the Communists while our older history teacher supported them. Or at home, my grandma would say, "Instead of communists, we're going to have speculators." My mother disagreed: "No, we're going to have a beautiful, fair life." She went to rallies, breathlessly recounted Yeltsin's speeches. But Grandma was unshakable: "They've swapped socialism for bananas. Chewing gum . . ." Their debates began in the morning, then Mama would go to work, and they would resume in the evening. Whenever Yeltsin appeared on TV, Mama would hurry over to watch: "What a great man!" Grandma would cross herself: "He's a criminal, may the Lord forgive me." She was a dyed-in-the-wool communist. She voted for Zyuganov.* Everyone had started going to church, and my grandma did, too. She'd cross herself and keep the fasts, but the only thing she ever really believed in was communism . . . [*Silence.*] She liked telling me stories about the war . . . When she was seventeen, she'd volunteered to go to the front, and that's where my grandfather had fallen in love with her. She'd dreamed of being a telephone operator, but the division she was assigned to needed a cook, so she became a cook. Grandpa was a cook, too. They fed the wounded in the field hospital. Delirious, the wounded would scream, "Come on! Forward! Advance!" It's too bad, she told me so many stories, but I only remember bits and pieces . . . Nurses would always have buckets of chalk so that whenever they ran out of pills and powders, they'd make chalk placebos to keep the wounded men from yelling and beating them with their crutches . . . There was no TV back then, no one had ever seen Stalin, but everyone wanted to see him. And my grandma did, too—she worshiped him until her dying day: "If it weren't for Stalin, we'd be licking the German's asses." She could swear like a sailor when she wanted. My mother didn't like Stalin, she called him a fiend and a

---

* Gennady Zyuganov (1944–) emerged as the leader of the reformed Communist Party after the dissolution of the Soviet Union, spearheading the opposition against capitalist reforms. He remains a political force to this day.

butcher . . . I would be lying if I said that I gave any of this very much thought at the time . . . I was just living my life, enjoying myself. My first love . . .

My mother was a dispatcher at a geophysics research institute. We got along well. I'd tell her all my secrets, even the kinds of things that you don't usually share with your mother. You could do that with her, she wasn't like a grown-up at all, she was more like my older sister. She loved books, music—that was her life. Grandma was the one at the helm . . . Mama said that even when I was very little, I was a golden child. I was never difficult, she never had to coerce me into doing anything. I really did adore her . . . I'm glad I look like her—the older I get, the stronger the resemblance. We have practically the same face. It makes me really happy . . . [*She is silent.*] We weren't well off, but we got by. Everyone we knew lived the same way we did. It was even fun. Mama's friends would come over all the time and they'd talk and sing songs. I've known Okhudzhava since childhood:

> There once was a soldier
> Handsome and bold
> But he was a toy:
> Paper soldier . . .

My grandma would put a bowl of *bliny* on the table, she also baked really good pies. A lot of men pursued my mother, they'd bring her flowers and buy me ice cream. One time, she even asked me, "May I get married?" I wasn't against it because my mother was beautiful, and I didn't want her to be lonely. I wanted a happy Mama. People always noticed her on the street, one man would turn around, then another. "What are they doing?" I would ask when I was little. "Come on! Let's go!" my mother laughed, a kind of special laugh. Not like her regular laugh. We really were happy. Later, after I was left all alone, I would come back to our street and look up at our old windows. One time, I couldn't help myself and rang our doorbell—a Georgian family was living in our apartment now. They probably thought I was a beggar, they tried to give me money and some food. I burst into tears and ran away . . .

Soon, my grandma got sick. Because of her illness, she was always hungry, every five minutes she'd jump out into the stairwell and shout that we were starving her to death. She broke dishes . . . Mama could have put her in a special clinic, but she decided that she would take care of her herself. She also loved my grandmother a lot. Often, she'd take her war photographs out of the china cabinet, look at them and weep. The woman in the photos was young, she didn't look like Grandma, but it was her. It seemed like it was a different person . . . Yes, well, so it goes . . . Up until her death, Grandma kept reading newspapers and remained interested in politics . . . but after she got sick, there was only one book on her bedside table: the Bible. She'd call me over and read it to me: "For then the dust shall return to the Earth and the spirit will return to God . . ." Death was always on her mind: "It's so hard for me now, Granddaughter. So wearisome."

It happened on a weekend . . . We were all home . . . I checked in on my grandma, she couldn't walk very much anymore, so she spent most of her time lying down. She was sitting in her chair, looking out the window. I gave her some water. A little while later . . . I went back into her room, called out to her, and this time she didn't respond. I took her hand, it was cold. Her eyes were open and staring out the window. I'd never seen death before, I got scared and screamed. My mother came running, burst into tears, and closed Grandma's eyes. We had to call an ambulance . . . They came fairly quickly, but the doctor wanted my mother to pay for a death certificate and wouldn't take Grandma down to the morgue. "What do you expect? It's 'the market economy'!" We didn't have any money at home . . . My mother had just been laid off from her job, she'd been looking for work for two months already, but no matter where she went, there was already a long line of applicants. Mama had graduated with honors from a technology institute. But there was no question of her getting a job in her field. People with university diplomas were working behind counters, as dishwashers. They cleaned offices. Everything was different now . . . I didn't recognize the people on the street anymore, it was as though everyone had changed into gray costumes. All the colors had faded. That's how I remember that time . . . "This is all because of your Yeltsin, your Gaidar . . ." Grandma had cried when she was still alive. "What have they done to us? If things get any worse, we'll be living in wartime conditions." Mama wouldn't say anything: To my great surprise, she had stopped arguing. We scoured our house, looking for anything we could possibly sell. But we had nothing . . . We'd been living off Grandma's pension. All we had to eat were the cheapest noodles . . . Her whole life, Grandma had saved up five thousand rubles. The money was in the bank. It should have been enough, as she said, to provide for her up to the end, for "a rainy day," and to cover her

funeral expenses. But now, all that would buy you was a trolleybus
ticket . . . a box of matches . . . Everyone's money had simply evaporated. They ripped off the entire country . . . My grandma's greatest
fear was that we were going to bury her in a plastic bag or wrap her in
newspapers. Coffins were prohibitively expensive, people were buried
in all sorts of ways. Grandma's friend Fenya, who had been a nurse at
the front, had been wrapped in old newspapers . . . Her daughter did
it herself . . . They put her medals directly into the grave. Her daughter was disabled, dug through garbage cans . . . It was all so unfair!
My friend and I would go to privately owned stores to ogle the salami.
All those shiny wrappers. At school, the girls whose parents could afford to buy them leggings teased the ones whose parents couldn't. I
was teased . . . [*She is silent.*] But Mama had promised Grandma she'd
bury her in a coffin. She'd sworn that she would.

The doctor saw that we didn't have any money, so they turned
around and left. Leaving us to deal with Grandma on our own . . .

We lived with Grandma's body for a week . . . Several times a day,
my mother would rub her down with potassium permanganate and
kept her covered in a wet sheet. She sealed all the windows and tucked
wet blankets under all the doors. She did it all on her own, I was afraid
of going in Grandma's room. I would run past it to the kitchen and
back as fast as I could. The smell . . . it was already there . . . Although, it's awful to say this, but we were lucky: Grandma had lost a
lot of weight during her illness, all that was left of her was skin and
bones. We called all our relatives . . . We're related to half of Moscow,
but suddenly it was like we had no one. They would come over with
three-liter jars of pickled zucchini, pickles, jam, but no one offered us
any money. They'd sit with us, cry a little, then leave. None of them
had cash. I think that's what it was . . . Instead of money, at his factory, my mother's cousin was paid in canned goods—so he brought us
canned goods. Whatever he could . . . In those days, soap and tooth-
paste were considered good birthday presents. We had nice neighbors,
really, they were good people. Miss Anya and her husband . . . They
were packing, getting ready to move out to the country to live with
their parents. They'd already sent their kids there, they simply didn't
have time for us. Miss Valya . . . What could she do to help us, when
her husband and son both drank? My mother had so many friends,
but none of them had anything but books at home. Half of them were
already jobless . . . The phone went dead. Everyone transformed the
moment communism fell. We all lived behind closed doors now . . .

[*She is silent.*] My dream was that I'd go to sleep, wake up, and Grandma would be alive again.

On a time when gangsters walked the streets and didn't even bother concealing their weapons

Who were these people? These strangers appeared out of nowhere—and they somehow knew everything. "We understand your trouble. We're here to help." They made a phone call, a doctor came over immediately and issued a death certificate, then a policeman arrived. They bought us an expensive coffin, there was a hearse and tons of flowers, every kind of flower imaginable. Everything was exactly as it should be. Grandma had asked to be buried at Khovanskoye Cemetery, and although it's impossible to get in there without bribing someone—it's an old, famous cemetery—they took care of that, too; they brought in a priest, he said some prayers. It was all so beautiful. My mother and I just stood there and wept. Someone called Miss Ira was in charge of everything, she was the leader of that crew. There were always these beefy guys with her, her bodyguards. One of them had fought in Afghanistan, and for some reason, this comforted Mama. She thought that if someone had fought in a war or done time in Stalin's camps, they couldn't possibly be a bad person. "How could he—he's been through so much!" And in general, our people have each other's backs—this was her conviction, based in part on Grandma's stories of how people had saved one another during the war. Soviet people . . . [*She falls silent.*] But these people were different. Not quite Soviet anymore . . . I'm telling you how I see things now, not how they seemed to me back then . . . We'd been taken in by a criminal outfit, but for me, at that time, they were just these nice men and women who drank tea with us in our kitchen and brought us candy. Miss Ira would buy us groceries whenever she saw our refrigerator completely empty. She gave me a denim skirt—everyone worshiped denim back then! They did all that for about a month, we got used to them, and then they made my mother an offer: "Let's sell your three-bedroom apartment and buy you a one-bedroom. That way, you'll have money." My mother agreed . . . She was working at a café, washing dishes, bussing tables, but we were still catastrophically short on cash. We had already begun discussing where we were going to move, what neighborhood. I didn't want to change schools. We were looking for something nearby.

And that's when the other gang appeared. The head of that gang was a man . . . Mr. Volodya . . . And he and Miss Ira started fighting over our apartment. Mr. Volodya shouted at my mother, "You don't need a one-bedroom! I'll buy you a house in the suburbs." Miss Ira drove an old Volkswagen, while Mr. Volodya had a stunning Mercedes. He also had a real gun . . . It was the nineties . . . Gangsters walked the streets and didn't even bother concealing their weapons. Everyone who could afford them installed metal doors . . . One night, in our building, a gang showed up at our neighbor's house with a hand grenade . . . Our neighbor owned a kiosk—basically just painted boards and plywood—he sold everything: groceries, makeup, clothes, vodka. The gangsters demanded dollars. His wife didn't want to hand over the money, so they put a hot iron on her belly. She was pregnant . . . No one called the police because everyone knew that the gangsters had loads of money, they could buy anyone off. For some reason, people had started respecting them. There was no one to turn to for help . . . Mr. Volodya wasn't drinking tea with us—he was threatening my mother: "If you don't give me the apartment, I'll take your daughter and you'll never see her again. You won't know what happened to her." Friends of ours hid me; there were days when I had to miss school. I cried day and night, I was so scared for Mama. Our neighbors saw them come by two times, looking for me. Cursing. Finally, my mother gave in . . .

The very next day, they moved us out. They showed up at night: "Hurry up! Come on! You'll go stay somewhere else while we find you a new house." They brought paint cans, wallpaper, they were all ready to renovate the place. "Let's go! Hurry up!" My mother was so scared, all she took were her documents, her favorite Polish perfume *Maybe,* which someone had given to her for her birthday, and a few of her favorite books. I brought my textbooks and another dress. They shoved us in a car and took us to what you could call an empty space: a room with two big beds, a table, some chairs, and nothing else. They strictly prohibited us from going anywhere, opening the windows, or talking loudly. God forbid the neighbors hear! It was clear that this apartment had constantly rotating residents . . . It was so filthy! We spent several days just cleaning it, scrubbing everything down. And then I remember my mother and I standing in some official place, being shown some typed-up documents . . . everything seemed legal enough . . . They said, "Sign here." My mother signed, but I broke down in tears. It hadn't really hit me before, but now I realized that they were about to send us to live in the country. I got sad about my school, my friends who I would never see again. Mr. Volodya came up to me: "Hurry up and sign it, or we'll take you to an orphanage and your mother will move anyway. You'll end up all alone." There were some other people there . . . I remember there were a few other people standing around us, including a policeman . . . Everyone was silent. Mr. Volodya had bought them all off. I was just a kid . . . What could I do . . . [*She is silent.*]

For a long time, I never talked about it . . . All of this is private— it's bad, but it's private. I never wanted anyone else to know . . . I remember when they took me to the shelter—this was much later, after my mother was already gone. They dropped me off and showed me to my room. "This is your bed. Here are your shelves in the closet . . ." I stood petrified . . . Toward evening, I came down with a fever . . . All of it reminded me so much of our old apartment . . . [*She is silent.*] It was New Year's Eve. The tree was all covered in lights . . . everyone was making masks . . . There was going to be a dance. A dance? What's dancing? I'd forgotten all about that . . . [*Silence.*] There were four other girls sharing the room with me: Two of them were sisters, very young, eight and ten years old, and then two older girls; one of them was also from Moscow, she had a bad case of syphilis, and the other one turned out to be a thief, she stole my shoes. That girl wanted to go back to living on the street . . . What was I talking about? Oh yes, about how even though we were always together, day and night, we never told each other anything about ourselves—we just didn't want to. I kept silent for a long time . . . I only started talking after I met my Zhenya . . . But all of that came later . . . [*She is silent.*]

That was only the beginning for my mother and me . . . After we signed the papers, they took us all the way out to the Yaroslavl region. "It doesn't matter that it's far away, at least you'll have a nice house." They lied . . . It wasn't a house, it was an old wooden peasant hut with one room and a big Russian stove, which neither my mother nor I had ever seen before in our lives. We had no idea how to use it. The hut was falling apart. Everywhere you looked, there were cracks in the wood. Mama was in shock. When she stepped into the hut, she got down on her knees in front of me and begged forgiveness for making me live like this. She beat her head against the wall . . . [*She cries.*] We had very little money, and it ran out fast. We worked in people's gardens— some people would pay us with a basket of potatoes, others would give us ten eggs. I learned the beautiful word "barter" . . . My mother traded her beloved perfume, *Maybe,* for a nice hunk of butter when I got really sick . . . I begged her not to do it, we had so little to remind us of home. I remember . . . One day, a farm administrator, she was a kind woman, took pity on me and gave me a bucket full of milk. I was afraid and walked home with it through people's gardens. On my way, I ran into a milkmaid and she laughed at me, "What are you sneaking around for? You could easily walk through the center of the village if you wanted. People steal all sorts of things around here—plus, you had permission to take it." Everyone helped themselves to whatever wasn't nailed down, and the head of the collective farm was the worst of all. He got things delivered to him by the carload. He came to see us . . . waged a whole campaign: "Come work at the farm! Otherwise, you'll starve to death." Should we or shouldn't we? We were forced to by hunger. We had to get up at four in the morning for the first milking, when everyone else was still asleep. I milked the cows while my mother washed troughs. She was afraid of cows, but I liked them. Each cow had a name . . . Hazy, Wild Cherry . . . I took care of thirty cows and two heifers. We pushed around wagons of sawdust, we were up to our knees in manure. It went up higher than our boots. We'd hoist the milk canisters onto the cart . . . How many kilograms were they? [*She falls silent.*] They paid us in milk and meat whenever a cow accidentally suffocated or drowned in the muck. The milkmaids drank just as much as the men, and my mother started tippling along with the rest of them. Things between us weren't like they used to be. I mean, we were still friends, but more and more often, I'd yell at her. She'd be hurt. Very rarely, when she was in a good mood, she would recite poems to me . . . Her beloved Tsvetaeva: "Touched with a red brush / The rowans flushed / Leaves on the ground / I was born . . ." In those moments, I would catch glimpses of the way my mother used to be. It was rare.

Winter arrived. The frost came down hard and fast. We wouldn't have survived the winter in that hut. One of our neighbors took pity on us and drove us all the way back to Moscow for free . . .

On a time when "mankind" doesn't have "a proud sound," it sounds all sorts of ways

I've been babbling away, and I've forgotten that there are certain things I'm afraid of remembering . . . [*She falls silent.*] What do I think of people? When it comes down to it, people aren't good or bad, they're just people, that's all. In school, we used Soviet textbooks. There weren't any new ones yet, and they would teach us: "Mankind! That has a proud sound." Actually, "mankind" doesn't sound proud, it sounds all sorts of ways. Me, I'm also all sorts of ways, I'm a little bit of everything . . . But if I see a Tajik—they're like slaves here now, second-class citizens—and I have the time, I'll always stop and talk to them. I don't have any money, but I can talk. Someone like that . . . They're my kind of people, we're in the same boat—I understand what it's like to be a stranger to everyone and completely alone. I've also lived in stairwells and slept in basements . . .

First, one of my mother's friends let us live with her, they were good to us, I liked it there. A familiar setup: books, records, a portrait of Che Guevara on the wall. Just like our old place . . . the same books, the same records . . . Olga's son was in grad school, he'd spend all day at the library and at night he'd unload freight trains at the depot. There was nothing to eat. All we had in the kitchen was a sack of potatoes. After we'd gone through the potatoes, it was one loaf of bread a day. All day long, we drank tea. And that was it. A kilo of meat cost three hundred and twenty rubles—Olga was an elementary school teacher, and she made one hundred rubles a month. Everyone ran around like crazy, desperate to make money any way they could. Stretching themselves to the limit . . . The old kitchen tap broke, we called the plumbers, and they turned out to have PhDs. Everyone laughed. As Grandma used to say, you won't get by on tears . . . Taking time off was a huge luxury, very few people could afford it . . . During vacations from school, Olga would go to Minsk to see her sister, a university lecturer. They'd sew pillows out of artificial fur and fill them with polyester batting, but only half full. Then, right before it was time to get on the train, they'd put tranquillized puppies into the pillows. They'd take them to Poland . . . That's how they brought German Shepherd puppies over the border . . . and rabbits. At flea markets there, everywhere you turned, you'd hear Russian . . . They'd pour vodka into thermoses instead of tea, hide nails and locks in their suitcases under their underwear. Olga would come back with a bag full of delicious Polish salamis. They smelled incredible!

In Moscow, you would hear gunshots and even explosions at night. Kiosks, kiosks . . . kiosks everywhere . . . Mama started working for an Azerbaijani, he owned two kiosks, one selling fruit and the other fish. "It's a job, and you don't get any days off. Not a single one." But here's the rub—Mama was too embarrassed to sell things. Who would have guessed! The first day was the worst: She arranged the fruit then hid, peeking out from behind a tree. She pulled her hat way down over her face so that no one could recognize her. The next day, she gave a little gypsy boy a plum . . . The owner noticed and yelled at her. Money knows no pity or shame . . . She couldn't hold down that job for long, she was no good at sales . . . I saw an ad on a fence: "Seeking a cleaning woman with a higher education." Mama went to the designated address and they hired her. The pay was good. It was some kind of American foundation . . . At that point, we were able to more or less feed ourselves so we rented our own room. Another room in the same three-bedroom apartment was being rented out by these Azerbaijanis. Young guys. They were always buying and selling things. One of them kept asking me to marry him and promised to take me to Turkey. "I'm going to kidnap you. That's one of our customs— kidnapping brides." I was afraid of being home alone without my mother. He kept giving me fruit and dried apricots . . . The man who owned the apartment would drink for weeks on end, he'd go completely berserk: "You fucking whore! You bitch!" He'd beat his wife . . . The ambulance would come and take her away . . . and then he'd come after my mother at night. He'd break down our door . . .

We ended up out on the street again . . .

On the street without any money . . . Mama's foundation had shut down, and she was getting by on odd jobs. We lived in hallways . . . in stairwells . . . Some people would walk right past us, others would scream at us; there were people who would kick us out onto the street. It could happen in the middle of the night. Or when it was raining or snowing. No one offered us any help, nobody asked us any questions . . . [*She is silent.*] People are neither good nor bad. Everyone has their own lot in life . . . [*Silence.*] In the mornings, we would walk to the train station—we didn't have money for the Metro—and wash ourselves in the bathrooms. Wash our clothes. We'd have our laundry days there. It was all right in the summer; when it's warm out, you could really live anywhere . . . we'd sleep on park benches. In autumn, we'd make big piles of leaves and sleep in them—that was warm, too. It's like a sleeping bag. At Belorussky Station . . . I remember . . . we'd always run into this old, practically ancient woman, she would sit by the ticket counters talking to herself. She always told the same story . . . about how during the war, wolves would come into her village because they sensed that all the men were gone. All the men were off fighting. If my mother and I had any money, we'd give it to her. "May the Lord protect you," she'd make the sign of a cross over us. She reminded me of my grandmother . . .

One day, I left my mother sitting on a bench . . . When I came back, she was no longer alone, there was a man with her. A pleasant man. "Meet Vitya," Mama said. "He likes Brodsky, too." The writing was on the wall. We know full well that if someone likes Brodsky, for Mama, it's like a code word, it means he's one of us. "He's never read *Children of the Arbat*? What a savage! Straight out of the forest! That's a stranger, not our kind." That's how she'd always categorized people, and that hadn't changed, even then. I, on the other hand, had changed a lot in the course of our two years of vagrancy. I'd grown serious, perhaps beyond my years. I'd realized that my mother couldn't do anything to help me, quite the contrary: I felt like I was the one who needed to take care of her. That's how it felt to me . . . Vitya was smart, he asked me instead of her: "So what will it be, girls? Shall we?" He took us to his house, he had a two-bedroom apartment. We always lugged all of our possessions wherever we went, and so, with our tattered bags, we suddenly found ourselves in paradise . . . His house was like a museum! Paintings on the walls, a magnificent library, a curved antique cabinet . . . a grandfather clock as tall as the ceiling . . . We were dumbfounded! "Don't be shy, girls. Take your coats off." We were embarrassed and worse for wear . . . the smell of railway stations and stairwells . . . "Don't be shy, girls!" We sat down to tea. Vitya told us about himself . . . He'd been a jeweler and had his own studio. He showed us his tools, his satchels of semi-precious gems, silver settings . . . Everything was so beautiful, interesting, and expensive. I couldn't believe we were going to live there. The miracles were really raining down upon us . . .

We ended up becoming kind of like a normal family. I started going to school again. Vitya was very kind, he made me a ring with a little stone. But the trouble was . . . he drank, too. And smoked like a chimney. At first, my mother would yell at him, but pretty soon, they were drinking together. They sold off his library at secondhand bookshops, I remember the smell of the antique leather bindings . . . Vitya also had a collection of rare coins . . . They just drank and watched TV. Political shows. Vitya philosophized. He spoke to me like I was an adult . . . He'd ask me, "What do they teach you in school, Yulia, now that communism is over? What are we supposed to do now with Soviet literature and Soviet history—just forget it ever happened?" Truth be told, I didn't understand very much of what was going on . . . Do you find this interesting? Well, I didn't think that I had anything to do with all those questions, but as it turns out . . . when I think about it now . . .

". . . Russian life is supposed to be evil and base, that's what elevates the soul, and forces it to recognize that it doesn't belong in this world . . . The cruder and bloodier life is, the more space there is for the soul . . ."

". . . The only way we know how to modernize is with criminal syndicates and executions . . ."

". . . The Communists . . . What can they do about it? Bring back ration cards and fix up the barracks out in Magadan . . ."

". . . Today, normal people are the ones who seem insane . . . This new way of life made short work of people like me and my mother . . ."

". . . In the West, capitalism is old, an established fact; here, it's fresh, with brand-new fangs . . . While the government remains purely Byzantine . . ."

And then one night, Vitya started having pains in his chest. We called an ambulance, but he never made it to the hospital. Major heart attack. His relatives showed up: "Who the hell are you? Where did you come from? Get out." One man was screaming, "Get those beggar women out of here! Out!" He looked through our bags as we were leaving . . .

We were back on the street . . .

We phoned my mother's cousin . . . his wife answered. "Come on over." They lived in a two-bedroom Khrushchyovka not far from Rechnoy Vokzal Station with their married son. The son's wife was pregnant. It was decided: "You can stay here until Alyona gives birth." Mama slept on a cot in the corridor, I slept in the kitchen on an old couch. Uncle Lyosha's friends would come over . . . from the factory where he worked . . . I would fall asleep to their conversations. It was the same as ever: the bottle of vodka on the table, the game of cards. Only the topics had changed . . .

". . . We've squandered it all . . . Freedom . . . Where the fuck is freedom? We're gnawing on raw grain without any butter . . ."

". . . The kikes . . . They killed the Tsar, then Stalin, and Andropov, too . . . Now they've trotted out this liberalism! Time to tighten the screws. We Russians have to keep the faith . . ."

". . . Yeltsin is on his knees, fawning in front of America . . . even though we were the ones who won the war . . ."

". . . When you go to church, people cross themselves but stand there like statues . . ."

". . . Soon enough, things will heat up again, then it'll get fun . . . We'll hang the liberals from the lampposts for bringing about the nineties. We need to save Russia . . ."

A few months later, she gave birth. There was no room for us there anymore.

We were back out on the street . . .

Railway station . . .

Stairwell . . .

Railway station . . .

Stairwell . . .

At the railway station . . . The policemen on duty, both young and old, would either march you out onto the street—and this was in the winter—or you would have to go to the storeroom with them . . . They had a special screened-off corner . . . A little couch. One time, my mother got into a fight with a cop who tried to drag me in there with him . . . They beat her up and threw her in jail for several days. [*She falls silent.*] I . . . what happened was . . . I came down with a bad flu. It took us a while to figure out what to do . . . I kept getting worse . . . Finally, we decided that I should go recover at our relatives' house while she stayed at the train station. A few days later, she called me up, "I have to see you." I came back and she told me, "I met a woman here who's offering me a place to stay. She has enough room, she owns a house. In Alabino." "Let me come with you." "No, you need to get better first. You can come later." I put her on the commuter train, she sat down by the window and looked at me as though she hadn't seen me in a long time. I couldn't stand it and jumped on board: "What's wrong with you?" "Nothing, don't mind me." I waved good-bye, and the train took off. That evening I got a phone call. "Is this Malikova, Yulia Borisovna?" "Yes, it's me." "This is the police. Can you tell us what your relation is to Ludmila Malikova?" "She's my mother." "Your mother was hit by a train. In Alabino . . ."

She was always extremely cautious whenever a train was coming . . . She was terrified of them. Getting hit by a train was her biggest fear. She would look a hundred times: Is it coming or not? Really . . . it couldn't have been an accident, like some random tragedy. She'd bought a bottle of vodka beforehand so that it would be less painful and frightening. She threw herself under the train . . . She was tired . . . just plain tired . . . of this life . . . of herself. Those were her words.

Afterward, I remembered her every word . . . [*She cries.*] The train dragged her a long way . . . They took her to the hospital, she was in the intensive care unit for an hour, but they couldn't save her. That's what they told me . . . I saw her when she was already in her coffin, dressed. It was all so awful . . . I didn't have my Zhenya back then . . . If I had still been little, she would never have abandoned me like that. Never . . . It never would have happened . . . In her final days, she kept saying, "You're a big girl now. You're all grown up." Why did I have to grow up? [*She cries.*] I was left on my own . . . I had to go on all by myself . . . [*After a long silence.*] If I ever have a baby, I simply have to be happy . . . so that it'll remember its mother as happy . . .

Zhenya . . . Zhenya saved me . . . I had always been waiting for him. When I lived at the children's shelter, we would all dream that, even though we were living here for now, soon we'd be like everyone else—we'd have families, husbands, children. We'd buy ourselves cakes, and not just for special occasions, whenever we wanted. We wanted it all so bad . . . I was seventeen . . . I'd just turned seventeen . . . The director called me into her office. "You're off the subsidized meal plan." And that was all she said. After seventeen, the shelter pushed you into the real world. Get out there! But where was I supposed to go? I didn't have a job, I had nothing. And no mother . . . I called up Aunt Nadia: "I'm probably going to come stay with you. They're kicking me out of the shelter." Aunt Nadia . . . if it hadn't been for her . . . She's my guardian angel . . . She wasn't actually related to me, but now she's more than close; she left me her room in the communal apartment. Now . . . Yes . . . She used to live with my uncle, but he died a long time ago. They were never officially married, they were just together, but I knew that they loved each other. You can always turn to a person like that . . . If somebody understands what love is, you can always turn to them . . .

Aunt Nadia never had kids, she was used to living alone, it was hard for her to live with anyone else. We had a rough time! The room we shared was sixteen square meters. I slept on a cot. Naturally, her neighbor started complaining: "She needs to go." She'd call the police on us. Aunt Nadia was unmovable: "And where exactly is she supposed to go?" It had probably already been a year . . . Aunt Nadia herself brought it up: "You said you were only staying for two months, but you've been here a whole year." I didn't say anything, I was crying . . . and she didn't say anything, either. She was crying, too . . . [*She is silent.*] Another year went by . . . everyone ended up getting used to me. I did everything in my power . . . even that neighbor got used to me . . . Miss Marina isn't a bad person, she's just had a hard life. She was married twice, and both of her husbands croaked, as she puts it, from the drink. Her nephew would visit her all the time, he and I would say hi to each other. A good-looking guy. Then . . . here's how it happened: I was sitting in our room reading a book, and Miss Marina came in, took me by the hand, and led me to the kitchen. "Let me introduce you: This is Yulia, this is Zhenya. Now get out of here and go for a walk!" Zhenya and I started dating. Kissing. Nothing serious. He was a trucker and often went away on long trips. One day, he came back and I wasn't there. What? Where is she? Well, I'd been having these episodes for a long time—sometimes I'd get short of breath or I'd faint from weakness . . . Aunt Nadia made me go to the doctor, they examined me and discovered that I have multiple sclerosis. You know what that is, of course . . . an incurable disease. I got it from grief, I came down with it because of all the sorrow. I really missed my mother. A lot. [*Silence.*] So they diagnosed me and put me in the hospital. That's where Zhenya found me. He started coming to see me every day. One day, he'd bring me a beautiful apple, the next, an orange . . . just like my father once had . . . Then it was May . . . One day, he appeared with a bouquet of roses. I gasped—a bouquet like that must have cost half of his monthly wages. He was in his best suit . . . "Marry me." I was dumbstruck. "What? You don't want to?" What could I say? I don't know how to lie, and I didn't want to lie to him. I had already been in love with him for a long time . . . "I want to marry you, but you have to know the truth: I have a very serious disability. Pretty soon I'm going to be like a little hamster and you're going to have to carry me around." He didn't understand, but it upset him. The next day he came back and told me, "Everything's going to be fine. We can make it work." When I was discharged from the hospital, we went straight to the marriage registration bureau. He took me to meet his mother. She's a simple peasant woman, she's spent her whole life in the fields. There isn't a single book in her house, but I loved it there anyway. It's peaceful. I told her everything, too. "It's all right, child," she put her arms around me. "Where there is love, there is God." [*Silence.*]

Now I want to live with every fiber of my being, all because of my Zhenya . . . I even dream of us having a baby some day . . . The doctors are against it, but that's my dream. I want us to have a home together; my whole life, I've wanted a home. I found out they recently passed a new law . . . According to the law, I could get our old apartment back. I filled out an application . . . They told me that there are thousands of people like me, they're able to help many of them, but my case is complicated because ownership of our apartment has already changed hands three times. As for those gangsters that robbed us, they are all long in their graves, they killed each other off . . .

. . . We went to see my mother. There's a portrait of her on her tombstone, and it makes it feel like she's there. We cleared away the debris. Cleaned her grave. We stood there for a long time, I couldn't bring myself to leave, and then there was this moment when it seemed like she smiled at me . . . like she was happy . . . But maybe it was just a trick of the light . . .

ON A LONELINESS
THAT RESEMBLES HAPPINESS

◆

Alisa Z., advertising manager,
35 years old

I went to St. Petersburg to get a different story but came back with this one. I'd struck up a conversation on the train . . .

A friend of mine killed herself . . . She was a strong and successful woman. Tons of friends and admirers. We were all in shock. Suicide? What is that? Cowardice or an act of courage? A radical transformation, a cry for help, or self-martyrdom? An exit . . . a trap . . . a punishment . . . I want to . . . I can tell you why I'll never kill myself . . .

Love? That's not even an option . . . I'm not against all that happy shiny stuff, but you're probably the first person to say that word to me in ten years. It's the twenty-first century: It's all about money, sex, and two smoking barrels, and here you are talking about feelings . . . Everyone finally got their hands on some dough, for the first time ever . . . I was in no hurry to get married, have kids, I've always put my career first. I value myself, my time, and my life. And where did you ever get the idea that men are looking for love? Ooh, love . . . Men consider women game, war trophies, prey, and themselves hunters. Those are the rules that have been developed over the course of centuries. And women aren't looking for their knight in shining armor to come galloping in on a white horse—they want him on a sack of gold. A knight of indeterminate age . . . even a "daddy" will do . . . So what? Money rules the world! But I'm no prey, I'm a huntress myself . . .

I came to Moscow ten years ago. I was wild, fired up, I told myself that I was born to be happy, that only the weak suffer, and modesty is nothing but adornment for the weak. I'm from Rostov . . . My parents work at a school, my father's a chemist, and my mother's a Russian language and literature teacher. They got married when they were in college, my father only owned one decent suit but had more than his share of ideas. Back then, that was enough to make a young girl swoon. They still love to remember how, for ages, they got by with one set of linens, one pillow, and one pair of slippers. They'd spend their nights reciting Pasternak—they knew it all by heart! "Anywhere is heaven with the one you love!" "Until the first frosts," I'd laugh. "You have no imagination," my mother would reply, hurt. We were your typical Soviet family: For breakfast, it was always buckwheat or noodles with butter; we only had oranges once a year, on New Year's Eve. I can still remember how they smelled. Not now, but back then . . . it was the smell of a different life, a beautiful life . . . Summer vacation meant a trip to the Black Sea. We'd go to Sochi as "savages"—without reservations—and all share a single nine-square-meter room. But we had something to be proud of, something we were very proud of: We were proud of our favorite books, which came from the underground, through some major connections. And the greatest joy of all: complimentary passes to premieres! My mother's friend worked at the theater. The theater! The eternal topic of conversation in decent company . . . Today, they write about the Soviet Union being one big penal colony, a communist ghetto. A world ruled by cannibalism. I don't remember anything scary . . . I remember that it was naïve, that world, very naïve and clumsy. I always knew that it wouldn't be how I was going to live! I wanted none of it! They almost kicked me out of school for that. Oh! You know us . . . "Born in the USSR" is a diagnosis . . . You're branded for life! We had home economics classes, for some reason, the boys were taught how to drive while the girls had to learn how to make meat patties. I'd always burn those damn meat patties. One day, the teacher, who was also our class teacher, started lecturing me: "You don't know how to do anything! How are you going to cook for your husband?" My snap reaction: "I'm not going to make anyone meat patties. I'm going to have a housekeeper." It was 1987 . . . I was thirteen . . . What capitalism, what housekeeper?! Socialism was still in full swing! They called my parents in to the principal's office, told me off at the general class assembly, then at the council meeting of the school *druzhina*.*

---

* A Voluntary People's *Druzhina* is a civil police organization that has the right to perform citizen's arrests for petty offenses such as hooliganism and drunkenness.

They wanted to kick me out of the Young Pioneers. The Pioneers, the Komsomol—it was a huge deal. I even cried . . . Even though I'd never had any rhymes in my head, only formulas . . . never rhymes. When I was left home alone, I would put on my mother's dress and heels and sit on the couch reading *Anna Karenina*. Society balls, servants, aiguillettes . . . romantic trysts . . . I liked everything up to the part when Anna throws herself under the train: What did she do that for? She was beautiful and rich . . . for love? Not even Tolstoy could convince me . . . I liked Western novels better because of the bitches in them, the beautiful bitches that men would shoot themselves over and suffer for. Fall at their feet. The last time I cried over unrequited love was when I was seventeen—I spent the whole night in the bathroom with the tap running. My mother consoled me with poems by Pasternak . . . I still remember, "Being a woman is a mighty feat, / To drive men mad— heroic." I didn't like my childhood or adolescence, I was always waiting for it to finally end. I pored over my textbooks and worked out at the gym. I was faster, taller, and stronger than everyone else! At home, they kept playing the same Okudzhava tapes: "Let's take each other's hands, friends . . ." Not me! That's no dream of mine.

To Moscow . . . oh, Moscow! I've always seen her as a competitor, from the moment I got there, she inspired a sporting rage in me. My kind of town! The crazy pace gets you high! A city big enough to spread my wings in! I showed up with two hundred dollars and a few lousy rubles in my pocket. That was it. The roaring nineties . . . My parents hadn't been paid in ages. We were so poor! Every day, Papa would repeat: "We need to be patient. Just wait and see. I trust Gaidar." It took a long time for people like my parents to realize that capitalism had already begun in earnest. Russian capitalism, young and thick-skinned, the same beast that had been put down in 1917 . . . [*She falls into thought.*] Do they understand it today? It's hard to say . . . There's one thing I know for sure: Capitalism was not what my parents ordered. No two ways about it. It's what I ordered, it's made for people like me, who didn't want to stay in the cage. The young and the strong. For us, capitalism was exciting . . . Adventures in enterprise, risk . . . It's not just about money. The mighty dollar! Now I'll reveal my secret: For me, capitalism, I mean modern capitalism, not Dreiser, is more interesting to read about than the gulag or Soviet shortages. The informants. Oh! Oh! Gosh, I've trod on the sacred. I wouldn't dare breathe a word of this to my parents. My lips are sealed. How could I! My father remains a Soviet romantic. August 1991 . . .

The putsch! They started playing *Swan Lake* on TV that morning . . . Tanks filled Moscow like it was Africa. So my father and around seven other people, all of his friends, took off from work, heading straight to the capital. To support the revolution! I sat glued to the television . . . The image of Yeltsin on the tank stayed with me. The empire crumbled . . . so let it crumble . . . We waited for my father as though he were coming back from a war—and he returned a hero! This must have been his shining hour. After however many years, I realized that this was indeed the most important event of his life. Like my grandpa . . . His whole life, he kept telling the story of fighting the Germans at Stalingrad. After the fall of the empire, life grew boring for Papa, he's lost all interest—he has nothing to live for anymore. Mostly, they're disappointed . . . His generation . . . they feel like they were defeated twice over: The communist Idea was crushed, and then what happened afterward is beyond them, they don't want to accept it. They wanted something different—if capitalism, then capitalism with a human face and a charming smile. This world isn't for them. It's an alien planet. But it is for me! It's all mine! I'm happy that the only time I ever see Soviets is May 9, Victory Day . . . [*She is silent.*]

I hitchhiked to the capital—it was cheaper. The more I saw out the window, the more riled up I got. I already knew that I would never return from Moscow. Not for all the tea in China! To either side of the road there were markets . . . People selling tea sets, nails, dolls—back then, everyone was getting paid in goods. You could trade frying pans or irons for salami—meatpacking plants paid workers in salami—candy or sugar. There was a fat lady sitting next to a bus stop wearing a bandolier full of toys. It was like a cartoon! When I got to Moscow, it was pouring rain, but I went to Red Square anyway. I just had to see St. Basil's Cathedral and the Kremlin walls—that power, that might, and here I am! In the very heart of it! I walked along limping. Shortly before I had left, I'd broken my little toe at the gym, but I was still in high heels and my very best dress. Of course, fate is just luck, the luck of the draw, but I also have good intuition and know what I want. The universe never grants you anything just because . . . for free . . . Here you go! And for you! You have to really want it. And I really did! All my mother brought me were little homemade pies, and then she'd tell me about how she and Papa were going to all the democratic rallies. The ration cards allotted each person two kilos of grain, one kilo of meat, and two hundred grams of butter a month. Lines, lines, lines; numbers scrawled on people's palms. I don't like the word "*sovok*"!

My parents aren't *sovoks,* they're romantics! Toddlers living adult lives. I don't understand them, but I love them! I went through life alone, all on my own . . . It wasn't a cakewalk . . . And I have good reason to love myself! Without any tutors or money or patronage I got into Moscow State University. The journalism department . . . In my first year, a boy from my class fell in love with me. He wanted to know: "Are you in love with me back?" My reply: "I'm in love with myself." I did everything for myself. Myself! My classmates didn't interest me, the lectures were boring. Soviet professors teaching Soviet textbooks. Meanwhile, non-Soviet life was roiling all around us at a fever pitch! The first used foreign cars appeared—awesome! The first McDonald's on Pushkin Square . . . Polish makeup, the creepy rumor that it was intended for corpses. The first commercial on TV, for Turkish tea. Everything used to be gray, but here came the bright colors, the eye-catching billboards. You wanted it all! And you could have it all! You could be anyone you liked: a broker, a hitman, gay . . . Ah, the nineties! To me, they came as a blessing . . . an unforgettable time . . . The era of technocrats, bandits, and venture capitalists! Only the stuff stayed Soviet, the people had a new agenda . . . With some luck and a bit of elbow grease, you might end up with everything you've ever dreamed of. What Lenin? What Stalin? That's all in the past, there's an amazing new life ahead of you: You can see the whole world, live in a gorgeous apartment, drive around in a luxury car, eat elephant steak for dinner every night . . . Russia's eyes darted in every direction . . . You could learn more on the streets and at parties, so I transferred to the distance-learning department and got a job at a newspaper. I started loving my life from the moment I got up in the morning.

I was looking up . . . to the top of the tall ladder of life . . . I never dreamed of being fucked in stairwells or saunas in exchange for expensive dinners. I had a lot of admirers . . . I didn't pay any attention to my peers—we could be friends, go to the library together. It was unserious and safe. I preferred older, more successful men who had already made it. They were interesting, fun, and useful. But I attracted . . . [*She laughs.*] For a long time, I was pegged as a girl from a good family—from a house full of books, where the most important piece of furniture is the bookshelf. Only writers and artists ever paid any attention to me. The unrecognized genius type. But I wasn't about to devote my life to some genius who's only acknowledged after his death, gently doted on by his followers. On top of that, I was already sick of all of those conversations from constantly hearing them at home: communism, the meaning of life, the happiness of others . . . Solzhenitsyn and Sakharov . . . They weren't my idols—they were my mother's. The people who read books and dreamed of flying, like Chekhov's seagull, were replaced by those who didn't read but knew how to fly. The entire former repertoire of gentlemanly charms fell by the wayside: *samizdat,* whispered conversations in the kitchen. How shameful that our tanks had entered Prague! But look: Today, they're in Moscow! Who are you going to impress with that now? Instead of your *samizdat* poems, show me a diamond ring, expensive labels . . . It was a revolution of desires! Wants!! I liked . . . and still prefer bureaucrats and businessmen. Their vocabulary inspires me: offshore accounts, kickbacks, barters. Internet marketing, creative strategies . . . At editorial meetings, my editor would tell us, "We need capitalists. We have to support Yeltsin and Gaidar's initiative to create capitalists. Urgently!" I was young, beautiful . . . They'd send me out to interview these capitalists: How did they make their fortunes? How had they earned their first million? Could socialists become capitalists? I had to describe this phenomenon . . . For some reason, it was the number "one million" that sparked the imagination. To make a million! We had gotten used to the idea that Russians don't want to be rich, they're even afraid of it. So what do they want then? The answer is always the same: They don't want anyone else to get rich. That is, richer than they are. The magenta sports coats, the gold chains . . . that's all from films, TV shows . . . The people I met had steely logic and an iron grip on reality. They were systematic thinkers. All of them were learning English. Management. The academics and postgraduates were leaving the country . . . the physicists and lyricists too . . . But the new heroes, they didn't want to go anywhere, they liked living in Russia. This was their time to shine! Their big chance! They wanted to be rich, they wanted it all. Everything!

And that's when I met him . . . You could say that I loved him. This sounds like a confession, doesn't it? [*She laughs.*] He was twenty years older than me, married with two sons. A jealous wife. He lived under a microscope . . . But we drove each other crazy, the ebb and flow was so strong . . . He told me that he started taking two sedatives in the morning so that he wouldn't burst into tears at work. I also did crazy things, I would have jumped out of an airplane for him. It was all . . . it's just how things are in the candy and flowers phase . . . before it starts mattering who's lying to whom, who's pursuing whom, and what anyone wants. I was very young, twenty-two . . . I would fall in love . . . and fall in love again . . . Now I see that love is also a kind of business, everyone is taking their own measure of risk. You have to be ready for new configurations—always! These days, few people go weak in the knees for love. Everyone saves their strength for the leap forward! For their career! In our smoking room, the girls gossip about their love lives, and if any of them has real feelings, everyone feels sorry for her—like, what an idiot, she's head over heels. [*She laughs.*] Idiot! I was such a happy little idiot! He'd send his driver home, we'd catch a cab, and we'd roll around nighttime Moscow in some Moskvich that reeked of gasoline. Kissing and kissing. "Thank you," he'd say. "You've made me a hundred years younger." Flashes of episodes . . . flashes . . . I was stunned by his pace . . . the pressure . . . I'd get a phone call in the evening: "We're going to Paris tomorrow morning," or "Let's swing by the Canary Islands. I have three days." We'd fly first class, get a room in the most expensive hotel—the floor would be made of glass, and there would be fish swimming around under it. A real shark! But the thing I'll remember as long as I live is the Moskvich reeking of gas, rolling aimlessly through the streets of Moscow. And how we'd kissed . . . like mad . . . He'd get a rainbow for me out of a fountain. I fell in love with him . . . [*She is silent.*] He was turning his life into a party. For himself . . . Yes, just for him! When I hit forty, maybe I'll understand . . . One day, I'll understand him . . . For instance, he never liked watches when they worked, he only liked them stopped. He had his own special relationship with time . . . Yep! Uh-huh . . . I love cats. I love them because they don't cry, no one has ever seen their tears. People who see me on the street think that I'm rich and happy! I have everything: a big house, an expensive car, Italian furniture. And a daughter I adore. I have a housekeeper, I never make meat patties or do laundry, I can buy whatever my heart desires . . . Mountains of knickknacks! . . . But I live alone. And that's how I like it! I am never as happy with anyone else as I am by myself. I love talking to myself . . . first and foremost about myself . . . I'm excellent company! What do I think . . . ? What do I feel . . . ? How did I see this yesterday and how do I see it today? I used to like the color blue, now I prefer lilac . . . So much happens inside each one of us. Inside. Within ourselves. There's an entire cosmos in there. But we barely pay any attention to it. We're all too busy with the surface, the external stuff . . . [*She laughs.*] Loneliness is freedom . . . Now, every day, I'm happy I'm free: Will he call or won't he, will he come over or not? Is he going to dump me? Spare me! Those aren't my problems anymore! So no, I'm not afraid of loneliness . . . What am I afraid of? I'm afraid of the dentist! [*She suddenly loses control.*] People always lie when they talk about love . . . and money . . . They're always lying in so many different ways. I don't want to lie . . . I just don't! [*She regains her composure.*] Excuse me . . . please forgive me . . . I haven't thought about any of this for a long time . . .

The plot? A tale as old as time . . . I wanted to have his baby, I got pregnant . . . Maybe it scared him? Men are such cowards! Whether they're bums or oligarchs—makes no difference. They'll go to war, start a revolution, but when it comes to love, they're traitors. Women are stronger. "She'll stop a galloping horse in its tracks, run into a burning building."* According to the clichés of the genre . . . "But horses keep galloping and galloping. And buildings keep burning and burning. . . ." For the first time in my life, my mother gave me some sound advice: "Men stop developing at the age of fourteen." I remember . . . It went like this . . . I broke the news to him before I was supposed to go on a business trip, they were sending me to the Donbass. I loved traveling for work, I loved the smell of railway stations and airports. It was always a pleasure to come back from a trip and tell him about it, discuss what I'd seen. Today, I realize that he not only showed me the world, amazed me, took me to mind-boggling boutiques, showering me with presents—he also helped teach me how to think. Not that he did this intentionally, it just happened on its own. From observing him, listening to him. Even when I thought we were going to stay together, it wasn't that I was planning on permanently moving into someone's abundant shadow and settling into a well-fed and glamorous life. You've got to be kidding! I had my own plans. I loved my job, I was quickly building a career. I traveled a lot . . . That particular trip was to a mining village. It's a gruesome story, but probably typical for its time: At a mining enterprise, the best miners had been awarded stereos, they were given them as holiday presents. That night, the entire family of one of those miners was murdered. The killer didn't take anything else—just the stereo. A plastic Panasonic! A box! In Moscow, there were luxury cars and supermarkets, but just beyond the Garden Ring, people marveled at the most basic stereo. The local "capitalists" that my editor had dreamed of walked around surrounded by men with machine guns. They wouldn't even go to the

---

* A line from Nikolai Nekrasov's 1863 poem "Red-Nosed Frost," which has become a proverbial description of the Russian woman.

bathroom without a bodyguard. So what if there's a casino here and there. The rare privately owned little bistro. The nineties . . . that's what they were like . . . The notorious nineties . . . I was gone for three days. When I got back, we saw each other. At first, he was excited— we're going to have . . . we're going to have a baby soon! He had two boys already, so he wanted a girl. But words . . . words . . . They don't mean anything, people hide behind them to protect themselves. It's the eyes! And in his eyes, I saw fear: Decisions had to be made, he'd have to change his life around. At that . . . he suddenly clammed up . . . There was a breakdown in communication. Oh! There are men who leave you right away, going off with their suitcases full of socks and shirts still damp from the wash. And then there are men like him . . . Coochie-coo, blah blah blah . . . "What do you want? Tell me what you want me to do," he'd plead. "Just say the word and I'll get a divorce. Just say the word." I'd just look at him . . .

I'd look at him and my fingertips would go cold, I had started to realize that I could never be happy with him. I was young and stupid . . . Today, I would have flayed him like a hunter skins a wolf, I know how to be a predator and panther now. Sewed him up with a steel thread! Back then, I just suffered. Suffering is a dance; there's bitterness, weeping, then acceptance. Like a ballet . . . There's a secret to it, and it's very simple: It's unpleasant being unhappy . . . humiliating. I was at the hospital overnight for a check-up. In the morning, I called him to tell him to come pick me up, they were going to discharge me by lunchtime. With a sleepy voice, he told me, "I can't. I can't do it today." And didn't call me back. That day, he went on a ski trip to Italy with his sons. December 31 . . . New Year's Eve. I called a cab . . . The city was blanketed in snow, I walked through the snowdrifts clutching my belly. Alone. Actually, no! The two of us walked together. My daughter and I. My little girl . . . My darling! I already loved her more than anyone else in the world! Did I love him? Like in a fairy tale: they lived happily ever after for a long, long time and then died on the same day. I was suffering, but I wasn't like, "I can't live without him. I'll just die." I haven't yet met a man who has made me feel that way . . . So yes! Yes, yes, yes! But I learned to lose, I'm not afraid of losing . . . [*She looks out the window.*] I haven't had any major relationships since then . . . a couple of flings . . . I'll go to bed with someone pretty easily, but that's not the same thing, that's something else. I don't like the smell of men—not the smell of sex, but the smell of men. In the bathroom, I can always tell if there's been a man in there . . . even if he

wears the most expensive cologne and smokes expensive cigarettes . . .
I am filled with horror when I consider how hard you have to work to
keep someone in your life. It's like breaking rocks at a quarry! You
have to forget about yourself, reject yourself, liberate yourself from
yourself. There is no freedom in love. Even if you find your ideal partner, he'll wear the wrong cologne, he'll like fried meat and mock you
for your little salads, leave his socks and pants all over the place. And
you always have to suffer. Suffer?! For love . . . for that harmony . . . I
don't want to do that work anymore, it's easier for me to rely on myself. It's better to just be friends with men, have men as business partners. I rarely even feel like flirting, I'm too lazy to put on a mask and
start playing a game. A trip to the spa, a French manicure, Italian hair
extensions. Makeup. It's like war paint . . . My God! Good Lord! Girls
from Bumblejekistan . . . from all over Russia—to Moscow! To Moscow! Wealthy princes await! They dream of someone transforming
them from Cinderellas into princesses. They expect nothing short of
fairy tales! Miracles! I've been through that already . . . I understand
the Cinderellas, and I feel bad for them. You know, there's no heaven
without a hell. Pure heaven . . . there's no such thing. But they don't
know that yet . . . They're blissfully unaware . . .

It's been seven years since we broke up . . . He calls me sometimes—
for some reason, it's always at night. He's not doing well, he's lost a lot
of money . . . says he's unhappy . . . He was dating this one young girl,
now he's with another one. He asks to see me . . . What for? [*She is
silent.*] I missed him for a long time, I'd turn off all the lights and
spend hours sitting in the dark. I'd lose myself in time . . . [*Silence.*]
And then . . . after him, it's been just flings. But I . . . I'll never be able
to fall in love with a man from a dormitory town who doesn't have any
money. From a prefab ghetto, from Harlem. I hate people who grew up
in poverty, their pauper's mentality; money means so much to them,
you can't trust them. I don't like the poor, the insulted and the humiliated. All those Bashmachkins and Opiskins* . . . the heroes of great
Russian literature . . . I don't trust them! So what? Does that mean
that there's something wrong with me . . . I don't fit the stereotype?
Just wait . . . nobody knows how this world really works . . . I don't
like men for their money, it's never just for their money. When it comes

---

* *The Insulted and Humiliated* is a novel by Dostoevsky. Bashmachkin is the main
character of Nikolay Gogol's story "The Overcoat." Opiskin is a protagonist in another novel by Dostoevsky, *The Village of Stepanchikovo*.

to successful men, I like the whole package: the way they walk, the way they drive, the way they pursue you—everything about them is different. Everything! Those are the ones I go for. And that's why . . . [*She is silent.*] He calls me up, says he's unhappy . . . What hasn't he seen, what can't he buy? He and his friends . . . they've already made their fortunes. Big money. Crazy money! But all that money isn't enough to buy happiness, that same love we were talking about. Love shmove. A poor student can have it but they can't. There's injustice for you! But they feel like there are no limits to what they can do: They fly their private jets anywhere they want just to see a football match; they'll jet over to New York for the premiere of a musical. They can afford it all! Take the most beautiful model to bed, or bring a whole plane full of them to Courchevel! We all read Gorky in school, we know how the merchants party—breaking mirrors, lying facedown in black caviar, bathing babes in champagne . . . But then they get sick of all that, it starts to bore them. Moscow travel agencies offer these kinds of clients special entertainments. For example, two days in prison. The advertisement even says, "Would you like to be Khodor-kovsky for two days?" They pick them up in a police van with the bars in it and drive them to the city of Vladimir, to the most terrifying prison, Vladimir Central. Then they dress them up in prisoners' uni-forms, chase them around the yard with the dogs and beat them with rubber clubs. Real ones! Pack them like sardines into a filthy, reeking jail cell complete with a shit bucket. That's what makes them happy—new sensations! Three to five thousand dollars will buy you a game of "bums": Clients are changed into costumes, made up, and driven around the streets of Moscow, where they stand, begging for change. Although they always have bodyguards around the corner—their per-sonal ones and the ones from the agency. There are even more titillat-ing packages for the whole family: The wife plays a prostitute and the husband, her pimp. I know a story . . . One night, the modest, Soviet-faced wife of the richest gourmet food merchant in Moscow got the most clients out of anyone. He was so proud of her! Then there are the amusements that you won't find in the brochures . . . Top secret stuff . . . You can arrange for a nighttime hunt for a human being. Some unlucky homeless guy is handed a thousand bucks—these dol-lars are yours to keep! He's never seen that kind of money in his life! All you have to do is pretend to be an animal. If you make it out alive, that's fate, and if they shoot you, no hard feelings, please! It's all fair and square! You can rent a girl for a night . . . Let your imagination run wild, the darkest parts, things the Marquis de Sade never even dreamed of! Blood, tears, and semen!!! That's what they call happiness . . . Happiness Russian-style, going to jail for two days so that you can get out and realize how good you have it. Awesome! To not only buy a car, a house, a yacht, and a seat in the Duma . . . But also a human life. To be, if not God, then a minor deity . . . An übermensch! Indeed—there you have it!!! Everyone was born in the USSR, everyone is still from over there. That's their disorder. It was all so . . . that world was so naïve . . . They dreamed of creating a good man . . . They promised: "With an iron fist, we'll chase humanity into happiness . . ." All the way to heaven on Earth.

I had this conversation with my mother . . . She wants to quit working at the school. "I'll get a job as a coatroom attendant. Or a security guard." She tells children about Solzhenitsyn . . . tries to teach them about heroes and righteous men . . . Her eyes burn with passion, but the children's don't anymore. My mother is used to children's eyes lighting up at her words, but today's children tell her, "We're interested in how you used to live, but we don't want to live like that. We don't dream about performing great feats, we want to live well." They're reading *Dead Souls* by Gogol. The tale of a swindler . . . That's what they taught us in school. Today, the children are a different breed: "What makes him so bad? Chichikov is like Mavrodi,* he built a pyramid scheme up out of nothing. It's a cool idea for a business!" For them, Chichikov is a positive character . . . [*She is silent.*] My mother is not going to help raise my daughter . . . I won't let her. If she had her way, my child would only watch Soviet cartoons because they're "humane." But when the cartoon is over, you have to go out on the street, into a completely different world. "I'm so happy I'm old," my mother confessed to me. "I can just stay home. In my fortress." Before, she used to always want to be young, she'd do tomato juice masks, rinse her hair with chamomile . . .

When I was young, I liked to toy with my fate, to tempt it. Not anymore: I've had enough. My daughter is growing up, I need to think of her future. And that means money! I want to make it myself. I don't want to ask anyone else for it, or take it from anyone. I have no desire for that! I quit the newspaper and went to work for an advertising

---

* Chichikov is the protagonist of *Dead Souls*. Sergey Mavrodi (1955–) is a businessman and former deputy of the State Duma famous for his massive, unapologetic pyramid schemes, successfully perpetrated in Russia, India, China, and South Africa.

agency, the pay is better. It's good money. People are interested in the beautiful life, that's the most important thing happening today. It's what's on everyone's mind. Just turn on the TV: the political demonstrations . . . Even if tens of thousands of people are going to them, what the millions are doing is buying elegant Italian plumbing fixtures. No matter who you ask, everyone is renovating and fixing up their homes and apartments. Traveling. Russia has never been like this before. We're not just advertising goods, we're selling needs. We create new needs—we are the ones who teach people to live beautifully! We run this era . . . Advertising is the mirror of the Russian revolution . . . My life is stuffed to the gills. I'm not planning on getting married . . . I have friends and all of them are rich. One got fat on oil, another on mineral fertilizers . . . We meet up and talk. Always at an expensive restaurant: a marble hall, antique furniture, expensive paintings on the walls . . . Doormen that deport themselves like nineteenth-century Russian nobles. I love being surrounded by sumptuous decorations. One of my closest friends is also single, and he doesn't want to get married, either. He likes being alone in his three-story house. He always says, "Sleep next to someone, but live alone." By day, his head swells from the fluctuations in base metal prices on the London market. Copper, lead, nickel . . . He has three cellphones, they ring every thirty seconds. Works thirteen to fifteen hours a day. No weekends, no vacation. Happiness? What happiness? It's a different world . . . Today, single people are the ones who are happy and successful, they're not the weak ones or losers. They have everything: money, careers. Being alone is a choice. I want to keep moving forward. I'm a huntress, not docile prey. I am the one making this choice. Loneliness is a kind of happiness . . . That sounds kind of like a revelation, doesn't it? [*She is silent.*] Really, it's not you I wanted to tell all this to, it's myself . . .

ON WANTING TO KILL THEM ALL AND THE HORROR OF REALIZING THAT YOU REALLY WANTED TO DO IT

◆

Ksyusha Zolotova, student,
22 years old

Only her mother showed up to our first meeting. She confessed, "Ksy-usha didn't want to come. She tried talking me out of it: 'Mama, who needs us? They only want our words and feelings, they don't care about us—they haven't been through what we've been through.'" She was very agitated, she would get up to leave, "I try not to think about these things. It's painful to put myself through everything all over again," but when she'd start talking, there was no stopping her. Mostly, she was silent. What could I do to comfort her? "Don't get upset. Please calm down." At the same time, I was eager to hear her recol-lections of that terrifying day, February 6, 2004, when there was a terrorist attack on the Zamoskvoretskaya line of the Moscow Metro, between the Avtozavodskaya and Paveletskaya stops. Thirty-nine peo-ple were killed and 122 hospitalized.

I pace and pace the circles of pain, I can't break out of them. Pain has everything: darkness, triumph. Sometimes I think that pain is a bridge between people, a secret connection; other times, it seems like an abyss.

I have several paragraphs in my notebook from that first two-hour session:

". . . Being a victim is so humiliating . . . It's simply shameful. I don't want to talk about it to anyone, I just want to be like everyone else, but then I'm alone and that's it. I'm capable of bursting into tears any-time, anywhere. Sometimes, I'll roam the city crying. One day, a man on the street came up to me and said, 'Why are you crying? You're so beautiful and here you are weeping.' First of all, my beauty has never gotten me anywhere, and second of all, beauty betrays me, it doesn't correspond with what's going on inside me . . ."

". . . We have two daughters, Ksyusha and Dasha. We've always lived modestly, but whenever we could, we went to museums, the the-ater, we read tons of books. When the girls were still little, their father would always make up fairy tales to tell them. We did whatever we could to shelter them from life's harsh realities. We believed that art saved people. And then it turned out that it didn't . . ."

". . . There's an old woman who lives alone in our building, she's religious. One day she stopped me, I thought she was going to try to comfort me, but instead, in this mean voice, she demanded, 'Do you ever think about why that happened to you? To your children?' Why . . . What did I do to deserve those words? I'm sure she re-pented . . . I think that afterward, she must have repented for what she said . . . I've never deceived or betrayed anyone. I had two abortions: Those are my only two sins . . . I know in my heart . . . Whenever I can, I give money to people on the street, even a tiny bit, whatever I have. I feed the birds in the winter . . ."

The next time, the two of them, mother and daughter, came to see me together.

THE MOTHER

Maybe some people consider them heroes? They have this idea, they're happy to die for it, they think that they're going to heaven. It makes them unafraid of death. I don't know anything about them: "We've created a composite sketch of the alleged terrorist . . ." and that's it. For them, we're targets—no one explained to them that my little girl is no target, that she has a Mama who can't live without her, that there's a boy who's in love with her. How can you kill someone who is loved? I think that's a crime twice over. Go to war, go up to the moun-tains and shoot each other, what are you shooting at me for? Why are you shooting at my daughter? They kill us in the midst of our civilian lives . . . [*Silence.*] Now I'm afraid of myself, frightened of my own thoughts. Sometimes you want to kill them all and then it horrifies you that you wanted that.

I used to love the Moscow Metro. The most beautiful Metro system in the world! It's like a museum! [*She is silent.*] After the attacks . . . I'd see people going into the Metro holding hands. Fear kept its grip on us for a long time afterward . . . It was scary to go out into the city, my blood pressure would skyrocket immediately. I was always scoping out suspicious passengers on the Metro. At work, it was the only thing we talked about. What's happening to us, dear Lord? One day, I was standing on the platform, and there was this young woman near me with a baby stroller. She had black hair, black eyes, I could tell that she wasn't Russian. I don't know what her ethnicity was— Chechen, Ossetian? Who was she? I couldn't help myself and peeked into the stroller: Was there a child in there? Or was it something else? Thinking about riding in the same car as her ruined my mood. "No," I thought. "She can go ahead, I'll wait for the next train." A man came up to me, "Why did you look into her stroller?" I told him the truth. "So you too, then."

. . . I see an unhappy girl curled up in a ball. It's my Ksyusha. Why is she all alone? Without us? No, it's impossible, it can't be true. Blood on the pillow . . . I cry, "Ksyusha! Ksyushenka!" But she can't hear me. She pulled a hat over her face so that I wouldn't see her, so that I wouldn't get scared. My little girl! She'd dreamed of being a pediatrician, but now, she's lost her hearing. She was the most beautiful girl in her class . . . and now her face . . . For what? I'm drowning in a viscous fluid, my consciousness is splintering into shards. My legs don't work, they feel like they're made of cotton, and I have to be led out of the ward. The doctor screams at me. "Get ahold of yourself, or else we won't let you see her again!" I get ahold of myself . . . and go back into the room . . . She didn't look at me, she looked past me, off somewhere, as though she didn't recognize me. The look in her eyes was like a suffering animal's, it was unbearable. It was barely possible to go on living after seeing it. Now she's hidden that look away somewhere, she's put on an armored shell, but she's holding all that inside of her. It's all been imprinted on her. She's always in that place where none of us were with her . . .

There was an entire hospital ward full of girls like her . . . They'd all ridden in the same Metro car, and there they all lay . . . lots of students, school kids. I thought that all of us mothers were going to march out into the street to demonstrate. All of the mothers with their children. There would be thousands of us. Now I realize that my girl is only important to me, only at home, just to us. People listen and sympathize . . . but without feeling the pain! There's no pain for anyone else!

I'd come home from the hospital and lay there feeling nothing. Dashenka would sit with me, she took time off of work. She'd stroke my head like I was a little child. Their father didn't scream, he didn't panic, then suddenly he had a heart attack. We found ourselves in hell . . . Again? What have we done to deserve this? My whole life, I've made my daughters read good books, tried to convince them that good is more powerful than evil, that good always wins in the end. But life is nothing like books. Will a mother's prayer be heard from the bottom of the sea? It's all lies! I'm a traitor, I couldn't protect them like I could when they were little, and they were depending on me. If my love alone was enough to protect them, they would be invulnerable to all harm and disappointment.

One operation . . . another . . . Three total! Ksyusha regained her hearing in one ear . . . then her fingers started working again . . . We lived on the border between life and death; between faith in miracles and utter injustice. It made me realize that even though I am a nurse, I know next to nothing about death. I've seen it many times, but only in passing. You put an IV in, listen for a pulse . . . Everyone thinks that medics know more about death than other people, but no. I worked with a pathologist, he was about to retire. "What is death?" he asked me. [*Silence.*] My previous life turned into a big white nothing. All I remember is Ksyusha . . . Every little detail—how she was brave and funny as a little kid. She wasn't afraid of big dogs and wanted for it to always be summer. The way her eyes sparkled the day she came home and told us that she had gotten into medical school! Without bribes or private tutors. We couldn't afford the tuition, it was beyond our means. How a day or two before the terrorist attack, she happened to come across an article in an old newspaper about what you should do in the event of an extreme situation on the Metro . . . That . . . I don't remember what exactly, but it was a set of instructions. Then, when it happened, before she lost consciousness, Ksyusha remembered that article. And on that morning, she had just picked up her boots from the cobbler's. When she had already put on her coat and was pulling them on, she couldn't get them on . . . "Mama, can I borrow your boots?" "Sure. Go ahead." We're the same size. My maternal intuition didn't tell me anything . . . I could have stopped her . . . Some time before, in my dreams, I'd seen big stars, a constellation. But there was no sense of alarm . . . It's all my fault and I feel crushed by the guilt . . .

If they'd allowed it, I would have slept at the hospital and been a mother to everyone. Some people wept in the stairwell . . . some needed hugs and for someone to sit with them. A girl from Perm cried because her mother was far away. Another girl's leg had been crushed . . . There's nothing more precious than a leg! There's nothing more precious than your child's leg! Who can blame me for wanting to be there?

In the first few days after the attack, it was all over the papers and on the news. When Ksyusha saw a photo of herself in print, she threw away the newspaper . . .

THE DAUGHTER

. . . There's a lot I don't remember . . . I choose not to keep it in my memory! I just don't want to! [*Her mother puts her arms around her. Comforts her.*]

. . . Everything is scarier underground. Now, I always carry a flashlight with me in my purse . . .

. . . I couldn't hear any screaming or wailing. It was completely silent. Everyone was lying in a big pile . . . It wasn't scary, no . . . Then, slowly, people started moving. At a certain point, it dawned on me that I had to get out of there, everything was covered in chemicals, and it was all on fire. I was looking around for my backpack, it had my papers in it for school, my wallet . . . Shock . . . I was in shock . . . I didn't feel any pain . . .

. . . I heard a woman's voice calling, "Sergey! Sergey!" Sergey wasn't responding . . . A few people were left sitting in the train car in unnatural poses. One man was hanging from a railing like a worm. I was afraid of looking in his direction . . .

. . . I started walking, it made me dizzy . . . All around, I heard cries of "Help! Help!" Someone in front of me was moving like a sleepwalker, he kept going forward then turning around and going back. Everyone went past the two of us.

. . . At the top of the escalators, two women ran up to me and plastered some rag to my forehead. For some reason, I was freezing cold. They got me a chair, I sat down. I saw them asking other passengers for their belts and neckties and using them to tie off people's wounds. The station attendant was shouting into the phone: "What do you want us to do? People are coming out of the tunnel and dying on the spot, climbing up onto the platform and dropping dead . . ." [*She falls silent.*] Why are you torturing us? I feel bad for my mother. [*Silence.*] Everyone is used to it now. They turn on the TV, hear a little bit about it, then go drink their coffee . . .

THE MOTHER

I grew up in a deeply Soviet time. Totally Soviet. Born in the USSR. But the new Russia . . . I don't understand it yet. I can't say what's worse, what we have today or the history of the Communist Party. My mind still functions according to the Soviet scheme, in the Soviet mold; after all, I spent half of my life under socialism. All of that is ingrained in me. You couldn't beat it out. And I don't think that I'd want to. Life used to be bad, now it's outright frightening. In the morning, we scatter: My husband and I go to work, the girls go to school, and then we spend the whole day bugging each other: "How's it going over there? What time do you think you'll be heading home? How are you getting there?" Only when all of us are together again in the evening do I begin to feel some relief, only then can I take a break from worrying. I'm scared of everything. I simply tremble with fear. The girls admonish me: You exaggerate, Mama . . . I'm perfectly sane, but I need that protection, that extra layer, my home. Maybe I'm fragile because my father died when I was little—my father loved me a lot. [*She is silent.*] Our daddy fought in the war, he made it out of two burning tanks . . . He marched through the war and came out alive. Then he got home and they killed him in an underpass.

I was brought up on Soviet books, the things they taught us were totally different. Just an example, for comparison . . . In those books, the first Russian terrorists are depicted as heroes. Martyrs. Sophia Perovskaya, Kibalchich* . . . They died for the people, they were on a holy mission. They threw a bomb at the Tsar. Those young people

---

* Sophia Perovskaya (1853–1881) was a Russian revolutionary and member of the Will of the People. She successfully orchestrated the assassination of Alexander II in 1881, for which she was executed by hanging. Nikolai Kibalchich (1853–1881) was also a member of the Will of the People and may have manufactured the bomb that killed the Tsar.

often came from the aristocracy, good families . . . Why are we surprised that people like them still exist today? [*She falls silent.*] In history classes, when they taught us about the Great Patriotic War, the teacher would tell us about the heroism of Belarusian partisan Yelena Mazanik, who killed the Nazi *Gauleiter* Wilhelm Kube by planting a bomb in the bed where he slept with his pregnant wife. While their children were sleeping in the next room, just on the other side of the wall . . . Stalin personally awarded her the Hero's Star. For the rest of her life, she went around to schools telling the story of her daring feat during bravery lessons.* No one, not the teacher . . . nobody told us that the children had been sleeping in the next room . . . Mazanik had actually been those children's nanny . . . [*Silence.*] After the war, people with consciences are ashamed of remembering what they were forced to do in battle. Papa struggled with this . . .

At the Avtozavodskaya Metro station, it was a boy who'd detonated himself, a suicide bomber. A Chechen boy. His parents later said that he read a lot. Loved Tolstoy. He grew up during a war, surrounded by bombing and shelling . . . He saw his cousins die. When he was fourteen, he ran away from home into the mountains to join Khattab's men.† He wanted to avenge their deaths. He was probably a pure boy with a passionate heart . . . They made fun of him, ha ha . . . little idiot kid . . . But he learned how to shoot better than anyone else and how to throw grenades. His mother found him and dragged him back to their village, she wanted him to finish school and become a tile setter. But after a year, he disappeared into the mountains again. They taught him how to detonate bombs, and then he came to Moscow . . . [*Silence.*] If he had done it for money, it would have all made sense, but he wasn't getting paid to kill. This boy was capable of throwing himself under a tank and blowing up a maternity ward . . .

Who am I? We're just people . . . nothing but faces in the crowd. Our life is mundane, insignificant, though we do our best to live. We love, we suffer. It's just not that interesting to anyone else, no one is going to write a book about us. The crowd . . . The masses. No one has ever asked me so many questions about my life before, that's why I'm talking so much. "Mama, put your soul away," my girls will say. They're always educating me. Young people today inhabit a world

---

* "Bravery lessons" were held during the 1970s and 1980s (and reestablished in 2011) to instill patriotism in children from a young age.
† Ibn al-Khattab (1963–2002) was a Saudi-born Chechen independence fighter.

that's much crueler than the Soviet Union . . . [*She is silent.*] It's like life's not for us anymore, it's not intended for people like us; it's somewhere else. Somewhere . . . things are happening, but they have nothing to do with us . . . I don't go to expensive stores, I'm too shy: The security guards give me bad looks because my clothes come from the regular market. Made in China from head to toe. I ride the Metro, it terrifies me, but I do it. People who are more well off don't ride the Metro. It's not for everyone—it's for the poor; it's princes, boyars, and the taxed masses all over again. I don't remember the last time I went to a café, I haven't been able to afford that in ages. And the theater is a luxury now, too, even though there used to be a time when I didn't miss a single premiere. It hurts . . . It hurts a lot. We lead this gray existence, and all because we're not allowed into the new world. My husband brings home library books by the bagful, that's the one thing we can still afford. We still have our strolls around old Moscow, through our favorite places, Yakimanka, Kitai-Gorod, Varvarka. That's our shell; these days, everyone has to grow armor. [*She is silent.*] We were taught . . . Marx wrote that "Capital is theft." And I still agree with him.

I've known love . . . I could always tell when somebody really loved me. I have an intuitive connection with the people who've loved me. It's wordless. I just remembered my first husband . . . Did I love him? Yes. A lot? Madly. I was twenty. With a head full of nothing but dreams. We lived with his beautiful elderly mother, she was jealous of me: "You're as pretty as I was when I was young." She would take the flowers he'd bring me and move them to her room. Later on, I understood her, perhaps I've only just understood how deeply I love my girls, realized just how close you can be with your child. My therapist wants to talk me out of it: "You have a hypertrophied love for your children. You shouldn't love them like that." No way, my love is normal . . . Love! My life . . . It's mine . . . There's no perfect recipe . . . [*She is silent.*] My first husband loved me, but he had a philosophy: You can't spend your whole life with just one woman, you have to know others as well. I gave it a lot of thought . . . shed many tears . . . Then finally, I found the strength to let him go. I was left alone with little Ksyusha. My second husband . . . He's like a brother to me, and I'd always dreamed of having an older brother. At first, the whole thing troubled me. When he proposed, I didn't know how we were going to live together. In order to have kids, the house has to smell like love. But he went ahead and moved me and Ksyusha in with him. "Let's give it a try. If you don't like it, I'll take you back to your old place." And we ended up figuring it out. Love comes in many different forms: There's mad love, and then there's love that resembles friendship. A friendly alliance. I like to think so, because my husband is a really good person. So what if I don't go around in silks . . .

I had Dashenka . . . We were always with our children. In the summer, we'd go to their grandmother's house in the country, in Kaluga Oblast. There was a river there. A meadow and a forest. Their grandmother baked them cherry pies that they still talk about. We never went to the sea, although that was our dream. As you know, honest work won't make you rich: I'm a nurse, and my husband was a researcher at a radiological institute. But the girls always knew that we loved them.

A lot of people glorify perestroika . . . Everyone had very high hopes for the future. I have no reason to love Gorbachev. I remember the conversations we'd have in the staff room: "Socialism is ending— what's next?" "Bad socialism is over, now we're going to have good socialism." We waited . . . pored over the newspapers . . . Pretty soon, my husband lost his job and they shut down the institute. There was a sea of unemployed people, all of them with college degrees. The kiosks appeared, then the supermarkets where they had everything, like in a fairy tale, only there was no money to buy any of it. I'd go in and come right back out. I'd get two apples and an orange when the kids were sick. How are we supposed get used to this? Accept that it's how things are going to be from now on? How? When I'm standing in line for the cash register, there'll be someone in front of me with a shopping cart full of pineapples and bananas . . . It hurts your pride. That's why people seem so tired these days. God forbid you were born in the USSR but live in Russia. [*She is silent.*] Not a single one of my dreams ever came true . . .

[*When her daughter steps into the other room, she tells me this in a half-whisper.*]

How many years has it been? Three years since the attack . . . No, longer . . . I have a secret . . . I can't imagine getting in bed with my husband and letting him touch me. All these years, my husband and I haven't had any relations. I'm his wife, and yet I'm not a wife to him at all anymore. He keeps trying to talk me into it: "It'll make you feel better." My friend who knows everything doesn't understand me, either: "You're amazing. You're so sexy. Take a look at yourself in the mirror, you're so beautiful. Your hair . . ." I was born with this hair . . .

The fact is, I've forgotten all about my beauty. When someone drowns, their body becomes completely saturated with water. That's how I am, but with pain. It's as though I've renounced my body and all that is left of me is my soul . . .

THE DAUGHTER

. . . The dead lay on the ground with their cellphones endlessly ringing . . . No one would brave going over and answering them.

. . . There was a girl sitting on the floor covered in blood, some guy was offering her chocolate . . .

. . . My coat wasn't completely burned, but it was charred all over. The doctor examined me, and right away she said, "Lie down on a stretcher." I even resisted: "I'll get up and walk to the ambulance." She had to yell at me: "Lie down!" I lost consciousness in the ambulance and only came to in the intensive care unit . . .

. . . Why am I silent? I had been seeing this guy, we were even . . . he'd given me a ring . . . but after I told him about what happened to me . . . maybe it's completely unrelated, but we ended up breaking up. I learned my lesson, it made me realize that you shouldn't confess things to people. You get blown up, you survive, and you end up even more vulnerable and fragile than you were before. You're branded a victim—I didn't want people to see that brand on me . . .

. . . Mama loves the theater, sometimes she'll manage to get her hands on a cheap ticket. "Ksyusha, let's go see a play." I decline; she and Papa go by themselves. The theater doesn't affect me anymore . . .

THE MOTHER

People often find it difficult to comprehend why something has happened to them, they want to be like everyone else. To hide. It's an instinct that doesn't turn off right away . . .

That suicide bomber boy, and the others like him . . . They come down from the mountains to tell us: "You don't see the way they're killing us. We're going to do to you what they do to us." [*Silence.*]

I'm thinking . . . I want to remember, when was I ever happy? I have to try to remember . . . I think it was only when the kids were little . . .

The other day, the doorbell rang, it was Ksyusha's friends . . . I sat them down in the kitchen. My first impulse is always to feed the guests, I get that from my mother. For a while, young people had stopped talking about politics. Now they're at it again. At first, they were arguing about Putin . . . "Putin is a Stalin clone . . ." "This isn't going to last . . ." "Our whole country is screwed . . ." "It's a question of oil and natural gas . . ." Here's a question: Who made Stalin Stalin? There's the problem of responsibility . . .

Should you only put people on trial if they actually murdered and tortured people or:

should it also be the informants . . .

the people who took the children of "enemies of the people" away from their relatives and sent them to orphanages . . .

the drivers who transported the arrested . . .

the cleaning women who washed the floors after people were tortured . . .

the director of the railways that conveyed political prisoners to the north in cattle cars . . .

the tailors who sewed camp guards' coats. The doctors who did their dental work, took their cardiograms, all so that they could better withstand the stresses of their jobs . . .

those who stood silent at assemblies while others screamed, "Let the dogs die like dogs!"

From Stalin, the conversation turned to Chechnya . . . It's the same thing, again: The ones who kill, who set the bombs off—surely they are responsible, but what about the people who make the bombs and shells at munitions factories, who sew the uniforms, who teach soldiers to shoot, award them medals—are they guilty, too? [*Silence.*] I wanted to cover Ksyusha with my whole body, hide her away from these conversations. She sat there with her eyes huge with terror. She looked at me . . . [*She turns to her daughter.*] Ksyushenka, I'm not guilty and Papa's not guilty, either—he teaches math now. I'm a nurse. They used to bring our wounded officers from Chechnya to the hospital where I work. We'd treat them and then, of course, they'd have to go back. To keep fighting the war. Few of them wanted to return, many of them openly admitted: "We don't want to fight." I'm a nurse, my job is to try to save everyone . . .

There are pills for headaches, toothaches, but there are no pills for my pain. The psychologist put me on a schedule: in the morning, half a glass of St. John's wort on an empty stomach, twenty drops of essence of hawthorn, thirty drops of peony . . . My whole day is like that. I down all those drops. I used to go to this Chinese guy . . . Nothing has helped . . . [*She is silent.*] Everyday tasks distract you, they keep you from going insane. Routine can be very therapeutic: laundry, ironing, sewing . . .

There's an old linden tree in our courtyard . . . One day, I was walking—it had already been a few years—and I noticed that it was in bloom. The smell . . . Until that moment, nothing had been quite as vivid . . . Things weren't how they used to be . . . The colors had grown muted, the sounds . . . [*She is silent.*]

In the hospital, I made friends with a woman who had been riding in the third car—Ksyusha had been in the second. She'd gone back to work, and it seemed like she'd gotten over it. Then something snapped, and she suddenly wanted to throw herself off her balcony. She tried jumping out of her window. Her parents put railings on all of the windows, they turned their apartment into a cage. She tried gas . . . Her husband left her . . . I don't know where she is now. Someone told me they saw her at Avtozavodskaya Station, walking up and down the platform, screaming, "We're going to pick up three handfuls of dirt with our right hand and throw them onto the coffin. Pick them up . . . and throw them." She screamed like that until nurses came and took her away . . .

I thought it was Ksyusha who'd told me this at some point . . . About how there'd been a man standing so close to her, she'd wanted to say something to him. She never got the chance. He ended up shielding her, a lot of the shrapnel coming at her hit him instead. Did he make it out alive? I think about him all the time . . . I can practically see him . . . but Ksyusha doesn't remember him . . . Where did that idea come from? I probably made him up. Someone had to have rescued her for me . . .

I know a remedy . . . Ksyusha needs to be happy. The only thing that can cure her is happiness. It has to be something special . . . We were at an Alla Pugacheva concert, our whole family are fans. I wanted to go up to her or pass her a note: "Dedicate a song to my daughter. Say that it's for her alone." So that she'll feel like a queen . . . raise her up to the heavens . . . She's seen hell, now she needs to see heaven so that her world may regain its balance. My delusions . . . my fantasies . . . [*She is silent.*] My love wasn't enough to cure her. Who can I write to? Who should I turn to for help? You people made your fortunes on Chechen oil, Russian credits, now help me take her somewhere. She needs to sit under a palm tree, watch a turtle crawl past, she has to forget that inferno. Her eyes are always filled with hell. There's no light, I never see any light in them.

I started going to church . . . Do I believe in God? I don't know. But I do always want to talk to someone. One day, the priest was reading a sermon about how great suffering either brings you closer to God or pushes you further away, and if someone turns away from God, you shouldn't judge them, because it comes from anger and pain. I felt like he was talking about me.

I observe people from the outside, I don't feel like I'm one of them anymore . . . I look at them as though I am no longer a person my-self . . . You're a writer, you'll understand what I mean: Words have very little in common with what goes on inside of you. Before, I was rarely in touch with what was happening inside me. Now, it's like I live down in the mines . . . I get upset, I fall into thought . . . I'm always chewing something over in my head. "Mama, put your soul away!" No, my darling girls, I don't want all my feelings and tears to simply evaporate. To disappear without a trace, without leaving a mark. This is what upsets me more than anything else. Everything that I've been through—I don't just want to leave it to my children. I want to share it with other people, I want it to be somewhere so that anyone who wants to can pick it up and see it for themselves.

September 3. The Day of Remembrance for Victims of Terrorism. Moscow is in mourning. People with disabilities fill the streets along with young women in black kerchiefs. Memorial candles burn on Solyanka, on the square in front of the Dubrovka Theater, by entrances to the Park Kultury, Lubyanka, Avtozavodskaya, and Rizhskaya Metro stations . . .

I'm also a part of that crowd. I ask questions and listen to people's conversations. How are we living with this?

Terrorist attacks took place in Moscow in 2000, 2001, 2002, 2003, 2004, 2006, 2010, and 2011.

—I was on my way to work. As usual, the train was overcrowded. I didn't hear the explosion, but for some reason, everything was suddenly orange and my body went numb. I tried to move my arm, but I couldn't. I thought I was having a stroke, then I passed out . . . When I came to, people were stepping over me without any regard for me, as though I were dead. I got scared that I was going to be trampled and raised my arms into the air. Someone lifted me up. Flesh and blood—that was all I saw . . .

—My son is four. How am I supposed to explain to him that his father is dead? He doesn't even know what death is. On the other hand, I don't want him to think that his father abandoned us. For now, we just say that he's gone on a business trip . . .

—I think about it all the time . . . In front of the hospital, long lines of people stood waiting to donate blood, carrying bags of oranges. They begged the exhausted nurses: "Take this fruit and give it to anyone who wants it. What else can I bring?"

—The girls from work would come see me, our boss would let them take his car. But I didn't want to see anyone . . .

—We need a war, maybe then we'll have real, upstanding people. My grandfather always said that he only ever met truly good people during the war. There's not enough kindness these days.

—Two women, strangers, were crying in each other's arms next to the escalator, their faces covered in blood. But I didn't even realize it was blood, I thought that it was just their makeup running from their tears. In the evening, I rewatched this scene, this time on TV, and that's when it finally hit me. When I was down there, it simply did not compute, I was staring at the blood in utter disbelief.

—At first, you think that you'll be fine going down into the Metro, you step into the train full of courage, but then, after one or two stops, you have to jump out, you're in a cold sweat. It's especially terrifying when the train stalls in the tunnel. Every minute stretches out to an eternity, it feels like your heart is hanging on by a thread . . .

—Every person from the Caucasus is a potential terrorist . . .

—What do you think, that Russian soldiers never committed any war crimes in Chechnya? My brother did a tour of duty there . . . You should hear some of the things he's told me about the glorious Russian army . . . They'd keep Chechen men down in pits, like they were animals, and demand that their relatives buy them out. They tortured people . . . pillaged their homes . . . These days, he's drinking himself to death.

—He's on the payroll of U.S. State Department? Provocateur! Who turned Chechnya into a ghetto for Russians? They fired Russians from their jobs, chased them out of their apartments, stole their cars. If you didn't hand it over to them, they'd kill you. Russian girls were raped just for being Russian.

—I hate the Chechens! If it weren't for us Russians, they'd still be up there in their mountains, living in caves. I also hate journalists who stand up for Chechens! Fucking liberals! [*Shoots a look of absolute hatred in my direction—I'm recording our conversation.*]

—Did we put Russian soldiers on trial for killing German soldiers during the Great Patriotic War? They also killed them in all sorts of ways. Partisans cut captured Polizei up into little pieces . . . You should hear the stories veterans tell . . .

—During the First Chechen War, back when Yeltsin was still in power, they would always show how things really were on TV. We saw the Chechen women crying. Russian mothers roaming the countryside in search of their sons who'd gone missing in action. No one laid a finger on them. The hatred we see today didn't exist yet, not on either side.

—First it was just Chechnya burning, now it's the whole North Caucasus. Mosques going up everywhere.

—Geopolitics has come home to us. Russia is falling apart . . . Pretty soon, all that'll be left of the empire is Muscovy . . .

—I hate them!!!

—Who?

—Everyone!!!

—My son was alive for another seven hours, then they shoved him in a body bag and put him on a bus with the other corpses . . . He was brought to us in a government-issue coffin along with two wreaths. The coffin was made out of some kind of wood shavings, it felt like cardboard, we lifted it up and it fell apart under the weight. The wreaths were cheap and pathetic. We ended up having to buy everything ourselves. The government doesn't give a damn about us mere mortals, and I spit on them in return. I want to get out of this fucked-up country. My husband and I applied to emigrate to Canada.

—Stalin used to kill people, and now the gangsters do. Is that freedom?

—I have black hair, black eyes . . . I'm Russian, Orthodox. The other day, my friend and I went down into the Metro, and the police stopped us and took me aside: "Remove your outerwear. Show us your documents." They paid zero attention to my friend because she's blonde. My mother said, "Dye your hair." But I'm ashamed to.

—A Russian stands on three legs: "perhaps," "perchance," and "sometime maybe." At first, everyone quaked with fear, but a month later, when I found a suspicious package under a bench in the Metro, I barely managed to convince the station attendant to call the police.

—At Domodedovo Airport, after the terrorist attacks, those fucking taxi drivers hiked up their prices. Sky high! People will try to make a buck off of anything. I'd like to pull them out of their cars and slam their faces into their hoods, those shitheads!

—Some people were lying in puddles of blood, while others were snapping pictures of them on their phones. Click, click. Couldn't wait to put them up on their blogs. The office plankton need their entertainment.

—Today it's them, tomorrow it's going to be us. And no one says anything, everyone is okay with it.

—As much as we can, we'll try to help the departed with our prayers. To beg the Lord for His mercy . . .

A group of schoolchildren begin a performance on an improvised stage. They've been bussed in. I get closer.

—I'm interested in Bin Laden . . . Al-Qaeda, their global project . . .

—I'm for individual terror. Pinpointed terrorism. For instance, against the police and the bureaucracy . . .

—Terrorism: Is it a good thing or a bad thing?

—It's what passes for good these days.

—I'm sick of freakin' standing here. When do we get to go home?

—Here's a cool joke . . . A group of terrorists is sightseeing in Italy. They get to the Leaning Tower of Pisa. "Amateurs!"

—Terrorism is a business . . .

Human sacrifice, like in ancient times . . .

A mainstream phenomenon . . .

A warm-up for revolution . . .

Something personal . . .

ON THE OLD CRONE WITH A BRAID
AND THE BEAUTIFUL
YOUNG WOMAN

◆

Aleksander Laskovich, soldier, entrepreneur, emigrant,
interviewed periodically between
the ages of 21 and 30

DEATH IS LIKE LOVE

When I was little, we had a tree in our courtyard . . . this old maple . . .
I'd talk to it, it was my friend. After Grandpa died, I cried for a long
time. Bawled all day long. I was five, and it had made me realize that I
was going to die and everyone I knew was going to die, too. I was
seized by terror: Everyone is going to die before me, and I will be left
all alone. Savagely lonely. My mother felt sorry for me, but my father
came up to me and barked: "Wipe those tears away. You're a man.
Men don't cry." But I didn't even know what I was yet. I'd never liked
being a boy, I didn't like playing war. But no one ever asked me what I
wanted . . . Everyone made the decisions for me. My mother had
dreamed of having a girl, and my father, in typical fashion, had wanted
her to get an abortion.

The first time I ever wanted to hang myself, I was seven . . . The
incident with the Chinese bowl . . . My mother had made jam in this
Chinese bowl we had and put it on a stool to cool; meanwhile, my
brother and I had been chasing our cat all over the house. Muska managed to fly over the bowl like a shadow, but not us . . . My mother was
still very young, my father was in military training. And there it was:
a puddle of jam all over the floor. My mother cursed her fate as an of-

ficer's wife forced to live out in the back of the beyond, on Sakhalin,* where there were ten meters of snow in the winter and in the summer, the burdock grew taller than she was. She grabbed my father's belt and chased us out into the street: "But Mama, it's raining and the ants in the barn bite." "Shoo! Get out of here! Beat it!!!" My brother ran to our neighbor's house, and I decided to hang myself. I clambered into the barn, found a rope in a basket. They'll come looking for me in the morning and find me dangling from the rafters—happy now, fuckers? Right then, Muska squeezed through the door . . . meow, meow . . . Sweet Muska! You've come to take pity on me. I hugged her, squeezed her, and that's how the two of us stayed until morning.

Papa . . . What was Papa? He read the paper and smoked. He was a political commander† in an air regiment. We moved from one military town to the next, always living in dormitories. Long brick barracks, exactly the same wherever we went. Even the way they smelled was identical: like shoe polish and Chypre, the cheap cologne. That's how my father always smelled, too. A typical scene: I'm eight, my brother is nine, and my father comes home from his shift. His belt squeaking, his calf boots creaking. In that moment, all my brother and I want is to become invisible, to fall off the face of the Earth! Papa takes *Story of a Real Man* by Boris Polevoy down from the shelf—in our house, it was like the Bible. "And what happened next?" He starts in on my brother. "The plane crashed. And Alexey Maresyev crawled away from it . . . Wounded. He ate a hedgehog . . . and fell into a ditch . . ." "What ditch?" "It was the crater from a five-ton bomb," I try to help him. "What? That was yesterday." We simultaneously shudder at the sound of my father's commander tone. "So you didn't read it today?" The next scene: We're running around the table like three clowns, one big one and two little ones; us with our pants down and Papa clutching a belt. [*A pause.*] We all grew up on movies, huh? The world in pictures . . . It wasn't books that raised us, it was movies. And music . . . The books my father brought home still give me a rash. My temperature rises whenever I see *Story of a Real Man* or *The Young Guard* on anyone's bookshelf. Oh! How Papa dreamed of throwing us under a tank . . . He wanted us to hurry up and grow up so we could

---

* An island in the Pacific Sea that has alternated between Russian and Japanese rule since the nineteenth century. The USSR seized Sakhalin from the Japanese during World War II.
† A political commander is a military political commissar responsible for the political education of the troops, lecturing on ideology and the Party line.

volunteer to fight in a war. He was incapable of imagining a world
without war. He needed us to be heroes! And you can only become a
hero at war. If one of us had lost our legs like that Alexey Maresyev of
his, he would have only been happy. It would have meant that his life
had not been in vain . . . Success! Everything had fallen into place!
And he . . . I think he would have carried out the verdict with his own
bare hands if I had broken my oath, if I had dared to waver in battle.
A regular Taras Bulba! "I begat you, and I shall be the one to kill you!"
Papa belonged to the Idea, he wasn't really a human. You must love
the Motherland with your entire being. Unconditionally! That was all
I ever heard, my entire childhood. The only reason we were alive was
so that we could defend the Motherland . . . But despite all this, I simply could not be programmed for war, instilled with a puppy-like
readiness to stick myself in a hole or a dike or throw myself on a land-
mine. I just never liked death . . . I'd crush ladybugs—on Sakhalin, in
the summer, there are more ladybugs than sand—and I'd crush them
like everyone else did. Then, one day, I had this terrifying realization:
Why have I made all these little red corpses? Another time, Muska had
had kittens, but they were premature . . . I brought them water, tended
to them. My mother saw what I was up to and asked: "Are they dead?"
And after she said that, they died. But no tears allowed! "Men don't
cry." Papa gave us army caps as presents. On weekends, he would put
on his records with army songs, and my brother and I were forced to
sit there and listen as a "modest manly tear" made its way down our
father's cheek. Whenever he got drunk, he'd tell us the same story:
The enemy had surrounded "the hero," he valiantly defended himself,
shooting at them until he was down to his last bullet, which he'd saved
for shooting himself in the heart . . . At that point in the story, my father would fall over cinematically, catching the leg of the stool with his
foot, which made it topple down with him. That was always really
funny. Then my father would suddenly sober up and turn stern:
"There's nothing funny about a hero dying."

I had no interest in dying . . . When you're little, thinking about
death is very frightening . . . "A man must always be prepared," "the
holy duty to the Motherland" . . . "What? You don't want to learn
how to take a Kalashnikov apart and put it back together?" There was
no way to say no to my father. The humiliation! Oh! How I longed to
sink my baby teeth straight into his calf boots and not let go, thrashing around, biting him. Why was he beating my bare ass in front of the
neighbor boy Vitka?! While also calling me a girl . . . Like I said, I

wasn't born to dance with death. I have high arches . . . I wanted to dance in the ballet . . . While Papa served the great Idea. It was as though everyone had been lobotomized, they were all terribly proud of living without any pants on, but clutching a rifle . . . [*A pause.*] We grew up . . . we all grew up a long time ago . . . Poor Papa! Life, in the meantime, changed genres . . . What used to be an optimistic tragedy is now a comedy and action flick. What crawls on its belly and gnaws on pinecones? Guess! Good old Alexey Maresyev. Papa's beloved hero . . . "In the basement, the boys were playing Gestapo, / Tortured the hell out the plumber, Potapov . . ." That's all that's left of Papa's Idea . . . As for Papa himself? He's an old man now, but old age has taken him unawares. He should be savoring every moment, gazing up at the sky, admiring the trees. Playing chess or collecting stamps . . . matchboxes . . . Instead, he's glued to the television: parliamentary sessions, leftists, rightists, rallies, demonstrations with little red flags. That's where you'll find my father! He staunchly supports the Communists. We'll get together for dinner . . . He'll throw the first punch, awaiting my response: "We lived through a great epoch!" Papa needs a battle; without one, life has no meaning. The only place for him is on the barricades, banner in hand! One day we were watching TV, a Japanese robot was extracting rusted landmines out of the sand . . . one and then another . . . A triumph of science and technology! Of human reason! But Papa's just sad for the fallen fortress—he's disappointed that it's not our technology. And then . . . In an unexpected turn of events, toward the end of the segment, the robot makes a wrong move and gets blown up. As the saying goes, if you see a sapper running, follow him. Robots aren't programmed to do that. Papa can't believe his eyes: "Destroying imported technology? What, do we not have enough men?" He has his own relationship with death. Papa's life's purpose was to complete any mission assigned to him by the government and the Party. His life was worth less than a hunk of metal.

On Sakhalin, we lived across from a cemetery. Almost every day, I'd hear funeral marches: A yellow coffin meant someone from the village had died; if it was draped in red calico, it was a pilot. More often, it'd be a red one. After every red coffin, Papa would bring home a cassette. Other pilots came over . . . On the table, chewed *papirosa* butts smoldered in the ashtray, glasses of vodka glistened with condensation. The tape rolled: "I'm craft number so and so . . . engine stalling . . ." "Switch to the second one." "That one is out, too." "Try starting the left engine." "It won't start . . ." "The right . . ." "The right won't start, either . . ." "Eject!" "The cockpit canopy is malfunctioning . . . Fuck!!! Ahhhh . . . Ughhh . . ." For a long time, I imagined death meant falling from an unfathomable height, ahhhh . . . ughhh . . . One of the younger pilots once asked me, "What do you know about death, kid?" I was surprised. I thought that I'd always known about it. A boy from my class died . . . He'd started a fire and thrown a bunch of ammunition on it . . . Ka-boom! And there he was, lying in his coffin like he was just faking. Everyone standing around him, looking at him, but he wasn't there anymore . . . I couldn't look away. It felt like I'd always known about death, like it was something that I was born knowing about. Maybe I've died before? Or maybe it's because when I was still inside of my mother, she'd sit by the window watching the cemetery gates: red coffin, yellow coffin . . . I was mesmerized by death, I'd think about it dozens of times a day. So often. Death smelled like *papirosa* butts, unfinished cans of sprats, and vodka. Does it have to be a toothless old crone with a braid or can it be a beautiful young woman instead? One day, I'd meet her.

Eighteen years old . . . I wanted everything: women, wine, travel . . . mysteries, secrets. I'd imagine all the lives I could lead, fantasize about what they'd be like. And that's when they get you . . . Goddamn it! I still want to dissolve into thin air, disappear so that no one will ever find me. Leave no trace. Go off and become a lumberjack or some passportless hobo. I have this recurring nightmare: They're re-enlisting me into the army, they've messed up the documents, and I have to do another term of duty. I scream, trying to fight them off: "I've already served, you bastards! Leave me alone!!!" I go berserk! It's a terrible nightmare . . . [*A pause.*] I never wanted to be a boy . . . and I especially never wanted to become a soldier, I have no interest in war. Papa said, "It's time you finally become a man. Or else the girls will think you're impotent. The army is the school of life." You have to go learn how to kill people . . . For me, as I pictured it, this meant drums beating, columns of marching soldiers, top-of-the-line death machines blazing, the whistle of hot lead, and then . . . shattered skulls, eyeballs ripped out of their sockets, digits blown off . . . the wailing and moaning of the wounded . . . and the battle cries of the victors. The ones who are better at killing . . . Kill! Kill! Use an arrow, a bullet, a shell, an atom bomb, whatever it takes, just as long as you kill . . . Kill them all . . . I didn't want to. I also realized that in the army, it would be other men making a man out of me. I was either going to get killed or be forced to kill someone. My brother had gone off with a head full of pink cotton candy, this total romantic, and come back a frightened man. Every morning, he'd get a kick in the face because he slept on the bottom bunk and his senior slept on top. A heel in your face every day for a year! Just try and hold on to your old self under those conditions. And what if you were to undress someone, can you imagine how many things you can do to them then? So much . . . You can make them suck their own dick while everyone laughs at them. And whoever doesn't laugh is the next one to have a go . . . How about cleaning the soldiers' bathroom with nothing but a toothbrush or a razor blade? "Make it shine like a cat's balls." Shit! There are two kinds of people: those who are incapable of being just meat and those who can't be anything else. Human pancakes. I realized that I would need to harness every ounce of passion I could muster just to survive. I signed up for the athletic division, hatha yoga, karate. I learned how to kick people in the face, between their legs. How to break spines . . . I'd light a match, place it in the palm of my hand, and wait for it to finish burning. Of course, I couldn't take it . . . I'd cry. I remember . . . I remember . . . [*He pauses.*] A dragon is walking through the woods. He comes across a bear. "Hey bear," says the dragon. "I eat dinner at eight. Come over and I'll eat you." And he keeps going. A fox runs by. "Hey fox," the dragon says. "I eat breakfast at seven in the morning. Come over and I'll eat you." Goes a little farther. A rabbit hops by. "Hold it right there, rabbit," says the dragon. "I eat lunch at two. Come over and I'll eat you." "Can I ask you a question?" the rabbit raised his paw. "All right." "Can I not come?" "Sure, I'll take you off the list." But few people are capable of asking a question like that . . . Shiiiiiiiiit!

My send-off . . . Two days of frying, boiling, steaming, stuffing, and baking in preparation. They bought two cases of vodka. All of my relatives came. "Don't embarrass us, sonny!" my father raised the first glass. And so it began . . . The same old shit: "Undergo harsh trials" . . . "Endure with honor" . . . "Prove your courage" . . . In the morning, next to the conscription office, there was an accordion, singing, and vodka being passed around in little plastic cups. Except I don't drink . . . "You sick or something?" Before taking us down to the station, they inspected our personal belongings. They made us take everything out of our bags and confiscated all the knives and forks and food. At home, they'd given me a little bit of money . . . We'd stuffed the bills deep into my socks and underwear. Shit! The future defenders of the Motherland . . . Finally, they put us on the buses. The girls waved, the mothers wept. Here we go! A bus full of men. I can't remember a single one of their faces. They gave everyone buzz cuts and dressed us all up in rags. We looked like prisoners. Voices: "Forty tablets constitute a suicide attempt . . . Unfit for service. If you want to be smart, play dumb . . ." "Beat me up! Hit me! So what, I'm shit, I don't care. At least at home I fuck girls while you go off to play war." "Yep, boys, we've traded our sneakers for calf boots, and now we'll go and defend the Motherland." "People with dough don't sign up for the army." We rode like that for three days. The whole way there, everyone drank. Except I don't drink . . . "You poor bastard! What are you gonna do in the army?" We had to sleep in our clothes. At night, everyone took off their shoes . . . Fuck! The stench! A hundred guys with their boots off . . . Some people hadn't changed their socks in two or three days . . . It made you want to shoot or hang yourself. The officers escorted us to the bathroom three times a day. If you need to go more, tough luck. The bathroom's off-limits. Who knows what could happen in there . . . We'd just left home . . . One guy still managed to kill himself in the night . . . Fuck!

People can be programmed . . . Some of them want to be. One-two! One-two! In step!!! In the army, they make you walk and run a whole lot. You have to run far and fast, and if you can't run, then crawl! What do you get when you strand hundreds of young men in the same place? Beasts! A pack of young wolves! Prison and the army are governed by the same law: total chaos. Rule number one: Never help the weak. The weak must be beaten! So the weak are weeded out right off the bat . . . Rule number two: no friends, every man for himself. At night, some people oink, others quack, some cry for mommy, others fart, but the same rule applies to everyone: "Bend over or bend others over." It's as simple as one, two, three. What good were all those books I'd read? I'd believed Chekhov . . . He's the one who said that you have to squeeze the slave out of yourself drop by drop, that everything about a man ought to be wonderful: his sweet little soul, his cute little clothes, his charming notions. But in lots of cases, it's just the opposite! The complete opposite! Some people want to be slaves, they like it. It's personhood that they want to squeeze out of themselves, drop by drop. On your first day, the sergeant explains that you're all swine, nothing but beasts of burden. He commanded us to "Lie down!" Then "Get up!" Everyone did what he ordered except for one person. "Lie down! Get up!" The guy just kept lying there. The sergeant turned yellow, then violet: "What's wrong with you?" "Vanity of vanities . . ." "What the hell?" "The Lord taught us: Do not kill, do not even grow angry . . ." The sergeant took him down to the squadron commander, and the squadron commander took him to the KGB officer. They opened a case against him: It turned out that he was a Baptist. How had he ended up in the army?! They cordoned him off from everyone else and then took him away somewhere. An insanely dangerous element! Imagine: He didn't want to play war . . .

A young warrior's training: aesthetic marching, learning Army regulations by heart, disassembling and reassembling a Kalashnikov with your eyes closed, underwater . . . There is no God! The sergeant is Lord, Tsar, and Commander-in-Chief all rolled into one. Sergeant Valerian: "Even fish can be trained to do tricks. You got that?" "When you're singing in ranks, shout loud enough to make your ass muscles shake!" "The deeper you dig yourself into the dirt, the less they'll kill you." Folklore!! The biggest nightmare was the imitation leather boots . . . The Russian army was only recently re-shod—they finally gave them short boots just a few years ago. In my time, it was still calf boots. To make them shine, you have to rub them with shoe polish and buff them with a taut woolen rag. Then you're expected to cover ten kilometers in them. In eighty-five degree heat . . . It's hell! The second-biggest nightmare are footwraps.* There were two kinds, one for the summer and one for the winter. The Russian army was the last to stop using them. They waited until the twenty-first century . . . They've given me more than my share of bloody blisters. Here's how you wrap your feet: You start from your toes and always go outward, not in. We fall into ranks. "Private . . . Why are you wobbling? There are no narrow boots, only wrong feet." Everyone speaks in profanities: they're not cursing, that's just how they talk, from the colonel down to the private. I never heard anything else.

The ABCs of survival: A soldier is an animal that is capable of anything . . . The army is a prison where men are required by the constitution to serve time . . . Mama, I'm scared! A new soldier is "fresh meat," a "serf," a "worm." "Hey serf boy! Fetch me some tea." "Hey you, shine my boots . . ." Hey, hey! "I see how it is, you're a proud little fuck." The persecutions begin . . . At night, four guys hold you down while two others beat you. They've mastered the technique—they can do it without leaving any marks. Nothing. For instance, with a wet towel . . . or spoons . . . One time, they messed me up so bad I

---

* Footwraps are pieces of cloth wrapped around the feet, serving the same purpose as socks. They were common before socks became widely available.

couldn't speak for two days. For every single ailment, the only treatment offered at the infirmary is antiseptic. When they get sick of beating you, they give you a "shave" with a dry towel or a lighter, and when
they get tired of that, they'll feed you feces, filth. "With your hands!
Pick it up with your pretty little hands!" Bastards! They can force you
to run around the barracks naked or dance . . . A new soldier has no
rights . . . Papa: "The Soviet army is the greatest in the world . . ."

And then . . . the moment arrives . . . You get this nagging little
thought, this low-down, base little thought that, all right, I'll wash
their underwear and footwraps for now, but one day, I'll be the one
making someone wash my underwear. Back home, I'd considered myself all clean and pure. I thought nobody could ever break my spirit or
kill my "self." That was all before . . . [A pause.] You were always
hungry, especially for anything sweet. In the army, everything gets
stolen—instead of the regulation seventy grams, they'd serve a soldier
thirty. One time, we had to go a whole week without kasha because
someone had made off with the freight car of barley at the depot. I
dreamed of bakeries . . . raisin cakes . . . I got to be a master at peeling
potatoes. A virtual virtuoso! I could get through three buckets of potatoes in an hour. They brought us soldiers the unsaleable goods, like
at a farm. You sit there covered in potato peels . . . Fuck! The sergeant
goes up to the soldier on kitchen duty: "Peel three buckets of potatoes." The soldier: "People have been going into space for a long time
now, funny they still haven't invented a machine for peeling potatoes."
The sergeant: "The army has everything it needs, Private. Even a machine for peeling potatoes: namely, you. You're the latest model." The
soldiers' cafeteria is a world of wonders . . . For two years, they served
us nothing but kasha, sauerkraut, macaroni, and meat soup with meat
from the military stores, stockpiled in case of war. How long had it
been in there? Five, ten years . . . Everything came greased with lard
out of these huge orange five-liter cans. On New Year's Eve, they'd put
condensed milk on the noodles—yummy! Sergeant Valerian: "You can
eat cookies at home and even share them with your whores . . ." According to the regulations, soldiers were not permitted to have forks or
teaspoons. The only utensil you get is a spoon. One time, someone
received a pair of teaspoons in a package from home. Christ! You
should have seen how giddy we were sitting around stirring our tea.
Civilian luxuries! You're constantly told you're swine and then, all of
a sudden, somebody hands you a teaspoon. Good God! I have a home
somewhere . . . The captain on duty walked in and saw what we were

up to. "What? What's going on here? Who gave you permission to have these items? Immediately clear the premises of that junk!" Spoons, and then what? A soldier's not a person. He's an object . . . a tool . . . a killing machine . . . [*A pause.*] Discharge. There were about twenty of us . . . They drove us to the railway station, let us out: "Well, good-bye! So long, boys! Good luck in civilian life." We just stood there. And half an hour later, we were still standing there. An hour went by . . . None of us had moved! We stood around, looking at one another. Awaiting orders. Someone had to give us the command: "Run! To the ticket counter!" But the orders never came. I don't remember how much time passed before it dawned on us that there weren't going to be any orders. That we had to decide for ourselves. Fuck! Those two years really screwed us up . . .

I wanted to kill myself about five times . . . But how? Should I hang myself? There you are, hanging, covered in shit, your tongue flopping out of your mouth. No one is going to shove it back into your throat for you . . . Like that guy on the train when they were transporting us to the base. They'll just insult you . . . your own guys. Jump off the top of a watchtower? You'll end up mincemeat. Get a machine gun and shoot yourself in the head at your post? Your head will burst open like a watermelon. When it came down to it, I felt bad for my mom. The commander told us: "Just don't shoot yourself. It's easier to deduct personnel than it is to account for missing ammunition." A soldier's life is worth less than a service pistol. A letter from your girlfriend— that meant a lot in the army. Your hands would tremble. You're not allowed to hang on to letters. They check your dresser: "Your women will be our women. You're not done serving yet . . . Dispose of your paper pulp in the toilet." You're allowed to have a razor, a pen, and a notebook. You sit in the can and read the letter one last time: "I love you . . . Kisses . . ." Fuck! Defenders of the Motherland! A letter from my father: "There's a war going on in Chechnya . . . You know what I'm getting at!" Papa expected me to return a hero . . . One of our warrant officers had served in Afghanistan, he'd signed up as a volunteer. The war had taken a major toll on him. He never told any stories, he just kept cracking jokes about it. Shit! Everyone laughed their heads off . . . A soldier is dragging along his heavy, wounded friend, the guy is bleeding everywhere. Dying. He begs, "Just shoot me! I can't take it anymore!" "I don't have any more bullets. I'm out." "So buy some." "Where am I supposed to buy ammunition? We're in the mountains, there's no one else here." "Buy them from me." [*He laughs.*] "Comrade Officer, why did you ask to go to Afghanistan?" "I wanted to get promoted to major." "Not general?" "No, I can never be general—the general already has a son." [*A pause.*] No one was volunteering to go to Chechnya. I don't remember a single volunteer . . . My father would come to me in my dreams: "Didn't you take the oath? You stood under the Red banner, 'I swear to faithfully observe . . . strictly obey . . . courageously defend . . . and if I should break my solemn oath, let me face harsh punishment . . . universal hatred and contempt . . . ' " In my dream, I kept running away, but he kept aiming at me . . . taking aim . . .

You stand there at your post with a gun in your hands. Your only thought is that in a matter of seconds, you could be free. No one will ever see you again. You fucks can't reach me there! Nobody . . . no one! If you want to find a reason, you can begin with the fact that my mother had wanted a girl and my father, in typical fashion, had wanted her to get an abortion. The sergeant called me a sack of shit . . . told me that I was a waste of space . . . [*A pause.*] The officers were all sorts of people—one of them was an alcoholic intellectual who could speak English—but mostly, they were faceless drunks. They'd drink until they started seeing things . . . They could wake up the whole bunk in the middle of the night and make us run around the square until soldiers collapsed. We called the officers "jackals." There were bad jackals and good jackals . . . [*A pause.*] Who's going to tell you about how ten guys gang up on one guy and rape him . . . [*Bitter laughter.*] This isn't fun and games, and it's definitely not literature . . . [*A pause.*] They'd load you in a truck like cattle and drive you out to the commander's dacha. To haul slabs of concrete . . . [*Bitter laughter.*] Come on, drummer boy! Play us the Soviet anthem!

I never wanted to be a hero. I despise them! Heroes either have to kill a lot of people or die beautifully . . . You have to be willing to kill the enemy at any price: after you get through your ammunition, when you run out of bullets and hand grenades, use your knife, your gun butt, your shovel. Rip them apart with your teeth if you have to. Sergeant Valerian: "Learn to use your knife. The wrist is a very valuable thing, it's better to stab it than slice it . . . Use a reverse grip . . . like that . . . Good . . . Steady your hand, go behind the back . . . Don't get distracted by complicated maneuvers . . . Excellent! Excellent! Now twist the knife out of your opponent's grasp . . . good . . . Very good . . . Now he's dead. Great job! You killed him! Scream, 'Die, motherfucker!' What are you so quiet for?" [*He stops.*] The whole

time, they try to drill it into your head: Weapons are beautiful . . .
Shooting is for real men . . . They train you by making you kill animals, they'd bring us stray cats and dogs to practice on so that afterward we wouldn't flinch at the sight of human blood. Butchers! I
couldn't handle it . . . I'd cry at night . . . [A pause.] When we were
kids, we'd play samurais. A samurai is supposed to die Japanese-style,
he has no right to fall face down, screaming. But I always screamed . . .
The other kids didn't like playing that game with me . . . [A pause.]
Sergeant Valerian: "Remember, the machine gun works like this: one,
two, three and you're out . . ." To hell with all of you!! One, two . . .

Death is like love. In the final moments, there's nothing but darkness . . . Terrifying, ugly convulsions . . . You can't come back from
death, but we do recover from love. And we can remember the way
things were before . . . Have you ever drowned? I have . . . The more
you resist, the less strength you have. Surrender and descend, all the
way down to the bottom. And then . . . if you want to live, you'll break
through the sky of water and return to the surface. You just have to hit
bottom first.

What's it like? There's no light at the end of the tunnel, and I didn't
see any angels, either. Just my father, sitting next to a red coffin. The
coffin was empty.

*Several years later, I once again found myself in the town of N——
(I won't name the town, per my protagonist's request). We reconnected
over the phone and decided to meet. He was happy and in love, so
that's what he talked about. I didn't realize right away that I should
turn on the tape recorder so as not to miss this transformation of
life—everyday life—into literature. I'm always listening for it, in every
conversation, both general and private. Occasionally, my vigilance
flags—a "fragment of literature" may sparkle into sight at any moment, even in the most unexpected places. Which is what happened
here. We'd only wanted to get coffee, but life had handed us a develop-
ment in the narrative. Here's what I managed to record . . .*

WE KNOW TOO LITTLE ABOUT LOVE

I found love . . . I understand what it is now. Before, I had thought that
love was nothing but two fools running a fever. Madness . . . Really, we

know too little about love. And if you start pulling on this thread . . . love and war seem to be of a piece, like they're made of the same cloth, woven from the same material. The man with a machine gun and the guy who climbs to the top of Mount Elbrus, the people who fought to victory, who built a socialist paradise—it's all the same thing, the same magnetism and electricity. Do you understand? There are things that no one can do, that you can't buy or win in the lottery . . . But people know they exist and they want them . . . They just can't figure out how to look for them, or where.

It's almost like being born . . . It begins with a shock . . . [*Pause.*] Perhaps it's no good unraveling these mysteries? You're not scared, are you?

The first day . . .

I'd gone to my friend's house, he was having people over. As I was taking my coat off in the foyer, I heard someone coming toward me from the kitchen. I had to let them through, I turned around and—it was her! For a moment, I short-circuited, like they'd suddenly switched off the electricity in the apartment. And that was it. I'm not usually one to be tongue-tied, but with her there, I just sat and stared, I couldn't even see her, like, it's not that I didn't look at her, but for a long, long time, it felt like I was looking through her. Like in a Tarkovsky film: Someone is pouring water from a pitcher, and it's flowing down just past the rim of a cup, and then, very slowly, it turns along the cup's contour. The way I'm telling it, it sounds like this went on for longer than it really did. It happened in a flash! That day, I learned something that made everything else seem insignificant. I won't even attempt to dissect it—really, what's the point? It happened and that's enough. It's a very solid thing. Her fiancé went out to walk her home— I gathered that their wedding was right around the corner—but I didn't care. As I was getting ready to go home, I realized I wasn't going home alone, she was with me now. She'd already started living inside of me. You fall in love . . . Everything suddenly changes color, there are more voices, more sounds . . . You don't get a chance to make sense of any of it . . . [*A pause.*] I'm trying to give an approximate impression of what it's like . . .

The next morning, I woke up convinced that I had to find her. I didn't know her name or address or phone number, but the important thing had already taken place, this major life event had already happened. She'd arrived. It was as though I had forgotten something, then suddenly remembered it . . . Do you understand what I'm getting at?

No? We're not going to derive any formula here . . . It'd all be artificial . . . We're accustomed to thinking that while our future is a mystery, the past is something that we can explain. It either happened or it didn't . . . For me, everything came into question . . . what if none of it had ever really happened? Like it was all just a film reel turning and then it stopped . . . I can pinpoint the moments in my life that feel like they never happened. Even though they did. For instance, I was in love several times before that . . . or at least I thought I was . . . There are lots of photos to prove it. But all of it has spilled out of my memory and washed away. There are things that never spill out of you, that you have to carry around with you forever. As for the rest . . . Do people really remember everything that happens to them?

The second day . . .

I bought a rose. I had practically no money, but I went down to the market and bought the biggest rose I could find. And here's another thing—can you explain it? A gypsy woman came up to me, "Let me tell your fortune, honey. I can tell by your eyes that . . ." I ran away from her. What did I need my fortune for? I could tell for myself that the mystery was standing right there in the doorway. The mystery, the secret, the shroud . . . First, I went to the wrong apartment—a man opened the door, an undershirt drooping off of his body, visibly wasted. He saw me standing there with the rose and froze: "Fuck!" I went up to the next floor . . . A strange old woman in a knitted beret peered out at me through the chain: "Lena, it's for you." That evening, she played the piano for us, told us stories about the theater. She was an old actress. They had a big black cat, the household tyrant, who took an immediate dislike to me, although I don't know why, I tried to get him to like me . . . Their big black cat . . . While the mystery is happening, it's like you're not there. Do you understand what I'm talking about? You don't have to be a cosmonaut, an oligarch, or a hero, you can just be happy and experience everything there is to experience in a regular two-bedroom apartment—fifty-eight square meters, a full bathroom—surrounded by old Soviet junk. It got to be midnight, two in the morning . . . I had to go, but I didn't understand why I should ever leave this house again. More than anything, it felt like a memory . . . I'm looking for the right words . . . It was as though I was remembering something that I had forgotten for a very long time; now it was all coming back to me. I reconnected. Something like that . . . I think it's like . . . what a person experiences after spending many days in a monk's cell. The world suddenly appears to you in all of its infinite detail. All of its contours. Its secret becomes as accessible as any other object—say, a vase—but in order to understand this, it has to be painful. How can you understand something unless it hurts? It has to come with a great deal of pain . . .

. . . The first time anyone explained anything to me about women I was seven, it was my friends . . . they were seven, too. I remember how excited they were when they figured out that they knew and I didn't—like, now we're going to open your eyes. They started drawing me diagrams with sticks in the sand . . .

. . . I realized a woman was a different kind of being when I was seventeen. Not from reading it in a book—I felt it on my skin, the feeling of something utterly different from myself so close to me, this huge difference that shocked me with its starkness. There's something hidden inside of the vessel of woman that I will never have access to . . .

. . . Picture the soldier's barracks . . . It's Sunday. No planned activities. Two hundred men are holding their breath in front of a television watching aerobics, women in skin-tight outfits exercising on the screen . . . The men sit frozen like the statues on Easter Island. It was a real catastrophe if the TV broke, the person whose fault it was could have been killed. Do you understand? This is all about love . . .

The third day . . .

You get up in the morning, and you don't have to run off anywhere because you remember that she exists, you've found her. Sorrow loses its hold on you . . . You're not alone anymore. You suddenly become aware of your body . . . your hands, your lips . . . You start paying attention to the sky and the trees outside your window. For some reason, everything appears very close, it has all grown claustrophobically close to you. Things like this only happen in dreams . . . [*A pause.*] In the evening paper, we found an ad for a dreadful apartment in a dreadful neighborhood in the new buildings at the edge of town. All weekend long, from morning till night, men sit around in the courtyard swearing, playing cards and dominoes for bottles of vodka. A year later, we had our daughter . . . [*A pause.*] And now, I'll tell you about death . . . Yesterday, the whole city buried one of my classmates, he was a police lieutenant . . . His coffin got shipped in from Chechnya and they didn't even open it, they wouldn't show his mother the body. What was in there? There was a gun salute and all that. Glory to the heroes! I went with my father . . . His eyes sparkled . . . Do you understand what I'm talking about? People aren't prepared for happiness, they're ready for war, for ice and hail. I don't know any happy people other than my three-month-old daughter . . . I've never met anyone else who's happy . . . Russian people don't expect to ever be happy. [*A pause.*] Everyone sane is taking their children out of this country. A lot of my friends have already left . . . They call me from Israel and Canada. I'd never thought about leaving before. Leaving, leaving . . . I started considering it only after my daughter was born. I want to protect the people I love. My father will never forgive me. That I am sure of.

A RUSSIAN CONVERSATION IN CHICAGO

We met again—this time, in Chicago. The family had more or less settled into their new home. A group of Russians got together, Russian food and Russian conversation. In addition to the eternal Russian questions, what is to be done and who is to blame, there was another one: to leave or not to leave?

—I left because I got scared . . . Every revolution we have ends in people taking advantage of the disorder to rob one another and pummel the kikes. There was a real war going on in Moscow. Every day, someone else would get blown up or murdered. In the evening, you couldn't go out on the street without a fighting dog. I got a bull terrier . . .

—Gorbachev opened the doors of the cage and we made a run for it. What did I leave behind? A shitty two-bedroom apartment in a Khrushchyovka. It's better to be a well-paid cleaning woman than a doctor scraping by on a bum's salary. We all grew up in the USSR: In school, we collected scrap metal and loved the song "Victory Day." We were raised on the grand fairy tales about fairness; on Soviet cartoons, where everything is clearly delineated: This is good and this is evil. A kind of corrected version of reality, a world where everything was in its right place. My grandfather died at Stalingrad for his Soviet Motherland, for communism. But what I really wanted was to live in a normal country. I wanted cute curtains, little cushions, for my husband to come home from work and put on his robe. The Russian soul isn't so strong in me, I don't seem to have very much of it. I skipped out to the States. Now I eat strawberries in the winter. There's tons of salami here, and it's not a symbol for anything at all . . .

—In the nineties, everything was fun and magical . . . You looked out the window and saw a protest on every street corner. But soon enough, the fun and magic ran out. We'd asked for the free market, and that's what we got! My husband and I are engineers, but so were half of the people in our country. They didn't stand on ceremony with us: "You're out with the trash." And yet we were the ones who had brought about perestroika, we were the ones who had dug communism's grave. Now we were useless. I'd rather not think about it . . . Our little girl would say she was hungry, but there was nothing to eat in the house. There were notices up all over town: I'll buy . . . I'll buy . . . "I'll buy a kilogram of food"—not meat, not cheese, but a kilogram of any kind of food at all. We were happy if we managed to get our hands on a kilo of potatoes. At the market, they started selling press cakes,* like in wartime. Our neighbor's husband was shot in the hallway of our building. He was a *palatochnik*.† He lay there for half a day, barely covered by a newspaper. In a puddle of blood. You'd turn on the TV: A banker was killed over here, a businessman over there . . . In the end, a gang of thieves took over everything. The time is coming when the people will descend on Rublevka. With axes . . .

—They're not going to go after Rublevka, they're going to attack the cardboard boxes at the markets, the ones that the migrant workers live in. They'll start murdering Tajiks and Moldovans . . .

—I don't give a fuck about anything! They can all drop dead. I'm going to live for myself . . .

—I decided to leave when Gorbachev returned from Foros and said that we weren't rejecting socialism. In that case, I'm out! I don't want to live under a socialist system! That way of life was boring. From a young age, we knew that first we would be Little Octobrists, then Pioneers, then join the Komsomol. Our first salary would be sixty rubles, then eighty, then, toward the end of our lives, it'd go all the way up to 120 . . . [*Laughs.*] Our class leader in school tried to spook us: "If you listen to Radio Liberty, you'll never get into the Komsomol. And what if our enemies learn of this?" The funniest part is that she lives in Israel now . . .

—I used to be on fire with the Idea, more than just your typical citizen. Thinking about it makes me want to cry . . . The putsch!

---

* A press cake is made of the solids that remain after something (grains, nuts, olives, etc.) has been pressed to extract the liquids. It is often used as animal feed.
† The owner of a tented stall selling everyday goods.

Tanks looked so crazy in the center of Moscow. My parents came into town from the dacha to stock up on groceries in case civil war broke out. That gang! That junta! They thought that all they had to do was call in the tanks and that would be enough. Like people only wanted one thing, food, and as long as you gave it to them, they would agree to anything. The masses swept the streets . . . The nation awoke . . . It was only for a moment, it lasted one second . . . Like some seed had suddenly germinated . . . [*Laughs.*] My mother is a flighty person, she goes around without a thought in her head. She's completely removed from politics and lives according to the principle that life is short, you have to take everything you can get in the moment. But even she went out to the White House with her umbrella slung over her shoulder . . .

—Ha, ha, ha . . . Instead of freedom, they gave us vouchers. That's how they divvied up the wealth of a great nation: our oil, our natural gas . . . I'm not sure how to express these thoughts . . . Some people get the bagel, others get the bagel hole. You were supposed to use the vouchers to buy stocks from various enterprises, but very few people actually knew how to do that. Under socialism, we were never taught how to make money. My father would bring home these weird advertisements for companies like Moscow Real Estate, Oil-Diamond-Investa, Norilsk Nickel. He and my mother would argue in the kitchen, and in the end they sold everything they had to some guy in the Metro and spent the money on a cool leather jacket for me. The whole lot. That jacket is what I wore to America . . .

—We still have our vouchers. In thirty years, I'll sell them to a museum . . .

—You can't even fathom how much I hate that country . . . I hate the Victory Day Parade! All those prefab concrete apartment blocks with their balconies crammed full of jars of pickled tomatoes and cucumbers. They make me sick . . . All that old furniture . . .

—The Chechen war began . . . Our son would have had to enlist the following year. Hungry miners showed up to the capital to bang their helmets on the Red Square cobblestones. In front of the Kremlin. It was hard to tell where all of this was headed. The people in Russia are magnificent, they're treasures, but you can't live there. We left for the sake of our kids, turning ourselves into the foundation for them to build on. But now they've grown up and they're terribly distant from us . . .

—Um—um—um . . . How do you say it in Russian? I forget . . . Emigration is the norm, Russian people can't live where they'd like to, where they'd be most interested in living. Some people leave Irkutsk for Moscow, others leave Moscow for London. The whole world has become a caravanserai . . .

—A true patriot can only hope for Russia to be occupied. That someone comes and occupies it . . .

—I worked abroad for a while and then returned to Moscow . . . I was conflicted: I wanted to live in a familiar environment where I could find any book on the shelf with my eyes closed, like in my own apartment, but at the same time, I wanted to blast off into a world without limits. Am I staying or going? I couldn't decide. It was 1995 . . . Then, one day, I was walking, as I remember it now, down Gorky Street, and there were two women in front of me having a loud conversation . . . I couldn't understand what they were saying—but they were speaking Russian! I was dumbfounded! There's no other word . . . It was bewildering . . . They were using these new words and, more importantly, unfamiliar intonations. Tons of southern dialect. Even their facial expressions were somehow different . . . I had only been gone a few years, but already I was a foreigner here. Time was moving at a clip, it simply bolted by. Moscow was filthy—what capital city sheen?! There were heaps of garbage everywhere. The dregs of freedom: beer cans, brightly colored wrappers, orange peels . . . everyone was munching on bananas. It's not like that anymore. They've all had their fill now. I realized that the city I used to love, where I had been so happy and comfortable, no longer existed. Real Muscovites were either sitting at home horrified, or they'd already left. Old Moscow had receded and a new population had moved in. I wanted to pack my bags and flee right then and there. I hadn't even been that afraid during the August putsch. When that happened, I was intoxicated! There was a photocopier at our college, we'd make copies of flyers, and then my friend and I would drive them down to the White House in my old Zhiguli; we went back and forth past the tanks. I remember how surprised I was to see the patches on their armor. Square metal patches, screwed on with regular screws . . .

In all the years I'd been gone, my friends had continued to live in a state of total euphoria: The revolution had succeeded! Communism had fallen! For some reason, everyone was positive that it would all end well simply because Russia was full of educated people. Plus, it's an incredibly wealthy country. But Mexico is rich, too . . . The thing is, you can't buy democracy with oil and gas; you can't import it like bananas or Swiss chocolate. A presidential decree won't institute it . . . You need free people, and we didn't have them. And they still don't have them there. In Europe, they've been tending to democracy for the past two hundred years with the same kind of care they devote to their lawns. At home, my mother cried: "You say that Stalin's bad, but he led us to victory. And now you want to betray your Motherland." One of my oldest friends came over. We were drinking tea in the kitchen. "What happens next? Nothing good, not until we shoot every last commie." More blood? A few days later, I submitted my application to leave . . .

—My husband and I had gotten divorced . . . I'd sued for alimony, but he just wouldn't pay it. My daughter had enrolled at a private college, we weren't making ends meet. A friend of mine knew an American who had started a business in Russia. He was looking for a secretary, but he didn't want a model with legs up to her neck, he needed someone reliable. My friend recommended me. He was very interested in our way of life, there was a lot that he didn't understand. "Why do all Russian businessmen wear patent leather shoes?" "What does 'grease a palm' mean, and 'it's all under control' or 'it's bought and paid for?'" Those kinds of questions. But he had big plans: Russia is a huge market! They put him out of business in a very banal way. In fact, it was child's play. He put a lot of stock in what people said. If someone told him something, he'd believe it. He ended up losing a lot of money and decided it was time to go home. Before he left, he invited me out to a restaurant with him. I thought that we were just saying goodbye, but he raised his glass: "Let's drink! Do you know what we're drinking to? I haven't made any money here, but I did manage to find myself a proper Russian wife." We've been together for seven years now . . .

—We used to live in Brooklyn . . . Surrounded by Russian speech and Russian stores. Here in America, you can be delivered by a Russian midwife, go to a Russian school, work for a Russian boss, confess to a Russian priest . . . Yeltsin, Stalin, and Mikoyan are varieties of salami they sell at the store . . . Next to the chocolate-covered *salo* . . . Old men sit around on the benches, playing cards and dominos all day long. Holding their endless debates about Yeltsin and Gorbachev. There are Stalinists and anti-Stalinists. You walk by and overhear them saying, "Did we need Stalin?" "Of course we did." Even as a little kid, I knew all about Stalin. When I was five . . . I remember my mother and I were at a bus stop, as I now know, not far from the district KGB offices, and I kept whining and crying. "Don't cry," my mother implored me. "Or else the bad people who took Grandpa and lots of other people away will hear us." And she began telling me all about Grandpa. Mama needed someone to talk to . . . When Stalin died, at our nursery school, they sat us all down to cry. I was the only one who didn't. Grandpa came back from the camps and got on his knees in front of my grandma. All those years, she'd done so much on his behalf . . .

—There are suddenly lots of young Russian guys here in America walking around in Stalin T-shirts. Putting hammer and sickle decals on their cars. They hate black people . . .

—We're from Kharkov . . . From over there, America seemed like paradise. The land of opportunity. My first impression when we got here was that back home, we'd been trying to build communism, but here the Americans had actually succeeded. A girl we knew took us to a store that was having a sale. When we got here, my husband only had one pair of jeans, and I needed a whole new wardrobe. A skirt cost three dollars, jeans were five . . . ridiculous prices! The smell of pizza . . . good coffee . . . In the evening, my husband and I opened a bottle of Martini and a pack of Marlboros. Our dreams had really come true! Although, at the same time, we were forced to start from scratch at the age of forty. When you get here, you automatically go down a few rungs—forget about the fact that you're a director, an actress, or graduated from Moscow University . . . My first job was as an orderly at a hospital, emptying bedpans, washing floors. I couldn't do it. I started walking dogs for these two old men. Then I was a cashier at a supermarket . . . It was May 9—for me, the most important holiday. My father fought through the whole war, he made it to Berlin. I was telling my coworkers, and the senior cashier goes, "We won the war, but you Russians did well, too. You helped us." That's what they teach them in school. I nearly fell off my chair! What do they know about Russia? That Russians drink vodka by the glassful and there's a lot of snow there . . .

—We came for the salami, but, as it turns out, the salami is not as cheap as we'd imagined . . .

—We leave Russia as brains and arrive here as hands . . . Migrant workers . . . My mother writes that the Tajik janitor back home has already managed to bring all of his relatives to Moscow. Now they work for him and he's the boss. Tells them what to do. His wife is always pregnant. They slaughter a ram for their holidays right in the courtyard. Under the windows of Muscovites. And they grill their kebabs out there, too . . .

—I'm a rational person. All that wishy-washy stuff about the language of our grandmothers and grandfathers is nothing but sentimental nonsense. I stopped letting myself read Russian books or look at the Russian web. I want to beat everything Russian out of myself. Stop being Russian . . .

—My husband was very eager to leave . . . We brought ten cases of Russian books with us so that our kids wouldn't forget their native language. In Moscow, at customs, they opened all of our suitcases, looking for antique books, but all they found was Pushkin and Gogol . . . The customs officials had a good laugh at us . . . I'll still put Radio Mayak on sometimes to listen to Russian songs . . .

—Oh Russia, my Russia . . . my beloved St. Petersburg! How I wish I could return! I'd go at the drop of a hat . . . Glory to communism! Home! Even the potatoes here taste like total garbage. And Russian chocolate is simply divine!

—Do you miss buying underwear with ration cards? I remember studying and taking tests on communism . . .

—The Russian birches . . . and then more birches . . .

—My sister's son speaks excellent English. He's a computer guy. Spent a year living here before going back home. He said that today, living in Russia's more interesting . . .

—I can also tell you that lots of people there also live well now. They have jobs, houses, cars, everything. But they're still afraid and want to leave. Their businesses could be taken away, they can be put in jail for no reason . . . get beaten up in the lobbies of their buildings at night . . . Nobody lives by the law over there, neither at the bottom nor at the top . . .

—The Russia of Abramovich and Deripaska . . . Luzhkov* . . . Is that really Russia? The ship is sinking . . .

—Where we really ought live is Goa . . . and go to Russia to make money . . .

*   *   *

---

* Oleg Deripaska (1968–) is a Russian businessman and the owner of the largest aluminum company in the world. Yuri Luzhkov (1936–) was the mayor of Moscow from 1992 to 2010 and co-founded United Russia, the ruling political party.

I step out onto the balcony. People are smoking and continuing the conversation: Are the people leaving Russia today the smart ones or are they dupes? At first, I didn't believe my ears when I heard someone inside singing "Moscow Nights," our favorite Soviet song. When I go back into the room, everyone is singing along. I am, too.

Nothing in the garden stirs,
Everything 'til morning is still,
If you only knew, just how dear they are
Oh, those Moscow nights . . .

ON A STRANGER'S GRIEF
THAT GOD HAS DEPOSITED ON
YOUR DOORSTEP

◆

Ravshan, migrant worker,
27 years old

AS TOLD BY GAFKHAR DZHURAYEVA,
DIRECTOR OF MOSCOW'S TAJIKISTAN FUND

"A man without his homeland is like a nightingale without a garden"

I know so much about death. Someday, the things I know will drive me insane . . .

The body is a vessel for the soul. A home. According to Muslim custom, a body must be buried as quickly as possible, preferably the same day, as soon as Allah has taken the soul. In the house of the deceased, we hang a scrap of white cloth from a nail, and it stays there for forty days. At night, the soul flies home and perches on the cloth. It listens to familiar voices and feels glad. Then it flies back.

Ravshan . . . I remember him well . . . the usual story . . . They hadn't been paid in six months. He had four kids back in the Pamir region, then his father got very sick. He went to the construction bureau, asked for an advance, and they refused him. That was the last straw. He went out onto the porch and slit his own throat with a knife. They called me . . . I went down to the morgue . . . That strikingly handsome face . . . Unforgettable. His face . . . We took up a collection. It's still a mystery to me, the workings of this inner mechanism: Nobody has a kopeck to spare, but if somebody dies they'll instantly raise the necessary amount, people will give the last of whatever they have to help the person get buried at home and rest in their native soil. So that they won't have to remain on foreign soil. For that, they'll give away their last hundred rubles. If you tell them that someone needs to go home, you'll get nothing; say a child is sick, they refuse; but if there's been a death, here you go. They gathered all those crumpled hundred-ruble bills in a plastic bag and brought them to me, placed them on my desk. I took the money down to an Aeroflot ticket office. To the manager. The soul will fly home of its own accord, but shipping a coffin is pretty expensive.

[*She picks up a stack of papers from her desk and begins to read.*]

. . . Police entered an apartment occupied by migrant workers, a pregnant woman and her husband. They started beating the husband in front of the woman because the couple didn't have the proper resident registration documents. She started hemorrhaging—both she and her unborn child died . . .

. . . In the suburbs of Moscow, three people went missing, two brothers and their sister . . . Their relatives, who had come from Tajikistan to search for them, turned to our organization for help. We called the bakery where they had been working. The first time, they told us, "We don't know anyone by those names." The second time, the owner himself came to the phone: "Yes, I had some Tajiks working for me. I paid them for three months and that same day, they all took off. I couldn't tell you where they went." That's when we went to the police. All three of them had been found bludgeoned to death and buried in the woods. The bakery owner started making threatening phone calls to the fund: "I have people everywhere. I'll bury you, too."

. . . Two young Tajiks were taken to the hospital in an ambulance from a construction site . . . They spent all night in a cold waiting room, and nobody helped them. The doctors didn't conceal their feelings: "Why do you black-asses keep showing up here?"

. . . One night, a group of riot policemen rounded up fifteen Tajik street cleaners, marched them out of the basement where they had been living, threw them down on the snow and started beating them. Stomping on them with their steel-toed boots. One fifteen-year-old boy died . . .

. . . A mother received her son's body from Russia. Without any of his internal organs . . . You can buy anything on the Moscow black market, everything a person has: kidneys, lungs, livers, pupils, heart valves, skin . . .

These are my brothers and sisters . . . I was born in the Pamir region myself. I'm a highlander. For us, good soil is worth its weight in gold; where we come from, they don't measure wheat by the bag, they measure it by the *tubeteika*.* We're surrounded by towering mountains. Compared to them, everything man-made seems childish. Like a toy. You live with your feet on the ground and your head in the clouds. You're up so high, it's like you're already in the next world. The sea is completely different, it draws you in like a magnet, but the mountains make you feel protected, they stand guard over you. Like a second set of walls for your home. Tajiks aren't warriors; when enemies invaded our land, our people would hide up in the mountains . . . [*She is silent.*] My favorite Tajik song is a dirge about leaving your native land. I cry every time I hear it . . . The most terrifying fate for a Tajik is leaving his Motherland. Living far away from her. A man without his homeland is like a nightingale without a garden. I've been living in Moscow for many years now, but I always surround myself with things that remind me of home: If I see a picture of the mountains in a magazine, I'll cut it out and put it on my wall. The same goes for pictures of flowering apricots and fields of white cotton. In my dreams, I often pick cotton . . . I open up the boll, it has very sharp edges, and there's a little white clump in it, like cotton, almost weightless. You have to take it out without scratching your hands. In the morning, I wake up tired . . . I always look for Tajik apples at the Moscow markets, they're the sweetest ones in the world; Tajik grapes are sweeter than sugar cubes. When I was little, I dreamed that one day, I'd see the Russian forest, mushrooms . . . I thought about how I would go and meet those people. That's the other half of my soul: the peasant hut, the Russian stove, *pirozhki*. [*She is silent.*] I'm telling you about our lives . . . about my brothers . . . To you, they all look the same: black hair, unwashed, hostile. From a world you don't understand. A stranger's grief that God has deposited on your doorstep. But they don't feel like they've come to live with strangers, their parents lived in the USSR; Moscow used to be everyone's capital. Now, they get jobs and shelter here. In the East, they say you shouldn't spit in the well you drink from. When they're in school, all Tajik boys dream of going to Russia to make money . . . They'll borrow from everyone in their village to buy their tickets. At the border, Russian customs officers ask them, "Who are you going to visit?" And they all answer "Nina." . . . For them, all Russian women are Nina . . . They don't

* Central Asian men's cap; Gafkhar is emphasizing the scarcity of grain.

teach Russian in school anymore. All of them bring their prayer rugs . . .

[*We're sitting in the foundation's offices, which are just a few small rooms. The telephones never stop ringing.*]

Yesterday, I saved a girl's life . . . She managed to call me from the car while a group of cops were driving her out to the forest. She called me and whispered, "They grabbed me off the street, and now they're taking me out of the city. All of them are drunk." She told me the license plate number . . . They had been too drunk to search her and confiscate her phone. The girl had just come from Dushanbe . . . a beautiful girl . . . I'm an Eastern woman, I was very little when my mother and grandmother began teaching me how to talk to men. "You can't fight fire with fire, you can only use wisdom," my grandma would say. I called up the police station: "Hello, my dear man, I've just been notified of a strange situation unfolding. Your boys are taking our girl somewhere she shouldn't be going, and they're drunk. Call them before things take a bad turn. We know their license plate number." On the other end of the line, it's a constant stream of obscenities: "These *churki,* those black monkeys who must have just climbed down from the trees, why the hell are you wasting your time on them?" "Darling, listen, I'm a black monkey myself . . . I'm your mother . . ." Silence! After all, the person on the other end is human, too . . . That's what I pin all my hopes on . . . Little by little, our exchange turned into a conversation. Fifteen minutes later, they turned the car around . . . they brought back the girl . . . They could have raped her, killed her. In the forest . . . I've had to pick girls like her up piece by piece on more than one occasion . . . Do you know what I am? I'm an alchemist . . . We run a nonprofit—no money, no power, just good people. Our helpers. We aid and rescue the defenseless. Our results materialize out of nothing: just nerve, intuition, Eastern flattery, Russian pity, and simple words like "my dear," "my good man," "I knew you were a real man and wouldn't fail to help a woman in need." "Boys," I say to the sadists in uniform, "I have faith in you. I know that you're human." I had this very long conversation with a police general . . . He wasn't an idiot or some one-track-mind military type, he seemed cultivated. "Did you know," I said to him, "that you have a real Gestapo man on your force? He's a master of torture, everyone is afraid of him. Every homeless person and migrant worker he comes across ends up crippled." I thought that he'd be horrified or at least get scared and start defending the honor of the uniform. But he just looked at me with a smile: "Tell me his last name. Good man! We'll promote him, reward him. We need to take good care of such members of our staff. I'll personally make sure that he gets an award." I went numb. He went on: "To tell you the truth . . . We intentionally create impossible conditions for you people so that you'll leave as soon as possible. There are two million migrant workers in Moscow, the city can't digest this many of you suddenly descending on us. There are just too many of your kind here." [*Silence.*]

Moscow is beautiful . . . You and I strolled through the city and you kept exclaiming, "Moscow has become so beautiful! It's a real European capital now!" I don't feel this beauty. When I walk along looking at the new buildings, I always remember: Two Tajiks died here, falling from the scaffolding . . . Here, a man drowned in cement . . . I remember how ridiculously little people were paid to dig these foundations. Everyone makes money off them: bureaucrats, policemen, building managers . . . A Tajik street cleaner signs a contract saying he'll earn thirty thousand rubles, but they only ever pay him seven. The rest is taken from him, redistributed among various bosses . . . Bosses and bosses' bosses . . . Laws don't mean anything— around here, it's all about money and muscle. The little man is the most vulnerable creature on earth, even an animal in the forest is more protected than he is. For you, the forest protects the animals; for us, it's the mountains . . . [*She falls silent.*] I spent most of my life under socialism. I remember how much we idealized man, I too used to hold human beings in high regard. In Dushanbe, I worked at the Academy of Sciences. I was an art historian. I thought that books . . . that what men had written about themselves was the truth . . . But actually, it's only a tiny sliver of the truth. I haven't been an idealist for a long time now, I know too much. This girl comes in to see me all the time, she's unstable . . . She used to be a famous violinist. What made her lose her grip? Maybe it was people constantly saying to her, "You play the violin—what good is that? You know two languages—what for? Your job is to clean up, sweep the floors. You're nothing but slaves here." This girl, she doesn't play the violin anymore. She's forgotten everything.

There was also this young man . . . One day, the police caught him somewhere in the suburbs of Moscow, took his money, but it wasn't enough for them. They got mad. Drove him out to the forest. Beat him. It was the middle of winter. Freezing cold. They stripped him down to his underwear . . . Ha, ha, ha . . . Tore up all of his documents. And yet, here he was, telling me the story. I asked him, "So how did you make it out of there alive?" "I was sure I was going to die, I was running barefoot through the snow. Then suddenly, it was like a fairy tale, I saw a little hut in the middle of the woods. I knocked on the window, and an old man came out. He handed me a blanket so I could warm myself, poured me tea, and served me jam. Gave me clothes to wear. The next day, he led me to a large village and found a trucker who would take me back to Moscow."

That old man . . . he is Russia, too . . .

She is called into the next room, "Gafkhar Kandilovna, someone is here to see you." I wait for her to return. I have time. I think about the things I heard in Moscow apartments.

IN MOSCOW APARTMENTS

—We've been overrun . . . That's the Russian soul for you, we're too kind . . .

—The Russian people are not at all kind. That's just a widespread misconception. They're maudlin, sentimental, but they're not kind. Someone killed a stray dog and made a video of it. The whole Internet blew up. People were ready to lynch the guy who did it. But when seventeen migrant workers were burnt alive at a market—their boss would lock them up in a metal wagon at night along with his goods—the only people who stood up for them were human rights advocates. People whose occupation it is to stand up for everyone. The general feeling was, "These people died, others will come to replace them." Faceless, voiceless . . . strangers . . .

—They're slaves. Modern-day slaves. All they have are their dicks and their sneakers. And back in their homeland, things are even worse than they are in the most rotten Moscow basement.

—A bear accidentally wound up in Moscow and survived the whole winter here. All he ate was migrant workers—because who counts them . . . Ha, ha, ha . . .

—Before the fall of the Soviet Union, we lived together like one big family . . . That's what they taught us in political literacy classes . . . Back then, they were "guests in the capital," now they're *"churkas"* and *"khaches."* My grandfather would tell me about how he defended

Stalingrad alongside Uzbeks. They all believed that they were brothers forever!

—What you're saying surprises me . . . They're the ones who decided to split off from us. They wanted freedom. Did you forget that? Remember how they'd murder Russians in the nineties? Rob them, rape them. Chase them out of their homes. A knock on the door in the middle of the night . . . They break in, some holding knives, others machine guns: "Get the hell out of our country, you Russian swine!" Five minutes to pack . . . and a free trip to the nearest railway station. People would run out of their apartments in their slippers . . . That's how it was . . .

—We remember the humiliations suffered by our brothers and sisters! Death to the *churkas*! It's hard to rouse the Russian Bear, but once he's up, there'll be rivers of blood.

—The Central Asians bashed the Russians' faces in with their gun butts. Whose turn is it now?

—I hate skinheads! All they know how to do is beat innocent Tajik street cleaners to death with hammers or baseball bats. At rallies, they shout, "Russia for Russians, Moscow for Muscovites." Well, my mother is Ukrainian and my father's Moldovan—only my maternal grandmother is Russian. So what does that make me? What criteria are they planning on using to "cleanse" Russia of non-Russians?

—Three Tajiks can do the job of one dump truck. Ha, ha, ha . . .

—I miss Dushanbe. I grew up there. Studied Farsi. The language of poets.

—I dare you to walk through the city holding a poster that says, "I love Tajiks." You'd get beaten up instantly.

—There's a construction site next door. *Khachi* scuttling about like rats. Because of them, I'm scared of walking home from the store at night. They could kill you for a cheap cellphone . . .

—Says you! I've been mugged twice—both times, it was Russians. The time I almost got killed in my building hallway—also Russians. I'm so fed up with those God-bearing people.

—So you would let your daughter marry a migrant?

—This is my hometown. My capital. And they've showed up here with their Sharia law. On Kurban Bayram,* they slaughter their sheep right under my windows. Why not on Red Square then? The cries of

---

* Another name for the Eid festival, a Muslim holiday celebrating Ibrahim's willingness to sacrifice his son as an act of submission to God.

the poor animals, their blood gushing everywhere . . . You go outside, and here, and there . . . you see red puddles all over the sidewalk. I'm out walking with my kid: "Mama, what is that?" That day, the city goes dark. It stops being our city. They pour out of the basements by the hundreds of thousands . . . The policemen press themselves against the walls in terror . . .

—I'm dating a Tajik. His name is Said. He's as beautiful as a god! At home, he was a doctor; here, he's a construction worker. I'm head over heels for him. What do I do? We go walking in the parks or get out of the city altogether so that we won't run into anyone who knows me. I'm afraid of my parents finding out. My father warned me, "If I see you with a darkie, I'll shoot you both." What does my father do? He's a musician . . . he graduated from conservatory . . .

—If a "darkie" is out walking with a girl . . . and she's one of our girls . . . People like that ought to be castrated.

—What do people hate them for? Their brown eyes, the shape of their noses. For no reason at all. Everyone has to hate someone: their neighbors, the cops, oligarchs, the damn Yankees . . . It doesn't matter! There's so much hatred in the air . . . You can't get through to people . . .

"The uprising I witnessed terrified me for the rest of my life"

[*It's lunchtime. Gafkhar and I drink tea out of Tajik bowls and continue our conversation.*]

Someday, the things I remember will drive me insane . . .

1992 . . . Instead of the freedom we had all been waiting for, civil war broke out. People from Kulob started killing people from Pamir, and Pamirites started killing Kulobites . . . People from Karategin, Hisor, and Garm all splintered off. There were posters all over the city: "Hands off Tajikistan, Russians!" "Go back to Moscow, Communists!" This was no longer the Dushanbe I loved . . . Mobs roamed the streets, armed with metal fixtures and rocks . . . Completely peaceful, quiet people turned into murderers overnight. Just yesterday, they were absolutely different, calmly drinking tea at the *chaikhana;* today they were walking around ripping women's stomachs open with metal rods . . . Shattering shop windows, smashing kiosks. I went to the market . . . Hats and dresses hung from the branches of the acacias, the dead lay on the ground—all in one heap, people and animals together . . . [*She is silent.*] I remember it was a beautiful morning. For a moment, I forgot about the war. It seemed like everything would go back to the way it was before. The apple trees were in bloom and the apricots . . . No signs of war anywhere. I opened the window wide. Immediately, I saw this roving, dark mob headed in my direction. They walked in silence. Suddenly, one of them turned toward me and we locked eyes . . . I could tell he was a poor man, the look in his eyes said, "I could come into your beautiful home right now and do whatever I want, this is my time . . ." That's what his eyes told me . . . I was completely horrified . . . I leapt away from the window, shut the blinds, one set, then another, locked the doors, bolted all the locks, and hid in the innermost room. There was fervor in his eyes . . . There's something satanic about a mob. I'm scared of even remembering it . . . [*She cries.*]

I saw a Russian boy being murdered in the courtyard. No one went out to help him, everyone just closed their windows. I ran outside in my bathrobe: "Leave him alone! You've already killed him!" He lay there without moving . . . They left. But soon, they came back to finish him off—they were just kids, all of them were the same age as him. Boys . . . just boys . . . I called the police. They stopped by, took a look at who was being beaten to death, and left. [*She falls silent.*] The other day, I heard some people in Moscow saying, "I love Dushanbe. What an amazing city it used to be! I miss it." I was so grateful to the Russian who said that! Nothing but love can save us. Allah will not hear prayers said with ill will. Allah teaches us that you shouldn't open a door that you won't be able to close . . . [*Pause.*] They killed a friend of ours . . . He was a poet. Tajiks love poetry, every single household has books of poetry, even just one or two of them. To us, poets are holy men. You mustn't harm them. And yet they murdered him! Before killing him, they broke his hands . . . because he wrote . . . Soon afterward, another one of our friends was killed . . . There wasn't a single bruise on his body, everything was perfectly intact because they only hit him in the mouth . . . for what he said . . . It was spring. It was sunny and warm out, but people were killing one another . . . It made you want to go up into the mountains.

Everyone was leaving. Running for their lives. We had friends in America. In San Francisco. They told us to come. We rented a small apartment there. It was so beautiful! The Pacific Ocean . . . wherever you go, you can see it. I spent entire days sitting on the beach and weeping, I was incapable of doing anything else. I had come from the war, where you could be killed for a bag of milk . . . One day, I saw an old man walking along the shore, his pants rolled up, wearing a brightly colored T-shirt. He stopped in front of me: "What happened to you?" "There's a war in my Motherland. Brothers are killing brothers." "Then stay here." He told me that I would be healed by the ocean and all the beauty . . . He comforted me for a long time. I wept. Kind words always had the same effect on me: Hearing them, I would be drowning in tears. Kind words make me cry harder than the gunshots had back home. Or the blood.

But I couldn't stay in America. I was dying to get back to Dushanbe, and if it was too dangerous to go home, I wanted to be as close to home as possible. We moved to Moscow . . . I remember how once we were over at our friend's house, she's a poet. I was listening to their endless grumbling: Gorbachev is all talk . . . Yeltsin's an alcoholic . . . The people are just cattle . . . How many times had I heard these things already? A thousand times! The hostess wanted to take my plate away to rinse it off, but I wouldn't let her—I can eat everything off the same plate. Fish and dessert. I've lived through war . . . Another writer had a refrigerator full of cheese and salami—Tajiks had long forgotten what these things were—and again, all evening long, that same grumbling: The government is evil, the democrats are no different from the Communists . . . Russian capitalism is cannibalism . . . And no one was doing anything about it. Everyone was waiting for a revolution which was expected to come at any moment. I don't like these disappointed people in their kitchens. I'm not one of them. The uprising I witnessed terrified me for the rest of my life; I know what it looks like when freedom falls into inexperienced hands. Idle chatter always ends in blood. War is a wolf that can come to your door as well . . . [*Silence.*]

Did you see those videos online? They wrecked me. I spent a week in bed after watching them . . . Those videos . . . They murdered people and filmed it. They had a screenplay, they wrote out the dialogue . . . like they were making a real movie . . . Now they just needed an audience. And we watched . . . they forced us to. There's a guy walking down the street, one of us, a Tajik . . . They call him over, he comes, and they knock him down. They beat him with baseball bats. At first, he struggles on the ground, then he grows quiet. They tie him up and throw him into the trunk of their car. In the forest, they tie him to a tree. You can see that the person filming is looking for the best angle so he can get a good shot. Then they cut off his head. Where did this come from? Decapitation is an Eastern ritual. Not Russian. It's probably from Chechnya. I remember . . . One year, they were killing people with screwdrivers, then they started using garden forks, then it was pipes and hammers . . . All death resulting from blunt force trauma. Now there's a new trend . . . [*She is silent.*] This time they actually found the people who did it. They're going to court. All of them were boys from good families. Today they're murdering Tajiks, tomorrow it will be the rich or those who pray to a different God. War is a wolf . . . It's already here . . .

IN MOSCOW BASEMENTS

We chose a building—a Stalinka right in the center of Moscow. These buildings are called Stalinkas because they went up during Stalin's time, built to house the Bolshevik Party elite. They're still upscale today. Stalinist Imperial style: elaborate moldings on the facades, bas-reliefs, columns, three- to four-meter ceilings. As the descendants of the country's former leaders have gone down in the world, the "new Russians" have been taking their places. The courtyard is full of Bentleys and Ferraris. On the street level, the lights are on in the windows of swanky boutiques.

Such is life above ground; underground, it's a completely different world. A journalist friend and I descend into the basement. We spend a long time winding among rusted pipes and mold-infested walls. From time to time, our path is obstructed by painted metal doors studded with locks and seals, but that's all for show. If you know the secret knock, you're in. The basement teems with life. A long, well-lit corridor is lined with rooms on either side; the walls are made of plywood, they have multicolored blinds for doors. Moscow's underground world is divided between the Tajiks and the Uzbeks. We've found ourselves among Tajiks. Seventeen to twenty people live in each room. It's a commune. Someone recognizes my guide—it's not his first time down here—and invites us into his room. There's a heap of shoes in the doorway next to a number of baby strollers. In the corner, a stove, a gas tank, and tables and chairs dragged here from nearby dumpsters, all packed tightly into the small common space. The rest of the room is taken up by homemade bunk beds.

It's dinnertime. About ten people are already sitting around the

*table. Meet Amir, Khurshid, Ali . . . The older ones, who attended So-
viet schools, speak Russian without an accent, while the young ones
don't speak any Russian at all. They just smile.*

They're happy to have guests over.

—We're about to have a bite to eat. [*Amir sits us down at the table.
He used to be a teacher. Here, he's like an elder.*] Try our Tajik pilaf.
You won't believe how good it is! The Tajik custom is that if you see a
stranger near your house, you have to invite them over and give them
a cup of tea.

*I'm not allowed to record them, they're scared. I get out my pen. They
respect people who write and that helps me. Some of them come from
villages, others came down from the mountains. Suddenly, they've all
found themselves in this enormous megalopolis.*

—Moscow is good, there's a lot of work. But living here is scary. When
I am walking down the street alone, even during the day, I never look
young men in the eye—they could kill me. You have to pray every
day . . .

—Three guys came up to me on the commuter rail . . . I was heading home from work. "What are you doing here?" "I'm going home."
"Where's your home? Who asked you to come here?" They started
beating me up. Pummeling me, screaming, "Russia for Russians! Glory
to Russia!" "Why are you doing this? Allah sees everything." "Your
Allah can't see you here. We have our own God." They knocked my
teeth out . . . broke one of my ribs . . . A train car full of people and
only one girl stood up for me. "Leave him alone! He didn't do anything to you." "What's your problem? We're beating a *khach*."

—They killed Rashid . . . stabbed him thirty times. Tell me, why
thirty times?

—It's all the will of Allah . . . A dog will bite a doomed man even
if he's on a camel.

—My father studied in Moscow. Now he laments the loss of the
USSR day and night. He dreamt that I would come here to study like
he did. Instead, the police brutalize me, my boss beats me . . . I live in
a basement like a cat.

—I don't feel sorry for the Soviet Union . . . Our neighbor Kolya
was Russian . . . He would scream at my mother when she'd speak

Tajik to him. "Speak normally. It's your country, but we're the ones in charge here." My mother would cry.

—I had a dream last night. I was walking down our street and the neighbors were all bowing to me, "*Salaam alaikum . . . Salaam alaikum . . .*" The only people left in our villages are women, old men, and children.

—At home, I made five dollars a month. I have a wife and three kids . . . In the villages, people go years without seeing sugar . . .

—I've never been to Red Square. I haven't seen Lenin. It's all work! Work! Shovel, pickaxe, wheelbarrow. All day long, I'm dripping in sweat like a watermelon.

—I paid this major for my documents: "May Allah grant you lasting health, good man!" But the documents he gave me turned out to be false! I ended up in a jail cell. They kicked me, beat me with their truncheons.

—Without ID, you don't exist . . .

—A man without his homeland is like a stray dog, anyone can have their way with him. The police can stop you ten times a day: "Your papers." You have this one document, but you don't have that other one. If you don't pay them off, they beat you.

—Who are we? Construction workers, freight loaders, street cleaners, dishwashers . . . You won't find us among the managers here . . .

—My mother's happy, I send her money. She found me a beautiful girl, although I haven't seen her yet. Mama arranged it all for me. I'll go back and marry her.

—All summer long, I worked in the suburbs of Moscow for this one rich guy, and in the end, he wouldn't pay me. "Scram! Scram! I fed you."

—If you're the one with one hundred sheep, you're right. You're always right.

—My friend wanted to know when his boss was going to pay him. It took the police a long time to find his body afterward. They'd buried it in the forest . . . His mother received a coffin from Russia.

—If they kick us out, who's going to build Moscow? Who'll sweep the courtyards? Russians would never work for this kind of money.

—When I close my eyes, I see the water running through the irrigation ditch, the cotton all in bloom, its flowers a gentle pink, it's like a garden.

—Did you know that we had a major war? After the fall of the USSR, they started shooting everyone . . . Only the people with machine guns lived well. I'd walk to school . . . Every day, on my way there, I'd pass two or three corpses. My mother stopped letting me go, so I stayed home and read Omar Khayyam. Everyone reads Khayyam. Do you know his poetry? If you do, you're a sister to me.

—They were killing infidels . . .

—It's for Allah to decide who is faithful and who is an infidel. He will be the one to judge.

—I was little . . . I never shot anyone. My mother told me that before the war, they lived like this: At weddings, there'd always be people speaking Tajik, Uzbek, and Russian. People who wanted to pray would pray, and those who didn't want to didn't. Tell me, sister, why were people so quick to start killing each other? They'd all read Khayyam in school. And Pushkin.

—The people are a caravan of camels that must be herded with a whip . . .

—I'm studying Russian . . . Listen: "pretty gurl, bred, maney . . . the boss is meen . . ."

—I've lived in Moscow for five years, and not once has anyone said hello to me on the street. Russians need "blacks" so they can feel "white." So they have someone to look down on.

—As every night has a morning, every sorrow has an end.

—Our girls are more radiant than the ones here. That's why it's said that they're like pomegranates . . .

—It's all the will of Allah . . .

We ascend from the underground. I look at Moscow with new eyes— its beauty now seems cold and uneasy. Moscow, do you care whether people like you or not?

ON LIFE THE BITCH AND
ONE HUNDRED GRAMS OF FINE
POWDER IN A LITTLE WHITE VASE

◆

Tamara Sukhovei, waitress,
29 years old

Life's a bitch! I can tell you . . . it's no picnic. I've never seen anything good or beautiful in this life. I can't think of a single thing . . . You could put a gun to my head, I still wouldn't be able to think of anything! I've tried poisoning myself, hanging myself. Three suicide attempts so far . . . Most recently, I slit my wrists. [*She shows me her bandaged arm.*] Right here, in this spot . . . I got rescued then slept for a week. Just kept sleeping and sleeping. That's how my body works . . . The psychiatrist came, she told me to talk, keep talking, just like you're doing right now . . . What's there to say? Death doesn't scare me . . . You shouldn't have come, and you shouldn't stay. Won't do you any good!

[*She turns to the wall and is silent. I want to leave, but she stops me.*]

Fine, listen . . . This is all true . . .

When I was still little . . . One day, I came home from school, went to bed, and the next morning, I couldn't get up. They took me to the doctor—no diagnosis. So then we went off to find a wise woman—a magic healer. Someone gave us an address . . . The wise woman laid out the cards and told my mother, "Go home and cut open the pillow your daughter sleeps on. You'll find a piece of a tie and chicken bones inside. Hang the tie from a cross by the side of the road and feed the bones to a black dog. Your daughter will get up and walk. Someone put a curse on her." I've never seen anything good or beautiful in this life . . . As for this slitting my wrists thing, it's nothing, I'm just sick of struggling. It's been like this since I was little: There's nothing but vodka in the fridge. In our village, everyone over the age of twelve drinks. Good vodka is expensive, so people drink moonshine and cologne, glass cleaner and acetone. They make vodka out of shoe polish and glue. Many young men die—from that vodka, of course—it's toxic. I remember how one of our neighbors used to get drunk and fire birdshot at the apple trees. Call his whole household to arms . . . Our grandfather also drank into old age. At seventy, he could put away two bottles in a single night. And he was proud of it, too. He'd returned from the war covered in medals—a hero! For a long time, he'd just parade around in his army jacket, drinking, carousing, having a gay old time. While my grandmother worked. Because Grandpa was a hero . . . He would beat my grandmother half to death. I'd crawl around on my knees in front of him begging him not to lay his hands on her. He chased us around the house with an axe . . . We'd sleep at the neighbors'. In their barn. He hacked the dog to pieces. My grandpa made me hate all men. I was planning on staying single.

When I moved to the city, I was afraid of everything: all the cars, all the people. But everyone moves to the city, so I did, too. My older sister lived here, she took me in. "You'll go to school and be a waitress. You're pretty, Tamara. You'll find yourself a nice army man to marry. A pilot." A pilot—yeah, right! My first husband was short and had a limp. My girlfriends tried to talk me out of it: "Why him? There are so many good-looking guys who are into you!" But I've always loved movies about war, women waiting for their husbands to return from the front, no matter what condition they were in—no arms, no legs, just as long as they were alive. My grandma told me how one man came back to our village without any legs, so his wife would carry him around everywhere. And still, he drank and raised hell. He'd pass out in a ditch and she'd pick him up, wash him off in the trough, and set him down on a clean bed. I thought that that must be what real love is . . . I don't really understand what love is . . . I took pity on him, coddled him. We ended up with three kids, but meanwhile, he'd started drinking. He'd threaten me with a knife. Wouldn't let me sleep on the bed . . . I'd lie there on the floor . . . I developed a reflex, like one of Pavlov's dogs: If my husband walked in, the kids and I would go out. Everything I can remember makes the tears run down my face . . . Or it makes me just want to say to hell with it all! I've never had anything beautiful or good happen to me, those things only happen in the movies. On TV. And that's it . . . so you can sit there with someone and dream . . . think about good things . . .

When I was pregnant with my second child, I got a telegram from the village: "Come to the funeral. Mother." A little while before that, a gypsy at the train station had told my fortune: "A long road awaits you. You're going to bury your father and weep for a long time." I didn't believe her. My father was healthy, a calm presence. It was my mother who drank, she'd start first thing in the morning, while he'd go out and milk the cow, make some potatoes—he did everything himself. He loved her deeply, she'd put a spell on him, she knew how to do that kind of thing. Some kind of potion was involved. I went home . . . I was sitting next to the coffin weeping when the neighbor girl came up and whispered in my ear, "She killed him with the cast-iron pot and told me not to tell. She promised that she'd buy me chocolates . . ." I felt sick, nauseated from fear . . . from the horror . . . When there was no one else home—everyone had gone out—I undressed my father and searched his body for bruises. There weren't any, but I did find a big wound on his head. I showed my mother, and she said that he'd been chopping wood when a stick flew up and hit him. I sat up all night weeping . . . While I was sitting there I got the feeling that he wanted to tell me something, but my mother wouldn't leave, she stayed sober all night and never left me alone with him. In the morning, I saw a tear of blood appear from underneath his eyelashes. Out of one eye, then the other . . . The tears streamed down his face as though he were alive . . . It was terrifying! It was winter. At the graveyard, they'd had to break up the frozen ground with a crowbar. They'd warmed the soil by building a fire in the grave pit, burning birch logs and old tires. The men demanded a whole case of vodka for their efforts. As soon as they buried my father, my mother got plastered. She sat there all happy. While I wept . . . Even now, all of this makes my tears come down like hail . . . My own mother . . . she gave birth to me. She's supposed to be the person I'm closest to . . . As soon as I left, she sold the house, burnt down the barn for insurance money and came out to live with me in the city. She found herself another husband immediately . . . She worked fast . . . He kicked out his son and daughter-in-law and put his apartment in her name. She lured men in, she knew how do that . . . She'd cast spells on them . . . [*She rocks her bandaged arm like it's a baby.*] Meanwhile, my husband would chase me around the house with a hammer, he fractured my skull twice. A bottle of vodka, a pickle in each pocket, and he's out the door. Where was he running off to? The children went hungry . . . All we had to eat were potatoes, and on holidays, potatoes with milk or a can of sprats. Try saying something to him about it when he gets home. All that will get you is a glass in the face and a chair flying at the wall . . . At night, he'd pounce on me like a beast . . . There's never been anything good in my life, not even some small thing. I go to work all beat up, my eyes red from crying, but my job is to smile and bow to people. The head manager at the restaurant will call me into his office: "I don't need any tears around here. My own wife has been paralyzed for a year already." And then he'll try to get in my pants . . .

My new stepfather didn't even last two years . . . She called me up one day: "Come over and help me bury him. We'll take him down to the crematorium." I almost passed out from the shock. But then I came to—I had to go. My only thought was: "What if she killed him?" She killed him so she could have the apartment to herself and drink and party. Right? Now she's scrambling to take him down to the crematorium. To burn the body. Before his kids get there . . . His eldest son is a major, he'll fly in from Germany, but all that'll be left is a handful of ashes . . . one hundred grams of fine powder in a little white vase. From all the shock, I stopped getting my period. For two years, I didn't bleed. When it started up again, I begged the doctors, "Cut everything female out of me, give me surgery, I don't want to be a woman anymore! I don't want to be anyone's lover! Or wife, or mother!" My own mother . . . She gave birth to me . . . I wanted to love her . . . When I was little, I'd ask her, "Kiss me, Mommy." But she was always drunk . . . My father would leave for work, and the house would fill up with drunken men. One of them dragged me into bed with him . . . I was eleven . . . I told my mother, but all she did was yell at me. She drank and drank . . . All she ever did was drink and party, her whole life. Then, all of a sudden, it came time to die! She didn't want to. Not for anything in the world. She was fifty-nine: One of her breasts was removed, then, six weeks later, the other. She was seeing this younger man, this guy fifteen years younger than her. "Take me to a wise woman!" she cried. "Save me!" But she kept getting worse and worse . . . Her boyfriend took care of her, emptied her bedpan, bathed her. She wasn't even considering dying . . . "But if I do," she told me, "I'm leaving everything to him. The apartment and the TV, too." She wanted to hurt me and my sister . . . She was cruel . . . and she loved being alive. She clung to life greedily. Finally, we took her to the wise woman, we had to carry her out of the car. The woman prayed, laid out the cards. "Oh?" And she got right up. "Take her away! I'm not going to try to heal her . . ." My mother yelled at us, "Leave. I want to be alone with her . . ." But the woman told us, "Don't move!" She wouldn't let us go . . . She looked at the cards again. "I'm not going to try to heal her. She's put more than one man in his grave. And as soon as she got sick, she went to the church and lit two candles . . ." My mother: "For the health of my children . . ." The woman: "No, it was for the peace of their souls. You prayed for your children's death. You thought that if you gave them up to God, He would let you live." After I heard those words, I made sure to never be alone with her. I lived in fear of her. I knew that I was weak and that she'd get the better of me . . . Whenever I went to see her, I'd bring my eldest daughter with me. My mother would get furious when my girl would ask me for something to eat: There she was dying, while somebody else was hungry, somebody else would get to keep living. She took scissors and cut up her brand-new bedcover and tablecloth so that no one could have them after she died. She smashed her plates. Everything she could, she destroyed. You couldn't get her to the bathroom, she would go on the floor or in her bed on purpose so that I would have to clean it up . . . She was taking revenge on us for staying alive. For the fact that we were going to get to keep walking around, talking. She hated everyone! If a bird flew up to her window, she would have killed it, too. But it was spring . . . Her apartment was on the ground floor . . . The smell of lilacs everywhere . . . She kept gulping for air, she couldn't get enough. "Bring me a branch from the courtyard," she asked. I brought her one, and the second she touched it, it shrivelled, the leaves curled up. Then she said to me, "Let me hold your hand . . ." The healer had warned me that a person who's done evil deeds has a long, tormented death. You have to either take apart the ceiling or pull out all the windowpanes—otherwise, their soul won't leave, it can't break free of the body. And no matter what, don't give them your hand, or you'll catch their disease. "What do you need my hand for?" She quieted down, lay low. The end was near, but she still wouldn't tell us or show us where she put the clothes that she wanted to be buried in. Where she'd stashed away the money to pay for her funeral. I was afraid that she would smother me and my daughter with pillows in our sleep. Anything seemed possible . . . I'd close my eyes, but kept peeking: How would her soul leave her body? What was it like, this soul of hers? Would there be a light or a little cloud? People have said and written all sorts of things, but no one has ever really seen a soul.

One morning, I ran out to the store and asked her neighbor to watch her. Her neighbor took her hand, and that's when she finally died. At the last moment, she cried out something incomprehensible. She'd called someone's name . . . Whose? The neighbor didn't remember. No one she'd ever heard of. I washed her and dressed her myself. I had no feelings, it was as though she were an object. A pot. No feelings, my feelings were hidden somewhere. It's all true . . . Some friends of hers came over, stole her phone . . . All of our relatives showed up, our middle sister came out from the village. My mother lay there . . . My sister started pulling her eyes open. "Why are you molesting our dead mother?" "Remember how she tormented us when we were little? She liked it when we cried. I hate her."

The relatives all got together, and the bickering began . . . They started divvying up her stuff that very night, while she still lay there in her coffin. Someone was packing up her TV, someone else, her sewing machine . . . They took the gold earrings off her dead body. Ransacked the house for money—didn't find any. I just sat there and wept. I even started feeling sorry for her. The next day, she was cremated . . . We decided that we'd take the urn to the village and bury it next to my father even though she hadn't wanted that. In fact, she'd ordered us not to bury her next to my father. She was scared. What if there was an afterlife? She and my father are bound to meet somewhere . . . [*She stops.*] I don't have many tears left in me . . . I'm surprised at how little I care about any of it anymore. Life and death. Good and bad people. I don't give a damn . . . When destiny doesn't take a shine to you, there's nowhere to run. You won't escape your fate. Yes . . . My older sister, the one I'd lived with, got married a second time and moved to Kazakhstan. I loved her . . . and I had this premonition. My heart told me that she should not marry this man. There was something I didn't like about her second husband. "No, he's a good guy," she assured me. "I pity him." When he was eighteen, he'd landed in prison for killing a guy in a drunken fight. They gave him five years, but he was out in three. He started coming around, bringing presents. Whenever his mother ran into my sister she'd start trying to talk her into it. Beg her. She'd say: "Men always need nannies. A good wife is a little like a mother to her husband. On their own, men become wolves, they'll eat off the floor . . ." And my sister bought it! She's the pitying kind, just like me. "I'll make him into a good man." I spent all night next to my mother's coffin with the two of them. And he was so nice to my sister, so gentle, I was even a little jealous. Ten days later, I got a telegram: "Aunt Tamara, come. Mama died. Anya." That was her daughter, the eleven-year-old, who had sent the telegram. We'd just carried out one coffin, and another one had already arrived . . . [*She cries.*] He'd gotten drunk and jealous. Stomped on her, stabbed her with a fork. Raped her dead body . . . He was drunk or high, I don't know what . . . In the morning, he told his work that his wife had died, and they gave him the money to pay for the funeral. He handed it to Anya, then went down to the police station to turn himself in. Now the girl lives with me. She doesn't want to go to school, there's something wrong with her, she can't remember anything. She's afraid of everything . . . afraid of leaving the house. As for him . . . They gave him ten years. Watch him come back to live with her after they let him out. What a dad!

When I got divorced from my first husband, I thought that I would never let another man into my house ever again. No man will set foot in here! I was sick of crying, walking around covered in bruises. What good are the police? They'll come once, but if you call again, they'll tell you: "You're just having family issues." On the floor above us, in the same building where we live, a man ended up killing his wife—only then did they show up in their cars with the flashing lights, write up a report, lead him away in handcuffs. He'd been torturing her for ten years . . . [*She beats her fist on her chest.*] I don't like men. I'm scared of them. I have no idea how I ended up married a second time. He'd returned from Afghanistan shell-shocked, twice wounded. A paratrooper. Still, to this day, he hasn't removed his striped undershirt. He'd been living with his mother in the building across from ours. In the same courtyard. He'd come out and sit there playing the accordion, or just songs on a stereo . . . songs about the Afghan war, sad stuff. I had war on the brain . . . I was always so scared of those damn mushroom clouds . . . Atom bombs. I used to like it when young people—a bride and groom—would go straight from the marriage registration office to pay their respects at the Eternal Flame with a bouquet. I loved it! It's so noble! One day, I sat down next to him on the bench: "What is war?" "War is when you really want to live." I felt bad for him. He'd never known his father, his mother had been disabled since childhood. If he'd had a father, they would have never sent him to Afghanistan. His father would have protected him, paid them off like other people do. But he and his mother . . . I went over to their apartment, and all they had was a bed and some chairs, his medal from

Afghanistan hanging on the wall. I took pity on him, I didn't think of myself. We moved in together. He came with a towel and a spoon. Brought his medal. And the accordion.

I made it all up . . . this fantasy that he's a hero . . . a defender. I'd crowned him myself and told the kids he was a Tsar. We're living with a hero! He'd performed his soldier's duty and really suffered for it. I'll melt his heart with my love . . . save him . . . A regular Mother Teresa! I'm not a very religious person, all I ever say is "Lord, forgive us." Love is a kind of wound . . . You start feeling sorry for the other person. If you love them, you pity them . . . that comes first . . . He'd "run" in his sleep: His legs wouldn't move, but his muscles twitched like he was really running. Sometimes he'd run like that all night long. In the middle of the night, he'd scream *"Dushari! Dushari!"* Those were the *dukhi*—the "spirits"—Afghan *mujahideen*. He'd cry out to the commander and his brothers-in-arms, "Pass them from the flank!" "Grenades ready!" "Make a smoke screen . . ." One time, he nearly killed me when I tried to wake him up: "Kolya! Kolya! Wake up!" The truth is, I even fell in love with him . . . I learned a lot of Afghan war words from him: *zindan, bochata, duval . . . Barbukhaika . . . "Khodahafez!"**—*"So long, Afghanistan!" For a year, we were happy together. We really were! He made a little money, he'd bring home canned meat, his favorite food. Since Afghanistan. They used to go up into the mountains and bring canned meat and vodka. He taught us how to perform first aid, which plants are edible, how to trap animals. He told us that turtle meat tasted sweet. "So did you really shoot people?" "You didn't have a choice out there, it's either you or them." I forgave him everything because of how much he'd suffered . . . I tied this burden onto myself . . .

And now . . . His friends will drag him home at night and leave him on the doorstep. Without his shirt or watch, lying there naked from the waist up . . . The neighbors will call me: "Come and get him, Tamara! Or he'll give up the ghost out there in the cold." I'll pull him into the house. He'll be crying, sobbing, rolling around on the ground. He can't hold down a job; he's been a security guard, a bodyguard . . . He always either needs a drink or he's hung over. He's drunk everything away . . . You never know if there's going to be anything to eat at

---

* A *zindan* is a kind of Middle Eastern and Central Asian prison. *Bochata* is a term Russian soldiers used for the young Afghan boys who would walk alongside them. A *duval* is a tall, thick clay fence. A *barbukhaika* is a large Afghan truck. *Khodahafez* is Persian for "God be with you," said in parting.

home. He'll either beat the shit out of me or plant himself in front of the TV. Our neighbors rent a room to this Armenian . . . Once, he said something that my husband didn't like, and the poor guy ended up on the ground covered in blood with his teeth knocked out and a broken nose. Kolya just doesn't like Eastern people. I'm afraid of going to the market with him because all the sellers there are Uzbek and Azerbaijani. Any little thing could set him off . . . He has this saying: "For every twisted asshole there's a threaded screw." They knock the price down for him, they want nothing to do with him. "An Afghanistan vet . . . a whack-job . . . a devil!" He beats the kids. My youngest son loves him, when he used to try to get close to him, he'd smother him with a pillow. Now, as soon as he comes through the door, my son runs to his bed and goes to sleep—closes his eyes so that he won't beat him. Or he'll hide all the pillows under the sofa. All I can do is weep . . . or . . . [*She points to her bandaged arm.*] On Paratroopers Day, his friends all get together . . . all of them in their striped shirts, just like him . . . They get completely trashed! Piss all over my bathroom. They're all messed up in the head . . . Delusions of grandeur: We fought in a war! We're tough! The first toast is always: "The world is shit, all people are whores, and the sun is just a fucking streetlight." And on it goes until the morning: "To resting in peace," "To health," "To medals," "Death to them all." Things haven't worked out for them . . . I couldn't tell you if it's because of the vodka or the war. They're mean as wolves! They hate the Jews and all people from the Caucasus. The Jews, because they killed Christ and ruined Lenin's plan. Home life is no fun for them anymore: Wake up, wash up, eat breakfast. It's boring! At the drop of a hat—just call 'em up—they'd all march straight to Chechnya. To be heroes again! There's this bitterness left over, they're mad at everybody: the politicians, the generals, and everyone who wasn't there with them. Especially the last category . . . more than the rest . . . Just like my husband, many of them don't have any sort of career. Or they all have the same career: walking around with a handgun. They say they drink because everyone here betrayed them . . . Boo-hoo! They drank when they were out there, too, and they don't try to hide it: "Without a hundred grams of vodka, the Russian soldier won't make it to victory," "If you leave one of our men in the middle of the desert, two hours later, he won't have found any water, but he will be drunk." They drank methyl alcohol, brake fluid . . . Drunk or high, they'd crash and burn . . . When they returned: One of them hanged himself, another one got shot in a street fight; one of them got beaten up so bad, he's paralyzed now. Another one was so mentally damaged, they locked him up in the nut-house . . . and these are just the ones I know about. Who knows what happened to the rest of them . . . The capitalists—you know, these new Russians—they hire them as thugs, pay them to shake their rivals down for debts. They're trigger-happy, and they don't feel pity for any-one. You think they'll feel the least bit sorry for some twenty-year-old, crazy rich little punk, while all they have are medals, malaria, and hepatitis? No one ever felt sorry for them . . . They feel like shoot-ing . . . Don't write this down . . . It scares me . . . Conversations with them are short: They'll put you up against the wall and shoot you in the head! They want to go to Chechnya because there's freedom there, plus Russians are getting hurt . . . They dream of bringing back fur coats for their wives. Gold rings. My guy was dying to go there, too, but they don't take drunks. There are plenty of healthy men willing to go. Every day, it's the same thing, "Give me money." "No." "Heel, bitch!" And he'll punch me in the face. Then he sits there crying. Throws himself on me: "Don't leave me!" I felt sorry for him for a long time . . . [*She weeps.*]

Pity is an ugly thing . . . I won't give in to it anymore . . . Don't look for pity from me! Eat up your own vomit with your own goddamn spoon. Pick up your own mess! Forgive me, oh Lord, if you really do exist. Forgive me!

I come home from work in the evening . . . I hear his voice. He's training my son. At this point, I know the routine by heart: "Stop! Remember: You throw the grenade at the window and somersault here. Get on the ground. And then another one behind the column . . ." For crying out loud! "Four seconds and you're out on the stairwell, you kick down the door and shift the machine gun to your left-hand side. The first guy goes down . . . the second one runs past . . . the third one covers him . . . Stop! Stop!!!" Stop . . . [*She screams.*] It terri-fies me! How am I supposed to save my son? I asked my friends for help, one of them told me: "You have to go to church. Pray." Another one took me to a wise woman . . . where else can I go? There's no one else to turn to. The woman was as old as Koschei the Deathless.* She told me to come back the next day with a bottle of vodka. She walked around the apartment with the bottle, whispered to it, swept her hands over it, and handed it back to me. "The vodka is enchanted now. Give

* The archetypical villain in Slavic folklore.

him a glass of it for two days in a row, on the third day, he won't want it anymore." And it really did work—for a month, he didn't drink. But then he started again: He'll stumble in plastered in the middle of the night, banging the pots and pans, demanding I feed him . . . I found another healer. That one read my cards, poured molten lead into a cup of water. Taught me simple spells to say over salt, over a handful of sand. Nothing helped! You can't cure war and vodka . . . [*She rocks her bandaged arm.*] I'm so sick of it all! I don't feel sorry for anyone anymore. Not the kids, not myself . . . I'm not asking her to come, but my mother keeps showing up in my dreams. Young and happy. She's always laughing. I chase her away . . . Other times, I'll see my sister, and she's always somber. Every time, she asks me the same question: "Do you really think you can just switch yourself off like a light-bulb?" [*She stops.*]

All of this is true . . . I've never seen a beautiful thing. And never will. Yesterday, he showed up at the hospital: "I sold the rug. The kids were hungry." My favorite rug. The one nice thing we had in the house . . . the one thing we had left. I scrimped and saved for an entire year to buy it. Kopeck by kopeck. I'd wanted that rug so bad . . . It's from Vietnam. And just like that, he drank it away. The girls from work ran over: "Oh, Tamara, hurry up and come home. He's fed up with your youngest, he's been beating him. And your eldest (my sister's daughter), she's twelve now . . . You know yourself what can happen . . . One night he'll be drunk and . . ."

I lie awake at night. I can't sleep. And then I'll drop into an abyss, fly off somewhere. I never know what I'll be like when I wake up. I have these terrifying thoughts . . .

[*She unexpectedly hugs me in parting.*]

Remember me . . .

A year later, she made another suicide attempt. This one was successful. I learned that her husband had soon found himself another woman. I called her. "I feel sorry for him," she told me. "I don't love him, but I pity him. The only trouble is, he started drinking again even though he promised he would quit."

Can you guess what she told me next?

ON HOW NOTHING DISGUSTS THE DEAD AND THE SILENCE OF DUST

◆

Olesya Nikolayeva,
junior police sergeant, 28

AS TOLD BY HER MOTHER

Sooner or later, telling my stories will kill me . . . Why do I keep doing this? There's nothing you can do to help me. You'll write it down, publish it . . . Good people will read it, they'll cry, but the bad ones, the important ones . . . they'll never read it. Why would they?

I've told this story so many times already . . .

November 23, 2006 . . . It was all over the news, the neighbors knew. It was the talk of the town . . .

But me and Nastya, my granddaughter, we'd been home all day. Our TV wasn't working, it'd been broken a long time, it was very old. We were waiting for Olesya to come home to get a new one. We'd been cleaning the house. Doing laundry. For some reason, we were having a lot of fun that day, we kept laughing and laughing. My mother came home . . . Olesya's grandma . . . She came in from the garden: "Oh girls, you seem to be having a little too much fun. Look out, the next thing you know, you'll be crying." My heart sank . . . How's my Olesya? We'd just talked to her the night before, it'd been a holiday—Police Day. They'd presented her with a decoration: "For Excellent Service in the Ministry of Internal Affairs." We congratulated her. "I love you all so much," she said. "I can't wait to see my native land again." Half of my pension went toward those long-distance calls. I'd hear her voice, and then I could get through the next two or three days, until the next phone call . . . "Mama, don't cry," she'd comfort me. "I carry a weapon, but I never use it. It's war on one side, and completely peaceful on the other. In the morning, I can hear the mullah singing, that's how they pray here. The mountains are alive, they're not dead—they're covered in grass and trees up to their very peaks." Another time: "Mama, the Chechen soil is saturated with oil. Dig around in any garden, you'll find oil everywhere."

Why did they send them down there? They're weren't defending the Motherland, they were fighting for oil derricks. These days, a drop of oil is worth a drop of blood . . .

One of my neighbors stopped by . . . an hour later, another . . . "What are they all dropping in for?" I wondered. They'd come by without any particular purpose. Just to sit for a moment, then leave. Meanwhile, they'd already played the story on TV several times . . .

We didn't know anything until the following morning. My son called: "Mama, are you at home?" "Why? I was about to go to the store." "Wait for me. I'll come after you send Nastya to school." "I was going to let her stay home. She has a cough." "If she doesn't have a fever, send her to school." My heart dropped, my whole body started shaking. My blood ran cold. Nastya ran off to school, and I went out onto the balcony. I saw my son coming, and he wasn't alone, my daughter-in-law was with him. I couldn't stand waiting for them, two more minutes would have pushed me over the edge! I ran out onto the stairwell and screamed, "What happened to Olesya?" Apparently, the way I was screaming, bellowing . . . they started shouting "Mama!" They came out of the elevator and just stood there, not saying a word. "Is she in the hospital?" "No." The whole world started spinning. Whirling. After that, I don't remember much . . . Suddenly, there were a lot of people standing around me . . . All of our neighbors had opened their doors, people were lifting me up from the cement floor, trying to calm me down. I was crawling around on the ground grabbing onto their legs, kissing their boots. "Kind people, my friends . . . She couldn't have abandoned Nastya . . . her sunshine . . . the light of her life . . . No . . ." I beat my head against the floor. At first, you don't believe it, you grasp at straws. She's not dead, she'll just return disabled. Without any legs . . . blind . . . It'll be all right, Nastya and I will lead her around by the hand. As long as she's alive! I wanted to beg someone—get on my knees and beg for her life back . . .

There were suddenly so many people . . . The house filled up with strangers. They pumped me full of sedatives—I'd lie there, come to, and then they'd have to call the ambulance again. The war had come into my home . . . but other people had their own lives to lead. No one understands a stranger's tragedy, God willing you might understand your own. Oh . . . Everyone thought I was unconscious, but I was lying there listening to them. It's bitter for me, very bitter . . .

". . . I have two sons. They're still in school. I'm saving up to buy them out of military service . . ."

". . . We are a patient people—that's for sure. People are nothing but meat, cannon fodder, and war, it's a job . . ."

". . . Renovating the house cost us a fortune. We're lucky we bought the Italian tiles before they changed the prices. We put in PVC windows. Armored doors . . ."

". . . And our kids keep growing . . . Enjoy them while they're still little . . ."

". . . A war here, and a war there . . . shootings every day. Explosions. Riding the bus is frightening, you're scared to get on the Metro . . ."

". . . Our neighbor's son was unemployed, he did nothing but drink, so he signed up as a contract soldier. A year later, he came back from Chechnya with a suitcase full of cash: bought a car, a fur coat for his wife, a gold ring. Took his whole family to Egypt . . . These days, without money, you're nothing. But how are you supposed to make it?"

". . . They're pillaging . . . tearing Russia into little pieces . . . slicing up the big pie!"

That godforsaken war! It had been going on somewhere far away . . . Far, far away . . . And then, it came into my home. I'd hung a cross around Olesya's neck . . . It wasn't enough. [*She weeps.*]

A day later, they brought us her body . . . The coffin was all wet, it was leaking . . . We wiped it down with bed sheets. The military administration kept telling us to hurry up, hurry up . . . Hurry up and bury her. "Don't open the coffin. Nothing but mush in there." But we opened it anyway. We clung to the hope that it had been a mistake. On television, they kept saying, "Olesya Nikolayeva . . . Twenty-one years old . . ." They had her age wrong. Maybe it was another Olesya? Not our girl. "Nothing but mush . . ." They issued us a death certificate: "Premeditated self-inflicted gunshot wound from a service weapon to the right side of the head . . ." What do I care about a piece of paper! I wanted to see her for myself, touch her. Caress her with my own hands. When we opened the coffin, her face was alive, it looked good . . . There was just this little hole on the left side of her head . . . so small, tiny . . . just big enough for a pencil. Another untruth, just like her age: The bullet hole was on the left side of her head and they said it was on the right. She'd gone off to Chechnya with a military police detachment with people from all around Ryazan, but only the ones from her police department helped with the burial. Her comrades. And all of them had the same question: What suicide? This is no suicide, she's been shot from a distance of two or three meters . . . While the administration kept putting pressure on us. They'd help us, rush us along. They brought her back to us late at night, and the very next morning, at noon, we were already burying her. At the cemetery . . . Oh . . . You should have seen how strong I was—I was possessed with superhuman strength . . . They'd nail the coffin lid shut but I could have ripped it right off, I would have pulled the nails out with my teeth. None of her superiors had come to the cemetery. Everyone turned their backs on us, starting with the state . . . Then the church: They didn't want to hold a service for her, she was a sinner . . . God wouldn't accept the soul of a suicide. How could they? How could they do that? I've started going to church . . . I'll light a candle . . . One day, I approached the priest: "Can it really be that the Lord only loves perfect souls? If that's true, then why do we need Him at all?" I told him everything . . . I've told this story so many times . . . [*She falls silent.*] The priest at our church is young. He broke down in tears: "How are you still alive and not in a madhouse? Dear Lord, grant this woman the heavenly kingdom!" He prayed for my little girl . . . But people kept gossiping, saying she'd shot herself over a man. Or that she'd done it because she was drunk. Everyone knows that they drink nonstop out there. Men and women alike. The pain, it's enough to drown in . . .

When she was packing, I'd wanted to tear everything up, smash it all to pieces. I had to hold myself back, I couldn't sleep. My bones felt like they were breaking, spasms went up and down my whole body. I would have these dreams . . . I wasn't quite asleep . . . Eternal ice, eternal winter. Everything a silvery blue . . . Sometimes, I'd see her and Nastya walking and walking over the water but never reaching shore. Nothing but water all around . . . I could always see Nastya, but Olesya would disappear . . . suddenly, she'd just be gone . . . I would get scared in the dream, too. "Olesya! Olesya!" I called to her. She'd reappear. But not as a living person, but as a portrait . . . a photograph . . . With a bruise on the left side of her face. In the same spot the bullet went through . . . [*She is silent.*] And that was just when she was packing her suitcase . . . "Mama, I'm going. I've already submitted my documents." "You're a single parent. They have no right to send you there." "They'll fire me if I don't go, Mama. You know how it is: Volunteering is compulsory. But don't cry, they're not shooting anymore, they're just rebuilding. My job will be to guard the construction sites. I'll go down there and make some money like everyone else does." Other girls from their department had already done their tours of duty, and everything had been fine. "I'll take you to Egypt and we'll see the pyramids." That was her dream. She wanted to make her Mama happy. We were poor . . . We barely had anything to our names. You go into town and everywhere you look, you see ads: Buy a car . . . take out a loan . . . Buy now! Just pick it up and take it home! In every store, there's a table in the middle of the sales floor, sometimes two, where you can sign up for credit. There's always a line in front of those tables. People are sick of being poor, they're all hankering to live a little. Meanwhile, I don't always know what I'm going to feed my family, even the potatoes run out. And macaroni. Sometimes, I wouldn't have enough for the trolleybus fare. After technical school, she enrolled at the teacher training college to study psychology. She went there for a year, and then we couldn't afford tuition anymore. She had to quit. My mother's pension is one hundred dollars a month, and that's how much mine is, too. The people at the top, they're pumping all that oil and natural gas . . . Those dollars aren't trickling down to us, they're going straight into their pockets. Regular people like us go to the store as though we're going to a museum, just to look. And on the radio—it's like subversive propaganda or something to incite the masses—they try to tell us to love the rich! That the rich are going to save us! That they'll give us jobs. They show us how they vacation, what they eat . . . their houses with their swimming pools . . . personal gardeners, personal chefs . . . like the gentry used to have in Tsarist times. In the evening you'll turn on the TV, and it's so gross you'll go straight to bed instead. A lot of people used to vote for Yavlinsky and Nemtsov[*] . . . I was a social reformer, I voted in every single election. A true patriot! I liked Nemtsov, I liked that he was young and handsome. Then everyone realized that the democrats had their eyes on the good life, too. They'd forgotten all about us. People are nothing but dust, specks of dust . . . Now the people have once again turned to the Communists. There were no billionaires back when they were in

[*] Grigori Yavlinsky (1952–) is an economist and politician, best known for the 500 Day Program, a plan for the transition of the USSR to a free market economy.

charge, everyone had a little bit, and that was enough for us all. We all felt like human beings. I was like everyone else.

I'm a Soviet, and so is my mother. We were building socialism and communism. Children were taught that selling was shameful and money couldn't buy happiness. Live honestly and give your life to your Motherland—the most precious thing we have. My whole life, I had been proud of being Soviet, but now I'm somewhat embarrassed about it, like I was dumb for believing in it. We used to have communist ideals, now the ideals are capitalist: "No mercy for anyone, because no one has any mercy for you." "Mama," Olesya would tell me, "you're still living in a country that hasn't existed for a long time. You can't help me." What have they done to us? What have they . . . [*She stops abruptly.*] There's so much I want to tell you! So much! But what's the most important thing? After Olesya's death, I found an old notebook of hers from school, it had an essay in it called "What Is Life?" "I want to describe the ideal that mankind should strive for . . ." she'd written. "The purpose of life is whatever makes you rise above . . ." I was the one who had taught her that . . . [*She bawls.*] She couldn't even kill a mouse, and yet she went off to a war zone . . . All I know is that it was all wrong, but I have no idea what actually happened. They're hiding it from me . . . [*She screams.*] My daughter died without leaving a trace. They can't do this! During the Great Patriotic War, my mother was twelve, they were evacuated to Siberia. Even though they were just children, they put them to work at a factory for sixteen hours a day . . . Just like the adults. All for a pass to the cafeteria where they would be served a bowl of noodles and a little piece of bread. Just a bit of bread! They were making shells for the front. Children would die at their work stations because they were so little. It made sense to her why people were killing each other back then, but she can't understand why they're doing it now. No one can. This filthy war! Argun . . . Gudermes . . . Khankala* . . . Whenever I hear those words, I turn the TV off . . .

I have the certificate right here: "Premeditated . . . gunshot wound from a service weapon . . ." Leaving Nastya behind . . . She's only nine . . . Now I'm both her grandmother and her mother. I'm sick, all cut up by surgeons. I've had three operations. My health is terrible, and how could I possibly be healthy? I grew up in Khabarovsk Krai. In the middle of the taiga. We lived in barracks. Oranges and bananas—

---

* Towns and villages in Chechnya.

we'd only ever seen pictures of them. To eat, we had noodles . . . macaroni and powdered milk . . . Every so often, canned meat. Mama was
recruited to the Far East after the war, when they called on the youth
to master the North. They recruited them as though they were sending
them to the front. Only destitute people like us went to the great construction sites. People without hearth or home. "For the fog and the
fragrance of the taiga"—that's the songs, the books. In reality, we
were bloated from hunger. It was hunger that drove us to great feats. I
got a little older, and then I too went to work at the construction
site . . . Mama and I helped build the Baikal-Amur Mainline. I have a
medal, "For the Construction of the Baikal-Amur Mainline," and a
whole stack of certificates. [*She falls silent.*] In winter, it would be
minus 50 degrees, the ground was frozen a meter down. The tall white
hills. When they're covered in snow, they get so white, you can't even
see them in good weather. Can't make them out. I loved those hills
with all my heart. Everyone has a big Motherland and their little
homeland. That's my personal homeland. The barracks had thin
walls, the bathroom was outside—but we were young! We believed in
the future, and our belief was unflagging. Plus, our lives really did
improve year after year: No one had a TV—no one!—and then, suddenly, they were everywhere. We lived in barracks, and then they
started giving people their own apartments. They promised: "The current generation of Soviets shall live to see communism." That meant
me . . . I was going to get to live under real communism?! [*She laughs.*]
I enrolled in a university distance-learning department and got a degree in economics. You didn't have to pay tuition fees back then—who
would teach me anything now? For that, I am grateful to the Soviet
state. I worked at the district executive committee in the finance department. I bought myself a beaver lamb coat . . . a nice goat down
shawl . . . In winter, you bundle up until all that's left is your nose
sticking out. I'd travel around to collective farms conducting audits.
At the collective farms, they raised sables, Arctic foxes, minks. By
then, we weren't too badly off. I bought my mother her own fur coat.
And that's when they decided it was time for capitalism . . . They
promised that when the Communists left power, everyone would be
happy. We're not a trusting people, we've been through too much. Everyone stocked up on salt and matches. "Perestroika" sounded like
"war" to us. Then, right in front of our eyes, they started pillaging the
collective farms . . . and the factories . . . After that, they bought them
all up for kopecks. We'd spent our whole lives building, just to watch

it all be sold for a five-kopeck piece. The people were given vouchers . . . They cheated us . . . I still have mine in the china cabinet. Olesya's death certificate . . . and those useless pieces of paper . . . Is this capitalism? I've seen plenty of our Russian capitalists, and they weren't all Russians, either; there were Armenians, Ukrainians. They took out huge loans from the government and never paid them back. Their eyes gleamed like the eyes of prisoners. That characteristic gleam I'm all too familiar with. Where I'm from is covered in camps and barbed wire. Who do you think mastered the North? It was the prisoners and us, the poor. The proletariat. But that's not how we thought of ourselves back then . . .

My mother made a decision . . . the only way out was to return to Ryazan. Go back to where we came from. There were already shootings, people were divvying up the wealth of the USSR. Grabbing whatever they could, tearing it to bits . . . The bad guys took over, and the smart ones became the idiots. We'd built it all then handed it over to the gangsters—that's what happened, right? We left the north empty-handed, with nothing but our household junk. Leaving the factories to them . . . the mines . . . We rode the train for two weeks, lugging back our refrigerator, our books, our furniture—the meat grinder, the dishes, all that stuff. For two weeks, I looked out the window: There is no end nor boundary to the Russian soil. This Mother Russia of ours is all too "great and bounteous" to ever be properly run. It was 1994. Yeltsin was already in power . . . What awaited us at home? At home, the school teachers moonlighted for Azerbaijani grocery stall owners selling fruit and *pelmeni*. In Moscow, the market stretched from the railway station all the way down to the Kremlin. Beggars seemed to have suddenly appeared out of nowhere. But all of us were Soviet! Soviet! For a long time, everyone was ashamed, uncomfortable.

I once had this conversation with a Chechen at the market . . . The war had been going on for fifteen years already, they'd come to escape it here. They're fanning out through all of Russia . . . getting into every corner . . . even while we're supposedly at war with them . . . Russia is fighting the Chechens . . . that so-called "special operation." What kind of war is this? The Chechen I talked to was young: "I'm not out there fighting, lady. My wife is Russian." I heard this story once— I'll tell it to you, too . . . A Chechen girl fell in love with a Russian pilot. This handsome guy. By mutual agreement, they decided he should take her away from her parents. He brought her to Russia. They got married. Everything was by the book. Their son was born.

But she kept crying and crying, she felt so bad for her parents. Finally, they wrote them a letter: "Please forgive us, we love each other . . ." And they sent them greetings from her Russian mother. But all those years, her brothers had been looking for her, they wanted to kill her for bringing shame on their family—she'd not only married a Russian, but a Russian who'd bombed them. Killed their people. The return address led them directly to her . . . One of her brothers murdered her, then another one showed up to take her body home. [*Silence.*] This filthy war—this catastrophe—has come into my home. Now I collect everything . . . I read everything I can about Chechnya. I talk to everyone I meet . . . I'd like to go there. So they can kill me there. [*She cries.*] I would be so happy. That's how strong my maternal love is . . . I know a woman . . . There was nothing left of her son, a shell had hit him head-on. "It would make me feel so much better," she confessed to me, "if his remains were resting in his native soil. Even if it was just a little piece of him . . ." That tiny bit would be enough to make her glad . . . "You got a son or something, lady?" that Chechen had asked me. "Yes, I have a son, but my daughter was the one who died in Chechnya." "Russians, I want to ask you: What kind of war is this? You kill us, disfigure us, and then you treat our wounds in your hospitals. You bomb and loot our homes, then you rebuild them. You try to tell us that Russia is our home, but every day, I have to bribe the police not to beat me to death for the way I look. Pay them not to rob me. I have to convince them that I haven't come here to kill them and that I don't want to blow up their houses. They could have killed me in Grozny . . . But they might also kill me here . . ."

While my heart is still beating . . . [*With despair.*] I will continue to search for her. I want to know how my daughter died. I don't believe anyone.

[*She opens up her china cabinet where, next to the crystal cordial glasses, she keeps her documents and photographs. She lays them out on the table.*]

My girl was pretty . . . popular at school. She liked ice skating. Her grades were fine, normal . . . In tenth grade, she fell in love with Roma. I was against it, of course, he was seven years older than her. "But Mama, it's love!" It was a mad love, if he wasn't calling her, she was calling him . . . "Why are you calling him?" "Mama, it's love!" She only had eyes for Roma. She forgot all about her Mama. One day, she was graduating, and the next, they were already married. Already had a baby. Roma drank, brawled, while all she could do was cry. I hated his guts. They lived like that for a year. He'd rip up her nice clothes when he got jealous. Grab her by the hair, wrap it around his fist, and slam her head against the wall. She just kept taking it . . . she didn't want to listen to her mother. Until, finally, by some miracle, she managed to get away from him. Where do you think she ran to? Her mother . . . "Mama, save me!" But then he went and moved in with us, too. One night, I woke up from the sound of sobbing . . . I open up the bathroom door, and he's standing over her with a knife. I grabbed the blade, cut my hands on it. Another time, he'd gotten ahold of some sort of gun, I think it must have been a gas pistol and not a real one. I was pulling Olesya away from him, and he pointed it at me, "This will shut you up!" I wept and wept until they finally broke up. I kicked him out . . . [*She is silent.*] It was . . . maybe not even six months had passed . . . Olesya came home from work one day and told me: "Roma got married." "How do you know?" "He gave me a lift." "And?" "And nothing." That was quick. But she'd had this childish love for him. She couldn't get over it. [*She picks up a sheet of paper from the pile of documents.*] The medical examiner put down that she was shot in the right side of the head, but the bullet hole was on the left. That tiny hole . . . Maybe he never even saw the body? They just told him what to write and paid him off.

I hoped . . . I waited for her unit to return. I'll ask them, I thought . . . Reconstruct the scene . . . The hole was on the left side of her head, but on paper, it was on the right. I needed to know . . . It was already winter. Snow on the ground. I used to love the snow. And my Olesya had loved it, too, she would get her skates out ahead of time and oil them up in anticipation. It seems so long ago, ages. It's bitter for me, very bitter . . . I look out the window, and people are getting ready for Christmas, they're running around with presents and ornaments. Carrying trees. In my kitchen, the radio was always on. Tuned to the local station. Local news. Waiting. Finally, it happened. They announced, "The Ryazan police division volunteers have returned from their tour of duty in Chechnya." "Our countrymen honorably fulfilled their soldierly duty." "They did not put us to shame." . . . They were welcomed with pomp at the railway station. An orchestra, flowers. Presented with medals and valuable gifts. Some of them got televisions, others wristwatches . . . Heroes . . . The heroes had returned! Not a single word about Olesya, no one even mentioned her . . . I waited . . . I held the radio right up to my ear. They have to say her name! They cut to a commercial for detergent . . . [*She breaks down*.] My little girl has disappeared without a trace. How could they! Olesya . . . She was our city's first coffin from Chechnya . . . A month later, they brought two more coffins, one was an older police officer, the other was very young. There was a ceremony for them at the theater . . . at the municipal theater named after Yesenin. They had a guard of honor. A wreath from members of the community, the mayor, speeches. They buried them in the Alley of Heroes, where the boys who had fought in Afghanistan lay. Now, the Chechnya boys are there with them . . . There are two main alleys in our cemetery, the Alley of Heroes and another one people call the Alley of Gangsters. Gangsters war among themselves, shoot one another. Bloody pere-stroika. They end up with the best plots in the cemetery. Their coffins are made of mahogany, encrusted with fake gold, outfitted with elec-tronic refrigeration systems. For tombstones, they have Mounds of Glory. The government is responsible for the heroes' monuments, and, to be honest, those soldiers' tombstones are pretty modest. And not everyone gets one, at that. Contract soldiers get nothing. I know one mother who appealed to the conscription office, and they refused her: "Your son fought for money." My Olesya, she lies apart from everyone else—after all, she's just a suicide . . . oh . . . [*She can't speak.*] Our Nastya . . . They give her 1,500 rubles a month in death benefits— that's fifty dollars. Where's the truth? Where is justice? They give her so little because her mother isn't a hero. It would be a different story if she'd killed someone, blown them up with a grenade, but her mother only killed herself, she didn't manage to kill anyone else. That's no hero! How do you explain this to a child? What am I supposed to tell her? In one newspaper, they printed Olesya's alleged words: "My daughter won't be ashamed of me . . ." In the first few days after the funeral, Nastya sat there listless, as though she wasn't there, or didn't know where she was. No one could bear to do it . . . It was me who finally told her: "Your Mama, Olesya . . . your Mama is gone . . ." She stood there, and it was as though she hadn't heard me. I was crying, but she wasn't. And then . . . whenever I brought up Olesya, it was as though she couldn't hear me. This went on for a long time, it even started making me mad. I took her to a psychologist. They told me that she was normal, but in a state of shock. We went to see her father. I asked him: "Are you going to take your child?" "Where do you want me to take her?" He's already had another kid with his new wife. "Then disown her." "Why would I do that? What if I need something in my old age? A couple of kopecks . . ." That's what her father's like . . . He doesn't help out with her at all. Only Olesya's friends visit. On Nastya's birthday, they always scrape together some money and bring it to us. They bought her a computer. Her friends remember her.

For a long time, I sat there waiting for the phone to ring. Her unit had returned, the commander and her fellow troops. They'll call me, I thought—they have to! But the phone was silent, so I started looking up their names and phone numbers myself. The unit commander was Klimkin . . . I'd learned that from the newspapers. All of them! They were all over the papers—the epic heroes of Russia! The Knights of Ryazan. One of the newspapers even had a little article by him where he expressed his gratitude to the unit for their excellent service. They had fulfilled their duty with honor, he said—with honor, even! I called the police department where he works: "Please ask Major Klimkin to the phone." "Who wishes to speak to him?" "Ludmila Vasilyevna Nikolayeva . . . the mother of Olesya Nikolayeva . . ." "He's not here." "He's busy." "He's out of town." You're a commander, you should be the one who comes and tells the mother what happened. Console her. Thank her. That's how I see it . . . [*She cries.*] I'm crying, but they're tears of rage . . . I never wanted to let Olesya go, I tried talking her out of it, but my mother told me: "If that's what she needs to do, she should go." "Needs"! I hate that word now! I'm not the same person I used to be . . . Why should I love my Motherland? They promised us that democracy would mean that everyone is happy. Everything would be fair. Honest. It was all a big fat lie . . . People are nothing but dust . . . specks of dust . . . The only good thing is that there's lots of stuff at the stores now. It's all yours! All yours for the taking! We didn't have that under socialism. Of course, I'm only a simple Soviet woman . . . No one listens to me because I don't have any money. If I had money, it would be a different story. They would be scared of me, the bosses . . . Today, money rules everything . . .

When Olesya was going away, she was happy. "Kormchaya is coming, too." They were the two women in their unit. Olga Kormchaya . . . I'd met her at the station when they were departing. "This is my mother," Olesya had introduced me. There was a moment as they were leaving, maybe I put too much stock in it now. After all the fanfare, the buses were just about to pull out, the national anthem had started up, everyone was crying. I was standing on one side and, for some reason, I ran over to the other side, Olesya had shouted something to me out the window, and I thought she had told me that the bus was going to swing around. I ran over to the other side so I could see her one last time. Wave to her. But then, the bus went straight ahead, and I didn't get to see her again. It broke my heart. At the last moment, her purse strap had broken . . . I'm probably just working myself up now . . . She was my heart and soul . . . [*She cries.*] I found Kormchaya's phone number in the phone book. I called her: "This is Olesya's mother . . . I want to see you." For a long time, she didn't say anything, and then, in a hurt and even angry tone, "I've been through so much. When are you all going to leave me alone!" And with that, she hung up on me. I called her back, "I'm begging you! I need to know . . . Help me, please!" "Stop tormenting me!" I called again, it was probably a month later . . . This time, her mother picked up: "My daughter's not home. She's gone back to Chechnya." Again! To Chechnya?! It's a war zone, but for some people, it's also a decent job. It's a matter of luck . . . They don't think about death, dying today is scary, but if it happens at some unknown point in the future, it's all right. For the six months they served there, they all got sixty thousand rubles. Enough to buy a used car. And that's on top of their salaries. Before she left, Olesya had bought a washing machine on credit, and a mobile phone . . . "I'll pay them off when I get back," she said. Now we're the ones who have to pay. With what money? The bills come, we pile them up . . . Nastya goes around in old sneakers, they're too small for her, she comes home from school crying because her toes hurt. My mother and I put our pensions together, budget our money, count every kopeck, and still, by the end of every month, there's nothing left. And you can't reach a dead person . . .

There were two people with her in her final moments, two witnesses. It happened at the security checkpoint, in a two-by-two-and-a-half-meter booth. During the night shift. It was the three of them on duty. The first one . . . "Well, you know, she came in," he told me over the phone, "we chatted for two or three minutes . . ." And then he had to go somewhere for some reason, maybe he had to use the toilet, or maybe someone had summoned him. From outside the door, he heard a bang. At first, it didn't even occur to him that it could have been a gunshot. He came back and found her lying on the floor. Her mood? What was she like that night? She was in a good mood, a regular mood . . . she came in, they said hi, joked around . . . The second witness . . . I called him at work. He didn't show up to our meeting, and they wouldn't let me anywhere near him . . . He was in there with her when she shot herself, but, according to the story, right at that moment, he'd turned away. Right at that very second . . . So, in a two-by-two-and-a-half-meter booth, he didn't see a thing. Would you believe it? I pleaded with them . . . Just tell me, I need to know . . . I won't go anywhere else with the information. I swear to God! They avoided me like the plague. They'd been ordered to keep their mouths shut. Defend the honor of the uniform. Their mouths were stopped up with dollars . . . [She weeps.] From the moment Olesya signed up with the police, I didn't like it. My Olesya, a cop? It just wasn't right! I hated it . . . But the thing is, she only ever went to technical college, then one semester of teacher training college. For a long time, she couldn't find a job. The police hired her right away. It scared me . . . Law enforcement is a business . . . They're a mafia . . . People are afraid of cops, there's someone who's suffered from police brutality in every family. They'll torture you, disfigure you. People are as scared of them as they are of the gangsters. God forbid! In the papers you read about the "werewolves in uniform"* . . . They rape people, kill people . . . The kinds of things that would never happen in Soviet times—not in a million years! And if they did happen . . . Many things were kept silent back then . . . No one wrote about them, so we all felt safe. [She falls into thought.] Half of the people on the force have seen combat. Some fought in Afghanistan, others in Chechnya. They've killed people. They are psychologically disturbed. They fought civilian populations because that's what the wars are like now: Soldiers don't just fight other soldiers, they fight civilians, too. Regular people. For them, everyone is an enemy—men, women, and children alike. When they come back, they'll kill someone here, at home, and then be surprised that they have to explain themselves. In Chechnya, no explanations were necessary . . . "Mama," Olesya would counter, "You're wrong. It all depends on the individual. A woman police officer is a beautiful thing. The blue shirt, the epaulettes."

Her last night at home, her friends came over to say goodbye. I remember it . . . These days, I dwell on every little thing. They stayed up all night talking . . .

". . . Russia is a great country, it's not just a gas pipeline with a tap on it . . ."

". . . We don't have Crimea anymore, we gave it away . . . There's a war in Chechnya . . . Tatarstan is starting to stir . . . I want to live in a great country. Our MiG jets will reach Riga . . ."

---

* A term coined by Russian Minister of Defense Boris Gryzlov during a series of major police corruption trials that took place between 2003 and 2006.

". . . They're slamming Russia's face against the table! Treating Chechen gangsters like heroes . . . Human rights?! Out there, they'd show up to Russians' homes with machine guns, demanding, 'Leave or we'll kill you.' A good Chechen says, 'Leave!' before killing you, a bad one kills you right away. Suitcase, station, Russia . . . On fences, the graffiti read: 'Don't buy apartments from Sergei, they'll end up ours anyway.' 'Russians, don't leave—we need slaves.' "

". . . Two Russian soldiers and an officer were captured by Chechens. They cut off the soldiers' heads but released the officer: 'Go lose your mind.' I've seen videos . . . They cut off people's ears, their fingers . . . They keep Russian prisoners as slaves in their basements. They're animals!"

". . . I'm going! I need to make money to pay for my wedding. I want to get married. She's a pretty girl, she won't wait around for long . . ."

". . . I have this friend, he and I were in the army together. He lived in Grozny. His neighbor was a Chechen. One fine day, the guy says to him: 'You have to leave—I'm begging you.' 'Why?' 'Because we're about to start butchering you.' They left behind a three-bedroom apartment. Now they live in a workers' dormitory in Saratov. They weren't allowed to bring anything with them. 'Let Russia buy you new stuff. All of this is ours now!' "

". . . Russia may be on her knees, but she's not dead yet. We're Russian patriots! We must fulfill our duty to Russia! You know the joke: Comrade soldiers and officers, if you prove yourselves in Chechnya, the Motherland will send you 'on leave' to Yugoslavia. You know, to Europe! Shit!"

My son put up with me until he couldn't take it anymore. He started giving me a hard time: "Mama, the only thing you're going to accomplish is giving yourself a stroke." They sent me to a sanatorium. By force, you could say, after a huge family quarrel. At the sanatorium, I made friends with a good woman, her daughter had died young from an abortion, we'd cry together. Became friends. The other day, I called her and found out she had died. In her sleep. I know in my heart that she died of grief . . . Why can't I die? I would be so happy to, but I keep on living. [*She cries.*] When I got back from the sanatorium, the first words out of my mother's mouth were, "Child, they're going to put you in jail. They won't forgive you for trying to find the truth." What happened was, the minute I left town, she got a phone call from the police: "You are to report to such-and-such an office at 2400 hours . . . There will be a fine for failing to appear . . . a custodial sentence of fifteen days . . ." My mother is a frightened woman—everyone in this country is frightened. Show me one elderly person who isn't. And that was just the beginning. They showed up here and questioned the neighbors. They wanted to know what kind of people we were, our behavior . . . They asked about Olesya, if anyone had ever seen her drunk, if she did drugs . . . They asked for our medical histories at the health clinic. They wanted to know whether any of us were on the psychiatric clinic registry. It was such a slap in the face! I was furious!! I picked up the phone and called the police department: "Who's been threatening my mother? She's in her ninth decade. Why was she summoned by the police?" A day later, they sent me a summons: "Come to such-and-such an office . . . Detective so-and-so . . ." My mother was in tears: "They're going to put you in prison." I wasn't afraid of anything anymore. I don't give a damn about them! Stalin needs to come back from the dead! I am calling on him to rise up from the grave! That's my prayer . . . He didn't put enough of our administrators in prison, more of them should have been executed. It wasn't enough! I have no pity for them. I want their tears! [*She cries.*] I showed up at that office to see this Detective Fedin. I started in on them from the doorway: "What do you want from me? You brought me my daughter in a wet coffin, wasn't that enough for you?" "You illiterate woman, you don't seem to understand where you are. We're the ones who ask the questions around here . . ." At first, it was just him, but then they called in Olesya's commander, that Klimkin . . . I finally got to see him in the flesh! He came in, and I pounced on him: "Who killed my daughter? I demand to know the truth . . ." "Your daughter was an imbecile, she was insane!" Oh, I can't handle it! I can't . . . He turned beet red, shouted at me, stamped his feet. Ugh! They were trying to provoke me, make me scream and scratch at them like a mad cat. Like I'm crazy and my daughter was crazy, too. They wanted to silence me . . .

As long as my heart is still beating, I will continue to search for the truth. I'm not afraid of anyone! I'm not a rag you can wipe the floor with or a bug you can crush. You're not going to scare me back into my corner. They brought me back my daughter in a wet coffin . . .

. . . I was on a commuter train. A man sat down across from me: "Looks like you and I are riding together, mother. Let's get acquainted . . ." He introduced himself: "I'm a former officer, former businessman, former member of the Yabloko party.* Currently unemployed." No matter what anyone asks me, I always tell them the same story: "My daughter died in Chechnya . . . She was a junior police sergeant . . ." He said, "Tell me the story." I've told it so many times already . . . [*She falls silent.*] He listened, and then he told me his . . .

"I was out there myself. I came back alive, but life at home isn't working out. I can't fit myself into these boxes. No one wants to hire me. 'I see . . . You were in Chechnya?' I'm afraid of people. They make me sick . . . But whenever I meet anyone who was also in Chechnya, they're like a brother to me . . .

"An old Chechen sees a carful of us discharged soldiers. He stands there wondering at the sight: Here are these guys who seem completely normal, just regular Russian guys, but not long ago they all had machine guns, they were snipers. We . . . we were all in new coats and jeans. Where did we get the money to buy them? We earned it in Chechnya. What was our job? Waging war . . . shooting . . . Children and beautiful women are struck down as well. But take away a soldier's weapon, dress him in civilian clothes, and you'll have a tractor driver, a bus driver, a student . . .

"We lived behind barbed wire, surrounded by guard towers and minefields. A cramped, sequestered world. A penal colony. You couldn't leave, they'd kill you. Death to the occupiers! Everyone drank, they'd drink until they were dumb beasts. Every day, you saw bombed-out houses, people looting, killing people. The things that start coming out of you! All of your boundaries break down—the boundaries of what you are capable of . . . You start allowing yourself to do all sorts of things . . . You're nothing but a drunken animal with a gun. Running on sheer testosterone . . .

" . . . It's executioner's work . . . We were dying for a mafia that wasn't even paying us what we were promised. Who cheated us. But it's not like I was here at home killing people on the street, I was at war. I saw a Russian girl that those jackals had raped. They burnt her chest with cigarette butts so that she would moan louder . . .

" . . . I came home with cash . . . I bought my friends some vodka, got a used Mercedes . . ."

[*She no longer wipes her tears away.*] So that's where my Olesya

---

* The Yabloko Party is a center-left Russian social liberal party founded by Grigori Yavlinsky.

landed! That's where she ended up! That filthy war . . . It had been somewhere far, far away, and now it's in my home. It's been two years . . . I knock on people's doors, meet with all sorts of officials. Write to the prosecutor's offices . . . district, regional . . . the Prosecutor General's office . . . [*She points to a stack of letters.*] And in response, I always get form letters—a mountain of form letters! "Regarding the death of your daughter we write to inform you . . ." And all of them lie: They'll say she died on November 13, when really, it was the 11th, or that her blood type is O, when it's actually B. In some, she was wearing her uniform, in others, she was in civilian clothes. The hole was on the left side of her head near the temple, but they keep saying it was on the right . . . I wrote a query to our State Duma representative—I'd chosen him, I voted for him. I used to have faith in our government! Somehow, I managed to get a meeting with him. I remember standing on the ground floor of the Duma . . . My eyes were like saucers! I saw their jewelry stall: gold rings with diamonds, silver and gold Easter eggs, pendants . . . The smallest diamond ring cost more money than I've made in my entire life. One little ring . . . Our deputies, the people's deputies—where do they get all this money? In all my years of hard labor, all I earned was a stack of certificates . . . same as my mother . . . While they all have shares in Gazprom . . . We get pieces of paper, and they get money. [*Angry silence.*] I shouldn't have gone there and wept in that place for nothing . . . Bring back Stalin! The people are waiting for him! They took away my daughter and brought me back a coffin. A wet coffin . . . And no one wants to speak to the mother . . . [*She weeps.*] Now I wish I could go work for the police department myself . . . Conduct a thorough investigation, write a detailed crime report. If it was a suicide, there should have been blood on the weapon and gunpowder on her hands. I know everything now . . . I don't like watching the news on TV. It's all lies! But the crime shows—murders, things like that—I never miss a single one. Some mornings, I can't get up, my arms and legs refuse to move, all I want to do is stay in bed. But then I remember Olesya . . . and I get up.

I pieced together the story . . . word by word . . . People would drunkenly blurt out bits of the truth. There were seventy of them there, word of what really happened must have spread. Our town isn't that big, it's not Moscow . . . Now, I have a partial picture of what happened . . . They all got outrageously drunk in honor of Police Day. Drunk to the point of blacking out, and things went downhill from there. If only Olesya had gone with the boys from home, from her own department. Instead, she was surrounded by strangers, in a combined unit, with people from everywhere. She ended up among the traffic police. These people, they live like kings, their pockets are always lined with bills. They stand on the roads with machine guns collecting tolls. Everyone has to pay them. A prime position! Boys like their fun . . . killing, drinking, and fucking—the three joys of war. They got tanked, they were sloshed . . . They turned savage . . . and supposedly raped every girl there. Their own girls. Olesya either resisted, or she threatened them afterward: "I'll make sure you all end up behind bars." So they wouldn't let her get away.

There's also another version . . . They were at the checkpoint letting cars through. Everyone out there is always hustling, trying to make some extra money however they can. Some people transport contraband—what and from where, I couldn't tell you, and I'm not going to make things up. Drugs or I don't know what . . . But this was a done deal. Everything had already been bought and paid for. A Niva drove up . . . everyone remembers it being a Niva . . . But Olesya dug her heels in. For some reason, she wouldn't let the car through . . . And that's why they shot her. A lot of money was on the line and she'd gotten in somebody's way. Apparently, some high-ranking official was involved . . .

My mother had had a dream about a Niva . . . When I went to see a clairvoyant, I put this photograph on her table . . . [*She shows me.*] She told me she saw a car, "Some Niva . . ."

. . . I'd struck up a conversation with this woman, a nurse. I don't know what she was like before she went to Chechnya, maybe she'd been a cheerful person. Now, she's full of rage just like I am. Many people today are very hurt, they don't say anything, but they're wounded. Everyone dreamed of winning big in this new life, but few have won anything at all, and almost no one has ended up with the golden ticket . . . Nobody was prepared to tumble all the way down to the bottom. Now, a lot of people live with this pain, harboring it. [*She is silent.*] And maybe Olesya, too, would have come back different . . . a stranger . . . Oh . . . [*Silence.*] This woman was very open with me . . .

". . . I went because I thought it was romantic! My friends laughed at me for a long time. To be perfectly honest, I was running from heartbreak. I didn't care whether a Chechen shot me or if I died of despair.

". . . People who don't handle corpses think that they're silent.

That they don't make a sound. Actually, they make all sorts of noises. Air comes out of them, their bones crack. Strange scratching sounds. It's enough to drive you crazy . . .

". . . I didn't meet any men out there who didn't drink and shoot people. They'd get drunk and shoot whomever they wanted. Why? No one can answer that question.

". . . He was a surgeon . . . I thought we were in love. Then, right as we were about to go home, he told me: 'Don't call and don't write. If I'm going to cheat, it better be with a beautiful woman, the kind that I'm not embarrassed to run into my wife with.' I'm no beauty. But he and I would spend three days at a time in the operating room together. It felt like . . . something even stronger than love . . .

". . . Now I'm afraid of men . . . The ones who came back from the war, I don't even want to see them, they're all pricks. Every last one of them! I was packing . . . thinking I want to bring this and that home . . . my stereo, my rug . . . The head of the hospital told me: 'I for one am leaving everything here. I don't want to take this war home with me.' But the war isn't in the things we brought home, it's in our souls . . ."

They gave us Olesya's things back: her pea coat, her skirt. Her gold earrings and necklace. There were some nuts and two little chocolates in the coat pocket. She must have been saving them for Christmas, collecting things to send to us. It's bitter for me, very bitter . . .

So write down the truth, who should be scared of that? The people in the government . . . We can't reach them anyway . . . Our last remaining option is to go on strike, brandishing our rifles. Lie down on the train tracks. Only we don't have a leader . . . Otherwise, the people would have risen up ages ago. There's no Pugachev! But if someone were to hand me a gun, I know exactly who I'd shoot . . . [*She points to the newspaper.*] Have you heard? You can go to Chechnya as a tourist now. They'll fly you around in a military helicopter over the ruins of Grozny, the burned-out villages. War and construction are happening side by side. They're shooting and building and showing it off all at once. We're still crying, but someone is already profiting off our tears. Our fear. Selling them like they're oil.

[*A few days later, we meet again.*]

I used to understand our way of life . . . The way we lived used to make sense to me . . . Now, I don't understand anything anymore . . . None of it makes any sense at all . . .

ON THE DARKNESS OF THE EVIL ONE
AND "THE OTHER LIFE WE CAN
BUILD OUT OF THIS ONE"

◆

Yelena Razduyeva, worker,
37 years old

It took me a long time to find a "guide" into this story, a narrator or interlocutor—I don't even know what to call the people who lead me on my travels through people's worlds. Through lives. At first, everyone refused: "This is a case for a psychiatrist." "Because of her sick fantasies, a mother abandons her three children—this is something for a court to examine, not a writer." "What about Medea?" I countered. "What about Medea, who killed her own children for love?" "That's a myth. These are real people." But artists don't live in a ghetto cut off from the real world. They're free, like everyone else.

Eventually, I learned that there was already a film about my protagonist—Suffering (Fishka Films). So I met the director, Irina Vasilyeva. As we watched the movie, listening to the characters tell their sides of the story, we would pause and Irina would tell me the rest.

AS TOLD BY FILMMAKER IRINA VASILYEVA

When I first heard the story, I didn't like it, it scared me. They tried to convince me that it would be a breathtaking film about love, that I had to go and start filming immediately. It's such a Russian story! A woman who's married with three kids falls in love with a prisoner—and a "lifer," at that—sentenced to life in prison for a particularly brutal murder. And for him, she abandons everything: her husband, her kids, her home. But something was stopping me . . .

Russia has loved its prisoners since the dawn of the ages—they're sinners, but they're martyrs, too. They need comfort and consolation. There's a whole culture of pity, and its traditions are carefully preserved, especially in the small towns and villages. The simple women who live there don't have the Internet, they use the mail. An ancient method. While the men drink and brawl, the women spend evenings writing each other letters. Their letters are filled with their artless tales alongside all sorts of ephemera—sewing patterns, recipes—and at the end, there'll always be prisoners' addresses. Someone's brother is doing time, he's spread word of his comrades on the inside. For others, it's their neighbor or former classmate. The addresses travel through the grapevine . . . Men will steal, raise hell, go to jail, get out, and then end up behind bars again. Always the same old story! In the villages, you'll learn that half the men have either already done time or are still serving out their sentences. But we're Christians, it's our duty to help the unfortunate. There are women who marry these habitual offenders, even murderers. I'm not judging, but if you were to ask me to explain this phenomenon . . . it's complicated . . . I can tell you that some men seem to have a nose for this kind of woman. Most often, it's women who come from bad situations, who haven't been able to realize their dreams. They're lonely. Suddenly, somebody needs them, they have someone to take care of. It's one way to change your life. A kind of medicine . . .

Finally, we decided to go out there and shoot a film. I wanted to show people that even in our pragmatic era, there are still people who live by a different logic. And that they're very vulnerable. We often speak about our people. Some idealize them, others consider them beasts. *Sovoks*. In reality, we don't even know them. There's a great gulf between us . . . I always film stories, and every story has everything in it. The two most important ingredients are love and death.

All this takes place in a remote village in the Kaluga Oblast . . . We drove there . . . Out the window, everything seemed endless: the fields, the forest, the sky. Churches shone on the hilltops. Power and peace. Ancient presences. We kept going and going . . . Finally, we turned off the main highway onto a country road . . . Oh! Russian roads are a special breed—some of them, not even a tank can pass. Two or three pits every three meters already counts as a good road. And villages on either side—gnarled, slanting huts with broken fences, dogs and chickens wandering the streets. Every morning, before it even opens, there's already a line of alcoholics outside the shop. Sights so familiar they give you a lump in your throat . . . In the center of the village, the plaster statue of Lenin still stands where it's always stood . . . [*She is silent.*] There was a time . . . It's hard to believe that it existed, but we all used to be that way . . . When Gorbachev came to power, we ran around mad with glee. We lived in our dreams, our illusions. Baring our souls to one another in our kitchens. We wanted a new Russia . . . Twenty years down the line, it finally dawned on us: Where was this new Russia supposed to have come from? It never existed, and it still doesn't today. Someone put it very accurately: In five years, everything can change in Russia, but in two hundred—nothing. Boundless open spaces and yet, a slave mentality . . . You won't refashion Russia in a Moscow kitchen. They brought back the Tsarist seal but left the Stalinist anthem. Moscow is Russian . . . a capitalist city . . . but Russia itself was and remains Soviet. They've never even set eyes on a democrat out there, and if they had, they would have ripped him to shreds. The majority of the people want equal shares and a leader. The cheap counterfeit vodka flows in rivers . . . [*She laughs.*] I get the sense that you and I both come from the kitchen generation, we started off talking about love, and five minutes later, we're discussing how to rebuild Russia. Russia doesn't care about what we have to say, it has its own life to lead . . .

A drunken little man pointed out our heroine's house. She stepped out of the hut . . . I knew that I liked her right away. Deep blue eyes, statuesque. You could say she's a beauty. A true Russian beauty! A woman like her will sparkle whether she's in a modest peasant hut or a luxurious Moscow apartment. And can you imagine—she's married to some murderer. We haven't met him yet, he has a life sentence and a case of tuberculosis. When we told her why we'd come, she laughed: "It's my little soap opera." I had been pacing around wondering how I would tell her that we were going to film her. What if she was afraid of cameras? But she said to me, "I'm such a little fool, I tell anybody and everybody my story. Some people cry, others curse me. If you like, I'll tell you, too . . ." And she told us . . .

YELENA RAZDUYEVA

On Love

I hadn't planned on getting married, but of course, I'd fantasized about it. I was eighteen years old. My man . . . What's he going to be like? One night, I had this dream: I was walking through the meadow, toward the river—there's a river behind our village—and suddenly a handsome and tall young man appeared in front of me. He took me by the hand and said, "You will be my bride. My bride before God." I woke up and thought: I better remember him . . . his face . . . So it stayed in my memory like it had been programmed into me. A year went by, two . . . I never came across him. Meanwhile, Lyosha had been courting me for a long time, he was a cobbler. He wanted me to marry him. I was honest with him, I explained that I didn't love him, that I loved and was waiting for the man I had seen in my dream. I was going to meet him one day, there was no other way, it just had to hap-pen—it was simply impossible that I wouldn't. Lyosha just laughed at me. And my mother and father laughed, too . . . They convinced me that I ought to get married and love would come later.

Why are you smiling? Everyone laughs at me, I know . . . If you live the way your heart tells you to, people will think you're crazy. You tell them the truth and people don't believe you, but when you lie, they eat up every word. One day, I was digging in my garden, and a guy I knew came walking by. I said, "Wow, guess what, Petya? You were in my dream the other night." "Oh no! Anything but that!" He ran from me like I was a leper. I'm not like everyone else, people are wary of me . . . I don't try to please anyone, I don't pay any attention to what I wear, I don't wear makeup. I don't know how to flirt. I only know how to talk to someone. For a while, I had wanted to go join a monastery, but then I read that you can lead a monastic life outside of one, at home. It can be how you live.

I got married. Dear Lord, what a good man Lyosha was! So strong, he could pick up a fire iron and bend it in half. How I loved him! We had a son. But after I gave birth, something happened to me, maybe it was the shock of giving birth . . . I became repelled by men. I already had a child, what else did I need my husband for? I could talk to him, wash his clothes, cook his food, make his bed, but I couldn't be with him . . . like you're supposed to be with a man . . . I'd scream! Go into hysterics! We suffered like that for two more years then, finally, I left him. I picked up my son and walked out the door. Only I had nowhere to go. By then, my mother and father had died. My sister is somewhere in Kamchatka . . . I had a friend named Yuri, he'd been in love with me since school but had never confessed it to me. I'm big and tall, and he's little, much shorter than me. He herded cows and read books. Knew all kinds of stories and was very fast at solving crosswords. I went to find him. "Yuri, you and I are friends. Can I stay with you? I'll live in your house, but please don't try to get close to me. Just please don't touch me." And he said, "Okay."

So that's how we lived . . . Except I kept thinking, "He loves me, he behaves himself so beautifully with me, doesn't demand anything, why should I keep tormenting him?" So he and I went down to the marriage registration bureau. He also wanted us to get married in a church, and that's when I confessed to him that I couldn't in a church . . . I told him about my dream, that I was waiting for my true love to come . . . Yuri laughed at me, too. "You're like a little child. You believe in miracles. No one is ever going to love you as much as I do." I had two sons by him. He and I lived together for fifteen years, and for all fifteen years, we walked around holding hands. Everyone marveled at us . . . So many people live without love or they only see love on TV. What is a person without love? Like a flower without water . . .

We have this custom . . . Girls and young women write letters to prisoners. All of my friends and I, we've done it since we were schoolgirls. I've written hundreds of letters to prisoners and received hundreds of replies. That time, it was the same as ever . . . The postman cried, "Lenka, there's a letter for you!" I ran over, grabbed the envelope. It had the prison stamp, a classified return address. And suddenly, my heart started pounding. All I'd seen was his handwriting, but I could already tell how dear he was to me. I became so agitated, I couldn't even read what it said. I'm a dreamer, but I have a grip on reality, too. It's not the first letter I've ever received from prison . . . The contents were simple: "Thank you for your kind words, sister . . . Of course, you are not my sister, but you are like a sister to me . . ." I replied that same evening: "Send me a photo, I want to see your face."

So he sent me his photo in his next letter. I looked at it—and he really was the one, the man from my dream—my true love! I'd waited for him for almost twenty years. I can't explain any of this to anyone, it's like a fairy tale. I told my husband immediately, "My love has arrived." He cried. He begged. Tried to talk me out of it. "We have three children. We need to raise them." And I wept, too: "Yuri, you're such a good man, I know the kids are in good hands with you." Our neighbors, my friends, my sister . . . everyone judged me. Now I'm alone.

At the station, when I was buying my ticket . . . there was a woman in line with me, and we struck up a conversation. She asked me, "Where are you going?" "To see my husband" (he wasn't my husband yet, but I knew that one day, he would be). "Where is he?" "In prison." "What did he do?" "Killed a man." "Oh, I see. Will he be in for a long time?" "Life." "Oh, dear . . . Poor woman . . ." "No need to pity me. I love him."

Everyone has to be loved by someone. Even if it's just one person. Love is . . . I can tell you what it is . . . He has tuberculosis, everyone in prison does. From the bad food, from melancholy. Somebody told me that what he needs is dog fat. I roamed the village, asking people. Managed to find some. But later, I learned that badger fat is actually better. So I bought some at the pharmacy—it cost me an arm and a leg! He needs cigarettes, canned meat . . . I got a job at the bread factory, they pay better than they did at the farm. The work is hard. Those old ovens get so hot, we have to take off our clothes and work in our bras and underwear. I haul fifty-kilo sacks of flour, pallets of bread weighing up to a hundred kilograms. I write to him every day.

AS TOLD BY IRINA VASILYEVA

So that's the kind of person she is. She's impulsive, determined . . . Something is percolating inside of her, she wants everything all at once. It's always extreme with her, overflowing, over the top. Her neighbors told me that one day, Tajik refugees were walking through the village. They had a lot of children, they were hungry, in tatters, so she gave them everything she had in her house: blankets, pillows, spoons . . . "We live too well while other people have nothing." Even when all they had in their hut was a table and chairs . . . You could say that they lived in poverty. They ate whatever they grew in their garden, potatoes, zucchini. They drank milk. "It's all right," she consoled her husband and children. "When the tourists go away in the autumn, they'll be sure to leave us something." Lots of Muscovites spend their summers out there, it's completely gorgeous—tons of artists, actors— all the deserted houses have been bought up. The villagers pick up every last scrap of whatever tourists leave behind, down to the plastic bags. The village is poor, full of old people, drunks . . . There was another story, too . . . Her friend had a baby, and they didn't have a refrigerator. So Lena gave them hers: "My children are grown up, and you have an infant." So that was that! Take it! She has nothing, and yet she still manages to have a lot to give. It's that Russian type . . . the kind of Russian person that Dostoevsky wrote about, who is as bountiful as the Russian land itself. Socialism didn't change him, and capitalism won't, either. Neither riches nor poverty . . . Three men sit in front of the store, they've managed to get their hands on a bottle to split. What are they drinking to? "Sevastopol is a Russian city! Sevastopol will be ours!" They're proud that a Russian can drink a liter of vodka without going cock-eyed. The only thing they remember about Stalin is that back when he was in charge, they were victors . . .

I wanted to film every moment . . . I had to hold myself back, I was afraid of getting sucked in so deep, I wouldn't be able to get back out . . . Every life story out there is like a Hollywood epic! A screenplay ready to go. For instance, her friend Ira . . . She's a former math teacher, she left the school because they barely paid her. She had three kids, they'd beg her: "Mama, let's go to the bread factory and sniff the bread." They'd go in the evenings, so no one would see them. Now Ira works at the bread factory like Lena, and she's glad that at least her kids can eat their fill of bread. They steal . . . Everyone out there steals, it's the only way they can survive. Their lives are ghastly, inhuman, but their souls are alive and well. You should hear what those women talk about—you wouldn't believe your ears! It's mostly love. You can survive without bread, but without love, you're dead . . . That's it . . . Ira read the letters from Lena's prisoner, and she got into it, too. She found herself a petty thief from the nearest prison. That one got out quick . . . Then the story developed according to the laws of tragedy . . . Vows of eternal devotion. A wedding. Soon enough, that Tolya, or maybe it's Tolyan, took up drinking. Ira already had three kids, and she had two more with him. He turns savage, chases her around the village, and then, in the morning, he sobers up and swears repentance. Ira—she's a beauty! And very bright. But that's how our men are, they always have to be kings of the jungle . . .

And now it's time to tell you about Yuri, Lena's husband. In the village, they call him the "reading cowherd," because he herds cows and reads. He has a lot of books by Russian philosophers. You can talk to him about Gorbachev or Nikolai Fedorov,* perestroika or human immortality . . . While the other men drink, he reads. Yuri is a dreamer . . . A watcher. Lena is proud of how quickly he can solve crossword puzzles. But Yuri is short . . . When he was little, he'd been growing very fast . . . Then, in sixth grade, his mother took him to Moscow. They gave him some sort of unfortunate injection into his spine, and he stopped growing completely—he's one meter fifty tall. He's a very handsome man, but next to his wife, he's tiny. In the film, we tried to make it so that the viewers wouldn't notice. I pleaded with the cameraman: "Just please think of something!" You can't let the viewer come to the simplistic conclusion that she left a little person for an attractive superman. Just like a woman would! And Yuri—he's a wise man, he knows that happiness comes in many forms. He's happy as long as Lena is near him no matter the circumstances, even if she's not his wife anymore and is just his friend. Who do you think she runs to with the letters? They read them together . . . It breaks his heart, but he listens. Love is patient . . . It does not envy . . . It doesn't complain, it thinks no evil . . . Of course, everything is not quite as beautiful as I'm telling you here . . . Their life is not all rosy. Yuri wanted to kill himself . . . To walk away wherever his feet would take him . . . There were real scenes between them, with flesh and blood. But he loves her . . .

YURI
———

On watching

I've always loved her, ever since we were in school. Then she got married and moved to the city. But I kept on loving her.

It was morning . . . My mother and I were sitting together drinking tea. I looked out the window and saw Lena coming with an infant in her arms. I told my mother, "See, Mama. My Lena has come. I think she has come to stay with me forever." Ever since that day, I've been cheerful and happy, I even got handsome . . . When we got married, I

* Nikolai Fedorov (1828–1906) was a thinker and philosopher nicknamed "the Russian Socrates." He was the founder of Russian cosmism, which combined elements of the Eastern and Western philosophic traditions, and was also influenced by Russian Orthodoxy.

was in seventh heaven. I kissed my wedding ring, which I managed to lose the very next day. It's amazing—it had fit my finger so well, but while I was working, I had to shake out my mitts, and when I was putting them back on, I noticed the ring was gone. I looked for it everywhere and couldn't find it. While Lena held on to her ring. Even though it was very loose on her finger, she never once dropped it until the day that she took it off . . .

We were always together, that's how we lived! We loved walking down to the spring together. I would carry the buckets, and she'd walk by my side: "Wanna listen to me prattle?" And she'd start telling me some story . . . Things weren't too good with money, but money is money and happiness is something else. As soon as spring was in the air, our house would fill with flowers. At first, it was just me who brought them, but then, when the children got a little older, we'd bring them to her together. We all loved our Mama. She was always cheerful. She played the piano—she'd gone to music school—and she sang. Made up fairy tales. For a little while, we had a TV, someone had given it to us as a present. The kids got sucked into the screen, it was impossible to tear them away, and it made them kind of aggressive, they started acting like strangers. So she went and poured water in it like it was an aquarium. The TV burnt out. "Children, go look at the flowers and trees instead. And talk to your mother and father." Our kids didn't even get upset because Mama had said so . . .

Our divorce . . . The judge asked us, "Why are you getting a divorce?" "We have differing views on life." "Does your husband drink? Does he beat you?" "He doesn't drink or beat me. And in general, my husband is an excellent man." "Then why are you getting divorced?" "I don't love him." "That's not a respectable reason." They gave us a year to reconsider, to let us think it over . . .

The men all laugh at me. They told me to kick her out, send her to a psych ward . . . What wasn't enough for her? You know, it happens to everyone. Melancholy, like the plague, descends on us all. You're riding the train, looking out of the window, and there it is: sadness. Everything's beautiful all around you, you can't look away, but the tears are running down your face and you don't know what to do with yourself. That Russian sorrow . . . Even someone who seems to have everything always wants more. That's how people live. They try to endure it. But she . . . She says, "Yuri, you're so wonderful, you're my best friend in the world. But even though he's spent half of his life in prison, I need him. I love him. If you don't let me go, I'll die. I'll do everything I'm supposed to do, but I'll be dead inside." Fate is a cruel joke . . .

She abandoned us and left. The children missed her, they cried for a long time, especially the little one. Our little Matvei . . . Everyone waited for Mama to come back, and they're still waiting. And I'm waiting, too. She wrote us, "Just don't sell the piano." It's the only expensive thing in the house, it'd been left to her by her parents. Her beloved piano . . . We'd sit around it in the evenings, and she would play for us. How could I ever sell it for money? She can't just throw me out of her life, leaving behind an empty space—it's simply impossible. We lived together for fifteen years, we have children together. She's a good woman, but she's not like anyone else. She's otherworldly . . . light . . . She's light . . . while I am an earthly person. I'm one of the people who live down here on Earth . . .

They wrote about us in the local paper. Then they had us come to Moscow to go on TV. Here's what it's like: They sit you down as though you're on a stage, and you tell your story in front of a live studio audience. Then there's a discussion. Everyone gave Lena a really hard time, especially the women, "You maniac! You nympho!" They were ready to stone her. "This is clearly pathological, it's just not right." The questions they had for me . . . It was knockout after knockout . . . "The dirty bitch who abandoned you and her children is not worth your little finger. You're a saint. On behalf of all Russian women, I bow at your feet . . ." I wanted to respond, but as soon as I opened my mouth, I'd be told: "We're sorry, your time is up." I ended up bursting into tears. Everyone thought it was because I was so hurt or angry. But actually, I was crying because they're all so smart, so educated, they live in the capital, and yet they don't understand a thing.

I will wait for her however long it takes. However long she wants . . . I can't imagine being with another woman. Although sometimes, it does occur to me . . .

FROM VILLAGE CONVERSATIONS

—Lena is an angel . . .

    —Wives like her used to get locked up in the pantry or whipped . . .

    —It would have been one thing if she had left him for a rich man. The rich lead more interesting lives. But what kind of relationship can she have with a criminal? And one behind bars for life, at that. Two visits a year, and that's it. That's their whole relationship.

—She's a romantic. Let her have her fun.

—Pitying the unfortunate is in our blood. Murderers and alcoholics. Some men can kill but still have the eyes of a baby. You feel sorry for them.

—I don't believe men at all anymore, and especially not prisoners. They're just bored in jail. That's their entertainment. They write the same thing to everyone: My white-winged swan, I dream of you, the light of my life . . . Some idiot falls for it and leaps at the chance to save him: Hauls packages for him in unliftable suitcases, sends him money. Waits. He gets out of jail, comes to her house—has a bite, takes a sip, gets her money, and instantly vanishes into thin air. Ciao! Bye-bye!

—It's such a powerful love, though! Girls, it's just like the movies!

—She left her good, kind husband for a murderer. Plus, her kids . . . three little boys . . . Just buying the ticket—she has to travel to the ends of the Earth to see him—where does she get the money? She's always taking the bread out of her children's mouths. She'll go to the store and face a dilemma: Should she buy them a roll or no?

—A wife must deeply respect her husband* . . . They're walking together in Christ. Otherwise, what's the point? Without that common purpose, why bother?

—Without me, the Lord says, you cannot create. But she's trying to create things out of her imagination. It's pure pride. Where there's no submission, there is always another force present. An evil spirit is involved.

—She ought to go to the monastery and seek a path to salvation. People save themselves through suffering. Even suffering has to be sought out . . .

AS TOLD BY IRINA VASILYEVA

I asked her myself: "Lena, do you understand that you're only going to see him twice a year?" "So what? That's enough for me. I'll be with him in my thoughts. In my feelings."

To see him, she has to travel to the far north. To Fire Island, Og-

---

* Ephesians 5:33.

nenny Ostrov.* In the fourteenth century, the disciples of Sergius of Radonezh journeyed through this region mastering the forests of the North. One day, as they broke through a thicket, they saw a lake and in the middle of the lake, there were tongues of fire. This was the spirit revealing itself to them. So they filled their boats with dirt and rowed out to the middle of the lake . . . They created an island, and on that island they built a monastery with walls a meter and a half thick. Today, this ancient monastery serves as a prison for the most violent offenders. It's death row. On the door of each cell, they hang a sign detailing the atrocities committed by the inmate: For stabbing Anya, six years . . . For murdering Nastya, twelve years . . . You read them and are seized with horror, but then you go into the cell and meet a more or less normal person. He asks for a cigarette, you give it to him. "What's it like out there? In here, we don't even know what the weather is." They live in a rock. Surrounded by nothing but forests and swamps. No one has ever tried to escape . . .

The first time Lena went, she didn't even consider the possibility that they might not let her in to see him. She knocked on the window where they issue passes, and no one even bothered listening to her: "That's the head warden over there. Go talk to him." She threw herself on the warden, "Please let me see him." "Who?" "Volodya Podbutsky." "Don't you know that our prison houses gravely dangerous criminals? They're on the strictest penal regime: two three-day visits a year, plus three short visits for two hours each. Only their closest relatives are allowed to see them—their mothers, their wives, their sisters. What's your relation to him?" "I love him." That was when the warden realized that he had a crazy person on his hands. He tried to get away, but she held on to him by a button: "You have to understand, I love him." "You're a complete stranger to him." "Then just let me take a peek at him." "What, you've never even seen him before?" Now, everyone thought it was funny, the guards had all come around to get a better look at the little fool. Ha ha . . . And there she goes telling them all about her dream, which she had when she was eighteen, about her husband and three kids and how her whole life, she's really only loved this one person. Her sincerity and purity can break down all walls. When they meet her, people start feeling like there's something off about their perfectly proper lives—they feel like they're coarse, not as sensitive as they'd thought they were. The warden was no spring

---

* A small island in Lake Novozero, in the region of Vologda.

chicken . . . In his line of work, he'd seen everything . . . He put himself in her shoes: "Since you've come such a long way, I'll give you six hours with him, but there will be a guard in there with you the whole time." "Make it two guards for all I care! I'm not going to see anybody but him . . ."

Everything that's extreme and unbounded about her, she dumped onto that Volodya. "Do you understand how happy I am . . . I've waited for you my whole life, and now, we're finally together." Naturally, he wasn't prepared for any of it. Some Baptist had already been visiting him, he was in a relationship with her. That story made sense to everyone—she was your typical young woman with a sad life story. She needed a man, a stamp in her passport that said she was married. But here, it was such an outpouring, this powerful blast of feeling! When someone wants you that bad, you're bound to get scared. His mind was reeling . . . "I'm begging you," Lena told him. "Let's get married so that they'll let me visit you and I can come to see you. That's all I ask." "Aren't you married already?" "I'll get a divorce. You're the only man I love." She'd brought a bagful of his letters with her, covered in drawings of flowers and maple pods. She couldn't bear to be apart from them for even a minute. They were the apogee of happiness for her: Her whole life, she'd sought out the absolute, and the absolute can only exist in written form, it can only be fully realized on paper. On Earth, in bed, it doesn't exist. You won't find the absolute here. Everything that involves other people—family, children—is a compromise . . .

It was as though someone had led her there . . . What force was this? What was the true nature of her dream?

. . . We also visited Ognenny Ostrov. It took a lot of paperwork and permits with seals. Phone calls. But we made it there . . . At first, Volodya was very hostile with us: "Why are you turning this into a spectacle?" For years, he'd been completely alone, he wasn't used to people anymore. He'd grown suspicious, he didn't trust anyone. It was good that Lena had come with us, she'd take him by the hand, "My Volodya." And he'd go all soft. Together, we convinced him to participate, or maybe he figured it out for himself, he's a smart guy: After twenty-five years, in special situations, prisoners may be eligible for reprieves, and if we shot a movie and he became a local celebrity, it might help him later on . . . All of the men out there want to live . . . They don't like to talk about death . . .

That's what we started with . . .

VOLODYA

On God

I was in solitary awaiting execution. It gave me a lot of time to think . . . But who's going to help you when you're trapped behind four walls? Time didn't exist, it was like an abstraction. I experienced such a deep sense of emptiness . . . One day, I burst out: "If you exist, God, please help me! Do not abandon me! I'm not asking for a miracle, just help me make sense of what has happened to me." I fell on my knees and prayed. The Lord does not make those who turn to Him wait too long . . .

If you read through my case file, you'll learn that I killed a man. I was eighteen. I had just graduated from high school, I wrote poems. I wanted to go to Moscow to study. To study to become a poet. I lived with my Mama, it was just the two of us. We had no money, I needed to make some in order to pay for tuition. So I got a job at a mechanic's. In the evenings, there'd be dances in the village . . . I fell in love with this beautiful girl. I was crazy for her. One night, we were coming home from a dance . . . it was winter, there was snow . . . The trees were lit up in people's windows, New Year's was just around the corner. I wasn't drunk. We were walking along, talking. Then she asked me: "So do you really love me?" "I love you more than life itself." "What would you be willing to do for me?" "I would kill myself." "Killing yourself—that's easy. But would you be willing to kill the first person we come across?" She might have been joking . . . or maybe, I'd found myself a real shrew . . . I don't remember her anymore, I've forgotten her face, and she's never once written to me the whole time I've been in prison. "Can you kill someone for me?" She said that and burst out laughing. But I'm a real man—a hero! I needed to prove my love. So I pulled a post out of the nearest fence . . . It was night. Dark. I stood there and waited. And she stood next to me, waiting too. For a long time, there was no one, and then finally, we saw someone coming toward us. I hit him over the head as hard as I could. Bam! I hit him once, then again . . . He fell. I finished him off as he lay on the ground. With that fencepost. It turned out that it had been our teacher . . .

Initially, I was sentenced to death by firing squad, but then, six months later, they commuted all death sentences to life in prison. My mother disowned me. My sister used to write to me, but then she stopped. I've been alone for a long time . . . locked up in this cell for the past seventeen years. Seventeen years! If you take a tree or an animal, they don't know a thing about time. God does the thinking for them. That's how I am, too . . . I sleep, I eat, they let us out into the yard . . . You only see the sky through bars. In my cell, I have a bed, a stool, a mug, and a spoon . . . Other people live off their memories, but what do I have to remember? Nothing ever happened to me, I never got the chance to live. When I look back, all I see is darkness, and sometimes, a little lamp burning. Most often, I see Mama . . . Standing by the stove, or in front of our kitchen window. Beyond that, it's all darkness . . .

I started reading the Bible and couldn't tear myself away . . . It made me tremble with excitement. I talked to Him: "Why have You punished me?" People thank the Lord for their joy, but when there's trouble, they wail, "What have I done to deserve this?" Instead of trying to understand the hardship they've been sent. Surrendering their lives to Him . . .

Then, suddenly, Lena appeared . . . She showed up and told me, "I love you." An entire world opened up before me . . . I could imagine anything I wanted for myself . . . A family, kids. Out from the darkest night, I found myself in the brightest day . . . I was surrounded by light . . . I admit that the situation is crazy: She has a husband, three kids, and then she goes and declares her love to another man, writes him letters. If I were in her husband's place—well, I know what I would do! "Who do you think you are? Some kind of saint?" "You can't have love without self-sacrifice. What kind of love would that be?" I didn't know that women like her existed. How could I have learned that in prison? I'd thought that women were either decent or bitches and that was it. Then suddenly she appears, the kind of woman you lose sleep over . . . She'll come here, she'll laugh and cry. And she's always beautiful.

Soon, we were legally married. Then we decided to have a real wedding . . . The prison has a prayer room. What if a guardian angel happened to glance in our direction?

Before I met Lena, I hated all women, I thought that love was nothing but hormones. Desires of the flesh . . . But she's not afraid of that word, she uses it all the time, "I love you! I love you!" When she gets like that, I just sit there, unable to move. All of this—how do I put it? I'm not accustomed to happiness. Sometimes, I believe her. I want to believe that it's true, that someone could love me, that the only difference between me and everyone else is the fact that they believe that they're good. But people don't actually know themselves, and if they found out what they were really like, they'd be terrified. Do you think I ever considered myself capable of . . . that a monster could leap out of me at any moment . . . Not in a million years! I thought I was a good person. Somewhere in Mama's house, you can find the notebooks full of my poems—that is, if she hasn't burned them. But other times, I'll get scared . . . I've been alone for too long, I'm stuck in this state. Normal life seems very far away. I've grown mean and feral . . . What am I afraid of? I'm scared that our story is just a movie, and a movie is something that I don't need. You could say that I've only now started to live . . . We wanted to have a child, she got pregnant. But then she had a miscarriage. The Lord reminded me of my sins . . .

It's scary . . . So scary that sometimes, I want to kill myself, or . . . "I'm afraid of you," she says. But she doesn't leave . . . There's a film for you! There you go . . .

FROM PRISON CONVERSATIONS

—It's madness! Madness! The girl ought to see a shrink . . .

—I've only ever read about women like her in books, the wives of the Decembrists . . . Pure literature! In real life . . . Lena is the only one I've ever encountered. Of course, I didn't believe it at first: "Maybe she's just crazy?" But then something inside me flipped . . . People thought Jesus was crazy, too. Why, she's more sane than anyone!

—One night, I couldn't sleep a wink, thinking about her. I remembered I too had once known a woman who loved me madly . . .

—This is her cross. She picked it up and bears it. A true Russian woman!

—I know that Volodya—the groom! He's the same kind of bastard as I am. I'm afraid for her. She's not the kind of person to get married and then drop it, she will do her best to be his wife. But what can he provide for her? We don't have the opportunity to give anyone anything. "And in my eyes the boys dripping in blood."* The only thing we can do is not take from people, not accept any sacrifices made in our

---

* A quotation from Alexander Pushkin's *Boris Godunov,* referring to the protagonist's lingering guilt after ordering the murder of his young rivals to the throne.

names. Our whole life's` purpose now is not to take anything. When you take things, it's like you're robbing someone all over again . . .

—But she's a happy person. And she's not afraid of being happy . . .

—In the Bible . . . God isn't called goodness or justice . . . God is love . . .

—Even the chaplain . . . He comes here and reaches his hand through the bars, but then he withdraws it as quickly as possible. He doesn't notice, but I do. I understand, there's blood on my hands . . . But she decided to marry a murderer, entrust herself to him, she wants to share everything with him. Now, every one of us thinks, "That means there might still be some hope for me." It would be so much harder for me in here if I had never heard of her.

—What does the future hold for them? I wouldn't pay a fortune teller a single kopeck to find out . . .

—You boneheads! Do you really believe in miracles? Life is no white ship with snow-white sails. It's all a pile of chocolate-covered shit.

—The thing she's looking for, what she actually needs, is not something anyone on Earth could ever give her—only God.

They got married in the prison. Everything was just as Lena had imagined: sparkling candles, gold rings . . . The church choir sang, "Rejoice, O Isaiah . . ."

The Priest: "Do you, Vladimir, of your free and good will and firm resolve take this Yelena, who you see before you, to be your wife?"

The Groom: "I do, Honest Father."

The Priest: "Did you promise to marry any other?"

The Groom: "I did not, Honest Father."

The Priest: "Do you, Yelena, of your free and good will and firm resolve take this Vladimir, who you see before you, to be your husband?"

The Bride: "I do, Honest Father."

The Priest: "Did you promise to marry any other?"

The Bride: "I did not, Honest Father."

"Lord, have mercy on them . . ."

AS TOLD BY FILMMAKER IRINA VASILYEVA

A year later, Irina Vasilyeva and I met again.

They played our film on TV . . . We received letters from viewers. At first, I was excited but . . . something is wrong with the world we live in. It's like that old joke: Mankind is good, but the people are mean. Some stick out: "I'm for the death penalty and recycling human waste," "Brutes like your superman murderer ought to be publicly drawn and quartered on Red Square. With breaks for Snickers ads," "They should be killed for their organs . . . used as human subjects for testing out new drugs and chemicals . . ." If you look in Dal's dictionary, you will find that the word for goodness comes from the verb that means to live in plenty, with many goods . . . It's when your life has dignity and stability . . . We don't have any of those things here. Evil doesn't come from God. In the words of St. Anthony, "God is not responsible for evil. He gave man the gift of reason, the ability to know the difference between good and evil . . ." But there were others, too . . . Beautiful letters like this one: "After watching your film, I started believing in love. I think God exists, after all . . ."

A document is an intrigue and a trap . . . For me, the documentary genre has one, I would call it, birth defect: The film is finished, but life goes on. My protagonists aren't fictional, they're real, living people; they aren't dependent on me, my will, ideas, or my professionalism. My presence in their lives is incidental and temporary. I'm not as free as they are. If I could, I would devote my entire life to filming a single person. Or just one family, day in, day out. Here they are walking along, holding their child's hand . . . going to the dacha . . . Drinking tea and talking about one thing one day, and something else the next . . . They've had an argument . . . bought some newspapers . . . the car broke down . . . summer is over . . . someone is crying . . . We live in the midst of all this, but so much happens without us. In spite of us. To capture a moment or observe some period of time is simply not enough for me. It's not enough! I can't tear myself away . . . I don't know how to . . . I become friends with the people I film, I write to them, I call them. We see each other. For a long time, I'll "shoot additional material," watching new scenes unfold before my eyes. I have dozens of "films" of this extra footage.

One of them is about Yelena Razduyeva. There's a whole notebook full of material. Something like a script for a movie that will never be made . . .

". . . She suffers from what she does, but she can't help herself."

". . . Several years went by before she decided to read the materials of his case. But it didn't frighten her: 'This doesn't change anything, I love him anyway. Now, I'm his wife before God. He killed someone, but it's because I wasn't with him. I need to take him by the hand and lead him out of there . . . ' "

". . . On Ognenny Ostorov, there's a former district prosecutor who, along with his brother, hacked two women to death with an axe, an accountant and a cashier. He's writing his memoirs. He doesn't even go out for walks, he can't spare the time. They ended up making out with a pretty paltry sum of money. So what did they do it for? He himself doesn't know . . . Then there's the locksmith who killed his wife and two kids. Before, he'd never held anything but a wrench in his hands, now the whole jail is covered in his paintings. Each one of them is haunted by his own demons, all of them want to unload their feelings. Murder is just as mysterious to murderers as it is to their victims . . ."

". . . Listen to the conversations they have . . . 'Do you think there's a God?' 'If He exists, then death is not the end. I don't want Him to exist.' "

". . . So is it love? Volodya is tall and handsome, and Yuri is a dwarf . . . She even told me that as a man, Yuri satisfies her more . . . Only she has to . . . her husband is the way he is, a tragedy befell him. She has to hold his hand . . ."

". . . At first, she lived in the country with her kids and visited him twice a year. But then he started demanding that she give it all up and go live near him. 'You're cheating on me, I can feel it, you're betraying me.' 'Volodya, how can I leave my kids? Matvei is very little, he physically still needs me.' 'You're a Christian . . . you must be submissive and obey your husband.' She wears a black kerchief and lives by the prison. There's no work out there, but the priest from the local church took her in. She cleans the church. 'And Volodya is nearby . . . I can feel it, I can feel his presence . . . "Don't worry," I write him, "I'm right here with you . . ." ' She's been writing to him every day for seven years now."

". . . As soon as they got married, Volodya started demanding that she write to all of the authorities saying that he's the father of multiple children and needs to get out to take care of his kids. That's his chance.

But Lena is pure . . . She sits down to write those letters and can't. 'He killed someone. There is no greater sin.' He throws insane fits, saying he needs a different woman. One who is richer, who has more connections. He's fed up with that holy woman of his . . ."

". . . He was locked up when he was eighteen . . . This was still during Soviet times, he only ever knew Soviet life. Soviet people. Socialism. He has no idea what the country he's living in is actually like. If he gets out, how is he going to deal with our new way of life? How will it hit him—he has no profession, his relatives have all turned their backs on him. And he's an angry guy. One time in jail, he got in a fight with one of his fellow inmates and nearly ripped the guy's throat out. Lena knows that she'd have to take him somewhere far away from people. She dreams of him becoming a logger. Living in the forest. As she puts it, among the trees and wordless beasts . . ."

". . . More than once, she's told me, 'His eyes got so cold, it was like they were empty. One day, he's going to kill me. I know what his eyes will be like when he's killing me.' And yet she's drawn to him, that abyss sucks her in. Why? Haven't I observed something similar in myself? The darkness pulls you in . . ."

". . . The last time we saw each other, she said, 'I don't want to live! I can't take it anymore!' It seemed like she was in a coma, neither dead nor alive . . ."

We decided to go see Lena together. But suddenly, she'd disappeared. She didn't respond to anything. There were rumors that she'd moved to a remote skete* and was living among drug addicts and people with AIDS . . . Many of those who live there take vows of silence.

---

* A Russian Orthodox hermit community.

ON COURAGE AND WHAT
COMES AFTER

◆

Tanya Kuleshova,
student, 21

A CHRONICLE OF EVENTS

On December 19, there was a presidential election in Belarus. No one was expecting a fair election, everyone knew the results ahead of time: President Lukashenko, who had run the country for the past sixteen years, would win again. They laugh at him in the global press, call him the potato dictator, but the reality is that he's taken his own people hostage. Europe's last dictator . . . He doesn't hide his sympathies for Hitler, who wasn't taken seriously himself for a long time; people called him "the little corporal" or "the Bohemian corporal."

That evening, tens of thousands of people went out onto October Square, the main square in Minsk, to protest the fraudulent election. Demonstrators demanded the annulment of the announced results, and that new elections be held without Lukashenko as a candidate. This peaceful protest was brutally suppressed by special operations forces and riot police. The forests surrounding the capital were filled with troops prepared for battle . . .

A total of seven hundred demonstrators were arrested—including seven former presidential candidates who technically still had the right to immunity . . .

Ever since the election, the Belarusian secret police have been working around the clock. Political repressions have swept the nation: arrests, interrogations, searches. They come to people's apartments, the editorial offices of opposition news outlets, human rights organizations; they confiscate computers and other office equipment. Many of the people being held at the jail on Okrestino Street or sitting in solitary KGB cells are facing four to fifteen years in prison for "organizing mass disorder" or "attempting to overthrow the government," which is what today's Belarusian government calls participating in a peaceful demonstration. Fearing persecution and the growing strength of the dictatorship, hundreds of people are fleeing the country . . .

From newspaper articles published between December 2010 and March 2011

A CHRONICLE OF FEELINGS

"We went for fun, it wasn't serious."

I'm not going to tell you my last name. I'm using my grandmother's . . . I'm afraid, of course . . . Everyone expects to see heroes, but I'm no hero. I was never prepared to become one. In prison, all I thought about was my mother, about how she has a bad heart. What's going to happen to her? Even if we win and they write about it in the history books, what about the tears of our loved ones? Their suffering? An idea is an incredibly powerful thing—it's terrifying because its power is not material, you can't measure it. There's no measurement . . . It's of a different kind of essence . . . It's capable of making something more important to you than your own mother. Forcing you to choose. But you're not ready . . . I now know what it means to walk into your room after the KGB has gone through your things, your books . . . After they've read your diary . . . [*She is silent.*] I was on my way to meet you when my mother called. I told her that I was meeting with a famous writer, and she broke down in tears. "Don't say anything. Don't tell any stories." Only strangers support me—my relatives, the people closest to me, do not. But they do love me . . .

Before the protest . . . we were hanging out at the dormitory debating. About life in general and also the topic of the day: Who's going to the protest and who isn't. You want me to recall what we talked about, right? It went something like this . . .

". . . Are you going to go?"

". . . No. They'll kick me out of university and force me to join the army. Have me running around with a machine gun."

". . . If I get kicked out, my father will make me get married immediately."

". . . Enough talk, it's time to do something. If everyone is too afraid . . ."

". . . You want me to turn into Che Guevara?" (Those were the words of my ex-boyfriend. More about him later.)

". . . It's a breath of freedom . . ."

". . . I'm going because I'm sick of living under a dictatorship. They consider us mindless beasts."

". . . I for one am no hero. I want to finish school, read books."

". . . You know what they say about *sovoks:* they're as mean as dogs and silent as fish."

". . . I'm the little man, I have no power over anything. I never vote."

". . . Well, I'm a revolutionary . . . I have to go . . . Revolution is cool!"

". . . So what are your revolutionary ideals? You think that the bright new future is capitalism? Glory to the Latin American revolution!"

". . . When I was sixteen, I was really hard on my parents, they were always afraid of something because of my father's career. I thought they were dumb. We knew what's up. We'll be on the streets! We'll tell them what we really think! Now I'm just like them, a conformist. A real conformist. According to Darwin's theory, it's not the strongest who survive, but those who are the best adapted to their environment. Average people are the ones who survive and carry on the human race."

". . . Going means being a fool, and not going is even worse."

". . . Who told you sheep that revolution means progress? I'm for evolution."

". . . Whites, Reds . . . I don't give a shit about any of it!"

". . . I'm a revolutionary . . ."

". . . It's hopeless! The war machines will show up full of boys in uniform, you'll get hit over the head with a club, and that's how the story ends. The authorities need to maintain their iron grip."

". . . Go fuck yourself, Comrade Mauser.* I never promised anyone

---

* Allusion to a famous revolutionary poem by Mayakovsky whose first stanza ends with the line, "It is your turn to speak, Comrade Mauser."

I'd be a revolutionary. I want to graduate from university and start my business."

". . . Mind blown!"

". . . Fear is an illness . . ."

We went for fun, it wasn't serious. We were laughing, singing. All of us were really into each other that day, everyone was so excited. Some people walked with posters, others with guitars. Our other friends would call us and tell us what they were saying online, keeping us in the loop . . . That's how we learned that the courtyards downtown were filled with military vehicles, soldiers, and police. That troops were surrounding the city . . . We believed it, but at the same time, we didn't. Our mood changed from moment to moment, but there was no fear. Fear had completely evaporated. First of all, look at how many people came—there were tens of thousands! All kinds of people. There had never been so many of us before. I can't remember ever seeing that many people . . . And second of all, we were at home. This was our city. Our country. Our rights are clearly laid out in the constitution: freedom of assembly, protests, demonstrations, rallies . . . freedom of speech . . . There are laws! We're the first generation that's never been scared. Never been flogged. Never been shot at. So what if they put us in jail for fifteen days? That's nothing! Something to write about in your blog. We can't let the authorities believe we're just a flock of sheep that blindly follows the shepherd! That we have TVs for brains. Just in case, I had a mug with me, because I'd heard that in jail there's only one mug for every ten people. I'd also brought an extra warm sweater and two apples. Walking along, we took lots of pictures, we wanted to remember that day. We were wearing Christmas masks and had these funny light-up bunny ears . . . Toys made in China. Christmas was right around the corner, it was snowing . . . What a beautiful night! I didn't see a single drunk person. If anyone spotted a can of beer, it was immediately taken away and poured out. We noticed this guy on the roof of a building: "Check it out, a sniper! A sniper!" That really got us going. We waved to him: "Come down! Jump!" It was so cool. Before, I'd been apathetic about politics, I never thought that there could be feelings like this and that I could experience them. The only thing that comes close is music. Music is everything, it's irreplaceable. But this was incredible. There was a woman walking next to me—why didn't I ask her last name? You could have written about her. I was busy with other things—having fun, it was all so new to me. This woman was marching with her son who looked to be about twelve. A school kid. A police colonel noticed her and started yelling at her through his megaphone, practically swearing, calling her a bad mother. Saying she's crazy. And everyone started applauding her and her son. It happened spontaneously, no one planned it. That's so important to me . . . so important to know about . . . because we're always embarrassed. The Ukrainians had the Orange Revolution, the Georgians had the Rose Revolution. But people laugh at us, calling Minsk a communist capital, the last dictatorship in Europe. Now I can at least be proud of the fact that we went out there. We hadn't been too afraid. That's what's most important . . . the most important thing . . .

We stood there, us and them. Face to face. One kind of people pitted against the other. It was a strange sight . . . One side had posters and portraits, and the other side was in full military regalia, with shields and clubs. These burly guys! Broad-shouldered hunks! Were they really about to start beating us? Beating me? They were my age, my peers, my admirers. Literally! There were boys I knew from my village among them, of course they were there. A lot of people from our village who went to Minsk ended up in the police, Kolka Latushka, Alik Kaznacheyev . . . regular guys. No different from us, except that they were in uniform. Were they really going to advance on us? It was hard to believe, impossible . . . We laughed and teased them. Tried to provoke them: "Are you boys really about to fight the people?" As the snow kept falling and falling. Then suddenly, it was kind of like a parade . . . There was an order: "Disperse the crowd! Hold ranks!" My mind couldn't adjust to the reality, not right away . . . It seemed impossible . . . "Disperse the crowd . . ." For a few moments, everything went totally silent. And then, the pounding shields . . . the rhythmic banging of the shields . . . They moved on us . . . advancing in ranks, banging their clubs against their shields like hunters chasing a wild animal. Their prey. They kept coming, and coming, and coming. I've never seen that many soldiers in my whole life, only on TV. Later, the boys in my village told me that they teach them that "the worst that can happen is if you start seeing the demonstrators as human beings." They train them like dogs. [*She is silent.*] Screaming, sobbing . . . People crying, "They're beating me! They're beating me!" I saw them beat people. And I must say it looked like they were enjoying it. Like they were doing it with pleasure. Great pleasure. I will always remember this: They took great pleasure in beating people . . . Like it was just another training exercise . . . A girl squealed, "What do you think you're doing, you animal!" She had this really high voice. It broke off. I was so terrified, I had to close my eyes for a moment. In my white coat and white hat, I stood rooted to the spot. All in white.

"Face down in the snow, bitch!"

A police van is an amazing machine. That was the first time I'd ever seen one. It's this special vehicle for transporting the arrested. It's all covered in steel. "Face down in the snow, bitch! One move and I'll kill you!" I lay there on the asphalt . . . I wasn't alone, all of my friends were down there with me . . . My mind went blank . . . no thoughts . . . The only real sensation was the cold. Kicking and prodding us with their clubs, they pulled us to our feet and shoved us into the police van. The guys got the worst of it, they'd go for their crotches: "Get his balls, get his balls! Hit him in the mouth!" "Break his bones!" "Beat the shit out of them!" They beat us, philosophizing along the way: "Fuck your revolution!" "How many dollars did you sell out your Motherland for, you piece of shit?" According to those in the know, a police van is two by five meters, intended for twenty people maximum. But they crammed more than fifty of us into a single vehicle. Asthmatics and anyone with a heart condition, hold on tight! "No looking out the window! Heads down!" Profanities, obscenities . . . Because of us "half-baked dipshits" that "sold out to the Yankees," they missed the football match that day. They'd kept them locked in covered trucks all day. Under tarps. They'd had to piss in plastic bags and condoms. When they were finally released, they came out hungry and full of rage. Maybe deep down they weren't such bad people, but they did the work of executioners. Really, they looked like normal guys. Minor cogs in a big machine. They're not the ones who decide whether or not to beat us, they just do the beating . . . First they beat us and then they think about what they've done, or maybe they don't. [*She is silent.*] We drove around for a really long time, going forward then turning around and going back. Where were they taking us? We were completely in the dark. When they opened the doors and we asked, "Where are you taking us?" they said, "Kuropaty." A mass grave for the victims of Stalin's repressions. Just a little bit of sadistic humor. They drove us around the city for a long time because the jails were all chock full. We ended up spending the night in the police van. It was twenty degrees below zero and there we were, locked in a metal box. [*She is silent.*] I should hate them. But I don't want to hate anyone. I'm not ready for that.

The guard changed several times that night. I don't remember their faces, they all look the same in uniform. Except this one guy . . . Even now, I would recognize him if I saw him on the street—I'd know him by his eyes. He wasn't young or old, just a regular man, nothing special. But what was he doing? He'd open the doors of the police van and leave them open for long stretches because he liked it when we'd all start shivering. Everyone was just in their jackets, cheap boots, fake fur. He'd watch us and smile. He wasn't acting on orders, this was his own free will. On his own personal initiative. But another cop snuck me a Snickers. "Take it. What the hell were you thinking going out on the square?" They say that in order to understand this, you have to read Solzhenitsyn. When I was in school, I took *The Gulag Archipelago* out from the library, but I couldn't get into it. It was this fat, boring book. I read about fifty pages and stopped . . . It seemed as distant from my reality as the Trojan War. Stalin was a played-out topic. My friends and I weren't all that interested in him . . .

The first thing that happens to you in jail . . . They dump your purse out on the table. What does it feel like? It's as though they're undressing you . . . Then they literally undress you. "Take off your underwear. Spread your legs shoulder width. Squat." What were they looking for in my anus? They treated us like we were prisoners. "Face to the wall! Eyes down at the floor!" They kept ordering us to look at the floor. They really hated it when you looked them in the eye: "Face to the wall! I said face to the wall!" We went everywhere in formation, they even took us to the bathroom like that: "Form a column with the backs of your heads to each other." In order to tolerate it, I created a barrier—this is us and that is them. Interrogation, the detective, the evidence . . . During interrogation: "You have to write, 'I fully acknowledge my guilt.'" "But what am I guilty of?" "What don't you understand? You participated in a mass riot . . ." "It was a peaceful protest." They started threatening me: They'd expel me from the university, fire my mother from her job. How could she keep being a teacher when she had a daughter like me? Mama! The whole time, the only thing I thought about was my mother . . . They noticed, so every interrogation began with the words, "Your mother is crying," "Your mother is in the hospital." And then, again: "Give us names . . . Who was with you? Who was handing out flyers? Sign this . . . Name names . . ." They promised that no one would ever know what I'd said and that they'd let me go home right away. I had to make a choice . . . "I'm not signing anything." But at night, I would cry. Mama was in the hospital . . . [*She is silent.*] It's easy to become a traitor out of love for your mother . . . I don't know if I could have endured another month in there. They'd laugh at me: "What's it going to be, Zoya Kosmo-demyanskaya?" These young, cheerful guys. [*She is silent.*] I was scared . . . We all went to the same stores, sat in the same cafés, rode the Metro together. We were together everywhere. In normal everyday life, there's no clear boundary between us and them. What makes them different? [*Silence.*] I used to live in a good, kind world, but it no longer exists, and it never will ever again.

I ended up spending a month in a jail . . . That entire time, I never once looked in a mirror. I'd had a small one with me in my purse, but after they searched me, a lot of things went missing. My wallet and cash, too. I was always thirsty. Unbearably thirsty! They only ever gave us something to drink with our meals, the rest of the time it was: "There's water in the toilet." And laughter. While they drank their Fantas. I thought that I would never get enough to drink, that when I got out I would buy a whole refrigerator full of mineral water. All of us stank . . . There was nowhere to wash ourselves . . . Someone had a tiny bottle of perfume and we would pass it around, sniffing it. While somewhere far away, our friends were writing papers, sitting in the library. Taking exams. For some reason, I kept remembering these little things . . . A new dress I hadn't had a chance to wear . . . [*She laughs.*] I learned that happiness can come from something as small as a bit of sugar or a piece of soap. In a cell intended for five people—thirty-two square meters—there were seventeen of us. You had to learn how to fit your entire life into two square meters. It was especially hard at night, there was no air to breathe, it was stifling. We wouldn't get to sleep for a long time. We'd stay up talking. The first few days, we discussed politics, but after that, we only ever talked about love.

CONVERSATIONS IN A JAIL CELL

"You don't want to believe that what they do is of their own free will."

". . . It's always the same scenario . . . Things keep going in circles. The people are a herd. A herd of antelopes. And the government is a lioness. The lioness picks out a victim from the herd and kills it. The rest keep chewing their cud, watching the lioness out of the corner of their eyes as she's picking out her next victim. Once she's bagged her prey, they all sigh in relief: 'It wasn't me! It wasn't me! I can keep living . . .' "

". . . I loved learning about the Revolution at the museum . . . I have a romantic bent. I made believe that I was in that fairy tale. No one had called on me to go, I went to the square on my own. I wanted to see for myself how people actually brought about revolution. For that, I got clubbed in the head and the kidneys. It was mostly young people who came out, they call it a "children's revolution." That's what they're saying now. Our parents stayed home. They sat in their kitchens talking about how we'd gone out there. Worrying. They were scared, but we have no memories of the Soviet era. We've only read about the Communists in books, we didn't have that fear. Minsk has a population of two million, and how many of us were out there? Thirty thousand, tops . . . But even more people were watching us: on their balconies, honking their horns, bolstering us. 'Come on, guys, you can do it! Go on!' There are always more people sitting in front of their TVs and drinking beer. That's how the majority of people are . . . And as long as it's only us educated romantics out in the streets, it's not a real revolution . . ."

". . . Do you really think the only thing holding all this together is fear? The police with their clubs? You're wrong. The victim and the executioner have an arrangement. That's something left over from communist times—there's a silent pact. A contract. The great unspoken agreement. The people understand everything, but they keep quiet. In exchange, they want decent salaries, the ability to buy at least a used Audi, to go on vacation to Turkey. Try talking to them about democracy or human rights—it's like you're speaking ancient Greek! Those who lived through Soviet times instantly start saying things like, 'Our children thought that bananas grew in Moscow. Take a look around . . . There's one hundred different kinds of salami! What more freedom do we need?' Even today, many people want to go back to the Soviet Union, except with tons of salami."

". . . I ended up in here by accident . . . I went to the square with my friends just for kicks, I was only curious about what it would be like in the middle of all those posters and balloons. To be perfectly honest . . . I had a crush on one of the guys I went with. In reality, I'm nothing but an indifferent spectator. I stopped thinking about politics a long time ago. I'm so damn sick of that battle between good and evil . . ."

". . . They drove us out to some kind of barracks. We spent the night on our feet facing the wall. In the morning: 'Get on your knees!' We got on our knees. 'Get up! Hands up!' They told us to put our hands on our heads and do one hundred squats. Then it was stand on one leg . . . What were they doing this for? Why? Ask them—they won't be able to tell you. Someone gave them permission . . . it made them feel powerful . . . Some girls got nauseated and fainted. The first time I got called in for an interrogation, I laughed in the detective's face until he finally snapped, 'Listen up, little girl, I'm going to fuck you in every hole, then throw you in a cell with real criminals.' I've never read Solzhenitsyn and I don't think the detective had, either. But we all knew the score anyway . . ."

". . . My interrogator was an educated man, he'd graduated from the same university as me. It turned out that we even liked the same books: Akunin, Umberto Eco . . . 'Why,' he said, 'did you have to become one of my problems? I'm used to dealing with corrupt officials. It's nice! You know exactly where you stand with them. But you guys . . .' He was doing his job reluctantly, he was ashamed, but still, it didn't stop him. There are thousands of people like him—officials, detectives, judges. Some do the beating, others spread lies in the press. Others arrest people, pass sentences. You need so little to start up the Stalinist machine."

". . . There's an old notebook we've kept in my family. My grandpa recorded his life story for his children and grandchildren. He wrote about what he lived through in Stalin's time. He was imprisoned and tortured: They would put him in a gas mask and turn off the oxygen. Or they'd strip him and put a metal rod or a doorknob into his rectum . . . I was in ninth grade when my mother gave me the notebook: 'You're old enough now. You have to know this.' But I didn't understand what for?"

". . . If they bring back the camps, there will be plenty of people who'll want to be guards there. Tons! I remember one of them . . . When you looked him in the eye, he seemed like a normal person, except that he was foaming at the mouth. They moved like sleepwalkers, as though they were in a trance. They kept swinging left, right, left, right. One man fell down and they put a shield on top of him and started dancing on it. These meatheads . . . two meters tall . . . eighty or one hundred kilos each, you know—they feed them well. Those riot police and special ops boys, they really are special . . . They're like Ivan the Terrible's *oprichniks** . . . You don't want to believe that what they're doing is of their own free will, you resist the thought with all your might. You fight it with the last of your strength. They need to eat. It's just some guy . . . all he's seen of life was school and then the army. Now he makes more money than a professor. Afterward, it's always the same old story . . . like clockwork . . . He'll say he was acting on orders, they didn't know anything, it has nothing to do with them. Even today, they find a thousand excuses: 'Who's going to feed my family?' 'I took an oath.' 'I couldn't break ranks even if I'd wanted to.' You can do this with anyone. Or at least with a lot of people . . ."

". . . I'm only twenty years old. How am I supposed to live now? I'm worried that when I get out and go into the city, I'll be too scared to raise my eyes off the ground . . ."

"You're having a revolution—over here, we're living under the Soviet regime."

They released us at night. Journalists, friends—everyone had been waiting for us outside the prison, but they put us in police vans and dropped us off all over the city outskirts. They let me out somewhere in Shabany. Next to a huge pile of rocks by some construction site. It was actually scary. I stood there, unsure of what to do, then started walking toward the lights. I had no money, my phone had been dead for a long time. The only thing in my wallet was a bill, all of us were handed bills for what we owed them for our bed and board in jail. It's my entire monthly stipend . . . I don't even know how . . . My mother and I are barely scraping by. My father died when I was in sixth grade, I was twelve. My stepfather drinks and parties away his salary every

* *Oprichniks* were sixteenth-century Russian secret police officers, serving Ivan the Terrible's secret police organization, the *Oprichina*.

month without fail. He's an alky. I hate him, he's ruined me and my mother's life. I am always trying to make some extra money: I stuff flyers in mailboxes—in the summer, I'll work at a fruit or an ice cream stand. I walked along with these thoughts . . . Some stray dogs were running around . . . No people anywhere . . . I was so happy when a taxi stopped for me. I gave the driver the address of my dormitory and told him: "I don't have any money." The driver somehow knew right away: "Ah, you're one of those Decembrists [we'd been arrested in December]. Get in. I've already picked up another one of you and taken her home. What are they doing letting you out in the middle of the night?" The whole ride home, he lectured me on common sense: "It's all bullshit! Nothing but idiocy! In 1991, I was a student in Moscow, I also ran around to demonstrations. There were more of us than there are of you. And we won. We dreamed that every one of us would start a business and get rich. And what do you think happened? When the Communists were in power, I was an engineer—now I'm a cabbie. We chased out one group of bastards, and another group of bastards took their place. Black, gray, or orange, they're all the same. In our country, power will corrupt anyone. I'm a realist. The only things I believe in are myself and my family. While the newest round of idiots tries to usher in the latest revolution, I just keep my nose to the grindstone. This month, I need to make enough money to buy my daughters new coats, and next month, my wife needs boots. You're a pretty girl. You'd be better off finding yourself a good man and getting married." We drove into the city. Music. Laughter. Couples kissing. The city had gone on with its life as though we didn't even exist.

I couldn't wait to see my boyfriend and talk to him. I really wanted to see him. We'd been together for three years, we were making plans for our future. [*She falls silent.*] He'd promised me that he would come to the demonstration, but he never showed up. I was waiting to hear why. Speak of the devil, he showed up, ran over as soon as I got home. The girls left us alone in our room. What kind of explanation was I expecting?! It was absurd. It turned out that I'm nothing but "a fool," a "prime example of a naïve revolutionary." He'd warned me—had I forgotten? He lectured me on how it was irrational to get worked up over things you can't control. There are people who believe we must live for others, but that's foreign to him, he had no desire to die on the barricades. It's not his calling. His primary objective was building a career. He wanted to make a lot of money. Get a house with a pool. You have to keep living and smiling. There are so many opportunities

these days, a dazzling array . . . You can travel the world, go on unbelievable cruises (though those are expensive), buy a palace if you like
(though it will cost you), order turtle soup and elephant meat at a
restaurant . . . Anything, as long as you pay for it. Cash money! The
big bucks! As my physics teacher always said, "My dear students! Just
remember that money solves all problems, even differential equa-
tions." It's the cold hard truth. [*She is silent.*] But what about ideals?
They don't exist? Maybe you know something about them? After all,
you write books . . . [*Silence.*] At a general assembly, they expelled me
from the university. Everyone raised their hands to vote "Aye," everyone except for my favorite elderly professor. Afterward, he was taken
away in an ambulance. When no one was looking, my friends comforted me: "Don't be mad, it's just that the dean threatened us, he said
that if we didn't vote against you, they'd kick us out of the dorms . . . !"
True heroines!

I bought a ticket home. When I'm in the city, I miss my village. Although I'm not quite sure which village I miss; it's probably the village
of my childhood. The village where Papa would take me along to
watch him take out the frames from the beehives, heavy with honey.
First, he would fill them with smoke so that the bees would fly away
and wouldn't sting us. When I was little, I was funny . . . I thought that
bees were little birds . . . [*She is silent.*] Do I still like the village? People here live the same way year in and year out. They dig for potatoes
in their vegetable patches, crawl around on their knees. Make moonshine. You won't find a single sober man after dark, they all drink
every single day. They vote for Lukashenko and mourn the Soviet
Union. The undefeatable Soviet army. On the bus, one of our neighbors sat down next to me. He was drunk. He talked about politics: "I
would beat every moron democrat's face in myself if I could. They let
you off easy. I swear to God! All of them ought to be shot. I wouldn't
have given it a second thought. America is behind all this, they're paying for it . . . Hillary Clinton . . . But we're a strong people. We lived
through perestroika, and we'll make it through another revolution.
One wise man told me that the kikes are the ones behind it." The
whole bus supported him. "Things wouldn't be any worse than they
are now. All you see on TV are bombings and shootings everywhere."

Finally, I got home. I opened the door. My mother was sitting in the
kitchen scrubbing dahlia bulbs. They'd frozen and gone a bit rotten
because they're so finicky. Afraid of the cold. I sat down to help her

just like I used to do when I was little. "So what's going on out there in the capital?" was the first thing out of Mama's mouth. "On TV, they showed a whole sea of people shouting things against the government. Lordy! It was terrifying! We got so scared out here, we thought that war was about to break out. Some people's sons are in the riot police, other people's kids were the students shouting in the square. In the papers, they call them terrorists and gangsters. People around here believe what they read in the papers. You're having a revolution—over here, we're living under the Soviet regime." The house smelled like valerian.

I learned all the village gossip . . . Two men in plainclothes showed up in a car and took Yurka Shved, a farmer, away in the middle of the night, just like they'd come for my grandpa in 1937. Ransacked his house. Confiscated his computer. A nurse, Anya N., had been fired because she'd gone to Minsk for the demonstration and signed up with an opposition party. She has a little kid. Her husband got drunk and beat her: "You little oppositionist!" The mothers of the boys who served in the Minsk police were going around bragging about the big bonuses their sons received. About how they'd brought home gifts. [*She is silent.*] The people have been split in two . . . I went to a dance at the club and no one would ask me to dance all night because I'm a terrorist . . . People were scared of me . . .

We ran into each other again a year later on the Moscow-Minsk train. Everyone else had been asleep for a while. We stayed up talking.

"It can turn red, too"

I'm a student in Moscow now. My friends and I go to protests together. It's so cool! I like the faces of the people I see there. They remind me of the faces I saw when we went out on the square in Minsk. That day, I didn't recognize my city or my people. They were different. Different people. I miss home, I miss it terribly.

I can never sleep on the train back to Belarus. I'm always half asleep, half awake . . . Sometimes I find myself in jail, sometimes in the dorms . . . Everything comes back to me . . . Men and women's voices . . .

" . . . They stretched me, pulled my legs over my head . . ."

". . . They put a piece of paper on top of my kidneys so that they wouldn't leave marks and started beating me with a plastic water bottle . . ."

". . . He would put a plastic bag or a gas mask over my head. You know the rest . . . Naturally, I would lose consciousness after a couple of minutes . . . And him . . . He had a wife and kids back home. He was a good husband. A good father . . ."

". . . They kept beating and beating and beating and beating me . . . With their boots, their shoes, their sneakers . . ."

". . . You think the only things they teach them how to do are parachute and fast-rope out of helicopters? They use the same textbooks as they did in Stalin's time . . ."

". . . In school, they told us, 'Read Bunin and Tolstoy, those books save people.' Why isn't this the knowledge that's passed down, instead of the doorknob in the rectum and the plastic bag over the head? Who can you ask this question?"

". . . If they double or triple their salaries, I'm scared that they're going to start straight out shooting people . . ."

". . . When I was in the army, I realized I liked guns. I'm a professor's son, I grew up surrounded by books, but I want to have a gun. It's a beautiful object! Over hundreds of years, they've refined them, adapted them to the human hand. They're so nice to hold. I would enjoy taking it out and cleaning it. Oiling it up. I love the smell."

". . . Do you think there's going to be a revolution?"

". . . Orange is the color of dog piss in the snow. But it can turn red, too . . ."

". . . We're coming . . ."

NOTES FROM AN

EVERYWOMAN

• • •

What's there to remember? I live the same way as everyone else. Perestroika . . . Gorbachev . . . The postmistress opened the gate: "Did
you hear? The Communists are out." "What do you mean?" "They
shut down the Party." No shots fired, nothing. These days they say we
used to have a mighty fortress and then we lost it all. But what have I
really lost? I've always lived in the same little house without any amenities—no running water, no plumbing, no gas—and I still do today.
My whole life, I've done honest work. I toiled and toiled, got used to
backbreaking labor. And only ever earned kopecks. All I had to eat
was macaroni and potatoes, and that's all I eat today. I'm still going
around in my old Soviet fur—and you should see the snows out here!

The best thing I can remember is getting married. We were in love.
I remember walking home from the marriage registration bureau, the
lilacs in bloom. The lilacs! If you can believe it, there were nightingales
singing on their branches . . . That's how I remember it . . . We lived
happily for a few years, we had a daughter . . . Then Vadik started
drinking, and the vodka ended up killing him. He died young, he was
only forty-two. Ever since, I've lived alone. My daughter is all grown
up, she got married and moved away.

In the winter, we always get snowed in, the whole village is blanketed in snow—the houses and the cars. Sometimes, the buses won't
run for weeks on end. What's going on out there in the capital? It's
a thousand kilometers from here to Moscow. We watch Moscow
life unfold on TV like it's a movie. I've heard of Putin and Alla
Pugacheva . . . The rest, I know nothing about. Rallies, demonstrations . . . Out here, we live the same way we've always lived. Whether
it's socialism or capitalism. Who's Red, who's White—it makes no
difference. The important thing is to make it to spring. Plant potatoes . . . [A long silence.] I'm sixty years old . . . I don't go to church,

but I do need someone to talk to. To talk to about other things . . . about how I don't feel like getting old, I have no desire to get old at all. It'll be too bad when it comes time to die. Have you seen my lilacs? I go out at night to look at them—they glow. I'll just stand there admiring them. Here, let me cut you a bouquet . . .

TRANSLATOR'S
ACKNOWLEDGMENTS

◆ ◆ ◆

I wouldn't have made it up this tall and craggy hill without the love and expertise of Ainsley Morse; my parents, Vadim Shayevich and Anya Raskin; my grandmothers, Ida Khait and Elena Raskin, my aunt Marina, my grandpa Moisey. For having walked the steep path from the 1930s to the present, through war, persecution, revolution, and immigration, for my invaluable inheritance—their memories—I dedicate this translation to my grandparents.

ABOUT THE AUTHOR

SVETLANA ALEXIEVICH was born in Ivano-Frankovsk, Ukraine, in 1948 and has spent most of her life in the Soviet Union and present-day Belarus, with prolonged periods of exile in Western Europe. Starting out as a journalist, she developed her own nonfiction genre, which brings together a chorus of voices to describe a specific historical moment. Her works include *The Unwomanly Face of War* (1985), *Zinky Boys* (1990), *Chernobyl Prayer* (1997), and *Secondhand Time* (2013). She has won many international awards, including the 2015 Nobel Prize in Literature for "her polyphonic writings, a monument to suffering and courage in our time."

ABOUT THE TRANSLATOR

BELA SHAYEVICH is a Soviet American artist and translator.

ABOUT THE TYPE

This book was set in Sabon, a typeface designed by the well-known German typographer Jan Tschichold (1902–74). Sabon's design is based upon the original letter forms of sixteenth-century French type designer Claude Garamond and was created specifically to be used for three sources: foundry type for hand composition, Linotype, and Monotype. Tschichold named his typeface for the famous Frankfurt typefounder Jacques Sabon (c. 1520–80).